Living Environments
and
Mental Retardation

Living Environments
and
Mental Retardation

EDITED BY

SHARON LANDESMAN
Department of Psychiatry
Frank Porter Graham Child Development Center
University of North Carolina
at Chapel Hill

PETER M. VIETZE
New York State Institute for Basic Research
in Developmental Disabilities

MICHAEL J. BEGAB
Consulting Editor

Proceedings of a Conference in the
Series on Mental Retardation
Sponsored by the National Institute of Child Health
and Human Development

NICHD-Mental Retardation Research Centers Series
AMERICAN ASSOCIATION ON MENTAL RETARDATION

Library of Congress Cataloging-in-Publication Data

Living environments and mental retardation.

    (NICHD — Mental retardation research centers series)
    Proceedings of a conference held in 1982 at Lake Wilderness, Wash., sponsored by the National Institute of Child Health and Human Development and the Child Development and Mental Retardation Center at the University of Washington.
    Includes bibliographies and index.
    1. Mentally handicapped—Institutional care—United States—Congresses.   2. Mental retardation facilities—United States—Congresses.   3. Mentally handicapped—United States—Deinstitutionalization—Congresses.   4. Mentally handicapped—United States—Family relationships—Congresses.   I. Landesman, Sharon, 1947— II. Vietze, Peter, 1944—.   III. Begab, Michael J.   IV. National Institute of Child Health and Human Development (U.S.)
HV3006.A4L62   1987   362.3′85′0973   87-26995
ISBN 0-940898-17-9

Printed in the United States of America

Contents

Introduction

Sharon Landesman

As a result of the vigorous expansion in residential services available to people with mental retardation, Peter Vietze and I invited a group of investigators to Lake Wilderness, Washington, to exchange findings about the effects of living environments on behavior. The theme of this conference, sponsored by the National Institute of Child Health and Human Development and the Child Development and Mental Retardation Center at the University of Washington, was simply "living with mental retardation." The purpose was twofold: (a) to assess our current knowledge about the everyday lives, especially at home, of individuals with mental retardation and of the other people who live and work in these same settings (e.g., parents, siblings, direct-care staff); and (b) to evaluate the research strategies and methods available to study the interactions between people and environments. The round of deinstitutionalization begun in the early 1970s coincides with a period of dramatic change in the ideology and in the location of residential services for mentally retarded individuals and their families. Yet, interestingly, the scientific interest in understanding the effects of home environments and the process of community adaptation has been apparent since the founding of special institutions in the 1800s (Landesman-Dwyer, 1981, Windle, 1962).

There are many possible ways to study the effects of environments on individuals and on groups, including epidemiological and descriptive studies, careful documentation of case histories, ethnographic and participant–observation studies, evaluation of model residential programs and family interventions, and more controlled longitudinal studies. The latter are especially valuable when investigators attend to sources of serious bias (most notably, significant differences in the types of individuals placed in alternative settings and major variation in the content and consistency of the programs delivered in various environments) and try to minimize these. Butterfield addresses these persistent design problems in his chapter. His cautionary words and strong critique warrant attention, once again, because the wave of zealous enthusiasm for new service-delivery philosophies has contributed to a general carelessness in the conceptualization and data analysis of some extremely important, naturalistic social experiments underway. In fact, the heated political controversies associated with the normalization movement have contributed to a blatant withdrawal from research on this topic by a number of first-rate investigators (Landesman & Butterfield, in press). The fine work presented in this volume, however, provides a testimony about "what's happening in the community and service delivery system" that is based on sound and truly multidimensional inquiry. Just as important, advances in the conceptualization of the issues—elevating the immediate applied questions to general ones about adaptation and development of individuals, across the lifespan—are exciting for the future of scientific investigation in this field.

In the studies presented here, the investigators have used almost all the tools of the social sciences—standardized tests, structured and open-ended interviews, mailed and self-administered questionnaires, record reviews, systematic direct observation, participant observation, clinical or therapeutic interventions, and experimental test situations. The collective goal has been to yield valid and reliable data relevant to understanding who lives where, what the ranges in residential settings and experiences are, and how home environments contribute to different patterns of behavior and subsequent development. The chapters represent an excellent sampling of the diversity in approaches to answering questions about transactions and interdependencies between people and places.

Over the past decade, one of the most impressive shifts in the field of mental retardation research has been the trend toward closer alliance with and appreciation of other fields of inquiry about *basic behavior processes* (Baumeister, in press; Landesman-Dwyer & Butterfield, 1983). This movement away from the insularity that characterized earlier research in mental retardation is welcomed because it expands the opportunities for sharing concepts and methods as well as for testing the robustness of the principles derived from studying special populations and special settings. The empirical findings presented in this volume demonstrate, in a compelling fashion, a fundamental truth that must be recognized at the levels of public policy and service delivery: *individuals with mental retardation, regardless of the severity of their mental and physical impairments, and those who live and work with them are affected significantly by their social and physical milieus.*

Remarkably, much of the earlier mental retardation research failed to acknowledge the importance of environmental variables. In studies that focused on individual differences and performance, investigators did not consider the types of environments from which mentally retarded subjects were selected. For many years, research subjects routinely were selected from institutions. The effects of such institutional settings on the subjects' behavior, typically evaluated only in experimental laboratory situations, were ignored until the classic studies of the Yale investigators (notably, Zigler, Butterfield, Balla, Belmont, and Klaber) and Baumeister (see Baumeister, 1967, for a superb early view of this field). Their findings forced a major re-evaluation of the role of the environment in determining response style, social motivation, and performance on standardized tests of intelligence and adaptive behavior. Moreover, this research provided the first major evidence in mental retardation of person–environment interaction. Specifically, they discovered that the types of homes children lived in *prior* to institutionalization affected their early adjustment to the institution: for those children who received relatively little cognitive stimulation in their homes, an institution was (surprisingly) a relatively enriched environment that elicited positive responses (e.g., as reflected in temporary gains in scores on intelligence tests), whereas just the opposite was true for children whose family life had been far more enriched than that in the institution. Similarly, other variables, such as the number of years individuals lived in an institution, significantly affected their behavior (e.g., responsiveness to social reinforcement). In a compelling fashion, this pioneering research on the effects of institutionalization demonstrated (a) that both current and long-term consequences of the environment must be considered when conducting any research in mental retardation, and (b) the effects of a given environment are not the same for everyone.

Meyers and Blacher provide a rich overview of the history of residential services for individuals with mental retardation. Bruininks, Rotegard, Lakin, and Hill add a valuable national picture, previously incomplete and of doubtful reliability, of the overall availability of different types of residential settings. Their survey research has been useful in elucidating some important service-delivery patterns that have been changing and that are of high priority for more rigorous study. Sulzbacher and Steinfeld remind investigators and clinicians that use of psychotropic and seizure control medications is prevalent among those in residential programs, and when assessing behavioral adaptation of residents, they must consider the current and cumulative effects of such drugs.

In this conference we sought to bridge a traditional gap in the field between the family researchers and those who study group care and community living. Apparent in the chapters is the similarity of questions asked and the data-collection strategies used, regardless of where people live. Coates and Vietze propose a definition of "family" that is broad and appropriately tuned to the reality of the everyday lives of many individuals with mental retardation. Neither biological affiliation nor generic place of residence (e.g., institution vs. group home) adequately identifies the important social variables or sources of long-term continuity for many mentally retarded persons. The experience of belonging to a "family" all too often is lacking in the lives of individuals, especially adults, with mental retardation. When a surrogate family is found, the members are likely to include peers who are mentally retarded and paid careproviders.

The section on parents, careproviders, and support systems underscores the problems associated with providing long-term high quality residential care. The chapters by Cherniss and by Baumeister and Zaharia provide a detailed analysis of the concepts of burnout, withdrawal, and commitment of direct-care staff. The concerns they address apply to many family situations as well, in which parents, relatives, and friends may experience mixed feelings about their daily responsibilities, may not be adequately trained for their "job", and may display inconsistent or even harmful behavior toward the person needing active care and supervision. Baker and Clark present findings about their intervention programs for parents of developmentally disabled children. They, like others, report that parent training programs are not effective with all parents. To understand why, they proceed to explore which variables best predict who will complete or drop out of training, who will learn what was taught, and who will apply the new information in ways to foster their child's development. They discover that relating parental training to differential child outcomes is extremely problematic, yielding weak evidence at best for "effectiveness." I think this reflects a larger dilemma inherent in evaluating the consequences of any social intervention that is embedded in a complex and changing context. For now, one major challenge appears to be developing alternative strategies that will maximize reaching a wider group of parents (e.g., single parents and less informed parents, two groups that Baker and Clark reported dropped out of existing programs) and direct careproviders and that will provide training and emotional/social support in ways like to enhance the developmental course and quality of life for those who are mentally retarded (Landesman-Dwyer & Knowles, 1987).

The chapter by Schroeder and MacLean is a particularly important one, with disturbing undertones related to clinical practice and the management of residential settings. Clearly, we have the theoretical framework, the assessment procedures, and the technological sophistication ("ecobehavioral technology") to understand the environmental variables that maintain so-called "maladaptive" behavior. The existence of *covariation effects*, however, must be recognized in the design and integrated into the evaluation of any systematic intervention concerning stereotyped or self-abusive behavior. Without adequate attention to transitional effects in the target behavior and to changes in collateral behaviors, behavioral intervention programs will continue to show minimal and short-lived success, at best. Faced with repeated failure to effect permanent change of such destructive and intrusive behavior patterns, therapists and careproviders (including parents) will be disheartened and accept weak excuses for failing to initiate and sustain sophisticated behavioral programs. More research is needed to understand how the overall social ecology of a residence contributes to problematic behavior and fosters or obstructs the success of individually tailored behavioral treatment.

Zetlin, Turner, and Winik gathered a rich set of participant observations concerning the relationships between adults who are mildly retarded and their parents. They identify three distinctive types of relationships: supportive, dependent, and conflict-ridden. The questions they ask about the significance of these relationships for retarded adults' independence and success are broad and warrant further study for all young adults, regardless of their level of intelligence. Similarly, the research by Lewis, Feiring, and Brooks-Gunn probes the social networks of young children (as perceived by mothers) in a way that may yield insights into socialization processes for all children. Whenever differences are detected between subjects with mental retardation and those with normal-range intelligence and adaptive behavior, careful exploration concerning the etiology and consequences of such differences is needed. The period of long debate about developmental differences versus deficits is ready to yield to alternative theories that incorporate the environment itself in the ontogeny of suboptimal, atypical, delayed, and/or undesirable behavior patterns (Berkson, 1978). Moreover, differentiating distinct combinations of behavioral, physical, and experiential components of mental retardation, as compared to normative patterns, may facilitate the creation of expanded theories of mental retardation—ones that can accommodate and help explain the complexity of the observed phenomenon.

Friedrich, Greenberg, and Crnic discuss many of the interesting conceptual issues and measurement problems in the study of families. They select three somewhat distinctive theoretical frameworks for consideration, each with applicability to understanding families with handicapped children. These frameworks—systemic/ecological, developmental, and coping—help identify variables of interest and hypothesized processes to account for different patterns of adjustment in families. The elements they posit as central—including the ecological setting with its physical and social resources, coping styles, and responses to perceived stressors, and how these change over time—are similar to those used by Bristol in her study of families with autistic children and in my research on institutional group care settings.

Several studies presented here depict noteworthy advances in methods and data analytic strategies. For example, Eyman, Borthwick, and Sheehy used several diverse ways of depicting the environment (PASS, Home Observation of the Environment, Home Quality Rating Scale) and then applied a path analysis to test their model of influences within foster care. Their analysis of the environmental variables and how these relate to caretaker characteristics further underscores the interdependence observed between persons and environments. They report that the factors explaining gains in adaptive behavior are not necessarily the same as those related to maladaptive behavior. Their findings support the broad conclusion that what fosters positive outcomes in some areas may be associated with negative or neutral outcomes in other areas. For example, foster parents with *less* education provided environments that reduced undesirable behavior, yet *more* careprovider education was associated with higher scores on several PASS factors that, in turn, correlated with significantly higher gains in adaptive behavior.

Another important point that Eyman, Borthwick, and Sheehy underscore is "the importance of classifying research subjects into mutually exclusive groups," based on their finding of highly significant differences in the behavior of those who moved and those who were affected by the relocation of others. In my research at two large traditional institutions undergoing a major transformation, I reached the same conclusion. That is, a major environmental change can best be evaluated by adopting a person–environment interaction perspective, one in which (a) initial (baseline) differences in everyday behavior are considered, (b) hypotheses are generated about the probable impact of selected changes in the environment, and (c) the observed changes over time are related to these hypothesized differences in environmental responses. Ironically, the service-delivery system mandates *individual* habilitation planning for citizens with mental retardation, yet the "solutions" offered concerning "ideal" residential programs tend to be simplistic and reflect an assumption that there is a "best" way to maximize the quality of life for nearly all retarded persons (Landesman, 1986b).

Excellent examples of the application of observational methods to the study of living environment are provided by Stoneman and Brody (who focus on a topic too long neglected—the relationships among siblings), Felce (who brings us an interesting view of community homes in England), and Repp, Barton, and Brulle (who challenge some of the observational approaches used to analyze behavior in naturalistic settings and suggest ways to correct the problems they identify). Similarly, in my chapter I describe a scoring method and the amount of observations needed to gather a fairly complete profile of individuals' everyday behavior in their homes. In contrast to these microanalytic approaches, much broader pictures are obtained from the statewide survey research conducted by Janicki, Jacobson, Zigman, and Lubin and from the research of Seltzer and Seltzer, who explore the relationship of the "home" to the wider community. Far more research is needed about the processes of community acceptance and resistance (perhaps independent rather than intertwined) and the extent to which the larger ecology affects the functioning of a residence.

This book is intended to be much more than a sampler. The contributions indicate that mental retardation research is emerging as strong and well-integrated with advances in other social sciences. The findings confirm that the environment is a significant determinant of behavioral and emotional patterns of adjustment. Increasing sophistication in the conceptualization of the environment has facilitated investigation of the *processes* hypothesized to account for differential effects associated with variations in residential environments. That no single theory has emerged is not surprising or particularly distressing. The questions demand reliance on different levels of theorizing. Given the scope of human adaptation to be considered, there is ample reason to benefit from the theoretical advances in the social sciences. A general taxonomy of residential ("home") environments—rather than a special one limited to the field of mental retardation—would be of great value (cf. Landesman, 1986a) in facilitating the integration of empirical findings about different groups of people. I hope that the contents of this volume will be as exciting and informative to you, the readers, as they have been to us as investigators.

REFERENCES

Baumeister, A. A. (Ed.), (1967). *Mental retardation: Appraisal, education, and rehabilitation.* Chicago: Aldine.

Baumeister, A. A. (in press). Mental retardation: Some conceptions and dilemmas. *American Psychologist.*

Berkson, G. (1978). Social ecology and ethology of mental retardation. In G. P. Sackett (Ed.), *Observing behavior, Vol. I: Theory and applications in mental retardation.* Baltimore: University Park Press.

Landesman, S. (1986a). Toward a taxonomy of home environments. In N. R. Ellis & N. Bray (Eds.), *International review of research in mental retardation* (Vol. 14). Baltimore: University Park Press.

Landesman, S. (1986b). Quality of life and personal life satisfaction: Definition and measurement issues. *Mental retardation, 24,* 141–143.

Landesman, S., & Butterfield, E. C. (in press). Normalization and deinstitutionalization of mentally retarded individuals: Controversy and facts. *American Psychologist.*

Landesman-Dwyer, S. (1981). Living in the community. *American Journal of Mental Deficiency, 86,* 223–234.

Landesman-Dwyer, S., & Butterfield, E. C. (1983). Mental retardation: Developmental issues in cognitive and social adaptation. In M. Lewis (Ed.), *Origins of intelligence: Infancy and early childhood* (2nd ed.). New York: Plenum.

Landesman-Dwyer, S., & Knowles, M. (1987). Ecological analysis of staff training in residential settings. In J. Hogg & P. J. Mittler (Eds.), *Issues in staff training in mental handicap.* London: Croon Helm.

Windle, C. (1962). Prognosis of mental subnormals. *American Journal of Mental Deficiency* (Monograph supplement), *66,* 1–180.

Residential Care: Fundamental Issues and Historical Facts

1

Historical Determinants of Residential Care

C. Edward Meyers
University of California at Los Angeles

Jan Blacher
University of California at Riverside

In this chapter the history of residential care for mentally retarded people is reviewed. Although many good histories of mental retardation exist, with one exception (Scheerenberger, 1983) they lack systematic treatment of how residency was provided in their accounts of pre-19th century history. That history contains here and there a reference to a special asylum or hospital or family-type care, but otherwise residency was not a topic until institutions developed in the 19th century. Our own examination of both primary and secondary sources indicates that those who wrote the histories had little to find. We are left only with the inference that few if any special residential arrangements existed to be described. Summarizing the history of residential care of the mentally retarded population is further complicated by changing definitions and variations in sensitivity to deviance across time and between cultures (Edgerton, 1970, 1981).

The history has two parts. The history of care before the 19th century is an unorganized collection of odds and ends found in historical, legal, and religious literature. It also contains scattered anthropological findings from the cross-cultural study of contemporary undeveloped societies. In contrast, the second part is a well-documented history of care in Western civilization since about 1790, replete with facts, numbers, and biographies of leaders from Itard to the present.

Acknowledgements. This study was supported by Grants No. HD-14612, HD-14680, and HD-14688 from the National Institute of Child Health and Human Development, U.S. Department of Health, Education, and Welfare.

BIBLIOGRAPHICAL NOTE

Scheerenberger (1983) provided a recent detailed history of mental retardation, particularly valuable in containing a good summary of what little is known of residential care prior to the 19th century. Kanner (1967) emphasized historical medical–psychiatric developments. Abt (1965) and Zilboorg (1941) also provided medical accounts, and Henry (1941), a history of mental hospitals. Fernald's history of caretaking in the United States is recommended reading (Bremner, 1974). Bremner's collection of reprints is exceeded by Rosen, Clark, and Kivitz's (1976) two volumes that include the famous Dorothea L. Dix *Memorial,* just one of her exposés of inhumane treatment of mentally different people in the mid-19th century. Elsewhere, Baumeister (1970) provided a thoughtful and foresightful review of then-current developments in residential situations. Other historical accounts were provided by Doll (1962) and Scheerenberger (1982). Edgerton (1970, 1981) produced a masterful collection and interpretation of the scattered cross-cultural information on how societies perceive and cope with feeble-minded individuals.

PRE-ITARD HISTORY

Our knowledge of past civilizations and cultures suggests that not everyone was created equal, that forms of mental illness, deviance, and deformity existed (Kanner, 1967; Scheerenberger, 1983; Zilboorg, 1941). Furthermore, we know that handicapped individuals were not viewed or treated the same as nonhandicapped people. When special care was provided, it often reflected the society's general philosophy toward dependent individuals (e.g., the sentiment of the ruler or leaders, current religious beliefs) or economic conditions.

Early references to defective individuals are in the Bible and the teachings of Christ and Mohammed. Jesus reportedly healed the blind, deaf, crippled, demonic, epileptic, dumb, and paralytic (Scheerenberger, 1983). Following his example, the Apostle Paul wrote, "Now we exhort you, brethren, warn them that are unruly, comfort the feeble-minded, be patient toward all men" (1 Thessalonians 5:14). Kanner (1967) pointed out, however, that no organized help or "care" existed.

In some primitive societies, residential care for handicapped or retarded children was not needed, because they did not survive. Inhabitants in the New Hebrides would not only kill any malformed child, but the mother as well (Sumnar, 1960, cited in Scheerenberger, 1982). Infanticide was practiced in other areas of the world, including ancient Egypt (in about 3000 B.C.). For the most part, however, Egyptian families treated handicapped children with love and affection. One account (Abt, 1965) reported that parents who did kill their children were condemned to hug the dead infant continually in their arms for 3 days and 3 nights, presumably to experience the full horror of it all (Scheerenberger, 1982).

The Spartans left their defective children on the Mount Taygetus to die. Presumably, however, some of the mildly or subtly handicapped children survived. The historian Caelius wrote about Soranus, who spoke out against infanticide. During the many centuries of the Roman Empire the attitudes toward handicapped individuals changed, usually reflecting those of the prevailing ruler (Zilboorg, 1941). The Romans set up colonies to house the poor, and Hadrian required parents to care for their own children, deporting any who killed or abandoned their sons (Scheerenberger, 1983). More notably, unwanted infants could be placed at the foot of the "Columna Lacteria," where the state provided wet nurses to suckle them.

Treatment Reflecting Religious Beliefs

Five hundred years before Hippocrates initiated the study of medicine in the 4th century B.C., society believed that divine power made people mad. There are reports that mental illness or "flagrantly queer behavior" existed in ancient Greece (Zilboorg, 1941). The Bible links certain afflictions to sinfulness: "The Lord shall smite thee with madness and blindness and astonishment of heart" (Deuteronomy 28:28).

During the Middle Ages treatment was variable, based on views of deformed children as "heavenly infants" (Wallin, 1955), or as witches who should be persecuted (Doll, 1962). The strong religious influence is reflected in some of the 15th century plays known as liturgical drama, in which Christ frequently heals crippled persons. At the time there were a few hospitals and religious homes for children who might otherwise be abandoned. Treatment reflected a combination of Christian doctrine, myth, custom, legend, and superstition (Scheerenberger, 1983). For example, Tuke recommended special drinks with herbs "for idiocy and folly" (cited in Scheerenberger, 1982).

Less-humane treatment included whipping, dunking, incarcerating, or tying to a church pillar. In 1346, mentally retarded persons in Hamburg were confined to a tower called the "Idiot's Cage." In other towns, such "idiots" were confined to home by family and friends; local authorities even provided money to assist this effort (Burdett, 1891, in Scheerenberger, 1982).

There were occasional bright spots during the Middle Ages. Mansur Hospital was established in Cairo. Patients had access to a dispensary, library, chapel, and lecture hall. Wards, cooled by fountains, had actors, musicians, and storytellers to provide entertainment. When discharged, patients were granted money to help make the transition to community life. A form of group home care appeared during the 13th century in Gheel, Belgium. Retarded and mentally ill individuals lived in family settings where they had separate living quarters but ate meals with the family and participated in the local community activities (Scheerenberger, 1982).

St. Paul advocated kindness, which gave way in the late Middle Ages to beliefs in witchcraft or Satanic theory, culminating in the Inquisition, the Salem witch trials, and the Satanic attributions of the great reformers (Zilboorg, 1941). Attitudes toward persons with mental retardation were harsh during the Reformation. Even Martin Luther appeared to be without compassion: "If I were the Prince, I should take this child to the Moldau River . . . and drown him" and "The devil sits in such changelings where their souls should have been" (Kanner, 1967, p. 7). Calvin also emphasized the devious ways Satan possessed individuals. The Satanic theory later gave way to Enlightenment, from which sprung the more recent concern for the welfare of behaviorally deviant persons.

Such accounts testify to the fact that behavioral deviance was recognized. Different types of deviance were discriminated and sometimes influenced treatment. In Talmudic law "persons who lack proper understanding—deaf mutes, idiots, and minors—were disqualified from acting as either principal or agent" (*Encyclopedia Judaica*, p. 351). The Koran required tolerant treatment of those who differed. An account of 19th century Egyptian practice followed Mohammed's preaching that those who were strange may be in special communication with God:

> An idiot or a fool . . . is considered an especial favorite of heaven.
> Whatever enormities a reputed saint may commit . . . such acts do not
> affect his fame or sanctity; for they are considered as the results of the
> abstraction of his mind from worldly things.

Individuals' behavior is to be tolerated except in those who are dangerous and to be "kept in confinement" (Hughes, 1885, p. 190). Edgerton (1970, 1981) provided several contemporary accounts of tolerance in other Moslem locations.

Drama

For information on early treatment and care of handicapped individuals, we also considered artistic sources. Drama, for example, is partially a mirror of reality and an important reflection of current practices and attitudes toward persons with handicaps (Blacher & Dixon, 1982). Although ancient Greek society emphasized beauty and health, playwrights also dealt with handicaps realistically and sympathetically as early as the 5th century B.C. Sophocles incorporated blindness in his Oedipus trilogy, with the theme of blindness versus insight in *Oedipus at Colonus*. Although Oedipus verbalized his helplessness ("Help me sit down, take care of the blind man" [line 21]), he also served as a leader ("Children, follow me this way: see now, I have become your guide, as you were mine" [lines 1542-1543]). Aristophanes' play *The Plutus* portrays a blind old man named "Wealth," who, when he regained his eyesight (through rather bizarre "medical" treatment), repaid his friends and society by eliminating poverty in Greece. Not surprisingly, the social institutions in Greece during this period reflected a positive attitude toward impaired individuals. One of the earliest mental hospitals, at Epidauros, was established around the 6th century B.C. and flourished for over 800 years. Epidauros was a sanctuary where residents were treated gently and humanely. Although it was not a hospital for mentally retarded or physically handicapped persons (Zilboorg, 1941), one can assume that some such individuals were treated there.

Early dramatic works from ancient Rome provide clues about treatment of various handicaps. Blindness again appears in the Roman versions of *Oedipus* by Seneca. Although wealthy Romans used deformed individuals as objects of amusement or entertainment in their homes (Wallin, 1955), the explicit mention of handicaps or the use of handicapped characters is missing from Roman comedies. Roman tragedies include a blind prophet in Seneca's *Oedipus* and the blind character, Oedipus, in Seneca's *Phoenissae*, however, these plays focus on issues of moral philosophy and tend to ignore the form or function of the characters' handicap (Blacher & Dixon, 1982).

The numerous references from religious, historical, and literary documents do recognize the existence of behaviorally deviant people and sometimes describe places of special care and treatment. What they lack is any description of systematic segregation of mentally retarded people, if they were permitted to live. Occasional mention is made of confining insane individuals; presumably, the insane population also included some mentally retarded individuals as well.

MENTALLY RETARDED PEOPLE IN NON-WESTERN SOCIETIES

Do non-Western societies identify the condition of mental retardation? As with the pre-Itard history, information on non-Western social attitudes is scattered and has no organizational principle to facilitate interpretation. According to Edgerton (1968), a true "anthropological study of mental retardation . . . does not exist" (p. 75).

Masland, Sarason, and Gladwin (1958) did summarize what little was known until Edgerton (1970) published a masterful collation of information on the views and practices of primitive societies in identifying and treating feeble-minded individuals. He secured data from existing descriptions of societies around the world, responses to inquiries from anthropologists in the field, and his own field studies. There is also an updated version of this review (Edgerton, 1981).

Edgerton focused more effort on describing the situation of mildly impaired individuals. He challenged the frequent assumption that a nonliterate society often fails to note mild degrees of retardation identified in literate societies. He theorized that even nonliterate cultures may require members to exercise discrimination and memory to detect subleties in nature and human relations and to conform correctly to sometimes highly abstract ritual expectations. So-called "nonliterate cultures" may indeed employ symbols such as stick-marks, knotted cords, or pebble arrangements that involve use of abstract intelligence (Price-Williams, 1981; Wober, 1975). Edgerton's account demonstrates that mental impairment is probably identified in all societies but may not be considered important in some. In others, mental impairment may invite maltreatment, social ostracism, or special attention. For example, if weak-minded persons get into mischief that requires compensation to those offended, their family or tribe may have to watch them closely or restrict them.

There are societies in which economic jeopardy may require drastic measures. Individuals who do not contribute, such as those who are lame, blind, elderly and helpless, or mentally impaired, may be abandoned or discarded, a practice similar to infanticide of those born with severe impairments. Yet such treatment is not universal, even in the most impoverished societies where this is more likely to occur. In some situations, imperfect physical or mental functioning may lead to demise, such as the inability to avoid a predator or to find sustenance. Edgerton concluded that primitive societies identify and care for retarded individuals in highly variable ways, both within and between the societies. Recently, Edgerton (1981) emphasized that the bothersome or intrusive behavior of retarded persons was a principal determinant of how they were treated.

We find *no mention whatsoever* in the anthropological literature of any residential segregation or seclusion of mentally retarded individuals. Edgerton (personal communication, 1982) checked with other anthropologists concerned with intelligence and mental retardation and confirmed that they know of no special living arrangements for mildly retarded family members. At most, some societies may confine individuals to a portion of such group quarters as "long houses," which were family or tribal residences. Otherwise, if not at home, the individuals may wander, gravitate toward population centers, or join the population of beggars. Segregation and asylum appear to be products of Western industrialized societies.

HISTORICAL DEVELOPMENT OF CARE IN MODERN WESTERN CIVILIZATION

The Age of Enlightenment caused a general reconsideration of human nature, of the relation to God to human beings, and especially a rejection of Satanic theory in favor of men and women as children of nature. Enlightenment characterized the 18th and early 19th centuries. For our purposes, it began in the 1790s, when Pinel struck the chains from incarcerated prisoners and insane persons in the Bicetre. Around this time Itard, a physician working with deaf and dumb individuals, tried to make Victor, the "Wild Boy of Aveyron," into a "normal" person. Itard, publishing his work in 1801, produced a revolution:

> Almost suddenly, interest in the mental defectives began to flare up in
> the first half of the 19th century, spreading from France and Switzerland
> to the rest of the civilized portion of Europe and to the United States of
> America. (Kanner, 1967, p. 9)

An almost religious movement, spread by evangelistic apostles, developed in the subsequent decades. The depravity of man and the belief in Satan's influence preached by Calvin and other reformers gave way to the belief in innate goodness preached by Rousseau, who taught that society corrupted the person who by nature was whole. An air of optimism developed among the physicians of the late 18th and early 19th centuries. In particular, the medical teachers of "deaf and dumb" individuals entertained hopes of improving their functioning. In Europe and the United States, many began to acknowledge that appropriate training could increase competency and thus permit handicapped children to live normal or nearly normal lives. These pioneers founded educational programs and schools, which then became residential institutions. Seguin's was first in 1838 at Salpêtrière, France, followed by his educational program for "idiots" in the Bicêtre, the hospital for insane persons in France. Guggenbuhl founded his famous Abendberg as probably the first residential center for retarded people, primarily to treat "endogenous cretins" in Switzerland. Others started residential schools in Germany, England, and elsewhere (for details see Baumeister, 1970; Fernald, 1974; Kanner, 1967; Rosen et al., 1976; Scheerenberger, 1982, 1983). All these centers provided good diet, exercise, medical care, and, above all, "sense training." Guggenbuhl's Abendberg initially was regarded as the model (it rapidly deteriorated, however), greatly influencing Howe of the United States, a physician and teacher of blind children.

In 1848, Wilbur founded the first private school in the United States (in Massachusetts) for mentally retarded children just months before Howe established the first public program, at the Perkins Institute. Howe's program later was moved to its own building in South Boston in 1855. Earlier, Massachusetts had established the prototype American hospital in Worcester for mentally ill persons, although an "asylum" for this population had already been founded in Williamsburg, Virginia, in 1773. Dorothea L. Dix provided some facts about New England in her famous "Memorial to the Legislature of Massachusetts, 1843" (reprinted in Rosen et al., 1976). She described the quality of care in almshouses, hospitals, and prisons. Frequently, she saw "idiots and insane persons" in the same residence, sometimes together with "harmless paupers." She provided no numbers but she used the term *idiot* about as frequently as *insane*.

Although the provision of hospital care for mentally ill individuals came a few years before the first residential schools for feeble-minded individuals, the two developments were parallel and responded to essentially similar demands. Grob (1966) described the forces behind the creation and expansion of Worcester, the first mental hospital. One was the new, optimistic philosophy that people could be helped. Accordingly, more humanitarianism had to be exercised. Another was that industrialization and urbanization undermined the informal care provisions that previously helped deviant people (Landis & Page, 1938).

Before Worcester and the early "schools" were developed, where did the feeble-minded or insane individuals live? Any answer is speculative. First, we note that a considerable, although unknown, proportion of severely impaired individuals would have died soon after birth or in early childhood. Less medically fragile individuals may have been permitted the run of the farm and the woods, provided they did not cause too much trouble. Urban living would be another, more difficult matter.

From Residential School to Institution

Other states, but not all, quickly followed Massachusetts in developing such schools. Age of Enlightenment doctors hoped to correct slow-mindedness by appropriate education and training, based on the belief that development was incomplete and that special training via the senses could cause physiology to mature. The trainers succeeded with many, who then joined the community. This early optimism, however, began to decline in the later 19th century. Not all mentally impaired persons, it was quickly shown, could be improved sufficiently to return to the community. Further, the egalitarian philosophy of the Age of Enlightenment gave way to a look at human beings from an evolutionary or Darwinian perspective (i.e., not all were born equal). Variations were a fact of nature, and Darwin suggested that fitness was required to survive. Galton, a disciple of Darwin, invented concepts and ways to depict individual differences. He also traced pedigrees of eminence, laying the groundwork for later emphasis on the inheritance of incompetence and criminality. The optimistic doctors lost part of their battle, training schools now had to keep many "incurables," and the return to the community was temporarily halted. White and Wolfensberger (1969) noted:

> As the early idealists were replaced by others, and as non-rehabilitated residents accumulated, the objective of the residential programs changed to one of protection. The period from about 1870 to 1890 emphasized *sheltering the deviant from society*. However, to shelter meant to isolate (p. 5).

Because budgets were always tight, one way to save money was to exploit the labor of the surplus population in the institution. White and Wolfensberger (1969) quoted Fernald in 1893 as boasting about cutting annual costs from $300 to $100 by fuller utilization of inmate labor. This quote can be matched more recently by the superintendent of Pacific Colony in California: "Actually the institutional workers of this type are of economic value to the State in that many contribute more to service to the institution than it takes to maintain them there" (Fenton, 1932, p. 302).

We would misinterpret both Fenton and his superintendent, Dr. Cutter, if we failed to consider their reports in the proper context. They described and showed pride in the humane treatment, diverse educational program, and recreational opportunities that they provided; however, they had to demonstrate their thrift, showing that they operated as stringently as possible and saved money by use of patients' labor.

Eugenic Segregation

The year 1877 witnessed the publication of Dugdale's genealogical survey of the apparently degenerate Jukes family, to be followed by other pedigree reports (Kanner, 1967). Thus came the era of "eugenic alarm," with the belief that feeble-mindedness and criminality were closely related and inherited. Institutions became places to put people to keep them from mischief and procreation. In White and Wolfensberger's (1969) continued figure of speech, the institution from 1890 to 1900 now protected society from deviant individuals. A "protect society" concept of residency prevailed, which included preventing retarded individuals from procreating, sterilizing them, and segregating them from members of the opposite sex. Indiana passed the first sterilization law in 1907, and by 1926, 23 states had such laws. In 1932, the superintendent of Pacific Colony noted that 187 sterilizations had been performed, a high proportion of their 810 patients in a 2-year period (Cutter, 1932). Sterilizations in California did not decline until later, when it became clear that they caused no reduction in overall incidence of retardation.

Increased Rate of Institutionalization and Deinstitutionalization

The various forces that enhanced the identification and the segregation of behaviorally different individuals (e.g., urbanization of the population, Darwinian theory, eugenic alarm) produced an increase in institutional commitment over and above that due to population increase alone (see chapter 2 by Bruininks et al. in this volume). Institutional population increased till the late 1960s when correctives measures began to occur under the influence of the "normalization principle." Since 1967, total institutional populations have declined along with the average size of populations in institutions; however, as Bruininks et al. indicated, this decrease reflects a build-up of alternative residential arrangements in the community.

Community Residential Care

Two forms of community care for mentally retarded dependents are discussed here: the *small-family* or *foster care plan*, generally defined as a home with an adult careprovider of not more than 5 or 6 developmentally disabled people, and the *group home* or *board-and-care plan*, typically housing 6 or more people, supervised by some responsible adult. We found little history on this topic. Foster care probably extends back as far as community care of any homeless child existed. Group home origin is confused with the development in the 19th century of residential schools and institutions. These early schools initially housed small numbers, often not more than found in today's larger group homes or mini-institutions. The principal difference is that by definition today the group home is in the community, not isolated (Lakin, Bruininks, & Sigford, 1981). However wispy the history of the group home, it is a burgeoning service of such significance today—whether operated by the state, proprietors, or not-for-profit auspices—that its history should be set down now (Flynn & Nitsch, 1980; Intagliata, Crosby, & Neider, 1981).

We know a little about the development of small family (foster) care. We assume that to some degree an organized society provided a way to take care of children whose parents died, abandoned them, or were found incompetent to continue as parents. If the extended family could not provide a home, the child would be assigned to foster care. This was true in Charles Dickens' England and otherwise in literature, the law, and history. Society thus possessed a system that could provide, and there is no a priori reason to assume that the care was not also extended to impaired children who otherwise could not be tolerated. We know that the foster care system has been easy to adapt to the placement of mentally retarded and other handicapped individuals.

Those who have probed for the origins of organized family care suggest that the first recorded instance was established for care of insane persons in Gheel, Belgium, during the 6th century (Caplan, 1969; Henry, 1941; Vaux, 1935). We may assume that just as individuals labeled "lunatics" and "idiots" were mixed in various incarcerations, so also some "idiots" were cared for in this community-wide endeavor. We further assume that such individuals were cared for in the late 19th century family care plans for mentally ill persons in the United States. Some of the physicians in the United States who initiated special residential programs for feeble-minded persons were known to have taken some students into their own homes (Rosen et al., 1976). In 1931, New York was the first state to enact family care as an alternative to institutionalization for mentally retarded persons (Vaux, 1935). Accounts also indicate that in the 19th century, many successful returns from institutions were able-bodied retarded persons who moved to a farm family, where labor was exchanged for the family care received.

Of the mentally retarded people who do not live in their own homes, what proportion live in other types of family care? The number was apparently small until past 1950. With the compelling moral and civil rights questions raised about institutionalization in the 1960s, community placement as an aspect of the normalization movement grew. An easy solution, quickly adopted by most states, was the extension of the foster care plan to mentally retarded people, either as a placement from the institution or as the initial placement from the natural home. Characteristics and numbers were provided by Borthwick, Meyers and Eyman (1981) who showed data for a three-state area in 1979. A total of 6,202 mentally retarded/developmentally disabled persons were on record for the areas in question. Of these, 16% of the total (24% of those not in natural homes) were in small family care. Those in group homes constituted 7% of the total.

CONCLUDING NOTES

Most of "the history of residential care" is a non-history. The institution as we know it developed in Western civilization from the boarding schools in Europe, the United States, and Canada. Residential care is simply not mentioned in the pre-Itard history. One exception is the care for insane persons in Epidaurus and Gheel, which we presume would include some feeble-minded persons. Another exception is the "hospitals," like Bedlam and Bicêtre, again housing together all individuals with unwanted or unmanageable behavior. As we have discussed, the anthropologists, too, report no contemporary segregation or special living arrangements specifically for mentally impaired individuals. On the other hand, foster care— some form of care in a household other than the natural home—most surely has occurred throughout history, with surrogate parenting and extended family responsibility probably universally exercised.

Students of history will note that the change from pre-Itard to post-Itard history coincides with the development of industrialization in Western civilization. It was not by chance that the large "hospital" for insane or deviant persons, represented by Bedlam and Bicêtre, was in relatively large cities. Indeed, the same movement affected residential care in those areas of the Pacific and Asia that show industrialization similar to that of Western civilization. Institutions exist in Japan, for example, though they have not reached the size of those in the United States (Nihira, personal communication, 1982). Residential schools operated by religious orders can be found in such undeveloped countries as Nepal and developing countries such as Taiwan.

Throughout history, quality of treatment of mentally impaired individuals was tempered by the religious or philosophical bent of society, whether marked by kindness and charity, demonic theory, enlightenment and the egalitarian ideal, Darwinian theory and its consequences, or the ideology of normalization.

Retarded Persons' Own Homes

The principal residence of mentally retarded persons was always and will continue to be their own home and neighborhood. That conclusion may startle readers after all the attention given to institutional development and contemporary clamor for deinstitutionalization. Yet the conclusion is valid. We note that some mentally impaired persons lived only short lives, and others historically were killed or exposed to death because they could not be tolerated or because the local law required it. Otherwise, the scattered information in pre-Itard history indicates that if mentally impaired persons lived, they lived at home or in the extended family and occasionally in the whole solicitous village, perhaps becoming beggars. A few were treated as saints; some others joined the ruling court as jesters or "fools," though we doubt that court fools who had to amuse the courtiers could have been too mentally retarded. The cross-cultural information about current undeveloped societies provides a similar picture: If permitted to live, the person lives at home.

But what of our own time in the United States? At its height around 1967, the institutionalized population did not reach 200,000 in the United States (a few more individuals who carried the retardation diagnosis probably also could have been found in hospitals for mentally ill persons, prisons, and nursing homes). If one assumes that from 1 to 3% of the population is mentally impaired, the 200,000 in custodial care is proportionally tiny and decreasing steadily. The majority of mentally retarded people live, as they have in the past, with their own families.

REFERENCES

Abt, I. (1965). *History of pediatrics*. Philadelphia: Saunders.

Baumeister, A. A. (1970). The American residential institution: Its history and character. In A. A. Baumeister & E. Butterfield (Eds.), *Residential facilities for the mentally retarded*. Chicago: Aldine.

Blacher, J., & Dixon, M. B. (1982). A history of the handicapped on stage. *Journal of Special Education, 16*(1), 21–35.

Borthwick, S., Meyers, C. E., & Eyman, R. K. (1981). Comparative adaptive and maladaptive behavior of mentally retarded clients of five residential settings in three Western states. In R. H. Bruininks, C. E. Meyers, B. B. Sigford, & K. C. Lakin (Eds.), *Deinstitutionalization and community adjustment of mentally retarded people* (Monograph No. 4). Washington, DC: American Association on Mental Deficiency.

Bremner, R. H. (Ed.). (1974). *Care of handicapped children*. New York: Arno.

Burdett, H. (1891). *Hospitals and asylums of the world*. London: Churchill.

Caplan, R. (1969). *Psychiatry and the community in nineteenth century America*. New York: Basic Books.

Cutter, J. B. (1932). *Report of medical superintendent of Pacific Colony*. California State Department of Institutions, 58-66.

Doll, E. (1962). A historical survey of research and management of mental retardation in the United States. In E. P. Trapp & P. Himmelstem (Eds.), *Readings on the exceptional child: Research and theory.* New York: Appleton-Century-Crofts.

Edgerton, R. B. (1968). Anthropology and mental retardation: A plea for the comparative study of incompetence. In H. J. Prehm, L. A. Hamerlynck, & J. E. Crosson (Eds.), *Behavioral research in mental retardation.* Eugene, OR: University of Oregon.

Edgerton, R. B. (1970). Mental retardation in non-Western societies: Toward a cross-cultural perspective on incompetence. In H. C. Haywood (Ed.), *Social-cultural aspects of mental retardation.* (Proceedings of the Peabody-NIMH Conference). New York: Appleton-Century-Crofts.

Edgerton, R. B. (1981). Another look at culture and mental retardation. In M. J. Begab, H. C. Haywood, & H. B. Garber (Eds.), *Psychosocial influence in retarded performance* (Vol. 1). Baltimore: University Park Press.

Encyclopedia Judaica, Vol. 2. (1971). Jerusalem: Keter.

Fenton, N. (1932). The Pacific Colony Plan. *Journal of Juvenile Research, 16,* 298–303.

Fernald, W. E. (1974). The history of the treatment of the feeble-minded. In R. H. Bremner (Ed.), *Care of handicapped children.* New York: Arno. (Reprinted Proceedings of the National Conference of Charities and Corrections, Vol. 20, Boston, 1893).

Flynn, R. J., & Nitsch, K. E. (1980). *Normalization, social integration, and community services.* Baltimore: University Park Press.

Grob, G. N. (1966). The state mental hospital in mid-nineteenth century America: A social analysis. *American Psychologist, 21,* 510–523.

Haskell, R. H. (1944). Mental deficiency over one hundred years. *American Journal of Psychiatry, 100,* 107–118.

Henry, G. W. (1941). Mental hospitals. In G. H. Zilboorg (Ed.), *A history of medical psychology.* New York: Norton.

Hughes, T. P. (1885). *Dictionary of Islam.* London: Allen.

Intagliata, J., Crosby, N., & Neider, L. (1981). Foster family care for mentally retarded people: A qualitative review. In R. H. Bruininks, C. E. Meyers, B. B. Sigford, & K. C. Lakin (Eds.), *Deinstitutionalization and community adjustment of mentally retarded people* (Monograph No. 5). Washington, DC: American Association on Mental Deficiency.

Kanner, L. (1967). *A history of the care and study of the mentally retarded.* Springfield, IL: Thomas.

Lakin, K. C., Bruininks, R. H., & Sigford, B. B. (1981). Early perspectives on the community adjustment of mentally retarded people. In R. H. Bruininks, C. E. Meyers, B. B. Sigford, & K. C. Lakin (Eds.), *Deinstitutionalization and community adjustment of mentally retarded people* (Monograph No. 5) (pp. 28-50). Washington, DC: American Association on Mental Deficiency.

Landis, C., & Page, J. D. (1938). *Modern society and mental disease.* New York: Farrar & Rinehart.

Masland, R. L., Sarason, S. B., & Gladwin, T. (1958). *Mental subnormality: Biological, psychological, and cultural factors.* New York: Basic Books.

Price-Williams, D. (1981). *A cultural approach to metacognition.* ERIC Document 210, 930.

Rosen, M., Clark, G. R., & Kivitz, M. S. (Eds.). (1976). *The history of mental retardation. Collected papers.* Baltimore: University Park Press.

Scheerenberger, R. D. (1982). Treatment from ancient time to the present. In P. T.

Cegelka & H. J. Prehm (Eds.), *Mental retardation: From categories to people.* Columbus, OH: Merrill.

Scheerenberger, R. C. (1983). *A history of mental retardation.* Baltimore: Brookes.

Vaux, C. L. (1935). Family care of mental defectives. *American Association on Mental Deficiency Proceedings, 40,* 168–189.

Wallin, J. E. W. (1955). *Education of mentally handicapped children.* New York: Harper.

White, W. D., & Wolfensberger, W. P. (1969). The evolution of dehumanization in our institutions. *Mental Retardation, 7*(3), 5–9.

Wober, M. (1975). *Psychology in Africa.* London: International African Institute.

Zilboorg, G. A. (1941). *A history of medical psychology.* New York: Norton.

2
Epidemiology of Mental Retardation and Trends in Residential Services in the United States

Robert H. Bruininks, Lisa L. Rotegard,
K. Charlie Lakin, and Bradley K. Hill
University of Minnesota

Although residential care for mentally retarded people consumes approximately five billion dollars annually (almost one half of the federal and state expenditures on mental retardation) (Lakin, Hill, & Bruininks, 1985), less than 5% of the retarded population actually receives such services at any one time. Because of their cost, visibility, and importance, residential care services warrant particular research regarding characteristics of residents, outcomes of habilitative programs and services, and movement of clients within the residential care system. These data provide a necessary link to effective service-delivery strategies and to scientific analysis of a major component of the mental retardation service system. Gathering such data is complex, in part because deinstitutionalization is associated with an increasingly decentralized, privately operated service system.

EPIDEMIOLOGY OF MENTAL RETARDATION

The 1980 United States Census estimated a national population of 227 million persons. The actual prevalence of mental retardation is not known, but authorities judge that about 1% of the population is labeled "mentally

Acknowledgements. Some material in this chapter is included in a technical report by Lakin, Bruininks, Doth, Hill & Hauber (1982). Preparation of this manuscript was supported in part by Grant No. 18-D-9087815-01 from the Health Care Financing Administration of the Department of Health and Human Services.

retarded" at a given time (Birch, Richardson, Baird, Horobin, & Illsley, 1970; Dingman & Tarjan, 1960; Farber, 1968; MacMillan, 1977; Mercer, 1973b; Tarjan, Wright, Eyman, & Keeran, 1973), whereas 2.27% may be so labeled during some period in their life (Haring, 1978; President's Committee on Mental Retardation, 1970). The Office of Special Education indicates that 1.8% of the 1980–1981 school age population was mentally retarded (National Center for Educational Statistics, 1982).

Several surveys of actual identified or certified cases of mental retardation, based on a clinical or subjective assessment of persons' adaptive behavior, have produced incidence rates only one half the rates estimated statistically (Dingman & Tarjan, 1960; Granat & Granat, 1973; Mercer, 1973b). Interestingly, actual prevalence rates of mental retardation reveal an excess of 400% in the profoundly retarded range and 125% in the moderately to severely retarded range (Dingman & Tarjan, 1960). Unlike mild retardation, this incidence of moderate to profound retardation is approximately the same across all socioeconomic strata and geographic areas (Abramowicz & Richardson, 1975).

DESCRIPTIVE STATISTICS ON RESIDENTIAL SERVICES

Since the United States Census of 1880, national studies of mentally retarded people in publicly operated facilities have been conducted. Most available data summarized trends in populations and programs in public facilities, with some recent attention given to describing the expansion of privately operated residential services (Lakin, 1979).

The recent increase in privately operated residences coincides with a dramatic change in social philosophy toward providing services to retarded citizens. The President's Panel on Mental Retardation in 1963 and the National Association of Superintendents of Public Residential Facilities for the Mentally Retarded (1974) have endorsed a deinstitutionalization policy comprised of three related aspects: (a) preventing admission to large public residential facilities by developing alternative community methods of care and training; (b) releasing all institutional residents who are prepared to function successfully in appropriate community settings; and (c) establishing and maintaining responsive residential environments that protect human and civil rights.

Since the first mental retardation institution in the United States opened in 1848, public residential facilities steadily grew in resident population through 1967. Fiscal year 1967–1968 saw the first drop in the average daily population, from 194,650 to 194,000 (Butterfield, 1976; Lakin, 1979); to 148,752 a decade later (Butterfield, 1976; Krantz, Bruininks, & Clumpner, 1979). Figure 1 shows the annual decrements subsequently (Lakin, 1979; Lakin, Krantz, Bruininks, Clumpner, & Hill, 1982; Scheerenberger, 1982).

Interestingly, the population of public institutions for mentally ill people peaked in 1955, and 20 years later had decreased 65% to 193,436 (Division of Biometry and Epidemiology, 1979). In 1976, 18,266 or 10.7% of the patients in mental health hospitals had a primary diagnosis of mental retardation (Division of Biometry and Epidemiology, 1978), whereas another 15.6% had mental retardation as a secondary handicap (President's Committee on Mental Retardation, 1981). The number of mentally retarded people in state and county mental hospitals peaked at about 40,000 in 1959. Based on 1980 and other data, an estimated 10,600 mentally retarded people presently reside in general state and county mental hospitals (Krantz, Bruininks, & Clumpner, 1980; Lakin, Bruininks, Doth, Hill, & Hauber, 1982).

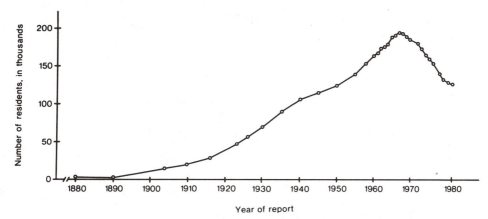

FIGURE 1.   Total population of mentally retarded people in public institutions (1880–1981). *Note.* From "One Hundred Years of Data on Populations of Public Residential Facilities for Mentally Retarded People" by K. C. Lakin, G. C. Krantz, R. H. Bruininks, J. L. Clumpner, and B. K. Hill, 1982, *American Journal of Mental Deficiency, 87,* 4. (Reprinted by permission.) Data also taken from Lakin (1979), Lakin et al. (1982), and Scheerenberger (1982).

Nursing homes have been used extensively in some states as major sources of placement for mentally retarded people. The National Center of Health Statistics' 1977 survey of nursing homes indicated that about 60% (48,000) of 79,000 mentally retarded nursing home residents were placed primarily because of their mental retardation rather than specific physical or health needs (National Center for Health Statistics, 1979). Although trend data are difficult to derive, the Center for Residential and Community Services conducted national surveys from 1977 and 1980 suggesting that nursing home placements for mentally retarded people declined between those years (Lakin, Bruininks, Doth, Hill, & Hauber, 1982).

In recent years, community-based residential services have increased in number and type. At least 40 different terms describe community residences for mentally retarded people (Developmental Disabilities Project, 1978). From 1969 to 1977, the number of privately managed community-based facilities increased five-fold to serve nearly three times as many individuals—from 24,355 to 62,397 (Bruininks, Hauber, & Kudla, 1979; Office of Mental Retardation Coordination, 1972). As Figure 2 shows, this means that the average number of residents per facility has decreased; also, the proportion of retarded residents in each facility has increased. As Figure 3 shows, nonprofit facilities increased from less than one third of all private facilities in 1967 to well over half by 1977.

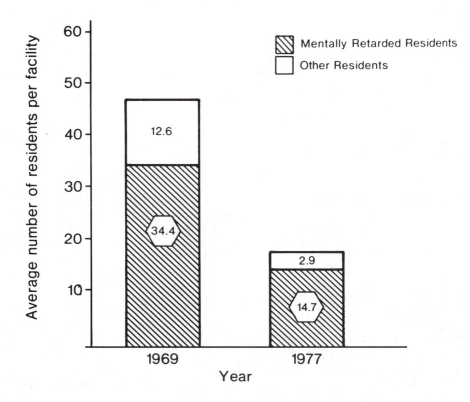

FIGURE 2.   Average number of residents in private residential facilities licensed for mentally retarded residents (1969 and 1977). *Note.* Data source, *Mental Retardation Source Book* by Office of Mental Retardation Coordination, 1972, U.S. Department of Health, Education, and Welfare.

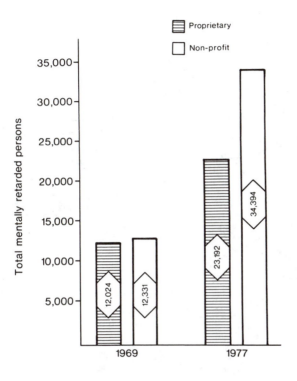

FIGURE 3. **Total mentally retarded residents in private proprietary and nonprofit facilities (1969 and 1977). *Note.* Data source, *Mental Retardation Source Book* by Office of Mental Retardation Coordination, 1972, U.S. Department of Health, Education, and Welfare and Bruininks et al. (1979).**

Another expanding type of residence is the specially licensed foster home. In addition to regular foster care licenses, providers of these homes are specially licensed or contracted by states or regions to provide residential and habilitative services to developmentally disabled people. A 1977 national survey of specially licensed foster care providers reported that 20 states operated 5,000 such specially licensed foster care homes (Bruininks, Hill, & Thorsheim, 1982). Twenty-six percent of the foster homes had been operating fewer than 18 months, whereas 44% had been providing foster care for 30 or fewer months (Bruininks, Hill, & Thorsheim 1982). Based on data from the Center for Residential and Community Services, we estimate an approximate 80% increase in foster residents between 1977 to 1980. Figure 4 summarizes all of these trends.

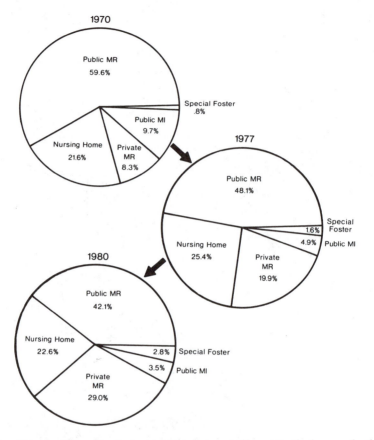

FIGURE 4. **Proportion of placements of mentally retarded people by facility type from 1970 to 1980. MR = mental retardation facility, MI = mental illness facility.** *Note.* **Data from Lakin, Bruininks, Doth, Hill, and Hauber (1982).**

An important factor in evaluating statistics on residential services is the change in the placement rates per 100,000 of the general population (see Figure 5). From 1970 to 1980, the placement rate number for mentally retarded persons decreased from 152.8 (105.9 in public institutions for mentally ill and mentally retarded individuals and 46.9 in other licensed residential facilities) to 136.8 (62.3 in institutions for mentally ill and mentally retarded people and 74.5 in other licensed facilities). These numbers reflect two factors: an approximate 10% increase in the total United States population and a general stability in the number of mentally retarded people in full-time, supervised residential settings (Lakin, Krantz, Bruininks, Clumpner, & Hill, 1982).

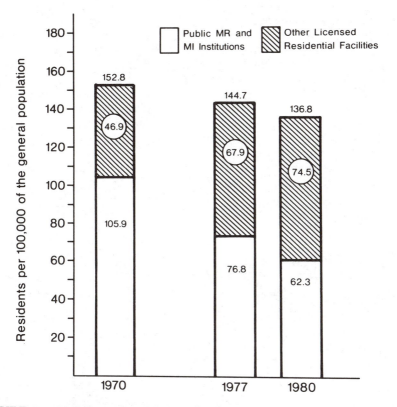

FIGURE 5. **Number of mentally retarded people in residential services systems per 100,000 general population, 1970, 1977, and 1980 (estimated).** *Note.* **Data from Lakin, Bruininks, Doth, Hill, and Hauber (1982).**

Data gathered from a national probability sample of residents in public and private residential facilities show that the average and median age at first admission to residential facilities rose significantly in the 1970s (Lakin, Hill, Hauber, & Bruininks, 1982). In 1967, people entering the residential care system averaged 13 years of age, with a median age of about 11 years. By 1976 through 1978, the mean age of first admissions rose to 18 years, and the median was 16 years. Direct causation cannot be confirmed for these trends, although the growth of education, training, and community and family-oriented community support programs undoubtedly contributed to these changes. When data are dichotomized into child (under 20 years old) versus adult admissions, the changing pattern is evidenced further. In the 1950s and 1960s, the percentage of children remained quite stable, from 83% to 89%. In the 1970s, however, that percentage dropped, so that by 1976 through 1978, only 65% of the first admissions were children (Lakin, Hill, Hauber, & Bruininks, 1982).

Only a small percentage of the mentally retarded population lives in licensed residential care settings, and the projected number of 314,000 in such settings clearly underestimates out-of-home placements. Many thousands more live in generic settings, notably boarding homes and regular foster homes. Estimates based upon prevalence figures cited earlier lead to the conclusion that from *6 to 15% of all mentally retarded people live in some form of supervised residential setting.* Increasingly, those settings are smaller, better staffed, and more likely to be privately operated than they had been in earlier decades. Even conservative projections indicated at least 85% of retarded individuals live with family members or in semi-independent or independent situations.

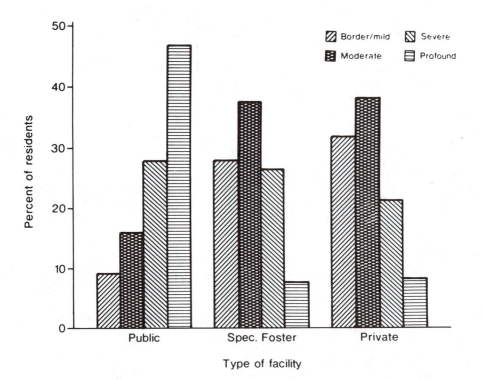

FIGURE 6. **Level of retardation of three modes of residential care for mentally retarded people in 1977.**

CHARACTERISTICS OF RESIDENTS AND SERVICES

Level of Retardation, Ability, Age, and Gender

Not unexpectedly, disproportionately more severely and profoundly retarded individuals receive out-of-home residential care. Figure 6 presents information on the average level of retardation of residents living in three models of residential care from national surveys conducted in 1977 (Bruininks, Hauber, & Kudla, 1979; Bruininks, Hill, & Thorsheim, 1982; Scheerenberger, 1978b). People residing in public institutions tended to be rated as more severely handicapped than those living in either private facilities or specially licensed foster homes. In 1977, about three fourths of the public institution residents were severely or profoundly retarded whereas nearly one third of the residents of both private and foster care facilities functioned at these levels. Clearly, the characteristics of residents overlap across different types of facilities, although the proportion of certain types of residents in diverse programs may differ. These trends have been maintained in later surveys (Hill, Bruininks, & Lakin, 1983).

Figure 7 further indicates a doubling of the proportion of profoundly retarded residents in public facilities since 1965, a finding with implications for treatment, services, and costs of providing future care.

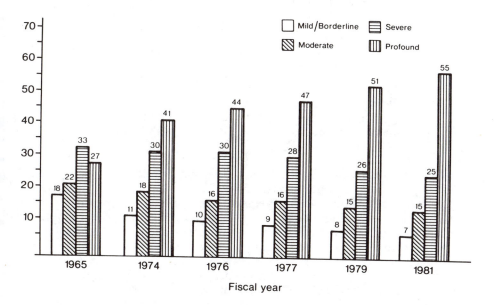

FIGURE 7.   Percentage of residents in public institutions by level of retardation (1965 through 1981).

Figure 8 presents the rated performance on selected adaptive behavior items by over 2,000 residents of public and private facilities collected in a 1978–1979 survey (Hill, et. al., 1983). As expected, residents in private facilities generally performed at higher levels than did residents of public institutions.

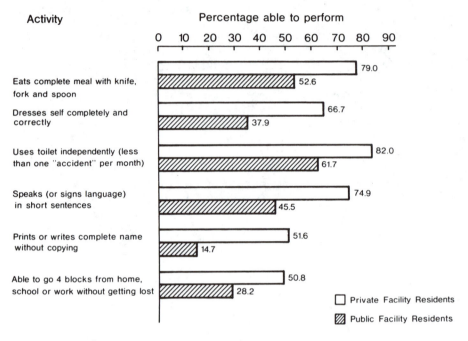

FIGURE 8. **Percentage of public and private facility residents able to perform specific daily activities (1978–1979). *Note.* Data from Lakin, Bruininks, Doth, Hill, and Hauber (1982).**

In 1980, the median age in the United States increased to 30 years, with only 22.5% of the population under 15 and 11.3% over 65 (U.S. Bureau of the Census, 1981). Similarly, the average age of mentally retarded persons in residential care facilities has increased. Besides the general demographic trend, this reflects the higher average age when such individuals enter residential care. The largest percentage of residents in both public and private facilities was between 22 and 39 years of age. Interestingly, there are some very young children in public facilities, with 15% of new admissions under 11 years of age (Lakin, Hill, Sigford, Bruininks, & Heal, 1982) and likely to be transferred to alternative, community settings. Whereas 0.5% of all institutionalized residents in 1979 were in the birth to 4-year range, 1.0% of all releases in 1978 were age birth to 4 years (Best-Sigford, Bruininks, Lakin, Hill, & Heal, 1982).

The prevalence of mental retardation is higher among males than females (Farber, 1968; Mumpower, 1970; Singer, Westphal, & Niswander, 1968). Relevant to more severe retardation, sex-linked recessive syndromes are more likely to occur in males. Also, because society has had different expectations and socialization practices for boys and girls, active and inattentive boys have been likely to be labeled "mildly retarded" during school years. Mercer (1973a) reported that girls must be slower intellectually than were boys to be placed in special education, suggesting more tolerance of lower intellectual ability in girls. Males historically have comprised the majority in public and private residential facilities: nationwide, 56% of all residents were male (Bruininks, Hauber, & Kudla, 1979). An exception occurred in specially licensed foster care, however, with females representing 54% of the population (Bruininks et. al., 1982). The percentage of males in public institutions increased from 54% in 1976 to 65% in 1981 (Scheerenberger, 1978b, 1982), even though males comprised only 49% of the total 1981 United States population (U.S. Bureau of the Census, 1981).

Concerning ethnic distribution, blacks in residential care (12%) are proportionate to their national representation (U.S. Bureau of the Census, 1981). Slightly higher percentages of blacks receive public compared to private residential care. Blacks appear disproportionately among admissions to public institutions, making up 21% percent of a newly admitted sample (Lakin, Hill, Sigford, Bruininks, & Heal, 1982). In contrast, retarded people of Hispanic, Native American, Native Alaskan, and Pacific Islander origin were underrepresented among new admissions.

Additional Physical and Health Disorders

Mental retardation is often accompanied by physically handicapping conditions (Hardman & Drew, 1977), limited motor skills (Bruininks, 1974), or health problems (Nelson & Crocker, 1978; Smith, Decker, Herberg, & Rupke, 1969). Earlier surveys of the health characteristics of retarded people in public institutions indicated higher incidence of medical problems (Wright, Valen, & Tarjan, 1962) and higher mortality rates compared to those for the general population (Balakrishnan & Wolf, 1976; Forssman & Akesson, 1970; Tarjan, Wright, Eyman, & Keeran, 1973; Wright et. al., 1962). Although physical handicaps and health-related problems clearly are not the reasons for most initial placements (Maney, Pace, & Morrison, 1964; Saenger, 1960), they are cited as reasons for reinstitutionalization of released residents (Keys, Boroskin, & Ross, 1973; Pagel & Whitling, 1978).

In our 1978-1979 national probability sample of facilities and residents, we found that more than 50% of the residents in private and public settings had some handicap in addition to their mental retardation (Hill et al., 1983). Overall, 60% of public facility residents and 44% of private facility residents had some secondary handicaps. Seizure disorders were the most common, with 36% of public facility residents and 21% of private facility residents receiving anticonvulsive medication. In addition, 15% of public facility residents and 11% of private facility residents reported a physical handicap. Scheerenberger (1978b, 1981) reported that individuals having two or more handicaps made up 33% of the publicly institutionalized population, with 44% of this group profoundly retarded and 29% severely retarded.

Approximately 20% of residents in both private and public facilities had some chronic health disorder (Hill et al., 1983). As with the general population (American Heart Association, 1982), the most common category of chronic health problems involved circulatory system disorders found among 7 to 8% of private and public facility residents, respectively.

Maladaptive Behavior

Although the number of first admissions to public facilities has decreased, the numbers of readmissions has increased (Conroy, 1977) to approximately equal the rate of new admissions (Krantz et al., 1979, 1980; Krantz, Clumpner, Rotegard, & Bruininks, 1982; Scheerenberger, 1978b, 1979, 1982). Behavior problems appear paramount in both new admissions and readmissions (Sternlicht & Deutsch, 1972; Windle, 1962). Next to severity of retardation, behavior problems probably are the single most important variable influencing placement in an institution (Eyman & Borthwick, 1980; Eyman, Borthwick, & Miller, 1981; Maney et al., 1964; Saenger, 1960; Spencer, 1976). In Minnesota, 8 of every 10 initial admissions were attributed to specific behavior problems.

Goroff (1967) found that the majority of critical behavioral incidents precipitating reinstitutionalization could be classified as "status offenses," that is, not severe enough to elicit similar penalties if performed by a nonretarded adult. Nihira and Nihira (1975) reported that only 16% of over 1,200 problem behavior incidents among 424 residents in community facilities were severe enough to jeopardize the health, safety, general welfare, or legal status of residents.

Over the past 15 years, government agencies and consumer and advocacy organizations have outlined a "minimum constellation of services" needed by developmentally disabled people (e.g., Accreditation Council, 1973; Galloway, 1974; President's Committee on Mental Retardation, 1976). The four areas are (a) health-related services (minimally, dental and medical care); (b) social, psychological, and rehabilitative therapies (minimally, counseling, physical therapy, occupational therapy, and speech therapy); (c) social and recreational programs outside the primary residence; and (d) transportation services. In a national survey of about 2,300 mentally retarded residents, Hill, Lakin, Sigford, Hauber, and Bruininks (1982) reported that medical services were provided nearly universally to residents of both private and public facilities. Residents probably receive more regular dental care (83 to 95% had seen a dentist in the past year) than the general population does. Medically related services are available to and utilized by mentally retarded people in the community, a finding corroborated by others (Gollay, Freedman, Wyngaarden, & Kurtz, 1978; Intagliata, Willer, & Cooley, 1979; Justice, Bradley, & O'Connor, 1971; Landesman-Dwyer & Butterfield, 1983; Landesman-Dwyer & Mai-Dalton, 1981; Willer & Intagliata, 1980).

Social, psychological, and rehabilitative therapies are generally provided to facility residents less universally than are health services (Hill, Lakin, Sigford, Hauber, & Bruininks, 1982; Landesman-Dwyer & Mai-Dalton, 1981). Residents in private facilities are more likely than are those in public residences to participate in planned social and recreational activities (61% vs. 35%) and to use public transportation services (68% vs. 16%). Generally, both private and public facility staff rate outside social and recreational services as the *least* adequately provided of all services for residents of their facilities (Gollay et al., 1978; Hill, Lakin, Sigford, Hauber, & Bruininks, 1982; Landesman-Dwyer & Butterfield, 1983). When primary care providers of a national probability sample of public and private facility residents were asked whether appropriate social/recreational programs existed for their particular client in the surrounding community, only 70% of the private facility care providers and 40% of the public facility care providers said "yes" (Hill, Lakin, Sigford, Hauber, & Bruininks, 1982).

In the past few years, a number of investigators have assessed therapeutic services available to, and utilized by, residents of public and private facilities (Butler, Bjaanes, & Horacre, 1975; Gollay, Freedman, Wyngaarden, & Kurtz, 1978; Hill, Lakin, Sigford, Hauber, & Bruininks, 1982; Landesman-Dwyer & Mai-Dalton, 1981; Landesman-Dwyer, Stein, & Sackett, 1976). Speech therapy is the most consistently available and utilized service used by mentally retarded people in residential care. Counseling, skills training, and physical and occupational therapies are available to most community residents who need such services. Concerning *frequency* of use of therapeutic services, about 20% of private facility residents take part in formal counseling sessions, with over 80% of these individuals receiving only one or fewer sessions per week. Furthermore, the *duration* of counseling was less than one year per resident, indicating that mere service availability does *not* lead to inappropriate or excessive levels of utilization.

Day Programs

In the normal rhythm of American life, physically healthy persons not fully occupied with domestic tasks leave their homes for some part of the day to participate in socially and/or personally beneficial activities. As legislators, advocates, and services providers have sought to "normalize" the lives of mentally retarded people, they have realized that an important part of this process is providing daily opportunities for residents to engage in creating, learning, and improving skills. Examples of increased attention to the developmental program needs of handicapped persons include the guaranteed inclusion of children in education programs no matter how severe their developmental impairment, the tripling of the sheltered work-shop placement between 1969 and 1977, and the near 4-fold growth in the number of adult day activity center placements (Bellamy, Sheehan, Horner, & Boles, 1980; Cortazzo, 1972; Lakin, Hill, Sigford, Bruininks, & Heal, 1982; Office of Mental Retardation, 1972). These programs are a cornerstone to efforts to depopulate large, publicly operated institutions, to prevent initial admission to such facilities, and to provide at least minimally adequate habilitation programs to persons who still remain institutionalized.

Figure 9 shows the use of day programs by mentally retarded people in residential care. In private facilities, about one third of the residents attend a work-related placement, nearly another third go to school, and one fifth participate in day activity centers. In public facilities, significantly fewer are engaged in these activities. Twelve percent of private facility residents and 28% of public facility residents did not participate in any formal day programs, a discouragingly large percentage.

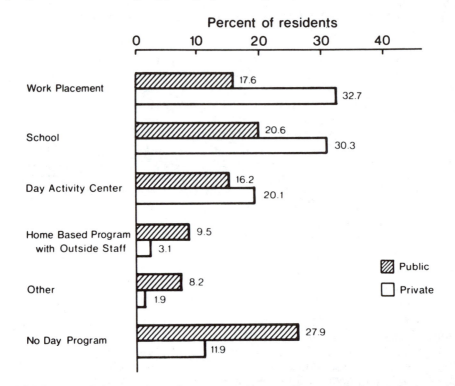

FIGURE 9. **Primary day placement of mentally retarded people in private and public residential facilities (1978–1979 national probability sample).** *Note.* **Data from Hill et al. (1982).**

Leisure Activities and Family Contact

It is often the case that leisure, family, and social activities are not viewed as priorities by program administrators or regulations that focus on physical and habilitative aspects. The quality of life within residential facilities is reflected partially in the nature and amount of interactions among residents and the members of the surrounding community, as well as in the opportunities to participate in rewarding leisure activities. Personal development of a repertoire of appropriate leisure activities is difficult for many mentally retarded people because of architectural or transportation barriers, a lack of structured programs for teaching leisure activities, and not enough suitable companions. Consequently, much free time is spent in activities that do not require interaction, such as watching TV, playing a radio or phonograph, or doing nothing (Bjaanes & Butler, 1974; Katz & Yekutiel, 1974; Landesman-Dwyer, 1984; Wehman, 1977).

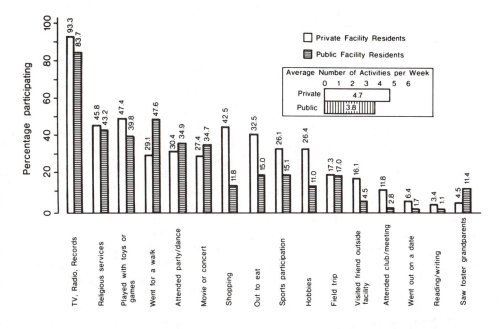

FIGURE 10. Leisure activities of private and public facility residents during a one-week period. *Note.* Data from Hill and Bruininks (1981).

Hill and Bruininks (1981) found that residents of private and public facilities generally participate in a wide variety of activities. Figure 10 represents the leisure activities of over 2,000 residents during a one-week period. The "average" resident participated in four or five different leisure activities during this period. Not unexpectedly, the most common leisure activity for both private and public facility residents was passive: watching television and/or listening to the radio or stereo. Other common activities for all residents were shopping; attending religious services, parties, or dances; playing with toys; or walking.

Providing opportunities for mentally retarded people to maintain some contact with natural families is considered important. Hill and Bruininks (1981) found that 66% of residents in private facilities, compared to 53% in public facilities, maintained some contact with their parents, although the percentages were higher when including any relative (84% and 69%, respectively). The frequency of contact with family members varied considerably, although most residents visited with relatives less than once a month. As expected, family characteristics (e.g., occupational level of father, no required maintenance payments to the facility, parental custody, and marital status) were correlated with family visitation patterns. In fact, Anderson, Schlottmann, and Weiner (1975) found that family characteristics were more important than resident characteristics (e.g., physical anomalies, high disparity between chronological age and social maturity) in predicting parental visitation patterns.

RESIDENT MOVEMENT

The residential services system always has been a dynamic system, but the rates of movement have been stimulated tremendously by deinstitutionalization. Public institutional care is provided to fewer individuals than at any time since 1950, with the 1981 number of public residents per 100,000 general United States population (56.5) being the lowest since 1930, compared to its high point of 99.0/100,000 in 1967 (Lakin, 1979; Scheerenberger, 1982). The number of discharges per 100 first admissions rose from an average of 61 in the 3-year period from 1963 to 1965 to an average of 283 in the period from 1978 to 1980 (Lakin, 1979; Krantz et al., 1979, 1980; Krantz et al., 1982). In the period from 1963 to 1965, there were 21.4 institution residents for every released resident. By the period from 1978 to 1980, there were only 9.0 institution residents for each released resident (Lakin, 1979; Krantz, et al., 1979; 1980; Krantz et al., 1982). Rates of new admissions to public institutions also have changed significantly. In the 5-year period between 1975/1976 and 1980/1981, new admissions to public institutions decreased a full 33% (Scheerenberger, 1977, 1982).

Changes in the residential services system are dependent in part on the number and characteristics of mentally retarded people served. In 1977, individuals newly admitted to both private and public facilities were most likely to be transfer residents from public institutions (35% and 49%, respectively), although many moved directly from their family homes (32% and 40%, respectively) (Bruininks et al., 1979; Scheerenberger,

1978b). Notably, in 1977, nearly half of the residents moving into public institutions were *transfers* from other public institutions. Since then, the number of transfer admissions to public facilities dropped to 30% in 1979 and 37% in 1981 (Scheerenberger, 1979, 1982).

Another important facet in understanding national trends in resident movement is the *new* place of residence for releases from residential facilities (see Figure 11). Most 1977 releases from both private and public facilities were to natural homes (25% and 27%, respectively) or private residential facilities (22% and 30%, respectively). Public institutions received about 40% of their 1977 new admissions from private facilities; they released about 30% of their total discharges to such facilities.

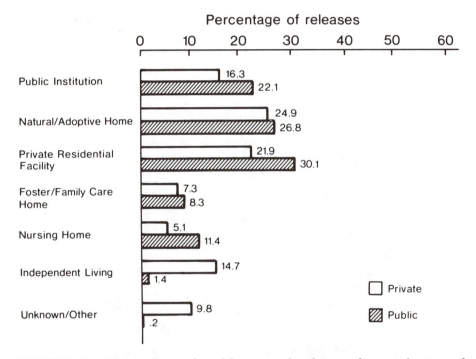

FIGURE 11. **New place of residence and releases from private and public residential facilities for mentally retarded people in 1977.** *Note.* **Data from Bruininks et al. (1979), Krantz et al. (1982), Lakin (1979), and Scheerenberger (1978b, 1982).**

In 1978, data were concurrently collected on national probability samples of the general population of public institutions and the three major movement categories: released residents, new admissions, and readmissions (Best-Sigford et al., 1982; Lakin, Hill, Sigford, Bruininks, & Heal, 1982). Residents in all movement categories were more intelligent than

those in institutions: 27% to 28% of the released and readmitted populations, respectively, had mild retardation compared to 9% of the general
institutionalized population. Newly admitted residents were somewhat
more severely retarded when the released and readmitted residents, but
still less handicapped than others in the institutions.

Data collected from state statistical offices on deaths, discharges, readmissions, and new admissions to state institutions for fiscal years 1978 to
1980 show that the most stable movement categories were deaths and new
admissions; the most fluctuating were discharges and readmissions. These
rates are shown for the years 1978 through 1980 in Figure 12. Careful
examination reveals that changes in institutional population suggested by
these data are not in complete agreement with the total institution population reported by the same agencies, *a problem that has been evident in resident
movement data since they were first collected in 1923* (Lakin, 1979).

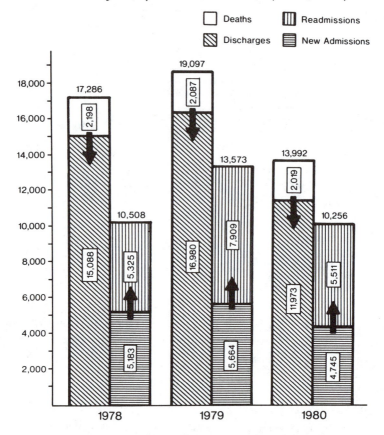

FIGURE 12.   **Changes in resident population of state institutions from
             1978 through 1980.** *Note.* **Data from Krantz et al. (1979,
             1980, 1982) and Lakin (1979).**

Between 1978 and 1980, the institutional mortality rate was stable, between 15.5 and 15.9 deaths per 1,000, which indicates a decline from 18.7 in 1975, 19.1 in 1965, 21.8 in 1945, and 40.2 in 1925 (Lakin, Krantz, Bruininks, Clumpner, & Hill, 1982). What makes this decrease striking is that profoundly retarded people comprised an ever greater proportion of the institutional populations over this time period, and their multiple health problems placed them at a higher than average risk for early death (Miller, 1975; Scheerenberger, 1975, 1977, 1982).

The 1981 data on deinstitutionalization for 9,464 mentally retarded people (179 state residential facilities) show that 68% were discharged to facilities reasonably assumed to be less restrictive. The most frequently used community placements were: group homes (23.5%), natural/adoptive homes (19%), and private Intermediate Care Facilities for the Mentally Retarded (14%). Remarkably, 26% of those "discharged" were merely transferred to other state institutions. These data indicate a decline in return of individuals to the homes of their relatives or to nursing homes (24.5% and 17%, respectively, in 1976).

The data on resident movement in private residential facilities are less extensive. In 1980, we conducted a one-year follow-up of 1,953 members of a national probability sample of 2,271. We found 256 residents (13.3%) no longer at the same facility, indicating higher resident movement rates in these private facilities than in public institutions. Of the surviving private facility residents, 17.2% compared to 9.9% of those in the public facility sample, moved elsewhere within one year. Of these, 7.1% of the private facility sample and 4.5% of the public facility sample were discharged to foster care, boarding care, or a group home; 4.2% percent of the private facility sample and 2.4% of the public facility sample went to a natural or adoptive home (Lakin, Bruininks, Doth, Hill, & Hauber, 1982).

According to administrators, the primary reason for release was the judgment that residents were prepared for a "less restrictive" setting and/or had completed their training program (29% and 37% for private and public facility discharges, respectively). A parent or resident-initiated request to move was the second most common reason (28% and 26%, respectively). Among private facilities there was a relatively high proportion (23%) of releases for mere administrative reasons (e.g., residents had reached maximum age for the facility's license, the facility had closed or moved).

CONCLUDING STATEMENT

In the past 2 decades, vast changes have occurred in the provision of residential care for mentally retarded citizens. The trends toward increased diversity in residential settings, smaller scale living arrangements, and greater attempts at community social and service integration is evident in recent statistics on licensed facilities and residents. The resident census in state-operated institutions for mentally retarded people has declined approximately 35% from a peak enrollment in the mid-1960s. Concomitant with this change has been rapid increase in number of smaller, mostly privately operated community-based family care homes and group facilities. In fact, the size of facilities in both the public and private sectors has significantly declined in recent years: public institutions dropped from an average of 1,516 residents in 1960 to 549 in 1980 (Lakin, Krantz, Bruininks, Clumpner, & Hill, 1982), whereas private facilities dropped from an average of 47 residents in 1969 to 17 in 1977 (Lakin, Bruininks, Doth, Hill, & Hauber, 1982). Our national study of residential care for mentally retarded people at the Center for Residential and Community Services, University of Minnesota, confirms the continuation of this trend toward smaller and more diverse living arrangements.

Despite the changing pattern of residential services in the United States and other western societies, the increased diversity, attractiveness, and apparent availability of services in the 1970s apparently has not resulted in greater proportions of retarded citizens being placed in licensed care arrangements. The relative number of retarded people in licensed residential care arrangements has actually decreased in the past decade according to all available statistics, from about 153 to about 137 per 100,000 of the general population. This decrease occurred during a period in which the national population base expanded by about 10%. It is doubtful that this decrease can be explained wholly by the difficulty of counting persons in less formally licensed care arrangements, changes in definitions, or treatment advances. The "woodwork" phenomenon of increasing numbers of out-of-home placements of retarded citizens, expected by many to accompany the creation of more attractive community-based residential alternatives, apparently has not materialized. Quite clearly, the extent to which the development of more palatable alternatives to institutions may have tacitly encouraged the out-of-home placement of retarded people has been more than compensated by programs, services, and attitudes that have encouraged families to keep their mentally retarded children at home or to assist their adult children in living independently.

Public and private facilities have important differences besides their size, location, and ownership. Generally, public facilities constitute the primary non-family placement for severely and profoundly retarded individuals, whereas private facilities increasingly serve more mildly and moderately retarded clients. In addition, public facility residents tend to display a proportionately higher rate of more severe behavior disorders, especially residents who are new admissions and readmissions to these facilities. These observations contain important implications both for planning residential environments and for conducting research that explores the impact of environments on human development. It is clear that deinstitutionalization will continue only to the extent that successful models of care for severely and profoundly retarded people and those with severe behavior disorders can be designed, implemented, and monitored. There are already many thousands of severely and profoundly retarded people in community-based placements. This fact allows us the opportunity to observe systematically what is already in operation. Our knowledge of the characteristics of effective treatment environments for severely and profoundly retarded people is only in an emergent state of development. Our sophistication in assessing behavior change in more severely handicapped people is likewise underdeveloped. Serious study of the effect of the environment on the development of retarded people must address these dual realities of changing residential patterns and the characteristics of residents in different settings.

Despite increased public support for human services in the past 20 years a surprising proportion of retarded people in licensed care facilities apparently receive no active treatment program. Of equal importance is the consistent finding that even in small community-centered facilities, the predominant leisure activities are passive and involve little apparent community integration. Again, many questions arise from these base-rate statistics regarding effects of various environments on friendship networks, community contacts, and the development of basic adaptive skills.

The coverage and attention given to formally licensed residential services within political and professional circles unfortunately obscures other important, and more common, living arrangements of retarded children and adults. Even using the most conservative prevalence estimates for mental retardation, only a small minority, *probably less than 15% of people defined as mentally retarded during their lifetimes*, receive specialized and supervised forms of residential care. Despite vastly increased public support for human services, the overwhelming majority of mentally retarded citizens in the United States live with their families, family surrogates, or on their own. Studies do report that many retarded adults often live marginal economic and social lifestyles (Edgerton, 1967, 1981, 1984; Goldstein, 1964), but many have adjusted well enough to meet basic life needs and social conventions (Bruininks, Meyers, Sigford, & Lakin, 1981; Edgerton, 1984; Edgerton & Bercovici, 1976; Schalock & Harper, 1978.)

The epidemiological facts about where retarded people live raise important questions about the direction of research strategies and public investment. The increased interest in research on the impact of retarded children upon families and the important impact of the family environment upon development, well represented by many of the chapters in this volume, is a promising recent development in the scientific study of mental retardation. At the same time, the large public expenditures that continue to support institutions must be reviewed carefully as to how effective they are in providing needed services for a highly disabled population.

Broad statistical trends, as presented in this chapter, provide a useful and necessary context for planning and evaluating the direction of public policies in residential services for retarded citizens. They can be equally useful in providing some perspective in guiding research on important environmental influences upon human development. The growing body of research exploring the dimensions of the person-environment interactions should serve as an important guide to the formulation and management of public policies. Such knowledge is greatly needed as program planners, policy-makers, and front-line staff seek to improve the rapidly changing system of social, educational, and residential services for mentally retarded citizens and their families.

REFERENCES

Abramowicz, H., & Richardson, S. (1975). Epidemiology of severe mental retardation in children: Community studies. *American Journal of Mental Deficiency, 80,* 18–39.

Accreditation Council for Facilities for the Mentally Retarded. (1973). *Standards for community agencies serving persons with mental retardation and other developmental disabilities.* Chicago: Joint Commission on Accreditation of Hospitals.

American Heart Association. (1982). *Heart facts.* Dallas: American Heart Association.

Anderson, V. H., Schlottmann, R. S., & Weiner, B. J. (1975). Predictors of parent involvement with institutionalized retarded children. *American Journal of Mental Deficiency, 79,* 705–710.

Balakrishnan, T. R., & Wolf, L. C. (1976). Life expectancy of mentally retarded persons in Canadian institutions. *American Journal of Mental Deficiency, 80,* 650–652.

Bellamy, G., Sheehan, M., Horner, R., & Boles, S. (1980). Community programs for severely handicapped adults: An analysis. *Journal of the Association for the Severely Handicapped, 1980, 5,* 307–324.

Best-Sigford, B., Bruininks, R. H., Lakin, K. C., Hill, B. K., & Heal, L. W. (1982). Resident release patterns in a national sample of public residential facilities. *American Journal of Mental Deficiency, 87,* 130–140.

Birch, H. B., Richardson, S. A., Baird, D., Horobin, G., & Illsley, R., (1970). *Mental subnormality in the community: A clinical and epidemiological study.* Baltimore: Williams & Wilkins.

Bjaanes, A. T., & Butler, E. W. (1974). Environmental variation in community care facilities for mentally retarded persons. *American Journal of Mental Deficiency, 78,* 429–439.

Bruininks, R. H. (1974). Physical and motor development of retarded persons. In N. R. Ellis (Ed.), *International review of research in mental retardation* (Vol. 7). New York: Academic.

Bruininks, R. H., Hauber, F. A., & Kudla, M. J., (1979). *National survey of community residential facilities: A profile of facilities and residents in 1977.* Minneapolis: University of Minnesota, Department of Psychoeducational Studies.

Bruininks, R. H., Hill, B. K., & Thorsheim, M. J. (1982). Deinstitutionalization and foster care: A national study. *Journal of Health and Social Work, 7,* 198–205.

Bruininks, R. H., Meyers, C. E., Sigford, B. B., & Lakin K. C. (Eds.). *Deinstitutionalization and community adjustment of mentally retarded people.* Washington, DC: American Association on Mental Deficiency.

Butler, E. W., Bjaanes, A. T., & Horacre, S. (1975, May). *The normalization process and the utilization of community agencies, services and programs by community-care agencies.* Paper presented to the annual meeting of the Academy of Mental Retardation and American Association of Mental Deficiency, Portland, Oregon.

Butterfield, E. (1976). Some basic changes in residential facilities. In R. B. Kugel & A. Shearer (Eds.), *Changing patterns in residential services for the mentally retarded* (rev. ed.). Washington, DC: President's Committee on Mental Retardation.

Conroy, J. W., (1977). Trends in deinstitutionalization of the mentally retarded. *Mental Retardation, 1977, 15*(4), 44–46.

Cortazzo, A. (1972). *Activity centers for retarded adults.* Washington, DC: President's Committee on Mental Retardation.

Developmental Disabilities Project on Residential Services and Community Adjustment. (1978). *Project overview* (Brief #1). Minneapolis: University of Minnesota, Department of Psychoeducational Studies.

Dingman, H. F., & Tarjan, G. (1960). Mental retardation and the normal distribution curve. *American Journal of Mental Deficiency, 64,* 991–994.

Division of Biometry and Epidemiology. (1978). *Additions and resident patients at end of year, state and county mental hospitals, by age and diagnosis by state, United States, 1976* (Mimeo). Rockville, MD: National Institute of Mental Health.

Division of Biometry and Epidemiology. (1979). *Data sheet on state and county mental hospital patients* (Mimeo). Rockville, MD: National Institute of Mental Health.

Edgerton, R. B. (1967). *The cloak of competence: Stigma in the lives of the mentally retarded.* Berkeley: University of California Press.

Edgerton, R. B. (1981). Crime deviance and normalization: Reconsidered. In R. H. Bruininks, C. E. Meyers, B. B. Sigford, & K. C. Lakin (Eds.), *Deinstitutionalization and community adjustment of mentally retarded people.* Washington, DC: American Association on Mental Deficiency.

Edgerton, R. B. (Ed.). (1984). *Lives in progress: Mildly retarded adults in a large city* (Monograph No. 6). Washington, DC: American Association on Mental Deficiency.

Edgerton, R. B. & Bercovici, S. M. (1976). The cloak of competence: Years later. *American Journal on Mental Deficiency, 80,* 485–490.

Eyman, R. K., & Borthwick, S. A. (1980). Patterns of care for mentally retarded persons. *American Journal of Mental Deficiency, 18,* 63–66.

Eyman, R. K., Borthwick, S. A., & Miller, C. (1981). Trends in maladaptive behavior of mentally retarded persons placed in community and institutional settings. *American Journal of Mental Deficiency, 85,* 473–477.

Farber, B. (1968). *Mental retardation: Its social context and social consequences.* Boston: Houghton Mifflin.

Forssman, H., & Akesson, H. O. (1970). Mortality of the mentally deficient: Study of 12,903 institutionalized subjects. *Journal of Mental Deficiency Research, 14,* 276–294.

Galloway, C. (1974). Guaranteeing growth in the community: ENCOR's developmental programs. In F. J. Menolascion & P. M. Pearson (Eds.), *Beyond the limits.* Seattle: Special Child Publications.

Goldstein, H. (1964). Social and occupational adjustment. In H. A. Stevens & R. Heber (Eds.), *Mental retardation: A review of research.* Chicago: University of Chicago Press.

Gollay, E., Freedman, R., Wyngaarden, M., & Kurtz, N. R. (1978). *Coming back: The community experiences of deinstitutionalized mentally retarded people.* Cambridge, MA: Abt.

Goroff, N. N. (1967). Research and community placement—An exploratory approach. *Mental Retardation,* (1973). *5*(4), 17–19.

Granat, K., & Granat, S. (1973). Below average intelligence and mental retardation. Washington, DC: *American Journal of Mental Deficiency, 78,* 27–32.

Hardman, M. L., & Drew, C. J. (1977). The physically handicapped retarded individual: A review. *Mental Retardation, 15*(5), 43–47.

Haring, H. (1978). Introduction. In N. Haring (Ed.), *Behavior of exceptional children* (2nd ed.). Columbus, OH: Merrill.

Hill, B. K., & Bruininks, R. H. (1981), *Family, leisure, and social activities of mentally retarded people in residential facilities.* Minneapolis: University of Minnesota, Department of Psychoeducational Studies.

Hill, B. K., Bruininks, R. H., & Lakin, K. C. (1983). Characteristics of mentally retarded people in residential facilities. *Journal of Health and Social Work, 8,* 85–95.

Hill, B. K., Lakin, K. C., Sigford, B. B., Hauber, F. A., & Bruininks, R. H. (1982). *Programs and services for mentally retarded people in residential facilities.* Minneapolis: University of Minnesota, Department of Psychoeducational Studies.

Intagliata, J., Willer, B., & Cooley, F. (1979). Cost comparison of institutional and community based alternatives for mentally retarded persons. *Mental Retardation, 17,* 154–156.

Justice, R. S., Bradley, J., & O'Connor, G. (1971). Foster family care for the retarded: Management concerns of the caretaker. *Mental Retardation, 9,* 12–15.

Katz, S., & Yekutiel, E. (1974). Leisure time problems of mentally retarded graduates of training programs. *Mental Retardation, 12,* 54–57.

Keyes, V., Boroskin, A., & Ross, A. T. (1973). The revolving door in an M. R. hospital: A study of returns from leave. *Mental Retardation. 11*(1), 55–56.

Krantz, G. C., Bruininks, R. H., & Clumpner, J. L. (1979). *Mentally retarded people in state-operated residential facilities: Year ending June 30, 1978.* Minneapolis: University of Minnesota, Department of Psychoeducational Studies.

Krantz, G. C., Bruininks, R. H., & Clumpner, J. L. (1980). *Mentally retarded people in state-operated residential facilities: Year ending June 30, 1979.* Minneapolis: University of Minnesota, Department of Psychoeducational Studies.

Krantz, G. C., Clumpner, J. L., Rotegard, L. R., & Bruininks, R. H. (1982). *Mentally retarded people in state-operated residential facilities: Year ending June 30, 1980.* Minneapolis: University of Minnesota, Department of Psychoeducational Studies.

Lakin, K. C. (1979). *Demographic studies of residential facilities for the mentally retarded: An historical review of methodologies and findings.* Minneapolis: University of Minnesota, Department of Psychoeducational Studies.

Lakin, K. C., Bruininks, R. H., Doth, D. W., Hill, B. K., & Hauber, F. A. (1982). *Source book on long-term care for developmentally disabled people.* Minneapolis: University of Minnesota, Department of Psychoeducational Studies.

Lakin, K. C., Hill, B. K., & Bruininks, R. H. (1985). *An analysis of Medicaid's Intermediate Care Facility for the Mentally Retarded (ICF-MR) Program* (Report No. 20). Minneapolis: University of Minnesota, Center for Residential and Community Services, Department of Educational Psychology.

Lakin, K. C., Hill, B. K., Hauber, F., & Bruininks, R. H. (1982). Changes in age at first admission to residential care for mentally retarded people. *Mental Retardation, 20,* 216–219.

Lakin, K. C., Hill, B. K., Sigford, B. B., Bruininks, R. H., & Heal, L. W. (1982). *New admissions and readmissions to a national sample of public residential facilities* (Brief #14). Minneapolis: University of Minnesota, Department of Psychoeducational Studies.

Lakin, K. C., Krantz, G. C., Bruininks, R. H., Clumpner, J. L., & Hill, B. K. (1982). One hundred years of data on populations of public residential facilities for mentally retarded people. *American Journal of Mental Deficiency, 87,* 1–8.

Landesman-Dwyer, S. (1984). Residential environments and the social behavior of handicapped individuals. In M. Lewis (Ed.), *Beyond the dyad*. New York: Plenum.

Landesman-Dwyer, S., & Butterfield, G. (1983). *Evaluation of specialized group homes for developmentally disabled persons*. Olympia, WA: Department of Social and Health Services.

Landesman-Dwyer, S., & Mai-Dalton, R. (1981). *A statewide survey of individuals receiving Case Management Services for the Division of Developmental Disabilities*. Olympia, WA: Department of Social and Health Services.

Landesman-Dwyer, S., Stein, J. G., & Sackett, G. P. (1976). *Group homes for the mentally retarded: An ecological and behavioral study*. Olympia, WA: State Department of Social and Health Services.

MacMillan, D. L. (1976). *Mental retardation in school and society*. Boston: Little, Brown.

Maney, A., Pace, R., & Morrison, D. (1964). A factor analyses study of the need for institutionalization: Problems and populations for program development. *American Journal of Mental Deficiency, 69*, 372–384.

Mercer, J. (1973a). *Labeling the mentally retarded*. Berkeley: University of California Press.

Mercer, J. R. (1973). The myth of the 3% prevalence. In R. K. Eyman, C. E. Meyers, & G. Tarjan (Eds.), *Sociobehavioral studies in mental retardation*. Washington, DC: American Association on Mental Deficiency.

Miller, C. R. (1975). Deinstitutionalization and mortality trends for the profoundly mentally retarded. In C. Cleland & L. Talkington (Eds.), *Research with the profoundly retarded*. Western Research Conference and Brown Schools, 1975.

Mumpower, D. L. (1970). Sex ratios found in various types of referred exceptional children. *Exceptional Children, 36*, 621–622.

National Association of Superintendents of Public Residential Facilities for the Mentally Retarded. (1974). *Contemporary issues in residential programming*. Washington, DC: President's Committee on Mental Retardation.

National Center for Educational Statistics. (1982). *Conditions of education: 1981 edition* (Number 065-000-00097-1). Washington, DC: Government Printing Office.

National Center for Health Statistics. (1979). *The national nursing home survey: 1977 summary for the United States*. Washington, DC: U.S. Department of Health, Education and Welfare.

Nelson, R. P., & Crocker, A. C. (1978). The medical care of mentally retarded persons in public residential facilities. *New England Journal of Medicine, 299*, 1039–1044.

Nihira, C., & Nihira, K. (1975). Jeopardy in community placement. *American Journal of Mental Deficiency, 79*, 538–544.

Office of Mental Retardation Coordination. (1972). Mental retardation source book. Washington, DC: U.S. Department of Health, Education, and Welfare.

Pagel, S. E., & Whitling, C. A. (1978). Readmissions to a state hospital for mentally retarded persons: Reasons for community placement failure. *Mental Retardation, 16*, 164–166.

President's Committee on Mental Retardation. (1970). *The six-hour retarded child*. Washington, DC: U.S. Government Printing Office.

President's Committee on Mental Retardation. (1976). *Mental retardation: Trends in state services*. Washington, DC: U.S. Government Printing Office.

President's Committee on Mental Retardation. (1981). *Characteristics of persons rehabilitated, summary by major disability for year 1980*. Washington, DC: U.S. Department of Health and Human Services.

Saenger, G. (1960). *Factors influencing the institutionalization of mentally retarded individuals in New York City.* Albany: New York State Interdepartmental Health Resources Board.

Schalock R. L., & Harper, R. S. (1978). Placement from community-based mental retardation programs: How well do clients do? *American Journal of Mental Deficiency, 83,* 240–247.

Scheerenberger, R. C. (1965). A current census of state institutions for mentally retarded. *Mental Retardation, 3,* 4–6.

Scheerenberger, R. C. (1975). *Current trends and status of public residential facilities for the mentally retarded, 1974.* Madison, WI: National Association of Superintendents of Public Residential Facilities for the Mentally Retarded.

Scheerenberger, R. C. (1977). *Current trends and status of public residential services for the mentally retarded, 1976.* Madison, WI: National Association of Superintendents of Public Residential Facilities for the Mentally Retarded.

Scheerenberger, R. C. (1978b). *Public residential services for the mentally retarded, 1977.* Minneapolis: University of Minnesota, Department of Psychoeducational Studies.

Scheerenberger, R. C. (1979). *Public residential services for the mentally retarded, 1979.* Minneapolis: University of Minnesota, Department of Psychoeducational Studies.

Scheerenberger, R. C. (1981). Deinstitutionalization: Trends and difficulties. In R. H. Bruininks, C. E. Meyers, B. B. Sigford, & K. C. Lakin (Eds.), *Deinstitutionalization and community adjustment of mentally retarded people.* Washington, DC: American Association on Mental Deficiency.

Scheerenberger, R. C. (1982). *Public residential services for the mentally retarded, 1981.* Minneapolis: University of Minnesota, Department of Psychoeducational Studies.

Singer, J. E., Westphal, M., & Niswander, K. R. (1968). Sex differences in the incidence of neonatal abnormalities and abnormal performance in early childhood. *Child development, 39,* 103–112.

Smith, D. C., Decker, H. A., Herberg, E. N., & Rupke, L. K. (1969). Medical needs of children in institutions for the mentally retarded. *American Journal of Public Health, 59,* 1376–1384.

Spencer, D. A. (1976). New long-stay patients in a hospital for mental handicaps. *British Journal of Psychiatry, 128,* 467–470.

Sternlicht, M., & Deutsch, M. R. (1972). *Personality development and social behavior in the mentally retarded.* Lexington, MA: Heath.

Tarjan, G., Wright, S. W., Eyman, R. K., & Keeran, C. V. (1973). Natural history of mental retardation: Some aspects of epidemiology. *American Journal of Mental Deficiency, 77,* 369–379.

U.S. Bureau of the Census. (1981). *Age, sex, race and Spanish origin of the population by regions, divisions and states: 1980* (PC80-51-1). Washington, DC: Government Printing Office.

Wehman, P. H. (1977). Research on leisure time and the severely developmentally disabled. *Rehabilitation Literature, 38*(4), 98–105.

Willer, B., & Intagliata, J. (1980). *Evaluation of the impact of deinstitutionalization of mentally retarded persons in New York State: Final report.* Albany: New York State Department on Mental Hygiene.

Windle, C. (1962). Prognosis of mental subnormals. *American Journal of Mental Deficiency, 66*(5 Monograph Supplement).

Wright, S. W., Valente, M., & Tarjan, G. (1962). Medical problems on a ward of a hospital for the mentally retarded. *American Journal of Disabled Children, 104,* 142–148.

3
Why and How to Study
The Influence of
Living Arrangements

Earl C. Butterfield
University of Washington

More can be learned from considering how and why one might study the effects of different living arrangements upon mentally retarded people than from reviewing what has so far been found by such studies. Most of what has so far been found is scientifically uninteresting because the methods used to find it are biased. It is time to ask why we want to know about the effects of living environments on mentally retarded people and how we might come to unbiased knowledge about these effects.

WHY STUDY LIVING ARRANGEMENTS?

Many nations provide living arrangements for some of their mentally retarded citizens. Their justifications vary, but, whatever the reasons, their practices occasionally come under scrutiny, as they have in the United States in recent years. Whenever this happens, government and private agencies want to know whether the official justification for special living arrangements is being fulfilled. If a nation justifies its special arrangements

Acknowledgements. The preparation of this paper was supported by U.S. Public Health Service Grant No. HD-16241. This chapter appeared earlier under the title "The Consequences of Bias in Studies of Living Arrangements for the Mentally Retarded" in D. Bricker and J. Filler (Eds.), (1985), *Severe Mental Retardation: From Theory to Practice*. Reston, VA: Division on Mental Retardation of the Council for Exceptional Children. Copyright by the Council for Exceptional Children. Reprinted by permission.

is being fulfilled. If a nation justifies its special arrangements for retarded people as ways to prolong and enhance their lives, there comes a time when it is necessary to determine whether the special living arrangements *do* prolong and enhance their lives. If a nation justifies its special arrangements as a way to habilitate retarded people so that they can return to more mundane living, there comes a time when it is necessary to determine whether the special arrangements habilitate them. One can argue that even before necessity arises, society should check to see whether the special arrangements for which it pays are providing fair returns on the investments. Thus, there are economic and social justifications for studying the effects of various living arrangements upon mentally retarded persons. The reasons are to protect taxpayers and recipients of the services and to provide factual bases for social policy.

People who provide special living and care arrangements for mentally retarded individuals occasionally want to know how effective the arrangements are or how to provide more effective arrangements. Sometimes simple pride motivates careproviders to search for the best way to do their jobs. Sometimes lack of resources or budget cuts motivate studies of alternative living and care arrangements. Sometimes changes in social policy motivate clinical studies of living and care arrangements. For example, the deinstitutionalization movement has raised questions about the relative efficacy of total institutional care compared to community-based care. Whatever the motivation, the methods for clinically justified studies are often different from those with social justifications. Thus, the methods for evaluating whether the special programs of an entire state are habilitating mentally retarded people will differ from the methods for determining whether the medical practices of a particular institution are prolonging the lives of its residents.

In addition to social policy and clinical reasons for studying living arrangements, there are scientific reasons. Although no scientist would set up special living arrangements just to answer a scientific question, many studies of existing service systems have been justified scientifically, thereby treating already established special living arrangements for mentally retarded people as natural experiments. Thus, there have been studies of the effects of institutional and other living arrangements on such variables as intellectual development (Balla, Butterfield, & Zigler, 1974), motivation (Zigler, Balla, & Butterfield, 1968), personality (Zigler & Butterfield, 1966), and social competence (Klaber, Butterfield, & Gould, 1969). Almost all scientific studies of special living arrangements have sought to answer specific forms of the general question, How does the environment influence behavior? Studies designed to answer this question need not focus on mentally retarded people nor upon special living arrangements. Studies with emotionally disturbed, deaf, blind, and nonhandicapped people, as well as laboratory studies of various animals, are as scientifically pertinent as studies of mentally retarded individuals. Pertinent environmental variations for scientific study include teaching methods, language experience, perceptual stimulation, and nutritional experience as well as living arrangements. Because the scientific reasons for studying special living arrangements for mentally retarded people are usually broader than the social and clinical reasons, the possibility of bias in such studies is always a problem for scientists. Bias is sometimes a problem, and it is sometimes quite unimportant to those who study special living arrangements for social and clinical reasons.

BIAS AND ITS CONSEQUENCES

The chief source of bias in studies of special living arrangements is that complex social, administrative, and clinical forces combine to select who enters the arrangements. Such selection biases create interpretative problems. When people who have lived in a special environment are found to differ from others, the question is whether the difference can be attributed to the living arrangement, to the characteristics of the people who were assigned to the living arrangement, or to an interaction of the arrangement with the people's characteristics. Unless people have been assigned randomly to the environments that are compared, no clear interpretation is possible. Subsequent differences between people assigned nonrandomly may have existed before the assignment or they may be the result of the living environment. The lack of random assignment always defeats the scientific purpose of comparing people in different living environments. It may or may not defeat the purpose of a clinically or socially motivated study.

Scientific studies are defeated by a lack of random assignment because the focus of such studies is upon the effects of different environments. Unless people are randomly assigned to environments, it is unreasonable to assume that they are comparable people, and unless they are comparable when they enter the environments, later differences among them cannot be attributed to those environments or any other known condition(s). This is true even when the effects of different environments are hypothesized to depend upon the characteristics of the people experiencing them. Such interactional hypotheses require the random assignment to all studied environments of people from groups that differ in known ways *in advance of the assignment*. It is not sufficient to identify people who have been nonrandomly assigned to different environments and to decide which people are comparable by some assessment procedure. The reason is that our assessment procedures are not able to detect all pertinent sources of variation among people. After-the-fact matching is not a satisfactory alternative to random assignment when the focus is on either main or interaction effects of environmental variables.

Some studies done for social or clinical reasons are not ruined by selection bias. For example, if the question is whether people who receive care in a special living arrangement advance to the point of being able to subsist outside the arrangement, then selection bias is irrelevant, because the question is about people who are selected for the arrangement. A service system might well want to answer this question; however, if the service system were interested in the more specific question of whether advances were due to the characteristics of the living arrangement, then random assignment to living arrangements would have to be arranged. In general, selection bias is not a problem when the question to be answered by studying a living arrangement pertains only to those people who live there.

COPING WITH BIAS IN SCIENTIFIC STUDIES

Despite the fact that random assignment to living arrangements is the only way to eliminate selection bias, many scientific studies without random assignment have been reported. In some of these studies investigators have employed designs intended to minimize the effects of nonrandom assignment on the interpretation of their findings. For example, Butterfield and Zigler (1965) studied the effects of two institutions located in the same state and having identical admission policies. The authors had observed marked differences in the management of children in these two facilities, and they expected that one institution would heighten the needs of its retarded residents for social reinforcement more than the other institution would. The data were consistent with the hypothesis: Children from one institution responded more to social reinforcement than did children in the other institution. The critical interpretative question is whether the difference in responsiveness should be attributed to differences between the living arrangements or to differential assignment of retarded people to the two arrangements. Had the assignment been random, this question would be irrelevant, so the question is whether the existence of identical admission policies is equivalent to random assignment.

The two institutions studied by Butterfield and Zigler (1965) served different halves of the state in which they were located. Therefore, although their admission policies were described as identical, the institutions drew from different populations. Although both halves of the state contained large urban areas, one half was more rural than the other, and the other half contained a greater density of highly affluent people. Other research has shown that the dependent measures employed by Butterfield and Zigler are influenced by socioeconomic background (Zigler, et al., 1968). Therefore, it is questionable whether the finding of greater responsiveness of social reinforcement can be attributed to the characteristics of the different living arrangements, even though the admission policies of the two arrangements were formally identical. Studies that compare children from different institutions are less likely to suffer from gross selection bias than are studies that compare institutionalized and noninstitutionalized children. Thus, the study by Butterfield and Zigler represents a methodological advance over studies that compared institutionalized and noninstitutionalized people. Still, only random assignment could have removed all question of selection bias in their investigation.

Klaber et al. (1969) reported results that seem to bolster the inference of Butterfield and Zigler (1965) that the depriving management style of one of their institutions heightened social motivation. Klaber et al. studied children from the depriving institution studied by Butterfield and Zigler. Some children were transferred to another living arrangement, and some remained in the depriving institution. The living arrangement to which children were transferred was judged in advance to manage children in such a way that their motivation for social reinforcement would be less than that of the children who remained in the original institution. The data showed that children in the new institution were less responsive to social reinforcement than those who remained in the original institution. Putting this finding together with the finding of Butterfield and Zigler seems to strengthen the conclusion that the original institution created greater needs for social reinforcement because children in that institution were more responsive to social reinforcement than were children in two other institutions, both of which were judged to have more nurturing management procedures and because the children studied by Klaber et al. were all admitted originally to the same institution. No selection bias could have operated at the time of original admission.

Although selection bias could not have operated when the residents studied by Klaber et al. were admitted to their original institution, it could have operated at the time of transfer to the other institution. Children were transferred in order to bring them nearer to their families, so that those who remained in the original institution came from one area of the state and those who were transferred came from another area. As in the study by Butterfield and Zigler, the socioeconomic characteristics of the areas were different, and as in that study, the children who were less responsive to social reinforcement came from an area with a higher socioeconomic status. Moreover, the study by Klaber et al. was designed after the decisions about who to transfer were made. This necessitated after-the-fact matching of children who were not transferred with those who were. Such matching is not a satisfactory substitute for random assignment (Kiesler, 1982). The comparability of the two groups in the study by Klaber et al. is still in question. This same concern remains about the much larger study by Klaber (1969).

Even though random assignment to living arrangements is the only way to ensure that differences among people in the arrangements are due to their living conditions and not to pre-existing differences in personal characteristics, the vast majority of studies of living arrangements have used nonrandom assignment. The temptation is great to interpret these studies as showing that living arrangements have different effects on mentally retarded people despite the possibility that their results stem from various selection biases. One way to justify such interpretation is to note that several studies of a particular effect (e.g., heightened social motivation) have yielded a coherent pattern of results and that different studies have different sources of bias. The logic is that if similar findings emerge from studies with different sources of bias, bias must not account for the results. This logic is compelling only when it can be shown that some of the biases do not influence the dependent variables studied. Unfortunately, we do not know enough about any dependent variable used in studies of living arrangements to be confident that any source of bias is irrelevant, and we do not usually have an analytic view of the sources of bias. Moreover, because the central hypothesis of such studies is that environmental variations influence behavior and because we cannot know all about the environmental experiences of any group of people before they enter a living arrangement, we can never satisfy the conditions needed to evaluate the logic of disregarding various sources of bias when a group of studies with different biases converge upon a single conclusion.

It can be taken as a given that mentally retarded people who are admitted through normal procedures to a special living arrangement are a biased sample of the mentally retarded population. This means that they are unsuitable subjects for studies in which such living arrangements are compared. It does not mean that every study of retarded people in special living arrangements is scientifically meaningless. Thus, people who have been admitted nonrandomly to one facility can be randomly assigned to each of several other facilities or experimental conditions, thereby allowing unbiased study of the effects of those facilities or conditions. Using this approach, investigators would simply not be able to generalize their results to the entire population of mentally retarded people. Similarly, whenever investigators can systematically assess the prior living conditions of a group of people assigned nonrandomly to a particular living arrangement, they can study those people while they are in the special living arrangement in order to assess the effects of the prior arrangement. As with the random assignment of people in a living arrangement to different conditions, the population to which investigators can generalize when comparing subjects from different prior arrangements is restricted to people like those admitted to the prior arrangement. The results for that population are unbiased as long as one does not try to establish an interaction between prior living arrangements and present living arrangements. A study by Zigler et al. (1968) illustrates the relevant issues.

Zigler et al. (1968) studied changes in social motivation among children who had come to an institution from different preinstitutional backgrounds. Preinstitutional background was assessed with an objective scale applied to information from social histories (Zigler, Butterfield, & Goff, 1966). Zigler et al. found that children from less supportive family environments had greater needs for social reinforcement shortly after institutionalization than did children from more supportive family environments. Moreover, children from less supportive environments showed marked decreases in social needs over 3 years of institutionalization, whereas children from more supportive environments showed very small changes in their social neediness. Is it safe to conclude from these findings that preinstitutional social deprivation heightens need for social reinforcement and that children with heightened needs become less needy the longer they are institutionalized? One necessary caveat on these conclusions is that they may not apply to all children who have depriving home environments. They may only apply to those who have depriving home environments *and*, for whatever reasons, are subsequently placed in a particular institution for mentally retarded persons. Another necessary caveat is that the source of the decrease in need for social reinforcement is unclear. It might simply be aging, it might be the fact of removal from the original environment, or it might be due to some positive feature of the institutional environment. Given these qualifications, the results can be taken as unbiased.

During the discussion of their results, Zigler et al. (1968) noted that their pattern of findings differed from that of a similar investigation in another institution for mentally retarded individuals (Zigler & Williams, 1963). In an effort to reconcile these findings, Zigler et al. noted that the two institutions appeared to differ in how supportive they were of their residents, and they suggested that preinstitutional environment interacts with institutional environment to create different sorts of changes in need for social motivation. This hypothesis seems reasonable, but the pattern of results that suggested it could be due to selection bias. That is, the two institutions may well have had different selection criteria, and these criteria could have dictated the pattern of results.

When studying the effects of preinstitutional environments, investigators must use different institutions appropriately to determine the extent to which particular findings can be generalized to people admitted to all institutions for retarded persons. If preinstitutional variables are found to have the same effect across several institutions, then one can conclude that the preinstitutional variable is an important one among people who are admitted to institutions; however, if a preinstitutional variable has different effects across institutions, the findings are not interpretable because they may be due to selection bias. Because there is a third study showing that the nature of the effects of preinstitutional environment varies with the institution studied (Balla, Butterfield, & Zigler, 1974), the appropriate conclusion is that preinstitutional living environment as assessed by Zigler and his collaborators has no demonstrated general effects on social motivation.

Bias in the assignment of mentally retarded people to special living arrangements has several effects. It invalidates comparisons among different living arrangements unless the bias is prevented by random assignment. It limits the generality of conclusions from studies done in particular institutions, unless the results of those studies are shown to be general across people in different institutions. As a rule, this latter result is more likely to be observed when the people who live in a particular institution are randomly assigned to subsequently administered conditions than it is when people who live in a particular institution are divided according to their preinstitutional experience.

Consumers of biased research are in the same position as consumers of a poisoned meal. It makes no difference that every dish may have a different poison; none of the dishes should be consumed. Bias is like poison, except that there is no antidote for bias. There is only prevention, in the form of studies that are unbiased.

UNBIASED STUDIES OF THE EFFECTS OF LIVING ARRANGEMENTS

In chapter 5 of this volume, Landesman reported on the only large study of the effects of living environments to which mentally retarded people were randomly assigned. Landesman began by constructing 49 trios of severely and profoundly retarded people ($N = 147$). The people in each trio were residents of a single multipurpose institution, and within trios they were matched for sex, adaptive behavior, age, length of institutionalization, and medical and behavioral characteristics. One member of each trio was selected by clinical and administrative staff members for assignment to a new living arrangement. A second member was randomly selected for assignment to the new arrangement, and the third member remained in the old arrangement. Baseline data were collected for one year before any residents were moved to a new living arrangement. Outcome data were collected for a year after residents moved from the old to the new living arrangements. The data were derived from observations of day-to-day behavior, standardized ratings of adaptive behavior, and assessments of health. Landesman found small but reliable effects of changed living arrangements. The nature of these effects varied with the behavioral characteristics of the residents prior to their move. Her findings highlight several methodological issues that are of great importance to future studies of living arrangements for retarded people.

Logically, there are two approaches to studying the effects of special living arrangements. One way is to examine the effects of such arrangements on people entering them from the community. No unbiased approach of this sort has been attempted with mentally retarded people, but 10 unbiased studies of this sort have been conducted with psychiatrically disturbed people. Kiesler (1982) has recently reviewed these studies, and I discuss them in a later section of this chapter. Another approach is to examine the effects of changing the living arrangements of people who already reside in a congregate living facility. Within this latter approach, one can examine the effects of moving from congregate living to community living or the effects of moving from one congregate living arrangement to another. Landesman used the latter approach.

Either variation on beginning with people already in a congregate living facility has several advantages over starting with people who reside in the community. The chief advantages are that any variance due to environmental differences when the study begins will be minimized by the fact that all subjects will have been in the same environment, and it is far easier to collect baseline measures on a large group of people when they are congregated together. There may also be some disadvantages of this approach. If congregate living has major adverse effects on mentally retarded people, and if these effects are difficult to overcome, then studying people who have already resided in congregate living for a long time may not reveal the effects of new living arrangements because the people studied will be resistant to the influence of the new environment. This could be especially true when examining the effects of moving from one congregate living facility to another. A related disadvantage could result from the fact that people who have resided in a congregate living facility will be older than those who are coming to one for the first time. If the effects of living arrangements are greater on younger people, starting with people already in a congregate facility could reduce the likelihood of observing effects of living arrangements. Landesman's subjects had a mean age of 35 years and a mean length of institutionalization of 22 years. Whether these facts reduced the size of her observed effects is impossible to determine now, but it could be determined by other unbiased studies in which age and length of institutionalization at the time of transfer were varied. Varying age and length of institutionalization, however, assumes that people of different ages and lengths of residence are comparable in all other respects. That is, it assumes that age and length of institutionalization are not confounded with other factors. It is unreasonable to assume unconfounded comparisons across age and length of institutionalization if admission policies have changed over time or if the policies are designed to make it easier to admit people of certain ages. In this country, admission policies have changed dramatically in recent years, and they are designed to militate against the admission of younger people.

Despite the disadvantages of beginning with people who have already resided in a congregate living facility, that seems the most reasonable approach in future studies. Many more retarded people are being released from congregate living facilities than are being admitted to them, so that studying large groups of newly admitted people will be impractical, and there will be relatively less clinical and social policy interest in such studies. Policy makers have already decided to keep admission down, but they remain interested in the question of the desirability of different placements for people who are already institutionalized. Moreover, Landesman's study establishes that there is an overwhelming methodologic advantage to studies of people who are already in a congregate living facility. The advantage lies in the ease of collecting baseline data prior to moving residents to different living arrangements.

Landesman's cluster analyses of her baseline data revealed five distinctly different groups of residents. These groups responded in different ways to their new living arrangements. Had Landesman lacked the opportunity to collect her baseline data, her findings would have been far less meaningful because she would not have had any premove basis for segregating her subjects into groups. Her findings illustrate the generally useful principle of grouping subjects according to measures that are directly related to the dependent measures employed in a study. Students of learning and memory have known for some time that their experiments have greater power and meaning when their subjects are grouped on empirically relevant variables. Thus, as early as 1969, Belmont and Butterfield could argue that studies of mentally retarded persons' memories are more powerful and informative when subjects are grouped according to their memory characteristics rather than according to some gross factor ' such as mental age or IQ. Landesman's findings indicate that the same is true for studies of living environments.

Although Landesman was able to define subgroups of retarded residents prior to changing their living environments, she did not take subgroup membership into account when assigning subjects to environments. That is, her matching within trios was based on characteristics such as age and sex rather than on baseline measures. In future studies, residents should be divided into subgroups according to baseline measures or some other directly pertinent indices before they are randomly assigned to living arrangements. One must, however, expect regression to the mean to attenuate or exaggerate some differences between pre- and postmove measures when premove subgroups are formed from measures that will also be used to assess the effects of a new environment. Landesman's findings indicate that such regression effects are not great when one has a large amount of baseline data to use for the subgrouping of subjects. Even further reduction and possible elimination of regression could be obtained by using one set of baseline measures for classification purposes and a subsequently collected set of the same measures for comparison with postmove measures. If this procedure is used, regression effects are reflected in the second premove measure rather than in the postmove measures alone.

Landesman found no differences between the residents who were moved as a result of clinical and administrative decisions and those who were selected randomly. This does not mean that clinical/administrative decisions are functionally random. If it did, then my prior arguments about random assignment and bias could be dismissed. If clinical/administrative decisions were random, then comparisons among different living arrangements would not be biased by subject-selection factors. The clinical/administrative decisions in Landesman's study were constrained by her trios design. That is, these decisions were not based on the retarded people's age, sex, adaptive behavior, length of institutionalization, or medical or behavioral characteristics, because the trios (from which the clinical/administrative selections were made) were matched on these variables. Such constraints do not apply to usual clinical/administrative decisions. The lack of differences between clinically selected and randomly selected residents in Landesman's study does not contradict the argument that selection bias invalidates comparisons among groups assigned by unconstrained administrative/clinical processes.

Landesman observed that the residents who remained in their original living arrangement changed some of their behavior from before to after the move of the *other* residents. It is difficult to judge the extent to which these changes are regression effects, but their occurrence suggests a refinement of the design for future investigations of the effects of moving residents from one congregate living arrangement to another. The refinement is to include two groups who remain in the original facility, one group of residents who might be influenced by the move of other residents from the facility and a second group who could not be so effected. To do this in an unbiased way, one would begin by taking baseline measures for purposes of matching subjects. Having decided how many groups were to be studied (e.g., four groups), one would then select groups of subjects (quartets in the case of a study with four groups) who were matched within groups (quartets) on the baseline measures. All residents in each quartet would then be moved within their place of residence. This movement would be random with the restriction that three members of the quartet would be moved to living units from which members in the study were to be drawn at placement time. The fourth member would go to a living unit from which no one in the study would subsequently be moved to new living arrangements. Prior to placement, additional baseline measures would be taken. Their purpose would be to allow for regression effects. These additional measures would be used as the premove measures in the study of changes in living environments, and they would allow a check on the possibility that different living units within the facility had different effects upon their residents. Following these measures, two of the three residents assigned to units from which residents were placed would be randomly selected for placement. Upon completion of the followup, comparisons among the residents who remained in the institution would allow the separation of further regression effects from the effects of remaining in an institutional setting from which other residents had been moved. Other variations on this design are possible, and they share the characteristic of allowing study of the extent to which regression effects occur and the extent to which the effects of a living arrangement are determined by the grouping of residents within it. One interesting implication of Landesman's findings is that even profoundly and severely retarded people may be influenced by changes in the cast of characters with whom they live, and variations on this design would allow evaluation of that implication.

ARE NATURAL EXPERIMENTS ENOUGH?

Landesman found that retarded people showed few large behavioral changes when the state of Washington moved them from one living arrangement to another. She viewed this as unsurprising, because both the new and old environments were unstimulating. Officials of the state of Washington built new facilities that were far more homelike than its older institutions. The new facilities met licensing standards that the old ones did not approach, and the new facilities had more staff members per resident. Never the less, when the residents were transferred from the older institutions to the new facilities, no new programming was provided nor were staff of the new facilities told or trained to behave differently than were staff in the old facilities. As Landesman noted, finding ways to create large behavioral changes "is likely to be more difficult than just building new buildings, meeting federal licensing standards, and providing more staff members to look after things" (p. 116). It follows that researchers who are looking for large effects of different residential arrangements will probably have to do more than study the effects of changes in residential arrangements that just happen to occur in an existing service system. It is not enough to arrange unbiased assignment of retarded people to residential arrangements. One should also guarantee that the residential arrangements are substantially different from one another in the demands and resources they place upon residents. Natural experiments are not enough.

Close (1977) did the only other study in which retarded residents were randomly assigned to living assignments. In his study, the new living arrangement differed from the old one not only physically, geographically, and in generic programming, but also in specialized programming. The new arrangement provided individualized training programs; the old arrangement did not. The effects observed by Close seem large compared to those observed by Landesman. This is consistent with Landesman's conclusion that large effects require more than a change in physical environment. Unfortunately, Close's study cannot be taken as affirmation of Landesman's conclusion, because his study confounded changed environments and changed programming. It is impossible to determine whether the difference in magnitude of results between Close's study and Landesman's stemmed from the fact that Close's study involved radical changes in programming whereas Landesman's did not or whether the particular environment to which Close's subjects were transferred somehow prompted larger gains than did the environment to which Landesman's subjects were transferred.

To sort out the effects of changed environments and changed programming, we need studies in which environmental and programming changes are varied orthogonally. Some residents of an institution should receive neither a new environment nor new programming, some should receive new programming in their old environment, some should receive a new environment alone, and some should receive both a new environment and new programming. The environmental and programming changes should be large according to some theory about how such changes should influence behavior, and residents should be assigned randomly to the environmental and programming conditions.

Scientifically, natural experiments fall short in two ways. First, they are plagued by selection bias. Landesman's and Close's studies show that this bias can be prevented but that prevention does away with some of the naturalness of the natural experiment. Their studies also suggest that natural experiments on residential arrangements for retarded people are not enough in the second way, which is that their environmental variations are not sufficiently pertinent to change behavior. Whether more pertinent environmental variation could be made is an open question, and we are unlikely to answer that question if we wait for a relevant natural experiment. Naturalness needs to be done away with. Close's experiment suggests that programming changes are powerful determinants of behavioral change, but further work is needed to eliminate the possibility that it was environmental change, not programming change, that produced Close's results.

I have mentioned two ways in which natural experiments are not enough. They provide too little control over selection bias and they too seldom vary factors that according to theory should have large effects. These are shortcomings from the vantage point of scientists, but in addition to scientific purposes, there are social and clinical purposes to be served by studying living environments for mentally retarded individuals. Are natural experiments enough to meet the needs of social planners and clinicians? Are they enough if the only modification in them is the elimination of selection bias? Or must social planners and clinicians not only eliminate selection bias but also arrange for theoretically powerful changes in living environments and programming? In other words, are planned experiments the only satisfactory bases for clinical and social action, or will observation of the outcomes of existing practices suffice?

Although there are only two unbiased studies of the effects of living arrangements on mentally retarded people, there are 10 unbiased studies comparing institutional care and alternative care arrangements for mentally ill people (Brook, 1973; Flomenhaft, Kaplan, & Langsley, 1969; Herz, Endicott, Spitzer, & Mesnikoff, 1971; Krowinski & Fitt, 1978; Levenson et al., 1977; Mosher & Menn, 1978; Pasamanick, Scarpitti, & Dinitz, 1967; Stein, Test, & Marx, 1975; Washburn, Vannicelli, Longabaugh, & Scheff, 1976; Wilder, Levin, & Zwerling, 1966). In all of these studies, mentally ill people were assigned randomly to total institutional care or to community-based alternative care arrangements. Kiesler (1982) assessed the clinical and policy implications of these 10 studies, and his assessments help answer the foregoing questions about the adequacy of natural experiments for clinical and policy purposes. My discussion of implications of these studies is heavily influenced by Kiesler's arguments. Note that it does not matter that these investigators used mentally ill instead of mentally retarded people. The issues are the same for the two populations.

The quality of the institutional care provided was high in the 10 unbiased studies of mentally ill people. The modes of alternative care were diverse. In every study, the outcomes for the patients were more positive in the alternative care arrangements than in the institutional arrangements. The outcome measures included psychiatric evaluations, subsequent employment, school performance, maintenance of social relationships, and success at independent living. The costs per day were lower for alternative care than for institutional care. The chief scientific claim that these facts

justify is that many mentally ill people who are currently receiving institutional inpatient care could be receiving alternative care that is more effective and less expensive.

Eight of the 10 studies provided follow-up periods during which information was collected about subsequent institutionalization. In every study,
the rates of subsequent institutionalization were significantly higher for
people who had been previously assigned to institutional care than for
people who had been assigned to alternative care. The scientific conclusion
is that institutionalization is self-perpetuating. Having once been an inpatient, one is more likely to be an inpatient again.

The policy implication of these results is that community-based alternative care should be provided for many mentally ill people who are now
being institutionalized. Community-based care should be provided because it is more effective, it is less expensive, and because institutional care
is self-perpetuating, which further raises the cost to society of treating
mentally ill people in institutional settings and which prolongs their recovery. Now consider some questions these studies do not answer.

*Could all mentally ill people be treated more effectively in community-based
programs?* Although the 10 unbiased studies establish that many mentally
ill people would fare better in community-based facilities, they do not say
whether all of them would do better in such facilities. The reasons are that
not all types of people treated in institutions were included in these 10
studies, and the investigators did not seek to find interactions between
patient characteristics and kinds of care. These questions could be
answered by further unbiased studies in which different types of patients
received either alternative or institutional living. Either existing or experimental living arrangements could be studied, but the chances of finding
large effects would be greater if experimental programs were studied. The
reason is that experimental programs can be tailored to the purposes of
the evaluation and to the characteristics of the patients under study.

Could institutional care be improved? Because the investigations in these
unbiased studies evaluated existing institutional programs and because
they did not examine dimensions along which institutions can vary, they
say nothing about untried programs. Neither do they say anything about
how difficult or easy it would be to change existing institutional programs.
These are pertinent questions for policy makers and clinicians alike, and
answering them would require planned experiments rather than natural
experiments.

Could alternative care be improved? None of the 10 unbiased studies
examined more than one type of alternative care, so they provide no
evidence about relative effectiveness of the different programs studied.
Furthermore, none evaluated any attempt to change or improve an alternative care program. Whether alternative care could be improved is an
experimental question that no natural experiment is likely to answer. Both
clinicians and policy makers would be interested in the answer.

How can alternative care programs best be implemented? Given that the 10
unbiased studies show that alternative care programs are better for many

mentally ill patients, and given that there are too few alternative care programs to accommodate many of the patients who are presently being institutionalized for mental illness, policy makers need to know how to establish new alternative care programs. Although something can be learned about this from retrospective reports of people who have established such programs, far more satisfactory answers could be obtained by an experimental program that tests various ways of implementing alternative care arrangements. Again, the clinical and policy questions require an experimental approach, and if such an approach were undertaken, it could answer other pertinent policy questions. *How can resistance to closing existing institutions be most effectively overcome? How can economic hardships that might fall on employees and communities of existing institutions if they are closed as a result of increased alternative care arrangements be prevented? How can community resistance to the establishment of community-based alternative care programs be overcome?*

Which features of institutional and alternative care programs are responsible for their positive effects? This is the chief clinical question about all complex service systems. It is also the chief question of policy makers who are interested in minimizing their costs or maximizing the return on their expenditures. Natural experiments in the form of observations of ongoing programs can provide important information on this question, but definitive information requires an experimental approach in which various features of existing programs are varied in unbiased ways. Despite their random assignment of patients to living arrangements, none of the investigators in the 10 studies provided any answers to this question, because they all addressed the grosser question of whether complexly different care procedures vary in their effectiveness.

THE COMMON GROUND OF SCIENCE, SOCIAL POLICY, AND CLINICAL PRACTICE

There are scientific, clinical, and policy reasons for studying living arrangements for mentally retarded people. In my introductory remarks I observed that policy and clinical questions about living arrangements could sometimes be answered by biased investigations, but that scientific questions could never be answered with biased investigations. I argued that selection bias was unimportant when policy makers or clinicians wanted an answer to the question of how well or poorly their services were doing for the people they were currently serving. For such questions, it does not matter whether the outcomes for the people being served are due to the services or to preexisting characteristics of the people. I should now say that it rarely happens that policy makers or clinicians are seriously interested in such questions. Scientists, clinicians, and policy makers share a large common ground, namely that they want to know the particular conditions that promote the welfare and adaptive behavior of the clients in their service systems. The reasons for their interest differ, but they share the desire to have unbiased knowledge because they wish to know how much the provided services contribute to the welfare of their clients. It follows that future investigations of the effects of living and care arrangements for mentally retarded individuals should result from a partnership among scientists, policy makers, and clinicians. The partnership should be devoted to eliminating selection bias from the study of living and care arrangements and to varying living and care arrangements systematically. The approach should be experimental in the sense that it seeks an analytic understanding of the effective elements of current care practices and in the sense that it seeks to understand innovative arrangements that would be more effective than existing arrangements.

If there is any seed of discord in this proposed partnership, it is scientists' desire to test general conceptions. It is possible to execute unbiased studies to analyze existing programs or evaluate innovative programs without testing any theory that would guide extrapolation of the findings to situations beyond the ones studied. Unless a study tests such a theory, it will be of little interest to scientists, though it could be of immense interest to policy makers or clinicians. Therefore, the challenge for scientists is to judge whether the independent variables that they would study for theoretical reasons are interesting enough to clinicians and policy makers to justify their cooperation. The challenge for clinicians and policy makers is to facilitate studies that will not only help to improve the service systems of their immediate concern but will also contribute to understandings that will make it possible to design systems for other needs, so that every new system will not require extensive experimental analysis.

REFERENCES

Balla, D. A., Butterfield, E. C., & Zigler, E. (1974). Effects of institutionalization on retarded children: A longitudinal cross-institutional investigation. *American Journal of Mental Deficiency, 78,* 530–549.

Brook, B. D. (1973). An alternative to psychiatric hospitalization for emergency patients. *Hospital and Community Psychiatry, 24,* 621–624.

Butterfield, E. C., & Zigler, E. (1965). The influence of differing institutional social climates on the effectiveness of social reinforcement in the mentally retarded. *American Journal of Mental Deficiency, 70,* 48–56.

Close, D. W. (1977, October). Community living for severely and profoundly retarded adults: A group home study. *Education and Training of the Mentally Retarded,* 256–262.

Flomenhaft, K., Kaplan, D. M., & Langsley, D. G. (1969). Avoiding psychiatric hospitalization. *Social Work, 16,* 38–45.

Herz, M. I., Endicott, J., Spitzer, R. L., & Mesnikoff, A. (1971). Day versus inpatient hospitalization: A controlled study. *American Journal of Psychology, 127*(10), 107-117.

Kiesler, C. A. (1982). Mental hospitals and alternative care: Noninstitutionalization as potential public policy for mental patients. *American Psychologist, 37,* 349–360.

Klaber, M. (1969). *Retardates in residence: A study of institutions* (Final Report, Project No. RD-1816-P, sponsored by the Social and Rehabilitation Service, U.S. Government). Hartford, CT: University of Hartford.

Klaber, M., Butterfield, E. C., & Gould, L. J. (1969). Responsiveness to social reinforcement among institutionalized retarded children. *American Journal of Mental Deficiency, 73,* 890–895.

Krowinski, W. J., & Fitt, D. X. (1978). *On the clinical efficacy and cost effectiveness of psychiatric partial hospitalization versus traditional inpatient care with six month follow-up data* (Report to Capital Blue Cross, Reading Hospital and Medical Center, Day Treatment Center).

Levenson, A. J., Lord, C. J., Sermas, C. E., Thornby, J. I., Sullender, W., & Comstock, B. A. (1977, April). Acute schizophrenia: An efficacious outpatient treatment approach as an alternative to full-time hospitalization. *Diseases of the Nervous System,* 242–245.

Mosher, L. R., & Menn, A. Z. (1978). Community residential treatment for schizophrenia: Two year follow-up. *Hospital and Community Psychiatry, 29,* 715–723.

Pasamanick, B., Scarpitti, F. R., & Dinitz, S. (1967). *Schizophrenics and the community.* New York: Appleton-Century-Crofts.

Stein, L. I., Test, M. A., & Marx, A. J. (1975). Alternative to the hospital: A controlled study. *American Journal of Psychiatry, 132,* 517–521.

Washburn, S., Vannicelli, M., Longabaugh, R., & Scheff, B-J (1976). A controlled comparison of psychiatric day treatment and inpatient hospitalization. *Journal of Consulting and Clinical Psychology, 44,* 665–675.

Wilder, J. F., Levin, G., & Zwerling, I. (1966). A two-year follow-up evaluation of acute psychotic patients treated in a day hospital. *American Journal of Psychiatry, 122,* 1095–1111.

Zigler, E., Balla, D. A., & Butterfield, E. (1968). A longitudinal investigation of the relationship between preinstitutional social deprivation and social motivation in institutionalized retardates. *Journal of Personality and Social Psychology, 10,* 437–445.

Zigler, E., & Butterfield, E. C. (1966). Rigidity in the retarded: A further test of the Lewin-Kounin formulation. *Journal of Abnormal Psychology, 71,* 224–231.

Zigler, E., & Butterfield, E. C. (1968). Motivational aspects of changes in IQ test performance of culturally-deprived nursery school children. *Child Development, 39,* 1–14.

Zigler, E., & Butterfield, E. C., & Goff, G. (1966). A measure of preinstitutional social deprivation for institutionalized retardates. *American Journal of Mental Deficiency, 70,* 873–885.

Zigler, E., & William, J. (1963). Institutionalization and the effectiveness of social reinforcement: A three-year follow-up study. *Journal of Abnormal and Social Psychology, 66,* 197–205.

4
Design of Research on Families

Deborah L. Coates
Catholic University of America

Peter M. Vietze
*New York State Institute for Basis Research
and Developmental Disabilities*

Research on families with mentally retarded members has recently become a topic of interest. The current interest in how a retarded family member might affect the family and how the family might, in turn, affect the behavior and well being of the retarded person comes about as a result of a number of trends. First, the normalization movement has meant that families must care for their retarded children at home with little or no chance for finding care in institutional settings, as was once the case. Second, research on family process and on families in general has been developing new methods and progressing so that investigators interested in applying some of these methods to families with handicapped members can do so. Finally, there has been an awareness that the family as an institution has been changing and, therefore, the knowledge base about families with retarded children is outdated. In this chapter, we consider some alternative conceptualizations about families with a retarded member and then describe some methodological implications of these conceptualizations.

Definition of Family

A first step in developing a new framework is to define the *family* as a social group with whom one resides. This would mean that rather than defining a family in terms of blood kinship or marital status, a family would consist of the persons who reside within one living unit or residential space.

This expansion of the definition of family has several important implications. First, by recognizing the importance of the social unit in which any person lives, this broader definition of family is sensitive to the psychological and behavioral world of retarded individuals who often "lose" or "leave" their families of origin. Second, this definition can provide a basis for bringing together two groups of researchers who traditionally have remained separate, namely, those who study institutional and out-of-home residential settings and those who study natural families. Third, this definition permits the development of an empirically based classification system and the study of which "family" variables mediate different outcomes. A distinction, similar to one made presently, would be made between one's birth family or family of origin and family of residence. This distinction would be made in order to mark the historical context of an individual's life cycle. Thus, one would have only one family of origin but could have a series of families of residence. In addition, because some children belong to a series of families due to adoption or temporary placement, families in which adults serve as the parent or in which they have served in an initiating capacity would be called *initiated families.*

To make clear where a particular family fits into an individual's life cycle, one could use subscripts. Thus, the family of origin would be designated as $family_0$ indicating that it is the first family the individual belonged to. Subsequent families prior to adulthood would be designated with a subscript numeral indicating which family is being referenced, e.g., $family_3$. After the individual reaches 21 years of age, families would be designated with a subscript *i* indicating that it was an initiated family but the numbering would continue from the earlier numbering, e.g., $family_{i4}$. Such an indexing system would decrease some of the confusion in discussing how many and what sort of families an individual has belonged to. Further elaborations (e.g., markers for adoptive families, foster families) could also be made but will not be discussed here. Suffice it to say that a taxonomy of family types with a numbering system would go a long way in clarifying the nomenclature used to describe families across the life cycle.

DIRECTION OF INFLUENCE IN THE FAMILY

Research on families traditionally has focused on how parents influence their children's development. This came about as a result of the strong environmental position that most child development researchers maintained. It might be seen as an extension of John Locke's and later J. B. Watson's view that children are shaped and molded by their experiences and that most of the earliest experiences are under the control of parents. The implication of this unidirectional model for parents of retarded children is that the way the children are developing is their responsibility. Even an enlightened version of this model positing that mental retardation is probably not the fault of parents failed to guide these parents in how they might raise their handicapped child.

During the last 15 years, there has been a shift in focus from how parents cause their children to act to how children's behavior and characteristics affect the parents. Thus, the interactional nature of family relationships and of the child developing in the family is now acknowledged. This change in conceptualization from the unidirectional model of child rearing—parent-to-child—to a bidirectional model made it possible for researchers to appreciate that families with handicapped children can make a substantial contribution to our knowledge of family functioning and family process. This shift in focus within the family led to the development of new research techniques to permit study consistent with this more complex conceptualization. In addition, methodological advances were made for analyzing data from these new techniques, especially from the complex interactional observations that have become the hallmark of family behavior research. These techniques are discussed more fully in the second half of this chapter. Suffice it to say that these methodologies do not rely on the competence of the actors being studied. This is a major breakthrough for the study of children in families because it is not necessary to develop special scales or techniques for them. It also allows comparative studies to be proposed in which the retarded child's competence does not affect the measurement of family functioning or family interaction per se.

CHANGES IN THE FAMILY

The family has been changing as a social institution in this country and in other countries as well. Since the early 18th century, the role of children in the family has changed drastically from economic resource and apprentice to protected property. Social and cultural as well as economic pressures have led to changes in the structure and architecture of families. As old external pressures that provided support for families have fallen by the wayside, new internal pressures must take their place in order to maintain the family as an institution. Thus, as the importance of children as an economic resource for the family has become obsolete, the importance of affectional bonds has come to occupy greater prominence as a cohesive force for the family.

Recent Changes in Family Demography

According to the 1980 census, there are a number of noteworthy trends in family structure in the United States. First, the family is diminishing in size. This is the result of a number of trends including decreasing fertility, increasing divorce rates, decreasing marriage rate for women, and delayed childbearing. In addition, there appears to be a new human life course emerging with more transitions than previously existed. This latter trend is due to the prevalence of divorce and remarriage, which often leads to second families with children.

Another important trend in the demography of the family is that larger numbers of children live in one-parent homes (usually with their mothers) below the poverty line. Half of the black children in the United States live in one parent homes that are usually maintained by the mother. Unfortunately, we do not have any recent complete demographic or epidemiological studies of retarded children living in families in the United States (Rowitz, 1985).

If the demography of the family is changing in the United States, how does having a retarded or handicapped child in the family affect family structure? We do not have a very good conception of what a "normal" family is like. We also may not know what the appropriate responses are to having a handicapped child in the family. It is most likely that there are different appropriate responses at different stages of a child's development and at different points in the family life cycle.

FAMILY LIFE-CYCLE THEORY

One of the current perspectives from which to view the family in modern society is that of family life-cycle theory. This perspective grows out of the view that there are specific stages in the course of a family's existence and the way in which the family passes through these stages will determine its success or failure as a social unit. The standard stages usually considered include the unattached young adult, the newly married couple, the family with young children, the family with adolescents, the family launching children, and the family in later life (McGoldrick and Carter, 1982). This is obviously an idealized middle-class version of the life cycle and leaves out single parent families and reconstituted families. Some writers have included many more stages in order to account for varieties of transitions and substages in the life course of a family. Many of these may have become necessary in the light of the new information reviewed previously about how the family is changing demographically in the United States. Thus, the prevalence of divorce and remarriage in recent years may add new stages of family development to the traditional family life cycle. In addition, some families may not go through the stages in the traditional family life cycle. For example, families with never-married single mothers follow a different life course than the traditional life-cycle course.

It is not clear how having a handicapped child alters the family life cycle. There really is no available evidence that considers what the family life cycle is like for families with mentally retarded members. Turnbull, Summers, and Brotherson (1986) proposed some theoretical formulations for considering the family life cycle for such families. They pointed out that although the essence of family life cycle is change, for families with a retarded youngster there is also the chronicity of the child's condition that may affect how the family evolves over the child's life course. Turnbull and her colleagues constructed an elaborate framework for considering the family in the context of demands and stressors to which they are subject. Their approach allows for many interesting and important questions to be asked about how handicapped children affect and are affected by the family and its eco-cultural niche. Their approach will no doubt lead to some very interesting and important findings that will contribute to answering the many questions about families of mentally retarded persons.

These authors, however, consider family in the more traditional sense of the term: that is, a nuclear family consisting of a father, mother, and children. In the context of the present volume, it seems important to propose a framework that would permit consideration of a broader definition of the family so that family means social group with whom one resides. This would allow a methodological approach bridging both traditional family configurations and such residential arrangements as group homes and even institutional residences. In the balance of this chapter we present a framework that we hope will lead to the possibility of comparing various family forms or residential settings in which mentally retarded children and adults live. Such comparisons will facilitate evaluation of placement decisions.

FAMILY CHARACTERISTICS

In order to compare different types of families or family settings in research on families with developmentally disabled members, we must adopt a uniform set of descriptors. These descriptors will represent independent variables that are necessary to make comparisons in multivariate studies. Three major categories are proposed here, but this is certainly not an exhaustive list. The first category, the setting in which the family lives, provides a designation of the context of the family residence. The other categories are reserved for describing the members of the family, with each category representing the major role classifications that are usually of interest to investigators studying families. First, caregivers are described. The subcategories here represent the most important dimensions that can be used to describe caregivers. The second category, family members, is used to characterize the members of the family other than the caregivers.

Setting

There are four major ways in which family settings may be characterized. The type of setting is the most basic category. This category is divided into family residence, group home–community setting, group home–institutional setting, and institutional dormitory. The second category is size of setting. This dimension, which refers to the number of people, is easily quantified and ranges from 2 to 100s. Another category that is considered under setting is organization. This refers to the social structure and functional organization of the residential setting. Under this heading are roles, staffing patterns, hierarchical structures, and power/dominance relationships. Finally, the physical design of the setting may be an important variable to consider. This may include number of rooms, density, room arrangement, and privacy.

TYPE

The family residence is the most prevalent setting for children growing up, although it is not clear that it has been the most prevalent one for mentally retarded children. This type could be subdivided into traditional nuclear families, single-parent families, large extended families, adoptive families, and foster families. The convention for classifying families that was just described can serve to identify what sort of family a child belongs to. Few investigators have compared a large variety of these family settings. In Chapter 20, Eyman, Borthwick, and Sheehy described a study of foster placement but did not compare the foster setting with the other types of families. The group home in the community is a type of setting that has grown in number in the era of deinstitutionalization. Such group homes vary along a number of other dimensions that describe family settings. Most group homes have house parents or counselors and a number of residences. Several authors in this volume discussed group homes, including Janicki, Jacobson, Zigman, and Lubin (Chapter 8), Seltzer and Seltzer (Chapter 9), and Felce (Chapter 6). Group homes in institutional settings are a relatively recent development, also in response to the deinstitutionalization trend in residential facilities. In Chapter 5 Landesman described the process of adaptation of retarded residents to such settings. The institutional dormitory is the setting that dominated the living arrangements for large numbers of mentally retarded persons until the trend to deinstitutionalization began. It is this setting that most people consider when they think of residences for retarded persons.

SIZE

This dimension is easy to measure because there is a continuum of number of persons in a setting. This variable is of interest because there is a literature on the number of people in a setting and how various psychological and biological processes are affected by size. Landesman has written about the relationship of number of people in a setting to many outcome variables. Although the basic finding regarding size is that "smaller is better," this is not always the case, and group size must be considered in conjunction with other factors. For example, Landesman-Dwyer, Sackett, and Kleinman (1980) found that residents of larger group homes had more social interactions and more sophisticated relationships than did those in smaller homes, although other factors were not related to group size.

ORGANIZATION

This factor may include social structure as well as functional organization of the setting. The roles different people in the setting assume constitute one type of organization structure. For example, in traditional families, one person often assumes the role of "mother." This person attends to the emotional needs of the other persons in the setting. Another person may have the role of "breadwinner," working outside the home to earn money to provide for the material needs of the family. These roles may also be shared among different people. There are many other roles that family members may assume that can describe the functional organization of the family. There are other ways to describe the structural organization of the family setting. The way in which family members utilize their influence and resources may define the family's power/dominance relationships. Thus, there may be one person who has the dominant influence, or there may be a number of people who maintain the power in the family. The power/dominance relationships may define a hierarchical social structure, or such structure may be imposed by some authority external to the group itself. For example, in the case of a group home, the authority is given to a leader by the agency who has established the home. Finally, in larger residential settings, the staffing patterns may define the organization. These are all important features of the setting that can be defined and may determine the way in which people behave and develop in the setting.

PHYSICAL DESIGN

The space in which a setting is located is one of the least understood features of settings. The number of rooms available may be an important determinant of behavior organization in family life. Although this factor is usually considered in conjunction with the number of people occupying the space, it can be a factor in itself. Having the space divided into a number of compartments may allow individuals to get away from one another without leaving the residence. A larger number of rooms may also provide needed variety and extra stimulation. When the size of the group or number of people is considered in relation to the number of rooms or the size of the space, then the density of the setting can be established. Research with animals and human beings has shown that the larger the number of people per space, the more abnormal behavior becomes. The arrangement of rooms may also be an important feature of the setting. Certain kinds of arrangements may be conducive to social interaction whereas others may lead to isolate behavior. The way in which rooms are furnished or decorated may also determine the quality of the behavior in the setting. Some of these foregoing factors (e.g., density and room arrangement) may also affect the privacy afforded to individuals. This can have a great impact on the well being and quality of life of the individuals in the setting.

Family Members/Residents

A number of dimensions may be used to describe the characteristics of residents or family members. Some of these characteristics are demographic factors, such as age and age mix, gender ratio of the residents, socioeconomic status of the residents, and ethnicity and ethnicity mix of the residents. Other characteristics are relevant to the residents' handicapping conditions, such as type, severity, and etiology of the disability; competence; learning potential; or work skills. Finally, a number of factors are social factors such as the person's length of time in the residence, social network, and personality traits.

Demographic Factors

The chronological ages of family members or residents may be important in understanding how the family group functions. In a family with very young children, biological needs may occupy a dominant place in family life, whereas a family with adolescents may be more concerned with providing guidance for the imminent launching phase. The mix of ages in a group may also take on significance, especially when individuals from different developmental periods are present.

Similarly, the homogeneity or heterogeneity of family composition with regard to gender, ethnicity, and socioeconomic status may have some significance for the quality of outcomes and expectations for adaptation of the individuals in the family. These factors are not often considered in research on families with retarded members. Nevertheless, some of them may be quite important. Although comparisons were not made with other ethnic groups, Edgerton (1984) reported that black families seem to have a greater acceptance of retarded family members than what has been reported more generally for white families. Anecdotally, Hamburg (1983) reported that in China there also seems to be better acceptance of retarded children in families and in schools. Likewise, there appears to be differential acceptance in families of retarded girls and boys, where the latter may be less acceptable. This, of course, may be due to the differential value placed on boys and girls by some families. It is not at all clear whether the socioeconomic status of a retarded individual's family of origin has any impact on his or her behavior or environment. We hope that greater attention will be paid to these demographic variables in the future.

HANDICAPPING CONDITION

Severity of disability is one characteristic that has been studied extensively. For example, Landesman-Dwyer, Stein, and Sackett (1978) showed that the level of retardation among group home residents was related to the amount of time spent in major activities. Mildly retarded persons spent more time in social activities and less time inactive than did severely or profoundly retarded individuals. Richardson, Koller, Katz, and McLaren (1983) also considered level of disability in their study of services to retarded young adults. They found that the level of impairment was related to the kind and length of day and residential services received.

We found few studies in which investigators made comparisons across family settings with regard to this variable. Likewise, there is little information regarding the relationships between etiological condition of mentally retarded individuals across family settings and outcome factors . Etiology may interact with severity of disability or level of retardation but, in some cases, it is of interest, especially if provision of services is under study. Brooks-Gunn and Lewis (1984) reported that etiology of handicap was related to the mothers' responding to their young children. There has been some interest in developmental level of handicapped infants and the way in which mothers interact with these children. Vietze, Abernathy, Ashe, and Faulstich (1978) found that developmental level did not seem to influence responsive vocal responding in retarded infants. Dunst (1984) reported differential responses to infants at different developmental levels by mothers in terms of communicative acts. Brooks-Gunn and Lewis (1984) found differential maternal responsiveness to infants with Down syndrome, general developmental delay, and cerebral palsy although this may have interacted with developmental level of the children. Nevertheless, it is rare to find comparisons across level of disability and across the age span in studies of parent–child interaction because of the inherent methodological problems in such research.

SOCIAL FACTORS

Social factors may also influence a variety of outcome variables in family studies. The length of time persons have been in a particular setting may be a marker for social experiences that shape their behavior and potential for adaptation. This variable is often overlooked as an independent variable. It may be determined by the age of the individual during the period of childhood, but in older individuals it can also be independent of age. Richardson et al. (1983) studied length of time that residential services were received but treated it as a dependent variable. Another social factor that may be considered as a predictor is the person's social network. This really is a set of variables that can be used to describe the degree of social isolation an individual experiences as well as the quality of social embeddedness the person enjoys. Turner (1983) described the social networks in a sheltered workshop using qualitative analytic techniques but provided no information about the quantitative dimensions or representativeness of these networks. In other research endeavors, investigators have studied social networks quantitatively as well as qualitatively so that the social network measures may be used as predictors or as outcome variables (e.g., Coates, 1985). Finally, the personality traits of individuals in relation to the family settings as we have construed them can be useful ways of characterizing persons. Although personality approaches often tend to label individuals and apply static classifications, it is possible to entertain a notion that personality is a dynamic construct capable of modification and change. In this context, we acknowledge the potential for personality measurement to facilitate the understanding of how retarded persons adapt to their family settings and how they might respond to different service patterns.

Caregiver Characteristics

There are three major categories under which caregivers may be described: demographic characteristics, management attributes, and social variables. These categories can be used to describe caregivers in a similar fashion to the use of social variables to describe family members.

DEMOGRAPHIC CHARACTERISTICS

The caregivers' age may be relevant to the quality of care provided. Very young and very old caregivers may be less able to provide adequate care to retarded persons, though for different reasons. The very young caregiver may be inexperienced and too focused on self-fulfillment to be able to provide patient and attentive caregiving to retarded children or adults. Older caregivers may just not have the stamina and physical strength to provide appropriate care. There has been little systematic attention paid to this characteristic in the literature on caregivers of retarded individuals. The major interest in caregiver age has been in the age of the parents and its influence on offspring with Down syndrome and in adolescent parents in general.

Ethnicity of caregivers in relation to family members or residents has also not been studied specifically, except by Edgerton (1984). This is probably a very important factor because the rapport of caregivers with their charges probably will determine the caregivers' effectiveness. Findings from other areas suggest that ethnicity of staff and clients may affect rapport. Thus, the match between caregiver and resident with regard to ethnicity may be the important issue.

Similarly, the sex of the caregiver may have an effect on the behavior of residents or family members. Considering parents as caregivers provides a built-in comparison of the sex of the caregiver. In the past, much of what was written on relationships between parents and children has focused on mothers. This has extended to the literature on handicapped children as well (e.g., Vietze et al., 1978; Vietze & Anderson, 1983). There is now a literature on fathers and their behavior with their children (Lynn, 1974; Parke, 1981). There has been a dearth of research on fathers of handicapped children. Anecdotal evidence has suggested that fathers of handicapped children tend to withdraw from the family and become less involved with their children, especially their handicapped children; however, Gallagher, Cross, and Scharfman (1981) found that fathers and mothers think that fathers should be involved with their handicapped children. Further, they found that fathers want to be more involved with their handicapped child, although they are often unsure of just how to express such involvement. In a more recent investigation, Gallagher and his associates found that although a handicapped child may impose greater demands on a family, the father is no more involved in helping the mother than are fathers in comparable families with nonhandicapped children (Gallagher, Scharfman, & Bristol, 1983). Sex of caregiver in nontraditional families has rarely, if ever, been considered, although it might be important to understand whether female caregivers are more likely to act more maternal with the children in their charge than are male caregivers and whether male caregivers are more likely to adopt paternal roles. The match between sex of caregiver and sex of residents might therefore be an important consideration in research on families because the behavioral manifestations of gender roles could affect outcome behaviors in those being cared for.

Finally, the socioeconomic status of the caregiver may be an important factor in the same way that other demographic variables might affect the behavior of family members or residents. Socioeconomic status probably would be influential in the way it determines values related to caregiving. In this case, it is also possible that the match between socioeconomic status of the caregiver and that of the resident may only be relevant when they do not match. It is evident that the importance of these demographic variables may depend on the similarity between caregiver and resident rather than the caregiver's demographic characteristics per se.

Management Attributes

A number of variables concerning the management of residential settings for retarded persons must also be considered. One of these is the educational and training of caregivers. This may apply to biological parents and foster parents as well as residential caregivers. In general, investigators have found that better-educated caregivers perform better in caregiving functions. Although this has been considered in studies of the latter two group of caregivers, there has been little attention paid to the training or parenting education of biological parents. One successful program of research and development in the training of parents of retarded children is that developed by Baker (see Chapter 12 for a summary description of this program). Parent training is an especially important issue when considering the adequacy of biological parents who are mentally retarded.

What to focus on in training mentally retarded parents raises the issue of minimal and maximal criteria for parenting adequacy. These issues are considered in detail by Greenspan and Budd (1986).

A second issue that must be considered and for which there is no adequate conceptualization is the attitudes of caregivers toward mentally retarded and handicapped persons. There is a long history of research and discussion regarding the relationship of attitudes and behavior in the social psychological literature. Indeed, attitudes and attitude change have been the bread and butter of social psychology. Nevertheless, little effort has been made to apply the vast technology of the social psychology of attitudes to the very important problems presented by mentally retarded and handicapped persons in our society. Much of the focus of research on attitudes toward mentally retarded children has been in school settings. Gottlieb (e.g., 1975) has provided a discussion of some of the problems of measuring and understanding the role of attitudes toward mental retardation. Among them is the assumption that the mentally retarded persons about whom attitudes are held are generally moderately or severely retarded. Thus, there is often little differentiation among the class of object referents in attitude studies. Increasingly, researchers in this area have begun to define the behavioral attributes of the object referents in attitude studies. Suffice it to say that extensive research is necessary in order to develop paradigms and measures that can characterize the attitude dimensions of caregivers of retarded persons.

The ratio of caregiver to resident is an issue that has been all but neglected in research on family settings for mentally retarded persons. In the long history of writing and research on infant and child day care, this issue has been among the most hotly debated. Growing out of a concern that young infants and children might not get sufficient high quality care in day care settings in which a caregiver had too many children to supervise, specific limits have been set for the caregiver to child ratio. Earlier, we considered the density of persons in a setting as an important variable. The ratio of caregivers to residents is related to person density but is considered here because the ability to provide optimal care may depend on the number of persons that caregivers supervise. It is difficult to find studies in which investigators have considered this variable specifically. There is some research in the family literature concerning the number of children in a family, though this literature is not as concerned with the quality of care issue. One reason in that in some types of families, older or more experienced children/residents may be given responsibility for the younger or less experienced ones. In institutional family settings, this may be less likely to happen. In her study of changing institutional settings, Landesman (Chapter 5) considered the optimization of the caregiver/resident ratio in the smaller home-like settings. Her findings show, however, that merely improving the ratio between caregivers and residents did not have much impact on the quality of interaction between the caregivers and the residents. She suggested that specific retraining should probably be provided in order to maximize the potential benefits of a favorable caregiver to resident ratio.

The last of the important management attributes concerns length of service of the caregivers. This variable may or may not be related to education and training of caregivers. In the case of biological or foster parents, the two factors may be confounded. In considering caregivers who work in institutional or community residence family settings, however, the length of service may be independent of training and education. In general, many researchers studying institutional and community care facilities have found that for caregivers who remain, length of service often improves the quality of care. Unfortunately, this is not a variable that is always considered, and therefore we are including it here as a factor that should be examined in family studies.

SOCIAL VARIABLES

There are four sets of variables that might be considered as social variables of caregivers. First, the marital status of caregivers may have an influence on the quality of their caregiving. This is especially the case in single-parent families where the fact that the caregiver may not have been married or where the caregiver is divorced could affect the social milieu of the family. Much has been written about the effect of divorce on nonhandicapped children (Hetherington, 1981), but little is known about how divorce affects the family life and the development of retarded or handicapped children. In families in which the biological parents are not the caregivers, the marital status of the caregiver might also be important.

A second social variable that might affect family outcomes is the family history of the caregivers. The quality of family life that caregivers experience could have an effect on how effective they are as caregivers. The aspect of family history that has received the most attention is whether the caregiver experienced abuse or neglect as a child. Although definitive evidence has not been uncovered to show a causal relationship between history of abuse of the caregiver and quality of caregiving, some correlation has been demonstrated. How such family history factors relates to the quality of care for caregivers in foster families, institutional settings, or community group homes is unknown. The whole continuum of caregiving behavior, not just the possible negative experiences and outcomes, might be affected by caregivers' own family experiences and should be considered.

The social networks of caregivers should also be considered in research on families. The caregivers' social network may be a marker for the relationship of the family to the community at large. It may also be an index of the social experiences that the family members/residents can have. The additional pressures of daily living that may exist in families with retarded members may make the social network factors especially important. Valid measures of social networks have been developed and could be applied to examining how families affect and are affected by retarded or handicapped members.

Finally, in the same sense that personality factors might provide some insight into the behavior of family members, the personalities of the caregivers might also be important. Such dimensions as dominance—submissiveness, internal–external locus of control, and introversion–extroversion might provide useful information regarding the quality of life of the family with retarded or handicapped members. If a caregiver tends to respond to stress with depressive behaviors or responses, the effect on the other family members might be devastating. Consideration of such personality traits, whether they are viewed as static or dynamic factors, could be significant in selecting and training caregivers.

RESEARCH ON FAMILIES WITH RETARDED MEMBERS

We have provided a definition of family that will permit the comparison of traditional families, adoptive families, foster families, group homes, and institutional residences, all settings in which retarded persons are found. We believe that in order to have a complete understanding of the impact of family life on retarded persons and of the impact of family configurations on the well being of retarded persons, similar variables and factors must be considered when studying these different residential settings. To that end we have provided a framework for describing independent and intervening variables that can be studied when conducting such research. This framework is considered necessary in light of our description of the changing structure of the traditional family in the United States, the research and conceptualization on direction of influence in families, and the emerging interest in family life-cycle theory. We have provided a framework for outcome variables for families and children in another book (Coates, Vietze, & Gray, 1985). That framework dovetails well with this one.

We expect that future research on families with retarded members, using our definition of family, will reflect this broader view of family variables. It is our belief that this research will begin to form a body of knowledge that may be more easily applied to problems facing retarded persons and the people responsible for their well being. We also expect that progress in this direction will contribute to facilitating the development of greater opportunities for independent living for retarded persons themselves.

REFERENCES

Brooks-Gunn, J., & Lewis, M. (1984). Maternal responsibility in interactions with handicapped infants. *Child Development, 55*, 782–793.

Coates, D. L. (1985). Relationships between self-concept measures and social network characteristics for black adolescents. *Journal of Early Adolescence, 5* (3) 19-338.

Coates, D. L., Vietze, P. M., & Gray, D. B. (1985). Methodological issues in studying children of disabled parents. In K. Thurman (Ed.), *Children of handicapped parents.* New York: Academic.

Dunst, C. (1984). Toward a social-ecological perspective of sensorimotor development among the mentally retarded. In P. Brooks, R. Sperber, & C. McCauley (Eds.), *Learning and cognition in the mentally retarded.* Hillsdale, NJ: Erlbaum.

Edgerton, R. (1984). *Lives in process: Mildly retarded adults in a large city.* Monographs No. 6). Washington, DC: American Association on Mental Deficiency.

Gallagher, J. J., Cross, A., & Scharfman, W. (1981). Parental adaptation to a young handicapped child: The father's role. *Journal of the Division of Early Childhood, 3,* 3–14.

Gallagher, J. J., Scharfman, W. & Bristol, M. M. (1984). The division of responsibilities in families with preschool handicapped and nonhandicapped children. *Journal of the Division of Early Childhood, 8,* 3–11.

Gottlieb, J. (1975). Public, peer and professional attitudes toward mentally retarded persons. In M. J. Begab & S. A. Richardson (Eds.), *The mentally retarded and society: A social science perspective.* Baltimore: University Park Press.

Greenspan, S. & Budd, K. S. (1986). Research on mentally retarded parents. In J. J. Gallagher & P. Vietze (Eds.), *Families of handicapped persons.* Baltimore: Brookes.

Hamburg, B. (1983). *Services for children and adolescents in China.* Paper presented to the Center for Research on Mothers and Children, NICHD, Bethesda, MD.

Hetherington, M. (1981). Children and divorce. In R. Henderson (Ed.), *Parent-child interaction: Theory, research and prospects.* New York: Academic.

Landesman-Dwyer, S., Sackett, G. P., & Kleinman, J. S. (1980). Small community residences: The relationship of size to resident and staff behavior. *American Journal of Mental Deficiency, 85,* 6–18.

Landesman-Dwyer, S., Stein, J. G., & Sackett, G. P. (1978). A behavioral and ecological study of group homes. In G. P. Sackett (Ed.), *Observing behavior, Vol. 1: Theory and application in mental retardation.* Baltimore: University Park Press.

Lynn, D. (1974). *The father: His role in child development.* Monterey, CA: Brooks/Cole.

McGoldrick, M., & Carter, E. A. (1982). The family life cycle. In F. Walsh (Ed.), *Normal family processes.* New York: Guilford.

Parke, R. (1981). *Fathers.* Cambridge: Harvard University Press.

Richardson, S., Koller, H., Katz, M., & McLaren, J. (1983). Severity of intellectual and associated functional impairments of those placed in mental retardation services between ages 16 and 22: Implications for planning services. In K. T. Kernan, M. J. Begab, & R. B. Edgerton (Eds.), *Environments and behavior.* Baltimore: University Park Press.

Rowitz, L. (1985). Proposal for information networks in mental retardation. *Mental Retardation, 23,* 1–2.

Turnbull, A. P., Summers, J. A., & Brotherson, M. J. (1986). Family life cycle: Theoretical and empirical implications and future directions for families with mentally retarded members. In J. J. Gallagher & P. Vietze (Eds.), *Families of handicapped persons.* Baltimore: Brookes.

Turner, J. (1983). Workshop society: Ethnographic observations in a work setting for retarded adults. In K. T. Kernan, M. J. Begab & R. B. Edgerton (Eds.), *Environments and behavior.* Baltimore: University Park Press.

Vietze, P., Abernathy, S., Ashe, M., & Faulstich, F. (1978). Contingent interaction between mothers and their developmentally delayed infants. In G. P. Sackett (Ed.), *Observing behavior, Vol. 1: Theory and application in mental retardation.* Baltimore: University Park Press.

Vietze, P. & Anderson, B. J. (1983). Styles of parent-child interaction. In M. J. Begab, H. C. Haywood, H. L. Garber (Eds.), *Psycho-social influences in retarded performance, Vol. 1: Issues and theories in development.* Baltimore: University Park Press.

Group Residential Settings

5
The Changing Structure and Function of Institutions: A Search for Optimal Group Care Environments

Sharon Landesman

University of North Carolina at Chapel Hill

Public residential facilities for mentally retarded individuals are a barometer of a society's beliefs, values, resources, and technology related to handicapping conditions. As such, these environments seldom are static. Over the past century, public institutions in the United States have changed considerably in terms of their size, the populations they serve, and their per capita cost (Lakin, Krantz, Bruininks, Clumpner, & Hill, 1982). Besides these documented changes, institutions have assumed a philosophy of care that emphasizes the active habilitation of each resident, replacing the earlier benevolent careprovider view (Berkson & Landesman-Dwyer, 1977). Since the mid-1960s, federal and state standards have become increasingly rigorous, in part to prevent the neglect and abuse that had been prevalent in many of the state facilities. The controversy about institutions still rages on, in courtrooms, legislative sessions, advocacy groups, and professional circles (e.g., Center on Human Policy, 1979; Ferleger & Boyd, 1979; Kaufman, 1981). The controversy centers on three primary issues: (a) Should there be institu-

Acknowledgements. The National Institute of Child Health and Human Development (HD 11551 and HD 00346) and the Department of Social and Health Services, State of Washington, supported this research. I extend special thanks to Gale Watts, who supervised the field data collection, and to Judy Bly, Al Cory, Christine Curtis, Karla Fredericksen, Pamela Garnett, Kathy Kipp Hauck, Kevin Isherwood, Jean Jameson, Susanne Keller, Charles Lund, Victor Morin, Darcy Polanecsky, Judith Schockit, and Ann VanderStoep, who helped gather and analyze data. Above all, I thank the residents and the direct care staff for their willingness to let us study their lives, day in and day out.

tions at all, given the evidence that all types of developmentally disabled individuals can be served in community-based settings? (b) Can institutions be re-vitalized, so that the quality and intensity of their services match or exceed those provided in good family or community-based special care homes? and (c) Are there some mentally retarded individuals who essentially show only minimal awareness of their environments and for whom active, daily training programs are meaningless exercises?

Such broad questions are difficult to answer, particularly in terms of objective evidence about the effects of alternative residential environments on the lives of mentally retarded individuals (Landesman-Dwyer, 1981; Landesman & Butterfield, in press). Clearly, the majority of states continue to commit major resources (in excess of three billion dollars) to the renovation and operation of their institutions. Although the social policies guiding the maintenance of institutions are not always explicit and rarely are tied to research findings (Baumeister, 1981; Butterfield, 1976; Etzioni, 1976), the actual changes implemented within institutions are amenable to systematic evaluation. With an increasing array of alternative residential services, the possibilities are greater than ever for conducting controlled and prospective studies of similar populations placed in diverse environments. The difficulties, however, in conducting such "real world" evaluations are many, and no single study can provide definitive answers about "what matters most" or whether what works today will work tomorrow.

The philosophy of normalization has provided the key impetus for re-designing many aspects of the social service-delivery system in mental retardation (e.g., Kugel & Shearer, 1969; Nirje, 1976; Wolfensberger, Nirje, Olshansky, Perske, & Roos, 1972). Normalization ideology reflects the belief that behavior is directly affected by the environment, an assumption consistent with the fundamental axiom in environmental psychology (e.g., Moos, 1973; Stokols, 1981, 1982). As Moos (1973) advocated:

> Essentially, every institution in our society is attempting to set up conditions that it hopes will maximize certain types of behavior and/or vectors of development. . . . In this sense, it may be cogently argued that the most important task for the behavioral and social sciences should be the systematic description and classification of environments and their differential cost and benefits to adaptation. (p. 662)

The key untested tenet in mental retardation policy is this: that providing more "normative" environments (i.e., as home-like and age-appropriate as possible) will result in more "normative" behavior among handicapped individuals. Conceptually, environmental variables may be divided into those that are primarily structural versus functional. Although the studies reported here concern structural and functional changes in institutional settings, there is no a priori reason to assume that the principles of behavioral adaptation in these environments are different than those operating in other places. What does distinguish both the traditional and the modern institutional environments is the naturally occurring constellation of correlated variables.

SETTING THE STAGE FOR A CONTROLLED, LONGITUDINAL STUDY

My prior research in residential settings involved detailed description of environments (Landesman-Dwyer, Stein, & Sackett, 1978), naturalistic observation of day-to-day behavior and friendships (Landesman-Dwyer, Stein, & Sackett, 1978; Landesman-Dwyer, Berkson, & Romer, 1979), and assessment of enrichment strategies, including increased physical contact between peers (Landesman-Dwyer & Sackett, 1978). These studies demonstrated the usefulness of observational methodology (Sackett & Landesman-Dwyer, 1977; Sackett, Landesman-Dwyer, & Morin, 1981) and provided a rich data base for generating hypotheses and challenging some widely held beliefs about what is "good" for retarded individuals (Landesman-Dwyer, Sackett & Kleinman, 1980). These studies were limited, however, by their lack of appropriate control groups, alternative environments, and a longitudinal perspective.

To correct these problems in future studies, I developed a collaborative relationship with those responsible for the delivery of residential services. As part of this collaboration, I agreed to help answer the questions that administrators, legislators, professionals, and parents' groups raised, such as, "What's really happening out there?" and "Do our programs work?" In return, I gained access to a wide range of programs, people, and plans; permission to negotiate for reasonable controls in subsequent studies; and new insights into the factors that might influence the social behavior of retarded individuals.

The first study to result from this collaboration was conducted in 1975 when we gathered data on all 2,550 residents in Washington state's institutions (Landesman-Dwyer & Schuckit, 1976). In 1976, we extended this study to a representative sample of 2,200 retarded individuals living in group homes, board-and-care facilities, nursing homes, and family or foster care settings (Landesman-Dwyer & Brown, 1976). We gathered descriptive data about what services were available and who was receiving them. In accordance with a legislative mandate, state decision-makers and a community advisory board used these data to design future residential programs. To make the data more useful for state administrators, we developed guidelines for judging the appropriateness of residential placements for different subgroups of developmentally disabled citizens (Landesman-Dwyer & Brown, 1977; Landesman-Dwyer, Schuckit, Keller, & Brown, 1977). In essence, these guidelines suggested the parameters for a "behavior-environment fit" (Barker, 1960, 1968).

By apply these guidelines to the statewide population, we identified a large group ($N = 1,027$) of residents who did not appear well matched to their environments. This group consisted mostly of severely and profoundly retarded adults in traditional institutions and in nursing homes. These individuals did not need the intensive 24-hour medical and/or protective services that characterized their living environments, yet their self-help and communication skills were far below those of most residents in community-based group homes or board-and-care facilities (Landes-man-Dwyer & Brown, 1977). As reviewed by Eyman (1976), these are the severely and profoundly retarded clients who show some minimal adaptive behavior skills and have few serious sensory or motor problems, but who require residential support services for most of their lives. Eyman noted the ineffective residential programming for this subgroup and Landesman-Dwyer and Sulzbacher (1981) observed that profoundly retarded individuals often are socially isolated or inactive when placed in group homes not tailored to meet their training needs.

The Department of Social and Health Services proposed a major remodeling of the state's two largest institutions and introduced an innovative community-based program to serve approximately half of the subgroup identified in the studies just mentioned. As Figure 1 shows, these changes were to be implemented into phases, by first adding new duplexes to the traditional institutions, then establishing small "specialized group homes" in community neighborhoods. This provided an opportunity to evaluate prospectively the effects of alternative residential environments on the lives of retarded individuals and their careproviders. In addition to the physical changes, the state planned to enrich the staffing patterns and to provide structured training programs for all residents.

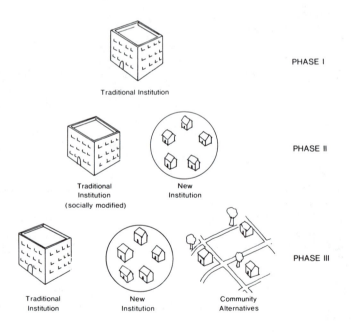

FIGURE 1. Phases of remodeling state-supported residences for severely and profoundly retarded clients.

The Design of a Natural Experiment

These plans set the stage for a natural experiment because the new living units would take 3 to 4 years to construct, the residents could not be relocated all at the same time, a large subject population was available, and the state needed a plan for assigning residents to the new institution-based duplexes and the special group homes in the community. When I proposed random assignment of matched pairs, I scarcely expected but was delighted to receive the support of the key state administrators. One year later, at the start of the study, I discovered that somewhere along the line the basic design had been "forgotten" and that for a variety of seemingly rational reasons, the institution would *have* to move certain residents into the first available beds. The reasons included not wanting to upset some influential parents of residents in the institution, hoping to let some staff members nominate residents to go or to stay, and complying with federal regulations (e.g., not moving residents from one old ward to another, even temporarily).

The state was willing to let about half the residents be randomly assigned, but I doubted whether this would be sufficient to permit certain statistical comparisons or meaningful conclusions about the program's effects. Nearly 20 years ago, Windle (1962) analyzed more than 100 place-ment studies of retarded individuals. He concluded that careless subject selection—often of very heterogeneous samples or of small sample sizes, assigned nonrandomly to treatment alternatives—led to contradictory findings and prevented making any valid predictions about outcomes. Not wanting to add another methodologically unsound study to the long list, I proposed a design called "matched trios."

The *matched trios design* involved a part-random and part-clinical/ad-ministrative assignment of subjects. First, trios of residents were matched on sex, adaptive behavior level, age, length of institutionalization, and medical and behavioral characteristics. Clinical staff reviewed these matches to see whether they thought that the residents were similar in their treatment needs and baseline characteristics. Six of 60 trios were judged poorly matched and were regrouped. Then, administrative and clinical staff members selected one resident from each trio to move into the new experimental units. The remaining two subjects were assigned randomly to either the new duplexes or the old (control) units. This matched trios design allowed the institution staff to select half the residents for the new units, thereby providing the opportunity to compare the clinically/administratively selected residents to those assigned randomly. If the clinical/administrative group fared differently than did the random group, it would be possible to study why. On the other hand, if no systematic differences existed, then I would have a much larger sample and would not have to worry so much about subject loss over time. In fact, any "lost" subject might be replaced with an already matched person upon whom baseline data had been collected. Statistically, the matched trios design ensured a stratified selection by clinical/administrative staff and avoided the bias that could have occurred if staff had placed only certain types of residents (e.g., highest functioning, most attractive) in the new settings. In exchange for approval of this design, I offered to collect outcome measures on the entire subject pool, rather than just on the randomly assigned individuals as originally proposed.

A few asides: First, direct-care staff and their supervisors did not know about the matched trios design, even though they provided information that the professionals and administrators used in the selection procedure. The randomly assigned subjects did not receive segregated or differential treatment at any time. Second, I did not use the term *random* when I interacted with program personnel. Instead, I spoke of "a systematic, fair assignment process," which I characterized as similar to a lottery system that gave all eligible residents an equal chance to participate in the new programs. Third, I felt a sense of relief that the study was not a pure random design. I had been worried that if the new living units were not a clear success, the subject-selection procedure might be blamed.

The *prospective feature* of the study involved 6 months of baseline behavioral observations and monitoring of program activities and health status, followed by 12 months of comparable data collection after residents were moved. In this chapter, I present data collected during the remodeling phase (Figure 1, Phase II) at the first institution, supplemented by measures obtained at the second institution. Follow-up in the specialized community group homes is still underway, although preliminary results from the first facility are included in this chapter.

Methodological Limits

When I proposed these studies, I recognized four limits that merit reiteration.

First, many variables are confounded because more than one variable is manipulated at a time. For instance, at the same time that living units were reduced in size, the staff:resident ratios were changed, so that isolating effects due solely to the residential environment was impossible. Such confounding seems unavoidable when studying the effects of changes in ongoing service-delivery systems. Are such studies useful?

The important issue is whether the type of confounding or correlated change is representative of what will happen when other states revise their service-delivery systems. It probably is, if only because of public pressure, national accreditation standards, and new legislation. Thus, most states are increasing staff:resident ratios in residential facilities in order to meet federal standards to receive matching funds, even though this variable in itself has failed to show beneficial effects on residents (e.g., King, Raynes, & Tizard, 1971; Klaber, 1969). Moreover, an entirely experimental study of each hypothetically influential variable would be inordinately expensive, time-consuming, and probably unethical.

The benefits of conducting such a study seem to outweigh its limits. The study does have random, stratified assignment of residents to different programs. Each residential program is described and monitored in sufficient detail to permit statistical control over uncontrolled or multiply correlated variables. At the practical level, questions that other designs could answer are simply unlikely to be relevant to the changing service-delivery system. For example, in a few years, Washington state will no longer have 40- to 60-bed wards, and it is doubtful that any research could have prevented the remodeling of the institutions because the facilities had been condemned as fire hazards and did not meet federal standards.

Second, there undoubtedly will be changes in residents, staff, and programming over the course of the study. From an experimental view, such changes complicate the research, but no service-delivery system will remain static, nor can guarantees be given that residents will be allowed to remain in any situation that appears unsuitable for them or is disruptive for others. Accordingly, the study was designed to include assessment of the effects of multiple placements. The data on residents who failed to adapt, according to clinical judgment and were moved elsewhere were analyzed separately. The effects on those residents who remained in the group, and who subsequently were exposed to a new group member can be evaluated as well. Concerning changes in the content of the residential programs, the observational methods permit describing what happens in the environments over time. Advance guarantees that a program will adhere to its original plans are not likely to be meaningful. More important, a constant and predictable residential program would not be representative of other ongoing service-delivery systems.

Third, the effects of observing these residential programs may influence what goes on. In all observational and evaluation studies, the presence of outsiders may contribute to observed outcomes. Unfortunately, we could not become invisible or mask the purpose of our presence. We did, however, observe residents and staff on a frequent basis (an average of 10 visits per week on each living unit) for 2.5 years, never announcing the specific observation periods in advance. Prior field experience indicates that people in group settings quickly adapt to observers and seem to ignore them and go about their business. Because Washington's institutions have had an open door policy for many years, the presence of visitors is not unusual. Although the effects of observers cannot be ruled out completely, these probably are diminished considerably after the first few weeks of routine observation. Indeed, if sustained behavioral improvement could be attributed primarily to observers' presence, then this would be a remarkably cost-effective treatment.

Fourth, a "Hawthorne effect" may contribute to improvement in all settings. The fact that something new and supposedly good is occurring is likely to have a positive effect on people regardless of the precise program (Cleland, Cochran, & Love, 1962). If such effects did occur, they should be detected in most new residential programs. Alternatively, the stress of even a beneficial relocation could produce some negative effects, at least during an early adaptation period (e.g., Heller, 1982; Richards & Dobyns, 1957). If either positive or negative effects were detected in the early post-move period, but changed over time, then more careful evaluation of the contributing factors would be needed. For example, if positive social interactions and exploratory play with objects increased in the new units at first, then returned to near baseline levels thereafter, then experimental addition of "new" program elements would be one means of assessing the value of novelty and positive expectations, independent of other variables associated with the first relocation.

STUDYING DAY-TO-DAY BEHAVIOR
AND QUALITY OF LIFE

This research was predicated on two closely related assumptions: that day-to-day behavior is an important barometer of the quality of one's life and that important changes in the environment will be reflected in day-to-day behavior. In part, this research tests the validity and generality of the popular social policy that endorses smaller and more home-like living units, higher staff:resident ratios, greater individual privacy and space, interdisciplinary planning for the habilitation of each resident, and the provision of daily training or education in structure situations. According to this policy, quality of life for almost all residents should be closely related to how well these objectives are met. If these basic assumptions are correct, then successful implementation of this social policy should result in observable and positive changes in residents' behavior. Specifically, residents should show an increase in prosocial behavior; a decrease in antisocial, disruptive, and stereotyped behavior; a greater diversity in their behavioral repertoires; and a higher level of adaptive behavior skills.

A competing theoretical view about the effects of residential environments is that places are not better or worse according to a priori or absolute criteria (e.g., the degree to which they are home-like and close to the norms of a society). Instead, the impact of a residential program would be predicted by the *match* of three elements: the availability of resources, the demands of the environments, and the ability of the individuals to perceive and to respond to the resources and demands.

Resources refer mostly to objects, people, places, and events. They may facilitate or hinder behavior. Resources may be measured systematically across environments, although an inventory per se does not indicate whether, when, or how the resources are used. *Demands* include those implicit and explicit factors that influence the behavioral goals of individuals and of groups. In part, environmental demands reflect the values and beliefs operating within a setting or a society; in part, they indicate the evolution of practical strategies for survival and adaptation. If new resources are introduced into an environment without a corresponding set of demands or expectations about how they are to be used and by whom, then their effects will be minimal or erratic. Similarly, a change in environmental demands will be relatively ineffective if adequate resources are not available. According to this view, the probability of behavioral change would be high when changes in major resources match changes in major demands. The third critical factor is the *ability of individuals* to perceive and to respond to their environments. Personal characteristics such as age, cognitive level, prior life experiences, sensory and motor capacities, and personal preferences are likely to contribute to persons' awareness of environmental changes and to their strategies for adaptation. External variables also may influence their perception of and response to the environment, such as freedom to come and go, rules governing direct actions upon the environment, and the response of other group members. This third factor underscores the fundamental interaction of persons and environments, a paradigm advocated by Cronbach in 1957, but only reluctantly and partly translated into action by the scientific psychology community (cf. Bem & Allen, 1974; Hunt, 1975).

Intuitively, almost everyone agrees that there are individual differences in responses and that environments do not have the same effects on all people. Despite this intuition, it is difficult to formulate precise predictions about who will show what types of responses under what conditions and to demonstrate that behavior is guided by fundamental principles rather than an inordinately large number of random and/or unspecifiable influences. In this conceptual framework, resources are like nouns, demands are like verbs, and individuals are the writers and speakers who generate different sentences, flavored with their own dialect and style, but essentially consistent with the grammar of their language, that is, the basic principles underlying their behavior.

METHOD

Subjects

To identify all residents meeting the criteria for the target group, we assessed all 606 residents living in a traditional institution. We collected demographic and diagnostic information from case records and interviewed direct-care staff about the current adaptive behavior skills of each resident, using items modified from the Adaptive Behavior Scale of the American Association on Mental Deficiency (Nihira, Foster, Shellhaas, & Leland, 1974). Table 1 shows the profile for the 390 severely and profoundly mentally retarded residents in terms of their medical, behavioral, and functional characteristics (see Landesman-Dwyer & Brown, 1976, for details about the method for subgrouping individuals). The 10 cells that are in italics identify the 191 residents who met the criteria for participation in the state's new residential program. None had serious medical or behavioral problems. All had some self-help and communication skills,

TABLE 1 Lakeland Village Residents, Severely and Profoundly Retarded, 17 Years and Older

		Functional Subgroups											
Medical Problems	*Behavior Problems*	*No Skills A*		*Very Limited Skills B*		*Limited Skills C*		*Moderate Skills D*		*High Skills E*		*Raw Totals*	
		%	No.	%	No.	%	No.	%	No.	%	No.	%	No.
None	None	.5	2	*2.3*	*9*	*4.9*	*19*	*10.3*	*40*	.5	2	18.5	72
Moderate	None	3.3	13	*7.7*	*30*	*7.7*	*30*	*6.9*	*27*	.8	3	26.4	103
None	Moderate	1.0	4	1.8	7	*1.3*	*5*	2.3	*9*	—	—	6.4	25
Moderate	Moderate	2.6	10	3.6	14	*2.1*	*8*	*3.6*	*14*	—	—	11.9	46
None	Serious	.5	2	1.0	4	3.3	13	3.9	15	—	—	8.7	34
Moderate	Serious	4.1	16	5.4	21	7.4	29	4.9	19	—	—	21.8	85
Serious	None	.8	3	.5	2	.3	1	1.0	4	.2	1	2.8	11
Serious	Moderate	.8	3	.2	1	—	—	.2	1	—	—	1.2	5
Serious	Serious	1.0	4	.8	3	.3	1	.2	1	—	—	2.3	9
Column Totals		14.6	57	23.3	91	27.3	106	33.3	130	1.5	6	100.0	390

Note Total institutional population was 606. Numbers in italics reflect target group.

but more than half needed assistance in dressing or toilet use. Most were nonverbal or spoke only in 2- to 3-word phrases.

The final subject group, with complete baseline and postmove data sets, included 147 individuals (67 females, 80 males) with a mean age of 34.9 years (standard deviation [*SD*] = 11.6). Their adaptive behavior and cognitive level ranged from that of a nonretarded 2.0- to 6.5-year-old, with a mean of 3.4 years (*SD* = 1.5) as estimated by psychologists at the institution.

Observational Procedures

Trained observers coded the behavior of each subject once every 30 seconds during a 3-minute session using the modified Home Observation Code (Landesman-Dwyer & Watts, 1979; Landesman-Dwyer, Morin, & Curtis, 1979). Each observation involved coding the following dimensions of the subject's behavior: (a) the major ongoing activity (one of 69 mutually exclusive and exhaustive codes), (b) vocalizations, (c) proximity to others, (d) expression of affect, (e) others with whom the subject was interacting, (f) the direction of the social interaction, and (g) the type of stereotype, if any. Table 2 summarizes the codes for these dimensions; full definitions for the major behaviors are provided in the Appendix.

TABLE 2 Listing of Behavorial Codes

A. Major Behavior Codes[a]

Basic Sleep & Wake
01 Sleep
02 Inactive Awake
03 Looking
04 Locomotion/Body
 Change
09 Other

Self-Care Activity
11 Eating/Drinking
12 Grooming/Dressing
19 Other Attention
 to Body

Externally Oriented Activity
21 Unfocused Activity
22 Focused Activity
23 TV/Radio/Stereo/Films
24 Fine Motor/Handicraft/Alone
25 Gross Motor/Recreation/Alone
26 Symbolic/Paper Work/Arithmetic
27 Household Maintenance
29 Other Externally Structured
 (Specify)

Stereotyped & Idiosyncratic Behavior
31 Destruction of Property
32 Self-Abusive Behavior
33 Loss of Temper
34 Major Stereotypy
35 Echolalia/Mimicking
39 Other Idiosyncratic
 (Specify)

Social Codes
41 Plan/Organize
42 Supervise/Direct
43 Instruct
44 General Social
45 Caretaking, Social
49 Social Nature/Can't
 Tell

Special Affiliative Behavior
51 Affection/Console/Care
52 Praise
53 Assist/Help
54 Share Resources
55 Social Play/Gross Motor
56 General Social with Objects
59 Other Positive Social
 (Specify)

Negative Social Behavior
61 Scold, Punish
62 Aggress
63 Inappropriate Sexual
64 Annoy/Obstruct/Upset
69 Other (Specify)

Unobservable/Not Coded
71 Interact with Observer
72 Couldn't Find
73 Left Premises
74 Unable to Observe, Other
79 Can't Code (Specify why)

89

TABLE 2 Listing of Behavioral Codes *(Cont.)*

Supplemental Dimensions[b]

B. Vocalizations	C. Proximity	D. Affect	E. Others as Objects of Interaction	F. Direction of Interaction
0 None	0 Greater than 1.5 m	0 Neutral	0 None or Self	0 Not Applicable
1 Talking to Others	1 Less than 1.5 m	1 Positive	1 Residents	1 Initiates
2 Talking Alone	2 Contact	2 Negative	2 Staff	2 Receives
3 Screaming/Aggressive Sounds	3 Can't Determine	3 Hostile	3 Nonhuman Animals	3 Mutual
4 Crying/Distress Sounds		4 Involved/Intense	4 Inanimate Objects	9 Can't Tell
5 Laughing/Gleeful Sounds		9 Can't Tell	5 Public (General)	
6 Singing/Whistling			6 Residents & Staff	
7 Vocalizing/Nonverbal	G. Type of Stereotypy *(Major or Minor)* [c]		7 Observer	
8 Listing to Other	0 None 5 Vocal		9 Other Human Beings	
9 Physical/Gestural	1 Facial 6 Complex		(to be specified)	
	2 Body 7 Minor Idio-			
	3 Locomotor syncratic			
	4 Object 9 Other			

[a] Only one major behavior code (01-79) entered per 10-second observation. Exact definitions for individual codes provided rules for hierarchial decisions when more than one behavior occurred. (Coding manual available by request to author).

[b] All six supplemental dimensions coded for each 10-second observation.

[c] Major stereotypies were identified by code 34 as major behavior. If major behavior was another code, then this supplemental dimension identified a minor stereotypy that accompanied the major behavior.

Table 3 presents two sample observation sessions, including the data recorded at the start of each session.

TABLE 3 Sample Data Entries From Two Observational Sessions

| Subject no.: 190 | Date: 05/14/79 | No. staff: 02 | No. residents: 08 |
| Observer no: 07 | Time: 1400 | Location: 290 | Setting: 60 |

Obser. no	Major behavior	Vocalizations	Proximity	Affect	Others	Direction	Stereotypy
1	02	0	1	0	0	0	0
2	03	0	1	0	4	0	0
3	03	0	1	0	6	0	0
4	44	1	1	0	2	1	0
5	04	2	1	0	0	0	4
6	04	0	1	0	0	0	4

| Subject no.: 164 | Date: 05/14/79 | No. staff: 01 | No. residents: 011 |
| Observer no: 07 | Time: 1405 | Location: 070 | Setting: 37 |

Obser. no	Major behavior	Vocalizations	Proximity	Affect	Others	Direction	Stereotypy
1	22	0	1	0	0	0	0
2	44	0	1	0	4	1	7
3	44	5	1	1	6	2	0
4	02	1	1	0	2	1	0
5	22	2	1	0	0	0	0
6	45	0	2	1	2	2	0

Interrater agreement on major codes exceeded 80% after 2 weeks of initial training. Every 3 months, interrater reliability was recomputed by having the six observers rotate in all possible pairs and simultaneously code the behavior of randomly selected subjects. To reduce the possibility of any systematic observer bias influencing the data, I assigned observers across subjects, times, days, and settings in a balanced manner.

In this study, I had the good fortune of being able to determine empirically how much observational data to collect. (This good fortune was caused by the delay in building the new living units, which allowed us to conduct some methodological studies.) A representative group of 14 subjects was observed for 2 weeks; their behavior was coded every 15 minutes from early in the morning (6:30 a.m.) until bedtime (9:30 p.m.). A behavioral profile was compiled for each of the subjects from their observed behavior codes and their proportionate occurrence. By randomly selecting subsets of the data and comparing these behavioral profiles with those from the larger data set, I identified the minimum number needed to approximate the larger set. For this population, eight 3-minute sessions generated similarly shaped profiles on those codes that occurred more than 2% of the time. Accordingly, I decided to observe each subject at least eight times every 2 weeks (across different times and days of the week) throughout the baseline and postmove period. This yielded 1,872 discrete observations per subject for 1.5 years, and more than a quarter of a million observations for the subjects collectively. These observations reflected the nature and distribution of social interactions, the relationship of social to solitary behavior, and the changes in day-to-day activities over time and across settings for each subject.

Environmental Measures

Each of the 37 living units was characterized in terms of its (a) physical space and resources; (b) staffing patterns, including the type of staff, their prior work and educational history, job satisfaction, attitudes toward mentally retarded individuals, perception of job responsibilities and autonomy, and ideas for improving the institution; (c) composition of the resident group, including heterogeneity of demographic and behavioral profiles and the number of changes in the group; (d) the degree to which environments were institutionally oriented versus resident-oriented, according to the King et al. (1971) revised Child Management Scale; (e) the amount of cognitive stimulation provided, as reflected on scores on the Caldwell (not dated) Home Observation for Measurement of the Environment (HOME), using the form for 3- to 6-year-olds (comparable to the developmental level of the subjects); and (f) the availability of activities, based on documentation of all special events on and off the living units.

RESULTS

The findings from this study depict changes in environments and their effects on observable behavior. Even during baseline, several basic principles about environment–behavior interactions appeared. Individual baseline differences predicted postmove adaptation strategies.

Baseline Profiles

Initially, all residents lived on large halls of 40 to 60 residents that had dormitory style bedrooms; open bathing and toileting areas; large common living rooms; and clearly identified staff offices, coffee rooms, and storage areas. Although the old units appeared "institutional," they had an ambiance and individuality, reflected in their decor, lighting, availability of things to do, and particular patterns ("culture") of staff–resident interaction. Staff morale and behavior, as well as attitudes toward mentally

TABLE 4   **Premove Baseline Behavioral Activities Across Settings for Control (Con.) and Experimental (Exp.) Groups**

Behavior Code	Living Units		Mealtime		Training Setting	
	Con. N = 60	Exp. N = 87	Con. N = 60	Exp. N = 87	Con. N = 43	Exp. N = 74
Sleep	3.8% (1.1)	3.5% (.9)	— —	— —	.2% (.2)	.2% (.2)
Inactivity	35.8* (2.2)	28.5* (1.8)	11.9* (1.3)	8.6* (1.0)	20.6 (2.2)	21.8 (1.7)
Looking	11.7 (1.0)	12.3 (.9)	6.6 (.8)	5.7 (.7)	10.0 (1.4)	12.7 (1.2)
Locomotion	9.1 (1.1)	9.8 (1.1)	3.4 (.5)	4.4 (.5)	1.8 (.5)	3.7 (.7)
Eating–drinking	.8 (.2)	.9 (.2)	60.2 (2.2)	60.5 (1.7)	.6 (.3)	.8 (.2)
Unfocused activity	6.6 (1.0)	5.0 (.8)	.6 (.2)	.8 (.2)	4.6 (.8)	3.6 (.5)
Focused activity	2.1* (.4)	4.0* (.6)	.3 (.1)	.5 (.1)	13.3 (2.0)	10.2 (1.7)
Watching TV, listening to music	6.1 (1.1)	6.6 (.9)	.1 (.1)	.0 (.0)	1.9 (.8)	2.9 (.6)
Fine-motor activity	.8 (.4)	.3 (.1)	— —	— —	2.9 (1.0)	1.8 (.4)
Gross-motor activity	1.0 (.5)	1.7 (.5)	— —	.1 .1	3.0 (1.2)	1.1 (.6)
Symbolic work	.3 (.1)	.3 (.2)	.1 (.1)	.0 (.0)	3.6 (1.0)	5.2 (.9)
Household work	.9 (.5)	1.5 (.4)	1.1 (.2)	2.4 (.3)	3.2 (1.5)	2.2 (.6)
Externally structured activity	1.0 (.2)	1.4 (.4)	.9 (.2)	1.5 (.3)	2.7 (.6)	2.6 (.4)
Stereotypy	2.7 (.9)	3.1 (.7)	.7 (.3)	.7 (.2)	.8 (.5)	.9 (.4)
Being supervised	.9 (.1)	.8 (.1)	2.2 (.4)	1.2 (.2)	6.7 (.9)	4.8 (.6)
Receiving instruction	.0 (.0)	.1 (.0)	.1 (.0)	.0 (.0)	4.5 (.7)	6.4 (1.1)
General social interaction	4.4* (.8)	7.4* (.9)	3.2 (.5)	5.2 (.8)	2.9* (.6)	6.8* (1.1)

**TABLE 4   Premove Baseline Behavioral Activities Across Settings
for Control (Con.) and Experimental (Exp.) Groups *(Cont.)***

Behavior Code	Living Units		Mealtime		Training Setting	
	Con. N = 60	Exp. N = 87	Con. N = 60	Exp. N = 87	Con. N = 43	Exp. N = 74
Receiving care	1.0	.8	3.3	2.3	.3	.7
(social)	(.2)	(.2)	(.9)	(.4)	(.1)	(.4)
Special affiliative	1.1*	2.4*	1.0	1.2	3.9	3.7
behavior	(.5)	(.8)	(.3)	(.4)	(1.7)	(1.0)
Unobservable	2.9	2.8	1.2	1.9	9.7	3.6
	(.5)	(.4)	(.4)	(.5)	(2.5)	(.9)

Note. Codes observed less than 2% of the time in all three settings were not included in this table. Standard error of measurement is presented in parentheses under the mean (in %).

* Group differences significant at $p < .05$, univariate analyses of variance. The overall group effect was significant only in the living units, based on multivariate analyses of variance for the 10 most frequently observed behavior codes.

retarded people, varied significantly across the living units. Generally, residents lived with others of similar adaptive behavior level, age, and temperament (e.g., aggressive vs. not aggressive residents), although there were a few notable exceptions.

Table 4 presents the baseline behavioral profiles for the residents, taken before any were transferred to new living arrangements. On the living units, inactivity or "doing nothing" occurred more often than any other behavior code, representing nearly one third of the observed behavior. The second most frequent behavior was "looking" (nearly 12%), followed by locomotion (about 10%). General social interaction represented just over 5% of the residents' behavior, whereas special affiliative behavior (e.g., assisting, sharing resources, social play) occurred less than 2% of the time. Note that control and experimental subjects had significant baseline differences on four major behaviors, including general social interaction and special affiliative behavior. These differences also existed for the randomly assigned pairs, indicating that matching on intelligence, age, and sex does *not* ensure similar patterns of day-to-day activities for subjects.

A key finding from the baseline observations is that severely and profoundly retarded residents do show setting-specific patterns of activity. That is, during mealtimes and training, subjects displayed quite different behavioral profiles than they did in their living units. The training setting is of particular interest for three reasons. First, this setting was novel for most residents because they had not been enrolled in outside training programs before. Second, these environments had far more physical and staff resources than did the living units. Third, specific environmental demands or expectations were made for individual residents and for staff members. Under these conditions, the residents tripled their "focused activity" and showed more object-related behavior (e.g., housework, symbolic behavior, fine motor activity). Not surprisingly, subjects received significantly more direct supervision, more than 5% versus less than 1% on the living units. Also, the residents displayed more frequent and diverse types of special affiliative behavior—especially sharing, assisting, and socially playing with objects. Unfortunately, those individuals who showed the greatest behavioral gains during training did *not* demonstrate similar changes in behavior on their living units (Sackett et al., 1981).

TABLE 5 Characteristics of Social Interaction in Different Environmental Settings (Baseline Rates)

Characteristic	Living unit Con.[a] N = 60	Living unit Exp.[b] N = 87	Mealtime Con. N = 60	Mealtime Exp. N = 87	Training Setting Con. N = 43	Training Setting Exp. N = 74
Target of interaction						
Peer(s)	6.6 (.7)	10.7 (.9)	3.1 (.4)	6.7 (.9)	4.2 (.8)	7.3 (1.0)
Staff members	7.0 (.7)	7.2 (.6)	10.2 (1.3)	6.9 (.7)	18.3 (1.6)	21.3 (1.6)
Other(s)	2.0 (.4)	2.0 (.4)	1.0 (.2)	.6 (.2)	.9 (.3)	.5 (.2)
Direction						
Initiates	3.3 (.5)	5.2 (.6)	2.3 (.4)	3.2 (.5)	2.4 (.6)	5.1 (1.0)
Receives	3.3 (.4)	3.9 (.5)	7.1 (1.0)	5.3 (.5)	13.7 (1.3)	14.3 (1.4)
Mutually engages in	1.7 (.4)	3.1 (.5)	.6 (.1)	1.7 (.4)	2.1 (.9)	3.3 (.5)
Distance						
Greater than 1.5 m	27.5 (2.4)	32.8 (1.9)	5.6 (.9)	5.7 (.8)	17.2 (3.0)	9.8 (1.7)
Less than 1.5 m (but no contact)	67.0 (2.4)	60.7 (1.7)	88.5 (1.7)	90.3 (1.0)	76.8 (3.1)	83.9 (1.8)
Physical contact	5.6 (.7)	6.5 (.8)	5.9 (1.2)	4.0 (.5)	6.9 (.9)	6.3 (.8)

Note. Means are in percentages. The standard error of measurement is presented beneath the mean in parentheses.

[a] Control subjects who continued to live in old wards.
[b] Experimental subjects who moved to new duplexes.

Table 5 summarizes some of the features of social interaction during the baseline period. On the living units, residents tended to interact with peers as much as or more than they did with staff members. During mealtime, they interacted more with staff, and this difference was even more pronounced in the training setting. These rates of interaction are attributable primarily to differences in staff-initiated behavior, rather than to residents' approaches to staff members. That is, the residents initiated contact with others at a rate of 3 to 5%, *regardless* of the environmental setting; however, they received significantly more interaction from others during mealtime and training, averaging 6 and 14% respectively, compared to only 3% in the living units. In both mealtime and training settings, residents spent proportionately more time in close proximity (less than 1.5 m) to others than they did on the living units, although their rates of physical contact with others remained similar across settings.

The baseline observations indicate that severely and profoundly retarded individuals do show environment-sensitive patterns of behavior, can engage in special types of affiliative behavior, have the ability to use objects constructively when in certain situations, and have notably high rates of inactivity and low rates of general social interaction.

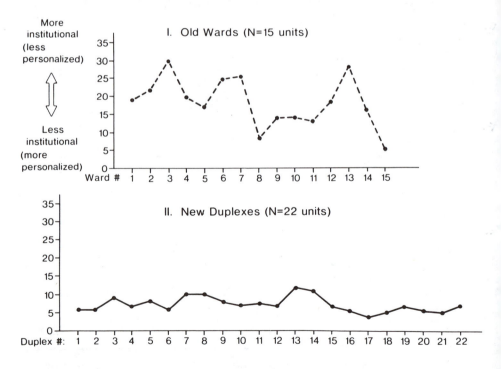

FIGURE 2.   Living unit routines as reflected by resident management scale.

Effects of Moving to New Living Units

The new living units were 14-bed duplexes (six to eight residents per side). Residents had single or double bedrooms, places for their own clothes and personal possessions, and private bathing and toileting areas. Each side had its own kitchen (although meals were prepared in a centralized kitchen), dining area, and small living room. The furniture was more home-like and colorful. On the outside, the duplexes appeared to be attractive single-story brick homes, identified by numbers rather than names, and surrounded by sidewalks, streets, and yards.

The management practices on the new duplexes tended to be significantly less institutional, according to scores on a revision of the Resident Management Scale (Raynes, Pratt & Roses, 1979). The maximum score possible was 30, reflecting the most institutional type of regime. As Figure 2 shows, none of the new duplexes had scores higher than 14, whereas all but 2 of the 15 old halls had scores above this level. The old units had a mean score of 18.2 (SD = 7.1) compared to that of 7.6 (SD = 2.0) for the new units, a highly significant difference, $F(1, 34)$, $p < .001$.

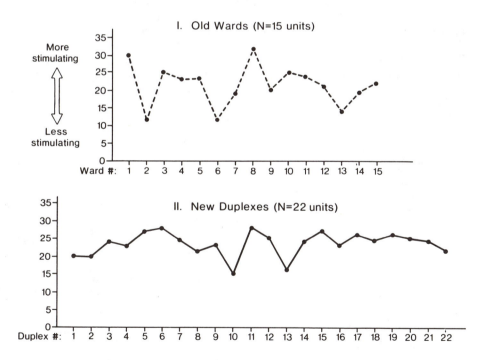

FIGURE 3.   Environmental stimulation as measured by the Caldwell HOME Scale.

Figure 3 indicates that the old wards and new living units also differed on the Caldwell HOME $F(1,34) = 22.9$, p .001, although their mean scores were fairly close together, at the lower (i.e., less stimulating) end of the scale. The new duplexes averaged 21.6 ($SD = 2.7$), whereas the old halls averaged 16.3 ($SD = 4.0$). In comparison, homes for nonretarded 4-year-olds in the greater Seattle area have a mean score of 68.4 ($SD = 5.7$) (Landesman-Dwyer, Ragozin, & Little, 1981). Interestingly, the two highest HOME scores were obtained in the old wards, one of which was fairly institutional in its management practices whereas the other was not so institutional.

In addition to these differences between old and new residential settings, the social contexts changed dramatically. Besides the obvious drop in the average number of residents living on each hall, there were significant changes in the average size of the resident group observed and in the number of staff present and visible. During the post move period, the average size of the resident group was 10.8 ($SD = 5.0$) on the modified old wards, and 3.65 ($SD = 1.0$) on the new duplexes, $F(1,34) = 42.6$, p .001. Figure 4 depicts the number of residents observed on both new and old units. On the old halls, residents were alone about 5% of the observed periods and spent 47% of their time in groups of more than 10 residents. A very different picture emerged in the new settings, where residents spent 19% of their time alone, 23% with only one other person, and only 22% with 5 or more individuals. In essence, residents in the new duplexes experienced two events that seldom occurred during their years of living on large wards: being totally alone and being with only one person at a time.

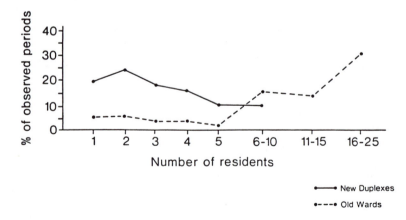

FIGURE 4.   Observed size of resident groups on old wards versus new duplexes.

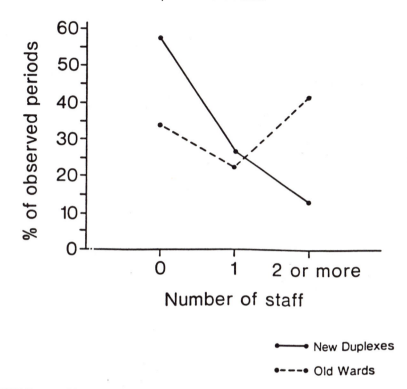

FIGURE 5. **Observed size of staff groups on old wards versus new duplexes.**

Although the formal assignment of staff to new duplexes resulted in a more than four-fold increase in the number of staff per resident, this change did not lead to an increase in the *functional* presence of staff near residents. As shown in Figure 5, no staff members were observed during 58% of the coded periods on the new duplexes, a rate much higher than that of 35% on the old units. Moreover, when a staff member was present on the new units, he or she was much more likely to be alone, whereas staff members usually were in pairs or trios on the old halls. The resident group size appeared to be an important influence on the probability of staff presence, as Table 6 indicates. In the old halls, a group of 11 or more residents was needed before the probability of staff presence exceeded 50%. In the new units, this critical group size was reduced to 5 residents. Moreover, when residents were alone in the new units, the probability of some staff presence was 21%, considerably more than that of 6% in the old units.

Group Settings

TABLE 6   **Distribution of Staff Presence as a Function
of Resident Group Size**

| Resident group size | % occur | Conditional probabilities | | |
		No staff	1 staff	2 or more staff
Old units				
1	5.1	.94	.03	.03
2	5.7	.76	.18	.05
3	4.8	.72	.28	.00
4	4.8	.56	.31	.13
5	2.7	.56	.33	.11
6-10	16.4	.56	.21	.23
11-15	15.1	.28	.27	.45
16-20	19.2	.14	.26	.61
21-25	13.0	.03	.17	.81
% occur	—	34.6	23.4	42.0
New duplexes				
1	19.1	.79	.15	.06
2	22.8	.69	.21	.10
3	18.0	.57	.32	.11
4	17.3	.52	.32	.16
5	11.3	.42	.40	.18
6-10	11.1	.19	.37	.43
11-15	—	—	—	—
16-20	—	—	—	—
21-25	—	—	—	—
% occur	—	58.1	27.8	14.1

To what extent did these changes in physical environments, resident management practices, and social opportunities affect the behavioral profiles of residents? Were the clinically selected subjects more or less sensitive to these environmental changes than were those randomly assigned to new units? Was there behavioral evidence of an initial period of adjustment after residents moved?

The question about the clinically selected versus randomly assigned subjects needs to be addressed first. These two groups did not differ significantly on any of the behavioral outcome measures, either from each other or in their within-group patterns over time. Accordingly, the results from these two groups have been combined in this paper. Furthermore, staff ratings about individual subjects failed to predict their adjustment to the new units. This finding should not be surprising, given the fact that staff had no prior experience with the new units and had only limited opportunities to observe the same individuals in more than one environment. A review of staff predictions indicates that factors such as intelligence, age, sex, or length of institutionalization were not contributing systematically to staff judgments about an individual's potential to benefit from a new, smaller living unit.

The question about the effects of new living units on daily patterns of activity may be answered by a variety of statistical and descriptive analyses. One approach is comparison by the residents transferred to those who were not, being sure to control for baseline behavioral differences between the groups (as shown in Table 4). Rather than using a repeated measures analysis of variance, I used a multivariate analysis of covariance (*cf.* Huck & McLean, 1975). The dependent measures were the 10 major behavior categories that accounted for 80 to 85% of the residents' observed activities. The independent measures were group (control vs. experimental) and time (in 3-month segments during the postmove year).

Group and Time main effects were significant, $F = 4.31$, p .001 and $F = 1.79$, p .01, respectively, although results from the univariate F tests showed that subjects in the old and new units differed significantly only in their television watching, $F = 22.14$, p .001, and stereotyped/idiosyncratic behavior, $F = 12.27$, p .001.

Table 7 presents the means for the groups at each of the postmove time periods. Although control subjects spent an average of 33% of their time inactive, compared to 25% for experimental subjects, this difference was not greater than that observed during the baseline period when all subjects lived on old wards. For all subjects, there was a small decrease (2.5 to 3%) in inactivity after major changes at the institution.

Despite the fact that experimental subjects were in novel environments, their looking behavior did not increase significantly, either above their own baseline rate or in comparison to that of control subjects. Similarly, although the opportunities to engage in unfocused and focused activities with objects was increased somewhat on the new units, based on Caldwell HOME scores, this was not sufficient to produce major behavioral changes. The most dramatic difference was in the amount of watching television by experimental subjects, averaging 10% of their time or twice the amount for control subjects and a 3.5% increase over their own premove rate. Concerning stereotyped and idiosyncratic behavior, residents in both settings showed an increase over the baseline rates. The control subjects, however, increased significantly more than did the experimental subjects, averaging 8.6% during the postmove year compared to 7.6% for the control subjects.

The initial group differences in general social interaction and special affiliative types of behavior persisted during the postmove period. Experimental subjects spent an average of 8.5% of their time in general social exchanges, a 1% increase over their premove rate. The control subjects' rate of 4.8% for general social interaction was less than .5% above their baseline rate. Special affiliative behavior continued to occur at low rates for both groups, 2% for experimental and 1.3% for control subjects.

TABLE 7   Postmove Behavioral Activities by Group

Behavior Codes	Time periods Postmove[a]	Control group		Experimental group	
		Mean	SEM	Mean	SEM
Sleeping	0- 3	4.88	1.03	3.08	0.70
	3- 6	4.34	0.82	3.12	0.85
	6- 9	4.19	0.99	2.60	0.79
	9-12	4.06	1.08	2.89	0.85
Inactivity[b]	0- 3	30.49	2.12	27.06	1.81
	3- 6	31.57	2.22	25.61	1.80
	6- 9	32.52	2.11	22.95	1.71
	9-12	35.55	2.29	26.32	1.76
Looking	0- 3	13.24	1.28	13.05	0.95
	3- 6	12.00	1.33	11.52	0.87
	6- 9	11.69	1.23	12.02	0.95
	9-12	11.94	1.31	9.67	0.86
Unfocused activity	0- 3	4.75	1.07	5.00	0.74
	3- 6	6.66	1.28	4.84	0.84
	6- 9	5.79	1.25	5.76	1.09
	9-12	5.49	1.22	5.32	0.99
Focused activity[b]	0- 3	3.37	0.74	2.64	0.43
	3- 6	3.62	0.92	3.49	0.61
	6- 9	3.46	0.91	4.33	0.64
	9-12	3.27	0.82	3.70	0.61
Watching TV	0- 3	4.30	0.87	8.99	1.21
	3- 6	5.90	1.12	10.66	1.28
	6- 9	5.46	0.87	11.53	1.43
	9-12	4.51	0.95	9.45	1.37
Housework	0- 3	1.27	0.78	1.83	0.43
	3- 6	1.94	0.77	2.50	0.89
	6- 9	1.30	0.91	2.01	0.65
	9-12	1.50	0.78	2.97	0.79
General social interaction[b]	0- 3	4.70	0.81	7.76	1.04
	3- 6	3.72	0.55	8.75	1.08
	6- 9	5.38	0.85	8.99	1.23
	9-12	5.44	1.11	8.54	0.97
Special affiliative behavior[b]	0- 3	0.94	0.17	1.55	0.21
	3- 6	1.78	0.32	2.87	0.40
	6- 9	1.21	0.25	2.26	0.41
	9-12	1.38	0.35	1.58	0.28
Stereotyped/ idiosyncratic	0- 3	9.38	2.31	7.44	1.50
	3- 6	7.57	2.12	7.37	1.58
	6- 9	9.55	2.17	7.80	1.74
	9-12	7.76	2.16	7.85	1.88

[a] In months.

[b] See Table 4: Groups differed significantly on these behavior codes during the premove period.

A different way of viewing behavioral change is to assess individuals' behavioral repertoires in terms of the emergence of new behaviors or the deletion of previously observed ones. As shown in Table 8, for both groups there was a significant number of subjects who demonstrated new behaviors, ones not seen prior to the time of the move. Within 3 months after the move, significantly more subjects in both settings slept during daytime hours, engaged in body stereotypy, interacted with objects, and actively listened to others. The latter two activities have apparent and positive values for adapting to new situations. Body stereotypy, however, is considered a typical institutional-type of behavior that has been related to factors such as lack of social and cognitive stimulation, stress, and seeking attention (Baumeister, 1978). Sleeping may be a side-effect of the new structured training programs in which subjects participated (cf. Landesman-Dwyer, 1976), indicating that individuals were tired from their busy programs.

TABLE 8 Significant Changes in Behavioral Repertoire: During First 3 Months Postmove

Unit/Behavior	No. of subjects	z
Old units (N = 60)		
Sleeping	15	3.25
Body stereotypy	11	2.22
Interacting with objects	18	2.25
Active listening	13	2.94
Focused activity	12	2.07
Fine motor	6	2.04
Major stereotypy	14	2.12
Idiosyncratic	13	2.58
General social	11	2.22
Nonverbal communication	6	2.04
Miscellaneous vocalizations	18	2.77
New units (N = 87)		
Sleeping	22	2.60
Body stereotypy	19	2.92
Interacting with objects	21	2.01
Active listening	20	3.62
Eating	31	3.32
TV/Radio	21	2.94
Housework	26	2.50
Receiving supervision	38	4.67
Crying	8	2.00
Interacting with visitors	29	3.94

In the new duplexes, there was a significant increase in the number of subjects who were observed for the first time to receive direct supervision, participate in household activities, interact with visitors to their homes, and eat at non-mealtime hours. Among control subjects, not as many showed positive additions to their behavioral repertoires, although 11 residents who previously were asocial began to engage in general social interaction and 18 began vocalizing general sounds. Two undesirable behavioral changes occurred for more than 20% of those who continued to reside in the old halls: major stereotypy and idiosyncratic behavior. These subjects had never shown these patterns prior to the changes at the institution.

TABLE 9   Significant Correlations Between Individual Characteristics and Major Behaviors for 147 Subjects

Behavior category	Adaptive behavior level		Age[a]		Length of institutionalization	
	Baseline	Postmove	Baseline	Postmove	Baseline	Postmove
Sleep				.30***		
Inactive	−.38***	−.31***	.28***	.28***	.20*	.19*
Looking				.22**		
Unfocused activity			−.17*			
Focused activity	.24**	.23**				
TV/radio/stereo	.22**	.19*				
General social	.40***	.44***				
Idiosyncratic	−.30***	−.39***	−.23**	−.24**		

[a] Age and length of institutionalization were significantly correlated, $r = .68$.
* $p < .05$.   ** $p < .01$.   *** $p < .001$.

Is There Evidence for Person–Environment Interaction?

An important issue is whether individual characteristics of the subjects influenced their behavioral patterns. Table 9 presents the correlations for adaptive behavior level, age, and length of institutionalization with the major behavior codes. Adaptive behavior level correlated significantly with five types of behavior, showing a similar patterns for both the baseline and the postmove periods. Subjects with higher adaptive behavior levels tended to be more social, have more focused activity, and watch more television, whereas those with lower levels of adaptive behavior were more likely to be inactive or to engage in stereotyped or idiosyncratic behavior. None of these correlations, however, accounted for more than 20% of the variance. (When entered as a covariate in the multivariate analysis of observed behavior, adaptive behavior level did not alter the findings reported previously concerning the effects of the new units.) Older residents showed more inactivity during the pre- and postmove periods and more sleep and looking after the transition. Younger residents demonstrated more stereotyped and idiosyncratic behavior. Length of institutionalization showed minimal association with observed behavior, correlating positively only with inactivity. Because this analysis did not reveal any person–environment interactions, an alternative way of classifying individuals, described next, was tried.

TABLE 10   Varimax Rotated Factor Matrix (After Rotation with Kaiser Normalization) for Major Behaviors, Baseline Period

Factor	Eigenvalue	% of variance	Highest loading variables
1. Social and verbal	2.94	33.3	Verbalization (.94), general social (.91)
2. Stereotyped/ idiosyncratic	1.53	17.4	Idiosyncratic (.95), stereotypy (.89)
3. Receives super-vision/contact	1.33	15.1	Physical contact (.95), special social (.48), social caretaking (.29), being supervised (.28)
4. Object-related activity	1.20	13.6	Inactive (–.86), TV/radio/stereo (.45), focused activity (.42), unfocused activity (.31)
5. Locomotion	.78	8.8%	Locomotion (.86)
6. Looking	.62	7.0%	Look (.78)

BEHAVIORAL CLUSTERS

Although the demographic characteristics and IQs of these retarded adult subjects were relatively homogeneous, factor and cluster analyses revealed great diversity in daily behavior profiles—even within the baseline institutional condition. Initially, 16 behavioral measures that were assumed to be socially or adaptively significant were selected. When factor analyzed, as shown in Table 10, six primary factors emerged, accounting for 95% of the variance. When each subject's scores on these factors were used to perform a cluster analysis by Ward's (1963) method with relocation (Everitt, 1980), five distinct behavioral clusters of subjects emerged. The mean factor scores of these subject clusters are presented in Table 11.

Before going further, I acknowledge the potential problems and difficulties faced when factor scores and clustering techniques are used. There is no best method for deciding how many factors to use or what is the optimal number of clusters. The program for clustering generated from 2 to 10 different clusters. By studying the computer printouts and reviewing which subjects were sorted into the clusters, I concluded that five clusters effectively separated subjects whom I knew to be different, whereas four or fewer clusters combined too many people into a large nondescript group, and more than five clusters resulted in a few peculiar, extremely small groups. I also applied a different statistical program that created the clusters from a randomized start. Because the two methods converged perfectly when five clusters were chosen (Everitt, 1980) (i.e., the same subjects clustered together), there was further justification for the choice of five clusters. Above all, the characteristics of the five clusters seemed to make sense behaviorally and clinically.

TABLE 11   Mean Factor Scores for Five Behavioral Clusters

Factor	Cluster 1		Cluster 2		Cluster 3		Cluster 4		Cluster 5	
	Mean	SD	Mean	SD	Mean	SD	Mean	SD	Mean	SD
1. Social & verbal	−.26	.44	−.27	.49	2.43[a]	1.11	−.30	.40	−.23	.19
2. Stereotyped/ idiosyncratic	−.17	.43	−.29	.36	−.20	.14	−.40	.50	2.57[a]	.92
3. Receives supervision/contact	1.49*	.83	−.50	.52	−.03	.62	−.41	.44	−.13	.65
4. Object-related activity	.18	.70	.76	.75	.03	.70	−1.18[a]	.58	−.30	.77
5. Locomotion	−.16	.42	.35	1.15	−.08	.60	−.34	.59	−.50[a]	.69
6. Looking	.33*	.94	−.08	.80	−.03	.59	−.03	.85	−.24	.37

Note.   Based on Ward's method with relocated clustering (Everitt, 1980). The same clusters resulted when analysis started with 10 randomized groups. Number of subjects for clusters 1 through 5, respectively, were 26, 47, 13, 31, and 13.
[a] Highest mean value for each factor across clusters.

Cluster 1 consisted of 26 residents who received lots of supervision and physical contact from staff and who mostly looked around as opposed to interacting with objects or other people in their environments. Cluster 2 was the largest group, with 47 residents who were not extremely high or low on any behavioral factor. In contrast, Cluster 3 contained the 13 most social and verbal individuals, who showed few maladaptive behaviors and not much interest in object-related activities. The 31 subjects in Cluster 4 represented the least active group, with high negative loadings on the factor of object-related behavior. Finally, Cluster 5 contained the 13 subjects whose behavioral profiles consisted mostly of stereotyped and idiosyncratic behavior.

TABLE 12 Social Behavior Characteristics of Clusters Over Time

Characteristic/ Time period[a]	Behavioral cluster										
	1. Supervised		2. Nondistinct		3. Social		4. Inactive		5. Stereotypy		F
	Mean	SEM	Mean	SEM	Mean	SEM	Mean	SEM	Mean	SEM	
No interaction with others[b]											
Baseline	68.2	2.2	81.9	1.6	57.8	1.4	82.0	1.8	89.9	1.3	27.4**
0-3	72.8	2.4	77.9	1.5	60.8	3.7	78.7	1.9	89.9	1.6	12.8**
3-6	74.2	2.2	76.9	1.7	59.5	3.8	81.6	1.8	91.0	1.7	14.4**
6-9	71.4	2.6	78.5	1.7	52.4	3.5	81.9	1.8	91.0	1.7	23.4**
9-12	74.6	2.0	78.8	1.6	63.7	3.7	81.5	2.3	93.5	1.5	12.8**
Interaction with peers											
Baseline	12.2	1.6	6.5	0.8	21.9	2.2	6.2	1.0	3.0	0.8	22.5**
0-3	10.0	1.6	6.7	0.8	17.8	2.5	6.1	0.7	2.0	0.4	13.6**
3-6	9.4	1.8	7.7	1.0	18.0	3.2	5.5	0.9	2.6	0.6	8.9**
6-9	12.7	1.9	7.2	1.0	19.4	3.3	6.5	0.9	2.0	0.6	12.1**
9-12	8.7	1.2	7.1	1.0	16.9	3.4	4.9	1.2	1.9	0.7	9.2**
Interaction with staff members											
Baseline	12.3	1.3	5.3	0.6	12.0	1.9	5.6	0.8	3.6	0.6	14.9**
0-3	10.2	1.5	7.7	0.8	14.0	2.5	7.2	0.9	4.5	0.8	5.0**
3-6	9.2	1.1	7.8	0.7	14.8	2.8	6.7	1.0	4.7	0.9	6.1**
6-9	10.2	1.2	7.8	0.8	20.8	2.7	6.1	0.7	5.6	1.3	17.6**
9-12	9.9	1.2	7.8	1.2	13.6	2.7	7.1	1.1	3.0	0.9	4.1*

[a] In months.
[b] Percentage of observed periods.
* $p < .01$.   ** $p < .001$.

107

TABLE 13 Direction of Social Behavior for Clusters Over Time

Characteristic/ Time period[a]	Behavioral cluster										
	1. Supervised		2. Nondistinct		3. Social		4. Inactive		5. Stereotypy		F
	Mean	SEM	Mean	SEM	Mean	SEM	Mean	SEM	Mean	SEM	
Initiates social contact with others											
Baseline	5.4	0.8	3.1	0.5	15.5	1.1	1.4	0.4	1.2	0.6	48.1***
0-3	5.1	0.9	4.1	0.5	15.1	2.5	1.9	0.5	1.6	1.2	23.3***
3-6	4.4	0.8	4.6	0.6	15.0	1.9	1.7	0.4	2.0	1.0	25.9***
6-9	6.2	1.0	4.1	0.8	18.6	2.6	2.0	0.4	1.4	0.8	27.0***
9-12	5.3	0.8	5.0	0.7	15.6	2.1	2.3	0.6	1.5	0.8	22.1***
Receives social contact from others											
Baseline	7.6	1.1	2.6	0.3	5.2	1.1	2.7	0.5	2.5	0.5	10.9***
0-3	4.9	0.6	3.9	0.4	5.1	0.6	3.3	0.4	3.0	0.6	2.2
3-6	4.8	0.7	3.7	0.3	6.0	0.9	3.4	0.5	3.0	0.7	3.2*
6-9	6.4	0.8	3.9	0.5	7.1	0.7	3.8	0.5	3.6	1.3	4.3**
9-12	4.8	0.8	4.1	0.5	4.6	0.5	4.7	0.9	2.2	0.6	1.2
Mutually engages in social exchange											
Baseline	3.1	0.6	2.1	0.4	8.9	1.8	1.1	0.3	0.3	0.1	17.7***
0-3	2.1	0.7	1.8	0.4	7.6	1.4	1.0	0.4	0.0	0.0	15.0***
3-6	4.3	1.2	3.1	0.6	9.3	1.7	1.2	0.3	0.1	0.1	10.4***
6-9	3.0	0.9	2.1	0.5	7.3	1.4	1.2	0.3	0.6	0.4	9.3***
9-12	1.9	0.6	2.3	0.8	6.6	1.2	1.0	0.4	—	—	5.6***

[a] In months.
[b] Percentage of observed periods.
* $p < .05$. ** $p < .01$. *** $p < .001$.

108

These subject clusters also differed significantly from one another on the majority of the behavior codes not entered into the factor analysis. Some of the social characteristics of these clusters are presented in Tables 12 and 13. Besides their initial baseline differences in social interaction, the subjects in these five clusters continued to be distinctly different during the postmove periods. These differences included the proportion of time they interacted with peers and with staff and their rates of initiating and mutually engaging in social contact with others. The one notable exception concerns "receiving social contact from others." Prior to the move, Cluster 1 subjects, who received much supervision from staff, had the highest rates of contact from others. After the move, however, this distinction disappeared. In fact, the subjects in Cluster 1 experienced more of a decrease in social attention than did subjects in the other clusters. For most subjects in the other clusters, the rates of receiving attention from others increased after their living environments were changed. Perhaps Cluster 1 residents were vulnerable to a loss of attention because of a disruption in particular friendships or dependency relationships. Certainly some regression to the mean may be expected, although such an effect tends to be rather weak in the entire data set.

Table 14 depicts the clusters in terms of their stereotyped and idiosyncratic behavior. The cluster differences remained highly significant across all time periods, yet significant time effects appeared as well. Most of the clusters showed increases in their maladaptive or undesirable behaviors (the social subjects in Cluster 3 only increased their minor body stereotypy), with the largest effects observed in Clusters 5, 1, and 4, respectively.

The cluster analysis was performed to see whether residents differed in their response to living environments as a function of cluster assignment. Based on repeated measures analyses of variance, performed separately for each cluster, for the 10 major behavior codes, the answer is "yes," the clusters do differ in their patterns of behavioral change. Two of the clusters showed significant main effects of treatment (old vs. new units) on several behaviors; two other clusters showed pervasive main effects of time, regardless of living environment; and one cluster showed no significant change over time or across settings.

The two clusters most affected by the new living units were Clusters 1 and 2. In Cluster 1, the supervised group, the 15 subjects moved to the new units showed significant increases in their object-related activity and television watching and a large decrease in the amount of time they spent "doing nothing"—23% versus 32% for the 11 subjects who continued to live in the old halls. There were also group trends, at $p = .06$, indicating that subjects in the new units engaged in somewhat more household activities and more social interaction, primarily with peers rather than staff members. A closer look at individual subjects in this cluster suggests that an important variable for these individuals was whether they move with familiar staff or whether their "favorite" staff members left. Because these residents initially were passive and received fairly high rates of attention

TABLE 14 Stereotyped and Idiosyncratic Behavior of Clusters Over Time

Characteristic / Time period[a]	Baseline behavioral cluster										F
	1. Supervised		2. Nondistinct		3. Social		4. Inactive		5. Stereotypy		
	Mean	SEM	Mean	SEM	Mean	SEM	Mean	SEM	Mean	SEM	
Major stereotypy[b]											
Baseline	0.6	1.4	0.9	2.2	—	—	1.5	2.5	18.1	9.7	68.9**
0-3	2.7	6.9	1.2	2.3	—	—	2.1	3.3	30.6	16.7	60.6**
3-6	2.5	5.5	1.2	2.9	0.3	1.0	2.3	5.1	36.6	20.6	63.5**
6-9	3.5	9.2	1.4	3.9	0.5	1.4	2.7	6.7	32.3	19.1	39.1**
9-12	4.1	11.4	1.6	3.4	0.2	0.6	2.3	6.0	38.7	25.9	38.2**
Idiosyncratic and disruptive behavior											
Baseline	1.7	3.0	0.8	2.2	0.1	0.2	2.7	4.9	13.5	7.3	31.1**
0-3	2.9	5.2	1.6	2.9	0.4	0.8	4.7	6.2	11.3	11.0	9.8**
3-6	2.3	4.7	1.0	2.8	0.2	0.5	2.3	2.7	6.3	8.0	5.4**
6-9	2.5	5.1	2.0	5.9	—	—	4.0	6.9	10.8	12.4	5.5**
9-12	2.3	5.3	0.7	2.1	0.1	0.3	2.0	3.5	6.4	10.3	4.6*
Minor body stereotypy											
Baseline	1.5	2.5	1.7	3.1	0.6	0.9	5.4	7.4	23.8	16.1	33.3**
0-3	4.5	9.2	3.8	5.7	1.4	2.3	6.3	9.6	30.9	20.6	23.0**
3-6	4.0	7.7	5.9	9.0	2.7	3.2	6.8	9.5	36.3	36.9	21.4**
6-9	6.6	11.1	7.3	10.9	3.9	5.2	7.9	14.2	35.8	23.7	14.3**
9-12	6.6	13.4	6.6	9.9	3.8	4.6	7.7	10.0	38.5	28.9	17.0**

[a] In months.
[b] Percentage of observed periods.
* $p < .01$. ** $p < .001$.

110

and supervision from staff, they were at risk for not being a favored resident when staff assignments or living conditions changed. Under such circumstances, however, Cluster 1 individuals in the smaller, more home-like environments seemed to take advantage of the situation and increased their proportion of object-related activities, whereas those remaining in the old wards did not. Furthermore, Cluster 1 subjects in the traditional institutional settings showed approximately a 20% increase in their rate of inactivity. A significant main effect of time appeared for all subjects in Cluster 1 regarding their stereotyped behavior, which increased substantially regardless of where they lived (refer to Table 14).

Cluster 2 subjects also showed differential response to the new versus old residential environments. These subjects initially had the least distinguished profiles in the baseline condition of the old units. When moved to smaller units, 30 residents from this cluster showed many positive behavioral changes. They slightly decreased their amount of inactivity, increased their television viewing, socialized much more, and engaged in more housework compared to the 17 residents who stayed in the old halls. Three main effects of time appeared as well: over time, subjects in this cluster showed increases in their general social and in their special affiliative behavior, regardless of where they lived; they also showed significant increases in stereotyped behavior, but not as large as those seen for subjects in other clusters.

The highly social and verbal individuals in Cluster 3 did not show any significant Treatment x Time effects. Because this was a fairly small cluster in which the majority of subjects moved to new units, statistical statements may be limited. The other small and very distinguishable cluster was Cluster 5. The residents in this group did demonstrate significant main effects of time on inactivity, which decreased from baseline rates of 32% to rates hovering around 22 to 25% after the move. Attentive looking also decreased over time. Unfortunately, these subjects showed large and significant increases in their stereotyped and idiosyncratic behavior. Whether these are direct responses to the changes at the institution or whether their rates would have shown a progressive increase regardless is difficult to evaluate.

Finally, subjects in Cluster 4, who originally were very inactive, became significantly more active, more observant of their surroundings, and more socially interactive in both the old and new living units.

These findings indicate that similar environments may have markedly different effects, depending to some degree upon the baseline behavioral profiles of the individuals living in them. A theoretical explanation for these differences in adaptation is postulated: The baseline behavioral profiles (reflected here in terms of clusters) are hypothesized to be valid, general indices of individuals' abilities to perceive and to respond to the resources in their environment. Accordingly, the degree to which their behavior is affected by changes in these environmental resources should be a dual function of (a) their initial dependence upon the immediate environment and (b) the availability of alternative behaviors in their repertoire, particularly ones that are adaptive or suited for responding to the changed resources. For individuals whose baseline profiles indicated a substantial degree of dependency on the immediate environment, either on other people (as observed for the subjects in Cluster 1) or on objects (as seen for Cluster 2 residents), even modest changes in social and physical resources theoretically should result in significant behavioral consequences. In fact, subjects in these two clusters showed behavioral benefits from their new, somewhat enriched living units. Conversely, subjects whose behavior appears relatively independent of their immediate surroundings should be less affected by comparable environmental modifications. Indeed, the highly verbal, social subjects in Cluster 3 had very low rates of passively receiving supervision or contact from others and had low amounts of interaction with objects in their living units. Given that these individuals were initiators whose modal activity was talking to and approaching others, it is not surprising that moving to new units did not significantly change their behavior. The only resources that these residents needed was the presence of others, which continued to be available in old and new units.

A similar prediction can be made for residents in Cluster 5, who initially engaged in high rates of autistic-like, repetitive, idiosyncratic behavior and who had low amounts of interacting with others or with objects. These subjects did not show signs of dependency on their immediate environments and thus did not benefit from modest changes in available social or nonsocial resources. Theoretically, the extent of the changes needed to influence the subjects in these latter two clusters would have to be much higher than what occurred in order to be noticed by them. Moreover, it is unlikely that the same types of resources would have been salient for these diverse clusters. Interestingly, Cluster 3 contained the most intelligent subjects, whose adaptive behavior level averaged that of a nonretarded 4.5-year-old ($SD = 2.0$), whereas Cluster 5 individuals functioned at the lowest level, about that of a 2.5-year-old ($SD = 1.3$). By selectively introducing different types of sensory, social, and cognitive stimulation, I could test specific hypotheses about stimulus saliency and their relationship to behavioral adaptation with these different subgroups.

Finally, the behavior of Cluster 4 subjects, who showed postmove changes in both the old and new environments, is consistent with this theoretical explanation. These subjects initially were the least active and least responsive to their baseline environments, indicating that the available resources were not effectively stimulating. By virtue of "doing nothing," these residents seemed to be independent of their immediate surroundings. Unlike subjects in Cluster 3 (social/verbal) and Cluster 5 (stereotyped/idiosyncratic), however, these subjects did not have competing or self-initiated behaviors that detracted from their ability to notice modest changes in their environments. Accordingly, given the changes in social and nonsocial resources that occurred to some extent in old and new settings—namely, an increase in staff and decrease in residents plus a per capita increase in availability of objects, toys, and games—these subjects were likely to increase their levels of activity. The observational data confirm such a hypothesis.

Concerning the relationship between subjects' behavioral repertoires—particularly the presence of alternative, suitable behavior for adapting to new environments—and subsequent changes, the findings indicate that the residents with more scattered or diverse repertoires were more likely to demonstrate positive effects of the small home-like units. Subjects in Clusters 1 and 2 had such profiles, although their baseline rates of certain environment-related behavior were moderately low. In contrast, subjects in Clusters 3 and 5 had somewhat narrower repertoires that did not appear as amenable to modification as did those of Cluster 1 and 2 individuals. Further testing of this relationship is critical. For example, subjects' baseline repertoires may be increased to determine whether this leads to more adaptive responses in new environments. Alternatively, the types of environmental changes introduced could be tailored to capitalize on the other positive behavioral activities seen in the baseline repertoires of certain clusters or types of residents.

Clearly, this prospective study warrants replication with independent samples of subjects in comparable types of changing environments (Windle, 1962). Such a study has been underway at another state institution in Washington. The subject population ($N = 126$) is somewhat more heterogeneous and includes children and some residents with serious behavioral problems. Unfortunately, the design is seriously constrained by lack of random assignment and by inadequate behavioral observations prior to moving to the new living units. The analyses of the data during the first 9 months in the new living units do confirm many of the general findings from the earlier and better-controlled study. First, the individual living units differed significantly from one another but did not show changes over time in overall activity profiles. Social interaction rates remained extremely low (mean = 3.7% during Time Period 1, 3.4% during Time Period 2,) whereas stereotyped/idiosyncratic behavior continued to be high at both time periods (means = 17.3% and 19.6% respectively). Similarly, residents spent more than a third of their time sleeping, inactive, or looking around (means = 40% during Time Period 1 and 34% during Time Period 2). Presently, analysis of cluster types is underway to determine whether (a) similar behavioral clusterings of subjects exist at the second institution and (b) there is further evidence of differential response over time to the new units. Estimates of subjects' initial dependence on the environment and the diversity of their behavioral repertoires will be the basis for predictions about styles of adaptation and response to new environmental demands.

SUMMARY AND CONCLUSION

The study reported in this chapter demonstrates what may happen when individuals living in large group settings move to smaller settings or

continue to live in groups that are modified socially. The subject population consisted of adults whose functional and cognitive abilities were
comparable to preschool children's levels and who had spent the majority
of their lives in situations that were nondyadic and highly variable in terms
of peer and staff group members.

In the new duplexes where the assigned staff:resident ratios had been
enriched considerably, there was no evidence that this led to increased
interactions among staff members and residents. In fact, residents actually
spent significantly more time totally alone or without any staff person
present than they had in the old halls. This finding is consistent with other
observations that the exact staffing patterns do not determine interaction
frequency or style (e.g., Grant & Moores, 1977; Harris, Veit, Allen, &
Chinsky, 1974) and with one prospective study in an institution, in which
Knight, Weitzer, and Zimring (1978) reported that in smaller settings staff
often isolate themselves from the residents. Knight et al. (1978) conclude
that:

> . . . the role of staff must be considered as central in any renovations
> or service-delivery system. Staff are also "institutionalized"; they are
> generally poorly paid, poorly trained, and beset by conflicting job
> pressures. As a result, staff may cancel any positive effect of homelike
> environments . . . they may also withdraw from residents altogether.
> (p. 8)

In the study reported in this chapter, the staff did not receive any new job
demands and did not receive any training to help them take advantage of
the new living spaces. In essence, the administrators had relied on the
normalization philosophy, which assumes that increased staffing patterns
will facilitate increased supervision and attention to residents. Clearly,
more than that was needed. Whether systematic training programs, such
as that demonstrated by Schinke and Landesman-Dwyer (1981) in community-based group homes, would be effective remains undetermined.

Another axiom in the normalization ideology is that physical environments are vital to promoting certain types of behavior and social interaction. A number of architects and professionals have discussed these ideas
(e.g., Gunzberg, 1973; Norris, 1969; Peterson, 1970), but empirical support
has been lacking. In this study, the new duplexes were markedly different
than the old traditional institutional halls. They offered considerably more
private spaces, smaller living and dining room areas, and easier access to
kitchen and bathing spaces as well as outdoor areas. More than this, the
management practices in the new duplexes were rated as significantly
more resident-oriented versus institutional. Similarly, the Caldwell HOME
scores reflected significant, although quantitatively small, increases in
stimulation. Despite these important changes, residents' daily behavior
was not affected dramatically. For residents in the new duplexes, dyadic

interpersonal situations did become more prevalent, whereas these had been rare on the old halls; however, these severely and profoundly retarded adults did not show spontaneous behavioral changes—even in the dyadic situation—and the nature of their social interactions did not change significantly.

Further analysis of possible person–environment interaction effects did show that certain clusters of subjects, based on their baseline patterns of behavior, were differentially affected by their environments. The most social and verbal residents did not show significant changes over time or across settings. In contrast, individuals who demonstrated high rates of stereotyped and idiosyncratic behavior got worse over time, regardless of where they lived—possibly reflecting stress effects or the lack of other behaviors to cope with the environmental changes. Those residents who previously had been passive recipients of staff attention or who oriented to objects, but who were not extreme on any behavioral dimension, seemed to benefit from the smaller living units—when successful adaptation is defined as interacting with objects and/or people in the environment. A theoretical explanation for these different Cluster × Environment effects was postulated: that individuals who initially are more dependent on the immediate, concrete environment are more likely to be affected by external changes than are those whose baseline behavior is less noticeably linked to their surroundings. Furthermore, positive adaptation to new settings will be influenced by whether individuals have the ability to perceive or to respond to the specific changes that occur. The importance of evaluating multiple outcome dimensions (Berzins, Bednar, & Severy, 1975) is underscored by the diverse results from this investigation.

Because there was a significant degree of heterogeneity among both the 12 old halls and the 25 new units, a more refined typology or categorization of environments is desirable (Landesman, 1986a). As noted in earlier studies of community settings, places that are classified as similar by one set of criteria may differ significantly along dimensions that are important from the viewpoint of those who live or work there (e.g., Baker, Seltzer, & Seltzer, 1974; Landesman, 1986b). Other factors that may influence ongoing behavior of staff and residents may include broader organizational factors (e.g., Holland, 1973) and the freedom of choice as perceived by staff members (Proshansky, Ittleson, & Rivlin, 1970). Basically, the study described in this chapter has many similarities to one in which Rutter and his colleagues tried to assess the influence of types of high schools on students; everyone knows that schooling probably does matter, but being able to identify what school features are critical for what types of outcome measures is a difficult and challenging task (Rutter, Maughan, Mortimore, & Ouston, 1979). In the Rutter et al. study, staff attitudes interacted with environmental features to produce learning environments that were more favorable. To date, I have not explored the relative contribution of the staff attitudes and opinions on each living unit.

Overall, the observational data revealed extremely low rates of any type of social interaction, across all settings and time periods. One finding during mealtime, after the move, was that staff and resident interactions did increase significantly when a very specific environmental demand had been changed. The demand related to how food was dispersed. On the old halls, residents were fed from preportioned trays in a large dining hall (often with more than 100 residents eating at a time, within 10 to 15 minutes). In the new duplexes, staff members had to serve the food to residents in a family style. In the course of serving food, the staff members spontaneously showed much higher rates of verbalization, instruction, and informal socializing with residents. In turn, residents increased their vocalizations and mutual interactions. Even the baseline differences observed for the same residents when in their structured training programs indicated that these individuals have the capacity for fairly sophisticated types of social behavior, just as preschool children do with their peers (e.g., Lewis, Young, Brooks, & Michalson, 1975). In the absence of any guidance or encouragement, however, these subjects do not show large differences in their social exchanges.

The general lack of large behavioral changes among residents is not surprising, given the fact that these environments, whether old or new, were still relatively unstimulating cognitively and had few salient resources available to subjects. What needs to be tested is whether changing the resources, the demands, or both, would result in more noticeable and long-term behavioral benefits to residents and staff. For this captive group of individuals, who have limited natural abilities to express their preferences or to exercise their rights to change their living environments, their social day-to-day worlds assume tremendous significance. Given the realities of the social service-delivery system, these individuals are likely to continue to face repeated fluctuations in where they live and who their careproviders and peers are. Finding the ways to achieve these desired outcomes is likely to be more difficult than just building new buildings, meeting federal licensing standards, and providing more staff members to look after things. By emphasizing the functional aspects of environments, and by studying the association between those variables hypothesized to have the greatest impact on daily adaptation—across the full range of living environments—professionals, in their search for optimal programming, are likely to make measurable progress. This would necessitate viewing each environmental variable, social or nonsocial, in terms of its functional role and its multiple influences on behavior. Accordingly, variables that are similar on the surface may differ functionally, and, conversely, different variables may assume similar function, depending on the overall context in which they occur and on the individuals involved.

REFERENCES

Baker, B. L., Seltzer, G. B., & Seltzer, M. M. (1974). *As close as possible: Community residences for retarded adults.* Boston: Little, Brown.

Barker, R. (1960). Ecology and motivation. *Nebraska Symposium on Motivation, 8,* 1–50.

Barker, R. (1968). *Ecological psychology: Concepts and methods for studying the environment of human behavior.* Stanford: Stanford University Press.

Baumeister, A. A. (1978). Origins and control of stereotyped movements. In C. E. Meyers (Ed.), *Quality of life in severely and profoundly retarded people: Research foundations for improvement* (Monograph 3). Washington, DC: American Association on Mental Deficiency.

Baumeister, A. (1981). Mental retardation policy and research: The unfulfilled promise. *American Journal of Mental Deficiency, 85,* 449–457.

Bem, D. J., & Allen. A. (1974). On predicting some of the people some of the time. The search for cross-situational consistencies in behavior. *Psychological Review, 81,* 506–520.

Berkson, G. B., & Landesman-Dwyer, S. (1977). Behavioral research in severe and profound mental retardation (1955–1974). *American Journal of Mental Deficiency, 81,* 428–454.

Berzins, J. I., Bednar, R. L., & Severy, L. J. (1975). The problem of intersource consensus in measuring therapeutic outcomes: New data and multivariate perspectives. *Journal of Abnormal Psychology, 84,* 10–19.

Bible, G. H., & Sneed, T. J. (1976). Some effects of an accreditation survey on program completion at a state institution. *Mental Retardation, 14*(5), 14–15.

Bruininks, R., Meyers, C. E., Sigford, B. B., & Lakin, K. C. (Eds.). (1981). *Deinstitutionalization and community adjustment of mentally retarded people* (Monograph 4). Washington, DC: American Association on Mental Deficiency.

Butterfield, E. C. (1976). Some basic changes in residential facilities. In R. B. Kugel & A. Shearer (Eds.), *Changing patterns in residential services for the mentally retarded.* Washington, DC: President's Committee on Mental Retardation, U.S. Government Printing Office, 1976, 15–34.

Caldwell, B. (undated). *Home Observation for Measurement of the Environment: Instrument and manual.* Little Rock: University of Arkansas.

Caldwell, B. M. (undated). *Home Observation for Measurement of the Environment, preschool version. Instruction manual.* Fayetteville: University of Arkansas.

Center on Human Policy. (1979). *The community imperative: A refutation of all arguments in support of institutionalizing anybody because of mental retardation.* Syracuse: Syracuse University, Center on Human Policy.

Cleland, C. C., Cochran, W. E., & Love, J. G. (1962). The "Hawthorne Effect" in an institution in transition. *American Journal of Mental Deficiency, 66,* 723–728.

Deutsch, C. P. (1981). The behavioral scientist: Insider and outsider. *Journal of Social Issues, 37,* 172–191.

Etzioni, A. (1976). Social science in the White House (lead editorial). *Science, 194,* 4970.

Everitt, B. (1980). *Cluster analysis* (2nd ed.). New York: Wiley.

Eyman, R. K. (1976). Trends in the development of the profoundly mentally retarded. In C. C. Cleland, J. D. Swartz, & L. W. Talkington (Eds.), *The profoundly mentally retarded* (Second Annual Conference Proceedings) San Antonio: Hogg Foundation.

Ferleger, D., & Boyd, P. A. (1979). Anti-institutionalization: The promise of the Pennhurst case. *Stanford Law Review, 31,* 101–135.

Grant, G. W. B., & Moores, B. (1977). Resident characteristics and staff behavior in two hospitals for mentally retarded adults. *American Journal of Mental Deficiency, 82,* 259–265.

Gunzburg, H. C. (1973). The physical environment of the physically handicapped: VII: "39 Steps" leading toward normalized living practices in living units for the mentally handicapped. *British Journal of Mental Subnormality, 19,* 91–99.

Harris, J. M., Veit, S. W., Allen, G. J., & Chinsky, J. M. (1974). Aide–resident ratio and ward population density as mediators of social interaction. *American Journal of Mental Deficiency, 79,* 320–326.

Heller, T. (1982). The effects of involuntary residential relocation: A review. *American Journal of Community Psychology, 10,* 471–492.

Holland, T. P. (1973). Organizational structure and institutional care. *Journal of Health and Social Behavior, 14,* 241–251.

Huck, S. W., & McLean, R. A. (1975). Using a repeated measures ANOVA to analyze the data from a pre-test-post-test design: A potentially confusing task. *Psychological* Bulletin, *82,* 511–518.

Hunt, D. E. (1975). Person-environment interaction: A challenge found wanting before it was tried. *Review of Educational Research, 45,* 209–230.

King, R. D., Raynes, R. V., & Tizard, J. (1971). *Patterns of residential care: Sociological studies in institutions for handicapped children.* London: Routledge & Kegan Paul.

Klaber, M. M. (1969). *Retardates in residence: A study of institutions.* West Hartford, CT: University of Hartford Press.

Knight, R. C., Weitzer, W. H., & Zimring, C. M. (Eds.). (1978). *Opportunity for control and the built environment: The ELEMR project.* Amherst: University of Massachusetts.

Kugel, R. B., & Shearer, A. (Eds.). (1976). *Changing patterns in residential services for the mentally retarded.* Washington, DC: President's Committee on Mental Retardation, U.S. Government Printing Office.

Lakin, K. C., Krantz, G. C., Bruininks, R. H., Clumpner, J. L., & Hill, B. K. (1982). One hundred years of data on populations of public residential facilities for mentally retarded people. *American Journal of Mental Deficiency, 87,* 1–8.

Landesman, S. (1986a). Toward a taxonomy of home environments. In N. R. Ellis & N. W. Bray (Eds.), *International review of research in mental retardation* (Vol. 14). New York: Academic.

Landesman, S. (1986b). Quality of life and personal life satisfaction: Definition and measurement issues. Guest editorial. *Mental Retardation, 24,* 141–143.

Landesman, S., & Butterfield, E. C. (in press). Normalization and deinstitutionalization of mentally retarded individuals: Controversy and facts. *American Psychologist.*

Landesman-Dwyer, S. (1976). Sleep patterns in the profoundly mentally retarded. In C. C. Cleland, J. D. Swartz, & L. W. Talkington (Eds.), *The profoundly mentally retarded.* Austin: The Hogg Foundation.

Landesman-Dwyer, S. (1981). Living in the community. *American Journal of Mental Deficiency, 86,* 223–234.

Landesman-Dwyer, S., Berkson, G. B., & Romer, D. (1979). Affiliation and friendship of mentally retarded residents in group homes. *American Journal of Mental Deficiency, 83,* 571–580.

Landesman-Dwyer, S., & Brown, T. R. (1976). *A method for subgrouping mentally retarded citizens on the basis of services needs.* Olympia, WA: Department of Social and Health Services.

Landesman-Dwyer, S., Morin, V. N., & Curtis, C. (1979). *Lakeland Village Study: Analyses of behavioral observation data with SPSS.* Seattle: University of Washington, Child Development and Mental Retardation Center (available on request).

Landesman-Dwyer, S., Ragozin, A. S., & Little, R. E. (1981). Behavioral correlates of prenatal alcohol exposure: A four-year follow-up study. *Neurobehavioral Toxicology and Teratology, 3,* 187–193.

Landesman-Dwyer, S., & Sackett, G. P. (1978). Behavioral changes in nonambulatory, profoundly mentally retarded individuals. In C. E. Meyers (Ed.), *Quality of life in severely and profoundly mentally retarded people: Research foundations for improvement.* (Monograph No. 3). Washington, DC: American Association on Mental Deficiency.

Landesman-Dwyer, S., Sackett, G. P., & Kleinman, J. A. (1980). Small community residences: The relationship of size to resident and staff behavior. *American Journal of Mental Deficiency, 85,* 6–18.

Landesman-Dwyer, S., & Schuckit, J. J. (1976). *Preliminary findings of the survey of state institutions for the mentally retarded.* Olympia, WA: Department of Social and Health Services.

Landesman-Dwyer, S., Schuckit, J. J., Keller, L. S., & Brown, T. W. (1977). A prospective study of client needs relative to community placement. In P. Mittler (Ed.), *Research to practice in mental retardation, Vol. II: Education and training.* Baltimore: University Park Press.

Landesman-Dwyer, S., Stein, J. G., & Sackett, G. P. (1978). A behavioral and ecological study of group homes. In G. P. Sackett (Ed.), *Observing behavior, Volume I: Theory and application in mental retardation.* Baltimore: University Park Press.

Landesman-Dwyer, S., & Sulzbacher, F. MacL. (1981). Residential placement and adaptation of severely and profoundly retarded individuals. In R. Bruininks, C. E. Meyers, B. B. Sigford, & K. C. Lakin (Eds.), *Deinstitutionalization and community adjustment of mentally retarded people* (Monograph 4). Washington, DC: American Association on Mental Deficiency.

Landesman-Dwyer, S., & Watts, G. (1979). *Behavioral coding manual for the modified home observation code.* Seattle: University of Washington, Child Development and Mental Retardation Center, (available upon request).

Lewis, M., Young, G., Brooks, J., & Michalson, L. The beginning of friendship. In M. Lewis & L. A. Rosenblum (Eds.), *Friendship and peer relations.* New York: Wiley.

Moos, R. H. (1973). Conceptualizations of human environments. *American Psychologist, 28,* 652–665.

Nihira, K., Foster, R., Shellhaas, M., & Leland, H. (1974). AAMD Adaptive Behavior Scale. Washington, DC: American Association on Mental Deficiency.

Nirje, B. (1976). The normalization principle. In R. B. Kugel & A. Shearer (Eds.), *Changing patterns in residential services for the mentally retarded,* Washington, DC: President's Committee on Mental Retardation.

Norris, D. (1969). Architecture and mental subnormality: V. The environmental needs of the severely retarded. *Journal of Mental Subnormality, 15,* 45–50.

Parke, R. D. (1979). Interactional designs. In R. B. Cairns (Ed.), *The analysis of social interactions: Methods, issues, and illustrations.* New York: Wiley.

Peterson, J. (1970). The physical environment of the mentally handicapped. *Journal of Mental Subnormality, 16,* 121–125.

Proshansky, H., Ittelson, W., & Rivlin, L. (1970). Freedom of choice and behavior in a physical setting. In H. Proshansky, W. Ittleson, & L. Rivlin (Eds.), *Environmental psychology: Man and his physical setting.* New York: Holt, Rinehart, & Winston.

Raynes, N. V., Pratt, M. W., & Roses, S. (1979). *Organisational structure and the care of the mentally retarded.* London: Croom Helm.

Richards, C. B., & Dobyns, H. F. (1957). Topography and culture: The case of the changing cage. *Human Organization, 16,* 16–20.

Rutter, M., Maughan, B., Mortimore, P., & Ouston, J., (1979). *Fifteen thousand hours: Secondary schools and their effects on children.* Cambridge: Harvard University Press.

Sackett, G. P., & Landesman-Dwyer, S. (1977). Toward an ethology of mental retardation: Quantitative behavioral observation in residential settings. In P. Mittler (Ed.), *Research to practice in mental retardation, Volume II: Education and training.* Baltimore: University Park Press.

Sackett, G. P., Landesman-Dwyer, S., & Morin, V. N. (1981). Naturalistic observation in design and evaluation of special education programs. In T. R. Kratochwill (Ed.), *Advances in school psychology.* Hillsdale, NJ: Erlbaum.

Schinke, S. P., & Landesman-Dwyer, S. (1981). Training staff in group homes serving mentally retarded persons. In P. Mittler (Ed.), *Frontiers of knowledge in mental retardation, Vol. 1: Social, educational, and behavioral aspects.* Baltimore: University Park Press.

Stokols, D. (1981). Group × place transactions: Some neglected issues in psychological research on settings. In D. Magnusson (Ed.), *Toward a psychology of situations: An interactional perspective.* Hillsdale, NJ: Erlbaum.

Stokols, D. (1982). Environmental psychology: A coming of age. In A. Kraut (Ed.), *G. Stanley Hall Lecture Series, Vol. 2.* Washington, DC: American Psychological Association.

Ward, J. H. (1963). Hierarchical grouping to optimize an objective function. *Journal of the American Statistical Association, 58,* 236–244.

Windle, C. (1962). Prognosis of mental subnormals: A critical review of research. *American Journal of Mental Deficiency Monograph Supplement, 66,* 1–180.

Wolfensberger, W., Nirje, B., Olshansky, S., Perske, R., & Roos, P. (Eds.). (1972). *The principle of normalization in human services.* Toronto: National Institute on Mental Retardation.

Zigler, E., & Muenchow, S. H. (1980). Principles and social policy implications of a whole-child psychology. In S. Salzinger, J. Antrobus, & J. Glick (Eds.), *The ecosystem of the "sick" child.* New York: Academic.

APPENDIX

Major Behavior Code Definitions for Home Observation Code

For each 10-second observation period, behavioral codes are entered for 7 dimensions of the focal subject's activity (see Table 2 for a complete listing). This appendix provides definitions for codes in Dimension 1, Major Behavior. The observational system was developed during a 2-year period of intensive cataloguing of behavior observed in a heterogeneous group of individuals with severe and profound mental retardation who ranged in age from 6 to 80 years and lived in traditional institutions, group homes, and family settings.

For mnemonic convenience, the numerical codes are grouped into categories that are identified by the first of 2 digits (e.g., all basic wake and sleep codes begin with a zero). Because only one code is entered for the period, a hierarchical rule is used to guide the observer: the first behavior that meets the coding criteria below is entered. In some instances, the criterion is simply that the subject spends at least half of the time period (5 seconds) engaged in that activity. In others, the subject's behavior qualifies as codable based on saliency or importance of certain events (e.g., even a brief physical attack is coded as 62, provided no other codable behavior preceded this in the same time period).

BASIC WAKE AND SLEEP BEHAVIOR CODES
(01 THROUGH 09)

All basic wake and sleep codes must occur for a least 5 seconds in the 10-second period and take place prior to or in the absence of any other observable behavior that qualifies for a higher level behavior code (10s through 60s).

01 *Sleep:* subject's body and head are in relaxed position and eyes are closed and/or shows other signs of sleep, including decreased body movements, rhythmic breathing, diminished response to environmental stimulation.

02 *Inactive awake:* subject has eyes open, although they may close or blink part of the time. Essentially, this code constitutes "doing nothing, but not asleep." Examples: waking up from sleep, sitting and intermittently making nonspecific sounds (note: vocalizations will be coded under Dimension 2), staring into space, looking at something for less than 5 seconds.

03 *Looking:* subject has eyes focused on or attending to specific aspect of environment but is not engaged in any other codable behavior. Observer must be able to identify the object, person, or event to which subject is attending. Small body movements may co-occur, as well as vocalizations (Dimension 2) or minor stereotypies (Dimension 7). When a subject's looking behavior is part of a higher numbered (i.e., more active) behavior code, such as TV watching (Code 23), these codes will be entered, rather than 03. Examples: staring out the window at birds in a tree, watching a group of residents, looking at a particular part of a wall.

04 *Locomotion/body change:* subject moves through space or changes body position in a way that is not part of any other codable behavior. Examples: just wandering around a room, getting up from reclining position and stretching, crawling or scooting across the floor, walking into another room, standing up and sitting down again in the same chair.

09 *Other low level activity:* subject engages in a very low level activity that does not fit above codes or any other codable behavior. Observer must provide a brief description of subject's behavior when using this code.

SELF-CARE ACTIVITY (10s)

11 *Eating-drinking:* subject consumes, appears to consume, or prepares to consume food and/or beverages as the major activity or talks about food, eating, table situation, etc. (e.g., asking to having a plate of food passed to him/her, preparation, etc.).

12 *Grooming/dressing:* subject gets dressed or undressed or attends to personal hygiene or physical appearance. Examples: washing face, brushing teeth, shaving, manicuring, brushing hair, applying makeup, staring at self in mirror and re-arranging clothing.

19 *Other attention to body:* subject attends to or manipulates body parts, either purposively or not. Examples: wiping nose, looking at body parts to see if injured, touching forehead as if checking temperature, or rubbing shoulders and arms.

EXTERNALLY ORIENTED ACTIVITY (20s)

21 *Unfocused activity:* for at least 5 seconds, subject engages in active attention to or manipulation of an object or component of the environment in a way that does not involve apparent rules, structure, or specific sequencing of behavior. Generally, unfocused activity may be characterized as nonspecific, informal, or free-play activity that is not focused on an identified goal or purpose from the observer's perspective (i.e., there is no common name to the observed activity, even though the subject is relating to an object). Examples: touching and intermittently exploring an object, rubbing face over the surface of a table, moving two objects back and forth and pausing to look at them, or picking at and rotating belt (but not related to Code 12, Grooming/dressing).

22 *Focused activity:* for at least 5 seconds, subject engages in play or recreation that (a) involves clear direction of attention, plus some structure or sequence of behavior related to objects or the environment in a form that can be described conventionally and (b) is not primarily social. If behavior has social component, refer to social categories below. Examples of Code 22 include turning the pages of a magazine, putting together a puzzle (whether or not subject succeeds), building with blocks, sorting beads. Note that many specified types of focused activity are given distinct codes below. Use Code 22 only if the focused activity does not qualify for these other externally oriented activities.

23 *TV/radio/stereo/films:* subject's behavior qualifies as focused activity (see above) and is directed toward television, radio, stereo, film, or video.

24 *Fine motor/handicraft/alone:* focused activity involving use of hands and usually related to making something. If subject is in a group, but not interacting with others who are engaged in a similar activity, then behavior is coded as Code 24 rather than the social Code 56, General social with objects. Examples: coloring in a book, making a wallet, sewing, cutting out pictures from a magazine, shaping clay.

25 *Gross motor/recreation/alone:* focused activity involving use of big muscle groups and participation in recognized forms of physical recreation. Code 25 may include practicing a component of a sports or game activity without actually playing with others. Examples: swinging a baseball bat, jogging, throwing a ball against a wall, riding a bike, dancing alone, skipping around the room, doing exercises, and swimming.

26 *Symbolic/paperwork/arithmetic:* focused activity involving manipulation of or attention to symbols such as letters, numbers, maps, pictorial signs. Examples: looking at charts, doing homework, telling time, spelling, playing flashcard or other preacademic game.

27 *Household maintenance:* focused activity involving cleaning and organizing of the environment. Examples: sweeping a floor, folding clothes, setting the table, preparing a food or beverage, rearranging furniture.

29 *Other externally structured activity:* focused activity that is structured by others and does not qualify for above codes. This is to be specified on the code sheet by observer. Examples: participating in a fire drill, waiting in a line as instructed by someone else.

STEREOTYPED AND IDIOSYNCRATIC BEHAVIOR (30s)

31 *Destruction of property:* subject engages in nonaccidental behavior that harms or threatens to damage objects or property, excluding mere verbal threats not accompanied by physical behavior indicating serious intent to harm property. Examples: throwing objects, kicking a wall, tearing clothing, yanking a light fixture from its mounting.

32 *Self-abusive behavior:* subject behaves in ways that inflict or threaten to inflict harm to the body. Examples: banging head against wall, jabbing fingers into eye sockets, vigorously scratching (sufficient to cause damage to skin), repeatedly biting own arm.

33 *Loss of temper:* subject shows active expression of anger, frustration, hostility, or resistance without any signs of potential damage to property, (Code 31), self-injury (Code 32), or aggression toward others (Code 62). Examples: yelling, stomping, kicking legs while lying on back, swinging or flailing arms in response to an event perceived as upsetting.

34 *Major stereotypy:* subject engages in repetitive body, limb, or face movements as the predominant ongoing activity (i.e., not accompanying any other codable behavior). To qualify, the subject must repeat the behavior sequence three or

more times in an invariant and mechanical-like fashion, and this behavior must not be part of a recognized adaptive behavior (e.g., repetitions of a physical exercise, dancing to music, chopping food). Examples: body rocking, pacing back and forth, rocking body to and fro, facial grimacing, flapping hands and arms in stereotyped manner, repeated verbal or vocal sequence with no apparent intent to communicate specific information to others, teeth grinding or mashing.

35 *Echolalia/mimicking:* at least twice, subject repeats what another person says or does, shortly after this occurs, in a way that appears automatic and nonpurposive.

36 *Other idiosyncratic:* subject engages in asocial behavior that appears bizarre, highly unusual, and not apparently related to specific goal (other than seeking attention, in some instances), or unacceptable, maladaptive behavior. Many behavior sequences that do not qualify as stereotypy are coded as 39. Examples: posturing body in strange position, making two full lunges then turning upside down, pulling one's clothes off in public (not related to Grooming/dressing—Code 12), drooling, and making strange sounds and twisting body.

SOCIAL CODES (40s)

All social codes must be accompanied by specification of the person with whom the interaction occurs (Dimension 5) and the direction of the interaction (Dimension 6) to indicate whether the subject is the initiator or recipient (or both) of the behavior.

41 *Plan/organize:* subject is involved in efforts with another to prepare for a future event or is participating in making choices about later behavior or activities. Examples: talking about a holiday party, pointing to items to order from a catalogue, listening to staff person make suggestions, and nodding approval.

42 *Supervise/direct:* subject is in situation with other(s) in which at least one person assumes a directive or supervisory role. Examples: telling another how to do a household task or how to behave, monitoring the activity of a group so that individuals comply with situational expectations (e.g., not disrupting or leaving the group without permission).

43 *Instruct:* subject participates in interaction that involves exchanging information, demonstrating a behavior, or directly teaching another a skill. Instruction may be verbal, physical, or a combination. The apparent goal of giving or receiving instructions should be to help the other person increase his or her skills or knowledge, rather than mere supervision or direction (Code 42). Examples: being shown how to tie a shoelace, giving clues such as pointing to help someone put together a form board, practicing a newly acquired skill with someone.

44 *General social:* subject engages in social interaction with one or more others in a rather general manner that cannot be coded as any other social behavior in the 40s, 50s, or 60s. General social interaction may include physical, verbal, vocal, visual, and/or spatial behavior related to others that is in the neutral to positive range.

45 *Caretaking/social:* subject is involved in social interaction while basic caretaking activity occurs. Examples: talking and laughing with someone about another event while also getting dressed or being dressed; affectionately smiling toward and verbally encouraging someone who is being fed.

49 *Social nature/can't tell:* subject clearly is involved in a positive or neutral social interaction, but its precise nature cannot be determined (due to problems in seeing or hearing content of exchange or inadequate information about the context to permit making a judgment).

SPECIAL AFFILIATIVE BEHAVIOR (50s)

51 *Affection/console/care:* subject gives or receives any highly personal and warm exchange, including flirtations, affectionate touching and/or conversation, courting, comforting, or other overt demonstration of special caring for another person.

52 *Praise:* subject engages in activity involving bestowal of positive consequences, direct verbal encouragement related to the individual, or acknowledgment of another's merit. Examples: staff member tells subject, "You've really made great progress. I'm very proud of what you've done," subject pats a friend on the back and nods in approval after he or she has finished a chore; subject is given a merit coupon for meeting conditions of a behavioral contract or program.

53 *Assist/help:* subject gives or receives assistance in carrying out instrumental acts or in coping with emotions associated with particular situation.

54 *Share resources:* subject participates in activity in which two or more individuals cooperatively use same resources or establish altruistic distribution of resources.

55 *Social play/gross motor:* subject engages with at least one other person in activities using gross motor skills, with or without formal rules. Note that the behavior cannot simply be parallel activity, but must include overt social exchange between two or more persons. Examples: playing game of tag, dancing with someone, wrestling, tickling, and gently pushing one another.

56 *General social with objects:* subject relates to or plays with other(s) in way that uses objects, excluding gross motor activities coded as 55. Examples: playing cards or board games, participating in play-like activity that uses props, making something together simultaneously.

59 *Other positive social:* subject shows other positive social activity that does not qualify for above codes. When using this code, the observer must specify the nature of the social exchange.

NEGATIVE SOCIAL BEHAVIOR (60s)

61 *Scold/punish:* subject gives or receives actions indicating that actions are not acceptable, liked, or permitted. Examples: reprimanding, scolding, threatening to withdraw another's privileges, physically moving someone to another area based on identified transgression by that person.

62 *Aggress:* subject initiates or receives verbal, physical, or gestural abuse; attack; or serious threat.

63 *Inappropriate sexual:* subject displays or receives behavior that clearly violates the sexual rights, feelings, or privacy of another person or subject masturbates in presence of others or in nonprivate spaces.

64 *Annoy/obstruct/upset:* subject behaves in manner that appears intended to create negative reactions in other(s) or continues behavior even when indications are provided that he or she is upsetting or displeasing other(s). Subject also may be object of such behavior from another. Examples: excessive clinging, teasing, following another.

69 *Other negative social behavior:* subject behaves in a negative way socially or is treated badly by another in a manner that does not meet criteria for other 60s codes. Observer must specify nature of exchange.

UNOBSERVABLE/NOT CODED (70s)

71 *Interact with observer:* subject approaches and interacts with observer.

72 *Couldn't find*

73 *Left premises*

74 *Unable to observe, other:* subject has gone to bedroom, bathroom, or other space where observer cannot code behavior (will vary with design of the study).

79 *Can't code (specify why):* some condition prevented observer from completing a particular observation.

6
The Planning and Evaluation of Community-Based Residences for Individuals with Severe and Profound Mental Retardation

David Felce
The University, Southampton, England

In recent years, concern has grown that deleterious effects are inherent in what Goffman (1961) termed *total institutions*. This fear has been strengthened by documentation of dehumanizing conditions in large public facilities for mentally retarded people both in the United Kingdom and in the United States (Blatt, 1970; Blatt & Kaplan, 1966; Department of Health, 1969; House of Commons, 1974; Morris, 1969; Shearer, 1968). Important research studies showing the considerable abilities of many adults living in these large facilities (O'Connor & Tizard, 1951, 1956) confirmed that severely mentally retarded people are capable of learning (Clarke & Hermelin, 1955). These findings directed attention to the possibility of alternative services.

In England, The Booklands study (Tizard, 1964) demonstrated that some severely mentally retarded children who lived in a community facility for up to 2 years developed favorably compared with similar children who remained in a hospital. Developing from this work, King, Raynes, and Tizard (1971) found care practices to be more resident-oriented in small group homes and more management-oriented in large hospitals. The elaboration of the concept of normalization (Wolfensberger, 1972; Wolfensberger & Glenn, 1975) logically endorses the delivery of residential services in very small community-based settings. Thus, at the same time as criticisms of large central institutions have been voiced, there has developed a substantial case for alternative community-based services.

Acknowledgements. The study on client progress was conducted by my colleagues John Smith and Albert Kushlick.

127

To some extent, these developments have influenced public policy. In England, the policy *Better Services for the Mentally Handicapped* (Department of Health, 1971) outlined a program for developing local services while reducing the size of existing institutions. Change in the pattern of provision has been slow, however, and has mostly affected the more competent people in residential care. The population now under consideration is severely and profoundly retarded citizens, and the provision of a network of small residences to meet their housing needs remains a contentious issue.

Despite the volume of opinion in support and in criticism of a community-care service model on the one hand and a large hospital model on the other, there have been few systematic investigations into the feasibility and quality of alternative ways of organizing residential care. Tizard (1964) concluded his important Brooklands study by stating a need for experiment and for the evaluation of results over a considerable period. An opportunity for such an investigation in England occurred in the 1960s and 1970s when the National Health Service in the Wessex Region commissioned research to plan and evaluate additional residential places. The Wessex Regional Hospital Board was created in 1959 to administer hospital services for a geographic region in the south of England with a population of about two million. At that time, hospital care for mentally retarded people was the major form of residential provision, and three institutions that served 200 to 700 individuals each existed in the region. There was, however, a need for 450 additional beds as judged by the application of provision estimates (Ministry of Health, 1962).

Table 1 shows the number of children and adults who were recognized as mentally retarded by health and social services agencies in the Wessex Region on July 1, 1963 (Kushlick & Cox, 1973) in terms of crude rates in a standard total population of 100,000. The low rates of children with mild handicaps are accounted for by low-referral rates of these children to the agencies surveyed. The survey showed that the majority of children under 16 years of age lived in the family home. Moreover, for every child with severe handicaps—rated as nonambulant, severely behavior disordered, or severely incontinent—living in residential care, there was almost one child living at home. In a standard total population of 100,000, 20 children were in residential care. Considerably more adults lived out of home—133 per 100,000. The data on behavioral characteristics, however, showed that nearly three quarters of these adults were continent, ambulant, and had no severe behavior disorder. In fact, one half of all severely mentally retarded adults in residential care were able to feed, wash, and dress themselves without help.

In 1966, an advisory group proposed that 400 of the additional 450 places should be provided in small hostels, each serving 20 to 25 previously institutionalized people. Specifically, they recommended 100 places for children who were continent, ambulant, and without severe behavior disorders and 300 places for adults who, in addition to being similarly free of incapacity, were able to feed, wash, and dress themselves. The remaining 50 places were to be provided in the form of two "experimental" 25-bed hostels to serve comprehensively the residential requirements for all children from a defined catchment area (100,000 total population), *no matter how handicapped.*

The two experimental units for children were given priority: the first in Southampton opened in 1969 and the second in Portsmouth, in 1970. The initial success of these two units, coinciding with changes in national policy (Department of Health, 1971) caused a broadening of the "experiment" in Wessex by providing two more units for children and one for severely and profoundly retarded adults.

TABLE 1   Characteristics of Population in Wessex Survey
(per 100,000 Total Population)

Group/residence	Nonambulatory	All SB[a]	SI[b]	CAN[c]
Children				
Severely retarded				
Home	4	4	2	20
Institution	5	5	3	5
Mildly retarded				
Home	1	1	1	7
Institution	—	1	—	1
Adults				
Severely retarded				
Home	2	2	1	45
Institution	6	14	6	53
Mildly retarded				
Home	1	—	—	69
Institution	2	4	1	45

[a] Severe behavior disorders, ambulatory.
[b] Severe incontinence, ambulatory, no severe behavior disorders.
[c] Continent, ambulatory, no severe behavior disorders.

CONCEPTUALIZATION OF THE RESEARCH

One response of researchers to help resolve the uncertainty in provision policy caused by the differences between the proponents of the large institution versus the small, integrated community facility has been to attempt to isolate the effects of separate features of residential settings, such as size, staffing levels, management structure, and client characteristics on the outcome for residents. For example, King et al. (1971) examined the correlation between the pattern of management of clients and size of institution, type of institution, staffing levels, staff continuity, and the performance and role definition of staff members. They concluded that the size of the institution and the assigned staff–client ratio were less important explanations of the quality of care than was the role of the head of the residential unit and the autonomy that person had to make decisions and manage the facility. Moreover, since that study, other investigators have also shown that size per se is not an important determinant of the quality of care (e.g., Landesman-Dwyer, Sackett, & Kleinman, 1980; McCormick, Balla, & Zigler, 1975).

Generally, these investigators used statistical rather than experimental methods for establishing the importance of variables. It became apparent, in the course of providing the experimental homes in Wessex, that there was a considerable interdependence in practice between variables that could be conceived in theory as separate independent variables. Thus, although researchers originally sought to assess the separate contribution of variables such as size, community location, domesticity, and autonomy, these variables could *not* be evaluated singly; rather, the locally based residence had to be compared as a whole to the traditional large hospital. Our research results in Wessex cannot be generalized to other settings unless they replicate the composite set of variables that constitute the two options evaluated. We do not view our conclusions as applicable to all small residences or to all community-based residences. It is unfortunately all too easy to countenance that there can be badly organized small community-based facilities that are indistinguishable in their day-to-day management of clients from badly managed, large, and more geographically isolated facilities.

WESSEX LOCALLY BASED HOSPITAL UNITS

The five experimental homes studied were the first of 12 now in Wessex. They were designed to be small, homelike settings in the community with an operational policy designed to avoid the negative characteristics of institutional life (Goffman, 1961; King et al., 1971). The first unit for children, a converted house, had 21 beds; the others were specially built and had 25 beds. Each was located in a residential area of the main town or city in the catchment area. Three children's units served all children from the catchment areas (approximately 100,000), whereas the fourth children's unit served only the most severely handicapped children from a large rural population base. The one adult unit was designed to meet the needs of the most severely handicapped adults (including those who were nonambulant; severely behavior disordered; incontinent; or unable to feed, wash, and dress) from a population of 50,000.

Many specific details were considered when formulating each service option. Emphasis was given to proximity to community resources: shops, leisure amenities, public transportation, and health and education services provided for the general public. The decentralized location of each unit affected variables that contributed to the unit's autonomy. The design of the unit included a fully equipped kitchen and laundry room, in contrast to the institution's central supply system. There was a single person-in-charge of each unit who was graded at the level of the most junior middle manager in the large hospital nursing structure. This person was responsible for the care of clients over the 24-hour day and possessed considerable authority over budget and personnel functions. In contrast, the large hospital model had three people in charge of the day-to-day care of clients: two people of equal status heading separate day-time shifts and a third at night. The immediate middle-management personnel also had responsibility limited to either day or night. Indeed, only at the senior echelons of management in the large hospital was there a person responsible for 24-hour client care; and this person had management responsibilities for many living units and a large number of clients. Establishing and monitoring consistent care of clients within this structure is problematic. Moreover, in the hospitals, the senior direct-care staff had little direct control over budgets, repair, upkeep of the building and equipment, and personnel decisions.

The separate locations of the local units determined that staff members worked solely in a given unit, whereas staff members in the large hospital were subject to transfer between living units on the hospital campus, both as planned personnel development and as an ad hoc response to staffing problems. The hospital staffing system thus had inherent staff turnover at the living unit level. Another important difference in staff policy was that the local unit required formal qualifications *only* for the three senior posts (person-in-charge and two deputies), whereas other staff, termed *houseparents*, did not need formal qualifications and were recruited generally from the local population. This de-emphasis on staff specially trained in the care of mentally retarded people also extended to visiting professional staff by the use of generic services, arising from the need to find a means of efficient staff deployment in a decentralized pattern of services. Apart from psychiatric services that were available from psychiatrists based in the large hospitals, who supplied psychiatric services to local unit clients, general medical and paramedical support for the units was obtained from generic services in the towns and cities in which the units were based. To ensure the required service (e.g., in the case of family practitioners and physiotherapists), professionals were contracted to serve unit clients on a sessional basis.

Each local unit had a written operational policy advocating care policies that would avoid aspects of block treatment, depersonalization, rigidity of routine, and social distance. Individual staff members had particular responsibilities for a small family-type group of clients on a permanent basis. Times for getting up or going to bed and types of food and clothing were to be related to client preferences and individual program objectives. Different activities were to be arranged in different rooms to allow a choice of activity and to prevent clients from necessarily being together all day. Similarly, staff members were encouraged to arrange outside activities, such as walks, shopping trips, visits to parks or cinemas, for individuals

or small groups rather than taking everyone at athe same time. The timing
of daily events was to vary for weekdays and weekends, school time, or
vacation. The fully equipped kitchen and catering staff permitted day-to-
day variation in meal routines corresponding to individuals' treatment
programs and leisure or social events.

In the local units, clients' clothing was personalized, kept in individual
wardrobes, and laundered within the unit. Clients helped shop for personal clothing and possessions, and families were encouraged to help
provide clothing and personal possessions for their relatives. Visits from
relatives were totally unrestricted; families were to be encouraged to join
in the day-to-day activities. Families could make arrangements for trips
out or overnight stays directly with the senior staff of the unit, usually just
involving a moment's notice to prepare what the client needed to take.
The staff members did not wear uniforms, and it was policy for them to
eat meals with the clients.

In summary, the locally based unit model and the traditional large
institution model differed considerably. The local unit was characterized
by small-scale client and staff groups, domesticity of design features,
greater autonomy and scope for control given to the senior care staff, a
staff policy that provided the opportunity for continuity and the programmed development of staff expertise (although initially starting with mostly
untrained staff), and a greater potential for outside influences from neighbors and clients' relatives, the recruitment of community residents as staff
members, and the use of generic specialist personnel. With regard to client
admission, there was a philosophy of catering to all people from the
catchment area, no matter what the extent of their physical or mental
handicap.

In contrast, the large hospital was characterized by large overall client
and staff groupings, generally larger living-unit client groupings, and
more institutional design. (Note: The living units for children recently
were physically remodeled to reduce their size to that of the locally based
hospital units and, as far as possible, to imitate the domestic design
standards. See Landesman, Chapter 5, for a description of a similar change
within United States institutions.) In the large hospitals, however, a higher
proportion of staff met formal qualifications in the specialty and a "center
of excellence" philosophy derived from the peer-support and occupational
groupings possible in these larger organizations. Control of resources and
decision making was more bureaucratic, and the institution was less
sensitive to or accessible by outside influences. Client placement within
the hospital was not related to previous address (or address of next-of-kin),
and an account was maintained of clients' functional grouping, although
for a number of local, practical, and historical reasons, this was not strictly
adhered to. In contrast to the local unit policy, however, client transfer
based on functional characteristics was endorsed as an important management strategy.

THE DESIGN OF THE RESEARCH EVALUATION

At the time of the Wessex experiment, claims were made that it would not be possible to set up homes for severely and profoundly mentally retarded people in community settings, staff them adequately, and provide an acceptable quality of care and development prognosis (e.g., Shapiro, 1970). The evaluation was designed to determine the feasibility of the local hospital unit. The comparative evaluation was conducted in two stages. An evaluation of *client progress* was conducted with data gathered prior to the opening of each unit and between 2 and 4 years subsequently. The evaluation of *quality of care, administrative feasibility*, and *costs* was undertaken after the final round of data collection on client progress. The level of client engagement in activity was taken to reflect many different aspects of the quality of care of a facility as well as being an important component of the quality of life of the residents themselves (Risley & Cataldo, 1973). The care received by the residents (e.g., health care, skill teaching, the structuring of opportunities for residents to engage in activity themselves, and social interaction with staff, relatives or other people) contributes to the degree to which individuals may become active participants in the social and physical environment.

Measures were taken of staff activities (time spent interacting directly with clients, preparing or clearing away client materials, or doing other activity) and frequency of client contact with family and/or friends. A number of indicators of administrative and cost feasibility were examined: the ease of recruitment and continuity of staff, the ability to provide a wide range of professional services, and the capital investment and operating revenue costs for the residential services.

Two distinct control groups were established for these studies. The Wessex locally based hospital units catered to clients from a defined geographical area, thus providing a population-based, representative sample for this area. For the study of client progress, control subjects were identified by selecting control territories and collecting data on those mentally retarded people receiving care. For the study of quality of care and cost, control living units were selected from a large hospital campus. The comparison groups of subjects for each study were not identical, although the characteristics of residents were somewhat similar.

Subject characteristics are described in general and comparative terms. The subjects eligible for the study of client progress were those who were in or required residential care from the identified experimental and control territories prior to the opening of each Wessex locally based hospital unit. The measure of client progress was successfully administered twice to 65% and 77% of the eligible experimental and control subjects, respectively. Data on the remaining subjects were not obtained due to death, mobility, and late identification of subjects. For experimental subjects, noninclusion also resulted from the fact that 11% of the eligible sample did not move into new units. For the majority of these subjects, this was because parents were content with their child's placement. There were no significant differences, however, in the distribution of major behavioral characteristics between the eligible and achieved samples, for the experimental and control groups of children and adults. (In all studies the Social and Physical Incapacity Scale and the Speech, Self-Help, and Literacy Scale were used to rate client characteristics [Kushlick, Blunden, & Cox, 1973]. This rating system allows a client to be rated one of the following: nonambulant; severely behavior disordered; severely incontinent, ambulant, and without severe behavior disorder in that order of priority. In addition, clients are rated as being literate or as having speech and self-help [can feed, wash, and dress without aid] or as having speech only or as having self-help only, or none of these abilities. The rating system was used in a survey of mentally retarded people in hospitals in England and Wales in 1970 [Department of Health, 1972].) The achieved experimental sample (n = 72) was representative of all mentally retarded children in hospitals in England and Wales in the distribution of ambulatory, behavior disorder, and incontinence characteristics. The control children (n = 61) differed in two areas: There were fewer nonambulant clients (30% as opposed to nearly 50%) and slightly more severely behavior disordered children (36% as opposed to 28%). The achieved samples of experimental (n = 23) and control (n = 24) adults were similar, with both groups displaying greater levels of disability than did severely mentally retarded adults in hospitals in England and Wales in general.

With respect to the studies of client engagement, staff performance, family contact, and staffing, the experimental groups included those clients living in the four experimental units for children and one adult unit. Two control units for children and three control units for adults were selected for study, all on the same large hospital campus.

For the observational studies of engagement and staff performance, the behavioral characteristics and age of the experimental children (n = 77) were similar to those of children in hospitals in England and Wales. The control children (n = 43) were more able and older. Of the three villas for adults, two were for severely handicapped people (Villa 3 for males and Villa 4 for females) and one (Villa 5) was for the most able group of clients in the hospital. The control villas for adults, therefore, included a much greater range of client abilities. As an overall group, the distribution of main behavior characteristics of the control adults (n = 119) was similar to the experimental group (n = 24); however, it is important to note that the proportion of severely behavior disordered adults in the experimental group had fallen below representative levels. When data on family contact were collected, the number of subjects differed somewhat, but the distribution of resident characteristics in the experimental group (90 children, 27 adults) and control group (55 children, 130 adults) was almost identical to that for the observational studies. Groups were comparable in length of stay.

MEASUREMENT

A client behavior profile was assembled using existing measures (e.g., Doll, 1953; Griffiths, 1954) that were augmented by direct observation and tested for reliability. The 100 items were grouped in 10 sections: mobility, speech, feeding, washing, dressing, toileting, social behavior to people (inappropriate and appropriate), inappropriate self-directed behavior, and appropriate object-directed behavior. For assessment of adults, 84 items were added in six additional sections: mealtime skills, bed making and cleaning, laundering, grooming, social skills (cognitive and interpersonal). The Client Development Schedules were administered as interviews with preselected answers and scores. Assessments occurred at Time 1, prior to opening each locally based hospital unit and 2.5 to 3.5 years later. Respondents were care staff who knew clients well in the residential setting. At Time 1, some evaluations were from parents if clients lived at home.

In English residential institutions, records kept routinely by nursing and medical staff include: staffing levels and continuity, the frequency of visits and trips out during the day and overnight stays clients had from or with their families and friends, and the frequency of contact clients had with professional staff. Data on staffing were collected in the locally based units from date of opening (various times between October 1969 through October 1972) to mid-1975. Staffing in the control villas was examined up to the same dates but for only half the previous period because of unavailability of past records. Data on family contact were collected over one year (1974) for all clients who spent a minimum of 30 days in a living unit during that year. In two living units (Local Unit 1 and Villa 4), staff did not record family visiting accurately. In Villa 4, an estimated annual frequency of visiting was obtained from senior staff. In the first locally based hospital unit, staff stated that the rate of family visiting was so great that they could not record it. No adjustment was made as recorded family contact still exceeded that of all other units. The frequency of specialist professional contact recorded in the notes was also abstracted for the year 1974. If clients received or attended therapy or treatment regularly (dental, physiotherapy, occupational therapy, speech therapy, education), statements by the responsible professional and senior care staff member were taken as corroborating evidence.

The activities of staff and clients were measured independently by direct observation. Observations were taken on all present in the living units at 5-minute intervals from 7:30 a.m. to 7:30 p.m. The data are limited in that they were collected over one day for each measure in each setting, so information on the stability or representativeness of the behavioral data within each unit over time is not available.

Client behavior was coded as *engaged* or *disengaged*. Engaged activity consisted of all interactions with people, materials, or furniture and defined activities such as watching television or singing. Disengaged activity consisted of all other behavior, such as passivity, stereotypy or repetitive behavior, or disruptive or damaging behavior. Within client disengagement, a distinction was made between time spent (a) passively receiving contact from other people or objects and (b) having no contact whatsoever. Staff activity was recorded as: (a) contacting clients, (b) handling materials provided for client use, or (c) other activity. Contacting clients included two categories: (a) praise or cue, which included physical or verbal rewards or encouragement to client engagement (spoken compliments, prompts, instruction, physical guidance, hugging); and (b) other client contact, which involved all other contact (general conversational remarks, physical contact such as holding hands, assisting in self-care, and suppressing a client activity). Materials handled by staff members were classified into health-care materials (those used for daily activities such as feeding, washing, dressing, toileting, sleeping, medication) versus recreational materials. Other staff codes described staff–staff contact, administration, general supervision, and no activity. Interobserver agreement on the distinction between engaged and disengaged client activity averaged 97%. Agreement between observers on different categories of staff behavior averaged 87% for praise or cue, 90% for other client contact, 87% for handling health-care materials, 82% for handling recreational materials, and 97% for other activity.

CLIENT PROGRESS

A Kolmogorov-Smirnov two-sample test was used to establish that there were no significant differences at Time 1 between the scores of experimental and control adults on the 16 checklist sections and for children on 8 of 10 sections. In two sections, feeding and dressing, the control children scored significantly higher than did the experimental children. Thus, although largely similar, the control children were slightly more competent than the experimental group.

The difference in client progress over time between experimental and control groups was compared by reference to the number of subjects who gained or lost skills for each section of the Child Development Schedule. For each section a sign test was used to establish the significance of the difference between the number who gained skills and the number who lost skills. Table 2 shows that there were six significant change sections for experimental children and only two for control children. There were seven significant sections for experimental adults compared with none for control adults.

Three separate experimental and control comparisons can be made for the children (the third and fourth experimental units had a joint control group). When sign tests were applied to the disaggregated data, a similar result is shown. For Local Unit 1, there were five significant sections compared with one among the control subjects. For Local Unit 2, there were three significant sections compared with two within the control group; for the Local Units 3 and 4, there were three and four, respectively, compared with none for the joint control group.

TABLE 2 Numbers of Children and Adults Who Gained
and Lost Skills Between Times 1 and 2

	Children				Adults			
	Experimental (n = 72)		Control (n = 61)		Experimental (n = 23)		Control (n = 24)	
Checklist	Gained skill	Lost skill	Gained skill	Lost skill	Gained skill	Lost skill	Gained skill	Lost skill
Morbidity	31 *	16	15	13	3	5	2	5
Speech	35	26	32	21	12	5	7	14
Feeding	61 **	5	32 **	13	15 *	4	7	13
Washing	39 **	14	25	17	15 *	5	9	8
Dressing	47 **	10	32 *	17	15 *	4	9	9
Toileting	40 **	14	30	16	8	7	5	11
SBPI[a]	41	25	30	22	5	14	12	9
SBPA[b]	42 **	15	25	24	14	8	9	11
SBSI[c]	35	26	27	26	8	10	7	12
SBOA[d]	38	24	25	27	13	5	10	11
Mealtime					14 **	1	3	6
Bedmaking & cleaning					7	3	2	5
Laundry					7 *	0	2	3
Grooming					16 **	3	10	4
Cognitive social skills					16	6	11	10
Interactive social skills					15 **	2	8	8

Note The difference between number gaining skills plus number losing skills and the total is the number who did not change. This table is from "Evaluation of Alternative Residential Facilities for the Severely Mentally Handicapped in Wessex: Client Progress," by J. Smith, C. Glossop, and A. Kushlick, 1980, *Advances in Behavior Research and Therapy, 3*, 5-11. Copyright 1980 by Pergamon Press. Reprinted by permission.
[a] Social behavior to people, inappropriate.
[b] Social behavior to people, appropriate.
[c] Social behavior to self, inappropriate.
[d] Social behavior to objects, appropriate.
* $p < .05$.   ** $p < .01$.

A higher proportion of the experimental children were nonambulant at Time 1, and a higher proportion of control children were categorized as severely behavior disordered. One possible interpretation of the differential progress is that experimental subjects merely increased their skills to the level of the control group; thereafter, both groups progressed at a similar rate. Moreover, the checklist may possess varying sensitivity for different developmental levels. Sign tests were therefore applied to the

TABLE 3 Percentage Levels of Client Engagement

Clients/living unit	% clients present engaged in activity						% clients present disengaged			
	Total	People	Health-care materials	Recreational materials	Furniture & fittings	Other activity	Total	Contact with people	Contact with materials	No contact with people or materials
Children										
LBHU[a] 1	42.3	9.9	10.4	13.3	6.6	2.1	57.7	7.3	4.4	46.0
LBHU 2	41.3	12.9	8.1	12.8	6.0	1.5	58.7	6.6	5.5	46.6
LBHU 3	38.4	11.0	5.2	13.6	7.2	1.4	61.6	7.0	2.8	51.8
LBHU 4	38.8	10.5	7.7	10.1	8.8	1.7	61.2	8.3	5.1	47.8
Villa 1	34.8	6.7	11.2	8.1	7.8	1.1	65.2	5.6	4.6	55.0
Villa 2	27.1	5.9	9.5	8.3	2.5	0.9	72.9	3.7	5.7	63.5
Adults										
LBHU 5	48.2	8.2	17.9	9.4	9.2	3.5	51.8	3.5	2.6	45.7
Villa 3	28.2	7.1	9.4	7.0	4.3	0.3	71.8	2.0	5.5	64.3
Villa 4	39.0	7.2	15.8	10.7	4.8	3.8	61.0	2.7	11.0	47.3
Villa 5	50.3	8.7	23.7	11.6	5.1	1.1	49.7	0.8	4.7	44.2

[a] Locally based hospital units.

differences between the numbers gaining in skill and losing skill for experimental and control subjects grouped according to their behavioral characteristics at Time 1. There were six significant sections for experimental children who were nonambulant at Time 1 compared with one for nonambulant control children. There were four significant sections for experimental children who were severely behavior disordered at Time 1 compared with one for behavior-disordered control children. Finally, there were four significant sections for nonambulant and severely behavior-disordered experimental adults compared to none for their control counterparts.

QUALITY OF CARE: CLIENT ENGAGEMENT AND STAFF ACTIVITY

As Table 3 shows, 40% of the children in the locally based hospital units were engaged throughout the day compared with 31% of the children in the villas. In the local unit for adults, 48% were engaged throughout the day, compared with 39% in the villas for adults. Severely mentally retarded adults in the locally based units were engaged in activity about as much as were the most able adults in the large hospital.

Table 3 shows engagement levels according to people, materials, furniture and fittings, and other activities. Children in the locally based units had more interaction with other people than did the children in the villas. Independent use of health-care materials was higher in the local unit than int he two villas for severely and profoundly handicapped adults. Experimental children engaged with recreational materials considerably more than did children in the control villas, and the use of furniture and fittings in the locally based units (particularly the one for adults) and in one of the "upgraded" villas for children was greater than in the three villas of institutional design for adults.

Table 4 shows the proportion of the time staff members spent attending to clients. Houseparent staff in the locally based units were observed to spend 42% of the observed periods attending to clients compared to 37% in the villas. This difference, however, was largely due to the high rates of staff involvement with clients in the first local unit only. The junior staff gave praise or cues more in the local units than they did in the villas (12% and 6%, respectively). In contrast, senior staff in the villas spent more than twice as much in time in direct client contact as did senior staff in local units.

It is important to note that the local units had more staff than did the villas. Table 5 presents the number of full-time-equivalent staff at any time of the day attending to clients and handling materials designed for client use. Clients in locally based hospital units received more staff contact and more praise and more cues than did villa clients, although handling of health-care materials was similar in most units, except Local Unit 2 (be-

TABLE 4 Percentage of Time Spent by Staff Attending to Clients

	Junior staff[a]		Senior staff[b]	
Clients/living unit	Praise or cue	Other	Praise or cue	Other
Children				
LBHU 1[c]	20.4	38.5	2.1	2.1
LBHU 2	11.7	32.5	5.2	6.5
LBHU 3	9.1	32.2	3.1	14.0
LBHU 4	9.1	25.8	3.4	8.0
Villa 1	6.0	34.3	11.0	21.2
Villa 2	7.8	34.6	7.4	27.3
Adults				
LBHU 5	8.8	23.8	—	2.3
Villa 3	3.2	32.1	1.5	16.3
Villa 4	7.3	31.8	0.8	14.2
Villa 5	6.4	23.6	9.4	17.0

[a] Houseparents in the locally based hospital units (LBHU) and nursing assistants, learner nurses, enrolled nurses, and staff nurses in the large hospital.
[b] Persons-in-charge and their deputies in the locally based hospital units and charge nurses and sisters in the large hospital.
[c] The deputy person-in-charge was mistakenly observed and coded as a houseparent; her performance is therefore included under junior staff.

TABLE 5 Number of Staff at Any Time of Day Attending to Clients and Handling Materials for Their Use

Clients/living units	Total contacting clients	Praising or cueing	Handling health-care materials	Handling recreational materials
Children				
LBHU 1[a]	2.6	0.9	1.6	0.4
LBHU 2	1.8	0.5	1.2	0.2
LBHU 3	1.9	0.4	1.8	0.2
LBHU 4	1.7	0.4	1.7	0.4
Villa 1	1.1	0.2	1.5	0.1
Villa 2	1.4	0.3	1.7	0.2
Adults				
LBHU 5	1.7	0.4	1.8	0.4
Villa 3	1.2	0.1	1.4	0.2
Villa 4	1.2	0.2	1.9	0.1
Villa 5	0.5	0.1	0.8	—

[a] Locally based hospital unit.

cause staff took clients out that day) and Villa 5 (lower staff level allocated because adults were very competent). Although staff in the local units spent more time handling recreational materials than did those in villas, this was still disappointingly low. The phenomenon of diminishing returns highlighted by other authors (e.g., Cataldo & Risley, 1972; Moores & Grant, 1976) was also apparent here; that is, the proportion of time spent by local unit staff in administrative duties, staff–staff contact, and no activity (43%) was greater than that spent by the more scarce villa staff (32%).

FAMILY CONTACT

As Table 6 shows, a greater proportion of children in the local units received family contact compared to the children in the villas (86% and 70%, respectively). Approximately equal proportions of adults in the local units and villas received family contact (63%).

TABLE 6   Client Contact With Family

Clients/living units	Proportion clients contacted (in %)	No. of nights out	No. of day trips	No. of visits
Children				
LBHU 1[a]	78	61	4	1
LBHU 2	88	24	7	27
LBHU 3	79	8	5	7
LBHU 4	96	21	4	13
Villa 1	63	6	3	4
Villa 2	76	6	5	—
Adults				
LBHU 5	63	14	7	29
Villa 3	67	16	1	12
Villa 4	74	5	0.5	15
Villa 5	50	10	6	6

[a] Locally based hospital unit.

The overall report rate of family contact in local units for children (47 times per client per year) and for adults (50 times) was greater than that in the villas for children (12 times) and adults (24 times).

MEDICAL CARE

Medical care differed in the two types of residences: In the local service family practitioners generally provided care, whereas in the larger hospitals junior hospital doctors assumed primary responsibility. Experimental children and adults received more frequent primary medical attention (7.1 and 8.7 contacts per client per year, respectively) as opposed to 6.1 and 4.8, respectively, per control child and adult. Specialist medical contact was rare, throwing doubt on the contention that mentally retarded people in hospital settings receive specialized services. Only one third of the children and one fifth of the adults had a recorded contact in the year from the consultant psychiatrist who was in charge of their clinical care. At the rate of contact found, the psychiatrist would, on the average, make one entry in each child's notes once every 3 years and in each adult's once every 5 years. A higher rate of recorded contact by pediatricians was found among experimental children, largely accounted for by one locally based hospital unit, where the consultant pediatrician also was the clinician-in-charge and shared primary medical care with the general practitioner. Children in this unit were recorded as being contacted by a pediatrician at a rate at least 16 times greater than were children in the other units where a psychiatrist was clinician-in-charge.

TEACHER AND PARAPROFESSIONAL INVOLVEMENT

A lower proportion of children in the local units attended school full-time compared to the control group (36% and 76%, respectively); however, a higher proportion attended part-time or were visited in the living unit by a teacher (6% and 57%, respectively). This did not occur for the control group, and, therefore, a higher proportion (24%) had no contact with teachers; however, contact by teachers visiting the local units varied from a full-time teacher and assistant in one unit to 12.5 hours per week in another. Moreover, the amount of contact was not directly related to the number of children not attending school. Substantially greater proportions of experimental than control clients were contacted regularly by a physiotherapist (29% compared to 10% for children and 50% compared to 0% for adults) and experimental children received more contact from speech therapists than did control children (16% and 5%, respectively).

STAFFING LEVELS AND STAFF CONTINUITY

Table 7 shows the extent to which day staff establishments were maintained in the five locally based hospital units from their time of opening up until mid-1975. Over a combined period of 19.17 years, staff were

TABLE 7 Proportion of Day Staff Establishment (in %) Maintained in the Locally Based Hospital Units (LBHUs)

Clients/unit	Time period[a]	Establishment maintained
Children		
LBHU 1	5–10	96
LBHU 2	4–5	99
LBHU 3	3–4	88
LBHU 4	2–11	91
Adults		
LBHU 5	2–8	96
Total	19–2	94

Note. This table is from "Evaluation of Alternative Residential Facilities for the Severely Mentally Handicapped in Wessex: Staff Recruitment and Continuity," by D. Felce, A. Kushlick, and J. Mansell, 1980, *Advances in Behavior Research and Therapy, 3,* 31-35. Copyright 1980 by Pergamon Press. Reprinted by permission.
[a] In years and months.

TABLE 8 Staff Numbers and Continuity

Client/unit	Time period[a]	Average no. of day staff[b]	No. of different staff	No. of staff allocations	Allocations per year
Children					
LBHU 1	5–10	11.6	41	47	8.1
LBHU 2	4– 5	12.5	55	55	12.5
LBHU 3	3– 4	11.9	49	51	15.3
LBHU 4	2–11	13.7	44	47	16.1
Adults					
LBHU 5	2– 8	14.8	59	62	23.3
Total	12–2	64.5	248	262	13.7
Children					
Villa 1	2– 3	8.2	126	376	167.1
Villa 2	1– 7	8.3	98	205	129.5
Adults					
Villa 3	1– 6	8.7	51	220	146.7
Villa 4	2–	7.3	73	144	72.0
Villa 5	2– 3	4.9	70	140	62.2
Total	9– 7	37.4	418	1085	113.2

Note This table is from "Evaluation of Alternative Residential Facilities for the Severely Mentally Handicapped in Wessex: Staff Recruitment and Continuity," by D. Felce, A. Kushlick, and J. Mansell, 1980, *Advances in Behavior Research and Therapy, 3,* 31-35. Copyright 1980 by Pergamon Press. Reprinted by permission.
[a] In years and months.
[b] For the locally based hospital units (LBHU), the figures represent staff-in-post and for the villas, staff actually working on the living unit; for comparability, the figures for the locally based hospital units should be deflated by 15% (an estimate of time spent on leave, sick, or otherwise absent).

maintained in 94% of established posts. The average number of staff was higher in the local units (see Table 8). The average day-time staff–client ratio in the experimental child units was 0.53 compared to 0.39 in the child villas and 0.62 in the experimental adult unit compared to 0.2 in Villas 3 and 4 for severely handicapped adults after allowing for leave, sickness, and absence in the local units. Villa 5 for mildly retarded people had an even lower staff–client ratio of 0.13.

Considerably more day staff worked in the villas (418) compared to the local units (248) in only half the time, despite higher staffing ratios in the locally based hospital units. The rate of staff allocation in the villas averaged eight times greater than did that in the local units, with a mean in the villas of 113.2 per year (range, 62.2 to 167.1) compared to 13.7 (range, 8.1 to 23.3) in the local units. These data reflect conservative assumptions in deciding what constituted a staff transfer between villas; thus, staff turnover in the villas should be considered as a minimum estimate. Contrary to the notion that staff are less stable in the community, these data show high turnover in the traditional setting.

CAPITAL COSTS

The capital costs of the first five and four subsequent Wessex locally based hospital units were compared to those of larger facilities to examine whether economics of scale exist in provision. As no new large hospital development had been pursued within Wessex, data were obtained on the cost of the Princess Marina Hospital, Northampton (built to provide 506 beds) and the Gloucester Centre, Peterborough (100 beds).

All facilities were completed during the 1970s, and the expenditure during different financial years was inflated to a common point (October 1, 1978) using an official index. Cost estimates of accommodation and services provided on the campus facilities but not in the local units (e.g., school, adult workshop, professional clinic, and treatment space) were derived from recent expenditure by health, education, and social services agencies for similar provision in the community, inflated to October 1, 1978, prices. Where accommodation on the hospital campus arose because of its size and separation from community resources (e.g., shops, parks, church, halls, gymnasia), however, no equivalent cost estimate was included for the more local service.

The Princess Marina Hospital provided 506 beds, staff accommodation for 30 families and 44 single staff, adult training and school facilities, office and treatment accommodation, a central kitchen and staff restaurant, and a range of amenities (pool, gymnasium, shops, library, hairdresser, chapel, cafe) at a total cost of £8,974,080, at October 1, 1978 prices, exclusive of the value of the land. Cost per bed was £17,735. A scheme consisting of Wessex locally based hospital units, separate local government training center and school facilities, and separate health centers to provide office and treatment locations is estimated for the same date at £6,233,290, exclusive of land, or at a price per place of £12,319. Considerable savings appear to accrue from the location of small clusters of residential places in urban areas where community amenities already exist.

The Gloucester Centre, a small campus hospital partially integrated into an urban area, had no cluster of client amenities that are common in larger institutions but considerable adult training departments and treatment and office facilities. At October 1, 1978 prices, exclusive of land value, the Gloucester Centre cost £1,633,527 to provide (£16,335 per bed). An equivalent scheme in Wessex was estimated as costing £15,657 per bed. The data do not show any evidence of economies of scale arising from grouping residential and day-care services and administrative and treatment facilities on the same site.

REVENUE COSTS

Revenue costs for the five Wessex locally based hospital units were compared with those for two large hospitals in Wessex for the financial years 1975–1976 and 1977–1978. Hospital A, the control site for much of the previously discussed evaluation, had 563 beds and Hospital B, 395 beds in 1977–1978, over 90% of which were for adults. They were representative of the range of revenue expenditures in large hospitals in England and Wales, being in the lowest quartile and highest quartile, respectively.

TABLE 9   Total Net Cost per Inpatient Day, After Adjustment
of Staff Costs

Hospital/Age Group	1975/76 £	1977/78 £
LBHU[a] 1, Children	9.54	13.08
LBHU 2, Children	10.05	12.62
LBHU 3, Children	10.72	14.49
LBHU 4, Children	10.49	17.56
LBHU 5, Adults	9.92	13.44
Hospital A, Wards for children	9.29	12.96
Hospital A, Wards for high- and medium-dependency adults	7.74	10.96
Hospital B, Wards for children and for high-dependency adults	12.30	16.74

[a] Locally based hospital unit.

The figures for the large hospitals were averaged over the resident population. The villas for children of all abilities and for high-dependency adults had higher staff–client ratios than did those for moderately dependent or competent adults. Table 9 shows the estimated total net cost per inpatient day in 1975–1976 and 1977–1978 in the villas of Hospitals A and B, which served clients of comparable ability to those in the local units, adjusted to take into account staff deployment. The costs of caring for children in Hospital A were little different than those for the local units, and Hospital B was, in fact, more expensive, thus challenging a supposition of economics of scale; however, care of adults in Hospital A was less expensive due to lower staffing costs, a factor that needs to be considered when judging the results of the evaluation.

DISCUSSION

The Wessex evaluation was designed to evaluate the feasibility of serving the most severely and profoundly mentally retarded children and adults in the community rather than in a large hospital setting. The experimental services were equal to or better than the existing large hospital services on almost all measures compared. The experimental residences had higher staff–client ratios, more favorable staff continuity, more staff contact with clients (although still low), higher rates of behavioral engagement, more client progress in skills, and more family contact. This consistency of results, although based on relatively crude or uneven sources of data (e.g., some missing data, inconsistent records, or only one day of observation) lends strength to the conclusion that alternative residences are possible.

Essentially, the research was *not* designed to be sensitive to within-group differences. One unfortunate limitation is that the observational data were taken over only one day in each setting. It is therefore not possible to comment on the variance of the estimate of client engagement for each setting; however, the design is a group design, and the results on client engagement were aggregated from a considerable number of observations. Mean engagement was remarkably stable across the locally based hospital units for children, a stability that is to be expected less than stability within the same unit over time. Further, in the case of the results on client engagement, indeed on all the main client welfare measures, the results from the locally based hospital units for children are better than their control counterparts. If the units are rated by this differential, the picture is one that approaches the most extreme possible, with the experimental units being clustered together and separated from the control units. This kind of nonparametric statistical treatment is appropriate to data where the statistic cannot be assumed to be continuous.

The results for children were established under conditions of approximately equal resource input, but because of considerably lower staff–client ratios in the large hospital, this was not the case for adults. It is therefore necessary to consider whether the outcome measures in the large hospital would have risen above those in the local unit had the number of staff been increased to a level that would have resulted in resource equality. Essentially, this is a question of how important staff–client ratio is to the quality of care. Many authors have reported that above a minimum level, staff–client ratio is unrelated to quality of outcome and that there are diminishing returns from increasing staff numbers (Kandler, Behymer, Kegeles, & Boyd, 1952; King et al., 1971; McCormick et al., 1975; Moores & Grant, 1976). Indeed, the data in this study support this opinion. The time spent in "other activity" by staff of the majority of the locally based units, especially among the senior staff, was greater than in the villas where staff time was scarce, confirming the pattern of diminishing marginal returns.

Cataldo and Risley (1972) presented data from a preschool day-care facility for nonretarded children showing that not only were there diminishing marginal returns from an increase in staff numbers but at a certain level there was an absolute fall in staff performance. This absolute fall was demonstrated to be preventable by assigning each staff member to separate duties. Cataldo and Risley therefore showed the positive effect of the interaction of two factors: staff numbers and staff assignment. It is likely that interaction effects were also substantially present in the translation of higher staff numbers in the locally based hospital units into a higher level of client-oriented staff performance. Staff continuity is a prerequisite of staff assignment to separate duties and allows for the development and improvement of the daily pattern of activities over time. Material resources are another prerequisite as may be argued are features in the architectural design and the provision of a kitchen and laundry facilities. Similarly, staff training and policy orientation will also mediate between staff numbers and observable staff performance. Given the number of differences between the experimental and control facilities, it is not likely that the alteration of one alone—the size of staff establishment—would bring equality in staff performance and thereby in the client outcome measures between the two types of setting. Therefore, I am disposed to conclude that the local service for adults was also shown to be a feasible alternative to a large hospital pattern of service.

What this study has not done is examine the effect of single differences between the services: size, community location, and staff qualifications. This was not done because such variables were not manipulated individually and because of a danger that a statistical analysis would yield spurious effects. It is doubtful whether any researchers will be able to test single independent variables experimentally. To test the change of one service component at a time will either not be practically possible or not considered sufficiently important to justify an evaluation that would have to compare favorably to this one in breadth of evaluative criteria and time span over which data are gathered. Empirical data, however, are not the only criteria. Common sense and a perception of citizens' rights also can be applied.

The right of every citizen to the opportunity to live in a community with fellow citizens and to have the consequent opportunity of free association appears to be a starting point that is departed from only with caution. Location within a residential community implies a certain smallness of scale for practical and integration reasons; urban location also implies a certain smallness of scale for practical and integration reasons; urban location also implies a certain level and proximity of community amenities.

This follow-up study of a "natural experiment" in residential options for a heterogeneous group of clients in England indicates that community residential options are a very sound possibility, even for clients previously judged to need institutional-level care. Moreover, some supposed advantages to the large-scale institution received *no* support, notably, the myth that such facilities provide more frequent and specialized medical care, more opportunities for activity because they are larger, or a more stable staff environment.

REFERENCES

Blatt, B. (1970). *Exodus from pandemonium.* Boston: Allyn & Bacon.

Blatt, B., & Kaplan, F. (1966). *Christmas in purgatory.* Boston: Allyn & Bacon.

Cataldo, M. F., & Risley, T. R. (1972). *The organization of group care environments: The infant day care center.* Paper presented at the annual meeting of the American Psychological Association, Honolulu.

Clarke, A. D. B., & Hermelin, B. F. (1975). Adult imbeciles: Their abilities and trainability. *Lancet. ii,* 337–339.

Department of Health and Social Security. (1969). *Report of the Committee of Inquiry into Allegations of Ill-Treatment of Patients and other Irregularities at the Ely Hospital, Cardiff. Cmnd 3975,* London: HMSO.

Department of Health and Social Security. (1971). *Better services for the mentally handicapped. Cmnd. 4683.* London: HMSO.

Department of Health and Social Security. (1972). *Census of mentally handicapped patients in hospital in England and Wales at the end of 1970* (Statistical and Research Report Series No. 3). London: HMSO.

Doll, E. A. (1953). *The measurement of social competence: A manual for the Vineland Social Maturity Scale.* Washington, DC, Educational Test Bureau.

Felce, D., Kushlick, A. & Mansell, J. (1980). Evaluation of alternative residential facilities for the severely mentally handicapped in Wessex: staff recruitment and continuity. *Advances in Behavior Research and Therapy, 3,* 31-35.

Goffman, E. (1961). *Asylums.* New York: Doubleday.

Griffiths, R. (1954). *The abilities of babies.* London: University of London Press.

House of Commons. (1974). *Report of the Committee of Inquiry into South Ockendon Hospital.* London: HMSO.

Kandler, H., Behymer, A. F., Kegeles, S., & Boyd, R. W. (1952). A study of nurse-patient interaction in a mental hospital. *American Journal of Nursing, 52,* 1100–1103.

King, R., Raynes, N., & Tizard, J. (1971). *Patterns of residential care.* London: Routledge & Kegan-Paul.

Kushlick, A., Blunden, R., & Cox, G. (1973). A method of rating behaviour characteristics for use in large scale surveys of mental handicap. *Psychological Medicine, 3,* 466–478.

Kushlick, A., & Cox, G. R. (1973). The epidemiology of mental handicap. *Developmental Medicine and Child Neurology, 15,* 748–759.

Landesman-Dwyer, S., Sackett, G. P., & Kleinman, J. S. (1980). Relationship of size to resident and staff behavior in small community residences. *American Journal of Mental Deficiency, 85,* 6–17.

McCormick, M., Balla, D., & Zigler, E. (1975). Resident care-practices in institutions for retarded persons: A cross-institutional, cross-cultural study. *American Journal of Mental Deficiency, 80,* 1–17.

Ministry of Health (1982). *Hospital plan for England and Wales.* London: HMSO.

Moores, B., & Grant, G. W. B. (1976). On the nature and incidence of staff–patient interactions in hospitals for the mentally handicapped. *International Journal of Nursing Studies, 13,* 69–81.

Morris, P. (1969). *Put away.* London: Routledge & Kegan-Paul.

Nirje, B. (1976). The normalization principle. In R. B. Kugel & A. Shearer (Eds.), *Changing patterns in residential services for the mentally retarded.* Washington, DC: President's Committee on Mental Retardation.

O'Connor, N., & Tizard, J. (1951). Predicting the occupational adequacy of certified mental defectives. *Occupational Psychology, 25,* 205–211.

O'Connor, N., & Tizard, J. (1956). *The social problem of mental deficiency.* London: Pergamon.

Risley, T. R., & Cataldo, M. F. (1973). *Planned activity check: Materials for training observers.* Lawrence, KS: University of Kansas, Center for Applied Behavior Analysis.

Shapiro, A. (1970). The clinical practice of mental deficiency. *British Journal of Psychiatry, 116,* 353–368.

Shearer, A. (1968 March 28). Dirty children in a locked ward: A children's ward in a mental hospital on a bad day. *Guardian.*

Smith, J., Glossop, C., & Kushlick, A. (1980). Evaluation of alternative residential facilities for the severely mentally handicapped in Wessex: Client progress. *Advances in Behavior Research and Therapy, 3,* 5–11.

Tizard, J. (1964). *Community services for the mentally handicapped.* London: Oxford University Press.

Wolfensberger, W. (1972). *Normalization: The principle of normalization in human services.* Toronto: National Institute on Mental Retardation.

Wolfensberger, W., & Glenn, L. (1975), *Program analysis of service systems: Handbook and manual* (3rd ed.). Toronto: National Institute on Mental Retardation.

7
An Applied Behavior Analysis Perspective on Naturalistic Observation and Adjustment to New Settings

Alan C. Repp
Northern Illinois University

Lyle Barton
University of Alberta

Andrew Brulle
Eastern Illinois University

The field of applied behavior analysis has developed from the operant psychology of B. F. Skinner and is the field-based analog of his laboratory-based work. As such, it has the same basic tenets or presumptions, one of which is that behavior is a function of both genetics and the environment. Although this is hardly a unique presumption, its translation into action in the 1950s and 1960s was somewhat unique. Behavior analysts developed new experimental designs (see Rock & Repp, 1983 for a review), insisted on the use of objective data in clinical settings, adapted time-sampling procedures generated by developmental psychologists in the 1920s, argued for the study of individuals as they behaved in their natural environments, and worked solely with behaviors that needed to be changed (hence, the original term *behavior modification*).

Because they could not control the genetic contributions to our behaviors, these applied behaviorists concentrated on the environmental contributions and categorized them in three ways: (a) *antecedent events* (i.e., those that come before the response and affect its probability of occurrence, for example, the question "What is 2 + 2?"), (b) *setting events* (i.e., those that are relatively continuous, natural to the setting, and affect behavior, for example, the relationship of ambient temperature to the way we dress), and (c) *subsequent events,* (i.e., those consequences that affect the probability of the recurrence of behavior, for example, confirmation that 2 + 2 is not 5). In all cases, those in this field are attempting to determine the extent to which any of these three types of environmental events affect the probability of a particular behavior. Similarly, in all cases, we are studying behavior as it occurs within the setting in which it naturally occurs and in which its probability is to be modified. Interestingly, however, the environmental events used to change behavior have often not been natural to the settings. For example, token economies have been introduced into preschool programs to increase behaviors such as being on task, time-out procedures have been used to control disruptive behaviors, and overcorrection procedures have been used to decrease stereotypic responding. The reason for this seeming discrepancy of sometimes using artificial procedures in natural settings is one of expediency: The behavior under study must be of significant social or clinical importance (Baer, Wolf, & Risley, 1968), and it must be changed rapidly. Hence, the environmental manipulations made are those that experimenters presume will be most potent rather than those that might be most natural or even scientifically elegant.

Although we certainly do not disagree with this position, we believe that a different line of study might be undertaken that combines the contributions of operant behaviorists with those of nonoperant behaviorists; this would be the study of socially important behaviors, described through time-sampling procedures in their natural settings, but as a function of *naturally* occurring antecedent, setting, or subsequent events. In this chapter we describe such a procedure by discussing our work and the work of others in two areas: (a) the extent to which recording procedures accurately describe the interaction of subjects' behavior with their environment and (b) the relationship of particular behaviors with naturally occurring environmental events.

RECORDING PROCEDURES

When one is recording behavior, the attempt quite obviously is to produce data that accurately represent the dimensions of the behavior during the period in which it was being observed. The two most basic and agreed upon dimensions of measurement are duration and frequency. So, for example, when behavior has occurred for 10 minutes of a 60-minute observation period, the recorded data should reflect that dimension; similarly, when behavior has occurred 20 times in that hour, the data should reflect that dimension also. The most accurate way to reflect these dimensions is, of course, to record both the frequency and the duration of the behavior in question, and this procedure is sometimes followed. More commonly (Kelley, 1977), however, one of three time-sampling procedures has been used: (a) *whole interval,* in which a session is divided into a number of equal-sized intervals and is scored if responding occurs for the whole interval; (b) *partial interval*, in which a session is divided into a number of equal-sized intervals and is scored if responding occurs during any part of the interval; and (c) *momentary time-sampling*, in which a session is divided into a number of (equal- or unequal-sized) intervals and is scored if responding occurs at the end of an interval.

Although these procedures have long been used either in these exact or in modified form (e.g., Arrington, 1932, 1943; Beaver, 1932; Goodenough, 1928, 1930; Olson, 1929, 1931), research on the accuracy of these methods has been conducted only in recent years. In an early study, Powell, Martindale, and Kulp (1975) examined the measurement error associated with each of these three recording methods by comparing the data obtained through these methods with a continuous record of the behavior in question (being in seat), Using the momentary time-sampling procedure with intervals of 10, 20, 40, 80, 120, 240, 400, and 600 seconds and the whole- and partial-interval methods with intervals of 10, 20, 40, 80, 120 seconds, they found that (a) at any value, whole interval underestimated the actual duration of the behavior, (b) partial interval consistently overestimated duration, and (c) momentary time-sampling both over- and underestimated behavior. In addition, they found that the accuracy of each method decreased as the size of the interval increased. Because the behavior recorded by Powell et al. was only of one duration (80% of the session), Powell, Martindale, Kulp, Martindale, and Bauman (1977) sought to replicate systematically the Powell et al. (1975) study by using three durations for their standard: 20%, 50%, and 80% of the session. They again produced the same findings, but by having added a 5-second value to their sampling procedures, they also found that all three procedures were equally accurate when the interval size was only 5 seconds. They concluded that neither whole- nor partial-interval recording should be used because neither accurately reflects the duration or the frequency of behavior and that momentary time-sampling was accurate at a 60-second value because it consistently over- and underestimated behavior (thus cancelling the errors).

Green and Alverson (1978) also examined the relative accuracies of whole interval, partial interval, and momentary time-sampling when used to record long-duration behaviors. They used computer-generated data and thus were able systematically to vary the mean durations and frequencies of the standards against which the accuracies of the time-sampling procedures were assessed. Again, these results showed that both the partial- and whole-interval methods were less accurate than momentary time-sampling.

Powell et al. (1975, 1977) and Green-Alverson (1978) examined what we might term *an enduring response* (i.e., one that occurs at least for many seconds and often for many minutes). Other behaviors, however, have extremely short durations, occurring for no more than 2 or 3 seconds at a time, and these might be termed *discrete*. In an effort to examine the accuracies of time-sampling procedures with a discrete behavior, Repp, Roberts, Slack, Repp, and Berkler (1976) compared estimates obtained through time-sampling and interval recording with the actual occurrence of an event with a 1-second duration. To do so, they summarized data in five ways: (a) the frequency of the event (as this information was produced by continuous measurement, it became the standard against which others were compared); (b) a time-sampling procedure (more common in animal research than is Powell's momentary time-sampling) in which behavior was ignored for 9 minutes and 55 seconds, observed for 5 seconds, ignored, observed, etc.; (c) the same procedure but with the off time being 9 minutes and 50 seconds and the on time being 10 seconds; (d) a 10-second/5-second partial-interval procedure in which the 10 seconds represented an observation period and the 5 seconds represented a nonobservation period in which the observer would record what had just been observed; and (e) a 10-second/0-second partial-interval procedure in which the observer would observe and record in the same 10-second period. Repp et al. found that (a) this time-sampling procedure was inaccurate, (b) the 10/0 and 10/5 procedures produced quite similar data (so studies using separate observe and record intervals were just as accurate as those that did not miss these alternating 5 seconds of observation), and (c) that partial interval was quite inaccurate for high rate (10 rpm) events, but accurate for moderate (1 rpm) and low rate (0.1 rpm) events when those events were of extremely short duration.

In another study of the accuracy of partial interval and momentary time-sampling, Dunbar (1976) recorded the grooming behavior of 11 gelada baboons in a manner that allowed him to note the exact onset and termination of each episode of behavior. With this continuous measure serving as the standard, Dunbar sampled the records using (a) the partial-interval method with 5-, 15-, 30-, 60-, and 120-second intervals, and (b) the momentary time-sampling procedure with 15-, 30-, 60-, and 120-second intervals. When he grouped the data from the continuous measure, Dunbar found that the 11 baboons had been grooming 24.8% of the time. When the data from the partial-interval method were averaged across animals at each of the interval values, the results showed behavior occurring 26.3% (5 seconds), 29.1% (15 seconds), 32.6% (30 seconds), 37.9% (60 seconds), and 46.1% (120 seconds) of the time. Dunbar then concluded that the 5- and 15-second intervals were sufficiently accurate when using partial-interval recording. When the data collected through momentary time-sampling were then averaged across the 11 animals at each of the values, the results showed behavior occurring 25.5% (15 seconds), 24.2% (30 seconds), 23.9% (60 seconds), and 24.8% (120 seconds). From these results, Dunbar concluded that momentary time-sampling was far more accurate than partial interval and was accurate up to and at a value of 120 seconds.

The results of these studies seem to show quite clearly and consistently that momentary time-sampling is much more accurate than partial or whole interval and that it is accurate at fairly high interobservation intervals (e.g., 120 seconds); however, with the exception of the Repp et al.

(1976) study, these studies averaged several sessions of observations and compared this *average* with the standard. Such a procedure is certainly viable when one is analyzing grouped data. Curiously, however, some of these studies were being conducted by single-subject researchers who were suggesting at least implicitly that the accuracy of momentary time-sampling would hold for both averaged and nonaveraged (i.e., time series) data.

The problem with this approach was suggested by the data (but not by the authors) in a study by Heward et al. (1980), who videotaped the rocking behavior of a retarded individual. These researchers, who were seeking to determine the relative accuracies of fixed and variable momentary time-samples, recorded five videotapes that they treated as five independent sessions. They then had trained observers record the behavior using fixed or variable 60-second time-samples, and compared the data from each of these procedures with the standard generated by a continuous measure of the duration of this behavior. They added a unique variation to their study, however, and the results were not entirely consistent with the results of prior studies on momentary time-sampling. They recorded data from each videotape several times, began these observations at various times within the tape, and plotted each of these measures for each session.

Although Heward et al. (1980) were apparently not interested in the accuracy of momentary time-sampling per se, we were and found that their graphs showed momentary time-sampling to be highly inaccurate at a 60-second interobservation time: in all cases, the time-sampling procedure overestimated the duration measure. This result was in striking contrast to the earlier studies that showed that this procedure both overestimated and underestimated the results produced by continuous recording. The results, however, could possibly be explained by an artifact in the way Heward et al. wrote their recording rules. They decided that rocking could not be recorded by duration recording until it had endured for at least 3 seconds. Their momentary time-sampling procedure, however, allowed rocking to be recorded when it occurred for only an instant. Thus, there must be instances when short-duration rocking would be recorded through the momentary time-sampling method but not through the duration method. As such, the momentary time-sampling procedure would be likely to overestimate the standard with which it was compared.

Although the results from Heward et al. (1980) could not be interpreted directly, the study seemed valuable to us in two ways: (a) it was the first to present each session's data without combining multiple observations at the same momentary time-sampling value, and (b) it was the first to suggest that momentary time-sampling might not be so accurate as others suggested. As we considered the latter, even with its recording-rule flaw, a possible problem with the results of prior research emerged. There had been a consistent finding with momentary time-sampling. It both overestimated and underestimated the standard an equal number of times and by an equal discrepancy. Thus, one might presume that when prior researchers averaged their data, they simply cancelled the errors and apparently made momentary time-sampling more accurate than it was.

This problem becomes an important one for some researchers, albeit less important for others. For those who would average data across subjects and discuss only the behavior of groups, the 60-second and 120-second interobservation intervals (which some researchers had been promulgating) would seem fairly accurate. For those, however, who would not be averaging data across individuals, who would instead present each subject's data for each session in a time-series fashion, these values might produce inaccurate data. Unfortunately, we could not make such an assumption straightforwardly, as there was a methodological problem with the Heward et al. (1980) study.

Therefore, Brulle and Repp (1985) conducted another study to examine more carefully the accuracy of momentary time-sampling at different interobservation intervals. They achieved their purpose by (a) recording observations on permanent line-chart records and treating the records as the data, thus obviating any concern over the adequacy of response definitions; (b) observing five behaviors for five sessions each; (c) using five delays (0, 12, 24, 26, and 48 seconds) in the starting time of the sampling so that multiple momentary time-sampling recordings could be compared with each other; (d) using six momentary time-sampling values (10, 20, 30, 60, 120, and 240 seconds); and (e) presenting data in both the common averaged form (of Powell et al., 1975) and the session-by-session form (of Heward et al., 1980).

For each of the momentary time-sampling values, there were 125 judgments (5 delays × 5 sessions × 5 behaviors) that could be made about the extent to which the momentary time-sampling data corresponded with the data from the continuous measure. Because there were five behaviors, each of which was measured for five sessions, the data from the continuous measure varied considerably, showing behavior to have occurred from 4 to 62% of the session. Some of the results of this study are presented in Table 1. From these and other data within the study, four conclusions can be drawn: (1) the 10-second and 20-second momentary time-sampling values were accurate for both single-subject and group research; (b) the 30-second value was moderately accurate for single-subject research (85% of the observations were within three percentage points of the standard) and quite accurate for group research; (c) the 60-, 120-, and 240-second values were inaccurate for single-subject research; and (d) the 60-, 120, and 240-second values were accurate for group studies in which researchers do not make statement about any of the individuals.

In order to learn still more about the accuracy of time-sampling, Olinger and Repp (1984) conducted a study to parallel recording efforts in applied settings. In those situations, an observer looks at one subject and records the behavior being emitted, then looks at a second subject, and so forth. In approximating such a situation, the authors chose to record the behavior of five subjects by sampling procedures and then to compare the sampled

TABLE 1   Accuracy of Momentary Time-Sampling

Interobservation interval	No. of cases within n% of standard				% error[a]
	±1%	±2%	±3%	±10%	
10	100	122	124	125	4
20	82	106	120	125	6
30	59	87	106	125	8
60	33	41	52	117	>10
120	20	33	43	99	>10
240	16	20	22	71	>10

[a] At which all 125 measures were accurate.

data with a continuous measure. The procedures chosen were (a) a 5-second partial interval in which each of the five subjects would be observed 5 of every 25 seconds; (b) a 5-second momentary time-sampling in which the observer would look every 5 seconds, but each of the five subjects would be observed once every 25 seconds; (c) a 10-second momentary time-sampling in which each of the five subjects would be observed once every 50 seconds; (d) a 20-second momentary time-sampling in which each of the five subjects would be observed once every 100 seconds; and (e) a 30-second momentary time-sampling in which each subject would be observed once every 150 seconds.

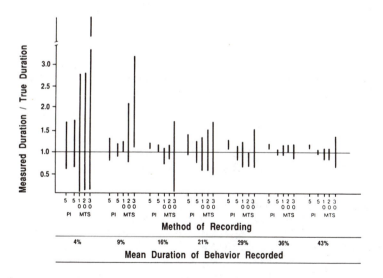

FIGURE 1.   Relationship of recording method and behavior duration to measured duration.

The results shown in Figure 1 allow a number of conclusions to be drawn: (a) each method became more accurate as the mean duration of the behavior being observed increases; (b) for durations up to 29%, none of the momentary time-sampling values produced data accurate enough to allow one to draw conclusions about individuals; (c) for durations of 36% and 43%, the 5-second momentary time-sampling produced data that might be accurate enough for some experimenters to gather data on individuals; and (d) for those conducting group research, the momentary time-sampling values up to 20 seconds would allow one to report accurate group data for all the durations in this study, whereas the 30-second momentary time-sampling produced accurate data for durations of 21% and above.

Summary

The research on sampling procedures clearly shows a difference for those making statements about individual subjects and for those making statements about groups of subjects. For the former, (a) the partial interval 5-second method accurately portrays the percentage of intervals in which responding was observed; (b) the partial interval 10-second method does so less accurately and should not be exceeded in value; (c) a 5-second record period after a 5-second or 10-second observation period will not markedly decrease accuracy when many observations are made; (d) momentary time sampling values up to 30 seconds are accurate when the behavior is of moderate duration and many samples are made; and (e) when observing across individuals in groups of five, momentary time-sampling values of 5 seconds on each subject should not be exceeded. For those doing group research, (a) the same restrictions on partial-interval recording would apply and (b) momentary time-sampling both overestimates and underestimates behavior an approximately equal number of times through momentary time-sampling values of 240 seconds provided many observations are made.

NATURALISTIC STUDIES OF
RETARDED PERSONS

The objective of conducting research on observational procedures is, of course, to improve the accuracy of our statements about the behavior of the subjects we observe. In the field of mental retardation, there have been enormous numbers of studies in which retarded persons have been observed in natural settings. Much of this research has been reviewed (from a group-research perspective) by Berkson and Landesman-Dwyer (1977) and Landesman-Dwyer (1981).

Our own work the last 5 years has been directed toward determining factors within the natural environment that influence the behavior of retarded persons. All of this information has been gathered in a single-subject format so that individualized changes in the environments of the subjects could be made. Because of the size of the data collection represented in these studies (more than 3,000,000 observations), only grouped data are presented.

Naturalistic Studies of Policy Decisions

Naturalistic studies can, of course, be conducted in many areas, with extremely varied purposes. In recent years, a number of movements have provided various bases, the efficacy of which can be tested. For example, one can examine the effects of instituting a functional curriculum, of adopting a normalization model, of teaching by massed instead of distributed practice, and so forth. Such work might loosely be grouped as those dealing with local or national policies. Other studies are more specific, dealing with less pervasive issues. Of the policy issues related to mental retardation, two of the most pervasive have been the quality of service and the deinstitutionalization movement. At the local level, great strides in programming have been made in many institutions in the last 2 decades, although much still remains to be done. Some of the efforts toward measuring the quality of service have been promoted by the federal government (U.S. DHEW, 1974), private agencies (Accreditation Council, 1971), and state governments (e.g., state licensure bureaus). Although these guidelines, regulations, and so forth vary, in general they attempt to (a) facilitate intellectual, affective, and sensorimotor development; (b) provide training experiences; (c) develop written training objectives; and (d) provide evidence that services have met those objectives. Although we certainly find these efforts to be laudatory, one can question their effectiveness and can in part answer that question through naturalistic observation. For example, Bible and Sneed (1976) found that the effects of an accreditation visit were ephemeral, with staff increasing the programming available to students by 276% of days a Joint Commission on the Accreditation of Hospitals team inspected the facility. In addition to questioning what immediate effects an inspection has on staff behavior, one can also question the long-term effects.

Such an opportunity was made available to us (Repp & Barton, 1980) by an institution in which some cottages had been licensed by the state whereas others had not. Thus, we had the opportunity to observe the behavior of staff and residents operating under the same administrators, within the same general environment, etc. The licensed group consisted of two cottages that housed 80 severely or profoundly retarded persons; the unlicensed group consisted of 150 severely or profoundly retarded persons. The differences in these groups were comprised of those items the examiners considered pertinent. In addition, however, there was a staff difference, with the licensed group having about twice as many staff per resident.

Both staff and residents were observed. The staff behaviors noted were: no interaction, verbal instruction, nonverbal instruction with physical assistance, social, and custodial. The client behaviors were of two types: One concerned habilitative programming, which consisted of on task, off task, and no programming. The other type included nonprogramming items and self-aggression, aggression toward others, and self-stimulation. The observations were made for 16 days for more than 4 hours per day according to a partial-interval 6-second program, resulting in more than 160,000 observations. Table 2 summarizes the results of these observations and suggests quite strongly that licensure did not mean that services would be adequate for these clients. Programming occurred seldom during these observation hours (9:30 to 11:20 and 1:00 to 3:50); self-stimulation occurred as much as 47% of the time; and self-abuse, as much as 3% of the time. Clearly, governmental licensures do not ensure that clients are being adequately programmed.

TABLE 2   Percentage of Observations per Category

Behavior	Licensed units	Unlicensed units
Staff		
No interaction	78 to 80	82 to 95
Verbal instruction	9 to 17	2 to 14
Nonverbal instruction	1 to 3	1 to 3
Physical assistance	1 to 4	1 to 2
Verbal instruction/physical assistance	1 to 2	1 to 2
Nonverbal instruction/physical assistance	1 to 3	0 to 3
Social	1 to 3	1 to 3
Custodial	1 to 2	1 to 2
Resident		
On task	2 to 20	2 to 6
Off task	1 to 3	0 to 3
No programming	77 to 98	92 to 99
Self-stimulation	27	7 to 47
Self-aggression	0 to 3	0 to 4
Aggression to others	0 to 2	0 to 2

Another major issue in the field of mental retardation has been deinstitutionalization. A number of investigators have examined this issue, and many of their studies have been reviewed by Landesman-Dwyer (1981) under nine categories. Her findings were in many cases provocative and suggest that some of our policy decisions are based on value judgments rather than on what is empirically best for clients. Some of the points she has made are that (a) the size of a residential setting is not directly related to the quality of care, (b) the frequency of staff-initiated positive statements does not increase when more direct-care staff are made available, (c) increased budget allocations do not guarantee appropriate services, (d) characteristics of the physical environment are more important than client characteristics in promoting successful residential transfers, (e) singular evaluation systems (e.g., PASS, Wolfensberger & Glenn, 1975; Intermediate Care Facilities for the Mentally Retarded) do not guarantee adequate services, and (f) residential transfers may result in a loss of adaptive behavior.

Landesman-Dwyer's (1981) position, and one with which we certainly agree, is that "Above all, systematic and objective evaluation of the programs and their influences on the clients must be implemented" (p. 228). Fortunately, there is increasing interest in researching the effects of transfers. Some of these investigators have relied on questionnaires (e.g., the Adaptive Behavior Scale, [ABS], and results of their studies have shown that (a) higher levels of maladaptive behavior are predictive of reinstitutionalization (Intagliata & Willer, 1982); (b) for a period of several months, higher level subjects increased their withdrawal and decreased the adaptive functioning (Cohen, Conroy, Frazer, Snelbecker, & Spreat, 1977); (c) for the measured 9 months, an intrainstitutional transfer resulted in a significant regression for these clients on Part One of the ABS (Spreat & Isett, 1981). Other studies have been observational in nature and have shown that (a) a transfer from an institution to the community produced increased activity levels both at home and away from home, with the family, and in one's own social/recreational areas (O'Neill, Brown, Gordon, Schonhorn, & Greer, 1981) and (b) relocation resulted in transitory decreases in social activity, task, and object interaction and more prolonged increases in sick days (Heller, 1982).

Although these and many other investigators have examined the effects of a residential transfer by various means, few have measured the effects of a large-scale educational transfer. Repp, Barton, and Brulle (1982) however, examined whether a least restrictive environment (LRE) transfer of institutionalized persons to a community school could be accommodated by these students.

Although there is a great deal of social literature on LRE, there is very little experimental literature. Although there are probably many reasons for this, two may predominate. The first is that many LRE moves are sociopolitical (i.e., they are the consequences of hearings, financial changes, or sweeping administrative changes, etc.). In most cases, these decisions result in the need for immediate transfers of students from one environment to another, and such action often obviates the possibility of using traditional experimental designs. A second reason is that the success of an LRE move goes against traditional experimental thought. In most cases, experiments are designed so that there are null hypotheses (no differences between conditions) and alternative hypotheses (differences between conditions), and researchers generally attempt to persuade us to accept the alternative hypothesis. In a successful LRE move, however, we often would like to demonstrate the null hypothesis. For example, we may want to show that even though children were moved from a segregated facility to an integrated facility and even though the student-to-staff ratio might have increased, the students are performing as well as they had in their prior environment: We want no more inappropriate responding and no less appropriate responding evidenced in the new environment.

Given these constraints, Repp et al. (1986) conducted a study to assess the effects of an educational transfer of 19 students from an institution to a community facility. Their purpose, to determine what effects this transfer had on appropriate and inappropriate responding of these students, was addressed in two ways: (a) the behavior of this group was assessed both in the community and in the institutional settings and appropriate comparisons were made and (b) the behavior of this group was compared with one other group through the method of social comparison advocated by Kazdin (1977), Wolf (1978), and others. In this procedure, data from direct behavioral observations for a target group and a reference group are compared. This comparison, however, is not made in the traditional control group vs. experimental group sense; rather, it is made to determine whether the experimental group is functioning as well as the reference group is functioning.

In this study, the experimental group was comprised of students whose educational services had been moved from an institution to a community facility; the reference group was comprised of students in the community classrooms to which the experimental group was moved. In summary, then, the primary question was: Are the members of the transferred group performing as well as they did while they were being educated in the institution? The secondary question was: Is this group performing about as well as the community group is performing?

The methodology (6-second partial interval) of the data collection as well as the categories of client and staff behavior scored were the same as those in the Repp and Barton (1980) study previously discussed. About 200,000 observations were made over four 2-month periods during consecutive summer, winter, spring, and summer seasons. Results are presented in Figures 2 and 3. If the students who were moved to the community environment did as well there as they had done at the institution's school, then the community program would be judged as not being too difficult for them. The results showed that this group did at least as well as when they were in an institution: Of each 4-hour period, they (a) had programming available 103 minutes in the institution and 132 minutes in the community; (b) were interacting with the staff 19 minutes in the institution and 103 minutes in the community; (c) were on task 67 minutes and 101 minutes, respectively; (d) displayed stereotypies 50 minutes and 46 minutes; and (e) displayed aggression 5 and 7 minutes.

In the social-comparison portion of this study, the behaviors of the transferred group were compared with the behaviors of the community group. These results showed that the transferred group performed at

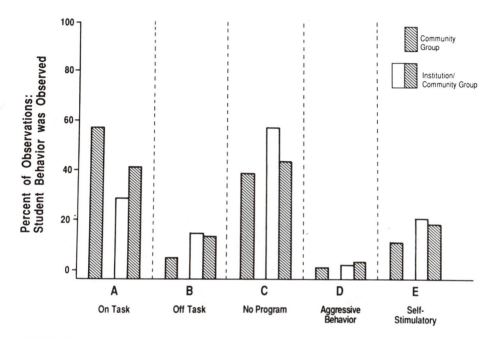

FIGURE 2. Behavioral observations of students in community and institutional settings.

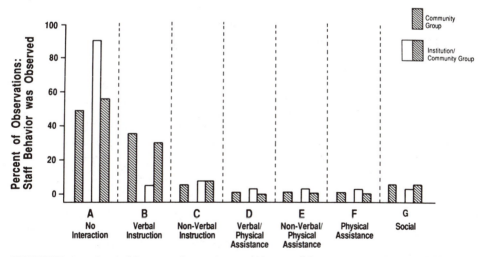

FIGURE 3. Social interactions, instruction, and assistance from staff in community and institutional settings.

lower levels and received less attention from the staff. More specifically, they (a) were on task 73% as much, (b) displayed stereotypies 148% as much, *but* (c) were presented programs 89% as much, and (d) were interacted with by staff 84% as much. These results suggest that when we transfer students such as these, we should consider focusing on their behavior, the relative behavior level of other students in the classes, and the staff. After all, if the latter group does not interact with the transferred students as much (even after a year), success might be less possible for these students.

Another approach to increase the probability of successful moves (discussed by Barton, Brulle, & Repp, 1982) is to assess beforehand (a) the behavior of students already in the environment to which the students will be transferred; (b) the teachers' expectations about the behavior of these students, and (c) the behavior of the students to be moved. In one such study, Nieminen, Barton, Brulle, and Repp, 1984) analyzed the behavior of students currently being educated in various classroom settings in order to characterize the patterns typically expected of students who might be placed in those settings in the future. The subjects were 500 students in 26 self-contained special education classrooms in rural and urban school districts in northern Illinois. All students had been classified educable mentally retarded (EMR), trainable mentally retarded (TMR), or severely/profoundly retarded by their local school districts, following state guidelines. These students were segregated for at least a majority of the day from nonretarded peers and from each other. Data were collected twice weekly by 50 trained observers over a 4-week period, using a 10-second sequential momentary time-sampling procedure in the urban districts and a 5-second momentary time-sampling procedure in the rural district.

Data were recorded on 10 student behaviors, 4 of which were subcategories of on task (using paper and/or pencil, verbalizing, attending, physical/motor), 5 of which were subcategories of off task (talking, out of seat, daydreaming/inactive, nontask, motor, self-stimulation), and one of which (imitates) was neutral. The results showed that the patterns of behavior observed in the three types of special education settings were consistent with traditional expectations. In both EMR and TMR classrooms, students spent a majority of their time (approximately 75%) attending to the teacher or to the task assigned and engaging in task-related activities. Important differences emerged, however, when a more-detailed analysis was made of the specific task-related behaviors on which students in these two settings spent their time. About 24% of total time in the EMR classroom, or about one third of their time on-task, was spent in paper and pencil activities, whereas in the TMR classroom only about 5%, or one-fifteenth of the time on-task, was spent in paper and pencil activities. Instead, a much larger part of the time in the TMR classrooms was spent in physical activities (15% of total time, or one fifth of time on-task) than was true of the EMR classrooms (2% of total time, or one thirtieth of time on-task).

In the classrooms for severely/profoundly retarded students, behavior patterns were very different from those reported in the other settings. Nearly 90% of these students spent their time in noneducation-related activities (e.g., fidgeting, daydreaming, self-stimulation) compared to about 25% of the time for the EMR and TMR students. Of the 10% of the time spent in task-related behavior in the classrooms for the severely/profoundly retarded students almost all of it was spent in physical activities.

These results demonstrate a workable technique for gathering objective data on classroom behaviors for the purpose of making placement decisions. The differing patterns of behavior observed in the three different special education settings have implications for differential placement of students, based on each student's current level of certain types of behavior. For example, in considering moving a student from a TMR to an EMR classroom, attention should be paid to whether that student is presently capable of spending about 25% of his or her time engaged in paper-and-pencil-type activities or whether this behavior needs to be shaped before such a move is carried out. The data also suggest that for severely or profoundly retarded students programming remains at a fairly rudimentary level in many public schools. Further efforts must be made to develop appropriate learning environments for these students if their full potential is to be reached.

Naturalistic Studies of Environmental Factors

As we have suggested previously, naturalistic studies can be of many types, two of which are those concerned with policies and those concerned with more immediate and individual factors in the environment. Certainly, there have been a large number of studies concerned with environmental factors influencing the behavior of retarded persons. Most of these have been in the genre of group research, in which factors such as group size and drugs have been examined. A few, however, have been flavored more by basic assumptions of operant behaviorists and single-subject researchers. The most basic of these assumptions is that some behaviors are a function of antecedents to and consequences of the target behavior, and a few investigators have conducted studies in which results suggest correlates between antecedents and target behaviors. For example, Pratt, Bumstead, and Raynes (1976) noted that informative speech (as an antecedent) produced the highest percentage of replies by institutionalized retarded persons.

Following up this work, we conducted a study to determine the relative effectiveness of five types of instructions on 268 retarded persons (Repp, Barton, & Brulle, 1982). Approximately 240,000 observations were made using 5-second intervals to record the type of staff instruction and then the type of student response. The former consisted of (a) verbal instruction, (b) nonverbal instruction, (c) verbal instruction with physical assistance, (d) nonverbal instruction with physical assistance, and (e) physical assistance. The student behaviors consisted of one correct-response and three incorrect-response categories (stops without completing task, does not respond, resists). Results were coded for each student so that they could be recalled. Grouped, however (in order to be quickly presentable), they showed that nonverbal instruction was the most successful (anteceding the correct response 83% of the time) and nonverbal instruction was the second most successful (77%). In addition, as expected, the categories including physical assistance resulted in the most resistance.

Although the instructions observed in this study could be considered an antecedent to the students' responses, the students' responses can be considered a consequence to the staff's instructing behavior. If we were to presume that a student's correct response were a reinforcer for the staff's behavior, then we might presume that a large proportion of the staff's instructions would be nonverbal. When we reanalyzed these data, however, we found that in only one setting (31 subjects) was this type of instruction the most prevalent. In others, verbal instructions were used 3 to 95 times as often. These results suggest that the natural results of instructions may not be sufficiently reinforcing for staff to differentiate their types of instruction. More directive information (perhaps feedback or direct staff training) might be necessary to produce appropriate changes in their behaviors.

In a continuation of this type of work, we were interested in the effects of natural interaction patterns of retarded persons, believing that the identification of natural interaction patterns among individuals can provide professionals with valuable information about these individuals (Barton, Brulle, & Repp, 1982). This process is particularly important for retarded persons as many of their interactions are contrived by their caregivers, who attempt to engineer an environment that promotes socially acceptable learning. Because a majority of the daily experiences of institutionalized retarded persons occurs in the presence of other retarded persons and ward personnel, the effects that a retarded person's behavior has on these other persons are important. The purpose of our study was twofold: to determine (a) whether the behavior of a retarded person had an effect on other retarded persons in the immediate area and, if so, what that effect was and (b) whether the behavior of a retarded person had an effect on a caregiver in the immediate area and, if so, what that effect was.

The subjects were 207 severely or profoundly retarded residents of a large rural institution for mentally retarded persons. They ranged in age from 6 to 21 years, and some exhibited associated disabilities of (a) visual impairment, (b) hearing impairment, (c) both visual and hearing impairments, or (d) physical and/or health impairments.

Extensively trained observers collected data on a daily basis at various sites throughout the institution using 6-second partial-interval and momentary time-sampling procedures. In the partial-interval method, the behavior of the target subject during any part of the 6-second interval was recorded at the end of the interval (in cases where two or more recordable behaviors occurred during the interval, only the first was recorded). In the momentary time-sampling method, the behavior of the nearest student and nearest staff member were recorded at the end of each interval. In this manner, the influence of the behavior of one person on the behavior of others could be observed.

An analysis of the nearest client's behaviors revealed that 99% of the time the targeting subject's behavior did not affect the nearest client's behavior. In almost all cases, the nearest client simply continued what he or she had been doing. This was true across all subjects, including those with varying secondary handicapping conditions. Staff behaviors varied, however, with the targeted subject's behavior. The client behaviors of aggression, self-aggression, self-stimulation, inactivity, wandering, and no-task communication resulted in the staff doing nothing. The behavior of on-task communication, however, generally resulted in the staff behavior of staff-instruction, whereas the behaviors of off-task communication and on-task, no communication resulted in either custodial guidance or staff-instruction. Finally, the client behavior of off-task, no communication prompted either custodial guidance or no program.

The results demonstrated that a client's behavior had no immediate effect on the other clients. This finding is probably relevant only to severely or profoundly retarded populations who may not attend to stimuli presented by other persons. This interpretation supports previous findings by the same authors regarding reactivity to observers (Brulle, Barton, Rose, Lessen, & Repp, 1981). In that study, the authors found that the presence of an outside observer in the classroom did not significantly affect the behaviors of profoundly, severely, and trainable retarded children.

The results also indicated that the staff generally did not react when the clients exhibited off-task behaviors characteristic of institutionalized retarded persons (e.g., self-aggression, self-stimulation). Many of the on-task client behaviors, however, prompted interactions on the part of staff members. This finding leads to the suggestion that staff members may be reinforced by appropriate client behaviors and thus respond to the clients. These responses (in the form of instructions) to the clients can, in turn, lead to appropriate responding on the part of the retarded clientele (Repp et al., 1981) and thus begin a circle of appropriate instructions. In earlier studies with institutionalized retarded persons, however, Repp and Barton (1980) and Repp et al., (1981) found that staff and clients did not interact more than 10% of the time. The implications of these findings point to the establishment of behavioral change procedures designed to increase staff responding, particularly during instances of off-task behaviors. This increased responding on the part of staff members should then lead to the retarded clientele's exhibiting more appropriate and less inappropriate behaviors.

Given these results, we were interested in studying the interactive effects of other behaviors of staff and students (Repp, Barton, & Brulle, 1982). Our earlier work (Repp, Barton, & Brulle, 1982) had shown that students generally attempt to comply with staff instructions. In this study, we attempted to assess the staff–student interactions of 268 subjects in classroom settings for TMR students. Using the same observational procedures previously described, we recorded three categories of staff behavior and four categories of student behavior: *Staff:* teacher approval (verbal, smiles, physical, eye contact), teacher disapproval (verbal, nonverbal), and instruction-related (instruction, discussion, correction, custodial, other, no programming, teacher preparation); and *Student:* on task (paper/pencil, verbal, attending, motor), Off Task (talking, out of seat, daydreaming/inactive motor), no program (daydream/inactive, motor, verbal), and other (self-stimulation, imitates, involuntary motor).

Data were collected twice weekly by trained observers over a 4-week period. A 5-second momentary time-sampling was used, and more than 300,000 observations were made. Data were analyzed in an antecedent–behavior–consequence fashion shown in Table 3.

Although these behavioral categories were grouped for presentation in this discussion, they are available separately for programming decisions. Quite apparently, there is a specific grouped relationship between student behaviors and staff behaviors that will hold for many but not all the students studied.

TABLE 3 **Significant Relations Between Staff and Student Behaviors**

Staff antecedents	Student behaviors increased		Staff consequences increased
Instruction	Verbal Attending Motor	on task	Verbal Physical Verbal
	Motor Daydreaming	off task	Correction
Discussion	Verbal Attending Motor	on task	
	Daydreaming, off task		Ignored
Custodial	Motor (no program)		
No program	Self-stimulation Daydreaming		Ignored
Eye contact	Motor, on task		

CONCLUSION

It is our position that naturalistic observations, when conducted in sufficient quantities, can produce significant information for those interested in general tendencies (i.e., when the data are grouped) as well as for those interested in specific student–staff relationships (when the data are separated for each subject). Because of our interest in the applied behavior analysis approach, wherein the behavior of individual subjects is changed to acceptable levels, we believe that such an approach is a valuable one. Currently, operant behaviorists do observe behavior within the context of natural environments; however, with very few exceptions (for representative discussions, see Rogers-Warren & Warren, 1977; Wahler & Fox, 1982), operant behaviorists record only one or two behaviors, thus losing considerable information. Our suggestion, consonant with the suggestion of other authors, is that we observe the natural interactions of our subjects in their environments, determine natural correlative or causal relationship between their behavior and environmental events, and alter these events rather than artificial ones in an attempt to modify the behavior of these individuals. In the present chapter we have addressed the first two of these objectives. In our current research, we are addressing all three.

REFERENCES

Accreditation Council for Facilities for the Mentally Retarded. (1971). *Standards for residential facilities for the mentally retarded*. Chicago: Joint Commission on Accreditation of Hospitals.

Arrington, R. E. (1932). Interrelations in the behavior of young children. *Child Development Monographs*, No. 8.

Arrington, R. E. (1943). Time sampling in studies of social behavior: A critical review of techniques and results with research suggestions. *Psychological Bulletin, 40*, 81–124.

Baer, D. M., Wolf, M. M., & Risley, T. R. (1968). Some current dimensions of applied behavior analysis. *Journal of Applied Behavior Analysis, 1*, 91–97.

Barton, L. E., Brulle, A. R., & Repp, A. C. (1982). Naturalistic studies of retarded persons: The effects of the behavior of retarded persons on other retarded persons and staff. *Mental Retardation Bulletin, 10*, 2–17.

Barton, L. E., Brulle, A. R., & Repp, A. C. (1982). The social validation of programs for mentally retarded persons. *Mental Retardation*.

Beaver, A. P. (1932). The initiation of social contacts by preschool children. *Child Development Monographs*, No. 7.

Berkson, G., & Landesman-Dwyer, S. (1977). Behavioral research on severe and profound mental retardation (1955–1974). *American Journal of Mental Deficiency, 81*, 428–454.

Bible, G. H., & Sneed, T. J. (1976). Some effects of an accreditation survey on program completion at a state institution. *Mental Retardation, 14*, 14–15.

Brulle, A. R., Barton, L. E., & Repp, A. C. (1984). Evaluating LRE decisions through social comparison. *Journal of Learning Disabilities 17*, 462–466.

Brulle, A. R., Barton, L. E., Rose, T., Lessen, E. I., & Repp, A. C. (1984). *Reactivity to observers*. Unpublished manuscript.

Brulle, A. R., & Repp, A. C. (1985). An investigation of the accuracy of momentary time-sampling procedures with time series data. *The British Journal of Psychology, 75*, 481–485.

Cohen, H. R., Conroy, J. W., Frazer, D. W., Snelbecker, G. E., & Spreat, S. (1977). Behavioral effects of interinstitutional relocation of mentally retarded residents. *American Journal of Mental Deficiency, 82,* 12–18.

Dunbar, R. I. M. (1976). Some aspects of research design and their implications in the observational study of behavior. *Behavior, 58,* 78–98.

Goodenough, F. L. (1928). Measuring behavior traits by means of repeated short samples. *Journal of Juvenile Research, 12,* 230–235.

Goodenough, F. L. (1930). Inter-relationships in the behavior of young children. *Child Development, 1,* 29–47.

Green, S. B., & Alverson, L. G. (1978). A comparison of indirect measures for long-duration behavior. *Journal of Applied Behavior Analysis, 11,* 530.

Heller, T. (1982). Social disruption and residential relocation of mentally retarded children. *American Journal of Mental Retardation, 87,* 48–55.

Heward, W. L., Test, D. W., Wegner, D. L., Cowardin, J. H., Olson, J. K., & Shrewsbury, R. D. (1980). *A comparison of fixed interval and variable-interval momentary time-sampling.* Unpublished manuscript, The Ohio State University.

Intagliata, J., & Willer, B. (1982). Reinstitutionalization of mentally retarded persons successfully placed into family-care and group homes. *American Journal of Mental Deficiency, 87,* 34–39.

Kazdin, A. E. (1977). Assessing the clinical or applied importance of behavior change through social validation. *Behavior Modification, 1,* 427–451.

Kelly, M. B. (1977). A review of the observational data-collection and reliability procedures reported in JABA. *Journal of Applied Behavioral Analysis, 10,* 97–102.

Landesman-Dwyer, S. (1981). Living in the community. *American Journal of Mental Deficiency, 86,* 223–234.

Nieminen, G. S., Barton, L. E., & Brulle, A. R. & Repp, A. C. (1984). *Naturalistic observations of retarded children in public schools: A comparison.* Unpublished manuscript.

Olinger, E., & Repp, A. C. (1984). *A study of the accuracy of sequential time-sampling procedures with unaveraged time series data of different durations.* Unpublished manuscript, Northern Illinois University.

Olson, W. C. (1929). The measurement of nervous habits in normal children. *University of Minnesota Institute of Child Welfare Monograph,* No. 3.

Olson, W. C. (1931). A study of classroom behavior. *Journal of Educational Psychology, 22,* 449–454.

O'Neill, J., Brown, M., Gordon, W., Schonhorn, R., & Greer, E. (1981). Activity patterns of mentally retarded adults in institutions and communities: A longitudinal study. *Applied Research in Mental Retardation, 2,* 367–379.

Powell, J., Martindale, A., & Kulp, S. (1975). An evaluation of time-sample measures of behavior. *Journal of Applied Behavior Analysis, 8,* 463–469.

Powell, J., Martindale, B., Kulp, S., Martindale, A., & Bauman, R. (1977). Taking a closer look: Time-sampling and measurement error. *Journal of Applied Behavior Analysis, 10,* 325–332.

Pratt, M. W., Bumstead, D. C., & Raynes, N. V. (1976). Attendant staff speech to the institutionalized retarded: Language use as a measure of the quality of care. *Journal of Child Psychology and Psychiatry, 17,* 133–143.

Repp, A. C., & Barton, L. E. (1980). Naturalistic observations of institutionalized retarded persons: A comparison of licensure decisions and behavioral observations. *Journal of Applied Behavior Analysis, 13,* 333–341.

Repp, A. C., Barton, L. E., & Brulle, A. R. (1981). Correspondence between effectiveness and staff use of instructions for severely retarded persons. *Applied Research in Mental Retardation, 2,* 237–245.

Repp, A. C., Barton, L. E., & Brulle, A. R. (1982). Naturlistic studies of mentally retarded persons: V: The effects of staff instructions on student responding. *Applied Research in Mental Retardation, 3,* 55–65.

Repp, A. C., Barton, L. E., & Brulle, A. R. (1986). Assessing a least restrictive educational environment transfer through social comparison. *Education and Training of the Mentally Retarded, 21,* 54–61.

Repp, A. C., Roberts, D. M., Slack, D. J., Repp, C. F., & Berkler, M. S. (1976). A comparison of frequency, interval, and time-sampling methods of data collection. *Journal of Applied Behavior Analysis, 9,* 501–508.

Rock, K., & Repp, A. C. (1983). *Multiple stimulus operant designs.* Unpublished manuscript, Northern Illinois University.

Rogers-Warren, A., & Warren, S. F. (1977). *Ecological perspectives in behavior analysis.* Baltimore: University Park Press.

Spreat, S., & Isett, R. (1981). Behavioral effects of intra-institutional relocation. *Applied Research in Mental Retardation, 2,* 229–236.

U.S. Department of Health, Education, and Welfare (1974). Regulations for intermediate care facilities. *Federal Register, 39,* 2220–2235.

Wahler, R. G., & Fox, J. J. (1982). Setting events in applied behavior analysis: Toward a conceptual and methodological expansion. *Journal of Applied Behavior Analysis, 13,* 327–338.

Wolf, M. M. (1978). Social validity: The case for subjective measurement or how applied behavior analysis is finding its heart. *Journal of Applied Behavior Analysis, 11,* 203–214.

Wolfensberger, W., & Glenn, L. (1975). *PASS III: A method for qualitative evaluation of human services.* Toronto: National Institute on Mental Retardation.

8
Group Homes
as Alternative Care
Settings: System Issues
and Implications

M. P. Janicki and J. W. Jacobson
*New York State Office of Mental Retardation
and Developmental Disabilities*

W. B. Zigmam and R. A. Lubin
Institute for Basic Research in Developmental Disabilities

Shifts in public policy during the past 20 years have promoted the development of a variety of community-based residential services (Braddock, 1981), with group homes emerging as the most prevalent form. Bruininks, Hauber, and Kudla (1980) reported that in 1977 there were approximately 4,400 group homes in the United States, and Janicki, Mayeda, and Epple (1983) indicated that in 1981 there were about 58,000 persons living in 6,300 discrete group homes. A paramount question is, How does the service system provide for the various needs of developmentally disabled persons residing in the community?

New York State has one of the largest, oldest, and most rapidly developing group home programs in the country (Janicki, Mayeda, & Epple, 1983; Merges, 1982). In 1982, close to 7,000 developmentally disabled persons resided in more than 700 community residences across the state. By 1985, more than 9,200 persons were residing in more than 900 group homes. Based on New York's varied history of group home development (Janicki, Castellani, & Lubin, 1982), many aspects of this community residential system can be evaluated. In this chapter we have focused on three issues: (a) How diverse are the residential services available to different types of disabled individuals? (b) What access do group home residents have to day programs and support services? and (c) Is the internal structure within the group home system adequate to sustain and promote the provision of quality services?

The data derive from two sources: the Living Alternatives Research Project (Living Alternatives, 1981) and New York's Developmental Disabilities Information System (Janicki & Jacobson, 1979, 1982). The first set of data is from a two-phase study of New York's group homes (1980–1981). The first phase surveyed 368 of the 499 group homes operating in New York. The second phase involved an intensive assessment of resident, physical/environment, occupational, and rehabilitative characteristics of a sample of 50 group homes. These data were augmented by a second survey in 1983 that provided data on 892 group homes (Janicki & Jacobson, 1985). The research instruments included the Demographic Questionnaire (Living Alternatives, 1981), the Demographic Questionnaire/2 (Office of Mental Retardation, 1983), a short form of the Program Assessment of Service Systems—PASS (Flynn & Heal, 1981), the Characteristics of the Treatment Environment (Jackson, 1964), the Group Home Management Schedule (Raynes, Pratt, & Roses, 1977), the Job Description Index (Smith, Kendall, & Hulin, 1969), and the Residence Personnel Opinion Scale (Living Alternatives, 1981).

The second data source was a needs assessment survey (Janicki & Jacobson, 1979, 1982) first administered in 1979 through 1982 by the New York State Office of Mental Retardation and Developmental Disabilities (OMRDD) to more than 55,000 persons identified as developmentally disabled or at risk for becoming so. The data gathered included sociodemographic, disability characteristic, functional skill level, and service-need information. Information on residents in New York's group homes and in other settings is updated continually and incorporated in the state's client information system.

The term *community residential facility* refers to a variety of residences that are not part of the state's institutional structure, encompassing a range of different program models (McCord, 1981). *Community residences* are defined here as small *privately* and *publicly* operated neighborhood-based group homes and apartments that provide a supervised living and learning environment for developmentally disabled children or adults. *Service patterns* refer to both day programs (vocational, activity, and habilitative) in which group home residents are enrolled and to the habilitative and support services (health care and therapies, social activities and recreation, advocacy and social services) that they receive.

WHAT IS THE DIVERSITY IN RESIDENT AND SERVICE CHARACTERISTICS IN AVAILABLE PROGRAM MODELS?

Initially, we analyzed characteristics of the residents in a variety of residential program models, ranging from public and private institutional care to natural family and independent living (Office of Mental Retarda-

TABLE 1 Characteristics of Mentally Retarded Persons Residing at Home and in Various Living Situations in New York

Characteristic	Family Living Situations		Group Living Situations			Congregate Care Situations	
	Natural family	Foster family	Group homes	ICF/MR	Supervised apartments	Skilled nursing facilities	State development centers
Age							
< 22	60	22	9	27	7	8	21
22-64	40	64	89	71	91	63	72
> 64	0	14	2	2	2	29	7
Gender							
Male	57	47	55	61	52	50	56
Female	43	53	45	39	48	50	44
Intellectual level							
Nonretarded	16	6	12	5	25	20	2
Mildly retarded	22	19	31	12	39	19	5
Moderately retarded	23	29	29	20	17	19	11
Severely retarded	14	29	20	32	7	15	23
Profoundly retarded	8	12	8	31	6	17	57
Unknown	18	5	7	3	6	11	2
Self-care skills[a]							
Toileting	76	95	89	64	98	51	59
Eating	80	95	85	61	98	66	61
Dressing	71	92	65	38	95	48	48
No. of individuals[b]	16,627	3,754	3,015	2,001	553	236	12,439

[a] % independent or needing minimal assistance.

[b] Numbers may not represent all individuals residing in these settings, only those appearing on the Developmental Disabilities Information Survey.

tion, 1980). The most prevalent residential care models include congregate care settings (e.g., developmental centers, residential treatment schools, skilled nursing facilities), surrogate family living settings (e.g., foster family care homes), group living settings (e.g., proprietary homes for adults, supervised and intermediate care facility type community residences [i.e., group homes], and supervised apartments), and independent living situations (e.g., minimally supervised apartments). Table 1 shows the sociodemographic characteristics of the residents of these program models (Janicki, Jacobson, & Scwartz, 1982; Jacobson, Schwartz, & Janicki, 1985). More detailed resident information has been presented by Janicki and Jacobson (1982).

New York's congregate care facilities, like those in other states, generally can be characterized as institutional environments wherein specialized residential, health, and habilitative services are provided. Individuals who reside in these facilities are among the most severely disabled. In developmental centers, for example, some 84% of the residents are severely or profoundly mentally retarded and need specialized health care, therapeutic interventions, and habilitative services. Many have significant deficits in basic self-care and communication skills, as well as major physical, emotional, or behavioral disabilities.

Surrogate family living settings are usually family-owned, limited size residences (mode = 1 resident) that provide board-and-care as well as some basic training experiences (Bruininks, Hill, & Thorsheim, 1980; Sherman, Frenkel, & Newman, 1984). These settings fulfill a variety of therapeutic purposes, primarily to employ the physical and social environment of the home and the psychosocial structure of the family to enhance interpersonal and group living skills. Most family care home residents have basic self-care skills and function in the mild-to-moderate range of mental retardation; in addition, a large proportion are either children or elderly. The predominant services being received by individuals in family living settings are basic health care (medical, nursing, dental), recreational diversion, religious/pastoral care, transportation, and specialized therapies (such as counseling and speech remediation). Most of the adults are enrolled in vocationally oriented day programs, and most of the children are in school programs. Their predominant service needs are reported to be in the areas of greater occupational training, leisure-time use, transportation assistance, and overall enhancement of community living skills.

Group living programs include a variety of alternatives, most notably the group home. These homes can be characterized as small neighborhood-based residences that provide a supervised living and learning environment. New York has two types of group home residence type programs: cooperative or supervised living facilities that provide board, supervision, and a range of training experiences; and intermediate care facilities for mentally retarded persons (ICFs/MR) that are specifically designed for residents with severe disabilities and specialized service needs. In general, cooperative group living is the goal for programs with more-intellectually-capable residents, whereas structured care is the goal for programs with more-severely-disabled residents (Silver, Lubin, & Silverman, 1984). The residents of group living programs represent a population with diverse characteristics and needs (Jacobson & Janicki, 1985; Jacobson, Sersen, & Schwartz, 1984). In most instances the level of impairment determines the extent of program services needed and provided (Jacobson & Ackerman, 1985; Jacobson, Silver, & Schwartz, 1984). These program models and their residents are addressed in more detail later in this chapter.

Independent living can be characterized as either maintaining one's own home or residing with family or relatives. Because these are natural settings, no specific program models are associated with them; however, some characteristics do differentiate individuals who reside in natural settings from those who reside in institutions or community alternatives. Persons living at home are most likely to be young, relatively more intellectually developed, and moderately more capable in basic self-care skills than are persons in other models of residential services. Persons living independently, most often in apartment programs that provide drop-in supervision or assistance, usually are minimally intellectually retarded and relatively more competent in basic skills. The predominant needs of persons living at home center around the use of recreation or leisure time and remedial training for occupational and communication deficits. The predominant needs of persons in apartment situations are related more to normative living demands, such as dental care, nutritional assistance, counseling, and improved use of leisure time. Most individuals living independently receive needed health care, such as routine medical and dental services. They also receive other generic services on an as-needed basis, such as specialized medical care and professional counseling. Their greatest unmet needs are usually in the areas of nutritional services and recreation or leisure-time activities. In comparison, more individuals living with their families need and receive a range of health care and therapy services. Where there are shortfalls, they are mostly in unmet needs for more recreational services, speech therapy, and occupational therapy. Among persons living at home or independently, our data show that practically all are enrolled in some form of day program or activity or receive an aggregate of services related to therapeutic care during the week.

We conclude that there is indeed diversity in resident characteristics and services (both needed and received) and that these are a function of the residential alternatives within the general system of developmental services as well as the needs of individuals (Jacobson, Silver, & Schwartz, 1984; Jacobson & Janicki, 1985). In general, statistical analyses have indicated that differences in the characteristics of individuals were associated with the type of residential model; in most instances, these differences were significant (Janicki, Jacobson, & Schwartz, 1982). As expected, persons residing in congregate care settings were the most disabled and persons living independently, the least disabled. Persons living in group homes had a diversity of disability characteristics that could be characterized as intermediate relative to persons residing in more- or less-structured settings and as varying widely from site to site (Jacobson & Janicki, 1985).

DO GROUP HOME RESIDENTS HAVE ACCESS TO A FULL RANGE OF DAY PROGRAMS AND SUPPORT SERVICES?

Sound rehabilitative practices call for placing individuals with social, vocational, and other adaptive deficits into a residential setting that provides adequate social experiences, training, and support (Anthony, 1977; Janicki, Castellani, & Norris, 1983). One way to assess whether group homes meet their residents' needs is to examine the support structure ensuring provision of a full range of social, health, and training services. We assumed that the boundaries of the group home extend beyond the walls of each residence and include the habilitative environment offered by a community living situation. This environment encompasses the formal day and evening habilitative services provided to residents on- and off-site, the more informally structured group activities afforded by a small group living situation, and the physical and social context of the surrounding community (White, Hill, Lakin, & Bruininks, 1984). According to Wolfensberger (1972), developmental growth and the normative practices of programs are dependent upon the extent to which residents of community residences participate in mainstream social activities and rely on services from generic providers (e.g., medical centers, rehabilitative programs, education programs, and private professional practitioners) rather than from specialized providers (a similar perspective was offered by Emerson, 1985).

As Martin and Laidlaw (1980) noted, residents require many support services, such as transportation, education and training, vocational rehabilitation, employment, leisure and recreation, medical services, psychological services, specialized therapies, and case management. It may not be correct, however, to assume that (a) generic service systems can provide these services or (b) that changes in these systems can be achieved such that this service capability can be realized. There is substantial evidence that out-of-home placement of developmentally disabled individuals often was the result of marked disability (Eagle, 1967; Windle, Stewart, & Brown, 1961) or problem behavior (Clark, 1959; Eagle, 1967; Sutter, Mayeda, Yanagi, & Yee, 1980) and that the generic service systems previously were unable to handle or appropriately serve these disabled individuals. Given national trends in the placement of increasingly disabled persons from institutions to community settings (Braddock, 1981), there is reason to question whether generic agencies that were unable, or refused, to serve an even less-disabled population will be able to provide and sustain the variety of special services currently needed by deinstitutionalized individuals. Even when services provided by private practitioners and generic agencies are available, there may be problems associated with ready access to private professional services because of the individual's dependence on third-party payment for services. Although utilization of generic resources is a critical component in the maintenance of a normalized residential setting (Janicki, 1981; Janicki, Castellani, & Norris, 1983; Janicki, Jacobson, & Schwartz, 1982), the needs of the residents may necessitate that many services will have to be provided by developmental disabilities professionals and agencies. Relatively little objective information is available on the services needed or utilized by group home residents or the strategies available for alternative delivery of needed services, although issues of health and other services delivery have received recent attention (Donnellan, LaVigna, Zambito, & Thvedt, 1985; Janicki, Jacobson, & Ackerman, 1985; McDonald, 1985; Spangler & Gilman, 1985; Schalock, Foley, Toulouse, & Stark, 1985).

Available information enabled us to examine a number of issues related to service provision for group home residents. These included: (a) the service needs of the general group home population and whether these services were being provided, (b) differences in the service structure of the two community residence models (the supervised living facility and the ICF/MR [service-intensive] group home), and (c) the relationship between service provision and characteristics of the group home residents.

Services and the General Group Home Population

Given the heterogeneity of group home residents (Jacobson, Silver, & Schwartz, 1984), we expected that service needs would be expressed in a variety of domains. We assumed that the primary service needs would be basic health care, maintenance and enhancement of psychological adjustment, and remediation of physical impairments and skill deficits. Table 2 shows the proportion of group home residents who needed and received various therapeutic services. Routine medical and dental care were provided to practically everyone, whereas specialized medical and nursing services were provided when a need was noted. Other diagnostic and remedial services (such as audiological and nutritional services), were provided readily, but the services designed to improve community abilities (e.g., speech therapy) were notably deficient. A small proportion of individuals reported to have motor impairments received occupational and physical therapy, although their needs were not fully met. Services directed primarily at personal growth (such as counseling and other psychological interventions) as well as services designed to increase the diversity of leisure-time use and recreational skills were not sufficiently available to residents. In addition to the pronounced need for more speech therapy and recreational therapy services, a variety of individual counseling services were the most noted deficits in service provision.

TABLE 2 Therapeutic Services Received and Needed Among Persons Residing in Various Residential Settings

| | Family Living Situations | | | | Group Living Situations | | | | Congregate Care Situations | | | |
| | Natural family | | Foster family | | Group home[a] | | Community apartment | | Skilled nursing facility | | Developmental center | |
Service	Receiving services	Needing services	Receiving services	Needing services	Receiving services	Needing services	Receiving services	Needing services	Receiving services	Needing services	Receiving services	Needing services
Dental	53[b]	17	89	7	90	8	82	19	71	9	97	3
Nursing	21	3	54	7	51	7	23	0	94	4	87	7
Nutritional	11	10	17	7	44	14	39	25	78	5	84	3
Occupational therapy	22	23	14	22	23	26	8	12	45	39	41	52
Physical therapy	24	19	7	8	17	18	3	9	57	32	24	30
Counseling	34	20	35	11	42	25	62	42	37	27	16	12
Psychological	38	17	40	19	58	22	37	26	32	20	78	26
Recreation therapy	26	40	49	52	62	36	34	26	62	43	77	52
Routine medical	83	7	96	3	96	3	93	12	92	3	98	2
Specialized medical	36	9	25	5	42	8	32	12	66	5	40	5
Speech therapy	42	35	28	38	35	40	7	20	26	30	34	45
No. of individuals	16,627		3,754		5,016		553		236		12,439	

Note. Information derived from the Developmental Disabilities Information System.

[a] Percentages represent all group home occupants for whom data were available; data in Table 4 differ in percentages as only persons for whom Demographic Questionnaire data were available are reflected in Table 4.

[b] Percentage receiving or needing.

180

TABLE 3 Types of Day Program Services Received by Persons Residing in Various Residential Settings

	Family Living Situations				Group Living Situations				Congregate Care Situations			
	Natural family		Foster family		Group home		Community apartment		Skilled nursing facility		Developmental center	
Day program	N	%	N	%	N	%	N	%	N	%	N	%
Educational	7815	47	713	19	652	13	0	0	17	7	995	8
Prevocational habilitation	3159	19	1051	28	1906	38	72	13	143	61	9703	78
Vocational	3990	24	1464	39	2157	43	381	69	0	0	746	6
Other	1663	10	526	14	301	6	100	18	76	32	995	8
No. of individuals	16,627		3,754		5,016		553		236		12,439	

181

Participation in a day program is required for all group home residents. Consequently, only about 1% of group home residents were without a specialized full-day activity (see Table 3). Most of the residents were enrolled in a formal sheltered work program (45%). Others were enrolled in Title XIX day treatment programs (18%), went to another type of work activity or training program (21%), or were competitively employed (4%). In addition, about 8% (i.e., children) were enrolled in school programs and 3% in a variety of other activities, including senior services.

Overall, the two major problems were inadequate coordination of the delivery of available services and unavailability of certain professionals and paraprofessionals to provide specific types of services. Coordination deficiencies were evident when staff members noted problems in making referrals to services known to be readily available. A recognized general shortage of available occupational and physical therapists to meet the identified client demands contributed significantly to the unavailability of these services.

Comparisons Between ICF/MR and Other Group Homes

We compared service-delivery patterns between supervised living facilities and intermediate care facilities (ICFs/MR) (Jacobson & Ackerman, 1985; Jacobson, Silver, & Schwartz, 1984). Data from the client information system denoted the proportion of persons who received and had unmet needs for professional services, regardless of whether services were provided by residential or day programs. Additional data from the later survey identified the proportion of programs (rather than persons) that provided each type of service on-site. Table 4 presents these data as a function of program model.

Program comparisons revealed the following statistically significant differences between the two residential models in 1981. First, programs serving persons with more-marked impairments provided more hours of service on-site, even when type of facility was controlled (supervised living facility vs. ICF/MR). Second, ICF/MR residents were more likely than were supervised living facility residents to receive each listed service—regardless of provider—with the exception of dental, educational, and vocational rehabilitation services; and to provide such services on-site, except dental and counseling. Third, ICF/MR programs provided significantly more hours of each service monthly, except for occupational therapy and specialized medical services, than did supervised living facility programs. In fact, the total monthly service hours provided on-site were roughly twice as high in ICFs/MR as they were in supervised living facilities. Fourth, and finally, the pattern of unmet needs was similar in both programs, notably, the previously reported shortfalls in occupational therapy, speech therapy, and recreation therapy services. In general, more recent data (i.e., Jacobson & Ackerman, 1985), although confirming earlier

TABLE 4 Services Received and Unmet Service Needs of New York's Group Home Occupants

Service	Developmental Disabilities Information System data				Demographic Questionnaire (DQ) data	
	Supervised residence		ICF/DD		Supervised residence, % sites providing service	ICF/DD, % sites providing service
	% receiving service	% needing service[a]	% receiving service	% needing service		
Audiology	43	3	77	4	—[b]	—[b]
Dental	88	4	87	5	26	29
Education	—[b]	—[b]	—[b]	—[b]	17	31
Nursing	47	4	57	3	57	89
Occupational therapy	22	13	23	14	12	24
Physical therapy	13	8	19	9	11	25
Professional counseling	45	15	34	11	21	13
Psychological	48	10	68	8	48	67
Recreational therapy	57	19	63	21	38	63
Routine medical	94	2	90	1	35	49
Specialized medical	39	4	55	3	14	26
Speech therapy	28	20	49	24	21	70
Transportation	68	8	70	2	—[b]	—[b]
Vocational rehabilitation	52	13	36	10	—[b]	—[b]
No. of individuals[c]	2,067		588		2,036	655
No. of sites	264		74		232	79

Note. Table adapted from Jacobson, Silver, and Johnson, 1984.

[a] Needing means needs but does not receive or needs more than now receives.

[b] Data element not present on DQ or Developmental Disabilities Information System.

[c] For DQ data, estimates from number of sites.

findings, also show an increase in the importance of program type (super-vised living facility vs. ICF/MR) compared to resident characteristics in determining hours of service.

Concerning patterns of day program use, residents from ICF/MR and supervised living facility programs were placed in day settings appropriate to their level of disability. Because individuals in ICF/MR programs were more-disabled, they were more likely to attend day habilitative (20%) and day training programs (19%) than were persons residing in supervised living facility programs (10% and 15%, respectively). Because sheltered workshops are designed for less-disabled persons, their greater use by supervised living facility residents (59%) compared to ICF/MR residents (25%) was expected. In general, the programs appear to be fulfilling their different missions.

Comparisons Among Residences by Resident Characteristics

We expected concordance between age-related functional needs and services received. To examine this, we related resident age, level of mental retardation, and extent of disability to the services residents received or needed (Jacobson & Janicki, 1985).

Regarding services that residents actually received, individuals with pronounced needs due to physical problems or with other needs for supervision, basic training in adaptive daily living, and behavioral mainte-nance received more nursing, occupational therapy, and psychological services. Individuals with higher intellectual capabilities and fewer major disabilities received more counseling services directed toward enhanced adjustment and life planning than did residents who were more severely retarded. As expected, more-capable individuals generally participated more in unstructured leisure-time/recreation activities, whereas more-dis-abled individuals engaged in more-formal recreation therapy and group activities (see also Gothelf, 1985). More-capable residents received generic health care services sufficient to meet most needs. Regarding services needed, but not met, more-intellectually-capable residents had a greater unmet need in the area of mental health and professional counseling services compared to less-capable residents. In contrast, both younger and more-disabled residents had more needs identified for specialized medical and remedial services (e.g., occupational and physical therapy).

The service support system within the community appears to provide at least minimal level of support services for many residents. Nevertheless, when individuals need more than minimal support services, deficiencies become more apparent in the service system. Occupational and physical therapy services were not readily available in the amount or manner required. Dental services for older and multiply disabled individuals were not sufficient. Transportation to access greater amounts of recreational, vocational, and health care services also was inadequate for older individuals. Finally, recreational and leisure-time activities were found to be insufficient to meet the needs of younger residents.

According to the data we had available, these deficiencies were attributable to two predominant factors: the unavailability of certain types of services and problems inherent in the referral and follow-through process. For example, with regard to unmet mental health or counseling needs, the mental health system may not be prepared to cope with providing counseling and other psychotherapeutic services to individuals with intellectual, communication, and mobility difficulties. System deficiencies, however, such as insufficient funding and lack of trained staff, do account for unmet needs in recreation and other therapies (e.g., occupational and physical therapy).

The implications of these system deficits are marked. To accommodate individuals with more-intensive service needs, a service-delivery system may need to provide more-complex services, and sometimes more-costly services, particularly to help divert institutional admissions or readmissions. Currently, financial cutbacks place serious constrictions on the amount and quality of support services.

IS THERE AN ADEQUATE INTERNAL STRUCTURE WITHIN THE GROUP HOME SYSTEM TO SUSTAIN AND PROMOTE THE PROVISION OF QUALITY SERVICES?

The image of the group home suggests that these residences are living, rather than service, environments. This is apparent in the literature on service system design (Hitzing, 1980; Janicki, Castellani, & Norris, 1983; Knowlton, 1980) and in empirical reports on the use of the generic services by community residential programs (Bjaanes & Butler, 1974; Butler & Bjaanes, 1977; Crapps, Langone, & Swaim, 1985; Eyman, Demaine, & Lei, 1979; Hull & Thompson, 1980, 1981; Martin & Laidlaw, 1980; Savage, Novak, & Heal, 1980). This developmental orientation means staff employed in group homes need to demonstrate behavioral competencies that would promote skill enhancement and acquisition of greater independent living ability for each resident. The internal structure of group homes thus gains prominence as a variable in assessing quality of care and differential client outcomes (Bersani & Heifetz, 1985; Cherniss, 1981; McCord, 1981). This is confirmed by studies demonstrating that the skills of staff and staff practices relate significantly to resident growth outcomes (Aanes & Moen, 1976; Burchard, Pine, Gordon, & Widrick, 1983; Close, 1977; Nihira & Nihira, 1975; Schalock, Harper, & Genung, 1981; Schinke & Wong, 1977). Substantive aspects related to the internal structure of group homes include the competence and job satisfaction of direct-care staff and management personnel.

Although definitive statements regarding the effects of internal structure cannot be made without adequate longitudinal study, current data permit description of some aspects of the existing internal structure, including both objective and subjective aspects of staff (McCord, 1981). Objective characteristics that include age, gender, experience, and education were available from questionnaires sent to all New York group homes (Jacobson & Janicki, 1984; Janicki, Jacobson, Zigman, & Gordon, 1984). Subjective data that include attitudes toward disabled people and their care in community residences and self-report of job satisfaction were based on data collected from a study of 50 randomly selected group homes.

Group home employees were mostly female (67%), young (mean age = 31 years), fairly well-educated (over 60% had 2 or more years of college, and 38% were college graduates), and had been employed in human services an average of 4.0 years. These direct-care staff members generally had received some specialized training related to their jobs. When asked to indicate what they perceived to be their greatest need for training, staff members identified areas related to enhancing skills for involvement with residents. The highest priorities included: additional training in goal planning, designing training and behavior modification programs, and medication management. These are the skill areas most linked to acquisition of new behaviors by group home residents (e.g., Close, 1977), although, theoretically, other areas may be as important (Landesman-Dwyer & Knowles, 1985).

For all group homes, a residence manager or administrator was identified as responsible for each group home program. Compared to direct-care staff, residence managers were more likely to be men, to have a higher level of education (78% had at least 2 years of college, and 58% were college graduates), to have worked for the host agency significantly longer, and, generally, to have had more years of experience in the field of developmental disabilities. Many managers had undergraduate or graduate degrees in psychology, special education, or health sciences fields. As expected, managers earned more (about $3,000) than did the staff members. Managers reported receiving training related to day-to-day performance of their duties, including staff supervision, general management, state policies, procedures related to the residence programs, fiscal management procedures, and neighborhood relations.

In sum, most group home employees in New York were both well-educated and experienced, at equal to or higher than levels reported elsewhere (e.g., George & Baumeister, 1981; Knowles & Landesman, 1986). Two opposing hypotheses may be proposed about the long-term consequences of these characteristics. One hypothesis is that well-trained, experienced, and educated staff will be more proficient in performing their jobs, thereby creating a more effective residential environment (McCord, 1981). Whether this staff "effectiveness" will result in improved resident outcomes has not yet been demonstrated. A second hypothesis is that the low wages paid to group home workers and the limited opportunities for advancement will be associated with job dissatisfaction levels and high turnover rates, which will reduce the actual effectiveness of these employees. Strikingly, comparisons of 1983 data (Jacobson & Janicki, 1984) with the 1980 data reported previously show an overall decline (from 34% to 22%) in college graduates and only a modest increase in total experience in providing services among staff. These findings suggest a changing character of the staff employed in community residential settings and further suggest that turnover is a problem and possibly more pronounced among better-educated staff providing direct supervision and training.

In another study we examined work attitudes and job satisfaction among group home employees (Silver, Lubin, & Silverman, 1984; Zigman, Schwartz, & Janicki, 1984). We used the Residence Personnel Opinion Scale, an instrument derived from the Attendant Opinion Scale (Bensberg & Barnett, 1966) to assess staff attitudes. The Residence Personnel Opinion Scale measures staff attitudes towards mentally retarded/developmentally disabled people and their care in community residential settings. Staff attitudes towards their jobs and the people they serve are hypothesized to be important for delivery of high-quality services to group home residents. Pratt, Luszcz, and Brown (1980) found a significant relationship between staff attitudes about equality with residents and certain care practices within residences. We found that staff members had generally positive regard for most aspects of residence employment, although there was some variation in attitudes. Our results also showed that most staff members reported positive attitudes toward the care of group home residents, including beliefs that they should not abridge resident autonomy. They reported mild-to-strong positive attitudes related to aspects of residence care such as comradeship with residents, equality, and residents' rights to freedom of expression. Staff members endorsed items portraying residents as positive and disagreed with those that were negative or critical. Although the relationships among staff attitudes, actual job behavior, and resident growth remain undetermined, there are intrinsic reasons for supporting staff attitudes that respect the rights of mentally retarded individuals.

Employee job satisfaction was assessed using the Job Descriptive Index (Smith, Kendall, & Hulin, 1969) with regard to five specific aspects of employment. Most staff members reported general satisfaction with three aspects: the work itself, supervision, and co-workers. They were less-satisfied with pay and promotional opportunities. Data from the Demographic Questionnaire indicated that about 70% of the direct-care staff members earned less than $10,000 per year and none earned more than $13,000. Administrators earned slightly more: 20% earned less than $10,000, 60% earned less than $13,000, and only 10% earned more than $16,000 per year. These salaries, given the job demands, are clearly low and a threat to staff stability and morale (George & Baumeister, 1981). Prolonged dissatisfaction with these aspects of employment in group homes may lead to a situation in which the most qualified staff members resign to seek enhanced employment, and the least-qualified staff members remain due to the dearth of alternative employment possibilities.

Although this hypothesis has not yet been tested, our 1983 data seem to be consistent with this idea that some of the most qualified and devoted staff members experience burnout and leave their jobs. Indeed, Lakin, Bruininks, Hill, and Hauber (1982) reported that over 20% of the staff members who separate from residence programs are rated as excellent employees by their former supervisors.

We next related attitudes regarding residents or their group home care to overall reported job satisfaction. If staff members identify specific job irritants that appeared to influence their satisfaction, modifications in the work environment might help alleviate dissatisfaction. Three areas of the Residence Personnel Opinion Scale significantly related to overall job satisfaction: job rejection, job insecurity, and institutional identification. Both job rejection and job insecurity inversely related to overall job satisfaction. Institutional identification positively related to overall job satisfaction (i.e., higher expressed support for and identification with the residence were associated with higher reported job satisfaction). Effective employee performance evaluations could be used to manipulate the job situation and increase role clarity, improve judgment about job security, and, perhaps, lead to more job satisfaction. Administrators should foster the development and maintenance of higher levels of positive identification with a residence because this attitude is associated with greater job satisfaction. For example, management strategies could emphasize staff becoming more involved in all aspects of group home life and management.

In addition to staff attitudes related to job satisfaction, certain resident variables also correlated with job satisfaction (Zigman et al., 1984). Specifically, reported job satisfaction related to residents' functional level. Staff in homes with more-intellectually-disabled residents showed less-positive job attitudes and were less-favorable about resident autonomy than were staff who worked with more-able clients (Silver, Lubin, & Silverman, 1984). Perhaps the latter "restriction of autonomy" attitude reflects realistic appraisal of the individuals' abilities and need for directed activities, rather than a devaluation of the individuals' activities and rights. On the other hand, as the number of severely and profoundly disabled persons residing in the community increases, it is vital that appropriate staff attitudes and expectations regarding significantly-disabled persons be fostered. The means may include training programs that acquaint staff members with the unique problems, responsibilities, and potential rewards associated with providing residential services to severely and profoundly disabled persons. Other approaches could include providing good role models, affording opportunities for establishing closer relationships with residents, and sharing experiences with direct-care staff members from other residential settings.

In summary, examining the internal structure of New York's group home system, as measured by subjective and objective staff characteristics, revealed a relatively well-educated and experienced employee group; staff who reported positive attitudes regarding staff–resident affiliation and encouragement of resident expression and staff–resident equality; occasional employee concerns regarding job security; job satisfaction positively related to resident level of intellectual functioning; and staff who were satisfied with most aspects of their jobs, except for pay and promotional opportunities.

DISCUSSION

Group homes clearly are an important component of each state's residential services, as both long-term and transitional care settings, for severely- to minimally-disabled persons. In New York State, these programs are multifaceted and represent a major residential option.

New York's network of residential services is one of the largest in the nation. The general characteristics of its group homes in terms of average size, type of auspice, and ages of persons served are similar to those reported for many other states (Janicki, Mayeda, & Epple, 1983). In this regard, what we have observed should then have relevance to other parts of the country. During the course of our studies, we have reported on the history and scope of the group homes (Janicki, Castellani, & Lubin, 1982), their general context and structure (Janicki & Zigman, 1984; Zigman, Lubin, & Janicki, 1984), employees (Janicki, Jacobson, Zigman, & Gordon, 1984; Zigman et al., 1982), their acceptance by the community (Lubin, Schwartz, Zigman, & Janicki, 1982), service-provision patterns (Jacobson & Ackerman, 1985; Jacobson, Silver, & Schwartz, 1984), fire safety provisions and self-preservation issues (Janicki & Jacobson, 1985), and patterns of adaptive behavior change (Jacobson, Sersen, & Schwartz, 1982).

In this chapter, we examined these homes and the nature of the services that group home residents receive by comparing group home program models and considering the strengths and weaknesses of the staff members employed. The data confirm a diversity of characteristics among residents in various residential settings. The group homes in New York rest easily among the variety of institutional and community residential options. In addition, these group homes, relative to other residential options, serve a wide range of functions, and their residents exhibit a variety of training and therapeutic needs. Residents participate in diverse day programs. Generally, service-provision levels appeared to be appropriately related to residents' disability levels, indicating that program services are attempting to meet individual needs. This diversity of program availability needs to be maintained. System administrators and planners should recognize that a diversity of program alternatives, both residential and day, increases the probability that appropriate treatment options will be available and that referral and admission decisions can consider individual needs in a practically implementable manner.

Most residents' needs appeared to be met, although certain deficiencies were detected for those with more complex problems, leading to difficulty in accessing the full range of needed services. Effective access to the generic health system, particularly mental health and dental services, was a problem. Similarly, there was a reported shortage in availability of certain types of allied health professionals, particularly occupational and physical therapists.

A number of potential internal strengths in the homes included their manageable size and the presence of young, fairly well-educated, and occupationally committed staff. Management personnel appeared to be trained for their job responsibilities. If any deficiency could be noted, the area would be lack of sufficiently intensive and appropriate training for group home staff.

Of the many suppositions that have been made about what aspects of the home contribute most to residents' growth, most have yet to be empirically verified (Landesman-Dwyer & Knowles, 1985). The findings that staff attitudes and job satisfaction are related open areas for further inquiry. Group home staff are committed to the types of rehabilitative practices that contribute to growth. They also have attitudes compatible with enhancing an improved quality of social and community life for residents.

In conclusion, group homes are growing as a national option for the residential care of persons with mental retardation. States need to provide a regulatory and administrative structure to foster the maintenance and continued monitoring of these homes. Staff members are an important resource, and training programs for them should be readily available to increase their skills and improve morale. A productive residential environment is not enough to ensure growth. Complementary day programs must be available, as well as a range of need-based health and therapeutic services. Group homes are living, not solely service, environments; services should be created with this in mind. A range of therapeutic models should be present within a state's group home system to offer community living to minimally, moderately, and severely disabled individuals. Administrators need to be sensitive to the relationships between resident and staff characteristics and procure, train, and nurture staff members with the realization that a variety of resident needs exist.

REFERENCES

Aanes, D., & Moen, M. (1976). Adaptive behavior changes of group home residents. *Mental Retardation, 14* (4), 36–40.

Anthony, W. A. (1977). Psychological rehabilitation: A concept in need of a method. *American Psychologist, 32,* 658–662.

Bensberg, G. J., & Barnett, C. D. (1966). *Attendant training in Southern residential facilities for the mentally retarded: Report of the AREB Attendant Training Project.* Atlanta: Southern Regional Education Board.

Bersani, H. A., & Heifetz, L. J. (1985). Perceived stress and satisfaction of direct-care staff members in community residences for mentally retarded adults. *American Journal of Mental Deficiency, 90,* 289–295.

Bjaanes, A. T., & Butler, E. W. (1974). Environmental variation in community care facilities for mentally retarded persons. *American Journal of Mental Deficiency, 78,* 429–439.

Braddock, D. (1981). Deinstitutionalization for the retarded: Trends in public policy. *Hospital and Community Psychiatry, 32,* 607–615.

Bruininks, R. H., Hauber, F. A., & Kudla, M. J. (1980). National survey of community residential facilities: A profile of facilities and residents in 1977. *American Journal of Mental Deficiency, 84,* 470–478.

Bruininks, R. H., Hill, B. K., & Thorsheim, M. S. (1980). *A profile of specially licensed foster homes for mentally retarded people in 1977.* Minneapolis: University of Minnesota, Department of Psychoeducational Studies.

Burchard, S., Pine, J., Gordon, L., & Widrick, G. (1983, October). *Manager competence and program quality of community residential programs.* Paper presented at the 13th annual conference of Region X, American Association on Mental Deficiency, Portland, ME.

Butler, E. W., & Bjaanes, A. T. (1977). A typology of community care facilities and differential normalization outcomes. In P. Mittler & J. deJong (Eds.), *Research to practice in mental retardation: Care and intervention.* Baltimore: University Park Press.

Cherniss, C. (1981). Organizational design and the social environment in group homes for mentally retarded persons. In H. C. Haywood & J. R. Newbrough (Eds.), *Living environments for developmentally retarded persons.* Baltimore: University Park Press.

Clark, M. J. I. (1959). A placement program for the mentally retarded. *American Journal of Mental Deficiency, 64,* 548–555.

Close, D. W. (1977). Community living for severely and profoundly retarded adults: A group home study. *Education and Training of the Mentally Retarded, 12,* 256–262.

Crapps, J. M., Langone, J., & Swaim, S. (1985). Quantity and quality of participation in community environments by mentally retarded adults. *Education and Training of the Mentally Retarded, 20,* 123–129.

Donnellan, A. M., LaVigna, G. W., Zambito, J., & Thvedt, J. (1985). A time-limited intensive intervention program model to support community placement for persons with severe behavior problems. *Journal of the Association for Persons with Severe Handicaps, 10,* 123–131.

Eagle, E. (1967). Prognosis and outcome of community placement of institutionalized retardates. *American Journal of Mental Deficiency, 72,* 232–243.

Emerson, E. J. (1985). Evaluating the impact of deinstitutionalization on the lives of mentally retarded people. *American Journal of Mental Deficiency, 90,* 277–288.

Eyman, R. K., DeMaine, G. C., & Lei, T. (1979). Relationship between community environments and resident changes in adaptive behavior: A path model. *American Journal of Mental Deficiency, 83,* 330–338.

Flynn, R. J., & Heal, L. W. (1981). A short form of PASS 3 for assessing normalization: Structure, interrater reliability, and validity. *Evaluation Review, 5,* 357–376.

George, M. J. & Baumeister, A. A. (1981). Employee withdrawal and job satisfaction in community residential facilities for mentally retarded persons. *American Journal of Mental Deficiency, 85,* 639–647.

Gothelf, C. R. (1985). Variations in resource provision for community residences serving persons with developmental disabilities. *Education and Training of the Mentally Retarded, 20,* 130–138.

Hitzing, W. (1980). ENCOR and beyond. In T. Apolloni, J. Cappuccilli, & T. P. Cooke (Eds.), *Achievements in residential services for persons with disabilities: Toward excellence.* Baltimore: University Park Press.

Hull, J. T., & Thompson, J. C. (1980). Predicting adaptive functioning of mentally retarded persons in community settings. *American Journal of Mental Deficiency, 85,* 253–261.

Hull, J. T., & Thompson, J. C. (1981). Factors contributing to normalization in residential facilities for mentally retarded persons. *Mental Retardation, 19,* 69–73.

Jackson, J. (1964). Toward the comparative study of mental hospitals: Characteristics of the treatment environment. In A. F. Wesson (Ed.), *The psychiatric hospital as a social system.* Springfield, IL: Thomas.

Jacobson, J. W., & Ackerman, L. (1985). Service provision in group homes: A replication. Unpublished manuscript, New York State Office of Mental Retardation and Developmental Disabilities, Albany.

Jacobson, J. W. & Janicki, M. P. (1981, March). *A demographic typology of community residence occupants.* Paper presented at the annual Gatlinburg Conference on Research in Mental Retardation and Developmental Disabilities, Gatlinburg, TN.

Jacobson, J. R., & Janicki, M. P. (1984, August). *Trends in staff characteristics in a large community residence system: 1980-1983.* Paper presented at the annual meeting of the American Psychological Association, Toronto.

Jacobson, J. W., & Janicki, M. P. (1985). Clinical need variations of disabled persons residing in group homes. *Journal of Community Psychology, 13,* 54–66.

Jacobson, J. W., Schwartz, A. A., & Janicki, M. P. (1985). Rehabilitative models and residential program services. In R. J. Brown (Ed.), *Rehabilitation education: Integrated programmes for handicapped adolescents and adults.* Kent, Great Britain: Groom-Helm.

Jacobson, J. W., Schwartz, A. A., & Silver, E. J. (1982, June). *Occupant characteristics and service environments of New York's community residences.* Paper presented at the annual meeting of the American Association on Mental Deficiency, Boston.

Jacobson, J. W., Sersen, E., & Schwartz, A. A. (1984). Characteristics and adaptive behaviors of New York's group home occupants. In J. M. Berg & J. M. deJong (Eds.), *Perspectives and progress in mental retardation: Social, psychological, and educational aspects.* Baltimore: University Park Press.

Jacobson, J. W., Silver, E. J., & Schwartz, A. A. (1984). Service provision in New York's group homes. *Mental Retardation, 22,* 231–239.

Janicki, M. P. (1981). Personal growth and community residence environments. In H. C. Haywood & J. R. Newbrough (Eds.), *Living environments for developmentally retarded persons.* Baltimore: University Park Press.

Janicki, M. P., Castellani, P. J., & Lubin, R. A. (1982). *Perspective on the scope and structure of New York's community residence system* (Technical Report 82-5). Staten Island, NY: Institute for Basic Research in Developmental Disabilities, Living Alternatives Research Project.

Janicki, M. P., Castellani, P. J., & Norris, R. N. (1983). Organization and administration of service delivery systems. In J. Matson & J. Mulick (Eds.), *Handbook of mental retardation.* New York: Pergamon.

Janicki, M. P., & Jacobson, J. W. (1979). *New York's needs assessment and developmental disabilities: Preliminary report* (Technical Report 79-10). Albany: New York State Office of Mental Retardation and Developmental Disabilities.

Janicki, M. P., & Jacobson, J. W. (1982). The character of developmental disabilities in New York State: Preliminary observations. *International Journal of Rehabilitation Research, 5,* 191–202.

Janicki, M. P., & Jacobson, J. W. (1985). A study of fire safety, self-preservation, and community residences for the mentally retarded in New York State. *Fire Journal, 79*(4), 38–41, 82–86.

Janicki, M. P., Jacobson, J. W., & Ackerman, L. J. (1985, July). *Patterns of health and support services among elderly mentally retarded persons living in community group home settings.* Paper presented at the annual meeting of the International Congress of Gerontology, New York.

Janicki, M. P., Jacobson, J. W., & Schwartz, A. A. (1982). Residential care settings: Models for rehabilitative intent. *Journal of Practical Approaches to Developmental Handicap, 6*(2/3), 10–16.

Janicki, M. P., Jacobson, J. W., Zigman, W. B., & Gordon, N. H. (1984). Characteristics of employees of community residences for retarded persons. *Education and Training of the Mentally Retarded, 19,* 45–48.

Janicki, M. P., Mayeda, T., & Epple, W. (1983). Availability of group homes for persons with mental retardation in the United States. *Mental Retardation, 21,* 45–51.

Janicki, M. P. & Zigman, W. B. (1984). Physical and environmental design characteristics of community residences. *Mental Retardation, 22,* 294–301.

Knowles, M. & Landesman, S. (1986). A national survey of state-sponsored training for residential direct-care staff. *Mental Retardation, 24,* 293–300.

Knowlton, M. (1980). The Pennsylvania system. In T. Apollani, J. Capuccilli, & T. P. Cooke (Eds.), *Achievements in residential services for persons with disabilities: Toward excellence.* Baltimore: University Park Press.

Lakin, K. C., Bruininks, R. H., Hill, B. K., & Hauber, F. A. (1982). Turnover of direct-care staff in a national sample of residential facilities for mentally retarded people. *American Journal of Mental Deficiency, 87,* 64–72.

Landesman-Dwyer, S. & Knowles, M. (1985). Ecological analysis of staff training in residential settings. In J. Hogg & P. J. Mittler (Eds.), *Issues in staff training in mental handicap.* London: Croom Helm.

Living Alternatives Research Project. (1981). *The identification and description of environmental conditions affecting growth in personal competence of persons with developmental disabilities: Phase one* (Technical Report 81-2). Staten Island, NY: Institute for Basic Research in Developmental Disabilities, Living Alternatives Research Project.

Lubin, R. A., Schwartz, A. A., Zigman, W. B., & Janicki, M. P. (1982). Community acceptance of residential programs for developmentally disabled persons. *Applied Research in Mental Retardation, 3,* 191–200.

Martin, J. E. & Laidlaw, T. J. (1980). Implications for direct service planning, delivery, and policy. In A. R. Novak & L. W. Heal (Eds.), *Integration of developmentally disabled individuals into the community.* Baltimore: Brookes.

McCord, W., T. (1981). Community residences: The staffing. In J. Wortis (Ed.), *Mental retardation and developmental disabilities* (Vol. 12). New York: Brunner/ Mazel.

McDonald, E. P. (1985). Medical needs of severely developmentally disabled persons residing in the community. *American Journal of Mental Deficiency, 90,* 171–176.

Merges, R. (1982). Checking the cycle: The decline of community-based residential programs in New York State. *Mental Retardation, 20,* 180–182.

Nihira, L., & Nihira, K. (1975). Jeopardy in community placement. *American Journal of Mental Deficiency, 79,* 538–544.

Office of Mental Retardation and Developmental Disabilities. (1980). *Comprehensive plan for services to mentally retarded and developmentally disabled persons in New York State: 1981–1984.* Albany: New York State Office of Mental Retardation and Developmental Disabilities.

Pratt, M. W., Luszcz, M. A., & Brown, M. E. (1980). Measuring dimensions of the quality of care in small community residences. *American Journal of Mental Deficiency, 85,* 188–194.

Raynes, N. V., Pratt, M. W., & Roses, S. (1977). Aides' involvement in decision-making and the quality of care in institutional settings. *American Journal of Mental Deficiency, 81,* 570–577.

Savage, V., T., Novak, A. R., & Heal, L. W. (1980). Generic services for developmentally disabled citizens. In A. R. Novak & L. W. Heal (Eds.), *Integration of developmentally disabled individuals into the community.* Baltimore: Brookes.

Schalock, R. L., Foley, J. W., Toulouse, A., & Stark, J. A. (1985). Medication and programming in controlling behavior of mentally retarded individuals in community settings. *American Journal of Mental Deficiency, 89,* 503–509.

Schalock, R. L., Harper, R. S., & Genung, T. (1981). Community integration of mentally retarded adults: Community placement and program success. *American Journal of Mental Deficiency, 85,* 478–488.

Schinke, S. P. & Wong, D. E. (1977). Evaluation of staff training in group homes for retarded persons. *American Journal of Mental Deficiency, 82,* 130–136.

Sherman, S. R., Frenkel, E. R., & Newman, E. S. (1984). Foster family care for older persons who are mentally retarded. *Mental Retardation, 22,* 302–308.

Silver, E. J., Lubin, R. A., & Silverman, W. P. (1984). Serving profoundly mentally retarded persons: Staff attitudes and job satisfaction. *American Journal of Mental Deficiency, 89,* 297–301.

Silver, E. J., Silverman, W. P., & Lubin, R. A. (1984). Community living for severely and profoundly retarded persons. In J. M. Berg & J. M. deJong (Eds.), *Perspectives and progress in mental retardation: Social, psychological, and educational aspects.* Baltimore: University Park Press.

Smith, P. C., Kendall, L. M., & Hulin, C. (1969). *The measurement of satisfaction in work and retirement.* Chicago: Rand McNally.

Spangler, P. F., & Gilman, B. (1985). The frequency of serious behavioral and medical incidents occurring in community based living arrangements. *Mental Retardation, 23,* 246–248.

Sutter, P., Mayeda, T., Yanagi, G., & Yee, S. (1980). Comparison of successful and unsuccessful community-placement mentally retarded persons. *American Journal of Mental Deficiency, 85,* 262–267.

White, C. C., Hill, B. K., Lakin, K. C., & Bruininks, R. H. (1984). Day programs of adults with mental retardation in residential facilities. *Mental Retardation, 22,* 121–127.

Windle, C. D., Stewart, E., & Brown, S. (1961). Reasons for community failure of released patients. *American Journal of Mental Deficiency, 66,* 213–217.

Zigman, W. B., Lubin, R. A., & Janicki, M. P. (1984). Characteristics of New York's community residences for developmentally disabled persons. *Applied Research in Mental Retardation, 5,* 375–384.

Zigman, W. B., Schwartz, A. A., & Janicki, M. P. (1984). Group home employee job attitudes and satisfactions. In J. M. Berg & J. M. deJong (Eds.), *Perspectives and progress in mental retardation: Social, psychological, and educational aspects.* Baltimore: University Park Press.

9

Community Responses to Community Residences for Persons Who Have Mental Retardation

Marsha Mailick Seltzer and Gary Seltzer

Boston University School of Social Work

A key objective of the community residence movement is to enable mentally retarded persons to interact to the greatest possible extent with the broader community. A problem commonly encountered by community residences is opposition from neighbors, local officials, or other community members who fear negative consequences resulting from locating a residence for retarded persons in their neighborhood. In response to community opposition, some state agencies have developed policies that encourage or require groups hoping to open a community residence to conduct public education activities. Interestingly, although public education is assumed to have a positive effect, there is little evidence about its true effectiveness in reducing community opposition.

Community opposition has occurred for at least 25 to 35% of the community residences in the United States (Baker, Seltzer, & Seltzer, 1977; Johnson, 1976; Lubin, Schwartz, Zigman, & Janicki, 1982; O'Connor, 1976), probably an underestimate of the problem's magnitude because community residences that failed to open or closed early are not included. Lubin et al. (1982) and O'Connor (1976) reported that opposition decreases dramatically after a community residence opens, although the reasons for this have not been studied.

At least five hypotheses can be advanced to explain community opposition. First, *client characteristics* may influence opposition. It is commonly hypothesized that younger adults, males, and more severely retarded clients with behavior problems will be viewed more negatively by the community.

Acknowledgements. Preparation of this chapter was supported in part by a grant from the National Science Foundation through a subcontract from the Boston Neighborhood Network.

Second, *staff characteristics* may contribute. Perceived inadequacies in staff-to-resident ratios, high staff turnover rates, and the presence of out-of-area staff members may increase community opposition. Third, *neighborhood characteristics*, especially socioeconomic profile, housing stock, and residential stability, may be related to opposition. We predicted that higher rates of opposition would be found in wealthy, stable neighborhoods. Fourth, the *relationship between the community residence and the neighborhood* may alter opposition, with opposition less likely when clients originally came from the local area. Fifth, the *entry strategy* utilized by the community residence may influence opposition. Some investigators have hypothesized that public education will minimize opposition (Luppacchino & Krishef, undated; Nelson, 1978) whereas others have suggested that a "low profile" approach may be more successful (Sigelman, 1976; Willms, 1981).

The evidence regarding each hypothesis, although scant, is as follows. Regarding client characteristics, clients' level of retardation was not related to opposition in the Baker et al. (1977) national study. Conroy (1980) reported that community members' attitudes toward *hypothetical* community residences were more negative when the residence was to serve severely retarded compared to mildly retarded persons; however, these expressed attitudes cannot be assumed indicative of real opposition. O'Connor (1976) reported no relationship between clients' age and community opposition. Johnson (1976) reported that community residences for children encountered more opposition than did those for adults; his sample, however, included residences for all types of clients, not just mentally retarded persons. Finally, Johnson (1976) found that sex distribution of the client group did correlate with opposition, with programs serving males more likely to encounter opposition from the community.

Johnson (1976) reported no significant relationship of staff characteristics to opposition. Regarding neighborhood characteristics, he found that higher socioeconomic status (SES) neighborhoods were more likely to oppose community residences than were lower SES areas. Lubin et al. (1982) reported no relationship between population density and community opposition. No published study could be located in which investigators examined whether community residences with a high proportion of local neighborhood clients were less likely to encounter opposition than those with a low proportion of neighborhood clients.

Finally, regarding entry strategies, both Baker et al. (1977) and Johnson (1976) found that the more advanced community education, the greater the opposition. Unfortunately, it is uncertain whether public education efforts increased the opposition or, alternatively, whether high levels of anticipated opposition led to education efforts. These studies do raise questions, however, about the assumed benefits of existing strategies of educating a local community.

The present study was designed to gather descriptive data about community opposition and to examine the five hypotheses stated previously.

METHOD

Sample

The sample of community residences consisted of 43 facilities, each of which (a) provided room and board to mentally retarded clients, (b) provided some staff supervision, (c) employed staff members, (d) did not give medical care to clients, (e) operated as a private nonprofit or proprietary facility, and (f) did not offer a formal treatment program on the premises during daytime hours. Included in the sample were such residences as group homes, halfway houses, staffed apartments, and transitional centers. Excluded were foster homes, emergency shelters, schools, residential treatment centers, and boarding houses.

These community residences represented 86% of all such residences for mentally retarded persons in the city of Boston and six neighboring cities and towns. The average number of residents per facility was 5.9, of whom 4.8 previously had lived in institutions. Most facilities (74.4%) had at least one moderately retarded client; fewer (41.9%) had at least one mildly retarded client, and only 11.6% had at least one severely retarded client. Nearly all community residences (98%) served adults, and over half (58.1%) served both men and women. During the year prior to the study, client turnover rate was 12.5%. Each residence had, on the average, four full-time staff members, one of whom came from the neighborhood in which the residence was located.

The community residences had operated for an average of 2.6 years (standard deviation [SD] = 2.4). They were evenly distributed between lower class/lower middle class neighborhoods (51%) and middle class/upper middle class neighborhoods (49%). The majority (61%) were located in rented buildings; the remainder were in buildings owned by the sponsoring organization.

Procedure

We developed a structured interview assessing characteristics of residents, staff, facility, neighborhood and the history of community reaction to the residence. Trained research assistants conducted telephone interviews (average = 37 minutes). Information was provided 85% of the time by the executive or program director of the residence, typically employed 3.3 years by the sponsoring agency (longer than the average time the residences had been open). In some instances, either the interviewer or the respondent asked another person, usually a board member, to provide supplemental information.

We did not contact neighbors or other community members, in part to avoid provoking latent opposition. The data reflect only administrators' perceptions about community opposition and support. To maximize accuracy, whenever we asked for global ratings, we also requested specific examples of opposition or support and estimates of the extent of opposition or support during specified time periods. Because all data were retrospective, respondents' memories may have been incomplete or in error to an unknown degree.

We relied on 1970 U.S. Census data for socioeconomic, housing, and demographic data for the census tracts in the study area. We grouped the 233 census tracts into (a) 151 with no community residences, (b) 35 with at least one community residence for mentally retarded clients, and (c) 47 with at least one community residence for a client group other than mentally retarded individuals, but no residence for mentally retarded clients. We analyzed the data for these three groups to identify distinctive neighborhood features of community residences for mentally retarded clients.

Operational Definitions of Community Opposition, Community Support, and Community Education

We constructed three operational definitions of community opposition. We asked respondents whether they encountered any of 17 types of opposition:

1. General lack of acceptance/cold attitude
2. Negative telephone calls to local officials and staff
3. Letters of protest/negative newspaper articles
4. Organized lobbying (by community groups) against the residence
5. Organized pickets or protests
6. Negative testimony at public hearings
7. Circulation of petitions to block residence
8. Legal action to block residence
9. City/town refusing to issue ordinance permit
10. Blocked access to community services and resources for staff and residents
11. Verbal threats to staff
12. Verbal threats to residents
13. Physical abuse of staff
14. Physical abuse of residents
15. Vandalism of facility
16. Neighborhood children not permitted to play near residence
17. Invoking of zoning or other exclusionary laws

Each residence was classified in terms of (a) whether opposition was reported, (b) the number of types of opposition encountered, and (c) the amount of opposition (ranging from 1 = none to 4 = a great deal) as experienced during four time periods: more than 6 months before the residence opened, 0 to 6 months before the residence opened, 0 to 6 months after the residence opened, and at time of interview.

Regarding community support, we assessed the availability of 11 dimensions of support:

1. Positive letters, newspaper articles, and media reports
2. Friendly attitude from neighbors towards staff and/or residents
3. Organized rallies (by community groups) in favor of residence
4. Organized lobbying (by community groups) in favor of residence
5. Positive telephone calls to staff and local officials
6. Staff and residents invited to community functions
7. Community extended assistance in gaining access to its services and resources
8. Positive testimony at public hearings
9. City/town grants, ordinance, or permit to open residence
10. Neighborhood children permitted to play near residence
11. Neighbors help staff/residents with facility, other (more than just friendly attitude)

Three operational definitions of support were constructed: (a) whether any support was provided, (b) the number of types of support, and (c) the amount of support at the same four time periods mentioned previously. The utilization of 11 community education activities was assessed:

1. Media (newspaper articles, TV, and radio)
2. Public information/discussion meetings
3. Distributing leaflets, posters of pamphlets describing the program
4. Open house at facility
5. Personal contact (i.e., phone calls, meetings, letters) with community/civic groups
6. Personal contact with local government officials
7. Personal contact with local business community
8. Personal contact with local churches
9. Personal contact with social service agencies
10. Personal contact with neighbors of residence
11. Personal contact with police/fire departments (other than that required to obtain a license)

Three operational definitions similar to those constructed for opposition and support were used.

FINDINGS

Description of the Facility and Neighborhood

The majority of the community residences (61%) were in multiple-unit dwellings reflecting the distinctly urban character of the geographic area.

About half (51%) of the facilities occupied the entire building. The building's exterior was reportedly in good or excellent condition for 95% of the residences. Residences had an average of 11.1 rooms (range = 5 to 32), with 5.1 used as bedrooms. No facility reported having an identifying sign (e.g., name of facility on lawn sign). When rented by the sponsoring agency, the monthly rent averaged $590.00. Facilities owned by the agency averaged $130,000 in property value.

The community residences were located within one mile from public transportation, shopping, and a fire station, and within 2 miles of a police station and a hospital. As noted earlier, neighborhoods were evenly divided between lower class/lower middle class and middle class/upper middle class. Regarding neighborhood turnover, most neighborhoods (74%) were characterized by respondents as either stable or somewhat stable.

Comparison of Census Tracts

As noted previously the 233 census tracts within the study's geographic area were classified as Group 1: 151 tracts that did not contain any community residences, Group 2: 35 tracts that contained at least one residence for mentally retarded persons, and Group 3: 47 tracts that contained at least one residence for a client group other than mentally retarded individuals but no residence for mentally retarded persons. Table 1 presents comparisons among these groups of census tracts on a variety of socioeconomic, housing, and demographic variables, using 1970 census data.

DENSITY OF POPULATION

The three groups of census tracts were found to be significantly different with respect to the number of persons who lived in the tract, with Group 2 containing the largest number of persons and Group 1 containing the smallest number of persons. Because of these differences, all other variables reflecting the number of persons in any subcategory were converted to percentages.

AGE DISTRIBUTION

The three groups of census tracts were significantly different with respect to the age distribution of residents. Group 2 contained the highest percentage of elderly persons (females aged 60 to 64 and males and females aged 65 to 74) and the lowest percentage of young adults (males and females aged 20 to 24). Group 3 contained the highest percentage of young adults, and Group 1 and 3 contained roughly the same percentages of elderly persons.

TABLE 1   Comparison Among Census Tracts *(CTs)*

Characteristic	Group 1	Group 2	Group 3	F	p
Density of CT					
No. of persons	4306.05	5706.60	4628.32	4.041	.019
Age distribution (in %)					
Males aged 20-24	0.11	0.09	0.13	3.414	.035
Females aged 20-24	0.11	0.10	0.15	6.407	.002
Females aged 60-64	0.05	0.06	0.05	3.370	.036
Males aged 65-74	0.06	0.08	0.07	5.527	.005
Marital status (in %)					
Married males	0.54	0.58	0.48	8.346	<.001
Married females	0.48	0.52	0.42	8.010	<.001
Single males	0.39	0.35	0.44	7.290	.001
Single females	0.33	0.33	0.39	4.962	.008
Divorced males	0.03	0.02	0.04	6.924	.001
Education					
Median years of education	11.52	12.09	12.02	3.094	.047
% high school graduates	49.73	57.68	54.76	3.996	.020
Occupation (in %)					
Managers, administrators	0.05	0.07	0.05	7.359	.001
Sales workers	0.05	0.07	0.05	3.493	.032
Laborers	0.05	0.03	0.04	3.358	.037
Operatives	0.14	0.10	0.10	5.415	.005
Transportation equipment workers	0.04	0.03	0.03	3.522	.030
Income					
Mean income–families	10238.02	12845.91	10682.40	6.380	.002
Median income–unrelated individuals	3218.75	3728.54	3524.89	3.329	.038
% families below poverty level	12.71	7.96	10.57	4.239	.016
Residential stability (in %)					
Persons in same house, 1965 and 1970	0.54	0.56	0.46	5.330	.006
Persons moved into house between 1968 and 1970	0.32	0.30	0.38	5.258	.006
Persons moved into house between 1960 and 1964	0.15	0.25	0.15	3.278	.040
Persons moved into house between 1950 and 1959	0.16	0.17	0.14	3.246	.041
Persons moved into house 1949 or before	0.18	0.18	0.14	3.937	.021
Housing stock					
% owner-occupied housing units	0.27	0.36	0.21	8.589	<.001

TABLE 1 Comparison Among Census Tracts *(CTs)* *(Continued)*

Characteristic	Group 1	Group 2	Group 3	F	p
Housing stock					
% renter-occupied					
housing units	0.66	0.59	0.73	7.706	.001
% single family homes	0.16	0.25	0.10	9.759	.001
% 2-family homes	0.20	0.24	0.15	3.806	.024
% homes with 5 to 49 units	0.27	0.19	0.35	4.832	.009
% structures built 1940-1949	0.10	0.08	0.05	3.235	.041
Median no. rooms	4.56	4.83	4.19	5.744	.004
Median no. persons/					
owner-occupied unit	2.83	3.08	2.80	3.827	.023
Median no. persons/					
renter-occupied unit	2.26	2.21	2.06	3.417	.035
Median value owner-occupied	17345.45	21717.65	20170.21	3.355	.037
Median rent renter-occupied	95.91	116.14	108.17	6.431	.002

Note. Group 1, census tracts with no community residences; Group 2, tracts with residence for retarded people; Group 3, tracts with residences for other groups.

MARITAL STATUS

The three groups were significantly different with respect to the marital status of residents. Group 2 contained the highest percentage of married men and women and the lowest percentage of singles and divorced men. Group 3 contained the highest percentage of singles and divorced men and the lowest percentage of married persons.

EDUCATION

Residents of Group 2 were better educated than the other two groups, and residents of Group 1 were the most poorly educated, as measured both by median number of years of education and percentage of high school graduates.

OCCUPATION

Group 2 contained a greater percentage of white collar workers in the occupations of managers, administrators, and sales workers and a lower percentage of laborers. Group 1 contained a greater percentage of laborers and transportation workers.

INCOME

The three groups were significantly different with respect to the income of residents. Residents of Group 2 had higher incomes. Also, the percentage of families and individuals below the poverty level was lower in Group 2. Residents of Group 1 had the lowest incomes as measured by most of these dimensions.

RESIDENTIAL STABILITY

The three groups were significantly different with respect to residential stability. Residents of Group 3 tended to be the least stable, with the highest percentage of persons moving into their houses during the 2-year period prior to the census and the lowest percentage living in the same house during the 5-year period before the census. Residents of Groups 1 and 2 were somewhat more stable than Group 3 residents. Groups 1 and 2 were generally comparable in residential stability.

HOUSING STOCK

The three groups of census tracts were significantly different with respect to housing stock. Group 2 tended to have the highest percentage of owner-occupied units and the lowest percentage of renter-occupied units. Similarly, Group 2 had the highest percentage of single and two-family homes and the lowest percentage of apartment buildings. Structures in Group 2 had the largest number of rooms in all types of units and the most people per room in owner-occupied units. Finally, owned units in Group 2 had the highest values and rented units in Group 2 had the highest rents among the groups.

In summary, census tracts that contained at least one community residence for mentally retarded persons (Group 2) were found to be the most stable neighborhoods in the area with respect to neighborhood turnover, with generally newer housing stock and more single family houses. The residents of these census tracts tended to be the best educated, with the highest proportion of white collar jobs, and the highest incomes. Persons who lived in these census tracts contained the highest proportion of married persons and of elderly persons. Together, these characteristics suggest that community residences for mentally retarded clients are located in the most middle class and most stable neighborhoods in the geographic area included in the study.

In contrast, the census tracts that contained at least one community residence for a client group other than mentally retarded persons (Group 3) were found to be less stable neighborhoods. Residents of Group 3 tended to be younger, were most likely to be single or divorced, and moved into their homes most recently. The housing stock was generally older and contained the most apartments. Residents of census tracts that contained no community residences (Group 1) were the most poorly educated, had the lowest incomes, and either paid the lowest rent or owned the least expensive homes.

Thus, with regard to many dimensions, community residences for mentally retarded clients were located in the most desirable neighborhoods of the geographic area of the study. Assertions made in the popular media that community residences are clustered in the worst neighborhoods of cities appear not to be true with respect to residences for mentally retarded clients in this metropolitan area, although perhaps these charges are more accurate for community residences for other client groups.

History of Community Opposition, Support, and Education

There was considerable variability as to when the community first became aware of the community residence. For 28% of the residences, the community knew about their planned location more than 6 months before opening; for 38%, community awareness occurred within 6 months of opening; and the remaining 35% reported no community knowledge until after opening.

Community opposition was reported by 51% of the residences. In general, the opposition encountered was relatively benign. For example, 33% reported a general "lack of acceptance" from the neighborhood, although 33% reported that neighbors made negative calls to officials. In contrast, fewer than 10% of the residences reported each of the following more active types of community opposition: protest letters, negative newspaper articles, lobbying, negative testimony at public hearings, petitions, legal actions, zoning disputes, vandalism, verbal threats, or picketing of the facility. The most commonly reported reason for community opposition was fear about resident behavior (35%). Concern about increased crime rate was reported by 7% of the residences. Interestingly, as many as 56% of the sampled residences previously attempted to locate in another neighborhood. In half of these cases, their changed location reportedly resulted from community opposition to their original choice.

Fifty-eight percent of the residences conducted some form of public education, typically informal contact with neighbors (40%), followed by open houses at the residence (30%), contact with civic groups (26%), and contact with local government officials (23%).

Most community residences (81%) reported some community support, and all of these noted that neighbors seemed friendly. Specific sources of support included help from neighbors with residence upkeep (58%), invitations to community activities (30%), and positive telephone calls to state or local officials (21%).

Respondents' estimates of the extent of opposition, support, and education at four points in time are presented in Table 2. Higher mean ratings indicated greater intensity on the 4-point scales. Community opposition increased slightly from Time 1 to 2 to 3 followed by a rather sharp drop-off

TABLE 2 Mean Ratings of Opposition, Support, and Public Education

Variable	Time 1	Time 2	Time 3	Time 4
Opposition	1.60	1.89	1.92	1.38
Support	2.17	2.57	2.68	3.15
Education	2.32	2.46	2.42	2.04

Note. Time 1, more than 6 months prior; Time 2, 0 to 6 months prior; Time 3, 0 to 6 months after; Time 4, present.

by the time of the study. Community education efforts followed a similar pattern. Community support predictably increased at each successive time period, with the largest increase between Times 3 and 4.

Table 3 presents ratings of the neighbors' first reaction to the residence and their current attitude. These data confirm a shift from negative to more positive attitudes. When asked how many months elapsed before community attitudes changed to their current level, interviewees reported an average of 11.8 months.

TABLE 3 Neighbors' Initial and Current Attitudes
Toward the Community Residence (in %)

Attitude	Initial attitude	Current attitude
Very negative	11.1	2.4
Somewhat negative	25.0	0.0
Neutral	36.1	31.8
Somewhat positive	22.2	51.2
Very positive	5.6	14.6

Community Residences That Encountered Opposition vs. Those That Did Not

We compared 21 residences encountering some community opposition to 22 that reported no opposition at any time. Table 4 presents significant differences between the two groups. Regarding client characteristics, no differences between the two groups were found in client age, number and the proportion of male residents, or clients' severity of retardation. The hypothesis that opposition is related to these resident characteristics was not supported.

Regarding staffing patterns, community residences with community opposition tended to have higher staff-to-resident ratios than did those without resistance. Higher staff-to-resident ratios were observed with full-time staff and part-time staff. Staff from residences with higher ratios may have spent more time with community members because these community residences conducted more public education than did those with lower staff ratios. The correlation between the direct-care staff-to-resident ratio and amount of education conducted more than 6 months prior to the opening of the residence was .526, $p = .053$.) The correlation with the amount of education conducted during the 6-month period prior to the opening of the residence was .486, $p = .019$.) Whether education efforts caused opposition or staff simply became more aware of community opposition cannot be determined from these data.

TABLE 4   Comparison Between Community Residences That
Encountered Opposition (Group 1) and Those
That Did Not (Group 2)

Variable	Group 1 (n = 22)	Group 2 (n = 21)	t	p
Staffing patterns				
Full-time staff-to-resident ratio	0.656	0.963	−2.07	.045
Part-time staff-to-resident ratio	0.556	0.868	−2.54	.015
Physical facility/neighborhoods				
Property value	51,250	175,000	−2.67	.032
Community education				
No. of public education activities	0.409	0.810	−2.87	.006
Meetings held	0.046	0.286	−2.17	.039
Open house held	0.091	0.524	−3.38	.002
Contact with				
Civic groups	0.046	0.476	−3.57	.001
Local government	0.091	0.381	−2.34	.024
Social service agencies	0.046	0.286	−2.17	.039
Neighbors	0.227	0.571	−2.14	.021

The property value of owned community residences was found to be higher among those residences experiencing opposition than those that did not. Interestingly, the SES of the neighbors did not relate to the likelihood of some versus no community opposition.

Regarding the relationship between community opposition and the extent of integration, several interesting findings emerged. The number and proportion of residents who originally came from the area did not relate to the presence of community opposition. This was contrary to the hypothesis that communities are more receptive to deviant persons who originally lived in their geographic area than to outsiders.

Community residences that encountered opposition made more attempts to involve the community through meetings or open houses or by contact with civic groups, local governmental officials, social service agencies, and neighbors than were residences with no known opposition. Once again, causal relationships were not determinable, although we believe that the present findings indicate that orientation alone does not have beneficial effects and may be potentially harmful, at least as typically conducted.

A number of variables hypothesized in the literature to affect community opposition did not relate to the residences in our study. Community residences that encountered opposition were not less likely to have had a site-selection committee, to have included local community members on planning committees or the board of directors, or to have designated staff members for public relations than were residents free of opposition. Thus, although public education strategies were more likely to be used by residences that encountered community opposition, strategies designed to involve community members directly in decision-making processes were not related to encountering opposition, contrary to the "conventional wisdom" that these strategies would be beneficial. Finally, we found a surprising degree of similarity in the extent of community support received by residences that encountered opposition and those that did not. The lack of a relationship between opposition and support is a provocative finding, supporting the view that relationships between communities and community residences are far more complex than we previously recognized.

Differences Between Residences That Encountered Support and Those That Did Not

As reported earlier, nearly all community residences received some community support. Because only 8 of 43 residences failed to receive community support, we reviewed possible differences. Only a few emerged, as Table 5 shows. Residences receiving no support had fewer staff members originally from the neighborhood and had a lower proportion of board members from the neighborhood. In addition, not one of these 8 residences was located in a facility previously used as a community residence compared to 11% of those that received support. Perhaps communities need time to adjust to the idea of having a community residence in their area. Support also was more prevalent in neighborhoods with a lower proportion of homeowners.

We found no differences between residences that received support and those that did not in their number or type of public education activities, unlike the situation regarding opposition. Such findings warrant further consideration and attempts to replicate in future research.

TABLE 5   Comparison Between Residences Receiving and Not Receiving Support (Mean Scores)

Variable	No support (n = 8)	Support (n = 35)	t
No. staff from area	0.500	1.314	−2.54*
Proportion of board members from area	0.128	0.350	−2.87**
Building used as a residence in the past	0.000	0.114	−2.09*
Homeowner/renters in neighborhood [a]	1.250	1.800	−2.06*

[a] This variable was coded 1 = 80% + homeowners, 2 = mixed owners and renters, 3 = 80% + renters.
* $p < .05$
** $p < .01$

Time of First Community Awareness and Subsequent Community Relationship With Community Residence

Approximately 28% of the community residences reported that the community first became aware of its intended existence more than 6 months prior to opening, 38% from 0 to 6 months prior to opening, and 35% within 6 months after opening. When residences in these three groups were compared, statistically significant differences were found in the amount of community opposition encountered. The lowest probability of opposition (.21) occurred for residences whose communities did not become aware until *after* the residence began operation, $F = 4.574$, $p = .02$. In contrast, those with the earliest community awareness had a .55 probability of opposition, whereas residences with community awareness 0 to 6 months before opening had a .73 probability. The number of types of opposition also varied in relation to timing of community awareness, $F = 3.27$, $p = .05$. Residences with the latest community awareness had fewer types of opposition than the other residences did. In our sample, very early awareness appeared not quite as problematic as awareness that occurred within 6 months of opening of a residence. Community support showed no significant relationship to time of first community awareness of the residence.

The desirability of early or later awareness on the part of the community is likely to remain a matter of local politics, judgment, and value preferences; however, our findings indicate that if the community becomes aware of the intended existence of the residence shortly before it opens, community opposition is very likely. It perhaps would be more prudent to either inform the community very early (more than 6 months before opening) or after the residents have moved in.

SUMMARY AND CONCLUSIONS

We investigated five hypotheses about communities and community residences. First, client characteristics were expected to relate to the likelihood of opposition, with more "threatening" characteristics associated with higher opposition levels. The findings failed to support this hypothesis, with no correlation between proportion of male clients, the level of clients' retardation, or the average age of clients and opposition. Furthermore, no relationship was found between any client characteristic and the receipt of community support.

Second, staff characteristics were hypothesized to be related to opposition, with less opposition expected when staff had lower turnover, when the staff-to-resident ratio was higher, and when staff originally came from the local area. We found no relationship between staff turnover and opposition. The effect of staff-to-resident ratios was opposite to that predicted, namely, residences with higher staff-to-resident ratios had more opposition. We suggested that when staff had more time they may have had more contact with the community, which somehow was associated with either (a) greater awareness of opposition or (b) increased levels of opposition. The number or proportion of staff members who previously lived in the local community did not relate to opposition. No relationship was found between any staff member characteristic and the receipt of support from the community.

Third, neighborhood characteristics were hypothesized to be important, with residences located in wealthier, more stable neighborhoods expected to encounter more opposition. Our findings provide mixed support for this hypothesis. The SES of the neighborhood did not relate to opposition; however, more stable neighborhoods did show more opposition to community residences, as did neighborhoods with a higher ratio of homeowners to renters.

Fourth, we hypothesized that opposition would be lower if clients originally came from the neighborhood. We found no support for this hypothesis.

Fifth, the entry strategy used by the residence was hypothesized to relate to opposition, although the direction of the relationship was not specified in the hypothesis (due to conflicting evidence in the literature). Increased public education efforts were associated with higher community opposition but were unrelated to community support. Although it is not possible to determine whether public education was the cause or the effect of community opposition, this association warrants careful consideration. Public education simply might not be as useful an entry strategy as has been commonly assumed. One purpose of this analysis was to attempt to identify those public education strategies that were used more often by community residences that did not encounter opposition; however, none of the 11 public education strategies analyzed in this study was used significantly more often by residences that did not encounter opposition than those that did.

Another finding pertinent to entry strategy concerned the time when the community first became aware of the intended or actual existence of the residence. The "riskiest" time for the community to become aware of the residence appeared to be the 6 months before opening. In contrast, opposition was least likely when the community became aware after the residence began operation, suggesting that a low profile entry approach may be more desirable.

On a descriptive level, we found that the overall picture is generally positive regarding the relationship between communities and residences, especially once the facility is established. Over time, opposition decreases and support increases, irrespective of any initial opposition encountered. The community residences in the present sample generally were located in middle class, stable neighborhoods. Thus, the goal of locating such residences for mentally retarded persons in favorable community locations appears to be achieved at least in one of the Eastern urban centers.

REFERENCES

Baker, B. L., Seltzer, G. B., & Seltzer, M. M. (1977). *As close as possible: Community residences for retarded adults.* Boston: Little, Brown.

Conroy, J. (1980). *Attitudes toward the mentally retarded in selected communities: Technical report of selected findings.* Philadelphia: Temple University, Institute for Survey Research.

Johnson, G. R. (1976). *Sources of neighborhood opposition to community residence programs.* Unpublished doctoral dissertation, Harvard University.

Landesman-Dwyer, S. (1982). *Residential environments and behavior: Implications for social policy.* Paper presented at the annual meeting of the American Association on Mental Deficiency.

Landesman-Dwyer, S., Stein, J. G., & Sackett, G. P. (1978). A behavioral and ecological study of group homes. In G. P. Sackett (Ed.), *Observing behavior, Volume 1: Theory and applications in mental retardation.* Baltimore: University Park Press.

Lubin, R. A., Schwartz, A. A., Zigman, W. B., & Janicki, M. P. (1982). Community acceptance of residential programs for developmentally disabled. *Applied Research in Mental Retardation, 3,* 191–200.

Luppacchino, R. W., & Krishef, C. H. (undated). *An analysis of barriers in establishing group homes for the mentally retarded.* Unpublished manuscript.

Nelson, R. (1978). *Creating community acceptance for handicapped people.* Springfield, IL: Thomas.

O'Connor, G. (1976). *Home is a good place (monograph).* Washington, DC: American Association on Mental Deficiency.

Seltzer, G. B. (1981). Community residential adjustment: The relationship among environment, performance, and satisfaction. *American Journal of Mental Deficiency, 85,* 625–630.

Sigelman, C. K. (1976). A Machiavelli for planners: Community attitudes and selection of a group home site. *Mental Retardation, 14,* 26–29.

Willms, J. D. (1981). Neighborhood attitudes toward group homes for mentally retarded adults. In P. Mittler (Ed.), *Frontiers of knowledge in mental retardation.* Baltimore: University Park Press.

Parents, Careproviders, and Support Systems

10
Staff Burnout:
Too Much Stress or
Too Little Commitment?

Cary Cherniss
Rutgers University

In this chapter I critically evaluate previous research and theory on burnout in the human services. In this evaluation I have focused on the basic assumptions on which this work is based, without attempting to summarize all studies and findings. The first and most fundamental question is whether the concept of burnout is necessary. I argue that it is but that we need a new paradigm—one that relates burnout to the sociological concept of commitment rather than to the psychological concept of *stress*. Adopting this new paradigm has direct implications for how to study burnout as well as for ways to organize formal systems of helping in our society.

It is not surprising that staff burnout is a concern in the field of mental retardation. Under the best conditions, helping another human being to learn and grow is a demanding, time-consuming process. When working with developmentally disabled individuals, the conditions rarely are ideal. Salaries are low and the work is not highly valued, relative to other occupations. Many clients' problems require that caregivers work long and hard, with few visible results on a day-to-day basis. Poor supervision, organizational conflicts, lack of autonomy, and many other factors commonly found in group care environments add to staff stress and frustration. Eventually, many dedicated workers give up. They leave the field or psychologically withdraw (Weinberg, Edwards, & Garove, 1981). Theoretically, this may diminish the quality of care and habilitation for clients. Whether or not we call this "burnout," we clearly must find ways to foster dedication and long-term commitment in caregivers. But does the burnout concept serve any purpose?

WHAT IS BURNOUT? IS THE CONCEPT NECESSARY?

There are many diverse definitions of *burnout* in the large literature on this topic (for a review, see Cherniss, 1980.) Before offering another, I will review its history briefly. Although Freudenberger (1974), a psychologist, usually is credited with coining the term, the word actually appeared much earlier. In fact, burnout was the theme of a story written by Graham Greene in 1962. Nevertheless, reference to the term in human services did not occur until the early 1970s.

One year before Freudenberger published his article, Maslach, a social psychologist, presented a paper on detached concern at the American Psychological Association's annual convention (Maslach, 1973). She described the process in which caregivers begin to dehumanize clients as a way of coping with role-related stress. Many traditional professionals viewed detachment as a necessary and even positive process to help caregivers remain sensitive and responsive without becoming overwhelmed by the emotional aspects of the helping process. Because of this fundamental disagreement, Maslach decided to change the label, expropriated Freudenberger's (1974, 1975) term *burnout* and used it in a popular article in the magazine *Human Behavior* (Maslach, 1976).

It is important to note that Maslach's definition differed considerably from Freudenberger's (1974), which was "to fail or wear out in response to heavy demands" (p. 161). Maslach's (1976) definition retained the "heavy demands" component, but she emphasized the *detachment* and *dehumanization* that had been her original interest. The waters became muddier in 1977 when the Berkeley Planning Associates (1977) conducted a study of staff burnout among protective services workers. This was the first empirical research on the topic and remains one of the best methodologically; however, their operational definition of *burnout* was almost synonymous with the concept of alienation, including withdrawal from the job and organization as well as from the client.

By the late 1970s, the burnout topic had achieved great popularity among teachers, nurses, social workers, and other human service groups. A steady stream of articles appeared. Researchers and writers often expanded the definition to fit their own work. Accordingly, the concept is not popular among many serious researchers; any topic that becomes such a fad tends to be regarded suspiciously by objective scholars. Exploiting a catchy term, however, is not new to psychology. Many currently accepted terms were once controversial when first introduced. A flamboyant new term probably often succeeds in gaining public visibility—for both the idea and its originator. I still remember a lecture by the late David Krech in 1968 in which he confessed that he chose the title "'Hypothesis' in Rats" for an article (Krechevsky, 1932) to stir controversy and thus to secure wide attention among experimental psychologists. That the article became a classic undoubtedly had something to do with the content as well as with the title; but Krech doubted that this work would have been as influential if he had used a more neutral term for the process that his rats engaged in while learning a discrimination task.

My own definition of *burnout* is a process in which a dedicated caregiver disengages from his or her work in response to job-related stress (Cherniss, 1980). Maslach and Jackson (1981) developed a standardized measure of burnout consisting of three subscales: emotional exhaustion, depersonalization, and personal accomplishment. They proposed that burnout is a process in which the first stage is emotional exhaustion. If no relief occurs, caregivers eventually attempt to escape from the strain by depersonalizing the clients. As this occurs, staff effectiveness declines, along with the caregivers' sense of personal accomplishment. Although Maslach and Jackson gathered much data on reliability and validity of the burnout inventory their developmental stage theory remains untested. The Maslach and Jackson instrument does not measure withdrawal from the job and does not distinguish burnout clearly from older concepts such as job stress, involvement, satisfaction, and turnover.

In fact, what is unique and potentially valuable about the concept of burnout is that it hypothesizes a psychological phenomenon that specifically links these earlier measures of reactions to the job. Burnout certainly relates to job stress as one particular response to such stress. Burnout, however, is just one of many ways people can respond to stress. Burnout also implies low job involvement but is not synonomous because burnout refers to the *loss* of involvement as a result of job-related stress. Low job involvement per se may be caused by many factors other than stress and also exists in jobs with low levels of stress.

Several studies confirm that burnout relates to job satisfaction and staff turnover (e.g., Maslach & Jackson, 1981; Weinberg et al., 1981). The highest correlation, however, between measures of burnout and of job satisfaction is .60, with somewhat lower correlations for turnover (below .50). Although this can be a function of the measuring instruments, a meaningful conceptual difference can be made. That is, job stress *may* make some workers dissatisfied, whereas others may like the stress and even thrive on it. Also, job dissatisfaction can occur even when there is no stress (e.g., because the pay is low); and, although the dissatisfied workers may burn out (i.e., withdraw from the job psychologically), this is only one of several responses available to them. Also, because burnout refers to *psychological* withdrawal and disengagement, it is distinct from turnover. People leave jobs for many reasons, both voluntary and involuntary; burnout is only one factor that may contribute to turnover rates.

Burnout can best be considered a syndrome (i.e., a set of symptoms that co-occur more often than predicted by chance and that theoretically relate to a dynamic process). No part of the burnout syndrome is new, and previous research and theory about job involvement, job stress, and job satisfaction could be relevant to the current study of burnout. Regrettably, many recent investigators of burnout have failed to review previous work in these closely related areas. Nonetheless, I believe that the concept of burnout has scientific merit, as reference to a distinct and important process that was not fully appreciated and studied before the term was used.

Finally, another compelling argument for using the term is that the plight of caregivers in the human services had been a neglected topic. When Sarata (1972) began his doctoral dissertation on job satisfaction in staff working in institutions for mentally retarded persons, he found only 19 published studies on job satisfaction in *any* human service occupation, despite hundreds of studies involving blue collar, white collar, and managerial workers. The popularity of the burnout concept has encouraged research on an important, previously neglected problem.

WHAT KIND OF ENVIRONMENT LEADS TO HIGH STAFF BURNOUT?

In addressing this question, researchers have been guided by a stress–coping paradigm. They have focused on specific organizational factors that may lead to stress (e.g., size of case load, type of leadership, and supervision) or may facilitate coping (e.g., social support). Not surprisingly, the findings tend to confirm what already is known about job-related stress (e.g., Caplan, Cobb, French, Harrison, & Pinneau, 1975).

One of the earliest studies examined protective service workers in 10 federally funded programs around the country (Berkeley Planning Associates, 1977). Their definition of burnout, as noted previously, differed somewhat from the popular ones used today, but the study remains one of the few to consider divergent classes of variables in a sophisticated, multivariate design. They examined structural variables (e.g., size, geographic dispersion), management variables (leadership, communication), and individual difference variables (age, sex, and education). The individual difference and structural variables accounted for little of the variance. In contrast, burnout was closely related to leadership and communication variables. Agencies with open communication styles in which the leadership provided structure, support, and autonomy to staff tended to have lower levels of staff burnout than did those with more closed communication or less-supportive highly controlling managers.

Autonomy, support, and communication have emerged as important environmental factors in other studies as well. For instance, Pines and Aronson (1981) studied burnout in a variety of service areas, including developmental disabilities. In one study of 198 mental retardation workers in Georgia, autonomy and social feedback were more strongly correlated with burnout than were any other aspects of the work environment, $rs = .32$. Work relations and social support also were related to burnout, $rs = .28$ and .26, respectively.

Weinberg et al. (1981) randomly selected 724 staff members from 14 residential facilities (11 states) for mentally retarded clients. They adapted the Pines and Aronson Burnout Scale, which emphasizes emotional exhaustion. "Overload" was the strongest environmental correlate of burn-out, $r = .39$, with "conflicting demands," $r = .37$, and "administrative hassles," $r = .33$, also significant.

Obviously, this research is problematic. First, different researchers use different measures of burnout. Second, the results are correlational and are based on self-report measures, which may reflect nonindependence in the data. For instance, a burned-out worker may begin to *perceive* less autonomy, less social support, and more administrative hassles because he or she is burned out, rather than vice versa. Third, the environmental variables tend to be highly intercorrelated, and seldom are appropriate multivariate techniques used to help identify the primary sources of the variance. Finally, the studies have not been theory-based, and experimental designs have not been used. Fundamental limitations, however, may be caused by the implicit assumptions guiding virtually all of these studies.

As noted previously, the research and writing on burnout has been guided by a stress–coping paradigm. The cause of burnout is seen as some set of stressors in the work environment. These may be mediated by individual differences that affect perceptions of stress. The employees then may experience strain (changes in attitudes as well as physiological changes) and may try to reduce strain through active coping strategies. If these fail, they may then attempt to withdraw psychologically by using defensive coping mechanisms. The individual differences assumed to be important are those presumably related to people's vulnerability to stress or tendency to create it for themselves (e.g., locus of control or achievement motivation). All of the most popular writings on burnout present some version of this model (Cherniss, 1980; Edelwich & Brodsky, 1980; Freudenberger & Richelson, 1980; Maslach & Jackson, 1981.) Researchers have followed this model, especially in the study of environmental factors. Researchers tend to focus on the most proximal causes of stress, such as high case loads or lack of "time outs"; and as we have seen, there have been positive results obtained from this approach. The actual stressors, however, vary with the sample, and the obtained correlations are never very high. Also, there has been no attempt to explain why the stressors vary from setting to setting. For instance, why is social support perceived as high in one program but low in another? Organizational context, structure, or history may be important, but studies of structural variables, such as size or span of control, have not produced very strong relationships either. These findings do not invalidate the stress–coping paradigm, but their lack of explanatory power suggests that alternative conceptions may be more productive.

I began to question the validity of the stress–coping paradigm after I conducted case studies of two rather unusual settings. One was a residential institution for mentally retarded people operated by a Catholic order of nuns. The core staff members were the sisters who lived and worked in the institution. Although I did not measure burnout formally, my discussions with some of the sisters; the low turnover rates; and the bright, clean, and attractive appearance of the facility all suggested that burnout was unusually low. Such positive signs cannot be construed to mean that burnout was totally absent in this facility. I did interview an individual who had left because of dissatisfaction, but her concerns were primarily with philosophical matters; she had not experienced burnout as usually defined.

What was intriguing about this setting was that burnout should have been high, given the prevailing ideas about its causes. The sisters worked 7 days a week, 52 weeks a year. Their autonomy was almost nonexistent: they were expected to obey any order received from their superior. Many of their jobs were not particularly varied or interesting. In fact, intelligent and well-educated individuals sometimes were required to do menial or demanding chores, such as working in the kitchen or doing janitorial work. As one of the sisters put it, "We do not have union cards here; we do whatever needs to be done." To compensate, the work loads did not seem heavy, and there clearly was a high degree of social support within the community. Yet, these two positive aspects seem unlikely to account for the low level of burnout, given such "adverse" working conditions. These women willingly, even joyfully, submitted themselves to work that the prevailing paradigm would regard as highly conducive to burnout.

Fascinated by this apparent contradiction, I looked for another setting in which there was a strong, guiding ideology. The one I found was secular rather than religious: a school for mentally retarded and emotionally disturbed children in one of the most notorious slums in Chicago. The children had been rejected by the public schools as too difficult to teach. This school was committed to taking any such child and operated all year. Its physical resources were far from ideal; it was situated in a former church plagued by bad plumbing, erratic heat, no air conditioning, and junkies sprawled outside the front door. Burnout did occur here, but turnover rates and interviews with staff members suggested that it was much lower than was the case for other schools in the city serving this type of population. Turnover, on the average, at this school was about 20%, compared to 50% for comparable schools.

Staff at the school pointed out that the director was one factor contributing to the sustained caring and commitment found among the teachers. She had been in charge for 15 years and was described as warm, nurturant, and supportive. She believed that caring for the staff members and their need for growth was as important as caring for the children; however, about 5 years before my visit, this positive leadership no longer seemed to be enough to keep staff morale high. The students represented increasingly higher functioning individuals with far more serious behavior problems. The strain on everyone was intense. At this point, they decided to become a Montessori school. Within 2 years, every teacher remaining on the staff received training and certification as a Montessori teacher. New staff began Montessori training shortly after they were hired, if they did not have prior certification. Although the school's problems did not magically disappear, staff morale was restored, and the difficulties in managing students lessened.

One thing these two settings had in common was a core ideology to which almost every staff member was committed. In most respects, the actual programs were no less "stressful" than were others serving similar populations. What differed was that staff did not *perceive* or describe their jobs as stressful, and when faced with problem situations, they were more able to cope. What really distinguished the staff members from those in other programs was their high level of *social commitment:* there was an ideology that people believed in and that organized their daily work. I began to wonder if burnout might be caused by the *absence* of social commitment as much as by environmental stressors.

THE SOCIAL COMMITMENT PARADIGM

Although subjectively perceived stress may be a proximal cause of burnout, vulnerability to stress may be a function of personal social commitment. Hypothetically, the absence or loss of social commitment may be a critical precursor to burnout within a human service setting. In this model, socially committed persons will tolerate significantly more stress, frustration, and lack of immediate success than will less-committed persons. Indeed, socially committed persons are less likely to regard certain conditions as "stressful," compared to less-committed persons.

This conception is inconsistent with the most popular notions of burnout, which regard loss of commitment as a *consequence* of burnout rather than as a *cause*. The sequence of changes in motivation, involvement, and commitment warrant careful empirical study. In uncommitted or undercommitted people, does stress lead to further withdrawal? Would an ideological framework for understanding job-related stress help to minimize reductions in commitment? Alternatively, some writers have argued that high commitment actually increases vulnerability to burnout. Freudenberger and Richelson (1980) referred to burnout as a "disease of overcommitment." Marks (1979), however, pointed out that: "Our energy tends to become fully available for anything to which we are highly committed, and we often feel more energetic after having done it. We tend to find little energy for anything to which we are *not* highly committed, and doing these things leaves us feeling 'spent,' drained, and exhausted" (p. 31).

This contradiction between Freudenberger and Richelson's (1980) notion and the view presented here in part may be based on two different ways of defining commitment. When Freudenberger and Richelson referred to a "committed person," they appeared to be thinking of an individual who becomes overextended, works too long and too hard, and does not know how to distribute work activities effectively. They also seemed to be referring to an individual whose commitment is primarily egoistic, a career-oriented achiever whose self-esteem is strongly affected by how well he or she performs and how quickly he or she rises up the career ladder. I, however, am referring to social commitment, by which I mean belief in a transcendent body of ideas and strong identification with a group, institution, or method that is based on those ideas. In other words, socially committed people believe in something greater than themselves; and when their work is based on this commitment, they are less likely to burn out.

Social commitment needs to be distinguished from simple altruism. Many people choose a helping occupation because they want to serve others (Cherniss & Egnatios, 1978). Socially committed persons serve others as a means of accomplishing a more transcendent goal, often by applying a particular approach to serving others. For instance, one of the sisters I interviewed said that helping retarded children was a way for her to come "closer to God." In other words, there was a well-defined, higher purpose on which her altruistic behavior was based.

Within the stress–coping paradigm, researchers ask, "What type of work environment contributes to stress?" Within the alternative social commitment paradigm, investigators pose a very different question: "What factors in a work environment promote commitment?" The commitment paradigm fosters a different direction for research that may broaden and improve our understanding of the burnout phenomenon.

The social commitment paradigm also directs us to a body of sociological research and theory previously ignored in the study of burnout. Kanter's (1972) work on commitment mechanisms in 19th century communes is a good example. Kanter used historical material to reconstruct the structure and practices of a large number of communes founded between 1780 and 1860. Her final sample consisted of 9 successful and 21 unsuccessful settings. Success was defined as surviving for at least 25 years. She found that successful communes more often used numerous mechanisms that generated and sustained personal commitment by members. Kanter divided these into six main types. The first she called *sacrifice*, defined as "giving up something considered valuable or pleasurable in order to belong to the organization" (p. 72). Examples include abstinence from certain foods or pleasures and austerity in living arrangements. A second commitment mechanism is *investment*, "a process whereby the individual gains a stake in the group, commits current and future profits to it, so that he must continue to participate if he is going to realize those profits" (p. 72). Investments include physical participation (time and energy requirements) as well as financial investment. Irreversible investments are particularly binding. An example is a commune that requires members to turn their wealth over to the community permanently when they join. *Renunciation* is "giving up competing relationships outside the communal group and individualistic, exclusive attachment within" (p. 73). This renunciation can be accomplished indirectly, as through geographic isolation and functional self-sufficiency of the community, as well as more directly, such as through renunciation of pair relationships. *Communion* refers to mechanisms that bring "members into meaningful contact with the collective whole" (p. 73). Examples would be homogeneity in religion; economic or educational status; communal sharing of property, clothing, or personal effects; communal labor through job rotation; communal work efforts; and shared persecution by an outside force. *Mortification* involves the "submission of private states to social control, the exchanging of a former identity for one defined and formulated by the community" (p. 74). Confession, mutual criticism, and public denunciation of deviants are well-known examples. Another mechanism placed in this category, spiritual differentiation, involves practices such as structure deference to those of higher moral status, a formal probationary period, and no status distinctions on the basis of skill or educational attainment. Another mechanism, deindividuation, refers to practices such as wearing a uniform and using communal dwellings and dining halls. Kanter's last general category is *transcendence*, "a process whereby an individual attaches his decision-making prerogatives to a power greater than himself, surrendering to the higher meaning contained by the group and submitting to something beyond himself" (p. 74). Ideology is a primary means by which social systems create transcendence. According to Kanter, the ideologies of the successful communities "legitimated demands made on members by reference to a higher principle, which gave meaning to the demands" (p. 114).

The more successful communities tended to have more comprehensive and elaborated ideologies that provided explanations and guidelines for many aspects of life. The less successful communities had very general, simple ideologies (e.g., the principle of brotherly love) or ideologies limited to one sphere of existence, such as economic organization. To be an effective commitment mechanism, ideology had to be translated into actions. Kanter found that in the successful communities, ideology was an integral part of the group's life, influencing many decisions and guiding everyday activities. In less successful groups, decisions often were justified on the basis of expediency. Kanter identified a mechanism of "guidance" concerned with specific behavioral norms: "By providing members with minutely detailed instructions for dealing with specific situations, nineteenth century communities rendered meaningful in terms of their values even the most minute and mundane behaviors and acts" (pp. 120–121). An example of this might be a fixed daily routine.

Few communes studied by Kanter (1972) used all of these mechanisms, and some of the commitment mechanisms probably could not be incorporated in contemporary human service programs. Other mechanisms may be useful, and some were observed in the two programs I described earlier. The religious order employed more commitment mechanisms, but even the Montessori school used several, including investment of time and energy in special Montessori training, regularized group contact through daily group meetings, an elaborate formal ideology, detailed guidance for the teaching routine, and strong tradition.

Another sociological study provides some additional ideas about the mechanisms that generate commitment in a social system. Clark (1970) studied a slightly less exotic social institution—elite liberal arts colleges. He was interested in learning why certain colleges, such as Antioch,

Swarthmore, and Reed, became distinctive. He studied the histories of these three schools and identified a number of factors that generated particularly strong loyalty and dedication in faculty, students, and alumni. This dedication helped promote excellence and put these schools at a competitive advantage. Like Kanter's commitment mechanisms, many of the factors identified by Clark seem to be institutional ways of generating strong social commitment and thus reducing burnout.

Clark (1970) identified at least six factors that seemed to enhance commitment. Several of these correspond closely to mechanisms identified by Kanter. For instance, Clark found that a *strong, clear, distinct ideology* was especially important:

> Career motives are not enough; an embodied idea is the institutional
> chariot to which individual motive becomes chained. When the idea is
> in command, men are indifferent to personal cost. They often are not
> even aware of how much they have risked and how much they
> sometimes have sacrificed. As ideologues, as believers, they do not
> care. They are proud of what they have been through, what they have
> done, and what they stand for. They feel highly involved in a
> worthwhile collective effort and wish to remain with it. (p. 262)

According to Clark, commitment is enhanced when "doctrine defines a straight line that rules out the zigs and zags of opportunism and where the theme of the institution becomes reflected in a thousand and one bits of statue and sidewalk, story and song" (p. 9).

Each college Clark (1970) studied developed a particular motif in which ideology was tied closely to distinctive programmatic elements. For instance, Clark reported that Antioch had a "philosophy of the whole man . . . expressed in a unique combination of work, study, and community participation" (p. 235). Clark called this the *program of work,* usually the curriculum, but sometimes extracurricular aspects as well. Clark suggested that the most effective program of work includes elements that are unique and unconventional. These set the institution apart and help ensure that those who choose to become part of it truly believe in its mission. The Swarthmore honors program exemplified this principle: When first adopted, no other American college had an honors undergraduate program. At Antioch, an unusual programmatic feature was the work–study program, and at Reed there was the interdisciplinary humanities program for freshmen and sophomores. These programmatic features vividly symbolize and reinforce the guiding ideology that establishes the individuality of the institution.

To give life to ideology and program, Clark (1970) stated his belief that *charismatic leadership* is essential. Charisma is a controversial concept in social psychology. Most contemporary studies of leadership avoid it and choose instead to examine variables such as task-centeredness versus person-centeredness (Burns, 1978; Stogdill, 1974). Sociologists and political scientists increasingly view charisma as a function of the group rather than of the leader (Burns, 1978). Nevertheless, the value of a certain type of leader is apparent in developing an institution that generates particularly high levels of commitment.

In looking for a good definition of *charisma*, I came upon one by the psychologist Murray (1968), who described it as "the capacity to put new and seductive ideas in metaphorical terms that tickle the senses, and the emotions even more. . . . The charismatic man must also be fervently committed to something greater than himself to bring others along with him" (p. 61). Charisma may be as valuable for generating commitment in a human service setting as in any other, although this has not been systematically studied. Its role in generating high levels of staff commitment was emphasized by Crissey (1975), who wrote: "It was Seguin's enthusiasm that inspired his teachers to work, to invent, and to influence from 5:30 in the morning when the children awoke to 8:30 at night when they went to bed" (p. 807).

Although charismatic leadership seems important, Clark (1970) concluded that a charismatic leader is not enough. To perpetuate the leader's zeal, there must be a dedicated *personnel core* that remains after the first leader departs. Selection, indoctrination, and retention are the mechanisms to facilitate such a core group. Selznick (1957) endorsed this view: "Elites play a vital role in the creation and protection of values . . . Specialized academies and selective recruiting are two devices for building up the self-consciousness and the confidence of present and potential leaders" (p. 14). Organizational structure also can facilitate developing a dedicated personnel core. For instance, because Reed College chose not to create the associate professor rank, there developed a small, exclusive faculty oligarchy made up of the full professors. They had great power and status; they towered over the rest of the faculty and perpetuated the original ideals.

Clark (1970) further hypothesized that there must be a group of dedicated partisans on the outside. He called this an *external social base*. These important individuals and groups provide necessary resources, political support, a receptive clientele, and a vehicle for making the ideology especially visible. In fact, *image-building through publicity* seems to be another important mechanism to generate commitment. All colleges studied by Clark launched particularly aggressive publicity campaigns during their early years. These publicity efforts created a powerful public image that helped sustain commitment and establish identity. Thus, the sociological work of Clark and Kanter (1972) revealed a number of factors in social institutions that promote commitment. Although their studies involved very different kinds of settings (colleges and communes), their ideas are relevant for other human service programs. The Montessori school and the Catholic residential program described previously employ many of these mechanisms.

Another example of an ideologically based program is l'Arche, an international group that develops and runs small residential programs for mentally retarded individuals (Shearer, 1976). In fact, l'Arche uses almost all the mechanisms Clark (1970) and Kanter (1972) identified. Its ideology is a blend of Christianity and "normalization." It is strongly based on spiritual belief and attracts people who share that belief. The goal is to create a "joyous, accepting community" in which the staff members receive not money but the intrinsic rewards that come from living a life of faith, religious observance, and giving. The staff "no pay" policy is a unique programmatic element that helps to reinforce the spiritual–humanistic ideology. Like the colleges studied by Clark, l'Arche's founder, Jean Vanier, is a charismatic figure who has become something of a legend among l'Arche's followers. L'Arche also has been effectively publicized in various forums, including Shearer's (1976) laudatory article in the influential *Changing Patterns in Residential Care for the Mentally Retarded.*

L'Arche has an especially interesting mechanism for creating a strongly committed personnel core: A new community only begins when two or three people receive a "call from God" and go to live in an existing community for about 2 years. After passing this "test," they are allowed to return home and begin the new community. They also are expected to make a lifelong commitment to l'Arche before beginning the new community. Although some of these core people do leave after a few years, this recruitment and induction process does ensure an unusually high degree of commitment in a core group of people. They then can share their own zeal with the staff members they recruit, train, and work with (Risse, 1980). Thus, there clearly are settings in the developmental disabilities field that employ many of the commitment mechanisms found in the sociological literature. Determining whether these mechanisms are, in fact, associated with lower levels of staff burnout is an important—and intriguing—task for future researchers.

THE COSTS OF STRONG COMMITMENT

Let us assume that strong commitment is associated with low burnout, that the religious zeal found in a "community" like l'Arche generates relatively high levels of staff dedication and care. Are there potential costs to pay for this type of commitment? Are there negative unintended consequences? Although burnout theoretically appears detrimental for the quality of care, "curing" burnout by creating ideological communities may have some drawbacks.

Perhaps the most obvious danger is fanaticism. There are many examples of extreme and harmful social commitment including Nazism, the community at Jonestown, the True Believer, and other destructive aberrations in social living. Even when strong commitment does not generate atrocities, it may lead to dogmatism, resistance to change, and intolerance of deviant viewpoints. The price of social commitment may be the subjugation of individuality and the degradation of human dignity. Even in human service programs such as those examplified here, the strong faith guiding them may cause their followers to reject useful ideas and practices simply because they do not fit their model.

Although a group or organization in which there is strong social commitment clearly can fall prey to "group think," this is not an inevitable outcome. In his classic work on group think, Janis (1972) suggested mechanisms that groups could adopt to avoid pitfalls associated with strong commitment. For example, Antioch College exemplifies a setting characterized by strong commitment but not antithetical to experimentation and nonconformity. Clark (1970) has shown that Antioch, early in its existence, defined itself as an "experimental college," always on the frontlines of academic innovation, thus tolerant of many educational practices.

Other risks of strong social commitment may be more pragmatic. Institutions such as communes and liberal arts colleges often alienate important segments of society because they emphasize one value and underplay or ignore others. Also, in committing an organization strongly to one path of action, it may be more difficult to adapt to new demands later.

Although strong social commitment clearly has costs and may not be desirable in every type of situation, human service settings may be instances in which social commitment is valuable. Those who must care for mentally retarded people do so in the face of great frustration and little extrinsic reward. Ideologies and the other commitment mechanisms I have identified may be ways of getting people to do what no "rational," economically motivated person would do. These institutional commitment strategies may be necessary to generate the high quality of care desired for retarded people.

IMPLICATIONS OF THE COMMITMENT PARADIGM

Adopting this commitment paradigm leads to significant changes in how burnout is conceptualized and studied. Rather than focusing on coping with stress, researchers would assess the *larger social context in which service workers function.* Without ignoring stress or the maladaptive ways helpers responded to stress, investigators could examine how *amount of social commitment* affects the level of perceived stress, the amount of strain generated by that stress, and the type of coping used in response to that stress. Most importantly, the extent to which social commitment mechanisms are associated with higher levels of staff involvement and care could be analyzed.

If strong social commitment is, in fact, associated with less burnout and better care, the policy implications could be profound. For over 100 years, the field of mental retardation has moved from the "moral treatment" approach that prevailed in the early 19th century to one that emphasizes rational professional, and scientific endeavors (Cherniss & Krantz, 1982). Care based merely on religious or ideological fervor has been suspect. Unfortunately, the rational approach has become associated with impersonal, degrading institutional care and growing concern with problems such as staff abuse, neglect, and burnout. In becoming highly analytic and rational in developing care systems for mentally retarded people, professionals unwittingly may have created conditions that foster low staff morale and neglect the importance of personal social commitment.

Most contemporary programs are based on a utilitarian rather than a normative staff reward system (French & Raven, 1959). Some staff members may choose this work in part because they derive satisfaction from helping needy people, but most staff are motivated by monetary, job security, and other extrinsic rewards. Unfortunately, helping the needy is not valued enough that we reward employees with relatively high salaries, status, or even security. Strong social commitment represents an alternative way of motivating people, which in turn fosters a normative reward system that may sustain motivation and caring even when extrinsic rewards are modest.

The social commitment conception also has implications for training programs. We tend to teach people to think rather than to believe (Cherniss & Krantz, 1982). We assume that if direct-care and managerial staff in a residential program are taught how to use effective techniques properly, their performance will improve. The most popular management training programs in the mental retardation field today offer rational "behavioral science" concepts, research findings, and techniques. The premise is that conscientious application of these behavioral principles will motivate staff members and organize their efforts. Without denying the potential value of these training approaches, the social commitment paradigm would suggest a different kind of training, one that emphasizes the use of commitment mechanisms and affords a guiding mission or inspirational theme.

These potential implications make it all the more important that we begin to study seriously the relationships between social commitment, stress, and burnout. Psychologists know a great deal about stress responses, and this knowledge increasingly is being used to enhance our understanding of staff burnout; however, that understanding ultimately will be limited if we remain attached to the stress–coping paradigm. We must begin to examine the larger social context in which stress and coping operate to produce burnout. Studying how social systems generate and sustain commitment may be a valuable way of expanding our horizons.

REFERENCES

Berkeley Planning Associates, (1977). *Evaluation of child abuse and neglect demonstration projects, 1974-1977. Volume XI: Project management and worker burnout.* Unpublished report, National Technical Information Service. Springfield, VA.

Burns, J. M., (1978). *Leadership.* New York: Harper & Row.

Caplan, R. D., Cobb, S., French, J. R. P., Harrison, R. V., & Pinneau, S. R. (1975). *Job demands and worker health.* Washington, DC: U.S. Department of Health,

Education, and Welfare, Public Health Service, Center for Disease Control, National Institute for Occupation Safety and Health.

Cherniss, C. (1980). *Staff burnout: Job stress in the human services*. Beverly Hills, CA: Sage.

Cherniss, C., & Egnatios, E. (1978). Is there job satisfaction in community mental health? *Community Mental Health Journal, 14*, 309–318.

Cherniss, C., & Krantz, D. L. (1982). The ideological community as an antidote to burnout in human services. In B. A. Farber (Ed.), *Stress and burnout in the human service professions*. New York: Pergamon.

Clark, B. R. (1970). *The distinctive college*. Chicago: Aldine.

Crissey, M. S. (1975). Mental retardation: Past, present, and future. *American Psychologist, 30*, 800–808.

Edelwich, J., & Brodsky, A. (1980). *Burn-out*. New York: Human Sciences Press.

French, J. R. P., & Raven, B. (1959). The bases of social power. In D. Cartwright (Ed.), *Studies in social power*. Ann Arbor: University of Michigan Press.

Freudenberger, H. J. (1974). Staff burn-out. *Journal of Social Issues, 30*, 159–165.

Freudenberger, H. J. (1975). The staff burn-out syndrome in alternative institutions. *Psychotherapy: Theory, Research, Practice, 12*, 73–82.

Freudenberger, H. J., & Richelson, G. (1980). *Burn-out*. New York: Anchor Press-Doubleday.

Greene, G. (1962). *The burnt-out case*. New York: Random House.

Janis, I. L. (1972). *Victims of groupthink*. Boston: Houghton-Mifflin.

Kanter, R. M. (1972). *Commitment and community: Communes and utopias in sociological perspective*. Cambridge, MA: Harvard University Press.

Krechevsky, I. (1932). 'Hypothesis' in rats. *Psychological Review, 39*, 516–532.

Marks, S. (1979). Culture, human energy, and self-actualization: A sociological offering to humanistic psychology. *Journal of Humanistic Psychology, 19*, 27–42.

Maslach, C. (1973). *Detached concern in health and social service professions*. Paper presented at annual meeting of the American Psychological Association, Montreal.

Maslach, C. (1976). Burned out. *Human Behavior, 5*(9), 16–22.

Maslach, C., & Jackson, S. (1981). A scale measure to assess experienced burnout: The Maslach Burnout Inventory. *Journal of Occupational Behavior, 2*, 99–113.

Murray, H. A. (1968, September). Interview with Henry A. Murray. *Psychology Today*.

Pines, A., & Aronson, E. (1981). *Burnout*, New York: Free Press.

Risse, J. (1980). Unpublished letter to C. McDowell, June 18, 1980.

Sarata, B. P. V. (1972). *Job satisfaction of individuals working with the mentally retarded*.

Selznick, P. (1957). *Leadership in administration*. New York: Row, Peterson.

Shearer, A. (1976). L'Arche. In *Changing patterns in residential care for the mentally retarded*. Washington, DC: President's Committee on Mental Retardation.

Stogdill, R. M. (1974). *Handbook of leadership: A survey of theory and research*. New York: Free Press.

Weinberg, S., Edwards, G., & Garove, W. E. (1981). *Burnout among employees of state residential facilities serving developmentally disabled persons*. Unpublished manuscript, University of Alabama, Birmingham.

11
Withdrawal and Commitment of Basic-Care Staff in Residential Programs

Alfred A. Baumeister
Peabody College, Vanderbilt University

Eric S. Zaharia
Caswell Center

Kirkbride, in 1912, referred to it as a "positive disgrace," and he was not talking about his salary. He was addressing an organizational problem that has plagued the operation of many residential facilities for mentally retarded persons ever since Guggenbühl opened Abendberg in the mid-1800s: the problem of staff instability. More recent surveys of administrators of both institutional and community facilities indicate that recruitment and retention of direct-care staff members are still considered major problems, second perhaps to inadequate funding for programs (Baker, Seltzer, & Seltzer, 1977; Bruininks, Kudla, Wieck, & Hauber, 1980; Lakin & Bruininks, 1981; O'Connor, 1976).

The generic literature regarding staff instability, particularly absenteeism and turnover, is enormous and historically represents one of the principal thrusts of organizational research by industrial psychologists. That industrial organizations are interested in understanding and controlling employee withdrawal hardly is surprising because staff instability may undermine an organization's ability to carry out its missions. Not only does employee withdrawal usually affect performance negatively, it is also increases financial costs.

With respect to human service organizations, such as residential programs for mentally retarded persons, it seems intuitively obvious that consistent job involvement of basic-care staff directly relates to program effectiveness and quality of care. In 1981, approximately 82% or about $3 billion (Scheerenberger, 1982) of the total operational budgets of public residential facilities was encumbered for salaries. Over 43% of institutional personnel are direct-care staff, representing an expenditure conservatively amounting to well over

229

$1 billion annually. Community residential programs are proportionately at least as labor intensive. Accordingly, it is reasonable to raise questions concerning the characteristics of this labor force, its effectiveness, and its stability. We focus here on what we have called "employee withdrawal," that is, disinclination to participate in the job (Zaharia & Baumeister, 1978b). Withdrawal takes numerous forms including applicant avoidance, tardiness, poor job performance, absenteeism, and termination.

ASSUMPTIONS

Before entering into a substantive account and analysis of the literature, we feel it necessary to identify the major assumptions in our approach to the problem of employee withdrawal. Some of these assumptions may be more tenable than others in terms of the available empirical evidence.

First, we assume that a stable work force is crucial to the ability of the organization to care for and provide effective treatment for its clients. There is, in fact, little direct evidence that quality of life and quality of care are highly dependent upon the stability of basic-care staff; but in light of logical considerations and a few scattered research reports, this seems to be a reasonable initial assumption. We suggest that personal relatedness or bonding mediates the quality of interaction between caregiver and recipient. For instance, Kahne (1968) observed a correlation between number of patient suicides and personnel turnover rates in psychiatric facilities. In other kinds of service organizations, such as general medical hospitals, there seems to be a clear relationship between turnover and quality of performance (Revans, 1964). At a philosophical level, the rapid rotation of caretakers in living units violates the principle of normalization (Lakin & Bruininks, 1981). Perhaps the most compelling argument to support the assumption that direct-care personnel represent the "bottom line" is the impression offered by a discouraged parent that "even a bad attendant is better than none" (Blatt, 1970, p. 236). We return to the question of impact of employee withdrawal in more detail subsequently.

Employee losses in the form of turnover, absenteeism, and tardiness create labor shortages within the organization. The impact and severity of these shortages is dependent upon three factors: (a) the relative strength of core staffing (i.e., maximal, minimal, or optimal numbers of personnel); (b) the cohesiveness and morale of core staff; (c) the time dimension of loss incidence, including when loss occurs (e.g., peak-period losses as contrasted with down-time losses) and its duration. We assume that dysfunction in these areas can further aggravate employee losses and reduce organizational effectiveness.

Second, we assume that the presence of withdrawal behavior within service programs is not necessarily a direct indicator of a dysfunctional organization. In fact, a certain amount of withdrawal sanctioned by the organization, such as sick leave and vacation time, represents job respite and may facilitate effective work behavior under some conditions. For instance, the high rates of turnover coupled with low rates of absenteeism in group homes (George & Baumeister, 1981) are likely linked as cause and effect. Further, movement of employees is positive to the extent that as poor performers exit, promotional opportunities are available, and "old timers" are replaced by more progressive workers. Clearly, even highly unstable work forces may be tolerated if conditions are such that the positive effects of withdrawal outweigh the negative effects or if the organization is in a transition (reform) cycle. Nonetheless, a minimum amount of worker participation is essential. The employee strike represents the nadir of worker participation.

Third, we assume that instances of withdrawal or failure to participate in the job can be represented roughly along a continuum that includes job applicant avoidance, poor job performance, tardiness, absenteeism, and termination. We do not suggest that each type of behavior is controlled or mediated by the same variables or that these events are ordered neatly along a dimension of less to more severe; however, these various behaviors all affect an organization's ability to carry out its missions and may be controlled and mediated by the same classes of variables (e.g., job satisfaction).

Fourth, we assume that employee withdrawal is costly to an organization in financial terms. In fact, we estimate that these "hidden" costs are enormous. Further, we assume that these costs can be measured and that, to some extent, they can be controlled by good administrative and management practice.

Fifth, we assume that agencies that serve mentally retarded persons are sufficiently unique to warrant separate study and analysis. Although broader theories of organizational behavior can be applied to human service agencies, the specific causes and effects of employee withdrawal must be understood in terms of the unique mission of these organizations.

Finally, we assume that the withdrawal/participation behavior of professionals in mental retardation facilities generally is controlled by the same type of variables that affect direct-care personnel. Professionals constitute one fourth to one third of most institutional work forces (Scheerenberger, 1982). Unlike support personnel (e.g., secretaries, dietary workers, mechanics) whose generic jobs are influenced only slightly by the characteristics of the clientele and the working environment, professionals probably are influenced by these factors. Notwithstanding that there are some differential determinants and effects relating to the stability of basic-care employees, withdrawal among professionals does occur and this affects the ability of the organization to achieve its goals. We limit our discussion in this chapter, however, exclusively to the front-line employee.

MEASUREMENT ISSUES

Turnover

At least 25 diverse indices of turnover have been used for various purposes (Price, 1977). The most commonly applied type of measure is rate, expressed as a percentage over time. Unfortunately, rates cannot always be compared directly. For instance, King, Raynes, and Tizard (1971) observed a positive relationship between staff stability and resident-oriented care practices. On the other hand, McCormick, Balla, and Zigler (1975) did not replicate this finding. One possible explanation of this discrepancy is that different measures of employee turnover were used in the two studies, each tapping a different feature of the phenomenon. The measure used by McCormick et al. was the traditional separation rate among employees who had been hired, whereas King et al. estimated the number of new employees, commonly called the "accession rate." Although both are commonly used measures of work-force stability, their correlation is far short of perfect (Price, 1977).

Aside from the problem of comparability, even the same measure can be subjected to multiple interpretations. For example, a separation rate of 100% over a specified period of time could mean that all employees are leaving once, half may be leaving twice, and so on. Quite obviously, implications for management may be different in the case where the organization is losing all its employees as opposed to the situation where a segment is highly stable and another segment is highly mobile.

It is not a simple matter to choose among the available measures because the purpose to which the information will be put is one crucial determinant. Other considerations are the size and type of organization and its mission. In any event, each of the measures that has been suggested has advantages and disadvantages, and it is no doubt the case that multiple measures ought to be used, at least for research as contrasted with management purposes. There is no "best" measure of turnover. We advocate using multiple measures, including who leaves, when, and under which conditions. For instance, it is useful to distinguish between controlled and uncontrolled turnover (e.g., retirement, illness, and death). Controlled separations include both voluntary terminations and dismissals, which probably are affected by different variables. The Bureau of Labor Statistics breaks down separations into quits, layoffs, and "other."

Actually, it is not easy to determine the reason for a particular termination. In instances such as death and retirement, there is little ambiguity. In contrast, most separations are not so clearly understood. A common procedure is for employees to report their reasons for leaving the organization. Clearly, departing employees are unlikely to indicate negative job conditions as the reasons for leaving because this may jeopardize their future employment (and recommendations from the organization). Then, of course, there are those who voluntarily leave just one step ahead of being dismissed. We conducted a follow-up interview in 1978 with 40 employees who had quit a large public institution, comparing their reasons for leaving 6 months after their initial exit interview with those given at the time they left. There was a marked contrast with respect to the reasons given for leaving. After 6 months, the reasons were decidedly much more negative. Quite aside from the issue of distinguishing between voluntary and involuntary turnover, this finding also has implications for understanding the causes of turnover within the organization.

Length of Service

Although general separation rates do characterize how much change occurs within a time period, their meaning is not precise and they do not control for other important variables, most notably length of service. This is an especially important consideration when the size of an organization is changing systematically. The "average length of service of leavers" can be a valuable measure particularly for research purposes because of its sensitivity. It is calculated by taking the median length of service of employees within a job category, separating voluntary terminations and involuntary ones. This measure tells us when, in terms of employment length, turnover occurs.

Beyond implications for management, study of the length of service provides an opportunity to analyze dynamics that may mediate employees' commitment to the job. Researchers at the Tavistock Institute in England were the first to conceptualize turnover as a social process (i.e., a function of the interactions between the individual and others across time). The Tavistock investigators focused on survival curves and predictable changes in these curves. They identified three distinct phases: (a) induction crisis, (b) differential transit, and (c) settled connection. In our own intervention research, we have focused on the first of these phases, although we prefer the term "critical initial employment period" as more descriptive of the array of events that the employee faces when entering the work context.

In our research we typically use two measures: labor turnover rate and average length of service of leavers. Together, these measures indicate the volume and timing of turnover in ways that permit some, however rough, comparison across studies. From a managerial viewpoint, these are necessary but not usually sufficient indices. For instance, the Skill Wastage Index provides a measure of attrition among the most skilled employees. When a more-thorough understanding of the nature of turnover within an organization is required, attention will necessarily be directed to a number of individual, organizational, and economic variables. Turnover is a multivariate phenomenon, and institutional "diagnosis" will necessarily require consideration of local factors.

Table 1 lists some of the more commonly used measures of turnover. These and others are described and discussed more extensively by Vander Merwe and Miller (1975) and Price (1977).

TABLE 1   Turnover and Absenteeism Measured

Measure	*Formula*
Turnover	
Labor turnover rate	$\dfrac{\text{Number of controllable separations}}{\text{Average of the number of workers at the beginning and end of the period}} \times 100$
Accession rate	$\dfrac{\text{Number of new members added during the period}}{\text{Average number of members during the period}} \times 100$
Median length of service of leavers	The length of service above and below half the separate workers fall
Uncontrollable losses	$\dfrac{\text{Number of uncontrollable separations}}{\text{Average of the number of workers at the beginning and end of the period}} \times 100$
Dismissal rate	$\dfrac{\text{Number of dismissals}}{\text{Number of controllable separations}} \times 100$
Skill wastage index	$\dfrac{\text{Number of workers with 1 or more years service}}{\text{Number of workers 1 year ago}} \times 100$
Stability rate	$\dfrac{\text{Number of beginning members who remain during the period}}{\text{Number of members at beginning of period}} \times 100$
Absenteeism	
Lost-time rate	$\dfrac{\text{Number of personnel hours lost}}{\text{Number of personnel hours scheduled}} \times 100$
Frequency rate	$\dfrac{\text{Number of instances of absences}}{\text{Number of workers}} \times 100$
Proportion of absentee group	$\dfrac{\text{Number of workers absent at least once}}{\text{Number of workers, minus persons with extended absences}} \times 100$
Average length of absences	$\dfrac{\text{Number of personnel hours lost}}{\text{Total number of instances}}$

Absenteeism

The recording of absences from work may appear to be rather straightforward, but choice of measure profoundly influences generalizations about absenteeism. For example, had Pierce, Hoffman, and Pelletier (1974) used more precise and sensitive measures of their primary outcome variable, unscheduled absences, they might have shown significant effects of variable work schedules. A major problem relates to the distinction between incidence and duration, that is, is measured absenteeism the result of many workers with few lost days or a few workers with many lost days? Distinctions also must be made between scheduled and unscheduled absences. Most researchers use the Department of Labor absenteeism definition that refers only to unscheduled absences, which excludes annual leave and educational leave but includes sick leave.

We assume that unplanned absence, whatever the reason, is disruptive to a program and expensive to an organization. Distinguishing between legitimate and illegitimate uses of sick time is futile, for the most part. In this regard, in our own research on institutional absenteeism, we seem to have found the source of a major health problem: The greater the amount of sick leave available, the more "illness" among the staff members.

Table 1 presents four measures of absenteeism that, in combination, permit rather precise discriminations within and between facilities. From a management perspective, identifying when and where absenteeism occurs in the organization is important.

Other measurement considerations

Employee withdrawal can be manifested in less direct ways than can turnover and absenteeism, and these other forms of withdrawal may influence an organization's performance. Tardiness, for instance, is accepted in some institutions as a fact of life and treated casually as a fixed cost. Yet tardiness can be disruptive to performance as well to staff morale if responsibilities are increased. Sensitive measurement requires identifying who is late, how often, and under what circumstances.

Perhaps the most insidious and difficult to quantify form of withdrawal is job performance itself. Lack of motivation to perform, poor work quality, and disinterest in clients undoubtedly affect outcome. Employee commitment has long been claimed by administration as the single most critical variable in achieving institutional goals of high-quality care and training (e.g., Barr, 1913). (The role of administrative and professional commitment and competence have received less attention, perhaps because direct-care staff members do not write journal articles.)

Unlike other jobs where productivity and performance can be assessed by simple counting (e.g., number of sales), measuring quality of direct-care staff is far more vexing, nebulous, and difficult (Butterfield, 1967). This job is obviously a complex one, although delineating precisely what the job entails, how it should be accomplished, and how performance should be evaluated is less clear.

Traditionally, supervisory ratings of performance have been relied on, despite dubious reliability and validity. A major problem is that good staff performance criteria are not explicit and remain largely subjective. Individuals at various levels within the organizational hierarchy have different conceptions of optimal staff behavior. Shotwell, Dingman, and Tarjan (1960) designed one of the first and best studies of this phenomenon. They constructed statements describing desirable job behavior and attitudes.

Half the statements pertained directly to the client and half related to other job aspects. Technicians, supervisors, and professionals each rated these statements as to their relative importance. Substantial differences in rater perceptions emerged. In particular, professionals valued client-related activities more than did direct-care staff members, who emphasized non-client-oriented activities.

A more satisfactory measure of performance involves direct observation of worker behavior across various aspects of the job. This approach requires an adequate, objective catalog of discriminable behaviors that define the job. Formal job specifications for direct-care staff in residential settings are usually available. The problem is that these job specifications typically bear only a superficial, general relationship to the employees' daily activities. In fact, using a number of procedures to identify the principal components of the job, we find surprisingly little correspondence between administrative definitions and actual daily activities. For instance, most job descriptions underscore "training" the resident in self-help and other skills. When we observe staff behavior, we discover that very little time is devoted to formal training activities, either in institutions or group homes. Others report similar observations, including many activities not related to the job in any direct way (Burg, Reid, & Lattimore, 1979), use of crude and ineffective training techniques (Repp, Barton, & Brulle, 1981), low frequency of social interactions with residents (Veit, Allen, & Chinksy, 1976), poor health-care practices (Iwata, Bailey, Brown, Foshee, & Alpern, 1976), and reliance on procedures that may increase rather than decrease dependence (Barrett, 1971).

In a recently completed study of 40 institutional aides and 10 group home workers over 2 months, we discovered that only about 10% of their time was devoted, in the broadest sense, to resident training facilities. A much greater proportion of time (about 25%) was spent in housekeeping chores, which were not even mentioned in the employees' job specifications. An additional 25% of staff time involved non-work-related activities. We conclude that formal job descriptions do not correspond closely to the actual job requirements, a mismatch that undoubtedly creates considerable dissonance and influences staff morale and job satisfaction.

Sound criteria for judging the effects of withdrawal will be based on an objective, systematic, and meaningful taxonomy of job-related activities. There are, however, other indices of employee performance. The most important effects are those on clients. We propose that these should be considered the ultimate criteria, recognizing that this is a value judgment.

EXTENT OF TURNOVER

The broad definition of turnover, accepted by organizational researchers and by the U.S. Department of Labor, is individual movement across the membership boundaries of an organization. The definition of an organization is important because this influences which moves are counted as turnover. For instance, in a public residential facility, staff members who move from one unit to another within the institution usually are not counted as turnover because they remain within the same organization. On the other hand, if the living unit were defined as the organization, then such moves would represent turnover. It probably matters very little to the individual resident whether the technician moved next door or to Botswana. Turnover rates generally consider the institution as a whole, however, rather than a collection of living units. Even within an institution, some units experience a high degree of turnover, whereas others experience very little. In some institutions, particularly where labor unions are strong, unit and shift assignments are based almost entirely on seniority.

Public Institutions

The most general question we may ask is what is the extent of turnover among direct-care staff in institutions and in group homes? At least five surveys, either regional or national, provide relevant data, summarized in Table 2.

TABLE 2   Turnovers Among Basic-Care Employees in Public Residential Facilities (Either Regional or National Surveys)

		Turnover [a]		Median length of service of leavers	
Source	N	Annual average	Range	Average	Range
Bensberg and Barnett (1966)	37	31[b]	2-102	N.A.	N.A.
Sheerenberger (1978)	193	26	3-126	N.A.	N.A.
Zaharia and Baumeister (1979)	12	29	7-50	15 mo.	(3-42)
Lakin and Bruininks (1981)	71	30[c]	2-157	10 mo.	N.A.
Scheerenberger and Jones (1980)	145	35[d]	5-164	N.A.[e]	N.A.

[a] In percentages.
[b] Regional sample, southeastern states, based on 1966 data.
[c] Average weighted for size of core staff.
[d] Includes licensed practical nurses, although the number of these must be relatively small.
[e] Although median length of service data were not provided, the authors did report that 28% of the leavers terminated within the first 3 months. If one extrapolates on the basis of our own survival curves, then we estimate the median length of service among leavers in this study to be between 8 and 10 months.

The first survey, in the southeastern region of the United States, involved 22 to 37 public institutions in 1962, 1963, and 1966 (Bensberg & Barnett, 1966). The precise measure of turnover is not explicit, but we infer from another article (Butterfield, Barnett, & Bensberg, 1966) that they used the crude separation index for both voluntary and involuntary terminations. In his 1977 national survey of public residential services, Scheerenberger (1978) collected data on turnover among technician-level staff in 193 institutions. The measure was the crude separation index without differentiation between voluntary and involuntary terminations. Neither study reported data on length of service.

Lakin and Bruininks (1982) surveyed a large number of both public and private facilities, gathering turnover data from 71 of 75 randomly selected institutions stratified according to census and geographical location. Demographic, personal, and organizational variables were gathered, as well as crude separation rate (both voluntary and involuntary separations) and mean length of service of leavers. Although administrators received a formula for computing turnover, they also had the opportunity to use data from their existing records or simply their "best estimate." Undoubtedly, some took the latter approach, contributing an indeterminate error of measurement in their turnover data. Lakin and Bruininks did try to obtain a more-precise turnover estimate by recording all direct-care terminations for one month. This measure, when expanded to an annual average, resulted in an estimated turnover rate of 36%, somewhat higher than that reported by administrators. One problem is that turnover shows seasonal variations, and the particular month selected may not have been representative.

In another retrospective national study, Scheerenberger and Jones (1980) reported on 145 public residential facilities for fiscal year 1978–1979. We surmise that their measure was the Labor Turnover Index without a distinction between controllable and uncontrollable terminations, although this was not stated.

In the only prospective study of turnover, we monitored 12 public institutions over a period of 9 months in 10 states representing 5 of the Federal Service Regions (Zaharia & Baumeister, 1979b). Measures used were labor turnover rate and median length of service of leavers, based on actual number of separations. A distinction was made between controllable and noncontrollable turnover.

Considering these variations in sampling and calculation, as well as historical period, the average estimates in Table 2 are remarkably consistent. From Bensberg and Barnett's study in 1966 to the most recent studies, the average remains about 30% per year.

It may be of some interest to compare turnover in these public institutions to that reported for other types of organizations. Compared to other industrial nations, the United States has been highly mobile; thus, turnover needs to be viewed in a relativistic context. The Bureau of Labor Statistics, Department of Labor, and the Bureau of National Affairs report monthly turnover rates (voluntary separations and layoffs) by region and type of industry. Reviewing the 1980 data (Bureau of National Affairs), we find an annual turnover rate of approximately 17% across all industries. In the health-care segment, the annual turnover rate of approximately 24%

is only 6% lower than rates for mental retardation institutions and represents the highest rate of turnover among all industries. Clearly, mobility of basic-care workers in institutions for mentally retarded individuals is high, although rates may be even higher among smaller private residential programs.

The average turnover rates represented in Table 2, although showing high consistency across studies and over time, also conceal a great deal of variation. All national studies except Zaharia and Baumeister's (1979b), revealed some institutions with turnover rates of more than 100% and others with virtually no employee movement. Even within the same state where common civil service regulations, resident living practices, and salary scales apply, considerable variation exists among institutions. Zaharia and Baumeister (1979b) observed a range from 10% to 53% for Tennessee's 3 public institutions in 1978. In the same year, 5 Massachusetts institutions ranged from 17% to 55% (Coleman, 1979), and 12 Texas institutions ranged from 38% to 88% (Ganju, 1979).

Local economic conditions, variations in living practices, differing managerial styles, the reputation of the institution, and a host of other external factors may contribute to variations, which we discuss more thoroughly later. We also have observed considerable differences across units within the same institution. For example, in one Tennessee institution in 1977, we found employee turnover rates among 16 living units that ranged from 14% to 108%. Apparently, employee attrition also is influenced by specific working conditions and intraorganizational factors.

Community Facilities

In their national study, Lakin, Bruininks, Hill, and Hauber (1982) gathered turnover data on 137 private residential facilities, most of which were group homes. Weighted for total sample size, mean rate of crude turnover in the nonpublic facilities was 55% (ranging from 0 to 400%), contrasted with 30% for the public residential facilities. Median length of service of separating personnel was 5.8 months, compared with 10.1 months among institutional staff. They also observed that very small facilities, housing six or fewer residents, experienced high turnover rates, averaging 87% annually.

These results are generally consistent with those reported by George and Baumeister (1981), who observed an annual controllable turnover rate of 73% among house managers in 47 group homes in Tennessee (1978–1979). (Owner-operated facilities, of which there were 33 in the Lakin study, were treated as a special case. Primary-care providers in this type of facilities were, as might be expected, highly stable. Of the 33 primary caretakers in this sample, 31 were still working after 1 year.) During the same period of time, Tennessee's three public residential facilities averaged about 28%. We further compared the 10 agencies that operated only one group home and 11 that operated more than one. Among the single-home agencies, the annual controllable turnover rate averaged exactly 100%, with a 5.5-month median length of service, whereas the multiple-home agencies averaged 65% turnover and an 8.0-month median length of service. Perhaps the multiple-home agencies attracted different types of applicants, or management practice may have affected employee turnover. About one third of the attrition among employees in multiple-base agencies was due to dismissal, which is a higher rate than that in single-home agencies or public institutions.

Additional studies of group homes have been reported in which staff turnover was measured. Landesman-Dwyer, Stein, and Sackett (1976) found that 42% of the group homes they studied in the state of Washington experienced annual turnover rates of 100% or greater. Dellinger and Shope (1978) also observed high turnover rates among group home personnel in Pennsylvania, with an estimated median length of service of 8 months. They concluded that staff retention is a greater cause for concern than staff recruitment, pointing to "stress" as a major contributor to attrition.

SURVIVAL

To capture the nature of attrition over time, an analysis that may be particularly useful for a theoretical account of the process of socialization of new employees into the organization, we plotted survival curves of cohorts of basic-care workers in both institutional and community settings. Figure 1 presents a survival curve for a cohort of 278 employees hired over a 1-year period by a fairly large public institution in the Southeast that experienced high turnover (about 50%). We tracked the cohort for only 36

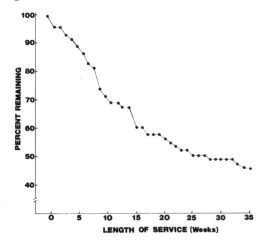

FIGURE 1.   Survival curve for a cohort of 278 employees in a public institution in the Southeast.

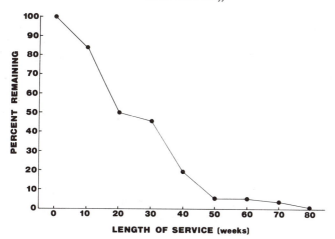

FIGURE 2. Survival curve for a cohort of group-home managers in Tennessee.

weeks, but the curve is similar to that observed in other industries. The major conclusion is that survival is characterized by two functions: a rapid drop over the first 15 weeks and a more gradual decline thereafter. These may indicate two distinct forms of turnover that are mediated either through a different set of variables or, more likely, a common set of variables that are differentially weighted. Accordingly, intervention strategies to curtail attrition would need to consider the variables that differentially influence separate segments of the curve.

In Figure 2 similar data are shown for a smaller cohort of group-home managers in Tennessee. Although the time course is much longer, essentially the same functions are evident as in Figure 1.

EXTENT OF ABSENTEEISM

Relatively little attention has focused on absenteeism, perhaps reflecting difficulty in distinguishing between avoidable and unavoidable absenteeism. We believe that most administrators view absenteeism (and tardiness) as a nuisance, but not as a major factor in the functioning of their organization. In fact, financial and performance costs owing to poor attendance may exceed costs associated with turnover. Studies in the generic literature show that turnover generally is highest among employees in whom the organization has the least investment, whereas absenteeism is higher among the employees in whom the organization has the greatest investment (Porter & Steers, 1973). Whether this generalization applies to mental retardation service organizations is uncertain, although our own data suggest that this is indeed the case.

As we have noted earlier, absenteeism is often regarded as a less-severe form of withdrawal than is turnover, but with different thresholds. Although this view may be too simplistic, some distinctions are important. From the employee's point of view, absenteeism usually carries far fewer negative consequences than quitting. Moreover, being absent from work is a relatively easy decision to make and, judging from our own observations, is more likely to be a spontaneous act than is termination. Absenteeism, for some employees, is a substitute for turnover, a sort of "release valve" that helps them avoid the decision to quit (George & Baumeister, 1981). What needs to be investigated is whether chronic absenteeism is a precursor to turnover or whether it is an alternative form of withdrawal.

In our prospective study of 12 public institutions (Zaharia & Baumeister, 1979b), we evaluated unscheduled absences. The average monthly lost-time rate was 6.7%, ranging from 4.7% to 11.0% across institutions, with absences per worker ranging from .3 to 2.6 days. The proportion of the absentee group (the percentage of the work force contributing to absenteeism) ranged from 26% to 100%. Finally, average length of absence ranged from 5.2 hours to 11.4 hours.

Do these results imply a management problem for public residential facilities? This is difficult to answer because it hinges on the question of what is "acceptable." Certainly, there are both programmatic and financial costs associated with absenteeism. Johnson and Peterson (1975) suggest that a lost-time rate in industrial organizations exceeding 5% to 6% is of serious concern. By this criterion, some of the facilities in our study have an absenteeism problem. The type of organization also must be considered. In labor-intensive service organizations, in which continuity of program is important, lost-time rates of this magnitude definitely impair organization functioning. One facility that we studied demonstrates this point. During a representative month, we found that 5,920 hours of 83,752 scheduled work hours were "lost" to unscheduled absences. This equals 740 shifts or an average lost-time rate of 7%. Frequency rate was nearly 6 absences for every 10 workers. The proportionate size of the group was 64%. This means that on any given day, supervisors could rely with confidence on only one third of their direct-care personnel. Not only did this cause a serious programming problem within a given living unit, but there was "ripple" effect when technicians were pulled from their assigned units to cover for this temporary labor shortage. There was a lost-time rate average of 2% to 16% among 16 units, but all units experienced serious program disruptions because employees were borrowed from the low loss-rate units.

Because this intrainstitutional mobility, caused by absenteeism, had become an institutional ritual over a long period of time, it was widely accepted as a "fixed cost." Accordingly, measures to increase attendance were minimal and nonexistent. Whether fewer absences would improve overall program integrity and client outcomes remains to be determined.

In our study, we classified absenteeism as occurring under sick-leave provisions versus leave without pay. We found that only 2 of 16 units had higher absenteeism rates in the latter category. Absenteeism correlated strongly with availability of sick leave; employees who had used up their sick leave were less inclined to get "sick."

Although absenteeism appears to be a major problem in public residential institutions, we have found markedly lower absenteeism rates in group homes (George & Baumeister, 1981). In a study of 47 group homes, we observed an absenteeism rate of less than 1% in a year. This figure is consistent with that from an earlier unpublished study of 10 group homes, in which we found much higher turnover rates than those found in 3 institutions in the same state. Although this inverse relationship between turnover and absenteeism may appear to contradict our assumption that the two forms of withdrawal are mediated by the same classes of variables, it is our impression that the group homes represent a special case. We believe that the live-in staffing patterns characteristic of group homes that we studied did not permit direct-care staff to take sick days. Moreover, there were few support staff to cover during absences. In interviews, staff reported remaining on duty when ill or tired for two reasons: no replacement staff and no place to go in any event. In these homes, employees appeared overworked. They reported a mean number of 60 work hours per week, which our observations (interval sampling) confirmed. The inability to "escape" coupled with an excessive and uncompensated work load probably triggers a great deal of turnover.

We suggest the hypothesis that part of the high turnover among house managers may be attributable to their inability to get any respite, a conclusion also reached by Dellinger and Shope (1978). In this sense, some absenteeism may be desirable to forestall more serious withdrawal behavior.

CONSEQUENCES OF WITHDRAWAL

Most of the generic research on the subject of turnover has focused on causes and correlates and what little there is in the mental retardation literature is no exception. Part of the reason, of course, is that negative effects are hard to calculate or evaluate. Perhaps there is also the assumption that some turnover is good for the organization—a natural sort of weeding out of malcontents and poor performers. Certainly some amount of turnover is desirable, for rather obvious reasons; but the extent and nature of the turnover problem observed in mental retardation service programs can hardly be viewed as wholesome. This is particularly true in view of the fact that turnover occurs most frequently among new employees, giving them little opportunity to infuse "new life" into the organization.

We divide turnover costs into (a) direct monetary cost, (b) direct program consequences, and (c) indirect effects on the organization and its employees.

Monetary Costs

Because 80% of the cost of service programs is in salaries, we must ask how turnover contributes to this. All new employees cost more than just their salary, although most managers tend to underestimate these costs. We hypothesize that employees whose jobs require learning through actual work experience are the most expensive to replace. In addition, we propose that the larger the bureaucratic system, the greater the position-replacement costs will be. Using the human resource accounting model described by Flamholtz (1974), we estimated turnover costs for institutional and group-home workers (George & Baumeister, 1981; Zaharia & Baumeister, 1978a). We considered the extent of replacement costs, including acquisition (advertising, screening, interviewing, health certification, vacancy coverage, and clerical processing), training (organization orientation, classroom teaching, work station orientation, on-the-job training by supervisors, and unearned salary up to proficiency), separation (unearned salary due to lost proficiency, clerical processing, and exit interviewing), and any purchased materials. The replacement costs then are apportioned on a per-inductee basis. Obviously, some costs can be measured more reliably than others. For instance, we did not differentially compute costs associated with replacing a highly competent employee with an equally skilled new employee.

TABLE 3   Technician Replacement Costs in Three
Southeastern Facilities

Component	Facility A		Facility B		Facility C		Average
Acquisition	$ 250.58	(16.1%)	$ 127.70	(8.8%)	$ 84.52	(5%)	$ 154.27
Advertisement	None		None		None		
Initial screening	12.58		64.94		11.27		29.60
Interviewing	27.82		6.24		53.01		29.02
Clerical processing	8.43		4.82		4.91		6.05
Health certification	74.00		27.42		None		50.71
Vacancy costs	127.75		24.28		15.33		55.79
Training	$1196.15	(76.8%)	$1260.08	(86.4%)	$1483.74	(88.6%)	$1313.32
Formal orientation	68.00		27.02		34.84		43.29
Work area orientation	36.04		25.52		57.42		39.66
Classroom training	None		260.30		101.66		180.98
On-the-job training	360.11		306.24		358.02		341.46
Time to proficiency	732.00		641.00		931.80		768.27
Separation	$ 110.63	(7.1%)	$ 69.72	(4.8%)	$ 105.00	(6.3%)	$ 95.12
Lost proficiency	102.20		62.92		99.65		88.26
Clerical processing	8.43		3.90		3.20		5.18
Exit interview	None		2.90		2.15		2.53
Totals	$1557.36		$1457.50		$1673.26		$1562.71

In Table 3, we present cost data for three public institutions in the Southeast (Zaharia & Baumeister, 1978a). Controllable turnover ranged from 10% to 53%. The absolute dollar figures grossly underestimate current costs of turnover nationally, because the base salary plus benefits for a new technician were only $483 per month. Even so, the average cost of replacement was over $1,500 per person. In one facility, over $412,000 (total budget of $9,000,000) was spent on replacement in one year. Projecting to the current situation, with an annual turnover rate of about 30%, this translates into sizeable expenditures for essentially avoidable emergent organizational behavior.

Just by way of example, Scheerenberger and Jones (1980) reported that 19,408 basic-care staff in 145 public institutions resigned during fiscal year 1978–1979. If we assume replacement costs per employee of $2,000, then almost $40 million was spent by the taxpayer simply to replace direct-care employees. During the same year, over 3,000 professionals also had to be replaced (costs unknown). Because residential care for mentally retarded individuals is a tax-supported industry, there may be little incentive for managers to reduce costs associated with turnover and other forms of withdrawal.

In addition to providing cost esimates, this type of force-cost analysis also reveals the nature of the expenditure process. Clearly, most of the costs associated with replacement of technicians arise from training, particularly in bringing new employees to proficiency.

A similar strategy was employed by George and Baumeister (1981) to estimate the cost of house-managers turnover in group homes. Estimates were made of recruitment costs (advertising, interviewing, processing), training (orientation, pre- and inservice, time to proficiency), separation (vacancy, exit interview), and processing. The number of applicants interviewed and hired were included in the calculation. Separate cost estimates were made for single-group-home agencies and multiple-group-home agencies. The average estimated cost to replace one house manager in the small organization was $466; for the larger organization the cost was $581. The two categories that accounted for the bulk of the replacement costs were acquisition and staff overload. The time to train to proficiency accounted for practically none of the expenditure. One interpretation of this finding is that simply having a staff member on the job, irrespective of quality of performance, was all that really counted in these group homes. This was not true in the institutional settings where staff training accounted for the largest proportion of the replacement costs. One might be tempted to conclude, from these data, that turnover is less costly in community settings than in institutions, and on an absolute basis that does appear to be the case. There are other considerations, however. One is that house managers received little more than perfunctory introduction to their jobs because the organization could not afford the costs associated with formal training of new employees. A second consideration is that turnover was much higher in these group homes than in the institutions we studied, perhaps because employees were given no formal systematic introduction to their jobs but were simply put "on the line." The primary consideration, however, is that, in the group homes, there seemed to be no formal acknowledgment of the likelihood that experienced house managers are more valuable than are inexperienced house managers.

Programmatic Impact

Research on the impact of employee withdrawal from mental retardation service settings is practically nonexistent. Nevertheless, it is possible to draw some tentative conclusions from generic literature on the topic (e.g., Mobley, 1982; Price, 1977). The most relevant outcome variable is the direct effects of employee withdrawal on client well-being. Clearly, a poorly motivated employee, or one unfamiliar with the needs of a client, or one unskilled in the caregiver role is not likely to be effective in implementing programs. Exactly how staff turnover influences the prevalence of such employees is not certain. Several observational studies of staff–resident interactions indicate that their quantity and quality are surprisingly low, at least in institutions, as noted earlier; that is, staff, whether new or old, simply do not interact very much with clients. Munro, Duncan, and Seymour (1983) recently reported that staff turnover has little direct effect on residents' behavior. The dependent measures were frequency and duration of time-out, as well as frequency of negative behavior recorded in ward incident logs. Several interpretations of this finding are possible. One is, obviously, that staff turnover has little actual effect on resident behavior, an interpretation with which Munro et al. are uncomfortable. Another possibility is that these dependent measures may be too global or insensitive to capture the subtle effects of employee turnover on interpersonal interactions. We believe that systematic, direct observation of staff and resident behavior would provide far more informative data about impact on clients. Alternatively, Munro et al. suggested that residents had been exposed to such high rates of staff turnover that they learned to cope with unstable relationships. Furthermore, we suspect that the client's age is an important variable, with effects of turnover being more devastating to children. It would be premature to conclude on the basis of this one study that staff turnover produces no negative consequence for residents; however, this is a valuable study in that it begins to address the nature of the relationship in measurable terms.

Indirect Effects on the Organization and Employees

RATED PERFORMANCE

From the point of view of program integrity, one of the most important questions concerns the performance of leavers and stayers. If poor performers are leaving, then turnover may enhance overall effectiveness. If leavers disproportionately include excellent employees, then the effects are more likely to be adverse. The generic literature (Price, 1977) indicates that good performers are more likely to leave, although this varies somewhat across vocations. What little data we have in the mental retardation literature suggest that there is no significant difference in rated performance of those who stay and those who leave voluntarily.

Typically, performance measures are obtained on the basis of supervisor ratings. That type of performance evaluation is apt to be highly biased. What the supervisor sees as good or bad performance may have little to do with client outcome. In any case, the few studies in the mental retardation literature relating turnover to performance have relied on this measure.

Brannon and Zaharia (1983) compared performance ratings of 144 separated institutional staff members with stayers, matched on length of tenure, sex, age, work area, and job classification. A summary evaluation score was obtained for each employee across several different performance domains. The mean performance score of the stayers was slightly but significantly superior to that of the leavers. If one accepts the supervisor ratings as a valid index of performance, then one may conclude that turnover occurs differentially relative to overall performance. Nevertheless, there was considerable overlap between the two groups; leavers had good performance ratings, and many stayers had poor ratings. Lakin and Bruininks (1981) also obtained supervisor performance ratings for separating staff members. On a 3-point scale, direct-care staff members who terminated were as likely to be rated as excellent (18%) as they were as poor (19%). We observed a similar pattern in our study of group-home staff, with 24% of terminating full-time house managers rated above average and 30% below average (George & Baumeister, 1981). Neither study, however, compared stayers and leavers within the organization. When leavers were stratified by age and education (Lakin & Bruininks, 1981), it appeared that separating employees who were older or better educated were more likely to be rated positively than were young or less educated ones.

If we accept these findings at face value, there is little reason to be sanguine about the high rates of turnover in either group homes or public institutions. The turnover process does not, on the whole, eject the poor performer and, therefore, increase organizational effectiveness.

ADMINISTRATIVE CONSEQUENCES

High turnover produces increased demands on administrative personnel, owing to the need to recruit, train, supervise, and terminate employees. Lakin and Bruininks (1981) reported small but consistent correlations between ratio of administrative staff to direct-care staff and crude turnover rates. We have observed the same phenomenon in our own studies, concluding that turnover and absenteeism increase administrative work load and intensity. This seems to be the case for virtually all types of organizations but is especially characteristic of direct-service organizations (Price, 1977). For instance, Kasarda (1973) evaluated consequences of teacher turnover in public schools and found that the proportion of administrative staff (and overhead costs) correlated directly with teacher turnover.

Other administrative consequences associated with high turnover may include (a) increased formalization of rules, regulations, and policies; (b) greater centralization of decision making; (c) disruption of communication patterns with concomitant decreases in cohesiveness; and (d) greater legal and advocacy problems for the institution. Such effects have been observed in other types of organizations (Mobley, 1982) but have not yet been evaluated in residential service programs.

VARIABLES RELATED TO TURNOVER

Personal Variables

A profile of leavers and stayers in any organization depends upon a variety of variables, including location, employment alternatives, management style, pay, job requirements. Nevertheless, there are some generalizations possible that may be of value for understanding the nature of the withdrawal process.

SEX

In the generic literature, considerable attention is directed to gender (e.g., Mobley, 1982). The conclusion that we draw from this literature is that it is not possible to make a generalization without taking into account, at the very least, the nature of the organization.

The job of direct-care worker in residential institutions and community settings is predominantly a female vocation. About 75% of the direct-care staff in public institutions and community facilities are women (Zaharia & Baumeister, 1978b). It therefore follows that more women will leave than men. The question is whether there is a disproportion of leavers between the two sexes. In our regional and national studies of institutions, we found that men are disproportionately represented among the leavers, by about 15% to 20%. In community settings, however, women were more likely than men to leave the position of house manager (George & Baumeister, 1981). Lakin and Bruininks (1981) reported a small, but nonsignificant sex disparity (more men than women) among leavers in their national survey of both public and private facilities.

Generally, when gender differences are found in turnover rates, economic explanations are invoked. We propose that social factors also may be implicated because we found significantly lower turnover rates and higher job satisfaction among both men and women when the unit work force was balanced between the sexes (Zaharia & Baumeister, 1978b).

AGE

Younger workers are significantly more likely to leave than are older workers, in both community and institutional settings (Lakin & Bruininks, 1981; Zaharia & Baumeister, 1979b). Age also correlates positively with length of service, as does age when first employed; that is, older employees are more likely to remain with the organization. Even controlling for length of service and sex, age and turnover continue to be correlated in our data.

Obviously, a number of explanations come to mind to account for this relationship between age and stability: (a) younger people are, as a group, more restless and mobile, (b) older workers have greater family responsibilities that encourage job stability (we have found that people who are married and/or own their homes are less likely to leave), (c) younger people have more difficulty accepting institutional routine and formalization of rules (we have found higher job satisfaction scores among older employees), and (d) younger workers are more likely to return to school. There is also the possibility that the relationship between age and turnover is modulated by other factors, such as education. The younger employees in the institutions we studied actually had higher educational levels (more grades in school) than did older workers.

EDUCATION

Another fairly consistent finding is that amount of formal education predicts turnover and length of service (Lakin & Bruininks, 1981; Zaharia & Baumeister, 1978b). Workers with some college education are two to three times more likely to terminate than those who have less than a high school education. Again, there are a number of possible explanations for this relationship, but it seems intuitively obvious that better educated employees are able to compete for higher paying jobs.

PERSONALITY VARIABLES

Many earlier studies of attendant tenure and job performance were focused on consideration of personality attributes of individual employees to improve selection. A common assumption was that personality predicts "success" (i.e., length of service) better than do other variables (e.g., Cliff, Newman, & Howell, 1959). The reasoning is that certain personality types may adjust better to institutional life and routine than do others. Cleland and Peck (1959) proposed the most extensive theoretical analysis along these lines. They characterized the institution as a hierarchical and patriarchal social system that demands certain types of behavior from its members. The technician was judged to be at the lowest level of the formal decision-making process and yet in the ward setting was perceived as a virtual ruler. Despite legal and professional challenges to institutions, many of which have wrought significant programmatic, structural, and demographic changes over the past 15 years, direct-care workers still have the least influence in the formal organization, yet maintain tremendous social significance in the residents' lives.

Relying largely on theories of authoritarianism, Cleland and Peck (1959) generated four basic hypotheses: (a) attendants with long tenure (10 years or more) will score higher on the California F-Scale (a measure of authoritarianism) than will those employed 6 months or less; (b) attendants with longer tenure will have stronger rural background and orientation than will short-tenure attendants; (c) long-tenure attendants will report greater acceptance of the standards and authority of their own parents, and (d) there will be other related personality differences between those who have short tenure and those who have long tenure.

To test these hypotheses, they controlled for age, measured IQ, socioeconomic background, and education. Despite a number of flaws, this is a competent and thorough study, both theoretically and methodologically. The results support the above hypotheses. (Note: these stayers had the highest mean F-scale score ever reported in the literature up to that time.) Whether this relationship between tenure and authoritarianism maintains today is uncertain, but it is still plausible.

Most studies of employee personality as a predictor of attendant tenure have lacked a theoretical basis, and their findings probably reflect alpha errors. Muchinsky and Tuttle (1979) concluded that personality variables, except at the extremes, have only a marginal impact on turnover. We doubt that standardized paper-and-pencil tests and personality inventories will ever he highly predictive of tenure. There may be greater benefits to be realized from using measures of such variables as job satisfaction and sociometric procedures (Schuk, 1967; Zaharia & Baumeister, 1978b).

There is less to be said about the relationship between personal variables and absenteeism. Based on our own unpublished studies in several southeastern institutions, we can suggest the following: (a) older technicians tend to have fewer, but more prolonged absences; (b) women have slightly poorer attendance records; (c) the greater the time and distance to get to work, the poorer the attendance record; (d) single workers with fewer family responsibilities have more absences; (e) the longer the tenure on the job, the better the attendance record, but the longer the absence when it does occur.

SELF-SELECTION

As in other fields, the people who apply for work in mental retardation settings do not necessarily represent a random sample of all persons who wish to work; that is, some type of self-selection occurs prior to application. Research is needed regarding this self-selection process. From our own informal observations, we believe that highly educated individuals are less likely to apply, and when they do, they tend to regard employment in residential settings as temporary. In many cases, job applicants have only a vague idea of what their jobs will be like.

Integration Variables

There are a number of important variables that could be considered "personal" but that directly interact with specific situational factors and surely affect the integration of the new employee into the organization. These variables have more theoretical appeal than do demographic ones.

JOB SATISFACTION

Job satisfaction, on face value, is a compelling variable to investigate. Locke (1976) described job satisfaction as an index of the discrepancy between what an organization provides and what an individual values. Price (1977) characterized satisfaction as the "degree to which members of a social system have a positive affective orientation toward membership in the system" (p. 79).

Lower job satisfaction is associated with higher turnover, although the correlations usually are less than .4 (Locke, 1976; Price, 1977). It is probable that poor performance and absenteeism also correlate with satisfaction. To discuss job satisfaction as a single measure, however, may be misleading. Jobs have diverse aspects that may be differentially satisfying and, in turn, differentially predictive of turnover. These include satisfaction with pay, promotion opportunities, job content, co-workers, supervision, and clients.

A number of instruments have been devised to measure job satisfactions. The Job Descriptive Index, developed by Smith, Kendall, and Hulin (1969), is probably the most carefully constructed and most thoroughly researched instrument of its kind. In addition to a job-in-general score, it provides subscale satisfaction scores regarding work, pay, promotional opportunities, and co-workers. Because a large data base exists on industrial norms, we selected this measure to study direct-care workers (Zaharia & Baumeister, 1979a).

Our sample consisted of 357 basic-care technicians (male:female ratio = 1:7) in four southeastern public institutions. Because no significant sex difference emerged on any subscales, we used norms for female workers in industry (Smith et al., 1969). The technicians we studied were significantly less satisfied on all subscales than were the industry employees. The most marked difference was on the pay subscale, where the institutional workers expressed extreme dissatisfaction. Other findings of interest were: (a) black technicians were less satisfied than were white technicians with their work and supervision, (b) satisfaction with work increased with age, (c) length of service was not correlated significant with satisfaction scores, (d) work satisfaction in units where both men and women technicians worked was higher than that of staff members in all male or all female units, and (e) the larger the basic-care staff, the less satisfied technicians were with their coworkers.

Despite the fact that the job satisfaction scores of these employees were generally depressed when compared with industrial norms, we also observed considerable variability among the four institutions. Three of these facilities were in the same state, with a common pay schedule and common civil service regulations. The variability among these institutions indicates the importance of organizational patterns and managerial practices. For instance, the finding that work satisfaction was higher in coed units suggests that the typical staffing pattern removes the collegial, heterosexual relationships found in most other occupations. This finding argues not only for modifications in living-unit patterns, but also for aggressive recruitment of men into what has historically been a matriarchal occupation. The discriminative power of the Work subscale, in particular, suggests that the design of the technician occupation is seriously lacking in motivating potential; that is, their jobs require fewer skills, allow less autonomy, and are less enriched than are other jobs in the typical residential facility.

Although we did not directly assess the relationship between job satisfaction and withdrawal in this study, given the fact that technicians generally view their pay and their work as unrewarding, it reasonably follows that dissatisfaction of this magnitude will be expressed in high-turnover and high-absenteeism rates. In an unpublished follow-up study, we found a significant negative correlation, $r = -.49$, between scores on the Work subscale and lost-time rate across 31 living units in two institutions. We also have observed that turnover is lower in small institutional units (Zaharia & Baumeister, 1978b), and those groups, as we have shown, are relatively more satisfied.

Porter, Steers, Mowday, and Boulian (1974) also used the Job Descriptive Index in a study of technicians in a large state institution on the West Coast over a 10.5-month period. The authors of this longitudinal study recognized that attitudinal factors were likely to change over time and that these patterns of change may be more important than any single measurement. The Job Descriptive Index was administered at four intervals 10 and 2 weeks prior to completion of training and 2 and 10 weeks after employees were assigned to work. Stayers and leavers were compared. On every subscale, at every interval, the stayers had higher satisfaction scores than did the leavers. Porter et al. demonstrated that the relationship between turnover and attitudes is strongest when an employee is close to quitting.

Another interesting finding was that pay satisfaction discriminated leavers versus stayers only on the first measure (i.e., just after being hired). This suggests that aspects of the job that trigger withdrawal may change over time. Our own results show exactly the same pattern across subscales of the Job Descriptive Index as that of Porter et al. On the other hand, their subjects were significantly more satisfied with pay and promotional opportunities than were ours, perhaps reflecting regional differences in these respects.

George and Baumeister (1981) also administered the Job Descriptive Index to house managers in community settings. The results were virtually identical with those that we had observed in our studies of institutional personnel. In this case, a weak but significant inverse relationship was observed between Pay scores and Length of Service. As in the case of the institutional technicians, pay and opportunities for promotion received the lowest ratings.

Another job satisfaction inventory that has been used extensively in the study of organization behavior is the Minnesota Satisfaction Questionnaire (Weiss, Dawis, England, & Lofquist, 1967), which purports to measure both intrinsic (e.g., feeling of doing something worthwhile, making contribution) and extrinsic (e.g., pay, policies, opportunity for advancement) satisfaction. Lakin and Bruininks (1981) used this scale with a stratified random sample of basic-care workers in 75 public residential facilities and 161 community residential facilities. They then determined whether any of the job satisfaction measures were related to tenure. The Extrinsic subscale scores significantly predicted the turnover among staff members separating from public institutions. In particular, these leavers were relatively dissatisfied with their pay and with the praise they received for doing a good job. The Extrinsic subscale also discriminated, but less clearly than among institutional employees, group-home personnel who seemed to be especially dissatisfied with their pay. Although turnover in public institutions could not be predicted on the basis of intrinsic factors, separating group-home personnel were significantly depressed on this particular factor.

The data are sparse, but some tentative conclusions seem warranted: (a) basic-care staff in both institutional and community settings are generally dissatisfied with their jobs when contrasted with workers in other industries: (b) a major source of dissatisfaction is the amount of pay, although other job aspects also produce dissatisfaction; (c) job satisfaction significantly relates to both turnover and absenteeism; (d) at least some sources of dissatisfaction could be alleviated by more creative job design and enlightened management practices; and (e) not all of the variance in withdrawal behavior can be attributed to measured satisfaction. We view the construct of job satisfaction as a person-oriented characterization of reaction to immediate circumstances that should not be considered in theoretical isolation from a constellation of other interactive variables that affect quality of care and treatment.

ORGANIZATIONAL COMMITMENT

Considerable interest has been focused recently on the strength of an employee's identification with the goals and values of a particular organization. Commitment includes job satisfaction among its specific components but also has to do with belief in and acceptance of the organization's goals, together with strong willingness to work hard in behalf of those goals. Most of the literature on the organizational commitment of mental retardation service providers is of an anecdotal and informal nature. The only systematic study of the relationship between turnover and technician commitment is that of Porter et al. (1974). They assessed commitment using a 15-item questionnaire that probed the employee's degree of loyalty to the organization, acceptance of its values, and willingness to exert effort. Scores on this scale correlated more strongly with turnover than did job satisfaction. Although satisfaction with pay predicted turnover early in the employment process, expressed commitment became a better predictor of turnover later on. Obviously, some time is required before an employee can develop an enduring sense of commitment to an organization.

AVOWED INTENTIONS

Perhaps the best way to predict turnover would be to ask employees about their intentions. If such an assessment were done periodically and done properly, it might serve useful diagnostic purposes. In the generic literature, behavioral intentions are among the best individual predictors of turnover (Mobley, 1982). Stated intentions to remain with the organization bear a strong inverse correlation with turnover (Atchison & Lefferts, 1972).

Extrainstitutional Factors

Some factors related to employee withdrawal are embedded in the broader social, historical, political, and economic fabric in which organizations exist. These determinants are not under the direct control of facility administrators, although through responsible planning the complex multivariate nature of organizations and the contextual systems that influence their effectiveness could be considered.

LOCAL ECONOMIC CONDITIONS

Generally, labor mobility is closely related to the economy and unemployment levels. In the aggregate, as unemployment increases, turnover decreases. This appears to be the case with respect to technicians in residential facilities as well. The first systematic study of this relationship was conducted by Butterfield et al. (1966) in 26 institutions in the southeast. Additional data from the Bureau of Census about the local counties included (a) percentage of labor force employed, (b) median income of all wage earners, (c) population per square mile, (d) percentage of land in farms, and (e) population increase or decrease from 1950 to 1960. County employment rate and population change together accounted for about half of the variance in turnover rates. The higher the unemployment and the faster the population growth, the lower the turnover rate. Butterfield and his associates attributed this relationship to low and noncompetitive salaries that attendant personnel are typically paid.

The importance of local economic conditions relative to turnover was confirmed by Lakin and Bruininks (1981), who found that county employment rate was the single best predictor of turnover in 71 public residential institutions. The correlation between crude turnover and unemployment rate was –.44. Starting salary was not far behind, $r = -.39$. Also, the larger the community, the greater the turnover, presumably owing to the availability of other employment opportunities. A similar pattern of correlations emerged among relatively large (65 or more residents) private residential facilities. When smaller (fewer than 65 residents) private facilities were considered, these types of economic and population variables did not predict turnover.

In a longitudinal study of 12 institutions, we failed to confirm a relationship between area unemployment and turnover, although we detected a significant difference between those institutions located in highly populated communities and those located in rural areas (Zaharia & Baumeister, 1979b). Employees in the rural area are more likely to remain on the job. Similarly, Ganju (1979) reported that the best predictor of turnover rates among Texas institutional staff was the size of the industrial sector in the surrounding community.

The relationship between local economic factors and turnover apparently is not as clearcut as commonly assumed. Although there is some evidence of an aggregate relationship between economic indices (e.g., unemployment rates) and turnover, there is still the question as to how the individual decision to quit is made. We have consistently observed as much variation in turnover between work units within the institution as between institutions. Obviously, given the pay structures used in most such service organizations, local economic variables cannot be directly implicated as a causative factor in intraorganization turnover. This is not to say that the effects might not be indirect or interactive. For instance, availability of other employment may be a "trigger" variable that lowers the threshold for leaving, depending on unit working conditions.

PAY

Pay includes salary and fringe benefits to employees for services rendered. Usually, pay and turnover are negatively related, whereas pay and satisfaction are positively correlated. In the presence of a tight job market, however, low pay may not lead directly to turnover but may produce other forms of withdrawal behavior.

By any standard, salaries for basic-care workers in the field of mental retardation are low, a circumstance long considered by superintendents of institutions and others to be a primary cause of employee turnover (Baumeister, 1970; Butterfield, 1967; McIntire, 1954). Lakin and Bruininks (1981) reported that administrators believed that poor pay and inadequate benefits were the major causes of turnover, a belief consistent with reasons provided by separating employees. Among all the types of facilities studied, pay correlated significantly with turnover.

In general, the conclusion is inevitably drawn that somewhere in the complex constellation of factors that contribute to employee withdrawal, pay must be accorded a prominent position. Studies already cited show that: (a) low pay is one of the most frequently given reasons for quitting,

(b) pay is the least satisfying aspect of the job among those still employed, and (c) a considerable disparity exists between pay for direct-care services and other jobs in the community with similar entrance requirements and performance demands. In addition, technicians regard poor pay as the preeminent reason for co-worker resignation (Minge & Bowman, 1969).

It probably would be an oversimplification, however, to assume a direct and nonmediated connection between pay and turnover. An examination of the extensive literature concerning pay and organizational effectiveness leads to the conclusion that pay variables affect worker behavior in a variety of ways for a variety of reasons. When applicants interview for technician positions, they learn about salary and benefits. Our studies indicate that about 35% of those who are offered employment never report for work. Thus, some self-selection related to salary must occur prior to employment. The low pay undoubtedly influences who applies for direct-care jobs and who accepts these positions. Theoretically, there may be important discrepancies between role expectations and reward for fulfilling this role. Salaries do have social as well as material significance, reflecting the worth attached to an individual's work.

SOCIAL STATUS

Another extrainstitutional factor that undoubtedly has an effect upon the nature of the applicant pool and the behavior of those who do accept employment involves the low social status of basic-care employees, particularly in institutional settings (Baumeister, 1970). Although this occupation has received no serious investigation in the status and prestige studies of occupations, our own unpublished data on occupational status rankings by 50 technicians place the job of institutional technician in the lowest 10%, factoring out such obvious variables as pay differential and advancement opportunities. This indicates that the direct-care workers judge their occupation to carry negative prestige, which presumably would encourage them to seek alternative employment. Not a single employee in this sample wanted his or her child to pursue this particular occupation, although 30% reported that a professional career in mental retardation could be a rewarding occupation for their own children. These attitudes are in sharp contrast to what appears to be the case in Scandinavian countries where institutional service is much more frequently regarded as a valued profession (McCormick, Balla, & Zigler, 1975).

Even within the institution itself, the technician job has extremely low status, despite hollow pronouncements from time to time by administrators and other professionals about how highly valued technicians are. In fact, direct-care employees have virtually no influence in developing organization policy, making programming decisions, or defining their own roles and responsibilities. Lakin and Bruininks (1981) found that approximately one half of the employees they interviewed expressed dissatisfaction with how institutional policy is formulated and implemented. Even in decisions involving individual clients, the technician tends to be the last consulted but the first blamed for program failure. To the extent that an organization is inefficient or ineffective, attributing the problem to a particular class of employee scarcely seems reasonable. Remedial actions must be understood in the context of the entire system.

There is a certain irony in all this because functional policy (i.e., day-to-day implementation of programming, care-giving, and decision making) is in the hands of ward personnel. Within every institution a potent subculture, involving direct-care employees and clients, with its own value systems, rewards, punishments, and contingencies operates independently of the formal organizational structure and rules. This is contrary to the impression of many administrators (and some judges) that they can control the institution.

In summary, low pay, low status, and the local economic climate seem to be the most influential external precipitants of the technicians' commitment to their jobs. Another interesting notion of external causation is the reputation an institution gains in the surrounding community (Butterfield, 1967; York-Moore, 1970). There is a question, however, as to whether this factor contributes to recruitment and withdrawal or whether it is a consequence.

Intrainstitutional Factors

A number of factors inherent in the organization itself are associated with employee stability and performance and are, more or less, under some degree of local control. Unfortunately, very little formal research has been conducted in this respect in mental retardation programs, and most of the generalizations that we can make derive from an analysis of the general literature.

MANAGEMENT STYLE

The manager as a source of employee dissatisfaction and withdrawal was considered by Cleland and Dingman (1970), who proposed that superintendents rely on outmoded, ineffective management practices and provide poor models for basic-care staff. Klaber (1969) found that 76% of the technicians blamed administrators for problems that aggravate employee withdrawal. Lakin and Bruininks (1981) reported that about half of the basic-care staff in their study were dissatisfied with the decision-making process, referring to a "static distrust" between basic-care employees and administrators. Recently, emphasis has been placed on developing effective management skills among administrators. It is possible that this sort of training makes a functional difference, although there are little data suggesting such an effect. Without doubt, considerable variability exists in institutional and community programs regarding how people-oriented versus organization-oriented a facility is.

The degree to which an organization's decision-making power is concentrated or centralized may relate to employee satisfaction, commitment, and stability. Practically every literature review indicates that high centralization of authority produces high turnover and other forms of withdrawal in virtually every type of organization. We think it safe to conclude that diffusion of decision and policy making throughout mental retardation service programs will have positive effects on employee performance and commitment. Raynes, Pratt, and Roses (1977) found that ratings by direct-care staff of their personal involvement in decision making correlated with degree of resident-oriented care practices. Furthermore, degree of perceived autonomy related to worker stability. Individual employees require independence and control over their work situation, within reasonable limits (Pettman, 1973).

Work Unit Size

In his review of the mental retardation literature, Balla (1976) stated that research is inconclusive as to whether institutional size relates to turnover. At the level of analysis he was using, it is probably the case that the relationship is weak at best. A better approach involves assessing the size of the functional work unit within the facility. Because most institutions have adopted some variant of the unit system, unit characteristics could be entered into an analysis. We have found a correlation of .62 between size of staff complement and turnover (Zaharia & Baumeister, 1978b), although the association is probably nonlinear. That is, work units that are either very large or very small generate excessive turnover. From our data we infer that the optimal number of employees to minimize turnover (and absenteeism) is around 30 staff members. We also observed a positive correlation, $r = .42$, between number of clients in a unit and turnover; however, interpretation of this correlation clearly involves other considerations. We concluded that small ($N = 30$) work groups (a) produce stronger interpersonal cohesiveness, (b) promote more rapid socialization of new employees, and (c) encourage closer and more supportive relationships between immediate supervisors and employees. Also, the greater the size of the work unit, the further the individual is from the functional decision-making process.

Client Characteristics

We are convinced that client characteristics, particularly level of independence, relate to worker satisfaction and stability. Lack of client progress is probably one source of worker dissatisfaction (Sarata, 1975). Clients who are aggressive, incontinent, and require a great deal of care may be less desirable ones with whom to work. Clients at the severe and profound levels of retardation may be regarded as the least desirable. Typically, new employees are not given any choice about their unit assignments and that probably does not help the situation. It is our impression that new employees are often dismayed by the sights, sounds, and smells they encounter in the living units. It is undoubtedly the case that unit assignment as well carries with it some sort of status differential. In one of our studies (Zaharia & Baumeister, 1978), we observed a correlation of $-.55$ between average client IQ in the unit and staff turnover; that is, the more severe the retardation, the higher the turnover rate for that unit. On the other hand, average resident IQ was not significantly correlated with absenteeism. Ganju (1979) has suggested that ambulatory ability may be more significant than cognitive ability. Severe physical disability may be more difficult for employees to accept than severe intellectual disability. In our study of staff turnover in group homes (George & Baumeister, 1981), we used another, more direct measure of adaptive behavior—the Community Skills Profile (Tennessee Department of Mental Health/Mental Retardation, 1979, a criterion-referenced adaptive behavior scale that is designed to assess the ability of retarded persons to function effectively in a particular community living environment. Scores on this scale were inversely related to turnover, r $-.43$; that is, the higher the functioning level, the lower the turnover rate. In addition, we found that the presence of severe behavior problems among clients was significantly correlated with turnover, $r = .31$. Whether this is a causal relationship, however, remains to be determined. Together, Community Skills Profile scores and behavior problems accounted for 29% of the turnover variance. Interviews with current staff also indicated that resident behavior problems are a major reason for quitting, a result Ganju (1979) also reported.

CONTROLLING WITHDRAWAL

Utlimately, the goal of organizations is to achieve their mission, not simply to reduce withdrawal. Ideally, management would attempt to increase turnover among employees whose performance is disruptive to the organization's goals, while decreasing turnover among those employees who contribute positively. As previously noted, however, objective methods for determining employee on-the-job effectiveness are not readily available. With respect to absenteeism, tardiness, and other forms of withdrawal, the negative consequences are more direct. Administrators of mental retardation service programs have paid scant attention to management strategies to enhance job commitment of basic-care personnel, despite the fact that the literature on effective human resource management is voluminous.

Exit Interview

The most common strategy employed by administrators of residential institutions to identify the causes of turnover is the exit interview. Sometimes, anonymous questionnaires are used, although the more common procedure involves an oral interview. Ostensibly, the purpose is to identify reasons that people leave and then to implement corrective interventions.

It probably does not matter that the exit interview is of dubious validity because in virtually all of the institutions that we have studied, administrators do not pay heed to this information anyway. Our own data (Zaharia & Baumeister, 1978b) indicate that after a 6-month interval, over half of our respondents reported reasons for terminating substantially different from those given at the time of initial interview. Furthermore, the reasons for quitting given later were decidedly more negative, particularly in the sense of being unappreciated for performing a stressful job under difficult conditions.

Inservice Training

Systematic inservice training programs for new employees is commonly believed to improve the quality of resident care and to increase staff motivation and job commitment (e.g., Stevens, 1963). Practically every public residential facility in the country now has some form of inservice training, if for no other reason than to meet accreditation and/or certification standards. As we have found (George & Baumeister, 1981), inservice training occurs more in institutions than in group homes.

Rather than evaluate the literature on· the effectiveness of inservice training programs, we refer readers to Butterfield's (1967) paper about effects of training on attendant behavior. His questions remain essentially unanswered today. Whether inservice training, in its present forms, minimizes turnover seems dubious. In fact, when turnover and other forms of withdrawal are high, quality inservice training is sacrificed because of the pressures to staff the facility.

An interesting model is provided by the Scandinavian National Preservice Training Centers. Employees undergo a 3-year training program focusing on practical issues of child development. Training features both classroom instruction and on-the-job training. These centers purport to: (a) raise and professionalize the status of direct-care workers, (b) screen out likely leavers, and (c) improve the quality of employees who remain (McCormick et al., 1975). Even if such a program did produce all these effects, given the nature and diversity of service-delivery systems we have developed in this country, it is unlikely that a comparable program could be initiated in the United States. Moreover, there may be social and economic constraints that militate against professionalization of the role of direct-care personnel.

Matching Employee and Job

We hypothesize that an important and practical time for intervention is during the critical initial employment period (Zaharia & Baumeister, 1978b). Among the major considerations are the following: (a) initial screening and selection procedures are of dubious validity and, furthermore, the complex government-imposed guidelines on employee selection place formidable barriers to screening on the basis of personality and demographic characteristics, those variables that are the best predictors; (b) survival curves that we have generated indicate that the bulk of turnover occurs early in the induction process; and (c) during this period an employee's experiences are still being assimilated and new accommodations formed. This entry process can be viewed as a period of socialization, the major result of which is to bring into alignment the expectations of the new employee and those of the organization (e.g., Wanous, 1980). Since the early 1950s, when Tavistock Institute investigators described this critical period and its relation to attrition, much research and theorizing have occurred regarding its component processes. Several general conclusions are: (a) early in employment, workers experience uncertainties with respect to job demands, peers, and supervisors; (b) new employees' assumptions about the organization's implicit values are often inaccurate; (c) the commitment of the new employee to the organization is tenuous and tentative; (d) new workers do not understand informal modes of communication well; (e) employee job satisfaction is not stable during this period; and (f) the speed with which new employees reach job proficiency partly depends on peer-group acceptance. If employee crisis during this transitional period are not resolved smoothly, a portion of the workforce will be constantly changing and/or the organization will have generally dissatisfied workers. If a goal of the facility, either institutional or community-based, is to recruit a stable cohort of workers, then the developmental foundation laid by formal and informal assimilation into the organization must be a primary concern.

The duration of this critical initial employment period varies with the type of organization (Wanous, 1980) but probably coincides with the point at which independent job proficiency is achieved by the new employee. From our own separation curves and from our interviews, we deduce that this process among institutional employees typically extends over the first 2 to 3 months of employment.

Both from a research perspective and from the management standpoint, the various processes, stages, and intervention events that occur within the critical initial employment period pose some important questions: (a) What are the observable episodes of the institutional critical initial employment period? (b) What criteria indicate when a new employee is considered socialized into the organization? (c) Are there identifiable crisis points in the socialization of a new employee? (d) What effect does job previewing have on a new employee? (e) What strategies during the critical period facilitate better performance of new technicians? (Zaharia & Baumeister, 1978b).

We have addressed some of these questions in our research, motivated by the idea that misaligned expectations between new employees and the organization produce dissonance that, in turn, is reflected in less-than-optimal performance, including withdrawal and turnover. In two experiments (Zaharia & Baumeister, 1981), prospective employees (N about 400) were randomly assigned to two groups. One group viewed a 12-minute color videotape designed to portray, as realistically as possible, the clients, the job tasks, pay, current employees, and other aspects of the job. The superintendent appeared on tape to state that this type of work is not rewarding to everyone. The other group was assigned to a control condition that involved the standard orientation. This method of intervention has been attempted in other types of organizational settings. Wanous (1978) proposed a model in which realistic job preview is expected to reduce staff turnover. In our study, we did not find conclusive evidence to support this hypothesis. Attrition among these employees was monitored over 9 months. After about 16 weeks, attrition was equal for the control and experimental subjects. From that point on, survival curves favored the experimental subjects by 6% to 17% on a weekly basis. Mean length of service for leavers, however, did differ significantly in favor of the experimental group. Job acceptance and hiring rates were equal for the two groups, indicating that the realistic preview did not "scare off" applicants. On the other hands, only 33% of those who applied and were offered employment actually reported for work. Considerable self-selection did occur, suggesting that the employees in this institution may be different in some important ways from those in the original applicant tool. A follow-up indicated that most of those who were eventually hired had tried but were unable to find other employment.

Another type of intervention is to help the new employee cope with stresses during this early transition period, including periodic professional and/or supervisory counseling. Assuming that the new employee is particularly vulnerable to social and job-related stress during the first few weeks, we arranged for institutional psychologists to meet weekly for 1-hour counseling sessions with new staff members. Forty new technicians received counseling focused mainly on client and peer problems on the job. This counseling was designed to provide psychological support and to convey a sense of the realities of the institutional environment. No effort was made to duplicate job training already included as part of the in-service training program. After 6 months, turnover rate in this cohort was compared with that of a group of 40 control employees who did not receive counseling. Turnover was significantly lower among counseled employees (14%) compared to control employees (26%). Lost-time rate (absenteeism) also was significantly lower in the experimental group. (10.7 days vs. 5.8 days per month). Those remaining in the experimental group also reported higher job satisfaction scores on the Job Descriptive Index, except on the Pay subscale; however, the mean subscale scores for the experimental group were still well-below industrial norms.

We believe such results indicate that withdrawal behavior can be reduced by proper attention to early, stressful events in an employee's assimilation process within an organization. We are persuaded that the most useful conceptual models of commitment and withdrawal will focus heavily upon the critical initial employment period.

CONCLUSIONS

We have summarized the findings on the causes, consequences, correlates, and control of withdrawal behavior among front-line personnel in residential programs serving mentally ·retarded clients. Further, we have added some conjecture, especially in the absence of empirical data, to support a particular viewpoint.

Our judgment is that preoccupation with univariate and simple relationships will not produce a coherent, useful conceptual model for understanding withdrawal and commitment as psychological processes. We have repeatedly referred to multivariate determinants and the multiplicity of effects that emerge from an analysis of the empirical literature, as well as the complexity of the social systems in which these services are delivered.

A number of models for conceptualizing the nature of withdrawal have been described in the broader organization literature. These are summarized well by Mobley (1982). As we examined the various conceptual models as they might apply to human service organizations in general and mental retardation agencies in particular, the most heuristic and analytic one is that proposed by Mobley, Griffeth, Hand, and Meglino (1979). Their theory integrates four major interacting processes: (a) present job satisfactions, (b) future expectations of the individual employees vis-a-vis the organization's goals and methods, (c) employment alternatives external to the particular organization, and (d) the employees' nonwork values and perceptions relative to how well the objectives and practices of the organization are consistent with their belief system. From our perspective, the advantages of this model are that most of the findings we have previously discussed are not only consistent with but predicted by this system. Furthermore, this conceptualization applies to alternative forms of withdrawal behavior, whereas other models are limited almost exclusively to turnover. Finally, a major emphasis is placed on value systems, which we view as central to any theory of an organization's effectiveness, especially when deviant groups are served. Attention to the nature of individual values has been conspicuously absent in the research literature on program effectiveness.

Initially, we assumed that service programs for mentally retarded persons can be effective and growth enhancing only when basic-care staff members are committed to these processes. Virtually all the behavioral technology that researchers can devise to produce behavior change is dependent for application on this large corps of service personnel. Given this fundamental consideration, it is disconcerting that so few researchers have been concerned with systematic analyses of variables that govern behavior of direct-care staff. These issues must be addressed in terms of an organizational framework, recognizing the complex formal and informal systems in which both staff and clients behave. Withdrawal is a process, not merely an outcome.

REFERENCES

Atchison, J. J., & Lefferts, E. A. (1972). The prediction of turnover using Herzberg's job satisfaction technique. *Personnel Psychology, 25,* 53–64.

Baker, B. L., Seltzer, G. B., & Seltzer, M. M. (1977). *As close as possible: Community residences for retarded adults.* Boston: Little, Brown.

Balla, D. (1976). Relationship of institution size to quality of care: A review of the literature. *American Journal of Mental Deficiency, 81,* 117–124.

Barr, M. W. (1913). *Mental defectives: Their history, treatment and training.* Philadelphia: Blakiston.

Barrett, B. H. (1971). Behavioral differences among an institution's backward residents. *Mental Retardation, 9,* 4–9.

Baumeister, A. A. (1970). The American residential institution: Its history and character. In A. A. Baumeister & E. C. Butterfield (Eds.) *Residential facilities for the mentally retarded.* Chicago: Aldine.

Bensberg, G. J., & Barnett, C. D. (1966). *Attendant training in southern residential facilities for the mentally retarded.* Atlanta: Southern Regional Education Board.

Blatt, B. (1970). *Exodus from pandemonium.* Boston: Allyn & Bacon.

Brannon, K. F., & Zaharia, E. S. (1983). *Organizational ejection: An analysis of the performance levels of leavers.* Unpublished manuscript.

Bruininks, R. H., Kudla, M., Wieck, C., & Hauber, F. (1980). Management problems in community residential facilities. *Mental Retardation, 18,* 125–130.

Burg, M. M., Reid, D. H., & Lattimore, J. (1979). Use of self-recording and supervision program to change institutional staff behavior. *Journal of Applied Behavior Analysis, 12,* 363–375.

Butterfield, E. C. (1967). The characteristics, selection, and training of institution personnel. In A. A. Baumeister (Ed.), *Mental retardation: Appraisal, education, and rehabilitation.* Chicago: Aldine.

Butterfield, E. C., Barnett, C. D., & Bensberg, G. J. (1966). Some objective characteristics of institutions for the mentally retarded: Implications for attendant turnover rate. *American Journal of Mental Deficiency, 70,* 786–794.

Cleland, C. C., & Dingman, H. F. (1970). Dimensions of institutional life. In A. A. Baumeister & E. C. Butterfield (Eds.), *Residential facilities for the mentally retarded.* Chicago: Aldine.

Cleland, C. C., & Peck, R. F. (1959). Psychological determinants of tenure in institutional personnel. *American Journal of Mental Deficiency, 64,* 876–883.

Cliff, N., Newman, S. H., & Howell, M. A. (1959). Selection of subprofessional hospital care personnel. *Journal of Applied Psychology, 64,* 876–883.

Coleman, T. E. (1979). *An investigation of staff turnover at five Massachusetts mental retardation facilities.* Boston: Massachusetts Department of Mental Health, Division of Mental Retardation.

Dellinger, J. K., & Shope, L. J. (1978). Selected characteristics and working conditions of direct service staff in Pennsylvania CLA's. *Mental Retardation, 16,* 19–21.

Flamholtz, E. (1974). *Human resource accounting.* Encino, CA: Dickenson.

Ganju, V. (1979). *Turnover trends among MHMR service employees in Texas state schools.* Austin: Texas Department of Mental Health and Mental Retardation.

George, M. J., & Baumeister, A. A. (1981). Employee withdrawal and job satisfaction in community residential facilities. *American Journal of Mental Deficiency, 85,* 639–647.

Iwata, B. A., Bailey, J. S., Brown, K. M., Foshee, T. J., & Alpern, M. A. (1976). A performance-based lottery to improve residential care and training by institutional staff. *Journal of Applied Behavior Analysis, 9,* 417–431.

Johnson, R. D., & Peterson, J. O. (1975). Absenteeism or attendance: Which is industry's problem? *Personnel Journal, 54,* 568–572.

Kahne, M. J. (1968). Suicides in mental hospitals: A study of the effects of personnel and patient turnover. *Journal of Health and Social Behavior, 9,* 255–266.

Kasarda, J. D. (1973). Effects of personnel turnover, employee qualifications, and professional staff ratios on administrative intensity and overhead. *Sociological Quarterly, 14,* 350–358.

King, R. D., Raynes, N. V., & Tizard, J. (1971). *Patterns of residential care: Sociological studies in institutions for handicapped children.* London: Routledge & Kegan Paul.

Kirkbridge, F. B. (1912). The institution as a factor in race conservation. In T. M. Mulry (Ed.), *New York City Conference on Charities and 'Corrections.* Albany, NY: Lyon.

Klaber, M. M. (1969). *Retardates in residence: A study of institutions.* West Hartford, CN: University of Hartford.

Lakin, K. C., & Bruininks, R. H. (1981). *Occupational stability of direct-care staff of residential facilities for mentally retarded people* (Developmental Disabilities Project on Residential Services and Community Adjustment, Project Report No. 14). Minneapolis: University of Minnesota, Department of Psychoeducational Studies.

Lakin, K. C., Bruininks, R. H., Hill, B. K., & Hauber, F. A. (1982). Turnover of direct-care staff in a national sample of residential facilities for mentally retarded people. *American Journal of Mental Deficiency, 87,* 64–72.

Landesman-Dwyer, S., Stein, J., & Sackett, G. P. (1976). *Group homes for the developmentally disabled: A behavioral and ecological description* (Report No. 2). Olympia, WA: State Department of Social and Health Services.

Locke, E. A. (1976). The nature and consequences of job satisfaction. In M. D. Dunnette (Ed.), *Handbook of industrial organizational psychology.* Chicago: Rand McNally.

McCormick, M., Balla, D., & Zigler, E. (1975). Resident care practices in institutions for retarded persons: A cross-institutional, cross-cultural study. *American Journal of Mental Deficiency, 80,* 1–17.

McIntire, J. T. (1954). Causes of turnover in personnel. *American Journal of Mental Deficiency, 58,* 375—379.

Minge, M. R., & Bowman, T. F. (1969). Attendants' view of causes for short-term employment at an institution for the mentally retarded. *Mental Retardation, 7,* 29–30.

Mobley, W. H. (1982). *Employee turnover: Causes, consequences, and control.* Reading, MA: Addison-Wesley.

Mobley, W. H., Griffeth, R. W., Hand, H. H., & Meglino, B. M. (1979). A review and conceptual analysis of employee turnover process. *Psychological Bulletin, 86,* 493–522.

Muchinsky, P. M., & Tuttle, M. L. (1979). Employee turnover: An empirical and methodological assessment. *Journal of Vocational Behavior, 14,* 43–77.

Munro, J. D., Duncan, H. G., & Seymour, L. M. (1983). Effect of front-line staff turnover on the behavior of institutionalized mentally retarded adults. *American Journal of Mental Deficiency, 88,* 328–332.

O'Connor, G. (1976). *Home is a good place: A national perspective of community residential facilities for developmentally disabled persons* (Monograph). Washington, DC: American Association on Mental Deficiency.

Pettman, B. O. (1973). Some factors influencing labor turnover: A review of research literature. *Industrial Relations, 4,* 43–61.

Pierce, P. S., Hoffman, J. L., & Pelletier, L. P. (1974). The 4-day work week versus the 5-day work week: Comparative use of sick time and overtime by direct-care personnel in an institutional facility for the severely and profoundly retarded. *Mental Retardation, 12,* 22–24.

Porter, L. W., & Steers, R. M. (1973). Organizational, work, and personal factors in employee turnover and absenteeism. *Psychological Bulletin, 80,* 151–176.

Porter, L. W., Steers, R. M., Mowday, R. T., & Boulian, P. (1974). Organizational commitment, job satisfaction, and turnover among psychiatric technicians. *Journal of Applied Psychology, 59,* 603–609.

Price, J. L. (1977). *The study of turnover.* Ames, IA: The Iowa State University Press.

Raynes, N. V., Pratt, M. W., & Roses, S. (1977). Aides' involvement in decision-making and quality of care in institutional settings. *American Journal of Mental Deficiency, 81,* 570–577.

Repp, A. C., Barton, L. E., & Brulle, A. R. (1981). Correspondence between effectiveness and staff use of instructions for severely retarded persons. *Applied Research in Mental Retardation, 2,* 237–245.

Revans, R. W. (1964). *Standards for morale.* London: Oxford University Press.

Sarata, B. (1975). Employees' satisfaction in agencies serving retarded persons. *American Journal of Mental Deficiency, 79,* 434–442.

Scheerenberger, R. C. (1978). *Public residential services for the mentally retarded, 1977.* Madison: Central Wisconsin Center for the Developmentally Disabled.

Scheerenberger, R. C. (1982). *Public residential services for the mentally retarded, 1981.* Madison: Central Wisconsin Center for the Developmentally Disabled.

Scheerenberger, R. C., & Jones, S. E. (1980). *Administrative problems: Resident abuse, salaries, turnover, overtime, and union activity.* Madison: Central Wisconsin Center for the Developmentally Disabled.

Schuk, A. J. (1967). The predictability of employee tenure: A review of the literature. *Personnel Psychology, 20,* 133–152.

Shotwell, A. M., Dingman, F., & Tarjan, G. (1960). Need for improved criteria in evaluating job performance of state hospital employees. *American Journal of Mental Deficiency, 65,* 208–213.

Smith, P., Kendall, L., & Hulin, C. (1969). *The measurement of satisfaction in work and retirement.* Chicago: Rand-McNally.

Stevens, H. A. (1963). The administrator looks at in-service training. *Mental Retardation, 65,* 208–213.

Vander Merwe, R., & Miller, S. (1975). The measurement of labour turnover. In B. O. Pettman (Ed.), *Labor turnover and retention.* New York: Halsted Press.

Veit, S. S., Allen, G. J., & Chinsky, J. M. (1976). Interpersonal interactions between institutionalized retarded children and their attendants. *American Journal of Mental Deficiency, 80,* 535–542.

Wanous, J. P. (1978). Realistic job previews: Can a procedure to reduce turnover also influence the relationship between abilities and performance? *Personnel Psychology, 31,* 251–261.

Wanous, J. P. (1980). *Organization entry: Recruitment, selection and socialization of newcomers.* Reading, MA: Addison-Wesley.

Weiss, D. J., Dawis, R. V., England, G. W., & Lofquist, L. H. (1967). *Manual for the Minnesota Satisfaction Questionnaire.* Minneapolis: University of Minnesota.

York-Moore, M. E. (1970). Paper No. 3. In E. Stephen (Ed.), *Residential care for the mentally retarded.* New York: Pergamon.

Zaharia, E. S., & Baumeister, A. A. (1978a). Estimated position replacement costs for technician personnel in a state's public facilities. *Mental Retardation, 16,* 131–134.

Zaharia, E. S., & Baumeister, A. A. (1978b). Technician turnover and absenteeism in public residential facilities. *American Journal of Mental Deficiency, 82,* 580–593.

Zaharia, E. S., & Baumeister, A. A. (1979a). Cross-organizational job satisfaction of technician-level staff members. *American Journal of Mental Deficiency, 84,* 30–35.

Zaharia, E. S., & Baumeister, A. A. (1979b). Technician losses in public residential facilities. *American Journal of Mental Deficiency, 84,* 36–39.

Zaharia, E. S., & Baumeister, A. A. (1981). Job preview effects during the critical initial employment period. *Journal of Applied Psychology, 66,* 19–22.

12
Intervention With Parents of Children With Mental Retardation

Bruce L. Baker
University of California, Los Angeles

Duncan B. Clark
Stanford University Medical School

Any consideration of the influences on a retarded child's development quite naturally begins with parents. Yet, despite the centrality of parents, especially mothers, in child development theory, parents and the home environment of mentally retarded children were long neglected in practice. Parents were felt to lack the ability to help their children learn, and the zeitgeist favored special methods in special places—institutions and schools. Even when investigators began to underscore the importance of early environment (Bronfenbrenner, 1974) provisions were seldom made for meaningful parent involvement (Strom, Rees, Slaughter, & Wurster, 1981).

Within the past 15 years, the emphasis has shifted dramatically toward extensive parent involvement (Baker, 1980; Turnbull, 1983). Federal legislation, especially the Education for All Handicapped Children Act of 1975, granted parents increased rights and responsibilities to make decisions about their child's education. Moreover, with a shift from a medical to a developmental view of retarded children (Wolfensberger, 1969) and the decreased use of institutional placement, professionals took a new look at parents and the home. Arguments were made in favor of enhancing the home environment's positive impact on the child's learning. Well-trained parents could carry over specific school programs and, hence, increase the child's learning rate and promote generalization. Also, there are some skills best taught at

Acknowledgement. Preparation of this chapter and the UCLA research reported herein were supported by Grant No. 5 R01 HD10962 from the National Institute of Child Health and Human Development.

home (e.g., toilet training) and many others that would benefit from a consistent school–home approach (e.g., language). Finally, by more effective home management of problem behaviors, parents could make the home a more pleasant place and better prepare the child for other social settings.

Services for retarded children are increasingly providing training in teaching and behavior management for their parents, and many promising programs have been described (Baker, 1984: Bricker & Bricker, 1976; Fraiberg, 1971; Fredericks, Baldwin, & Grove, 1974; Harris, Wolchik, & Weitz, 1981; Horton, 1976; Sandler, Coren & Thurman, 1983; Shearer & Shearer, 1976). Although these programs generally indicate benefits from parent training, they often lack the controls necessary for more specific conclusions. Indeed, the majority of controlled studies of parent training effectiveness have involved programs for parents of nonretarded but troublesome children. With retarded children there is a need for better controlled study of questions such as the nature of benefits, the active program ingredients, and the characteristics of families that are helped.

In this chapter we selectively review evidence concerning training for parents of mentally retarded children. Our primary focus is on the parent training activities of the Project for Developmental Disabilities (University of California, Los Angeles). We begin with a consideration of parent training approaches and then address three important questions about training effectiveness: Who participates in training? What outcomes result? Which families benefit from training?

PARENT TRAINING APPROACHES

Training programs for parents differ in overall orientation and in format. We describe training with a behavioral orientation, although programs with a reflective counseling orientation are also widespread. In behavioral programs the aim is to train teaching strategies systematically, whereas reflective programs are oriented more toward parents' feelings and attitudes. A choice between orientations is based mainly on personal values and objectives because there is little empirical basis for a decision. Tavormina (1975) compared reflective group counseling with behavioral training groups for parents of retarded children and found the latter produced more positive outcomes on measures of attitudes toward childrearing, perceptions of the child, evaluation of training, and parent and child behavior. A great deal more research, however, needs to be conducted to determine which orientation will best meet a given family's needs.

A common format of behavioral training for parents of mentally retarded children is individual consultation, wherein the trainer has a series of meetings with parent(s) and child. Sessions usually take place at an agency, although in many programs for parents of infants and preschool children, trainers employ home visits (Shearer & Shearer, 1976). In the individual format, the trainer typically demonstrates teaching methods and supervises the parent's teaching. Individual training sometimes follows a well-defined curriculum that aims at teaching specific knowledge and skills, although it more often proceeds loosely, with the trainer helping parents to solve specific problems, with little attention to general social learning principles.

Reports of successful individual training led to experiments with groups of 5 to 10 families (Hirsch & Walder, 1969; Rose, 1974; Salzinger, Feldman, & Portnov, 1970). The advantages of group training include greater parent-to-parent exchange and support, more stimulation for trainers (who usually work in pairs), a wider range of training techniques possible, and, most importantly, reduced cost per family. Using the first 53 families in the development sample, Brightman, Baker, Clark, and Ambrose (1982) investigated whether the less costly group format produces results comparable to individual training. Parents were randomly assigned to group ($n = 37$) or individual ($n = 16$) training formats, with essentially the same 10-session curriculum. In individual training, the child was usually present, so the parent could practice and obtain feedback. The groups only included the child for one meeting, thereby placing a greater burden on parents to apply what they had learned to their interactions with their children at home. Both conditions employed live and video modeling and a series of homework assignments. We hypothesized that group training would result in greater acquisition of knowledge but that individual training would produce greater gains in teaching ability. Two conclusions were apparent. First, both training conditions produced significant changes in parent knowledge, parent skills, and child behaviors. Second, group and individual training produced virtually identical outcomes. These and similar findings (Christensen, Johnson, Phillips, & Glasgow, 1980; Salzinger et al., 1970) led us to concentrate on training with a group format.

Parents-as-Teachers Curriculum

The UCLA project's studies have used the "Parents as Teachers" program, which was developed for families with moderately to severely retarded children ages 3 to 13. Training typically involves an initial assessment followed by 10, 2-hour group sessions and a postassessment. Training is conducted in groups of 8 to 10 families, with both parents encouraged to attend. The first 4 sessions focus on teaching self-help skills. Parents learn assessment and basic teaching methods, such as setting behavioral objectives, breaking skills down into components, and using reinforcement. In the 5th session parents bring their children and receive feedback on their teaching from trainers and other parents. The next 3 sessions are focused on strategies for behavior problem management and the final 2 sessions, on play skills, incidental teaching, and future planning.

Trainers do only limited didactic presentation; they rely on demonstrations, role playing, videotapes, and consultation with and between parents about progress and problems. Parents read several of the nine manuals in the *Steps to Independence Series* (Baker, Brightman, & Blacher, 1983; Baker, Brightman, Carroll, Heifetz, & Hinshaw, 1978; Baker, Brightman, Heifetz, & Murphy, 1976; Baker, Brightman, & Hinshaw, 1980). A cognitive–behavioral variation on this curriculum, which teaches parents to identify and replace maladaptive thoughts about teaching, has been used recently (see later discussion on validation sample).

PARTICIPATION IN TRAINING

Parents who join a training program are likely a select group, thereby limiting the generalization of research findings. The majority of published studies are based upon small numbers of volunteer families, and investigators rarely report on recruitment procedures or how many families were invited to participate. It is instructive to examine several reports of recruitment with larger numbers of parents of retarded children. Even when recruitment has involved personal invitations, a majority of families has declined. In Ireland, McConkey and McEvoy (1984) invited 101 families with moderately to severely retarded children to join a short-term group on teaching play skills; 39 enrolled. Morris (1973) reported that of 80 families who were sent letters inviting them to participate in group behavioral training, 41 agreed to participate but only 14 (18%) attended the initial meeting. Hetrick (1979) mailed letters to invite parents of 369 students to participate in a group communication-skills training program; 11% came to the first meeting.

Yet programs typically offer training with one particular focus and little choice of meeting time or place. A greater proportion of parents would likely participate if they were given options. Fredericks et al. (1974) offered school-based training that was individualized in content and meeting times and reported that about half of parents of children in special education classes participated. Still, reports of training are based upon a subsample of parents, and these differ from others in motivation to participate and probably in other ways as well.

In fact, we know little about how participating families do differ from others, except that middle-class families are overrepresented in most programs (Hargis & Blechman, 1979). This may in part reflect self-selection. Baker, Clark, and Yasuda (1981) offered parent training to all 74 families with moderately to severely retarded children in a public school. The 18 (24%) who joined were more educated that were the nonjoiners. McConkey and McEvoy (1984), however, did not find that parents who enrolled were different from nonjoiners on socioeconomic variables. Joiners may also be more involved with their child's activities. McConkey and McEvoy found that joiners spent more time in play activities than did nonjoiners, and Baker, Clark, and Yasuda found that joiners attended more school activities. Baker et al. also found that children of joiners were more retarded and had more behavior problems that interfered with learning. These greater child difficulties may have been one reason these parents were motivated to seek training. The implication of these findings is that outcome results have limited external validity. To the extent that parents who join a training program are better educated, more involved with their child, experience more difficulties, and perhaps are different in other ways, their results may not readily generalize to other parents of developmentally disabled children.

PARENT TRAINING OUTCOME

The choice of outcome measures is influenced greatly by the researcher's own values and goals. After training, our ideal family would be able to select skills to teach, develop strategies that are systematic and managable, implement these in a way that maximizes success, and know whether they are working. This requires that parents are knowledgeable about behavioral principles, that they are able to apply them in teaching interactions with their child, and that they actually do so. These goals have, in turn, led us to adopt measures of parent knowledge, skills, and implementation. We do not deny that altering attitudes and child-rearing beliefs also may be critical; we have not, however, made these a major focus of assessment.

TABLE 1 Family Demographics and Selected Prediction Variables

Demographics	Development sample (n = 103)	Validation sample (n = 44)
Family income category [a]	5.3	6.4
Primary parent's education [b]	13.6	12.5
Primary parent's age [b]	36.3	32.4
Child's age [b]	6.5	5.6
Single parent (in %)	16.5	20.4
Primary parent employed (in %)	41.7	40.6
Parents' behavior modification experience [c]	2.1	1.2
Parents' expectation of problems in teaching [d]	12.7	20.8

[a] 1 (low) to 8 (high).
[b] In years.
[c] 0 (low) to 5 (high).
[d] 0 to 60.

In this chapter we primarily report outcomes for two independently recruited and trained samples of families with moderately to severely retarded children 3 to 13 years of age. Aside from age and ability level, there were no exclusion criteria. The first 103 families, which we call "the development sample," were recruited from the Los Angeles area through newspaper and television coverage and letters from several Regional Centers for the Developmentally Disabled from 1977 through 1979. The second 44 families, which we call "the validation sample," were recruited entirely by Regional Center staff from 1980 through 1982. This second sample was obtained to validate results found in the development sample. Some demographic characteristics of these families are shown in Table 1.

We considered outcome of training at four levels: program completion, parents' knowledge and skills acquired, parents' implementation of programs, and child behavior change. We summarized the literature for each outcome level, highlighting the UCLA project's assessment and results and considered attempts to predict successful and unsuccessful outcomes.

Program Completion

For parents who begin training, the first outcome measure is whether they complete the program, a necessary condition for other gains. When dropout rates are high, we need to be concerned clinically about parents who are dissatisfied and scientifically about the generalizability of findings. Measurement of whether parents continue in training and adhere to the program demands is straightforward, and yet this has been the least examined of the four outcomes. When dropout rates are reported, they differ widely, from 0% (Hirsch & Walder, 1969) to over 50%. Some of the highest (40% or more) have been in programs stressing communication skills and parental attitudes, areas perhaps of less relevance to the needs of parents of developmentally disabled children (Hetrick, 1979; Miller, 1980).

The criterion for completion in the UCLA program has been attending at least half of the meetings and the posttraining assessment. In the development sample, 94 of 103 families (91%) were designated completers. Training outcome for the development sample is shown in Figure 1. In the validation sample, 35 of 44 families (81%) completed the program. Recruitment may partly account for the difference in completion rates; in the development sample families were self-referred and in the validation sample, they were referred by agency staff. The difference in dropouts between the two samples, however, was small and not statistically significant. (Differences between completers and dropouts are discussed in a later section.)

Parents' Knowledge and Skills Acquired

Many behavioral programs use a questionnaire to assess parents' knowledge of behavior change principles, and gains have been found consistently. Some programs assess general knowledge of behavioral terms and principles without special reference to mental retardation (O'Dell, Tarler-

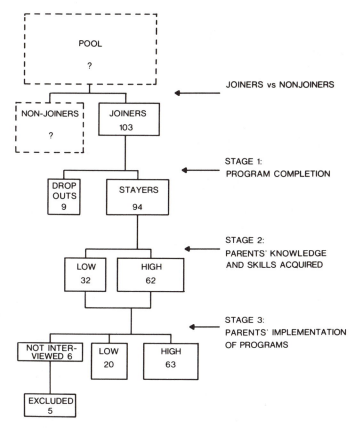

FIGURE 1. Categorization of families in the development sample.

Benlolo, & Flynn, 1979). The UCLA project uses the Behavioral Vignettes Test, which assesses knowledge of behavior modification principles as they apply to teaching retarded children (Baker & Heifetz, 1976). Twenty brief vignettes describe situations that reflect a range of common problems in the formulation and implementation of skill teaching and behavior problem management programs. Parents select from four alternatives the one they think would be the most effective response for each vignette. Studies using the Behavioral Vignettes Test have found significant gains from pre- to posttraining (Baker & Heifetz, 1976; Feldman, Manella, Apodaca, & Varni, 1982; Feldman, Manella, & Varni, 1983). Figure 2 shows changes in Behavioral Vignettes Test scores from about 50% pretraining to 70% posttraining for the development and validation samples. Moreover, in studies with no-treatment control groups, investigators have consistently found greater changes in trained families on a variety of knowledge measures (Baker & Heifetz, 1976; Brightman et al., 1982; Prieto-Bayard & Baker, 1986; Sandler et al., 1983).

Many programs also assess whether parents can apply what they have learned in interactions with their child. Measures developed for rating interaction in families with conduct-disordered children (Christensen, 1979; Patterson, Reid, Jones, & Conger, 1975; Zebiob, Forehand, & Resnick, 1979) have limited applicability to families with retarded children because the emphasis for the latter must be on skill teaching more than on behavior problem management. In several measures for parents of developmentally disabled children, teaching is scored according to a checklist of behavioral techniques employed (Koegel, Russo, & Rincover, 1977; Weitz, 1981). The UCLA project uses the Teaching Proficiency Test (Clark & Baker, 1982), a 15-minute standardized assessment of parents' ability to apply behavior modification techniques in teaching self-help and play skills to their retarded child. Rather than simply tally techniques used, the rater considers their relevance for the particular child and task. A videotaped session is scored on four dimensions: arrangement of the environment, task presentation, reinforcement, and behavior problem management. Figure 3 shows changes in Teaching Proficiency Test scores from before to after training for the development and validations samples. The results in Figures 2 and 3 indicate that parents trained in the Parents as Teachers program as a group made significant gains in behavioral knowledge and teaching ability.

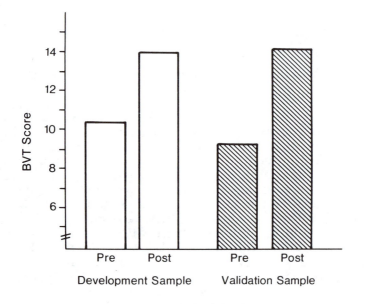

FIGURE 2. Behavioral Vignettes Test scores.

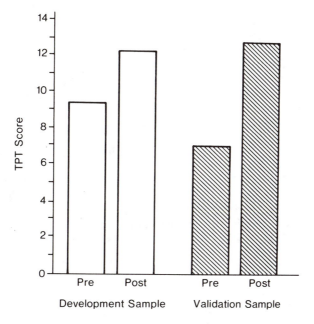

FIGURE 3. Teaching Proficiency Test scores.

Parents' Implementation of Programs

The next outcome level is amount of implementation: whether parents maintain and use these teaching skills after training. One year after training, Baker, Heifetz, and Murphy (1980) found that parents had retained their knowledge of behavioral principles and children had maintained and further developed skills learned when their parents were in training. Yet knowledge of teaching principles is of limited value unless parents also use what they have learned to teach new behaviors, and the evidence for this is more mixed. Only 16% of families continued to do "formal" teaching, where they set aside time for regular teaching sessions. Yet most families (76%) reported "incidental" teaching, incorporating behavioral principles into daily activities. Uditsky and MacDonald (1981) found very similar results when they assessed three groups of families with developmentally disabled children 3, 12, and 24 months after group training.

A 30-minute Teaching Interview (Ambrose & Baker, 1979) was administered to the development and validation sample families before training, after training (validation sample only), and at a 6-month follow-up. The interview was conducted in the parents' home by a staff member not known to the family; parents were asked about teaching during the preceding 3 months. Interview categories in this measure included regular systematic teaching programs, teaching that is more loosely integrated into daily routine, and behavior management. The interviews were taperecorded, and raters blind to condition or time of testing scored for extent of teaching and teaching sophistication (how well behavioral principles are used). Interrater reliabilities on total scores have been very good, $rs = .84$ and $.97$ in two recent samples.

Several investigators have found higher posttraining Teaching Interview scores for trained parents than for no-training control parents (Prieto-Bayard & Baker, 1986) or attention placebo control parents (Baker & Brightman, 1984). Follow-up results are more difficult to evaluate, however, because we have not continued a no-training control group through the follow-through period and hence cannot say how much the typical family would be doing without training. Compared with their pretraining levels, families in the development and validation samples were not doing much more teaching 6 months after training. They did receive significantly higher teaching sophistication scores, however, indicating that teaching was being done better.

Child Behavior Change

The demonstration of success of parent training on child change depends in part on the specificity of the measure. On one extreme, parent training programs assess changes in specific child behaviors that parents have targeted and, typically, good results are found. Rose (1974) reported that 90% of parents modified at least one child behavior "to their own satisfaction," and O'Dell, Blackwell, Lareen, and Hogan (1977), using a stricter criterion for outcome, found that 68% of parents completed one full modification project. Such specific measures, however, do not indicate whether training effects generalized to other child behaviors. On the other extreme some investigators who have used standardized intellectual or developmental measures have failed to show change in trained parents relative to control parents (Clements, Evans, Jones, Osborne, & Upton, 1982; Dorenberg, 1971; Sandler et al., 1983). These measures have tapped too much beyond what the program targeted and have, perhaps, masked successful albeit more narrow outcomes.

Standard measures have consistently shown significant child gains when they were directly related to the content of training. For example, Harris et al. (1981) used a language hierarchy to assess the effectiveness of their language training program for parents of autistic children. The UCLA Project has similarly assessed within domains targeted in training. The Performance Inventory Self Help Scale measures child performance on 38 specific skills in the areas of dressing, eating, grooming, toileting, and housekeeping. The component parts of each skill are arranged in a hierarchical scale (ranging from "Child cannot do any part of this skill" to

"Child can perform this skill completely independently"), and parents check the step that most accurately reflects the child's performance. Reliabilities between staff members' and parents' scores have been consistently above .90 (Baker & Heifetz, 1976; Brightman et al., 1982).

On the Performance Inventory Behavior Problem Scale, parents estimate the frequency or duration of 51 behavior problems commonly reported for retarded children. Items cover areas such as aggressive behavior, stereotyped behavior, and fears. Several investigators have found increases in self-help skills and decreases in behavior problems on the Performance Inventory following training (Baker & Heifetz, 1976; Brightman et al., 1982; Feldman et al., 1982, 1983). Feldman and her colleagues used a multiple-baseline design to show the relationship of gains to training, whereas Baker and Heifetz (1976) found gains on nontargeted as well as targeted behaviors by trained parents relative to nontrained parents. These child changes were corroborated in both the development and validation samples. At least by this measure, which relies on parent report, children benefit from their parents' participation in training.

PREDICTION OF TRAINING OUTCOME

Despite promising outcome findings, behavioral training programs do not benefit all families: Some do not complete training, others do not achieve teaching proficiency, and still others do not implement the skills that they have learned after training ends. Identifying predictors of outcome would help service providers develop alternative interventions for parents predicted to fare poorly in a standard group curriculum.

The relatively few investigators who have addressed correlates of outcome in behavioral training for parents have focused on socioeconomic variables, such as income and education. Rinn, Vernon, and Wise (1975), using group training for parents of behaviorally disordered children, found that lower-income parents attended fewer sessions and achieved considerably fewer targeted behavioral goals than did middle-income parents. With parents of retarded children, Salzinger et al. (1970) found that successfully carrying out a program was related to parents' education, reading ability, and pretraining knowledge of behavioral principles. Similarly, Rose (1974) reported that middle-income families benefitted more from group training in behavior problem management than did those who received Aid to Families With Dependent Children. Sadler, Seyden, Howe, and Kaminsky (1976) replicated these findings with a multiple-regression approach, finding income level and parents' education to be positive outcome predictors.

Clark, Baker, and Heifetz (1982), using parents of retarded children, considered a wider range of predictors (parents' socioeconomic status, education, pretraining experience, and performance during training as well as child characteristics) and two outcome variables (mother's knowledge of behavioral principles after group training and amount of implementation one year after training). They used a discriminant analysis with a two-group categorization of posttraining knowledge of behavioral principles as the outcome variable. In the resulting formula, mothers with previous group experience and previous behavior modification exposure were predicted to be in the high-knowledge group. With this simple rule, 75% of the low-knowledge group and 77% of the high-knowledge group were correctly predicted. In another discriminant analysis they utilized a two-group categorization of amount of implementation and produced a prediction formula using posttraining knowledge of behavioral principles and the number of teaching sessions with their children that parents entered in a daily log during the program. With this equation, 69% of the low-implementation group and 77% of the high-implementation group were correctly predicted.

In the remainder of this chapter, we report findings about prediction of training outcome with parents of mentally retarded children. The studies we report were designed to improve upon former prediction results in four ways: (a) the outcome measures were more comprehensive; (b) the prediction variables were more inclusive; (c) the development sample was twice as large; and (d) a validation sample was utilized.

Prediction Measures and Analysis

Prediction measures covered a broad range of child, parent, and family characteristics. Individual parent measures were taken from the parent primarily involved in teaching. The measures were as follows:

Family Demographics
   Primary parent's age
   Primary parent's education
   Primary parent's occupation
   Primary parent's number of working hours
   Marital status (single/married)
   Marital adjustment (Locke-Wallace Marital Adjustment Test)
   Number of older siblings
   Number of younger siblings
   Social class (Hollingshead, 1957, Index), using father's education
      and occupation
   Income (categories from 1 [0 to $2,999] to 8 [over $35,000])
   Distance family lives from meeting place

Parent Expectations
   Success in the program
   Problems expected and ability to overcome them
   Responsibility for teaching own child
   Commitment to teaching own child

Parents' Prior Related Experience and Skills
  Membership in past groups
  Membership in current groups
  Group leadership
  Previous behavior modification experience (0 to 5)
  Knowledge of behavioral principles (Behavioral Vignettes Test)
  Ability to teach in a simulated situation (Teaching Proficiency Test)
  Previous teaching at home (interview)

Child Characteristics
  Age
  Diagnosis
  Age at diagnosis
  Sex
  Self-help skills (from Performance Inventory)
  Self-quotient (score divided by age)
  Behavior problems (from Performance Inventory)

For program completion and child behavior change univariate relationships between prediction measures and outcome are reported. (Prediction formulas were not developed, due to the small number of dropouts and the few significant relationships between predictor measures and child change). For parent proficiency and implementation, prediction formulas were developed using discriminant analyses. Prediction analyses were first done with the development sample and then tested on the validation sample. To limit the variables in the prediction equation and thereby avoid the statistical problem of "overfitting" common in prediction research, we allowed only variables that were significantly related to the outcome variable individually to enter the equation, $p < .05$, two-tailed.

The equation predicting outcome category was developed by a forward step-wise discriminant analysis computer program (Brown, 1977). A description of this method is found in Kleinbaum and Kupper (1978). The formulas were cross-validated by the leaving-one-out method (Lachenbruch, 1975). (This procedure is a variant on the split-sample method of error estimation. In that method half of the sample is used to derive the equation, and accuracy is estimated by applying it to the other half. The leaving-one-out procedure is conceptually similar, in that it takes all possible splits, each consisting of one subject in one group and the remainder in the other. An equation is derived for this latter group of $N - 1$ subjects, and the left out subject is classified using this equation. This procedure is repeated for all subjects. For each $N - 1$ group, a discriminant function is constructed to classify the left-out observation, and the error estimate is based on the accuracy of these independent classifications. Thus, a given observation is not used in the construction of the discriminant function used for its classification, and the error estimate is unbiased. The leaving-one-out method is superior to the split-sample method with relatively small samples).

Program Completion

Families in the development sample who dropped out of training were compared on all variables with those who completed training. Completers ($n = 94$) and dropouts ($n = 9$) did not differ on measures of socioeconomic status, parent's age or employment, distance families lived from the meeting place, marital adjustment, parent expectations, previous group membership, prior teaching, or child characteristics. Dropouts were, however, significantly more likely to be single parents (56% vs. 13% of completers), and they were less knowledgable about behavior modification prior to training (Clark & Baker, 1983).

Families in the validation sample who dropped out of training ($n = 9$) and those who completed training ($n = 35$) were compared on these same measures. Again, dropouts were more likely to be single parents (33% vs. 17% for completers) but not significantly so. Dropouts again scored lower on pretraining behavior modification knowledge, $t = 3.85$, $p < .001$, and in this sample dropouts were doing significantly less prior teaching, $t = 2.09$, $p < .05$. Dropouts and completers did not differ on the remaining measures. With some minor differences, these results were consistent with those of the development sample.

Correlates of program completion must be considered tenuous because dropout rates were low. With larger samples and/or with higher dropout rates, other variables might also differentiate those who stay and those who do not. From these limited results, however, it appears that parents who drop out of our training are more likely to be single and to have limited prior knowledge of the content covered by the program. These characteristics may make parents ill-at-ease in a group of primarily married and better informed parents. An alternative method would be to conduct separate groups for single parents, although Hall and Nelson (1981) found that single parents continued to drop out at a high rate even in groups specifically tailored for them.

Child Behavior Change

To determine relationships with prediction variables, we considered child self-help skill and behavior problem change measures as continuous variables and computed Pearson correlation coefficients. Improvement in self-help and behavior problems were correlated, though not highly, $r = .25$, $p < .01$. Two predictors related to both child measures. Children with a higher self-help quotient (number of self-help skills divided by age) improved more in self-help skills, $r = .22$, $p < .02$, and behavior problems, $r = .24$, $p = .01$. Parents who perceived greater responsibility for teaching (from the Parent Expectancy Scale) had children who improved more in both self-help skills, $r = .25$, $p < .01$, two-tailed, and behavior problems, $r = .38$, $p < .001$, two-tailed. In addition, expectation of success in the program and expectations regarding teaching were significantly correlated with self-help skill change. There were other significant correlations, but they were not high and involved only one outcome measure; given the number of correlations computed, they may well have been chance relationships.

Although predictors of child change were in the expected direction, they were generally weak. In large part, this is a function of the measures used, which made global assessments of self-help and behavior problem levels. Such measures are adequate for demonstrating group change but do not adequately differentiate among children. A better measure would be changes in only the skills actually targeted for programming during training. A further difficulty in measuring changes in retarded children's behavior is that such changes come slowly and may not be sufficiently in evidence to be measurable until months after training. A better time for assessment of child change might be at follow-up. By this time, however, a great many other influences will have been active, and to keep an untreated control group waiting this long does not seem clinically appropriate. The difficulties in obtaining an accurate and meaningful measure of child change have led us to place more weight in our research on parent behaviors, seeing good parent teaching as a necessary condition for child change, no matter how retarded the child.

Parents' Knowledge and Skills Acquired

For prediction analyses, parents were categorized as either low or high in teaching proficiency on the basis of the Behavioral Vignettes Test, the Teaching Proficiency Test, and the trainer's evaluation of performance during training. Families were classified as high-proficient if the parent primarily involved in teaching scored above the median on two or three of these measures; remaining families were classified as low-proficient.

In the development sample's demographic characteristics, parent expectations and prior related experiences differentiated high-proficient from low-proficient families. Parents who did not attain proficiency were significantly lower on socioeconomic status variables and were significantly older than proficient parents. Their prior expectation was that they would encounter more problems in training and be less able to overcome them. Prior to training they had less experience with behavior modification and were doing less teaching with their child at home.

The resulting prediction formula incorporated four variables: family income, primary parent's education, expectation of obstacles to teaching, and previous behavior modification experiences. We used the leaving-one-out validation procedure, and the formula correctly classified 25 out of 32 low-proficient parents and 47 out of 62 high-proficient parents, for a total rate of 77% correct. This result was statistically significant, χ^2 corrected for continuity $= 23.0$, $p < .001$, one-tailed (Clark & Baker, 1983). The proficiency prediction formula and the distribution of prediction scores is shown in Figure 4.

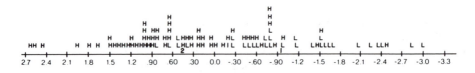

FIGURE 4. Histogram of canonical variable for proficiency prediction: (.24 × income) + (.21 × primary parent's education) + (.13 × expectation of problems) + (.22 × previous behavior modification experience) − 10.8. H = actual high-proficiency. L = actual low-proficiency.

Families in the validation sample, classified as high- or low-proficiency, were compared using one-tailed t tests. Low-proficient parents were again significantly lower on socioeconomic variables, including income, $t = 1.83$, $p < .05$, the primary parent's education, $t = .4.08$, $p < .001$, and socioeconomic status, $t = 2.42$, $p < .05$. Low-proficient parents also had less experience with parent groups, $t = 2.08$, $p < .05$, a result not found in the development sample but found in previous research (Clark et al., 1982). None of the other differences found between high- and low-proficient families in the development sample, however, even approached significance.

Parents in the validation sample were assigned prediction scores based upon the development sample formula. The formula correctly classified 13 out of 14 low-proficient parents but only 8 out of 21 high-proficient parents, for a total rate of 60% correct. This result was borderline statistically significant, χ^2 corrected for continity = 2.75, $p < .05$, one-tailed.

Socioeconomic variables appear to be the most consistent predictor of low proficiency, a finding that is quite consistent with results of other studies. To understand why the formula did not predict better, we considered ways in which the validation sample differed from the development sample. In the validation sample parents were less educated and less familiar with behavior modification, and they expected more problems in teaching. Hence, the formula predicted a high percentage of these families to be low-proficient. Yet their training produced greater gains than for the development sample, so that a high percentage of families met criteria for high proficiency. These contrasting percentages set a limit on possible accuracy of prediction. Why was training more effective? We cannot say, except to note that a variable used in the equation that failed to replicate was "parents' expectations of obstacles to teaching." A cognitive–behavioral curriculum that we describe in a later section was used with the validation sample to address such expectations and counter them. We do not have the appropriate comparative evaluation, but it seems that the cognitive–behavioral curriculum may produce better outcome than the standard training used with the developmental sample and, thus, may eliminate parental expectations as a predictor.

Parents' Implementation of Programs

For prediction analyses, we classified families as either low- or high-implementation on the basis of the follow-up teaching interview. Families were classified as low-implementation if they scored one standard deviation (*SD*) below the mean on either subscale; all others were classified as high-implementation. Development sample low-implementation families (*n* = 20) were compared with high-implementation families (*n* = 63) on measures gathered before and after training. The strongest finding was that low-implementation parents were less likely to have attained post-training proficiency. They also had lower socioeconomic status, less education, and were more likely to be single parents. Low-implementation parents expected more obstacles to teaching before training began. They also had had less behavior modification principles, and were doing less teaching with their child.

The resulting prediction formulas included three variables: parent proficiency, marital status, and pretraining teaching of the child. We used the leaving-one-out validation procedure, and the formula correctly classified 14 of 20 low-implementation families and 49 of 63 high-implementation families, for a total of 76% correct. This result was statistically significant, χ^2 corrected for continuity, 13.4, p χ .001 (Clark & Baker, 1983). The implementation prediction formula and the distribution of prediction scores is seen in Figure 5.

```
              H
              H  HH                                      H
           HH H  HHHH HH                              H H H
           HH H  HHHH  LH   H HH H                    HL H
     H   HH H H  HHHH  HHLH LHH H HL H      H      L  H HL H  HH        L    H L    L L  L  L
    +----+----+----+----+----+----+--2-+----+----+----+----+--I-+----+----+----+----+----+----+
   2.1  1.8  1.5  1.2  .90  .60  .30  0.0 -.30 -.60 -.90 -1.2 -1.5 -1.8 -2.1 -2.4 -2.7 -3.0 -3.3
```

FIGURE 5. **Histogram of canonical variable for follow-through prediction: (1.74 × proficiency) + (1.60 × marital status) + (.15 × previous teaching at home) – 4.6. H = actual high-implementation. L = actual low-implementation.**

Using the same criteria as in the development sample, we classified families as low-implementation (*n* = 9) or high-implementation (*n* = 23) and compared with one-tailed *t* tests. Posttraining proficiency replicated as a predictor, including knowledge of behavior modification principles, *t* = 2.50, *p* < .01, teaching proficiency, *t* = 1.99, *p* < .05, and, marginally, the proficiency category *t* = 1.59, *p* < .06. The differences between groups on these variables were not, however, as substantial as before. Marital status was not significant in this sample; however, the number of families was quite small bcause only 6 of the 9 single parents completed training. In all, only 3 single parents completed training and were classified as high-implementation (33%) compared with 66% of married families. This is consistent with our findings in the development sample, where the comparable figures were 14% and 59% for single and married parents, respectively.

Socioeconomic status, mother's education, expectation of problems, previous behavior modification experience, and pretraining knowledge of principles did not approach significance. In this sample pretraining teaching also was not related to implementation; however, teaching during training, a measure not available for parents in the development sample, was lower for low-implementation families, $t = 2.42$, $p = .01$. This finding was consistent with Clark et al. (1982), who found that performance during training related to follow-through.

Parents in the validation sample were assigned prediction scores based upon the development sample formula and classified as to implementation status. The prediction formula correctly classified 4 out of 9 low-implementation families and 18 out of 23 high-implementation families, for a total of 69% correct. This result was not significant. Thus, although there were no drastic inconsistencies between the two samples on relationships between prediction variables and implementation, the prediction formula did not replicate with this small sample.

Further Analyses

Although the overall accuracy of predictions was less than we had hoped for, most mispredicted families received predicted scores near our rather arbitrarily determined cut-off scores. Consider the distribution of predicted scores for proficiency (see Figure 4). Values between 0 and -1.00 had virtually no predictive utility, whereas predictions outside this range were quite accurate. When we combined the development and validation samples ($N = 129$) and excluded this middle group ($n = 36$), the proficiency prediction formula correctly classified 24 of 38 low-proficiency parents and 52 of 55 high-proficiency parents, for a total of 82% correct.

For implementation prediction (see Figure 5), values between -0.50 and -1.50 had virtually no predictive utility, whereas again predictions outside this range were quite accurate. When we combined the development and validation samples ($N = 115$) and excluded this middle group ($n = 32$), the implementation prediction formula correctly classified 10 of 15 low-implementation families and 65 of 68 high-implementation families, for a total of 90% correct. These accuracies, although still not ideal, are high enough to have some clinical usefulness.

IMPLICATIONS FOR PARENT TRAINING

The ability to predict which parents will benefit from group training has obvious practical significance. Parents predicted to do well in groups such as the Parents as Teachers program can be assigned to this relatively inexpensive intervention, whereas predicted low-benefit families can be offered a potentially more effective, although perhaps more costly, alternative. Attention to predictors of outcome can aid in designing training alternatives by redesigning training in minor ways to change modifiable parent characteristics and/or designing very different training approaches that accommodate better to more static parent characteristics.

As an illustration of changing modifiable characteristics, consider parents' expectation of obstacles. We were concerned with this variable because it predicted low-proficiency and low-implementation families in the development sample. Such an expectation may reflect a negative cognitive set as much as an accurate perception of real obstacles. There is evidence that negative cognitions can have enormous and often unrecognized effects on mood and actions (Beck, 1976).

The standard curriculum did not address parents' cognitions that precede, and too often prevent, the everyday act of teaching. For instance, parents may voice a generalized expectation such as "My child can't really learn anyway" and this thought, often unspoken, would impede teaching. Other cognitive obstacles are more situation-specific. Consider, for example, the parent who thinks, "Having a session today would be too much bother" or "It would be easier to do this for my child than to teach him to do it."

Following the lead of developments in other areas of parent education (e.g., abusive parents: Ambrose, Hazzard, & Haworth, 1980), we revised our curriculum to address maladaptive cognitions directly. For example, we now ask parents to list and discuss particular thoughts that help or hinder their teaching efforts. We also teach a scheme for solving problems that includes self-monitoring, self-reinforcement, and coping strategies following less than optimal performance by parent or child. this cognitive–behavioral curriculum is aimed at uncovering negative expectations and teaching alternative coping thoughts in order to alter expectations and perhaps, in turn, increase proficiency and implementation.

Although we have not yet experimentally tested this cognitive–behavioral curriculum, we have piloted it with the validation sample. With these families, as noted previously, the expectation of problems measure no longer predicted outcome. This is encouraging, but a direct assessment of changed expectations is yet to be done.

As an illustration of accommodating training to relatively static characteristics, consider mother's education and family socioeconomic status. The present curriculum is, in many respects, like an academic course in its use of manuals and homework assignments. A different direction is suggested by evidence that lower socioeconomic status persons learn better from active training approaches than didactic ones. With lower socioeconomic status families, we have experimented with several adaptations in training format that employ videotaped models and supervised teaching. Described in detail elsewhere (Baker, Prieto-Bayard, & McCurry, 1984; Brightman, Ambrose, & Baker, 1980), these programs have utilized: (a) a modified group approach, with incentives for participation and an ongoing child group for active teaching; and (b) school-based training, with parents involved as classroom observers and teachers. These more active training programs, although more costly, have produced reasonably good gains even among parents with very limited education.

FINAL THOUGHTS

Is training for parents of retarded children effective? From our review of findings from the UCLA project and related studies, we can conclude with a guarded "yes." We have considered four outcome levels: program completion, parent gains, subsequent implementation, and child gains. The majority of parents who begin parent training programs complete them. When parents' knowledge of teaching principles and skill in teaching have been assessed, training has consistently produced positive group changes; and when assessments of child gains have not been unrealistically broad, they too have shown positive changes.

We have reservations, however, and these suggest five areas in which training for parents of retarded children should be studied further. First, we have seen that families who participate in training are a select group; to the extent that this is so, results are not generalizable to other parents. Further comparisons of families who take advantage of training programs and those who do not would help in interpreting research findings and designing more responsive programs.

Our second and third points both relate to generalization — over time and across behaviors — and both bear on policy decisions about whether parent training services should be continued and expanded. Long-term benefits of parent training have not been adequately studied. We know that most parents do not continue daily formal teaching sessions with their child. That may be too much to expect. We do not know very conclusively, though, the extent to which participation in parent training affects more informal daily interactions or how to enhance long-term benefits. A related point is that we know little of generalized program impact on parental adjustment and attitudes, marital relationships, or family interactions. It is sometimes argued that increased involvement of families in their handicapped child's education will result in increased family stress. We argue the opposite: that for most families a sensitively conducted parent training program will decrease family stress. Yet at this point neither argument has much empirical basis.

The fourth and fifth points relate to prediction of outcome. On our measures roughly one third of parents fail to meet proficiency criteria, and perhaps one quarter do little useful teaching following training. So, although group results are significant and most parents show gains, a sizable minority fail to reach specific criteria of proficiency or useful implementation. We can now predict at better than chance level the families who will do less well. One point is that further studies of correlates of outcome are needed, with different training models and broader predictors that include individual and family adjustment. A related point is that prediction results should lead to development and evaluation of alternative intervention models for predicted low-benefit families. An ideal service-delivery system should have several types of intervention programs available for families and have a basis for determining the best match between a given family and programs.

REFERENCES

Ambrose, S. A., & Baker, B. L. (1979, September). Training parents of developmentally disabled children: Follow-up outcome. In A. Christensen (chair), *Maintenance of treatment effects following behavioral family therapy.* Symposium presented at the annual meeting of the American Psychological Association.

Ambrose, S. A., Hazzard, A., & Haworth, J. (1980). Cognitive-behavioral parenting groups for abusive families. *Child Abuse and Neglect, 4,* 119–125.

Baker, B. L. (1980). Training parents as teachers of their developmentally disabled children. In S. Salzinger, J. Antrobus, & J. Glick (Eds.), *The ecosystem of the "sick" child.* New York: Academic.

Baker, B. L. (1984). Intervention with families with young severely handicapped children. In J. B. Blacher (Ed.), *Families of severely handicapped children: Research in review.* New York: Academic.

Baker, B. L., & Brightman, R. P. (1984). Training parents of retarded children: Program specific outcomes. *Journal of Behavior Therapy and Experimental Psychiatry, 15,* 255–260.

Baker, B. L. Brightman, A. J., & Blacher, J. B. (1983). *Steps to independence series: Play skills.* Champaign, IL: Research Press.

Baker, B. L., Brightman, A. J., Carroll, N. B., Heifetz, B. B., & Hinshaw, S. P. (1978). *Steps to independence series: Speech and language, Level 1 and Level 2.* Champaign, IL: Research Press.

Baker, B. L., Brightman, A. J., Heifetz, L. J., & Murphy, D. (1976). *Steps to independence series: Behavior problems, early self-help skills, intermediate self-help skills, advanced self-help skills, toilet training.* Champaign, IL: Research Press.

Baker, B. L., Brightman, A. J., & Hinshaw, S. P. (1980). *Steps to independence series: Toward independent living.* Champaign, IL: Research Press.

Baker, B. L., Clark, D. B., & Yasuda, P. M. (1981). Predictors of success in parent training. In P. Mittler (Ed.), *Frontiers of knowledge in mental retardation.* Baltimore: University Park Press.

Baker, B. L., & Heifetz, L. J. (1976). The Read Project: Teaching manuals for parents of retarded children. In T. D. Tjossem (Ed.), *Intervention strategies for high risk infants and young children.* Baltimore: University Park Press.

Baker, B. L., Prieto-Bayard, M., & McCurry, M. (1984). Lower socioeconomic status families and programs for training parents of retarded children. In J. M. Berg (Ed.), *Perspectives and progress in mental retardation, Vol. 1—Social, psychological, and educational aspects.* Baltimore: University Park Press.

Beck, A.T. (1976). *Cognitive therapy and the emotional disorders.* New York: International Universities Press.

Bricker, W., & Bricker, D. (1976). The infant, toddler and preschool research and intervention project. In T. D. Tjossem (Ed.), *Intervention strategies with high risk infants and young children.* Baltimore: University Park Press.

Brightman, R. P., Ambrose, S. A., & Baker, B. L. (1980). Parent training: A school-based model for enhancing teaching performance. *Child Behavior Therapy, 2,* 35–47.

Brightman, R. P., Baker, B. L., Clark, D. B., & Ambrose, S. A. (1982). Effectiveness of alternative parent training formats. *Journal of Behavior Therapy and Experimental Psychiatry, 13,* 113–117.

Bronfenbrenner, U. (1974). *Is early intervention effective? A report on longitudinal evaluations of preschool programs (Vol. II, DHEW Publication No OHD 75-25).* Washington, DC: U.S. Dept. of Health, Education, and Welfare.

Brown, M. B. (Ed.). (1977). *Biomedical computer programs: P-series.* Los Angeles: University of California Press.

Christensen, A. (1979). Naturalistic observation of families: A system for random audio recordings in the home. *Behavior Therapy, 10,* 418–422.

Christensen, A., Johnson, S. M., Phillips, S., & Glasgow, R. E. (1980). Cost effectiveness in behavioral family therapy. *Behavior Therapy, 11,* 208–226.

Clark, D. B., & Baker, B. L. (1982). *The Teaching Proficiency Test: A measure of skill in applying behavior modification techniques for parents of retarded children.* Unpublished manuscript, Department of Psychology, University of California, Los Angeles.

Clark, D. B., & Baker, B. L. (1983). Predicting outcome in parent training. *Journal of Consulting and Clinical Psychology, 51,* 309–311.

Clark, D. B., Baker, B. L., & Heifetz, L. J. (1982). Behavioral training for parents of retarded children: Prediction of outcome. *American Journal of Mental Deficiency, 87,* 14–19.

Clements, J., Evans, C., Jones, C., Osborne, K., & Upton, G. (1982). Evaluation of a home-based language training programme with severely mentally handicapped children. *Behaviour Research and Therapy, 20,* 243–249.

Dorenberg, N. J. (1971). *The differential effect of parent-directed and child-directed part-time educational intervention on the level of social functioning of young mentally ill children on waiting lists.* Unpublished doctoral dissertation, New York University.

Feldman, W. S., Manella, K. J., Apodaca, L., & Varni, J. W. (1982). Behavioral group parent training in spina bifida. *Journal of Clinical Child Psychology, 11,* 144–150.

Feldman, W. S., Manella, K. J., & Varni, J. W. (1983). A behavioral parent training program for single mothers of physically handicapped children. *Child: Care, Health, and Development, 9,* 157–168.

Fraiberg, S. (1971). Intervention in infancy: A program for blind infants. *Journal of American Academy of Child Psychiatry, 10,* 381–405.

Fredericks, H. D., Baldwin, V. L., & Grove, D. (1974). A home-center based parent training model. In J. Grim (Ed.), *Training parents to teach: Four models.* First Chance for Children, *3,* 11-24.

Hall, M. C., & Nelson, D. J. (1981). Responsive parenting: One approach for teaching single parents parenting skills. *School Psychology Review, 10,* 45–53.

Hargis, K., & Blechman, E. A. (1979). Social class and training of parents as behavior change agents. *Child Behavior Therapy, 1,* 69–74.

Harris, S. L., Wolchik, S. A., & Weitz, S. (1981). The acquisition of language skills by autistic children: Can parents do the job? *Journal of Autism and Developmental Disorders, 11,* 373–384.

Hetrick, E. W. (1979). Training parents of learning disabled children in facilitative communication skills. *Journal of Learning Disabilities, 12,* 275–277.

Hirsch, I., & Walder, L. (1969). Training mothers in groups as reinforcement therapists for their own children. *Proceedings of the 77th annual convention of the American Psychological Association,* 561–562.

Hollingshead, A. B. (1957). *Two-factor index of social position.* Unpublished manuscript, Yale University.

Horton, K. B. (1976). Early intervention for hearing impaired infants and young children. In T. D. Tjossem (Ed.), *Intervention strategies for high risk infants and young children.* Baltimore: University Park Press.

Kleinbaum, D. G., & Kupper, L. L. (1978). *Applied regression analysis and other multivariate methods.* North Scituate, MA: Duxbury Press.

Koegel, R. C., Russo, D. C., & Rincover, A. (1977). Assessing and training teachers in the generalized use of behavior modification with autistic children. *Journal of Applied Behavior Analysis, 10,* 197–205.

Lachenbruch, P. A. (1975). *Discriminant analysis.* New York: Hafner Press.

Miller, J. H. (1980). Structured training with parents of exceptional children. *Dissertation Abstracts International, 40(08),* 3908-B.

McConkey, R., & McEvoy, J. (1984). Parental involvement courses: Contrasts between mothers who enroll and those who don't. In J. M. Berg (Ed.), *Perspectives and progress in mental retardation. Volume I. Social, psychological and educational aspects.* Baltimore: University Park Press.

Morris, R. J. (1973, August). *Issues in teaching behavior modification to parents of · retarded children.* Paper presented at the annual meeting of the American Psychological Association, Montreal, Quebec, Canada.

O'Dell, S. L., Blackwell, L. J., Lareen, S. W., & Hogan, J. L. (1977). Competency-based training for severely behaviorally handicapped children and their parents. *Journal of Autism and Childhood Schizophrenia, 7,* 231–242.

O'Dell, S. L., Tarler-Benlolo, L., & Flynn, J. (1979). An instrument to measure knowledge of behavioral principles as applied to children. *Journal of Behavior Therapy and Experimental Psychiatry, 10,* 29–34.

Patterson, G. R., Reid, J. B., Jones, R. R., & Conger, R. E. (1975). *A social learning approach to family intervention: Volume 1: Families with aggressive children.* Eugene, OR: Castalia.

Prieto-Bayard, M., & Baker, B. L. (1986). Behavioral parent training for Spanish-speaking families with a retarded child. *Journal of Community Psychology, 14,* 134–143.

Rinn, R. C., Vernon, J. C., & Wise, M. J. (1975). Training parents of behaviorally-disordered children in groups: A three years' program evaluation. *Behavior Therapy, 6,* 378–387.

Rose, S. (1974). Group training of parents as behavior modifiers. *Social Work, 19,* 156–162.

Sadler, O. W., Seyden, T., Howe, B., & Kaminsky, T. (1976). An evaluation of "Groups for Parents": A standardized format encompassing both behavior modification and humanistic methods. *Journal of Community Psychology, 4,* 157–163.

Salzinger, K., Feldman, R. S., & Portnoy, S. (1970). Training parents of brain-injured children in the use of operant conditioning procedures. *Behavior Therapy, 1,* 4–32.

Sandler, A., Coren, A., & Thurman, S. K. (1983). A training program for parents of handicapped preschool children: Effects upon mother, father, and child. *Exceptional Children, 49,* 355–358.

Shearer, D. E., & Shearer, M. S. (1976). The Portage Project: A model for early childhood education. In T. D. Tjossem (Ed.), *Intervention strategies for high risk infants and young children*. Baltimore: University Park Press.

Strom, R., Rees, R., Slaughter, H., & Wurster, S. (1981). Child-rearing expectations of families with atypical children. *American Journal of Orthopsychiatry, 51*, 285–296.

Tavormina, J. B. (1975). Relative effectiveness of behavioral and reflective group counseling with parents of mentally retarded children. *Journal of Consulting and Clinical Psychology, 43*, 22–31.

Turnbull, A. P. (1983). Parental participation in the IEP process. In J. A. Mulick & S. M. Pueschel (Eds.), *Parent-professional participation in developmental disability services: Foundation and prospects*. Cambridge, MA: Ware.

Uditsky, B., & MacDonald, L. (1981). Behavioral training for parents of developmentally-delayed children: A two year follow-up. *Journal of Practical Approaches to Developmental Handicap, 5*, 5–8.

Weitz, S. E. (1981). A code for assessing teaching skills of parents of developmentally disabled children. *Journal of Autism and Developmental Disorders, 12*, 13–24.

Wolfensberger, W. (1969). The origin and nature of our institutional models. In R. B. Kugel & W. Wolfensberger (Eds.), *Changing patterns in residential services for the mentally retarded*. Washington, DC: President's Committee on Mental Retardation.

Zebiob, L. E., Forehand, R., & Resnick, P. A. (1979). Parent-child interactions: Habituation and resensitization effects. *Journal of Clinical Child Psychology, 8*, 69–71.

13
Socialization Effects on the Community Adaptation of Adults Who Have Mild Mental Retardation

Andrea G. Zetlin
University of Southern California

Jim Turner
California State University, Long Beach

Lesley Winik

Galinsky (1980) reported that parents begin thinking about and preparing for their child's eventual departure from the family home as far back as they can remember. As their son or daughter gradually matures and demonstrates an increasing ability to handle him or herself, the authority relationship they have with their child undergoes a change, moving from more to less control. When the child enters the world of the adult, the reins of parenthood are loosened even further so as to make the task of parents that of caring, of being available, and of helping without corresponding control. The parental relationship is redefined for the newly emerged adult to that of resource, and the concept of family derives its meaning mostly through rituals such as regular Sunday dinners, weekly telephone calls, and the celebration of birthdays, holidays, or family events.

The parents of mentally retarded children, however, may have far less to look forward to than do parents of nonretarded children. The doubts and despair they have always felt, including the concern of what will happen to their child after their death, will often continue in some way for the rest of their lives. As one parent stated, "I feel responsible for this child forever. My

Acknowledgements. National Institute of Child Health and Human Development Grant No. HD 11944. We gratefully acknowledge the contributions of Tom Brauner, Marsha Bollinger, Melody Davidson, Pauline Hayashigawa, Sandra Kaufman, and Dave Tillipman to the collection of data.

other children will grow and leave on their own, this child will always be my burden" (Murphy, 1981.) Even for mildly retarded children who are expected to develop into adults capable of assuming some of the roles established by society, the need for continued care and attention by parents is anticipated (Farber & Ryckman, 1965.)

Few investigators have actually examined the range and nature of parental involvement in the lives of their retarded offspring, once grown and living on their own. Koegel and Kernan (1983) focused on the relationship of attitudes of mildly retarded adults toward competitive employment and corresponding levels of family support. Haas (1979) examined the influence of parents in retarded adults' decision to undergo voluntary sterilization. Zetlin, Weisner, and Gallimore (1985) reported that parents and other family members provide the extensive support required in childcare and survival needs (e.g., housing, food, money management) by their retarded offspring who become parents and, moreover, match their degree of involvement to the perceived or demonstrated needs of their retarded child and grandchild. Finally, Kaufman (1980) related her and her husband's experiences as the parents of a mildly retarded woman who had moved out on her own, as they struggled to maintain their strong-willed, independent-minded daughter in a middle-class lifestyle similar to their own. Although limited, these studies portray parents as uncertain of their grown son or daughter's ability to handle the personal and social responsibilities of adult life. They tend to perceive their retarded offspring as "no longer a child, yet not fully an adult" and their actions reflect their hesitancy to "cut their grown child loose" (Kaufman, 1980).

The present study was designed to examine the nature of the parent/ child relationship for mildly retarded adults living in the community and to identify patterns of interaction between parent and child that relate to the adult adaptation of these retarded individuals. More specifically, we permitted parents and offspring to present their perspectives on perceived needs and desired levels of support and involvement as well as their assessment of the quality of the existing relationship between them. For those retarded persons whose parents were no longer accessible, we examined the nature of their personal and social adjustment and the adaptive strategies evoked to cope with the demands of independent living.

METHOD

Subjects

Over an 18-month period, beginning in July, 1980, 46 individuals (25 males, 21 females) living independently in the greater Los Angeles area were intensely studied using participant-observation techniques. They ranged in age from 22 to 60 years (mean = 35.37, standard deviation

[*SD*] = 10.08); 44 were Anglo and 2 were of Mexican descent. All of the subjects were specifically selected so as to be free from major behavioral or emotional problems, although we later learned that one sample member did have a history of psychological disturbance.

Although most sample members spent their childhood years living at home with family members, 7 spent some time in a state institution: 1 was admitted at age 12 and stayed for 18 years, whereas another spent as little as 10 months in an institution at 9 years of age; 5 attended private special education residential schools for various periods of time; and 3 resided in foster care or board-and-care homes from very young ages. Although the socioeconomic status (SES) of the families of the sample members was not a controlled variable, the parents of all but 4 individuals were middle class; the remaining 4 sample members were from lower SES families.

During the period of observation, all subjects resided in their own apartments in the community, either alone, with roommates, or spouses. Twenty-two had been involved in independent-living training programs before the move to independent apartment living, and another 5 had lived in board-and-care facilities as adults for a short period before their move to independence. At the time of contact, 27 sample members had been living independently for less than 4 years; 7 had been on their own between 4 and 9 years; and 12 had lived independently for 10 or more years. There were 12 married couples, and in all cases both husband and wife had been identified as mentally retarded. Two of the couples had children: one had one child and the other had three children. One other sample member had been married for 21 years when widowed.

Twenty sample members were competitively employed either full or part time, 9 were clients at sheltered workshops, and 17 were unemployed. Of those unemployed, 2 were caring for their children, 1 was suffering from a terminal illness, some took classes at junior colleges, some performed volunteer work, others sought employment, and some were content to remain unemployed. Thirty-two of the sample members received Social Security Income or Survivor benefits (SSI), and 35 were California Regional Center clients currently receiving on-going services.

Although IQ data were not available for all sample members, all had been classified as mentally retarded at some point in their development by local or state agencies serving developmentally disabled individuals. All except 4 sample members had been placed in special education classes during their school years and remained there until they graduated or left school. Of the 4 who were not enrolled in special education, 1 attended regular classes in a Catholic school until seventh grade and then remained at home; 2—identical twins—spent one month in a special class until their parents discovered that much of the day was spent coloring and had them transferred back to regular classrooms; and 1 had been expelled from a series of kindergartens at the age of 6 because of an uncontrollable seizure condition and was never re-enrolled.

In only 24% of the cases, however, did the schools encounter parents who prior to the official contact that led to labeling the child, were unsuspecting of any problems in their child's development. In 38% of the cases, parents were concerned during the early childhood years with how their child's development was proceeding (i.e., slowness, excessive crying, hyperactivity) and sought medical advice. For some this occurred as early as 6 months, for others at the toddler stage, and for others at 3 or 4 years, when comparisons with peers made their child's "differentness" very apparent. For another 13% of the sample members, it was evident from birth that they would be disabled; for 6%, a trauma to the head was experienced at some point during childhood resulting in brain damage and significantly impairing performance; and in another 4%, a major seizure occurred during the childhood years without any prior symptoms. For the remaining 15% of the cases, no information was available.

Procedure

Sample members were located through a variety of sources including California Regional Centers for the Developmentally Disabled, residential facilities, sheltered workshops, social groups, and training programs. A pool of potential sample members was identified and approached by the various agencies for permission to be contacted by our researchers. Participant observation began once a potential sample member agreed to become involved in the research.

The technique of participant observation allows for the field researcher and sample member to engage in intensive interactions over a prolonged period of time. During that time discussions take place and observations are made as the sample member is involved in various typical activities. Given the continuing and long-term nature of the contact, close relationships develop between the researcher and sample member, resulting in intimate conversations on a range of topics, such as personal feelings, past events, and hopes or fears for the future.

A field researcher was assigned to each sample member, and visits were scheduled approximately once a month. In fact, contact was much more frequent, as sample members often invited researchers to special social occasions, telephoned just to talk to or report on some significant incident in their lives, or dropped by the office to visit. Over the course of 18 months, these meetings took place in the homes of the sample members as well as in other settings (e.g., a relative's home, amusement parks, bowling alleys, church, restaurants, work locations) to permit observation of the individual in a variety of natural settings. Tape recordings of conversations and the researcher's notes on other observations were then used to construct a detailed narrative account of each contact. The resulting fieldnotes provide a record of everyday concerns, behaviors, and skills and are extremely detailed, allowing us to examine a number of features of the sample member's lives. At approximately 6-month and 18-month intervals, field researchers were asked to summarize their knowledge to date of each of the sample members they had followed. Three major areas of focus were included in the structured format provided for their comments: the saliency of the handicapping condition to the sample member's self-evaluation; current relationships with family members and peers; and characteristic ways that sample members handled problems—both large and small—that confronted them.

In addition, structured interviews were conducted with the parents or other close family members of 37 sample members to obtain information on past and current issues in the lives of these retarded individuals. Family contacts were initiated by field researchers, and a total of 120 questions were asked, typically requiring two or three interview sessions and 7 to 9 hours for completion. A range of topics, including the impact of the retarded child on family members' lives, the developmental history of the retarded child as well as school, social, residential, and work histories, were covered. For the other 9 sample members, such information was inaccessible because family members were either deceased or for other reasons unavailable (e.g., in very poor health, living out of state).

RESULTS

Sample members were placed into one of two groups based on whether parents were accessible as providers of support. Each group was then examined to identify the various styles of adaptation made by sample members as they struggled to maintain themselves in the community. For those with parents, adaptation styles were related to the existing parent–child relationship because parental support was so pervasive.

For the 32 sample members whose parents are currently involved in their lives, three sources of available data were examined: (a) the ethnographic data of sample members' lives in process; (b) field researchers' perceptions of the parent–child relationships that emerged out of the process of interactive fieldwork; and (c) the background information obtained from the family interviews. Three distinct types of parent–child relationships were identified: supportive, dependent, and conflict-ridden, which varied in the kinds of support/assistance provided by parents (e.g., socioemotional support vs. instrumental assistance) and in the manner in which parents' intervened when needs were perceived (e.g., parent vs. child initiated; authoritative vs. noncontrolling.) Independent judgments were made by two researchers familiar with the data as to the nature of the relationship between sample members and their parents, which resulted in 84% interrater agreement across subjects.

Because little background information was available for the remaining 14 sample members whose parents are inaccessible (i.e., deceased, seriously ill, residing out of state) to supplement the general ethnographic data, researchers questioned them directly about their childhood histories and relations with family members. The ethnographic records were then examined as were reports from field researchers on the on-going relationships of sample members with relatives and/or other supporters. Two groups emerged from the analysis: those who were largely independent/ periodically dependent and those who were heavily dependent. Interrater agreement averaged 86% across subjects.

Once sample members had been classified as to characteristic adaptation styles, which either included or excluded parents as supporters, the data were analyzed to determine the corresponding relationships with other indices of community adjustment, including employment patterns, affiliative relationships, relationships with the service-delivery system, self-maintenance skills, and well being. The results of the analysis follow.

Coping with Parental Support

Supportive Relationships

The 16 sample members (8 males, 8 females) who made up this group had a mean chronological age (CA) of 33 years and had been living independently for a mean of 5 years. The parent–child relationship of these sample members can best be characterized as close, warm, and supportive yet not overprotective. For the most part, these parents saw their role as that of resource for their grown child and, therefore, maintained a respectful distance while their son or daughter forged their own way. They provided on-going emotional support, encouragement, and security in knowing that they were there if needed, but had ceased making decisions for their child. Rather, they subscribed to the belief that as an adult, their son or daughter needed to be the architect of his or her own existence and needed to run his or her own life. As the mother of retarded twins stated, "We avoid directing our sons too much but they know they can always come to us for help," and another parent noted, "I let my daughter and her husband be, but I'm there if needed."

From the sample members' perspective, they tried to handle most of the everyday affairs of their life without assistance, and only in times of crisis turned to their parents, who had yet to fail them. As one man put it, "Don't bother me, but be there when I need you." All were proud of their independence and self-sufficiency, which they had learned from their parents were integral components of adulthood, and they readily identified themselves to others in terms of their normative accomplishments (e.g., managing their own apartment, being married, having a job.) One sample member, for example, when asked to describe herself, proudly recited how she had a job, paid the bills, supported herself, and had an apartment. By the same token, they saw nothing troublesome about their reliance on parents when times were difficult and comfortably juggled their independent status with a willingness to accept the short-term assistance of parents when problems were encountered. Confronted by SSI foul-ups, running short of money at the end of the month, or difficulty in getting the landlord to do repairs, they asked their parents for advice and counsel. One woman, for example, consulted her parents when she was denied sick leave to recover from an injury sustained while working. Her step-father arranged for a lawyer to handle the case. These sample members, on their part, were grateful for the assistance they received from their parents and reciprocated by performing acts such as housesitting while their parents vacationed elsewhere, doing the gardening at their parents' home on a regular basis, chauffering a sick mother to the doctor.

Some of the younger sample members in this group, who were also the least experienced in independent living, received more extensive support from their parents in such practical matters as shopping, housekeeping, and money management. These parents, however, recognized the need for their son or daughter to be more self-sufficient and continued to push him or her toward increasing independence. One woman's parents, for example, noted how they were careful not to have their daughter come home too often as she started depending on them again. They intentionally kept her at a distance so that she continued her progress toward greater self-reliance. Another parent wanted to make himself less accessible to his daughter, so he refused to give her his new home telephone number. She was then only able to contact him when he was at work and had to seek support from her counselor or rely on herself at other times.

Parents in this group saw their child as capable of managing the routine demands of day-to-day life; however, when out-of-the-ordinary problems arose, most expected that assistance would always be required. With this in mind, they had arranged for a sibling or other family member to assume the position of overseer or for the relationships with counselors and support agencies to be strengthened as preparation for the future.

Examination of the background data from these sample members revealed that most of their parents had been accepting and open about their child's condition from the start and had made it a practice of speaking with their retarded child about his or her disability. Clarifying explanations, such as "Everyone learns at a different rate," "It's harder for some to learn and they have to work harder," and "Everyone has unequal abilities," were offered by the parents to assist their child in understanding of his or her condition. They made a point of emphasizing that with effort their child could progress, and they intentionally employed growth-promoting practices to develop skills leading to greater self-sufficiency. This included the encouragement of normal activities and risk-taking and setting realistic goals despite the fact that some of these retarded children had difficult temperaments. One mother, for example, reported how she taught her daughter to use the bus system. She described how she would specify which number bus to board and where to get off and then would drive behind the bus to make sure her daughter did not miss the stop. Another parent described how he had been informed by the doctor that his son would not be able to ride a bicycle because of his poor depth perception; however, the scene of his son running alongside his friends as they peddled along on their bikes was too much for him, so he bought him a bicycle. Within a short time he had taught him to ride and from that day

on decided he would never set arbitrary limits on opportunities for normative experience. His son now had a job, was married, and drove his own
car, accomplishments even his father admitted were beyond his expectations.

These parents thus came to believe that their retarded child could
achieve significantly if helped, and toward this goal they enrolled their
child in special training programs or, if none were available, developed
programs of their own. Many worked as volunteers in special education
classes and joined organizations to learn from other parents and professionals how to maximize their child's potential for normative development.
Further, they emphasized that they treated all their children equally and
made special efforts to ensure positive relationships between other siblings
and the retarded child. All of these parents thus reported having been
guided by the principles of normalization long before they became public
policy. Indeed, most actively resisted the recommendation of family physicians and others to institutionalize their retarded child.

**TABLE 1   Selected Family and Demographic Characteristics
of Subjects by Adaptation Group (in %)**

Characteristic	Supportive	Dependent	Conflict-ridden	Largely independent	Heavily dependent
Marital status	50	50	50	50	63
Employment status					
Competitive	69	40	33	50	12
Workshop	12	10	17	50	38
Unemployed	19	50	50	0	40
Out-of-home placement[a]					
State hospital	0	20	17	83	12
Foster care	0	0	33	17	0
Boarding school	19	20	17	0	0
Delivery-system involvement					
Supplementary income[b]	56	70	100	83	75
Regional center client	81	90	100	100	88
Independent living training program graduate	44	50	67	33	38

[a] Before age 21.
[b] SSI, survivor benefits or family trust fund.

Their sons and daughters were, in turn, the most successful of the
sample members in terms of their personal and social adjustment (see
Table 1). This group had the largest percentage of employed individuals,
either competitively or in sheltered workshops, and their employment

histories were the most stable. Many enjoyed large friendship networks in which associations were stable, enduring, and mutually satisfying. Those who were married had warm, caring relationships with their spouses, with a minimal amount of conflict. Their relationships with parents, siblings, social workers, and other supporters were generally positive and nonproblematic, and they were generally less involved and less dependent on professional service agencies (e.g., SSI, Regional Center, the Department of Rehabilitation) than were other sample members. These individuals also reported feeling good about themselves and the quality of their lives, and they maintained a balanced self-appraisal of their strengths and limitations, allowing them to do most things on their own while secure that their families would provide needed support when special problems arise.

DEPENDENT RELATIONSHIPS

There were 10 sample members (5 males, 5 females) in this group. Their mean CA was 28 years and mean number of years living independently was 5. They looked to their parents for protection and guidance in virtually every dimension of everyday life. They deferred to parents for almost any decision and continuously solicited parental assistance and support. They viewed this parental intervention as both necessary and desirable. The parents, in turn, were willing providers, and most viewed their child as incompetent to handle the basic self-maintenance tasks of an independent life style. Moreover, they typically reported feeling sorry for their grown child and the life he or she was forced to live and sought to shield them from any unpleasant or potentially harmful experience.

These sample members had come to expect extensive parental involvement not only for major problems, such as medical emergencies, marital conflicts, and employment hassles, but also in routine self-maintenance tasks, such as money management, housekeeping, grocery shopping, food preparation, and minor home repairs. One young man, for example, had problems controlling his spending once he had been given a major credit card and checking account. His solution was to turn both over to his mother and to allow her to monitor his expenditures. Another man, although 46 and married for 22 years, insisted that his mother accompany him when he shopped for clothes. He contended that, "If I buy something on my own, my mother may not like it. So she has to go with me to see if it looks good on me, if it's the right color or shade, if she thinks it's the right type of thing I should wear. If she doesn't like it, I can't buy it. It has to be up to her standards." The parents of these dependent adults kept a tight rein on significant decisions that needed to be made by their son or daughter and, in most cases, were responsible for the final outcome. Most maintained total control over their child's finances; assumed an active role in mediating any personal problems or conflicts with friends, spouses, or others; exerted a highly active influence over their child's attitude toward marrying and childbearing; encouraged or discouraged all

friendships and affiliations; and discouraged all activities that they considered to be beyond their son or daughter's capabilities. For example, one
mother discouraged her daughter from continuing to enroll in special
courses at the local junior college. She believed that the added tension of
school was increasing her daughter's nervousness and irritability.

As would be expected, there was variation in the degree of dependence
these 10 individuals actually had on their parents. At one extreme was a
man who called his mother at least two times a day, spent every weekend
at his parents' home, was assisted in all areas of self-maintenance, was
provided financial assistance to supplement his social security income,
and was expected to be present at all family social outings. At the other
extreme was a woman who at various times in her adult life had been
estranged from her parents and completely self-sufficient (e.g., when ties
with her parents were severed due to their disapproval of the men she
dated.) Now, however, the birth of her son had renewed her need for
extensive parental involvement in her life, and both she and her parents
accepted this dependent pattern of interaction. There were also several
members of this group who had begun to reduce their extreme dependence
on parents, the result of active encouragement by agency counselors who
stressed increased self-reliance as being in their best interest. One man,
for example, 40 years of age and the father of three daughters was now
being encouraged to assume some responsibility as "man of the house."
Until recently, all family decisions were made by his more-competent wife
and his mother, both of whom treated him as a fourth child. Regardless
of their degree of dependency, most members of this group apparently
attached little value to personal autonomy, and they accepted their parents
as the rightful arbiters over all aspects of their existence. They appeared
to be convinced that resistance to parental control would incur disapproval
or abandonment and, therefore, complied with their demands without
questions or protest.

When their children were growing up, these parents reported having
been concerned with promoting forward progress; however, in most cases
they adopted rearing practices that were characteristically highly protective. They apparently had not fully come to terms with their child's
condition, and their unresolved feelings of guilt were reflected in their
attitude and practices. One mother, for example, confessed that she had
felt sorry for her son knowing how hard life was for him and so babied
him a lot as he was growing up. Another mother admitted that because
her child appeared so helpless and pitiful, she did many things for him
that he could have done himself (e.g., she dressed him until he was 7 and
bathed him until much later.) These parents provided so much warmth
and care that they inadvertently socialized their son or daughter into
dependency, compliance, and incompetence. Unable to bear watching
their child fail, they discouraged risk-taking and spontaneity, made all
decisions for their son or daughter, and encouraged extensive reliance on
family members for advice on all matters. In most cases, there were
significant differences in the way parents handled their retarded and

nonretarded children. For the most part, the retarded child was given very little responsibility in the home in contrast to his or her nonretarded sibling, who in some cases was even responsible for caretaking. When it came to dating, most parents either discouraged such relationships for their retarded teenager or closely supervised associations with members of the opposite sex. One mother, for example, set up a strict curfew for her daughter, and another mother always chauffered her son and his similarly retarded girlfriend (an "arranged" relationship) during their 2-year courtship. Some sample members were unaware of the differential treatment or accepted it without protest. Some were frustrated by it, which resulted in continued uneasiness in their relationship with their "more successful" siblings, who, they argued, were given more opportunities.

Parents of these dependent sample members did not expect their grown child to ever attain an autonomous life style. Unlike the supportive parents, they did not encourage their son or daughter to develop even those skills necessary for managing their practical everyday affairs. Rather, they seemed to accept a considerable degree of dependence, the consequence of which was a grown child who lacked the capacity to maintain himself or herself without the active intervention of parents or significant others.

That these dependent sample members had been rendered less capable of being all that they could be was evident in their community adjustment (see Table 1.) Only half of these individuals were employed (although those that worked were conscientious and reliable employees). They were more socially immature than were members of the supportive group, tended to have fewer and more shallow peer relationships, and relied largely on their families for social interaction and recreational opportunity. They were also more involved with the service-delivery system and more dependent on agency counselors than were members of the supportive group. Contact with counselors and other agency personnel was maintained by both sample members and their parents, and, in some cases, private communication between parents and counselors was ongoing to encourage and support parental efforts to decrease dependency ties. For the most part, these individuals felt that they led a good life and had no plans or desires for change. They accepted their parents' overprotectiveness and the concomitant value of compliance/dependency as being what was best for them. They gave little thought as to the future, and for the time being remained secure knowing that family members would support them as they had always done.

CONFLICT-RIDDEN RELATIONSHIPS

There were 5 males and 1 female in this group. Their mean CA was 27 years and mean number of years living independently was 5. For each of the six families who made up this group, the sources of conflict stemmed primarily from two issues: the amount of support and assistance considered necessary and expectations concerning autonomy. The sample members seemed to prefer extensive resource and instrumental assistance but resented accompanying attempts by parents to exert control over their activities. The parents stated that they would prefer less time- and energy-consuming involvement but insisted on maintaining control over major decisions affecting their grown child's life. The result was an ongoing dialogue in which sample members negotiated for assistance and parents negotiated for control, with dissatisfaction being expressed by both parties with regard to the existing relationship.

Embedded in the parent–child struggle was also a personal struggle, in which both sample members and their parents vacillated in their commitment to their own ideas about independence and self-sufficiency. For although the sample members may have publicly expressed their wish to be more independent and may have asserted as one did that "parents are there to help you but basically should let you do as you please when you're grown," their actions revealed a lack of desire to sever their dependency ties with parents. One man, for example, continually demanded help from his parents to extricate him from the many messes he got himself into (e.g., making a bad deal with a used car salesman, initiating and canceling divorce proceedings from his schizophrenic wife, being evicted from his apartment because of noisy arguments with his wife) and smugly asserted, "I don't care what happens, my mother and father will take care of it." Similarly, parents insisted that they would like to see their grown son or daughter more self-reliant and voiced disappointment at their lack of independence to date but, nevertheless, continued to intervene in the everyday affairs of their child. One mother, for example, threatened time and time again to cut her son off from her and the family house but continued to prepare lunch and dinner for him daily (he lived a few blocks away), drive him to the grocery store, do his laundry, and give him large sums of money.

The exchange of warmth and affection between these parents and their adult offspring, for the most part, was kept at a minimum. Rather, there were numerous complaints by parents concerning their son or daughter's incompetence, laziness, childishness, or demanding nature. For example, one mother described her daughter as "a barely marginal adult who is dull company to be with." Another parent considered her son "an asshole, a pest, and an incessant talker" and was irritated by the fact that "he does nothing with himself." On their part, sample members referred to their parents as interfering, nagging, and meddlesome, and most expressed the desire to be rid of them. As one man stated, "I'll be glad when they die as then they won't bug me anymore." Both parties saw each other's actions as manipulative and were resentful of such behavior. Sample members put themselves in situations in which they were dependent on their parents but then either complained when their parents took control or became upset if they seemed reluctant to respond. Parents, as controllers, often made the provision of assistance contingent on meeting their demands or wishes. One mother, for example, offered to supplement the rent of a luxurious apartment and to buy a dog for her "animal-lover" daughter if she consented to a tubal ligation. Regardless of their constant bickering, sample members continued to see their parents as their most reliable supporters, and parents, in turn, recognized their responsibility and generally responded to the neediness of their imperfect child.

There was, in fact, a tremendous amount of assistance requested by sample members and provided by parents across a range of areas. Telephone contact occurred often and was initiated by both parties for advice or counsel on almost anything, including marital problems, housekeeping concerns, bureaucratic misunderstandings. One sample member, for example, called her mother one night at midnight, concerned whether the oven cleaner smell would asphyxiate her, her husband, and their rabbit. One parent called her asthmatic son often when she suspected that he was having a difficult time breathing. Many sample members were given financial assistance, some were relieved of all dealings with the service-delivery system, and some were assisted with subsistence needs (e.g., food, clothing) and material desires (e.g., a color TV, a car, a vacation to Hawaii, restaurant outings).

The parent–child relationship appeared to have always been strained in these six families. Parents tended to perceive their young retarded child as difficult, easily frustrated, and hyperactive. Most were resentful of the extra attention that was demanded of them, and some even blamed their retarded son or daughter for disrupting the normal household routine and for creating problems in their marriage. In fact, 3 of the 6 sample members were placed out of the home for extended periods of time before age 10: 1 to prevent marital discord and 2 so that a more normal home climate could be maintained for their nonretarded siblings (a fourth was placed at age 18 when his emotional problems and threats of violence became too much for his parents to handle.)

In all cases, relationships with siblings had been poor and continued to be so. Sample members were aware of and disturbed by the differential treatment shown them and their nonretarded siblings. They referred to having been sent away to school while their siblings remained at home or having been denied a variety of life experiences unlike their nonretarded brothers or sisters (e.g., not being allowed to ride their bicycle to school, to view late night or violent movies on TV, to purchase a motorscooter.) Siblings, in turn, were sensitive to special privileges and attention made available to the retarded child and denied them. At present, siblings were not viewed as potential caretakers (unlike the siblings of sample members from the supportive and dependent groups), despite the fact that parents expected close supervision to always to be required. Rather, they wanted to spare their nonretaded offspring from inheriting such a burden and preferred that agents of the delivery system assume the responsibility.

In terms of present day community adjustment, members of this group were the least successful to date (see Table 1). Their employment records, independent living situations, and friendship patterns were marked by instability. Only one man was employed competitively at the time of this study, although he, too, left his job for a time until his mother learned of the situation and arranged for him to be rehired. The others worked on and off at part-time jobs or in sheltered workshops or spent periods of time enrolled in job-training programs. Most seemed to be indifferent to their unemployed status and appeared to prefer unscheduled time and a guaranteed income (i.e., SSI). Most had not remained in one residence or the same living situation for any length of time. The transitory nature of their lives can be attributed to eviction because of excessive noise or untidiness; loss of a roommate or, in one case, a spouse (due to divorce); or unaffordable rent hikes. Their peer relationships, in general, were marked by shallowness, conflict, and instability. They were either domineering and manipulative toward their associates (e.g., one man forbid his friend from seeing him when he felt that his friend had misbehaved) or were unaware of the give-and-take aspect of such relationships and, thus, appeared too demanding. Finally, they maintained very dependent relations with counselors and agents of the delivery system, whom they regarded as additional sources of support (e.g., one man called his Regional Center counselor about "40 times a week" during crises.)

Counselors, however, regarded these individuals as "users" who sought their assistance to avoid undesired responsibilities (i.e., work) or to untangle them from problems or situations they become enmeshed in. One man, for example, tried to enlist the help of his counselor whom he contended "could speak the same language" as the social security people who were insisting he return money received from overpayments. Another man involved his counselor in negotiations with a used car agency after he learned that he was expected to pay exorbitant monthly installments. Previous attempts to counsel him against large purchases without consultation had been ignored. Although these 6 sample members reported dissatisfaction with the quality of their life, they failed to look honestly at how their own actions perpetuated the same problems and crises over and over again. They, therefore, were unable to make any significant changes in their day-to-day existence and could not construct a sense of personal worth from features of their adult life.

Coping Without Parental Support

The remaining 14 sample members who were relatively older than the other sample members, were without the support of parents. In 11 cases, both parents were deceased, and in the other 2 cases, fathers were deceased and mothers were not perceived as viable resources (one had been completely incapacitated by a stroke, and the other had alienated her son over the years and currently resided out of state). For all 14 sample members, however, support needs were on-going, and they had turned to others, such as siblings, service agency counselors, church associates, neighbors, or co-workers, to continue the assistance that they required. Variation did exist in the nature and range of activities for which they sought assistance, and, in fact, these individuals were divided into two groups: those who are largely independent/periodically dependent and those who are heavily dependent. Composite portraits of both groups follow.

LARGELY INDEPENDENT/PERIODICALLY DEPENDENT

Like sample members of the supportive group, the 6 individuals (5 males, 1 female, mean CA = 48 years) who made up this group had a high regard for independence and self-sufficiency. They had been living independently a mean of 23 years. They usually coped with the demands of everyday living themselves, and only in times of crisis turned to supporters for consultation or assistance. These individuals, however, unlike members of the supportive group who typically came from homes in which parents worked hard to foster personal growth, were removed from the family home early in their development and placed in state hospitals or foster homes (2 were placed out because parents were unable to afford their medical expenses, 3 were considered unmanageable by the courts, and 1 was orphaned at age 8.) For them, ideas about autonomy and self-maintenance appeared to have developed more as a result of their early distancing experience and premature "independence" than from parental attitudes and practices. They did not, however, harbor resentful feelings toward family members and, as adults, those who could made attempts to renew contact with their parents while they remained alive.

Without the availability of parents for advice and counsel, these sample members had located other dependable resources to whom they could turn in times of need. In most cases, nonretarded siblings had responded when called upon, but they preferred to be kept in reserve, with service agencies providing for most on-going needs. At least two sisters did maintain regular contact with their retarded brothers and tried to keep abreast of the goings on in their lives (e.g., medical ailments, problems with neighbors). They spoke frequently on the telephone, invited them to their homes for dinner, handled business matters (e.g., filling out forms for SSI, housing subsidies), and assisted when money was tight. In those cases where siblings were not comfortably accessible, agency counselors, ministers or church members, and in-laws often functioned as benefactors. Requests for assistance were made on an "as needed" basis when such matters as marital disputes, problems at work, financial difficulties, and delivery-system foul-ups were encountered. One man, for example, sought help from his minister when he received an eviction notice. Another man accepted help from his field researcher to negotiate him through the UCLA Hospital labyrinth in search of medical assistance for a back ailment. A third man enlisted the support of his father-in-law to prevent his scheming mother and stepfather from forcing his move to another state, where they planned to take control of his money.

For the most part, however, these sample members regarded themselves as their most reliable resource and, as such, had devised distinct ways of adapting to the practical difficulties of everyday life: Some adhered to routines that then regulated their activity, and others were planners, with self-maintenance as the major goal guiding their actions. Three of the sample members (each of whom had spent over 10 years at a state hospital) had adopted highly routinized, well-ordered lifestyles and derived comfort from the few demands and diminished risk-taking afforded by such a narrow and defined mode of existence. For example, they did their laundry, grocery shopping, and banking on the same day each week, were regular customers at the same restaurants, spent each night vigilantly glued to the television set, had set times when they telephoned or visited family members or associates. One woman was so accustomed to the life she and her husband had carved for themselves, when questioned as to what she would do if her husband was no longer around, replied, "I guess I'll have to die too."

The 3 other group members led more self-regulated lifestyles; however, they were self-absorbed in their struggle to survive on their own, which significantly influenced behavior and actions relevant to their day-to-day lives. One man, for example, subscribed to cable TV and rented films from the public library for evening entertainment because his modest budget did not provide for more extravagant forms of eventfulness. Moreover, he always included his two friends in these media events and assigned them the responsibility of supplying food and drink. Another man had worked out little arrangements with the many people in his neighborhood that he knew and trusted. For example, a waitress at the corner cafe gave him coffee and donuts in exchange for occasional use of his bus pass, and the owner of a local laundromat paid him "under-the-table" for a few hours of guard duty each night.

In terms of the community adaptation of these 6 sample members, they all appeared to be doing well on typical indices of adjustment (see Table 1). All were employed (3 competitively and 3 in sheltered workshops), and all had strong work ethics. One man who had worked at the same workshop for over 20 years spent 3 hours walking to and from work during a 2-week long bus strike so as not to miss a day. Another sample member who was fearful of riding the bus alone and who had always traveled to work with her co-worker husband had him accompany her on the bus even when he was on sick leave.

Their peer relationships, although typically small in number (3 related almost solely to spouses, and 2 had a small network of close associates), were characteristically stable, enduring, and satisfying. One man, for example, had one friend whom he met a number of years ago in a board-and-care facility. They spoke on the phone nightly, ate dinner together every week, and spent nearly every weekend together at amusement parks or other local recreational sites. One sample member was the exception, having developed a benefactor role for himself among a wide circle of fellow residents in the downtown slum hotel where he lived. For example, he regularly lent money to others, took care of his friends when they got drunk, and did the grocery shopping for elderly neighbors who feared going out by themselves.

This group had minimal contact with the delivery system. Although most had received SSI at one time or another, and some had been assigned social workers or counselors, they rarely initiated contact with service agencies and generally viewed any dependency of this sort as demeaning. One man, for example, was adamant that he and his wife would eventually be free from all delivery-system involvement in their lives. Another man chose to work at a low paying menial job rather than accept SSI and Medi-Cal, which he viewed as stigmatizing. He believed that this type of aid was "for people who are weak and can't do anything" and that he had little need for such services. These individuals took great pride in their independent lifestyle, and self-sufficiency was the primary attribute used in defining their sense of self-worth. Indeed, most were prone to self-aggrandizement, fabricating, and/or embellishing their accomplishments in order to enhance their presentation of self as more fully autonomous.

HEAVILY DEPENDENT

For the remaining 8 sample members (2 males, 6 females, mean CA = 43), routines as well as major problems were largely managed for them because without such intervention, they would most likely be unable to maintain themselves in the community, in which they had been living independently a mean of 12 years. As with members of the dependent group, these individuals had been dominated and overprotected by parents who believed that they were acting in the best interests of their child. All were placed in roles based on dependency and restricted freedom, which apparently socialized them into perceiving other-regulation as a preferred way of life. Three sample members, for example, had been confined to their parents' home from early on, where they spent their time in virtual isolation, listening to music and watching television. Little opportunity was provided for them to leave the house, to interact with other children or to assume responsibility—everything was done for them. Another sample member, an only child, was indulged by doting parents who made no demands on him whatsoever. For example, they accepted his refusal to help around the farm, his reluctance to assume responsibility for personal grooming (his mother even bathed him well into the teen years), and his disinterest in participating in church functions (although his parents were devout Mormons.) For most, it was not until their parents' death or incapacitation that opportunities for self-development (i.e., independent-living training) were made available.

As parents aged and their ability to "supervise" became increasingly more difficult, most made arrangements for siblings or other relatives/family friends to assume the burden of care. These benefactors loyally provided the rather extensive guidance and support demanded by their charge, and sample members had, in turn, come to expect their assistance and take it for granted. In all cases, regular and frequent contact was maintained. One sample member, for example, called her sister every evening when she returned from work "just to check in." Benefactors typically assumed responsibility for all money management and were actively involved in all phases of self-maintenance, including the purchase of clothing and personal grooming. One sibling called a couple of times a week to check that her retarded sister had clean clothing, was bathing, and had taken her pills (for a seizure condition.) They were generally consulted about decisions that needed to be made (e.g., how much the sample member could afford to spend on Christmas gifts, whether they should become a subject in our research project.) They had, as needed, located new apartments and handled arrangements with utility companies and landlords.

Some sample members had developed relationships with others (i.e., more competent co-workers, neighbors, church members) who provided additional support. One woman was helped by church members with transportation, home repairs, financial assistance, and babysitting. Another woman had consulted neighbors when her purse was snatched, when she received a problematic letter from Medi-Cal, when she had an ill-functioning refrigerator. A number of sample members made the rounds to "friends" when they ran short of money each month.

Although most of these individuals felt fortunate that these "benefactors" were willing to help them, at least 2 were uneasy about the lack of independence and need for constant supervision. Both had been closeted at home for so many years that they were now protective of their new found freedom. They resented having to continue their dependence on others and, thus, tried to project an image of self-sufficiency. One woman contended that her progress since living on her own confirmed that she was "no longer a kid. I feel like a woman now. I really have grown up." In both cases, however, years of confinement without responsibility had taken its toll, for they lacked the basic skills and judgment necessary for independent living. For example, one, when given a checking account after weeks of instruction, began writing checks without recording them, including a $1,500 check for carpeting (a purchase made without consulting anyone first.) The other sample member was unrealistic in assessing the depth of her relationships with members of the opposite sex. She was quick to identify anyone who paid the least bit of attention to her as her boyfriend and to say of them, "he loves me." Whether their desire to become master of their own lives was enough to overcome the effects of years of overprotectiveness at this point is unknown.

DISCUSSION

Over 18 years ago, Zigler and Harter (1969) emphasized the need to study how patterns of socialization interact with adult adaptation to permit identification of those experiences that optimize the potential for social adequacy. Our data demonstrate that even within what initially appeared to be a relatively homogeneous sample (all were living independently in the community, most were individuals known to delivery-system agencies and were receiving services designated for handicapped individuals, and all except 4 were receiving services designated for handicapped individuals, and all except 4 were from middle-class families) distinct patterns in past environment and circumstances were evident and can be linked to the social adjustment of these retarded individuals at the adult level. For the most part, sample members who had been most successful in their community adaptation and who sought normative accomplishments came from homes in which parents were supportive and worked hard to maximize their retarded child's self-confidence and social adequacy. Sample members who had adapted poorly to community living and who demanded the continual support of family and agencies came from homes in which the values of dependency and compliance were ingrained by highly protective or overregulating parents. Those few sample members who were removed from the influence of the family early on, like those from supportive families, strove for self-sufficiency; however, they either created insulated realities that were regulated by routine or applied their practical intelligence to ensure "here and now" self-maintenance. (Further research on this last group is warranted because the inaccessibility of in-depth background information prohibited identification of factors that may have influenced their ideas and attitudes.)

The most striking aspect of the data presented in this chapter is the relative lack of self-maintenance displayed by sample members across all groups. Although they may vary in their degree of dependence, what is portrayed is a group of mildly retarded adults who are maintaining themselves in the community with continuing support and aid. Even members of the supportive and largely independent groups who most resembled nonretarded counterparts, although very much on their own and quite competent, required support to cope with the exigencies of everyday life. Moreover, with few exceptions, parents were generally perceived by these individuals as their most reliable and unfailing supporters (whether relations were comfortable or uneasy). When parents were no longer accessible, other "benefactors" were located—from prior arrangements by parents (e.g., siblings, extended family members, family friends) or through the efforts of sample members themselves (e.g., more competent co-workers, friends, neighbors)—to satisfy their on-going support needs.

It is also the case that although there was relative consistency in the nature of relationships between caretakers and their charges, there have been instances of both temporary and more permanent shifts. For some, the adolescent period was marked by uncharacteristic conflict, as retarded teenagers—like their nonretarded counterparts—rebelled against parental attempts to restrict their freedom. For example, the reluctance of some parents to permit dating led at least 4 female teenagers to sneak out of the house. As these individuals matured, for the most part, the parent–child struggle subsided, and supportive or dependent relationships were resumed. There were also a few individuals within all groups, who sought increased independence. Some were pushed by parents who believed that they were doing what was best for their child; others were encouraged by counselors and agents of the delivery system to reduce dependency ties. Still others, upon the loss of a parent or as the result of an "awakening" experience, begin exerting more control over their life. One woman, for example, severed relations with her "benefactor" sister for insisting that she assume half of their mother's medical expenses and for refusing to give her a memento to remember her deceased mother by. Another sample member broke off contact with his mother after she tried to take control of his money. There were also instances of individuals who, under certain circumstances, increased their need for support by others. Two women had become more dependent on family members and agency counselors since the birth of their child(ren). Another 2 women, upon marrying, assumed traditional wife roles and began deferring major responsibility and decision-making to their husbands. What will happen to these dependent spouses if widowed, is unanswerable at this time. Another member of our sample, upon the death of her husband, transferred her support needs to her sister.

Clearly, this research cohort and their respective families are not representative of the entire mildly retarded adult population who are living independently in the community. Rather, they are a unique group of individuals from middle-class homes in which parents were committed to supervising their children closely as they were growing up. These parents adopted practices and interaction styles that they believed were in the best interests of their son or daughter and that they continued to rely upon as they assisted their adult offspring with the problems of everyday life. How these interaction styles evolved (whether in response to specific temperament or emotional states characteristic of the child, as a result of attitudes held by parents toward their child's condition and the associated stigma, or the consequences of other factors) still remains unclear and is in need of further investigation. These data do seem to indicate, nevertheless, that it is because of the willingness of these parents (and other benefactors) to continue their commitment of support that these retarded men and women were maintaining themselves in the community. In fact, many parents, concerned about their retarded child's continued welfare, had made plans to ensure on-going protection after their death. Depending on what resources were available to them, some set up trust funds to guarantee a minimum income; some made arrangements for siblings, other family members, or family friends to assume the role of benefactor; and/or others encouraged strengthening relationships with service agencies. So what we have, then, are a number of "successful" adaptations to independent living in which varying levels of support/assistance from parents and others is integral to the "self-maintenance" of these mildly retarded adults.

One final note is in order. There are other groups of mildly retarded adults living in the community who because they are less inclined to use delivery-system services have been overlooked by our sampling procedure. Previously, Kernan and Walker (1981) reported that mildly retarded adults from minority families are more likely to shy away from public agencies and to perceive the extended family as their major support system. Similarly, older retarded men and women tend to rely on family members as resources and thus are difficult to locate for study. These individuals grew up during an era in which few community services were available to them, so as adults they are less accustomed to relying on delivery-system agencies for support (Zetlin & Turner, 1984). But what of the adaptations of these other retarded individuals to the community niche they occupy? What of the adaptations of those who move into group homes or board-and-care facilities? Surely more research is called for if prescriptions for normalizing the lives of these mildly retarded individuals are to be developed. Moreover, included in the list of research needs is a better understanding of how to guide parents of retarded children so as to optimize their child's potential for self-reliance as well as information on how the delivery system can best be used to support the family's efforts. Further, counselors and agency personnel need to begin experimenting with how they can best tailor the delivery of services to the specific needs implied by the adaptations of their mentally retarded clients so as to move them toward increased self-sufficiency.

REFERENCES

Farber, B., & Ryckman, D. B. (1965). Effects of severely mentally retarded children on family relationships. *Mental Retardation Abstracts, II,* 1–17.
Galinsky, E. (1981). *Between generations: The six stages of parenthood.* New York: Times Books.
Haas, L. M. (1979). The mentally retarded and the social context of fertility control (Working Paper No. 9). Los Angeles: University of California, Los Angeles, Socio-Behavioral Group, Mental Retardation Research Center, School of Medicine.
Kaufman, S. Z. (1980). Research in progress: A retarded daughter educates her mother. *The Exceptional Parent, 10,* 17–22.
Kernan, K. T., & Walker, M. W. (1981). Use of services for the mentally retarded in the African-American community. *Journal of Community Psychology, 9,* 45–52.
Koegel, P., & Kernan, K. T. (in press). Issues affecting the involvement of mildly retarded individuals in competitive employment. In K. T. Kernan, M. J. Begab, & R. B. Edgerton (Eds.), *Settings and the behavior of retarded persons.* Baltimore: University Park Press.
Murphy, A. T. (1981). *Special children, special parents: Personal issues with handicapped children.* Englewood Cliffs, NJ: Prentice-Hall.
Zetlin, A. G., & Turner, J. L. (1984). Self-perspectives on being handicapped: Stigma and adjustment. In R. B. Edgerton (Ed.), *Lives in process: Mildly retarded adults in a large city* (Monograph No. 6). Washington, DC: American Association on Mental Deficiency.
Zetlin, A. G., Weisner, T. S., & Gallimore, R. (1985). Diversity, shared functioning, and the role of benefactors: A study of parenting by retarded persons. In K. Thurman (Ed.), *Children of handicapped parents: Research and clinical perspectives.* New York: Academic.
Zigler, E. F., & Harter, S. (1969). The socialization of the mentally retarded. In D. A. Goslin (Ed.), *Handbook of socialization theory and research.* Chicago: Rand McNally.

14
If It Isn't One Thing, It's Another: Experimental Analysis of Covariation in Behavior Management Data of Severe Behavior Disturbances

Stephen R. Schroeder
Ohio State University

William MacLean
Vanderbilt University

"If it isn't one thing, it's another." How often have we, as children, heard our parents use this aphorism to describe their frustration over our resourcefulness in misbehaving? How often do we now, as parents, use it to describe our own children's behavior, and, as behavior analysts, use it to describe the misbehavior of our clients? It strikes us that it is a rather profound statement. It is an expression of a problem that has plagued behavior analysts (e.g., Skinner's notion of reflex reserve, 1938, Hull's, 1943, notion of oscillation threshold) down to more contemporary analyses (e.g., Lewis & Baumeister's, 1982, neural oscillator theory of stereotyped behavior). It has bothered clinicians as well under the headings of "symptom substitution" and "covariation." It is an acknowledgement that most behavior management problems have multiple antecedents, and most behavior interventions have multiple

Acknowledgements. We acknowledge National Institute of Child Health and Human Development Grant No. HD-10570, "The Neuropharmacology of Developmental Disorders, "George Breese and C. T. Gualtieri, principal investigators; National Institute of Environmental Health Sciences Grant No. ES-01104; U.S. Public Health Service Grant No. HD-03110 to the Biological Sciences Research Center; and Maternal and Child Health Project 916 to the Division for Disorders of Development and Learning. A slightly different version of this paper was presented as an invited address at the annual meeting of the Association for Behavior Analysis, Milwaukee, May 1982.

effects. Usually, behavior analysts are only one member of an assessment or treatment team. Their job is to define, measure, and analyze the behaviors so that treatment can be more specific and systematic within the resource system that is available. This is what Wahler, Berland, Coe, and Leske (1977) called "social systems analysis" (i.e., dealing with the short-term *and* long-term consequences of behavior). It seems to us that covariation is more of a long-term consequence, the one that parents and caregivers need help with over the entire life-span of handicapped persons. It is why we will always have a job as behavior analysts.

Could we do a better job with covariation than we have in the past? Until recently, the most distinctive feature about it was its unpredictability; however, Kazdin (1982), as usual, had done an excellent job in summarizing and presenting the issues related to covariation. Our objectives in this chapter are to review some operant animal and human literature that bear on several definitions, analyses, and models of covariation and some data that illustrate the different models and then to draw implications for treatment. We have taken most of our examples from severely retarded, behavior-disordered clients, so caution in generalizing our conclusions across populations is recommended.

WHAT IS COVARIATION?

Covariation exists as two distinct behavioral phenomena: (a) Transitional changes may occur in the target responses as a function of a change in stimulus conditions or reinforcement contingencies (i.e., the contrast effect [Reynolds, 1961]); for example, rebound effects in follow-up baselines, end-of-session effects, and extinction bursts; and (b) changes in collateral behaviors may occur as a function of changes in the target behaviors and vice versa (Kara & Wahler, 1977). As Sajwaj, Twardosz, and Burke (1972) have pointed out, there are four possible kinds of "side effects": (a) desirable behaviors may increase, (b) undesirable behaviors may decrease, (c) desirable behaviors may decrease, and (d) undesirable behaviors may increase. The result in any given situation might be a function of: (a) the reinforcing or punishing effects of a particular contingent stimulus used, (b) the membership of a given target behavior in a wider response class, and (c) alterations in setting conditions to the extent that other behaviors are now affected by existing reinforcement contingencies. Because there are so many possible ways in which covariation can occur during a behavioral intervention, perhaps the best way to begin a discussion of the phenomenon is by giving an illustrative case history.

Subject

Pearl was a 25-year-old woman who lived in a nursing unit of a residential center for severely and profoundly retarded individuals. She had been totally blind from birth and totally deaf for the 2 years prior to our intervention; however, her senses of touch and smell did not appear to be impaired. She was admitted to the facility because her parents could no longer manage her self-injurious behavior (SIB), the two most frequent of which were headhitting and pinching. She also reportedly pulled out her hair and ingested it. Shortly after her arrival at the institution, her SIB became much worse. Kicking herself, kneeing her head, and butting objects were then observed. Behavior management efforts at that time quickly escalated until physical and chemical restraint became the primary intervention methods. As far as can be determined from records, she had been restrained to her bed by having her wrists and ankles tied to the bed frame for at least 11 years except for feeding, dressing, and bathing periods.

Procedure

PHASE A

Withdrawal Time-Out: The first systematic attempt to suppress Pearl's SIB by behavioral means was conducted by a psychologist at the Center who rearranged her room, placing vinyl mattresses on the floor and dangling toys from the ceiling. He stayed with her 10 hours per day trying to engage her in simple conditioning tasks (e.g., turning her head when tapped on the collar bone). If SIB occurred, he timed her out by moving away from her until she stopped. This exhausting regime led to a reduction of SIB over a 2-week period, but the rates were still very high — up to 1,500 hits per day (see Figure 1). During this period, Pearl injured herself and was hospitalized. The treatment was discontinued.

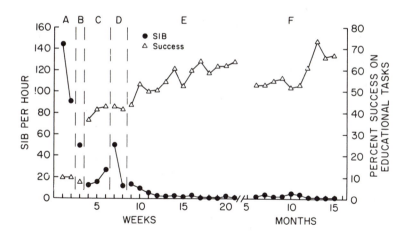

FIGURE 1. Average SIB per hour and percentage successful completion of educational tasks over different phases (A through F) of treatment.

PHASE B

Restraining Mittens: Upon release from the hospital, she was placed in a specially constructed wheelchair and required to wear mittens (two, 30-cm pillows sewn together for each hand) for approximately 5 months preceding our work with Pearl. This plan reduced SIB considerably (Figure 1B), but seriously hampered programming efforts because she could not use her hands.

In the first author's consultation visit to Pearl's Center, it appeared that she was using SIB very systematically to shape the behavior of the staff to meet her needs. The type and pattern of SIB varied according to activity and time of day. Our first task, therefore, was to break down her day into structured and unstructured times and concentrate our efforts on meeting Pearl's survival needs through forms of communication alternative to SIB.

For this program the institution assigned three full-time, direct-care staff members. They rotated so that one trainer and observer were always working together on Pearl's structured tasks. Figure 2 provides a breakdown of 40 activities in Pearl's day, together with the behaviors that were recorded and indicates some of the training activities aimed at self-feeding, fine- and gross-motor training, prelanguage, and training Pearl specifically not to hit herself but to touch herself appropriately.

PHASE C

Contingent Restraint was employed to control the SIB (Schroeder, Peterson, Solomon, & Artley, 1977). If Pearl hit or attempted to hit herself, her hands were held down manually in her lap by a staff member until she relaxed for 10 seconds. The educational task was then continued. If she hit or bit herself 10 times per minute within a 2-minute interval, the mittens were replaced for several minutes. During unstructured activities, Pearl was allowed to wear her mittens.

Figure 1, *Phase D* shows that, after a good start, Pearl's SIB began to increase. We, therefore, made three modifications in the program. Whenever the trainers took Pearl out of the mittens, they replaced the mittens with women's gloves. Also, the criterion for putting the mittens back on changed. If she hit or attempted hitting 20 times in the training period, the mittens were replaced until the next training period. If SIB reached 400 within one day, the mittens were replaced and training ceased for the rest of that day.

The results were an initial rise in SIB then a rapid decline (Figure 1D). In fact, by the end of 2 weeks, both gloves and mittens had been successfully faded out so that she wore them only at night while asleep.

During Phase E, Pearl's performance on educational tasks improved tremendously, and her SIB almost totally disappeared.

During Phase F, follow-up, the staff coverage for Pearl's program was reduced. She received fine-motor training and self-feeding for 1.5 hours in the morning. On an average of 2 days a week, SIB was recorded for the 13-hour day. A slight increase in SIB and a decrease in educational performance resulted initially but recovered over the following months. After 12 years, Pearl was still maintaining her skills, and no SIB was observed. Nevertheless, during such times as periods of illness or emotional distress, she is still at high risk for SIB, and the program remains ready for use if needed.

Discussion

The contingent restraint procedure was very effective in decreasing Pearl's SIB. It was possible to fade the restraint and provide alternative activities for her. Figure 1 suggests a negative relationship between the amount of SIB

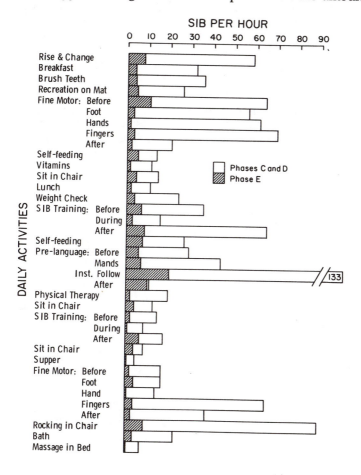

FIGURE 2. Average SIB per hour as a function of different daily activities during Phases C, D, and E.

observed and success on a variety of educational tasks (Figure 3). This result supports the view that SIB is a learned antisocial behavior, because the training of more socially acceptable forms of communication and enhanced educational performance was accomplished by a concomitant decrease in the amount of SIB observed. Although this finding is entirely consistent with the general feeling that behavior interventions designed to suppress undesirable behavior are typically not effective unless the client has a repertoire of more positive responses, it is apparent that if such alternatives do not exist, they must be specifically trained.

Figure 2 also presents the rate of SIB as a function of the particular ongoing activities. The open bars represent SIB during Phases C and D when the rates were high; the hatched bars show SIB during Phase E, when the rates were considerably lower. The distribution of SIB across activities is highly correlated for both phases. This graph shows a variety of environmental contextual effects. For example, the rate of SIB during SIB training, which followed a weight check, a highly undesirable activity for Pearl, was considerably higher than during the same activity following a quiet period in her chair later in the afternoon. Likewise, the rate of SIB during fine-motor training in the morning after a period of recreation on a mat was much higher than during the same activity after supper in the evening.

Contrast effects are apparent during baseline periods before and after training sessions (see Figure 2). There was a large rebound in postbaseline over prebaseline after SIB training. On the other hand, postbaseline after

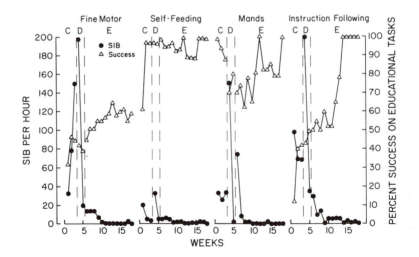

FIGURE 3. Average SIB per hour and percentage success on educational tasks during Phases C, D, and E across different activities.

prelanguage training and fine-motor training in the morning was lower than prebaseline on these tasks. These effects are important because they suggest that this client's SIB varied as a function of the organization of her daily routine. Contrast effects may reflect subjects' preference or dislike for certain tasks, as was apparent in Pearl's SIB. Transitional periods between activities are frequently occasions for SIB. Perhaps SIB enroute to and from different treatment settings should be recorded as carefully as the one after arrival.

Topographical covariation over the course of treatment is apparent in Figure 4. When hand-to-head hitting was consequated with mitten restraint in Phases C and D, footpounding increased to become the dominant SIB; however, when restraints were faded out, hand-to-head hitting again became the dominant topography in Phase E.

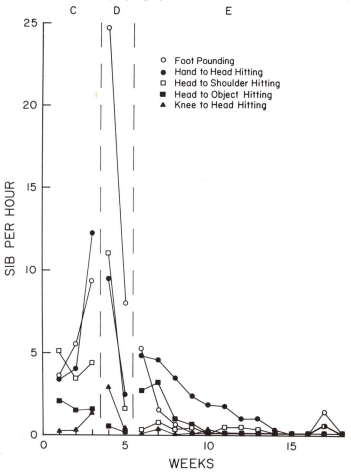

FIGURE 4. Average rate of different SIB topographies for Phases C, D, and E.

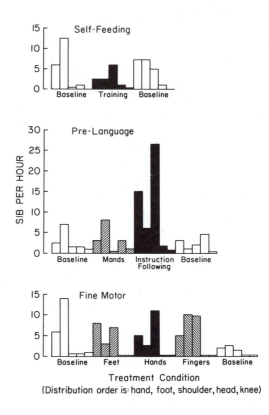

FIGURE 5. Change in frequency distribution of SIB topographies as a function of the task performed.

Figure 5 shows that the type of SIB that Pearl exhibited also varied with the nature of the ongoing activity. During mand training, head-to-object hitting increased, whereas during instruction-following, hand-to-head and head-to-shoulder hitting increased. During self-feeding, hand-to-head hitting and foot-pounding decreased, whereas head-to-shoulder hitting increased. To a great extent, these topographies varied as a function of the body parts required for an activity and the educational tasks involved. Thus, in fine-motor training, although the feet were involved in training, footpounding decreased and hand-to-head hitting increased. With hand training, hand-to-head hitting decreased and head-to-shoulder hitting went up. With finger training, footpounding again increased, while head-to-shoulder hitting remained high. The orderliness of Pearl's covariations eventually became interpretable by the staff as a type of nonverbal communication. Since that time Pearl has been taught several manual signs that she uses today to circumvent her deaf–blind handicap. She is one of only two clients out of a total of 52 whom we have been following since 1977 who have maintained their behavioral control of SIB beyond a 2-year period following the termination of treatment (Schroeder, et al., 1982).

ANALYSES OF COVARIATION

A notable precursor to current notions of covariation was *symptom substitution*. The psychodynamic notion (Spiegel, 1967) was that if a symptom was suppressed without treating the underlying cause, a new symptom would occur. This was the focal point of more heated debate than research among psychodynamic and behavior theorists for many years, even though Cahoon (1968) had clearly pointed out that this was largely an empirical question. The more modern view is that symptom substitution is the appearance of new behaviors as a function of changes in old behaviors already in one's repertoire. "Underlying causes" are viewed as antecedent conditions or what Kantor (1959) called "setting factors". No inferences related to "closed energy" systems or internal states are made; instead, the referrents are objectively specifiable classes of independent variables (Baumeister & Rollings, 1976).

Even so, the more operational definition of symptom substitution also has its problems, as Kasdin (1982) pointed out: (a) The analogy of dichotomizing symptoms and underlying causes limps, once one moves from the medical model to the behavioral model. The dream of surgical removal of a keystone behavior, as one does in a gallstone operation, is very unusual because most problem behaviors have multiple antecedents. (b) When a new problem emerges after treatment, how do we know it was not there all along, but that we just failed to observe it? Resemblance of the old and the new "symptoms" may be superficial and coincidental. (c) What is a suitable time constraint for testing symptom substitution: weeks, months, years? I know of several SIB cases (Schroeder, et al., 1982) where the "symptoms" were suppressed for months but returned years later. (d) How does one determine that a new problem is a substitute symptom or just something that arises from a change in antecedent conditions? (e) There appear to be some "symptoms" that *seem to be* rather functionally autonomous in that they are reinforced and maintained by multiple sources or they are maintained by higher order classical conditioning, as in the case of avoidance behavior, such that reduction of one symptom does not make symptom substitution any more predictable. These conceptual problems render the phenomenon of symptom substitution, as originally proposed, nearly impossible to investigate empirically; however, there has been some empirical evidence of behavioral covariation.

Response Generalization

If an organism reacts with one response to a given stimulus and then responds to that same stimulus with another response that is topographically unlike the first response, but, in some respects, equivalent to it, this is called "response generalization" (Kimble, 1961). It was used originally in the symptom substitution literature by Dollard and Miller (1950) to account for the ego defense mechanism of displacement. The key notions were that: (a) just like stimulus generalization, there is a gradient of response generalization based on similarity of responses and (b) the strength of the generalized inhibiting responses fall off more rapidly than that of the responses they inhibit. Thus, a transfer surface among different response probabilities based on gradients of similarity could be generated. This notion, although possible, has not as yet made its way out of the animal laboratory over the past 30 years. The reasons for this are probably many, but, in my view, the model is too simplistic to take into account the many different situational variables that might affect response generalization in a natural setting. Therefore, the notion of response generalization by itself is of little use in predicting response selection.

Response Differentiation and Induction

A more fruitful tactic would be to study response differentiation and induction (i.e., how chains and sequences of responses cluster and co-occur). Many of the terms we use (e.g., self-injurious behavior) imply the notion of "response class." Yet, we do not yet have a good taxonomy of SIBs (Schroeder, Mulick, & Rojahn, 1980): (a) the consequences specified by the term do not pertain functionally to the reinforcing stimuli responsible for maintaining the behaviors, (b) researchers disagree about the membership of various topographies in the response class of SIB, and (c) no single intervention strategy is indicated for a particular "class" of SIB as differentiated from other behaviors. Research on functional taxonomies of behavior disorders is needed.

Response Covariation

Response covariation is the most assumption-free of the three terms. When responses covary, a change in one response affects the other responses. No presuppositions are made about the direction of correlated changes. Whether they are "positive or negative side effects" is a value judgment imposed externally. A major source of ambiguity is in deciding a priori which responses should be target behaviors and which should be viewed as collateral behaviors. Some disorders have multiple effects on a client's level of functioning. In practice, the decision of what constitutes the target behavior is usually shared by a variety of caregivers, but from an empirical standpoint, a good operant baseline is still the best predictor. With the recent explosion of behavioral assessment research, a wide variety of new tools is available. Yet, a recent review of the behavioral intervention literature in mental retardation by Konarski (1982) showed that a high percentage of authors did not include adequate baseline procedures. Fortunately, the technological quality of this work is improving (Konarski, Johnson, Crowell, & Whitman, 1980).

A second area of ambiguity around the definition of covariation is the level of specificity with which the categories should be defined. In at least two studies, investigators have shown that interobserver agreement was higher on observational categories that were defined more globally than when they were reduced to more narrow operational definitions (Rojahn & Wool, 1979; Wahler & Leske, 1973). In such cases, the increase or decrease in covariants may be due to observers' and clients' drift from an observed standard. Presumably, research on standardized categories and assessment instruments for different behavior problems, clients, and settings would mitigate these problems.

A third area of inquiry on covariation is the question, what is actually modified by a behavioral intervention? The answer depends upon one's model of how multiple-response repertoires are organized for a particular client.

MODELS OF COVARIATION

The *psychodynamic interpretation* is that symptom substitution comes about when some libidinal impulse is blocked. Dollard and Miller (1950) translated this process behaviorally: "Symptoms often are comprised of responses that are produced by both of the drives in a conflict" (p. 192). Factors determining which symptom will occur depend on: (a) the innate hierarchy of responses to drives and cues, (b) the response previously learned or generalized to them, (c) the structure of the stimulus situation, and (d) reinforcement conditions. This would seem to be a reasonable attack on the problem, and it is curious that the only research it stimulated was on the contingencies of reinforcement. Perhaps this analysis was superseded by the advent of applied behavior analysis, which emphasized analysis of reinforcing consequences rather than apparently less-potent antecedent conditions (Sidman, 1978).

The *stochastic model of covariation* in behavior management was first proposed by Lovaas, Freitag, Gold, and Kassorla (1965) to help account for stereotyped and self-injurious behavior. This view was elaborated by Baumeister and Rollings (1976). Self-injurious behavior in a given situation is seen as a probabilistic event. Proponents of this model assume that the subject's repertoire is arranged stochastically in a hierarchy, such that with the cues available in Situation A, reinforcement is predicted following

Behavior B. If B is not reinforced, then C occurs, and so on, until reinforcement occurs. Position in the hierarchy is related to the relative probability of reward and punishment. If one behavior is punished, the relative probability of another is increased. The order of relative probabilities can be increased through learning or be mutually inhibited if one precludes the other. A good example of the latter is Jackson, Johnson, Ackron, and Crowley's (1975) food satiation procedure for chronic ruminative vomiting. They hypothesized that rumination was the terminal link in a chain of reinforced responses (i.e., hunger pangs, reverse peristalsis, vomits in the mouth, and rumination). By giving the client a thick milkshake 90 minutes after mealtime, they averted the hunger pangs and thereby precluded the rest of the chain. Another commonly held but meagerly supported notion related to the stochastic model is that decelerative behavior interventions are more effective when used in a program with positive rewards for alternative behavior. Empirical support for this notion has been forthcoming only recently (Horner, 1980; Solnick, Rincover, & Peterson, 1977; Williams, Schroeder, Rojahn, & Eckerman, 1983).

A major problem with the stochastic model is how well it fits most contexts in which behavior management problems occur. Usually, by the time behavior analysts are consulted, clients have more maladaptive than adaptive behaviors to work with. No rules are available that behavior analysts can use to decide were to begin most effectively. The old response-generalization model of Dollard and Miller (1950) has not been tested adequately and, frankly, seems unlikely given the wide diversity of response topographies that have been found to covary in the research literature on behaviorally disturbed retarded persons.

The work of Dunham and his colleagues on changes in the multiple-response repertoire of gerbils as a function of punishment and response restriction poses some challenging suggestions that we might try in our behavioral interventions. After observing a stable baseline repertoire of eating, digging, running, and paper shredding, Dunham (1978) then suppressed eating by punishment. As a result, the most probable unpunished alternative *increased* in probability during punishment sessions, whereas the other unpunished alternatives maintained their baseline levels or decreased slightly. Dunham called this effect the "hierarchical rule." In a clever set of experiments involving a noncontingent constraint on responding, Dunham and Grantmyre (1982) were also able to show that the *response most likely to follow* in sequence the punished or restricted responses during baseline sessions was also suppressed during subsequent punishment or response-restriction treatment (e.g., removal of food). Thus, sequential relationships among alternative responses observed during baseline reduced the extent to which the most probable unpunished alternative response increased during treatment.

There are many reasons why it would be attractive to generalize the hierarchical rule and the sequential dependency rule directly from gerbils to human beings, not the least of which is the inherent elegance of the data just described. Most important, there are ethological analyses of response hierarchies (Dawkins, 1976), operant probability models concerning choice behavior and substitution rules (Rachlin & Burkhard, 1978; Staddon, 1979), and problems of time sharing (McFarland, 1976) that would be fertile soil for exploration. Unfortunately, human beings do more than eat, run, dig, and shred paper, especially in social situations where behavioral interventions are needed. Moreover, not only is human behavior more varied, but it also becomes more difficult to establish which behaviors are relevant for study. For example, we recently learned of an extremely aggressive, severely retarded male who would frequently tear up mattresses to the point that they were rendered useless and had to be discarded. In an exhaustive effort, the institutional staff searched endlessly for the antecedent and consequating conditions that maintained this apparently purposeful, albeit aberrant, behavior. It was not until a visiting consultant noticed that the client spent a great deal of time gazing out of the window that it became apparent that the client was admiring his handiwork, for he was looking at the stacked remnants of the mattresses in a nearby dumpster. Moreover, the client was waiting for the dumpster truck that would lift the mattresses high into the air and then dump them into the back of the truck. When the destroyed mattresses were no longer placed within his view and the dumpster relocated, the behavior ceased completely without further intervention.

Although determination of target and collateral behaviors is not a new problem, the search for naturally occurring contingencies results in a bit of a nightmare in that investigators typically attempt to record every behavior, in sequence, and are frequently overwhelmed by the observational task as well as the resulting reams of data. Of course, that nightmare is not inherent in observational studies per se; it results because investigators have shunned the laboratory model for extensive environmental analyses. This shift is due to the growing sensitivity for ecological validity in the analysis of performance of retarded persons in general (Brooks & Baumeister, 1977). Adherence to this model obligates investigators to consider multiple sources of data (people and environment) simultaneously. The sequential analysis method and multivariate techniques permit this, however, only at the expense of time, effort, sanity, and, frequently, tenure.

Investigators who have examined the hierarchical relationships of aberrant response topographies have found that for some children a hierarchical arrangement is manifest, wheres for others intervening variables appear to be operating that influence the hierarchy from one time to the next or from one situation to another (Baumeister, MacLean, Kelly, & Kasari, 1980; MacLean &Baumeister, 1981; Wahler, 1975; Whaler & Fox, 1980). A similar result was found for sequential dependencies (Baumeister et al., 1980; Johnson & Baumeister, 1982), although it is clear that dependencies do exist among the various behaviors, and it is likely that intervention upon one target behavior would have multiple effects. What remains is the empirical test of the apparent relationships. We are currently gathering a great deal of descriptive data in an effort to characterize the observed variability in the aberrant behavior of retarded individuals. As Kazdin (1982) noted, "At this stage it may be premature to demand that a conceptual framework elaborate the bases of response covariations without more systematic descriptive information about how behaviors are in fact organized" (p. 360). Meanwhile, comparing frequency measures in a descriptive correlational way is still a useful exercise.

The correlational model of covariation makes no assumptions about hierarchical stochastic organization or sequential dependencies within the clients' repertoires. Behavioral clusters that are relatively stable across time, settings, and occasions are used as baseline predictors in a probabilistic model. The study of these taxonomic behavioral clusters is a preparatory phase to developing the probabilistic model. Two outstanding examples of such research in nonretarded clinical populations are studies by Patterson (Patterson, 1979) and Wahler and his colleagues (Wahler et al., 1977), all of whom have been working with just one clinical population for more than 15 years. There has been no comparable work on behavior taxonomies among retarded persons until recently (Landesman-Dwyer & Sackett, 1978a, 1978b; MacLean & Baumeister, 1981; Repp, Barton, & Brulle, 1981; Sackett, 1978a, 1978b; Schroeder et al., 1980; Schroeder et al., 1982). Much more descriptive work is needed in this area.

VARIABLES THAT AFFECT COVARIATION

Decreasing the Target Behavior

Contingent suppression of behavior has often been shown to result in a reorganization of clients' repertoires. The classic demonstrations were performed by Sajwaj, et al. (1972) and Twardosz and Sajwaj (1972) with hyperactive retarded children in classrooms. Even more dramatic demonstrations with stereotyped behavior have been reported by Koegel and Covert (1972), Koegel, Firestone, Kramme, and Dunlap (1974), and Rollings, Baumeister, and Baumeister (1977).

Noncontingent suppression of behavior, such as the use of self-protective devices like helmets or straitjackets (Rojahn, Schroeder & Mulick, 1980) and adaptive clothing like jumpsuits or jackets that permit self-restraint (Rojahn, Mulick, McCoy, & Schroeder, 1978) have all been shown to be setting factors for changing the probabilities of covariants.

Interaction with or proximity of certain people were also shown to differentially affect which covariants of self-injurious or stereotyped behavior occurred both in the Rollings et al. (1977) study and the case study of Pearl, which we discussed previously.

Type of contingent intervention procedure (e.g., reward vs. punishment) would also seem to be an important variable affecting covariation, but we are aware of only two studies (Mulick, Schroeder, & Rojahn, 1980; Tarpley

& Schroeder, 1979) in this area in which investigators compared extinction, extinction plus reinforcement for alternative responding, differential reinforcement of other behavior, and differential reinforcement of incompatible behavior and found them all to be differentially related to covariation.

In all of the studies just mentioned, there is no clear evidence for a hierarchical or sequential dependency rule for predicting the position of covariants in the response hierarchy. Because most of these studies were only descriptive or correlational, the direction of the relationship between the affected target and collateral behaviors is not clear. If topographically distinct and independent behaviors had covaried with the target behavior, one might be able to propose that both target and covarying behaviors comprised a larger functional "response class." Such a possibility is implied in labels such as "stereotype" or "self-injurious behavior." Conversely, if other behaviors had increased in frequency as the target behavior decreased, one might propose that these behaviors were maintained by avoidance of the target behavior or were substituted for it. In judging this possibility, however, we must acknowledge that the frequency of covariants might increase even if the rates remained constant because more time would be available for these behaviors once the target behavior was suppressed. Thus, an increase in frequency can be taken as evidence of avoidance or substitution only when the increase results from an increase in *rate* of the covariant and not just the extra opportunity to do it.

This functional analysis of covariants has practical implications. Risley (1968), Lovaas, Litrownik, and Mann (1971), and Koegel et al. (1974) have argued that stereotyped behavior may be functionally incompatible with appropriate behavior, especially among autistic children. Therefore, stereotypy must be suppressed before learning can occur. This is an empirical question that has far-reaching implications for management of stereotyped behavior, because some investigators see stereotyped behavior as an adaptive response with biological significance (see Lewis & Baumeister, 1982, for a thorough review of this topic). The nature and parameters of how stereotyped behavior helps or interferes with adaptive behavior is an important area of future research on covariation.

Antecedent Setting Factors

We have recently reviewed a wide variety of antecedent conditions that affect the occurrence and management of behavior problems (Mulick & Schroeder, 1980; Schroeder, Mulick, & Schroeder, 1979; Schroeder, Schroeder, Rojahn, & Mulick, 1981), and we will not repeat the findings here. Environmental antecedents that have been shown to affect covariation are: (a) the subjects' available response repertoires (Baumeister et al., 1980; Mulick, Hoyt, Rojahn, & Schroeder, 1978; Wahler & Fox, 1980); (b) body position among infants who exhibit stereotypies (MacLean & Baumeister, 1981); (c) type of activity being performed (Baumeister et al., 1980; MacLean & Baumeister, 1981; see also Figure 5); (d) contingent environmental enrichment (Williams et al., 1983), such as contingent caretaker interactions and availability of appropriate toys and educational materials; and (e) changes in stimulus conditions (Schroeder et al., 1982), such as adding or removing a disruptive person from a group and behavioral contrast related to transitions between activities.

Environmental Enrichment

The Williams et al. (1983) study is a good example of the importance of the environmental conditions in time-in conditions to the effectiveness of time-out contingencies on stereotyped and self-injurious behavior. This was a complex design involving a multiple baseline of reversals across covariant behavior problems across days and alternating environmental enrichment sessions within days.

The effectiveness of contingent restraint time-out was compared under four conditions of environmental enrichment and adult interaction in a class for four profoundly retarded, self-injurious adolescent boys. The teacher timed-out the misbehavior of the students in a counterbalanced multiple-schedule design for each of the environmental enrichment conditions, which were: (a) Custodial care: The teacher and students were in the classroom with only a wrestling mat on the floor and time-out device in the corner. The teacher performed only a caretaker role; the students were minimally supervised in whatever activity they initiated. The teacher interacted with students only when it was necessary to prevent them from hurting themselves or others. (b) Free toy play: This condition was the same as the custodial care condition with respect to teacher-initiated interaction, but stimulating toys with which students were free to play were added to the classroom. (c) Contingent adult and toy play: The same as the previous condition, except that the teacher assumed an active interpersonal role with the students by prompting and praising toy play and contingently attending to appropriate peer interactions. (d) Contingent adult and custodial environment: The teacher assumed the same role as in the previous condition but without stimulating toys in the classroom. This form of social contact required initiation of simple social games involving direct physical contact between teachers and peers.

The time-out procedure consisted of requiring the students to stand for 90 seconds in a stand-in chair, a device commonly used to train cerebral-palsied children to stand. During the time-out, the students could see and/or hear all classroom time in activities but not participate in them. At the end of the time-out, the subjects were released if they had been calm for 15 seconds.

Williams et al. (1983) found that (a) time-out procedures were less effective in custodial-care types of environments than in enriched time-in environments, (b) noncontingent enrichment of the environment by itself was not sufficient to inhibit antisocial behavior and increase prosocial behavior in this setting, (c) the most important component in the enriched environment was a contingently rewarding and/or punishing caretaker or activity to supplant the inappropriate behavior, and (d) negative covariations occurred among all four of the clients and were distinctly related to the time-out contingencies for three of the four clients, more pronouncedly in the custodial than in the other conditions. The blindness of one subject may have been related to his failure to discriminate the environmental conditions as well as the others did. Incidentally, two subjects seemed to have followed Dunham and Grantmyre's (1982) hierarchical rule for covariants, whereas two subjects did not (i.e., negative covariation during time-out was seen most in the most probable alternative covariant and least in the others). Appropriate behaviors (i.e., toy contact and positive social interactions) were not reliably affected by time-out for inappropriate behaviors.

These results are consistent with the notion that in order for time-out to be effective, alternative sources of reinforcement are necessary. The larger question of whether punishment effects rely on strengthening of particular competing responses is, of course, a long-standing question (e.g., Dunham, 1978). It is not clear, however, that suppression of the punished behavior in the present study depended on the strength of the other inappropriate behaviors because the relationship observed here was only a correlational one. That appropriate behaviors were not affected by the time-out contingency may be related to the highly discriminative properties of punishment stimuli (Azrin & Holz, 1966). For instance, Horner (1980) found an increase in adaptive behavior and a decrease in maladaptive behavior in his enrichment program when he used differential reinforcement.

Behavioral contrast is a type of transient covariation that is widely researched in the operant animal literature, but it has been underutilized in applied behavior analysis. It occurrence is readily observable in behavior management data (see Figure 2) as postbaseline rebound effects and schedule-induced behaviors such as the frequently observed increase of self-injurious behavior when chronic self-protective restraints are removed (Favell, Mcgimsey, & Jones, 1978). According to Reynolds (1961), a change in behavior is called a contrast when the change in the rate of responding during the presentation of one stimulus is in a direction away from the rate of responding generated during the presentation of a different stimulus. This is useful programming information, as well as support for the notion that clients do distribute their problem behaviors sequentially as well as topographically in a probabilistic manner. Two examples can be drawn from data replotted from Mulick et al. (1980) and Tarpley and Schroeder (1979) so that contrast effects can be seen. Both were experiments, the former on chronic ruminative vomiting and the latter on headbanging, in which various types of reinforcement techniques were compared with a baseline (extinction) condition in a counterbalanced alternating treatment design. Both experiments showed heightened SIB during baseline after sessions involving techniques that yielded a higher density of reinforcement (Figures 6 and 7). These data are useful in helping to choose a technique that can be adjusted to a client's behaviorally

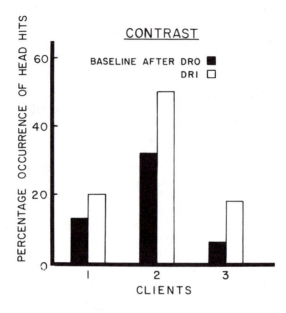

FIGURE 6. Behavior contrast in SIB using the alternating treatments
          design: baseline following DRI treatment was higher than
          baseline SIB following DRO.

indicated preferences. Similarly, such transitional behaviors may be useful
as signals to behavior managers as to which behavioral situations are likely
to be highrisk for undesirable behavior.

IMPLICATIONS FOR TREATMENT

Research on covariation suggests that traditional approaches to behavioral assessment and management of behavior problems need to be
expanded to take into consideration the long-term as well as the short-term
antecedents and consequences of behavior interventions. For instance,
before we decide to intervene with self-injurious or stereotyped behaviors,
we need to do a broader ecological assessment in an attempt to predict
whether such an intervention may lead to an even more undesirable
behavior, such as aggression. It is highly probable that some behavioral
interventions are more likely than others to set the occasion for such

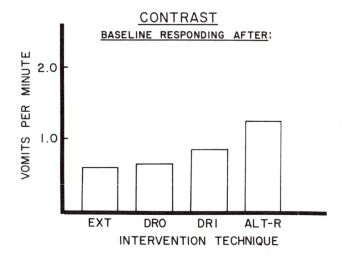

FIGURE 7. **Behavior contrast in chronic ruminative vomiting using the alternating treatments design. Baseline responding following ALT-R treatment was much higher than baseline following EXT (extinction) alone.**

covariation. For instance, coercive seclusion time-out is more likely to produce inappropriate behavior during time-out than is a noncoercive, nonexclusionary form of time-out (Williams et al., 1983). In order to achieve this new goal, it will be necessary to assess not only target behaviors but also their covariants and their setting characteristics, patterns, and sequential dependencies over more extended periods than has been done in the past. It may be that greater knowledge of temporal and topographical sequences of behavior problems will allow us to intervene more indirectly when direct attempts at intervention are unsuccessful or impractical. For instance, combined psychopharmacological and behavioral intervention for some behavior problems (e.g., hyperactivity and stereotypy) may be more successful than either alone (Schroeder, Lewis, & Lipton, 1983).

To some we may seem to be opening Pandora's Box by espousing this ecobehavioral technology; however, the interaction of covariant responses is not a new problem. It was recognized by Skinner (1938) in the *Behavior of Organisms* under the title of "the Interaction of Reflexes," which preceded his discussion of the concepts of stimulus and response. His introductory remarks on this topic are a fitting closing to this chapter:

A description of behavior would be inadequate if it failed to give an account of how separate units exist and function together in the ordinary behavior of the organism. In addition to processes involving reflex strength, a description of behavior must deal with the interaction of its separate functional parts. Interaction may be studied in a practical way by deliberately combining previously isolated units and observing their effect upon one another. In this way we obtain a number of laws which enable us to deal with those larger samples of behavior sometimes dubiously if not erroneously designated as 'wholes'. That great pseudo-problem — Is the whole greater than the sum of its parts? — takes in the present case this intelligible form: what happens when reflexes interact? The effects of interaction are in part topographical and in part intensive. (p. 29)

The same could be said about covariation in the management of problem behavior.

REFERENCES

Azrin, N. J., & Holz, W. C. (1966). Punishment. In W. K. Honig, (Ed.), *Operant behavior: Areas of research an application*. New York: Appleton-Century-Crofts.

Baumeister, A. A., MacLean, W. E., Kelly, J., & Kasari, C. (1980). Observational studies of retarded children with multiple stereotyped movements. *Journal of Abnormal Child Psychology, 8,* 501–521.

Baumeister, A. A., & Rollings, P. (1976). Self-injurious behavior. In N. E. Ellis (Ed.), *International review of research in mental retardation* (Vol. 9).

Brooks, P. H., & Baumeister, A. A. (1977). A plea for consideration of ecological validity in the experimental psychology of mental retardation. *American Journal of Mental Retardation, 81,* 407–416.

Cahoon, D. D. (1968). Symptom substitution and behavior therapies: A reappraisal. *Psychological Bulletin, 69,* 149–158.

Dawkins, R. (1976). Hierarchical organization: A candidate principle for ethology. In P. P. G. Bateson & R. A. Hinde (Eds.), *Growing points in ethology. Cambridge:* Cambridge University Press.

Dollard, J., & Miller, N. E. (1950). *Personality and psychotherapy.* New York: McGraw-Hill.

Dunham, P. J. (1978). Changes in unpunished responding during response-contingent punishment. *Animal Learning and Behavior, 6,* 174–180.

Dunham, P. J., & Grantmyre, J. (1982). Changes in a multiple-response repertoire during response-contingent punishment and response restriction: Sequential relationships. *Journal of the Experimental Analysis of Behavior, 37,* 123–133.

Favell, J. E., McGimsey, J. F., & Jones, M. L. (1978). The use of physical restraint in the treatment of self-injury and as positive reinforcement. *Journal of Applied Behavior Analysis, 11,* 225–241.

Horner, R. D. (1980). The effects of an environmental "enrichment" program on the behavior of institutionalized profoundly retarded children. *Journal of Applied Behavior Analysis, 13,* 473–491.

Hull, C. L. (1943). *Principles of behavior.* New York: Appleton-Century-Crofts.

Jackson, G. M., Johnson, C. R., Ackron, G. S., & Crowley, R. (1975). Food satiation as a procedure to decelerate vomiting. *American Journal of Mental Deficiency, 80,* 223–227.

Johnson, W. L., & Baumeister, A. A. (1982). Self-injurious and other behavior of two profoundly retarded, institutionalized women and related staff and peer interactions. *Analysis and Intervention in Developmental Disabilities, 2,* 41–66.

Kantor, J. R. (1959). *Interbehavioral psychology.* Bloomington, IN: Principia.

Kara, A., & Wahler, R. G. (1977). Organizational features of a young child's behavior. *Journal of Experimental Child Psychology, 24,* 24–39.

Kazdin, Z. E. (1982). Symptom substitution, generalization, and response covariation: Implications for psychotherapy outcome. *Psychological Bulletin, 91,* 349–365.

Kimble, G. A. (1961). Hilgard and Marquis' conditioning and learning. New York: Appleton-Century-Crofts.

Koegel, R. L., & Covert, A. (1972). The relationship of self-stimulation to learning in autistic children. *Journal of Applied Behavior Analysis, 5,* 381–387.

Koegel, R. L., Firestone, P. B., Kramme, K. W., & Dunlap, G. (1974). Increasing spontaneous play by suppressing self-stimulation in autistic children. *Journal of Applied Behavior Analysis, 7,* 521–528.

Konarski, E. A. (1982, April). *Research trends across twenty years of behavior modification with the severely and profoundly retarded.* Paper presented at the annual Gatlinburg Conference on Research in Mental Retardation and Developmental Disabilities, Gatlinburg, TN.

Konarski, E. A., Johnson, M., Crowell, C. R., & Whitman, T. L. (1980). Response deprivation and reinforcement in applied settings: A preliminary analysis. *Journal of Applied Behavior Analysis, 13,* 595–609.

Landesman-Dwyer, S., & Sackett, G. P. (1978). Behavioral changes in nonambulatory, mentally retarded individuals. In C. E. Meyers (Ed.) *Quality of life in severely and profoundly mentally retarded people: Research foundations for improvement* (Monograph 3). Washington, DC: American Association on Mental Deficiency.

Lewis, M. H., & Baumeister, A. A. (1982). Stereotyped mannerisms in mentally retarded persons: Animal models and theoretical analyses. In N. R. Ellis, (Ed.), *International review of research in mental retardation* (Vol. 11). New York: Academic.

Lovaas, O. I., Freitag, G., Gold, V., & Kassorla, I., (1965). Experimental studies in childhood schizophrenia: Analysis of self-destructive behavior. *Journal of Experimental Child Psychology, 2,* 67–84.

Lovaas, O. I., Litrownik, A., & Mann, R. (1971). Response latencies to auditory stimuli in autistic children engaged in self-stimulatory behavior. *Behavior Research and Therapy, 9,* 34–49.

MacLean, W. E., & Baumeister, A. A. (1981). Observational analysis of the stereotyped mannerisms of a developmentally delayed infant. *Applied Research in Mental Retardation, 2,* 257–262.

McFarland, D. J. (1976). Form and function in the temporal organization of behavior. In P. P. G. Bateson and R. A. Hinde (Eds.), *Growing points in ethology.* Cambridge: Cambridge University Press.

Mulick, J., Hoyt, P., Rojahn, J., & Schroeder, S. (1978). Reducction of a "nervous habit" in a profoundly retarded youth by increasing toy play: A case study. *Behavior Therapy and Experimental Psychiatry, 9,* 381–385.

Mulick, J., & Schroeder, S. (1980). Research relating to antisocial behavior in mentally retarded persons. *The Psychological Record, 30,* 397–417.

Mulick, J., Schroeder, S. R., & Rojahn, J. (1980). Chronic ruminative vomiting: A comparison of four procedures for treatment. *Journal of Autism and Developmental Disorders, 10,* 203–213.

Patterson, G. R. (1979). A performance theory for coercive family interaction. In R. B. Cairns (Ed.), *The analysis of social interactions: Methods, issues, and illustrations.* Hillsdale, NJ: Erlbaum.

Rachlin, H., & Burkhard, B. (1978). The temporal triangle: Response substitution in instrumental conditioning. *Psychological Review, 85,* 22–47.

Repp, A. C., Barton, L. E., Brulle, A. R. (1981). Correspondence between effectiveness and staff use of instructions for severely retarded persons. *Applied Research in Mental Retardation, 2,* 237–246.

Reynolds, G. S. (1961). Behavioral contrast. *Journal of the Experimental Analysis of Behavior, 4,* 57–71.

Risley, T. R. (1968). The effects and side effects of punishing the autistic behaviors of a deviant child. *Journal of Applied Behavior Analysis, 1,* 21–34.

Rojahn, J., Mulick, J. A., McCoy, D., & Schroeder, S. R. (1978). Setting effects, adaptive clothing, and the modification of head banging and self-restraint in two profoundly retarded adults. *Behavioral Analysis and Modification, 2,* 185–196.

Rojahn, J., Schroeder, S., & Mulick, J. (1980). Ecological assessment of self-protective restraints for the chronically self-injurious. *Journal of Autism and Developmental Disorders, 10,* 59–65.

Rojahn, J., & Wool, R. (1979). Inter- and intra-observer agreement as a function of explicit behavior definitions in direct observation. *Behavior Analysis and Modification, 3,* 211–228.

Rollings, J. P., Baumeister, A., & Baumeister, A. (1977). The use of overcorrection procedures to eliminate stereotyped behaviors in retarded individuals. *Behavior Modification, 1,* 29–46.

Sackett, G. P. (Ed.), (1978a). *Observing behavior* (1972). (Vol. 1). Baltimore: University Park Press.

Sackett, G. P. (Ed.). (1978b). *Observing behavior* (Vol. 2). Baltimore: University Park Press.

Sajwaj, T., Twardosz, S., & Burke, M. (1972). Side effects of extinction procedures in a remedial school. *Journal of Applied Behavior Analysis, 5,* 163–175.

Schroeder, S., Kanoy, R., Thios, S., Mulick, J., Rojahn, J., Stephens, M., & Hawk, B. (1982). Antecedent conditions affecting management and maintenance of programs for the chronically self-injurious. In J. Hollis and C. E. Meyers (Eds.), *Life-threatening behavior: Analysis and intervention* (Monograph 5). Washington, DC: American Association on Mental Deficiency.

Schroeder, S., Lewis, M. H., & Lipton, M. (1983). Interactions of pharmacotherapy and behavior therapy among children with learning and behavior disorders. In K. Gadow & I. Bialer (Eds.), *Advances in learning and behavioral disabilities* (Vol. 2). Greenwich, CT: JAI Press.

Schroeder, S. R., Mulick, J. A., & Rojahn, J. (1980). The definition, taxonomy, epidemiology, and ecology of self-injurious behavior. *Journal of Autism and Developmental Disorders, 10,* 417–432.

Schroeder, S., Mulick, J. A., & Schroeder, C. (1979). Management of severe behavior problems of the retarded. In N. R. Ellis (Ed.), *Handbook of mental deficiency,* (2nd ed.). New York: Erlbaum.

Schroeder, S. R., Peterson, C., Solomon, L., & Artley, J. (1977). EMG feedback and the contingent restraint of self-injurious behavior among the severely retarded: Two case illustrations, *Behavior Therapy, 8,* 738–741.

Schroeder, S., Schroeder, C., Rojahn, J., & Mulick, J. (1981). Analysis of self-injurious behavior: Its development and management. In J. L. Matson & J. R. McCartney (Eds.), *Handbook of behavior modification for the mentally retarded*. New York: Plenum.

Sidman, M. (1978). Remarks. *Behaviorism, 6,* 265–268.

Skinner, B. F. (1938). *The behavior of organisms*. New York: Appleton-Century-Crofts.

Solnick, J. V., Rincover, A., & Peterson, C. R. (1977). Some determinants of the reinforcing and punishing effects of time-out. *Journal of Applied Behavior Analysis, 10,* 415–424.

Spiegel, H. (1967). Is symptom removal dangerous? *American Journal of Psychiatry, 10,* 1279–1282.

Staddon, J. E. R. (1979). Operant behavior as adaptation to constraint. *Journal of Experimental Psychology: General, 108,* 48–67.

Tarpley, H., & Schroeder, S. R. (1979). A comparison of DRI, DRO, and extinction procedures in the modification of self-injurious behavior. *American Journal of Mental Deficiency, 84,* 188–194.

Twardosz, S., & Sajwaj, T. (1972). Multiple effects of a procedure to increase sitting in a hyperactive, retarded boy. *Journal of Applied Behavior Analysis, 5,* 73–78.

Wahler, R. G. (1975). Some structural aspects of deviant child behavior. *Journal of Applied Behavior Analysis, 8,* 17–42.

Wahler, R. G., Berland, R. M., Coe, T. D., & Leske, G. (1977). Social systems analysis: Implementing an alternative behavior model. In A. Rogers-Warren & S. F. Warren (Eds.), *Ecological perspectives in behavior analysis*. Baltimore: Univrsity Park Press.

Wahler, R. G., & Fox, J. (1980). Solitary toy play and time-out: A family treatment package for children with aggressive and oppositional behavior. *Journal of Applied Behavior Analysis, 13,* 23–29.

Wahler, R. G., & Leske, G. (1973). Accurate and inaccurate observer summary reports: Reinforcement theory interpretation and investigation. *Journal of Nervous and Mental Disease, 156,* 386–594.

Williams, J. L., Schroeder, S. R., Rojahn, J., Eckerman, P. A. (1983). Time-out from positive reinforcement procedures with mentally retarded persons: An ecobehavioral review and analysis. In S. Breuning & J. Matson (Eds.), *Advances in research in mental retardation and developmental disabilities*. Greenwich, CT: JAI Press.

15
Interaction Effects of Psychotropic and Seizure Control Medication On Behavior in Different Environmental Settings

Stephen Sulzbacher and Bradley Steinfeld
University of Washington

In his classic large scale study, Lipman (1970) found that about 50% of the mentally retarded residents in institutions in the United States received psychotropic medication. In subsequent research, investigators have reported similar usage rates. Kirman (1976) found that 60% of 617 institutionalized individuals in London were receiving such medication. Sewell and Werry (1976) reported a 40% rate in a New Zealand institution. Tu (1979) surveyed five institutions in Canada and found that 42% of 2,238 residents were receiving psychotropics; 27%, anticonvulsants; and 11% a combination of both. Wilson (1981) studied drug usage patterns in the five institutions for mentally retarded persons in Washington State, detecting considerable variation in psychotropic medication usage, ranging from 27 to 64%.

Little comparable data on psychotropic drug use in community settings are available. Gadow (1977, 1981) found that only 7.5% of 3,300 children in public school classes for moderately mentally retarded students were receiving psychotropic medication. Direct comparison of drug usage in community facilities versus institutions is not possible given the differences in the populations studied, although case control studies could be designed.

Certainly, staff members' philosophy on use of medications might differ across facilities, as would their knowledge about medication effects. In their evaluation of medication management in community-based facilities in Nebraska, Schalock, Foley, Toulouse, and Stark (1985) noted that:

> Clients frequently take multiple drugs prescribed by different physicians who are unaware of one another's prescriptions; personnel are unaware of the initial reason for the prescriptions, the desired effects, or the

possible contraindications; and generic physicians frequently do not provide meaningful data regarding desired effects and time lines within which to evaluate the drug's effects. (p. 504)

Serious questions remain regarding possible overuse and inadequate monitoring of psychotropic medications (Sulzbacher, 1973). Sprague and Baxley (1978) observed that the advent of widespread use of psychotropic drugs led to a dramatic decline in psychiatric institutionalization, but no comparable effect occurred in institutions serving mentally retarded individuals. That is, mentally retarded individuals did not show the dramatic therapeutic improvement that mentally ill individuals did. One hypothesis is that medication for mentally ill patients reduced the frequency of undesired behaviors *and* allowed increased desired behavior *that preexisted in the behavioral repertoire of these persons.* This is consistent with the notion that psychotropic medications, like chlorpromazine, selectively affect aggressive behavior and impulse control more than they do other types of behavior. Mentally retarded individuals, however, often lack a sufficient repertoire of those "other" behaviors needed for independent community living. Medication may reduce further retarded persons' ability to interact with the environment. What remains undetermined is what proportion of the acting out and aggressive behavior for which medication is usually prescribed is related to the institutional environment in contrast to the individual's traits. An excellent opportunity now exists to do research on this question as more and more institutions move toward smaller residential units and more stimulating environments (see Chapter 5 by Landesman).

Objective study of the behavioral effects of psychotropic medication is a complicated methodological problem. After reviewing the use of psychotropic medication with children, Sulzbacher (1973) suggested that only a small percentage of the published studies were adequately controlled or used objective direct measurements of behavior. Since then, there has been an increase in well-controlled studies using objective measurement of specific behaviors, but not many investigators have considered possible interaction effects with the residential environment (Schroeder, Lewis, & Lipton, 1981). When looking at combined versus separate use of two interventions, one must be able to determine whether the combined effect is greater than the sum of their individual effects (potentiation), less than the sum (inhibition), or equal to the effect of the more potent intervention (reciprocation). The conceptual model developed by Schroeder et al. (1981) provides a valuable framework for studying the interaction of pharmacotherapy and behavior therapy in various environmental settings.

The variables that should be included in evaluating drug-environment interactions are (a) medication variables: type of medication, dosage as related to body weight, time since the last administration of medication, duration of chronic administration, and possible placebo effects; and (b) environmental variables: length of treatment, effects of termination or withdrawal from treatment, generalization or maintenance of treatment effects, and placebo or transference effects. A single research design rarely can evaluate all these variables, but it is possible. Capitalizing on research opportunities afforded by legislative mandates, as has been done by Landesman (see Chapter 5), provides an ethical and feasible way to observe effects on treated versus untreated individuals in a multiple-baseline design.

The most persuasive research demonstrating that medication effects differ depending on the environment is that by Whalen, Henker, and colleagues (Whalen et al., 1978; Whalen & Henker, 1980; Whalen, Henker, Collins, Finck, & Dotemoto, 1979). Their research, primarily with the effects of methylphenidate on hyperactive children, illustrates the principle of Person X Environment interaction. For example, medication had a greater effect on a child's disruptive behavior relative to placebo in a noisy classroom than in a quiet classroom. Appropriate social behavior, however, was not differentially affected by ambiant classroom noise but, rather, showed significantly greater medication effects when students were doing individual classroom work versus being engaged in group instruction.

Sprague and Baxley (1978) categorized the kinds of behavioral disturbances by retarded individuals for which drugs have been prescribed as: (a) acting out and aggressiveness, (b) impulse control, (c) self-abusive behavior, and (d) stereotyped behavior. Although such behavioral excesses can be modified significantly by medication (Davis, 1971), the research failed to address etiological factors responsible for such maladaptive behavior. An implicit assumption is that such behavior by retarded individuals is part of an underlying pathological or psychiatric disorder, similar to that among mentally ill patients (Sprague & Baxley 1978). An alternative explanation is that much disruptive behavior is the result of faulty environments (Lindsley, 1964) and that the theoretical basis for treatment should focus on environmental manipulation rather than pharmacological manipulation (Butterfield, Chapter 3, this volume; O'Leary, 1980; Winett & Winkler, 1972). Here again, research with hyperactive children provides strong evidence for including behavioral or environmental approaches. Whalen et al. (1978) found systematic variation in task attention, out-of-seat movement, and classroom fidgeting, depending upon difficulty of instructional materials and the child's ability to control the presentation order of these materials. Jacob, O'Leary, and Rosenblad (1978) found differences in observed hyperactive behavior between hyperactive and nonhyperactive children in a formal classroom setting where the teacher specified the tasks, but these differences disappeared in an informal setting where the children had considerable flexibility in selecting tasks.

The foregoing research is relevant to the ongoing debate about the relative merits of pharmacological treatment versus behavioral treatment (Sprague, 1978) and makes clear the need for a more accurate assessment of how environmental variables interact with medications intended to alter behavior disorders of retarded individuals. Such an assessment is critical because environmental manipulation may be sufficient to produce desired changes in behaviors previously treated primarily with medication.

Case law on evaluating medication effects. Another reason for more research on environmental and pharmacological methods is the legal challenge to current medication practices in institutions. In *Wyatt v. Stickney* (1972), the judge specifically declared that institutional residents have a right to be free of excessive medication and ordered the monitoring of behavioral effects of medications. This decision implied that preexisting practices of administering medications and monitoring their effects were inadequate. A far more specific ruling was issued by Judge Larson in the case of *Welch v. Likins* (1977), who indicated that tranquilizing medication was not adequately supervised or monitored and was used as a form of chemical restraint at Cambridge State Hospital in Minnesota. In addition to specifying rules for the use of medications, the judge recognized the contribution of environmental factors by directing the institution to employ additional staff members with behavior-modification expertise. The court discovered that 70% of the residents of Cambridge State Hospital were given psychotropic medications, many in dosages exceeding the manufacturers' recommended maximum dose. The court specified that each resident's record must contain the following information if any medication is used to control or modify behavior: (a) a description of the objectionable behavior, (b) records showing the number of times the objectionable behavior occurred during a period of at least one month prior to administration of the medication, (c) the actual medication prescribed, (d) records showing the number of times the objectionable behavior occurred after the administration of the medication, (e) a written statement indicating what increase or decrease in dosage of the medication or other change in the resident's prescription was made as a result of comparing the pre and post drug records, (f) an ongoing record of frequency of objectionable behavior after any change is made in dosage or type of medication, and (g) a written plan for periodic "drug holidays" during which the resident receives no major tranquilizers, together with a requirement of recordkeeping during these periods to determine whether the medication is still needed.

Because overmedication may be considered by some to be a "cost effective" method of managing a residential facility that is understaffed or facing budget cuts, it is all the more urgent that we increase our scientific understanding of how environments, staffing ratios, and medication interact to decrease undesirable behaviors and to facilitate more socially appropriate behaviors in a treatment setting.

RESEARCH ON INTERACTION EFFECTS

Although interaction effects between environmental conditions and medication dosages almost certainly occur, researchers typically have *not* documented the expected *additive* effects when behavioral approaches are combined with medication (Christensen, 1975; Gittleman et al., 1977; Shafto & Sulzbacher, 1977; Wulbert & Dries, 1977). These studies do not comprise a comprehensive assessment or definitive test of this possibility.

The populations under study varied in age and diagnoses, and medication dosages often are not reported in standard milligram per kilogram format. Sprague and Sleator (1977) observed several types of behavior as they varied dosages systematically in a standard fashion and found that even in the same individual, specific behaviors respond differently at different dosages.

Treatment effects may appear to be different depending upon choice of dependent measure (Pelham, Schnedler, Bologna, & Contreras, 1980) and how changes in the behavior being observed are measured (Sulzbacher, 1973). In measuring effects of stimulant medications, Whalen, Henker, Collins, McAuliffe, and Vaux (1979) found that the measures that best differentiated drug from placebo conditions were not simple frequency counts but, rather, were the global impressions of behavior as rated by teachers. If this is true, then more careful consideration is needed regarding quality, form, intensity, and/or sequence of behaviors, rather than frequency counts. Schroeder et al. (1981) also noted that the interpretations of the nature of drug and behavior therapy interactions differed substantially depending on the measurement approach for documenting changes. The possible role of setting always needs to be included. For example, Whalen, et al. (1978) showed that hyperactive children did not improve on a relatively easy task when given stimulant medication, but did when task difficulty was increased. Theoretically, combining drug and behavior-modification strategies could result in a negative rather than positive interaction. Paul, Tobias, and Holly (1972) found that long-term adult psychiatric inpatients receiving placebo medication plus a social learning treatment responded better than did a comparison group receiving concurrent psychotropic medication and behavioral intervention. Sprague and Baxley (1978) suggested that psychotropic medication actually may interfere with or reduce the effectiveness of institutional programming efforts. Institutions are usually highly regimented during certain periods (e.g. wake-up, meal times, school schedules, physical therapy appointments) but can be very loosely structured during leisure times on the living units. Institution residents can depend on staff members to get to scheduled activities and meals at the prescribed time. Such environmental assistance from staff members may be more available during leisure time in smaller, more home-like, community placements. Such issues underscore the need to evaluate differential interaction effects of medication with environments when residents change their living arrangements.

Staff expectancy is another variable that interacts with medication. Whalen and Henker (1980) found that teachers responded differently to children they knew were taking placebos than they did to those receiving medication or those identified as a control group. A number of researchers have expreessed concern about staff "peeking through the double blind" when they learn to recognize some of the side-effects of the drugs. It is very likely that staff members in institutions and in community facilities may perceive and/or treat differently individuals whom they know are receiving medication, particularly if they anticipate a recurrence of behavior problems when they know individuals are being weaned from medication. Similar expectancies have been documented in children themselves. In interviews with children taking stimulant medication, Whalen and Henker (1980) learned that children tend to attribute *positive* changes in their behavior specifically to the medication, but they blamed their *bad* behavior on themselves and often claimed that they misbehaved because they forgot to take their medication. This effect has particularly important ramifications for deinstitutionalized retarded persons. Because a major goal in treatment of retarded persons is to increase independence and self-control, individuals need to accept more responsibility for their behavior and not view medication as a "crutch." *Dependence* on medication, whether real or imagined, is one more element in the mental set of many retarded persons that can interfere with the ability to develop independent-living skills.

A pioneering study of drug–environment interactions with a mentally retarded population was done by McConahey, Thompson, and Zimmerman (1977). They instituted a token-economy behavior-modification system in the morning on a women's ward. Chlorpromazine was alternated with placebo every month for 6 months. One of their results was a decrease in aggressive behavior in the morning during the more structured token-economy environment, but no detected medication effect on aggression in the afternoon. These researchers also measured time spent lying on the floor, which was significantly greater during the medication months than during placebo periods. "Lying on the floor" occurred even more frequently in the unprogrammed afternoon than during the morning token-economy time.

The effects of chlorpromazine on retarded individuals *across settings* have been studied by Marholin and Phillips (1976) and Marholin, Touchette, and Stewart (1979). They found considerable individual differences in drug response. In a highly structured workshop setting, there were minimal behavioral differences between drug and placebo conditions. In the less structured ward setting, however, individuals spent significantly more time in bed when they were on medication versus placebo. Conversely, they exhibited more eye contact, greater proximity, and increased interaction with others during placebo conditions compared to drug conditions.

In a single case study of a girl with Gilles de la Tourette syndrome, Sulzbacher and Liberty (1979) demonstrated several environment–drug interaction effects using haloperidol to treat verbal tics. Among the variables manipulated were level of difficulty of school work, medication dosage, teacher versus patient responsibility for administrating medication, and the reinforcement system in the classroom. Teacher control of drug-taking reduced verbal tics and improved school performance. Lowering medication dosage by one third led to a 10-fold decrease in verbal tics. Totally eliminating medication, however, produced a dramatic increase in tics to more than double the original tic rate. Academic performance improved as the assigned work became more difficult, whereas verbal tics declined. In other words, effective total care for this girl's problems required the close collaboration of the teacher and physician over a period of months to find the optimal combination of dosage and classroom contingencies. Simple drug treatment of tics neither controlled the disease adequately nor did it lead to satisfactory school and social adjustment.

Schroeder, Schroeder, Smith, and Dalldorf (1978) reviewed the records of severely retarded self-injurious persons and found that behavior therapy was the most effective treatment and that administration of neuroleptics resulted in little additional improvement.

In one of the few controlled double-blind studies of drug-therapy interactions in children, Campbell et al. (1978) evaluated the effects of haloperidol and a language-training program on the behavior problems of autistic children in an inpatient facility. There were two levels of drugs (placebo vs. optimal dose) and two reinforcement conditions (noncontingent and contingent reinforcement). Their results revealed that the combined program of medication and reinforcement was more effective than was either treatment alone in promoting language performance. Performances on a cognitive test battery, on-task behavior, and ratings of maladaptive behavior were not affected by any of the treatments.

Breuning and colleagues have conducted a series of drug–behavior interaction studies comparing neuroleptic withdrawal and contingent reinforcement. Two studies compared the effects of medication and reinforcement on repeated intelligence testings (Breuning & Davidson, 1981; Breuning & Poling, 1982). Results revealed that the reinforcement group not receiving medication improved significantly more on cognitive measures than did groups receiving medication alone or reinforcement and medication. Yet follow-up data revealed that the reinforcement/no-medication group also showed a large increase in inappropriate behavior.

In another study, Breuning, O'Neill, and Ferguson (1980) compared the effects of drug withdrawal, with or without a behavioral intervention, among institutionalized retarded adults. Results revealed that the drug plus behavior-management procedure was more effective than was drug treatment alone. Unfortunately, there was no behavior-management-only condition to permit determining how much drugs added to the effectiveness of the behavioral treatment.

Thus, although there is an increasing recognition of the need to evaluate combined drug–behavior treatment strategies, this effort needs to be extended to examining interactions of combined treatment across different environmental settings. The setting variable is a critical issue that may explain the failure to find consistent additive effects when combining treatments, yet it has not been assessed directly (Campbell et al., 1978; Conners & Wells, 1979).

INTERACTIONS WITH OTHER MEDICATIONS

Accurate assessment of interaction effects is further complicated for individuals receiving anticonvulsant medication as well as psychotherapeutic medication (Gadow & Kalachnik, 1981). In a British epidemiological study, Richardson, Koller, Katz, and McLaren (1980) found that 27% of the mentally retarded population studied had a seizure history; but this percentage increased to 50% among the more severely retarded individuals (those with IQs less than 50). In his survey of five institutions in Washington State, Wilson (1981) found that from 32 to 71% of the population at these institutions were receiving anticonvulsant medication. Well over half of these individuals were receiving two or more different anticonvulsant agents. In another survey, Tu (1980) found that 80% of institutionalized persons with epilepsy were given multiple anticonvulsants. Tu presented data on 26 patients who had been receiving 80 different drugs. Following a "drug holiday" for these patients, during which seizures and behavior problems were assessed, it was possible to maintain 9 of the patients (35%) completely without anticonvulsants and 14 patients (64%) free from psychotropic medication. Forty-seven of the 80 drugs were withdrawn in Tu's sample, with no increase in seizures or behavioral problems noted on follow-up. These data certainly provide provide persuasive evidence that anticonvulsants, as well as psychotropics, are monitored inadequately in some institutional populations.

Furthermore, Reynolds (1978) pointed out that polypharmacy (combining several medications to treat the same disorder) and inadequate monitoring of drug levels are a major problem for nonretarded persons with epilepsy in the community as well. He stressed problems of maintaining drug levels when patients do not comply with prescribed regimes for taking the medication. For deinstitutionalized retarded persons, the move from a more to less regimented environment is very likely to cause serious variations in drug levels. Furthermore, some community-based group-home staff members may be less sophisticated in drug administration than are their counterparts in institutions. Even among nonretarded populations, Kutt (1975) has pointed to the inevitability of serious drug interactions occurring when several anticonvulsants and nonanticonvulsants are taken at the same time. Sorting out the various drug–drug and drug–environment interactions and their separate effects on deinstitutionalized retarded individuals appears nearly impossible unless these effects are assessed prior to community placement and the number of medications and times of administration are carefully specified and monitored.

A CASE EXAMPLE

The problems of accurate assessment of the effects of several anticonvulsant medications on behavior and seizure frequency are illustrated in the case of Andy, who was 15 years old when this study was conducted. He had been diagnosed as mildly mentally retarded and had been showing satisfactory progress at school until he developed a seizure disorder at age 13. The seizure disorder proved to be intractable to treatment with a variety of medications, and Andy began to complain more about his medication levels than about his seizures. In collaboration with Andy and his parents, a program was devised to monitor seizure frequency and arithmetic homework performance as an index of cognitive functioning. Because complete seizure control did not appear to be possible, the goal was set to find the medication level at which Andy perceived the least discomfort, both from his seizures and from his medications.

The data presented here are clearly clinical data, recorded by the patient and his mother in an attempt to make rational drug-dosage decisions about the process of a disease that proved to be incurable. The data should not be interpreted to suggest anything about the relative merits of the drugs employed, but only as an argument for using objective behavioral data, in addition to accurate monitoring of seizure frequency, as a basis for adjustments in drug-treatment regimens.

Although Andy's cognitive and verbal abilities were clearly not representative of those of deinstitutionalized mentally retarded individuals, his regimen of three to four different anticonvulsants was typical of the drug regimens described by Tu (1980) and Reynolds (1978). Bennett, Dunlop, and Ziring (1983) have shown that as many as 78% of institutionalized mentally retarded epileptic individuals can remain seizure-free after switching from multiple drugs to a single anticonvulsant. They also noted that 20 to 40% of the individuals in the institutions they surveyed were taking anticonvulsants, a figure consistent with the previously cited studies. Glick, Guyer, Burr, and Gorbach (1983) found that 75% of deinstitutionalized multiply handicapped children had seizure disorders, which they judged to be inadequately monitored. The behavioral probes used in the following case were relatively easy to collect and helped guide certain dosage decisions.

Figure 1 shows the changes in the amount and the accuracy of Andy's performance during a daily 45-minute homework session. It is difficult to pinpoint precise behavioral changes as a function of specific medication changes (as Sulzbacher & Liberty, 1979, were able to do) because of the need to make gradual changes in medication levels. Data were not gathered throughout the entire course of changing drug levels; one week probes at regular intervals when new drug levels were thought to have stabilized were deemed sufficient. A clear overall trend, however, is apparent: the rate per minute of correct and error reponses showed great variability during the initial probe; deteriorated on the second probe (while error rate exceeded correct); varied on the third probe, and stabilized on the fourth probe. On the final probe, Andy showed consistent rapid performance with few errors. Seizures recorded during these homework sessions increased slightly during the course of the medication changes. Andy was making more errors than correct responses on 6 of the initial 11 sessions, but after Session 11, his error rate was never higher than his correct rate. This improvement in academic performance coincided with a gradual reduction from four to two anticonvulsants and reduction in dosage of one of the remaining medications.

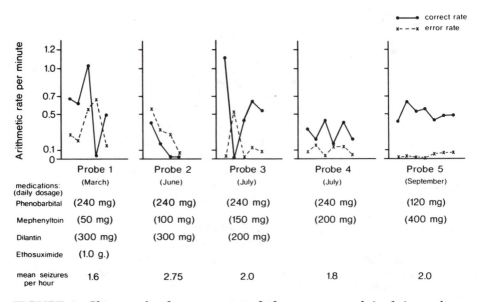

FIGURE 1. Changes in the amount and the accuracy of Andy's performance during a daily 45-minute homework session.

Andy's mother recorded his seizure frequency during the homework
sessions, which increased somewhat as medication was reduced; however,
both Andy and his parents felt that the academic data supported their
contention that he was "doing better" at the end of the last probe than he
had been previously. Although his seizure disorder worsened over time,
the family continued to use similar objective checks on Andy's cognitive
functioning in their ongoing monitoring of medications.

Andy's situation had no fully satisfactory solution, a situation quite
similar to that of many deinstitutionalized multiply handicapped individuals. A program of systematically monitoring cognitive and social functioning as these persons' complex medication regimens are adjusted to
minimize the effects of medical conditions is essential for their overall well
being.

WHAT ARE THE IMPLICATIONS OF THIS RESEARCH?

There are still too few studies in which investigators examine drug–
environment interactions among retarded individuals. Clinical research
should be directed at the implications of environmental versus medication
interactions for persons who have spent a long time in institutions and are
being moved into community residential facilities. There are four issues
toward which such research should be directed.

1. INTERACTION EFFECTS OF MAJOR TRANQUILIZERS

A commonly noted effect of these compounds is that day-dreaming, lethargic individuals receiving this medication can be roused from its effects quite easily when challenged, and will then interact appropriately with other people for a reasonable period of time. When the environmental stimulation is removed, medicated persons will resume their lethargy. In other words, what appears lost due to drug effect is the persons' initiative to act on their own; but, given a more moderate dosage, the same individual might respond appropriately in a classroom situation. The lethargic behavior pattern may be well suited to the environmental situation in a residential institution, but is not as appropriate in a community setting where individuals are likely to be required to show some initiative in getting from place to place. Because it is probably the case that undesired acting-out or aggressive behavior occurs more frequently in unstructured environments than in structured environments, one must give serious consideration to observing the behavior of deinstitutionalized persons on *and* off medication in a new environment before making an arbitary decision to either continue or discontinue medication (or to alter dosage).

2. DOSAGE AND MAINTENANCE OF ACCURATE COMPLIANCE TO MEDICATION REGIMES

As noted by Sulzbacher and Liberty (1979), the behavioral effects of psychotropic medication can be significantly altered simply by ensuring that the medication is taken at the actual times prescribed. The role of the environment in fostering careful adherence to prescribed administration of medication must be considered. Because up to 20% of individuals receiving psychotropic medication in institutions may have a daily dosage that exceeds the maximal FDA guideline amounts, and most have been long-term users, tolerance effects also must be assessed. These are overwhelmingly important factors in managing the transition from an institutional to a community residential placement. We are aware of no investigators who have systematically examined dosage changes as individuals move to new residential settings.

3. "ADEQUATE" MEDICAL MANAGEMENT FOR SEVERELY AND MULTIPLY HANDICAPPED CHILDREN AND ADULTS IN COMMUNITY SETTINGS

There is considerable difference of opinion about how to manage medical treatment (Conroy, 1985). The research and legal findings just reported suggest that there is room for improvement in the monitoring of medications by case-mangement teams. It appears that moving severely and profoundly retarded individuals with multiple medical problems into diverse community placements has resulted in less rather than greater attention to behavioral effects of drug dosages, drug–drug, and drug–environment interactions (Schalock et al., 1985). Because many individuals do not have the communication skills to signal discomfort, some of these effects may go unnoticed in less restrictive community settings with reduced levels of medical care. Clearly, the health-care delivery system must be considered an important part of the environment in any analysis of drug–environment interactions among deinstitutionalized individuals.

The deinstitutionalization process in most states has progressed to the point where only the lower functioning, more medically involved individuals remain to be placed in community facilities. Glick et al. (1983) studied 421 cases of severely and profoundly retarded, multiply-handicapped children placed in privately run, community-based nursing homes in Massachusetts and concluded that "low standards of care and financial disincentives have resulted in less than optimal educational and rehabilitative services" for these individuals. In their sample, 72% had seizures and 14% had cerebral palsy without known seizures, leaving only 14% free of complicating medical conditions. Nevertheless, Glick et al. found no mechanism for transfers between skilled-nursing and intermediate-care facilities as the medical or behavioral condition of these individuals changed. They cited high average annual death rates (between 3 and 6%) and low discharge rates at these community nursing homes as evidence of substandard case-management procedures. These researchers also reviewed the situation in five other states and found similar problems.

The current practice of simple office-visit medical care from local practitioners in the absence of continuous coordinated monitoring of the interaction effects of medications is not adequate. Community-care agencies should be funded and regulated to meet the standards mandated in the *Welch v. Likins* (1977) decision for institutional drug management.

4. EFFECTS OF GROSS VERSUS FINE CHANGES IN ENVIRONMENT

Research in which effects of residential placement are investigated would ideally involve studying individuals before and after movement to a new physical and social environment. Finer grain analyses are necessary to determine which specific environmental features affect behavior and which impact the effectiveness of psychotropic medications and vice versa. Room size, number of individuals in the house, size of bathrooms, stairs, and proximity of neighbors are all examples of such finer grain environmental features.

Most psychotropic medications (and all anticonvulsants) are prescribed to *reduce* the frequency of some behavior or behaviors. Particularly when individuals are moving to less structured or more enriched living environments, specific assessments need to include a listing of the types of behavior that could be influenced, in either positive or negative directions.

In summary, further research is needed to identify precise behaviors for which medication is being prescribed and the settings in which individuals reside and receive treatment. Both objective and subjective monitoring of changes in behavior, as a function of dosage and variables in the environment, are essential and ethical for maximizing improvement in the quality of life for persons who are retarded. Although the evidence to date is mixed, we remain confident that psychotropic medication in appropriate doses, responsibly monitored, can have favorable effects on the behavior of individuals and enhance the quality of their interactions with the physical environment and with the people in their social milieu. The guidelines specified in *Welch v. Likins* (1977) must be applied in community settings as well as in institutions and extended to include anticonvulsants as well as psychotropic medications. In addition, behavioral researchers studying other aspects of development of mentally retarded individuals must consider the possible contributions of medication effects, which may unknowingly vary with the setting or treatment being studied to their findings.

REFERENCES

Bennett, H. S., Dunlop, T., & Ziring, P. (1983). Reduction of polypharmacy for epilepsy in an institution for the retarded. *Developmental Medicine and Child Neurology, 26,* 735–737.

Breuning, S. E. & Davidson, N A. (1981). Effects of psychotropic drugs on IQ Test Performance obtained under standard and reinforcement conditions with institutionalized retarded adults. *American Journal of Mental Deficiency, 85,* 575–579.

Breuning, S. E., O'Neill, M J., & Ferguson, D. G. (1980). Comparison of psychotropic drug, response cost, and psychotropic plus response cost procedures for controlling institutionalized retarded persons. *Applied Research in Mental Retardation, 1,* 253–268.

Breuning, S. E., & Poling, A. D. (1982). *Drugs and Mental Retardation.* Springfield, IL: Thomas.

Campbell, M., Anderson, L., Meier, M., Cohen, I., Small, A., Samit, G., & Sachor, E. (1978). A comparison of haloperidol and behavior therapy and their interaction in autistic children. *Journal of the American Academy of Child Psychiatry, 17,* 640–655.

Christensen, D. E. (1975). Effects of combining methylphenidate and a classroom token system in modifying hyperactive behavior. *American Journal of Mental Deficiency, 80,* 266–276.

Connors, C. K., & Wells, K. C. (1979). Method and theory for psychopharmacology with children. In R. Trites (Ed.), *Hyperactivity in children.* Baltimore: University Park Press.

Conroy, J. W. (1985). Medical needs of institutionalized mentally retarded persons: Perceptions of families and staff members. *American Journal of Mental Deficiency, 89,* 510–514.

Davis, K. V. (1971). The effect of drugs on stereotyped and nonstereotyped operant behaviors in retardates. *Psychopharmacologia, 22,* 95–213.

Gadow, K. D. (1977). *Survey of medication usage with children in trainable mentally handicapped programs and teacher role in drug treatment.* Unpublished doctoral dissertation, University of Illinois.

Gadow, K. D. (1981). Effects of stimulant drugs on attention and cognitive deficits. *Exceptional Education Quarterly, 2,* 83–93.

Gadow, K. D., & Kalachnik, J. (1981). Prevalence and pattern of drug treatment for behavior and seizure disorders of TMR students. *American Journal of Mental Deficiency, 85,* 588–595.

Gittleman, R., Abikoff, H., Pollack, E., Klein, D., Katz, S., & Malts, J. (1980). A controlled trial of behavior modification and methylphenidate in hyperactive children. In C. Whalen & B. Henker (Eds.), *Hyperactive children: The social ecology of identification and treatment*. New York: Academic.

Glick, P. S., Guyer, B., Burr, B. H.. & Gorbach, I. E. (1983). Pediatric nursing homes: Implications of the Massachusetts experience for residential care of multiply- handicapped children. *New England Journal of Medicine, 309*, 640–646.

Jacob, R., O'Leary, K. D., & Rosenblad, C. (1978). Formal and informal classroom settings: Effects on hyperactivity. *Journal of Abnormal Child Psychology, 6*, 47–59.

Kirman, B. (1976). Drug therapy in mental handicap. *British Journal of Psychiatry, 127*, 545–549.

Kutt, H. (1975). Interactions of antiepileptic drugs. *Epilepsia, 16*, 393–402.

Lindsley, O. R. (1964). Direct measurement and prosthesis of retarded behavior. *Journal of Education, 147*, 62–81.

Lipman, R. S. (1970). The use of psychopharmacological agents in residential facilities for the retarded. In F. J. Menolascino (Ed.), *Psychiatric approaches to mental retardation*. New York: Basic Books.

Marholin, D., & Phillips, D. (1976). Methodological issues in psychopharmacological research: Chlorpromazine—A case in point. *American Journal of Orthopsychiatry, 46*, 477–495.

Marholin D., Touchette, P., & Stewart, R. M. (1979). Withdrawal of chronic chlorpromazine medication: An experimental analysis. *Journal of Applied Behavior Analysis, 12*, 159–171.

McConahey, O. L., Thompson, T., & Zimmerman, R. (1977). A token system for retarded women: Behavior therapy, drug administration, and their combination. In T. Thompson & J. Grabowski (Eds.), *Behavior modification of the mentally retarded*. New York: Oxford University Press.

O'Leary, K. D. (1980). Pills for skills for hyperactive children. *Journal of Applied Behavior Analysis, 13*, 191–204.

Paul, G., Tobias, L., & Holly, B. (1972). Maintenance psychotropic drugs with chronic mental patients in the presence of active treatment programs: A "triple-blind" withdrawal study. *Archives of General Psychiatry, 27*, 106–115.

Pelham, W., Schnedler, R., Bologna, N., & Contreras, J. (1980). Behavioral and stimulant treatment of hyperactive children: A therapy study with methylphenidate probes in a within-subject design. *Journal of Applied Behavior Analysis, 13*, 221–236.

Reynolds, E. H. (1978). Drug treatment of epilepsy. *Lancet, II*, 721–725.

Richardson, S. A., Koller, H., Katz, M., & McLaren, J. (1980). Seizures and epilepsy in a mentally retarded population over the first 22 years of life. *Applied Research in Mental Retardation, 1*, 123–138.

Schalock, R. L., Foley, J. W., Toulouse, A., & Stark, J. A. (1985). Medication and programming in controlling the behavior of mentally retarded individuals in community settings. *American Journal of Mental Deficiency, 89*, 503–509.

Schroeder, S., Lewis, M., & Lipton, M. (1981). Interactions of pharmacotherapy and behavior therapy among children with learning and behavioral disorders. In K. Gadow & I. Bialer (Eds.), *Advances in learning and behavioral disabilities* (Vol. 2). Greenwich, CT: JAI Press.

Schroeder, S., Schroeder, C., Smith, B., & Dalldorf, J. (1978). Prevalence of self-injurious behaviors in a large state facility for the retarded: A three year follow-up study. *Journal of Childhood Schizophrenia, 8*, 261–269.

Sewell, J., & Werry, J. S. (1976). Some studies in an institution for the mentally retarded. *New Zealand Medical Journal, 84,* 317–319.

Shafto, F., & Sulzbacher, S. (1977). Comparing treatment tactics with a hyperactive preschool child: Stimulant medication and programmed teacher intervention. *Journal of Applied Behavior Analysis, 10,* 13–20.

Sprague, R. L. (1978). Principles of clinical trials and social, ethical and legal issues of drug use in children. In J. S. Werry (Ed.), *Pediatric psychopharmacology: The use of behavior modifying drugs in children.* New York: Bunner/Mazel.

Sprague, R. L., & Baxley, G. B. (1978). Drugs used for management of behavior in mental retardation. In J. Wortis (Ed.), *Mental retardation* (Vol. 8). New York: Brunner/Mazel.

Sprague, R. L., & Sleator, E. (1977). Methylphenidate in hyperkinetic children: Differences in dose effects on learning and social behavior. *Science, 198,* 1274–1276.

Sulzbacher, S. (1973). Psychotropic medication with children: An evaluation of procedural biases in results of reported studies. *Pediatrics, 51,* 513–517.

Sulzbacher, S., & Liberty, K. A. (1979). Interaction effects of medication and classroom contingencies on verbal tics and school performance. In L. A. Hammerlynck (Ed.), *Behavioral systems for the developmentally disabled* (Vol. 2). New York: Brunner/Mazel.

Tu, J. B. (1979). A survey of psychotropic medication in mental retardation facilities. *Journal of Clinical Psychiatry, 40,* 125–128.

Tu, J. B. (1980). Drug holiday for the disturbed-retarded epileptics. *Journal of Clinical Psychiatry, 41,* 324.

Welsch v. Likins, 550 F. 2d 1122 (8th Cir., 1977)

Whalen, C., Collins, B., Henker, B., Alkus, S., Adams, D., & Stapp, J. (1978). Behavior observations of hyperactive children and methylphenidate effects in systematically structured environments: Now you see them, now you don't. *Journal of Pediatric Psychology, 3,* 177–187.

Whalen, C., & Henker, B. (1980). *Hyperactive children: The social ecology of identification and treatment.* New York: Academic.

Whalen, C., Henker, B., Collins, B., McAuliffe, S., & Vaux, A. (1979). Peer interaction in a structured communication task: Comparison of normal and hyperactive boys and of ritalin and placebo effects. *Child Development, 50,* 388–401.

Whalen, C., Henker, B., Collins, B., Finck, D., & Dotemoto, S. (1979). A social ecology of hyperactive boys: Medication effects in structured classroom environments. *Journal of Applied Behavior Analysis, 12,* 65–81.

Wilson, J. (1981). Drug utilization review in five institutions for the mentally retarded — A preliminary report. Unpublished memorandum, Department of Social and Health Services, Olympia, WA.

Winett, R. A., & Winkler, R. C. (1972). Current behavior modification in the classroom: Be still, be quiet, be docile. *Journal of Applied Behavior Analysis, 5,* 499–504.

Wulbert, M., & Dries, R. (1977). The relative efficacy of methylphenidate (ritalin) and behavior modification techniques in the treatment of a hyperactive child. *Journal of Applied Behavior Analysis, 10,* 13–20.

Wyatt v. Stickney, 344 F. Supp. 387 (1972).

Families Affected
by
Mental Retardation

16
The Effects of Developmental Disabilities on Children and Families: Measurement Issues and Conceptual Frameworks

William N. Friedrich
Mayo Clinic

Mark T. Greenberg and Keith A. Crnic
University of Washington

Ramifications of long-term illness are not restricted to the individual affected. Members of the nuclear and extended family are affected by serious physical or psychological illness, which in turn may influence the patient's illness and the family's health and happiness (Litman, 1974). Bentovim (1972) stated that "satisfactory emotional development of the handicapped child depends more on the way in which parents and family relate to the child than to the extent of the handicap itself" (p. 581).

Some handicapping conditions or illnesses may be more difficult for families than are others. Barsch (1964) asked professionals, nonprofessionals, and parents with and without a handicapped child to rate the perceived severity of coping with 10 handicapping conditions of childhood. The 4 rated as most severe were cerebral palsy, brain injury, mental illness, and mental retardation. Whether these rankings directly relate to actual increases in family stress has not been reported.

The handicapped child's impact on the family is mediated by the family's *coping resources* (Lazarus & Folkman, 1984), including the family's health and energy, problem-solving skills, social support, material resources, social skills, and positive beliefs. This impact may be observed in a number of *psychosocial contexts* (Bronfenbrenner, 1977) and includes individual, familiar, social network, and cultural variables. Because coping is a process, this model also allows for a *developmental focus*, which is essential to any area of research involving children.

Adequate assessment of both coping resources and psychosocial contexts is critical to understanding how families function over time. Yet this is rarely the case in any research to date in this area. For example, one major problem in research on families with handicapped children is the anticipation of continued pathology and the failure to interpret findings within a coping paradigm. A second problem is that researchers often ignore psychosocial contexts and focus only on an individual (e.g., the ill child, mother, or, more rarely, the father or sibling). Finally, despite the fact that the research focus is on developing children and families, cross-sectional and/or longitudinal research is only infrequently reported.

This neglect of the psychological issues of disability in children is somewhat surprising in view of its staggering prevalence. If visual and hearing impairments; mental retardation; and speech, learning, and behavior disorders are included, an estimated 30 to 40% of children up to the age of 18 suffer from one or more long-term disorders. If only serious chronic illnesses of primary physical origin are included, an estimated 7 to 10% of all children are affected (Mattsson, 1972).

This chapter is not intended to be a thorough review of the literature in the area of familial coping with developmental disabilities. An earlier paper has accomplished that (Crnic, Friedrich, & Greenberg, 1983). Rather, we have targeted three broad theoretical formulations—systemic/ecological, developmental, and coping theories—and selectively reviewed published works from the developmental disability literature that are pertinent to each of these areas. The literature reviewed may be pertinent to more than one theoretical formulation because the three theories chosen share a number of significant features. We then identified gaps in the research to date and outlined a methodology for future research.

SYSTEMIC / ECOLOGICAL THEORY

Bronfenbrenner (1977) proposed an ecological model of human development. An ecological model is founded in systems theory, the study of the interrelations of organisms and environment. A basic tenet of systems theory is that a change in any part of the system affects the system as a whole and its various subparts, creating the need for system-adaptation rather than simply attending to a single part.

Family systems are constantly coping and adapting to changing internal and external conditions. In so doing, families experience periods of growth and integration, periods of relative balance and stability, as well as periods of disorder and disintegration. As segments of the family system or the environment change, the system's equilibrium alters, calling for counterbalancing changes. In the meantime, stress or tension is created within the system. This stress, when within normal limits, is natural and even necessary. It serves as an activating force for change. When the stress is overwhelming, it may create disruption, and the system breaks down (Bubolz & Whiren, 1984).

The presence of a developmentally disabled child is a chronic stress that may place excessive demands on the energy and resources of the family. Yet, depending on the type or degree of handicapping condition and the actual amount of input (e.g., money, services) into the family, a particular family could be functioning with a relatively high energy expenditure and still remain intact; however, this family may be vulnerable to other sources of stress, such as inflation, unemployment, or school problems of siblings. Researchers must look outside the family to appreciate fully both the potential inputs, the stressors, and the arenas within which the family with a handicapped child must operate.

Bronfenbrenner's (1977) ecological model is not restricted just to the family. Rather, it encompasses four levels of influence on individual development: interactions with immediate settings (e.g., home, family, school, workplace), or the microsystem; the interrelations among major settings containing the individual, the mesosystem; the formal and informal social structures that impinge on the individual (e.g., neighborhood, media, government agencies), or the exosystem; and the ideological institutional patterns of the culture and subcultures, the macrosystem. Each of these contexts exerts considerable influence on the individual's development. Several previous investigators have suggested the importance of focusing on specific ecological factors (Farber, 1959; Rowitz, 1974); and Schoggen and Schoggen (1981) have noted the importance of various ecological factors in the prevention of psychosocial retardation. Yet much of the previous research has focused exclusively on individual family members, ignoring ecological levels as a moderator of behavioral response.

Presently, no descriptive base exists detailing the environments in which families with retarded members function and by which they are influenced. It appears that the ecology of these families could differ markedly from those of families with nonretarded children. For example, siblings of mentally retarded individuals describe their family environment as characterized by greater emphasis on control and organization and lowered tolerance of the expression of emotion. Yet these siblings did not differ on other psychosocial variables (e.g., depression) from comparison subjects with no mentally retarded sibling (Friedrich, Cohen, & Sather, 1985).

Families with retarded children operate under the same influences as do families with nonretarded children (especially if there is a nonretarded sibling), but they are likely to have greater involvement with schools and teachers, social agencies, and service-delivery professionals as well as more limited social contacts (Farber, 1970; Watson & Midlarsky, 1979). Furthermore, they must cope with a set of cultural attitudes regarding the stigma of the handicap (Goffman, 1963). The behavior and attitudes of others in these various settings seem likely to influence the individual and familial response to the retarded child. These are relationships that must be assessed if familial patterns of adaptation are to be understood. We now examine some of the research that is pertinent to several of these ecological levels.

Microsystem

Included in this level is the home setting, where the parenting process occurs. As predicted by systems theory, it seems logical that if stress is associated with parenting a handicapped child, the marital relationship will be vulnerable to the effects of that increased stress as well.

The marriages of the parents of retarded children have not been systematically researched. The research to date is not definite about their marital functioning, and has actually focused only on the issues of relative divorce rate and marital satisfaction, rather than other issues such as communication, decision-making, and role flexibility (Sabbeth & Leventhal, 1984). Farber (1959) studied the effects of having a severely retarded child on marital satisfaction in 240 families. He did not use comparison families, but found that although marital satisfaction declined with the presence of a severely retarded child, outcome was more strongly related to the marital satisfaction of the parents prior to the child's birth. Parents with high satisfaction early in the marriage seemed to do better than those whose satisfaction had been initially lower. Sex of the child was also important to marital satisfaction, as retarded male children had a more significant negative impact on the marriage.

In several recent studies, investigators have assessed marital relationships with the Locke-Wallace Marital Adjustment Inventory (Locke & Wallace, 1959), with conflicting results. Friedrich and Friedrich (1981), comparing matched groups of mothers of handicapped and nonhandicapped children, found a significant difference in marital satisfaction, with the former group reporting lower satisfaction. Using multiple regression to predict stress scores of 98 mothers of handicapped children, Friedrich (1979) found that marital satisfaction, accounting alone for 33% of the total variance, was the most significant predictor. In contrast, Waisbren (1980) found no differences in marital satisfaction between two groups of well-matched couples, half of whom were parents of developmentally delayed infants, nor did Kazak and Marvin (1984), using the Dyadic Adjustment Scale (Spanier, 1976) between two larger groups, one of which was composed of parents who had a child with spina bifida. The conflicting results of the three studies may be attributable to sample differences, as the children in the Friedrich study averaged 9.8 years of age, as opposed to 7.5 years in the Kazak and 13 months in the Waisbren report. Marital satisfaction may decrease over time in families with retarded children.

The variability in the findings on marital satisfaction suggests that marital response is not uniform and may be dependent upon factors other than the presence of a retarded child. Such factors would include the severity of the handicap, the age and sex of the child, and the quality of the marital relationship prior to the presence of the child. The conflicting results noted may also reflect the differences in subject samples on these characteristics. Again, however, it seems likely that the marital relationship will also be influenced by individual coping styles and ecological variables that have yet to be studied.

Also included in the microsystem are parent–child interactions. Very few investigators have actually observed such interactions in families of retarded children. This is especially surprising in view of the fact that parent–child interaction studies are a staple of the nonretarded child development literature.

Several interaction studies measuring responsiveness and communication between groups of mothers with retarded and nonretarded children have meaningful differences. In a pioneering study, Kogan, Wimberger, and Bobbitt (1969) compared a group of 6 retarded children and their mothers with a control group of 10 mother–nonretarded child pairs on parameters of relative status, affection, and involvement. Mothers of retarded children displayed extreme degrees of warmth and friendliness less frequently. The retarded children generally displayed a more neutral status (neither dominant nor submissive). Several subsequent investigators measuring interactive behavior during free play and/or structured situations (Breiner & Forehand, 1982; Eheart, 1982; Terdal, Jackson, & Garner, 1976; Thoman, Becker, & Freese, 1978; Vietze, Abernathy, Ashe, & Faulstich, 1978) found a general asynchrony in the interaction behavior of mother–retarded child dyads. Mothers of retarded children tend to be more active and directive with their children. Retarded children tended to be less responsive and less compliant to their mothers than were nonretarded children.

The interactive patterns of mother–retarded child pairs suggest difficulties in reciprocity within the relationship. Vietze et al. (1978) found that developmentally delayed infants' vocalizations were not as contingent on maternal speech as were the vocalizations of nondelayed infants. Similar findings were reported by Cunningham, Rueler, Blackwell, and Deck (1981), and Terdal et al. (1976), with older retarded children responding less contingently to maternal social behavior than did nonretarded mental age (MA) matched children.

The paucity of interaction studies is distressing; the sample sizes of those that have been conducted are usually too small to permit generalization, and fathers, siblings, or triadic interactions have been generally ignored. Further, the settings and conditions under which interactions have been observed are few. Basic descriptive research on interactions among family members is needed before more than tentative conclusions can be reached.

There are other members in this ecological level—siblings, extended family, teachers—but they will not be discussed in this chapter. For a comprehensive presentation of microsystem issues of retarded children see Fewell and Vadasy (1986).

In an excellent study, Bolstad (1975) compared in-home behavior between parents and children for 10 families who had a cerebral-palsied child between 4 and 9 years of age and 10 families with a healthy child in that age range. The parents were well-matched and observed in the home for 50 minutes per day for 5 consecutive days. In general, no differences were noted between parental behaviors toward the handicapped and nonhandicapped siblings, except that mothers were more responsive and exhibited more positive behaviors overall than did the fathers to the handicapped child. This difference did not hold for the nonhandicapped siblings. Between-family behavioral differences were very few, a principal one being that mothers in the families with a handicapped child exhibited more commands than did mothers in the families without a handicapped child. Bolstad's findings seem to contradict the prevalent view of the handicapped child as inadequate, disturbed, and destructive.

Broad-based assessment of the functioning of families of retarded children as a unit, or system, is the area that has received the least attention. Only one study was found in which such a comprehensive approach was taken in delineating the impact of a retarded child on the family (Nihira, Meyers, & Mink, 1980; Mink, Nihira, & Meyers, 1983). Nihira et al. (1980), studied 268 families of educable and trainable mentally retarded (EMR and TMR) children living at home, using numerous measures of the home environment, family adjustment, and child characteristics. Their results indicated that family adjustment and functioning were related not only to the severity of the child's retardation and degree of maladaptive behavior but to family demographic characteristics, the psychosocial climate of the home (e.g., family cohesion, expressiveness, and harmony) and specific kinds of parental behavior toward their retarded children. In addition, the perceived impact was related to marital disharmony, family conflict, and maladaptive behavior of the retarded child.

Nihira et al. (1980) also demonstrated the interactional and reciprocal nature of the family–retarded child system, as the parents' feelings of impact were related to the retarded children's lack of adaptive competency, and the children's adaptive competency was related to the parents' successful coping with the problem of mental retardation. This study suggests both the difficulties these families face as well as the variability of this impact within groups of families with retarded children. This is certainly a needed and promising direction for research and represents an initial step in integrating measures of child and family to identity outcomes within the family system.

In a later study, Mink et al. (1983), using some of the same subjects, utilized a cluster analytic approach to create a typology of family life styles. The five clusters identified, which clearly underscore the heterogeneity of families with a mentally retarded child, were, in decreasing order of frequency: cohesive–harmonious, control-oriented–unharmonious, child–oriented–expressive, disadvantaged–low morale, and low disclosure–unharmonious. The authors speculated that the differences among clusters were possibly due to differential availability of support systems. Because these studies did not have a developmental focus, however, it is impossible to answer questions about whether family clusters change over time, for example, or if one type is more related to successful development than is another type.

Mesosystem

This ecological level refers to those interrelations among the various settings within which the individual interacts. In a few recent studies, investigators have begun to examine these relationships. In their study of the interrelationships of home environment and school adjustment of TMR children, Nihira, Mink, and Meyers found that family harmony and cohesiveness, quality of parenting, emotional support for learning, and cognitive stimulation available at home were significantly related to the child's school adjustment. These results suggest that familial coping within a specific home environment influences the retarded child's adaptation in a related ecological context. Although Nihira et al. (1981) focused on a child outcome, several investigators have shown that social relationships and support available from several sources has a positive impact on parental functioning (Farber, 1959; Friedrich, 1979; Friedrich & Friedrich, 1981).

We do not mean to diminish the two remaining ecological levels, the exosystem and macrosystem. Rather, our failure to include them in our discussion reflects the lack of research in this area pertinent to mental retardation. We do expect that researchers will soon document the role of these two levels and their relation to familial functioning (Garbarino, 1982). For example, public policy decisions that affect educational funding and that are not supportive of parents contribute to the quality of parental coping in the same way that social beliefs about parents of mentally retarded children are impactful but difficult to assess. Whatever the case, we have demonstrated the need for future research to be ecologically valid and, hence, more clinically relevant to the parents and children we are helping.

DEVELOPMENTAL ISSUES

In a recent paper on family stress and coping, McCubbin et al. (1980) discussed developmental processes, including normative transitions and family stress. Surprisingly, in a field of study that involves developing children and families, truly developmental research in this area is a rarity. There have been a variety of interesting, mostly clinical papers on the initial parental grieving process that occurs upon the discovery of their child's handicap. These investigators have described stages that presumably reflect a process that occurs over a period of time (Fortier & Wanlass, 1984). A central issue in research in this area, however, namely, the effect of stress events germane to developmental disabilities on the developmental process and on subsequent functioning more generally is not well-understood.

Rutter (1983) discussed five main ways in which early experiences (e.g., prematurity, chronic illness) might be linked to later disorders. First, early events could lead to disorder in the individual, which then persists and is maintained by further events that may be largely independent of the initial causation. Second, early events may lead to physical changes in individuals that in turn influence later functioning. A third reason is that early events might lead to altered behavior patterns that manifest as an overt disorder only many years later. Fourth, early events may lead to changes in the family system that later predispose to behavior disorders. Finally, at their onset, early events may alter sensitiveness to stress on coping styles. These may then "steel" or "sensitize" toward disorder later when stressful events again occur. These possible outcomes, steeling or sensitizing, were intriguing to Rutter (1983) and at the core of his writings on stress, coping, and development, as he wrote, "the key question, in all cases, is what determines whether sensitizing or steeling occurs?" (p. 31).

There are some methodologically practical issues that immediately present themselves when doing research with a developmental focus. A developmentally relevant issue is the choice of comparison groups. For example, can a sample of 3-year-old mentally retarded children and their parents realistically be compared with a same-age, nonretarded sample? The problem may be particularly true when comparisons of parent–child social interaction are made and the two groups of children differ so significantly in their play sophistication. This would automatically contribute to differences in parental behavior that are a function of the child's developmental age and that might disappear if these children were compared to an MA equivalent sample.

The chronic nature of the disability and the accumulation, or "pile up," of family stress over time (McCubbin et al., 1980) and the steady increase in parental "role strain" (Pearlin & Schooler, 1978) also makes studies that combine older and younger subjects and their parents less readily interpretable. Supporting this contention is a study by Suelzle and Keenan (1981), who collected survey data cross-sectionally on 330 families of retarded children. Parents of younger retarded children utilized more support networks and were more supportive of mainstreaming, whereas parents of older retarded children had less support, were more isolated, and yet had a greater need for expanded services.

Related to Suelzle and Keenan's (1981) findings is a study in which the concept of chronic sorrow in families of handicapped children was explored more fully (Wikler, Wasow, & Hatfield, 1981). These authors borrowed the term *chronic sorrow* from Olshansky (1962), who originally used it as a descriptor of the ongoing, affective state of parents of retarded children. Wikler and colleagues saw chronic sorrow somewhat differently. They agreed that sadness, or sorrow, persists, but believed that it clustered at the various change-points, or stages, of the child's development. It is at these times that the parents are reminded once again of the shortcomings of their child as the new stage is either not negotiated or done so only after some delay.

These interesting studies support the need for researchers of families to be sensitive to the family life cycle. Patterson and McCubbin (1983), in a very interesting chapter on family stress and coping with chronic illness, identified the various responsibilities and challenges in the care of a handicapped child over stages of the family life cycle. Central to their family coping theory, the Double ABCX Model, is the concept of time, and they stressed the importance of viewing family coping efforts over time. They identified five normative transitions in family life. These events are viewed as normative because they occur in most families and are predictable in that families can anticipate their occurrence at certain scheduled points in the family life cycle. Discussion of two of these transitions follows.

Infancy

During this period, which includes the period of time through the first 2 years of the child's life, the family has to organize around the initial crisis of discovery that their child is different. This includes a period of mourning, and the time during which the family will probably be involved in pursuing diagnostic services and dealing with possible medical interventions. The parents and the child bring particular behavioral characteristics together for the first time, and these determine the success of the family relationship.

Bell and Harper (1977) documented the importance of the infant's behavior in establishing the reciprocal parent–child relationship. Young children with a mild degree of neurological immaturity can place great stress on the mother's ability to love and care for them. These children may be colicky, difficult to feed, and have erratic sleeping patterns, behaviors affecting the quality of parent–child interactions. The developmentally disabled child may not produce behavior that either maintains a parent's attention or elicits supportive or teaching behaviors from the parent. In addition, the presence of unattractive behavioral repertoires or limited social responsiveness probably reduces the naturally reinforcing aspects of parent–child contact, and comparison of the handicapped child's behavior and development with those of nonhandicapped children can result in inappropriate expectations for the child and frustration for the parent (Embry, 1980).

Allen, Affleck, McGrade, and McQueeney (1982) identified some of the early distresses that parents of a handicapped infant have that differ from those of parents of a healthy infant. They compared mothers of infants with genetic disorders to mothers of infants with perinatal medical complications (that were successfully resolved). Upon discharge from the hospital, the genetic-group mothers seemed to focus on the stigma attached to the child's disorder and reported greater anger, whereas the medical-complications group of mothers reported greater joy and hopefulness. The genetic-group mothers indicated that telling others of the child's condition was the hardest thing they faced. Accordingly, many withdrew from friends and neighbors, and there was a greater tendency for them to quit their jobs. They felt less anxious about leaving their child with a babysitter but often cited concerns about the babysitter's reaction to the handicap.

Two-year-old nonretarded children are definitely able to ambulate and speak words, and most show some initial steps toward toilet training. Each of these new progressions creates a potentially more capable, independent, and normally rewarding child. Parents of nonretarded children are beginning to think about the next phase in the life cycle, the preschool stage, extending from the ages of 3 to 5 years. In addition, the availability of preschool is a support to the parents, possibly allowing the mother to return to employment or allowing for a greater social network with other parents of preschoolers. The parents may begin to plan another child, feeling confident about their ability to have healthy children.

For parents of a retarded child, the progress of development is slower, and the movement toward independence is not as steady. This has an impact on how the parents feel about themselves, the child, and their ability to continue their own development, vocationally and socially. It would be at this delayed transition time into the preschool years that a return bout of "sorrow" is activated (Wikler et al., 1981).

School Age

According to Patterson and McCubbin (1983), the school-age family life-cycle phase includes the age period when the child is 6 to 12 years old. A variety of very important responsibilities and challenges present themselves at this phase. The first includes a focus on school programming (e.g., finding an appropriate school, contending with additional and necessary services, adjusting to the absence of resources). The advent of this developmental phase also brings an added variable that may be a chronic stressor. As part of the child's school involvement, ongoing evaluation and testing of the child's development occurs. This may present continued reminders of the child's deficiencies and the steadily widening gap between what is expected of children at that age and what the school-age developmentally-disabled child can do.

During this phase, the family is beginning to establish and solidify the various family members' roles within the family unit. An aspect of this emerges when the parents have to deal with obvious discrepancies that may exist between siblings regarding intellectual and social abilities. This may present problems in terms of differential privileges or discipline afforded to each child, particularly when the children are similar in chronological age or the retarded child is the oldest. Other problems in role establishment may be an even greater than usual difference in the parents' respective involvement with child rearing. Kazak and Marvin (1984), for example, found that mothers of children with spina bifida are the stressed parents and that fathers of these children report no more stress than do mothers and fathers of nonretarded children. This imbalance in roles may add to current or later problems in the marriage and, again, is a stressor that may not be as profound in other families without a retarded child.

Finally, the school-age child life-cycle phase exposes another difficulty in the retarded child's life, the relative absence of normal, age-appropriate, social engagements. This can have a reciprocal effect on the parents' social relationships, particularly in the "child-centered" cluster identified by Mink et al. (1983). Here again, an ecological perspective could identify relationships among family members that contribute to family development or dysfunction and the ability of the family to negotiate this life-cycle phase successfully by making use of its relations to other ecological levels.

Our discussion of these two life-cycle phases, from the perspective of a family with a retarded child, illustrates the variety of tasks and strains that present themselves to families at different stages. A family dealing in the infancy phase may not rate school-agency support as important; rather, immediate and extended family is more critical. Yet to a school-age family, the availability of quality school programming may stabilize, support, and offer hope to the family to a significant degree and be the most important support network in operation. If investigators are not aware of these potential developmental differences in social support utilization, their research would lose much explanatory power.

Short-Term Longitudinal Research

It is also important in a section that focuses on development to discuss briefly the importance of studying these families over time. To assess a family at Time A and never again fails to account for the developmental course of the family. McCubbin et al. (1980) discussed the family's response to a crisis as characterized by a period of disorganization with a subsequent angle of recovery and, finally, a new level of organization. The assessment of very young families may capture them still operating in the denial phase of the initial disorganization. How the family is coping during the preschool phase may be a far cry from the reorganization that they have reached during the school-age life-cycle phase. Recently, Friedrich, Wilturner, and Cohen (1985) followed a large sample of mothers of retarded children over a period of time averaging 10 to 11 months. Of interest was the variable maternal depression, particularly if it changed over time with these mothers of school-age children and if the change was related to any individual or ecological variable. The mothers did demonstrate a significant increase in depression, and, interestingly, the increase was related to a decrease in reported marital satisfaction. This study underscores the fact that the families studied at Time A will be different in a variety of ways at Time B, and these differences are not random but related to the family's role structures and ecological relationships.

To summarize what Rutter (1983) so clearly stated, researchers must study how stressors influence both the developmental process and later functioning. In this way, they can determine how early events in the system of the mentally retarded child activate mechanisms for later disorder or alter coping styles that successfully protect from disorder. In addition, a developmental and systems approach, in combination, becomes even more useful to the study of families coping with mentally retarded children (Garbarino, 1982).

COPING THEORY

Coping is a complex phenomenon. Pearlin and Schooler (1978) defined coping as any response to external life strains that serves to prevent, avoid, or control emotional distress. This framework is basically the same as that of Folkman, Schaefer, and Lazarus (1979), who distinguished two main coping functions: the alteration of the ongoing person–environment relationship (problem-focused) and the regulation of stressful emotions (emotion-focused). An understanding of coping in family systems involves an understanding not only of the sources of stress but also the mediators of stress. As mentioned earlier, the contrasting approach to a coping-based model is a pathology-based model, which does not allow for the possibility of positive outcome. The pathology-based model, although identifying the various sources of stress, ignores the investigation of its mediators. A competence or coping-based framework should be considered as an alternative to the pathology concept (Drotar, 1981), as it emphasizes the tasks and strategies involved in living with a retarded child. Coping is a process not readily operationalized, as it varies in mode (information-seeking or action), function (problem-solving or stress reduction), and outcome (more or less adaptive). Yet the strategies involved in coping with the stresses of having a retarded child should reveal the process as well as dictate the outcome of a family's adaptation. In this section, we first examine the stressors encountered in families of mentally retarded children and then discuss a coping framework.

Stressors

A social stressor is any set of circumstances that requires change in the individual's ongoing life pattern (Gallagher, Beckman, & Cross, 1983). It is important to study those circumstances germane to parenting mentally retarded children. Families of children who are retarded are often faced with a unique set of problems as they attempt to adapt to the presence of this child within the family unit. Patterson and McCubbin (1983) identified a variety of stressors experienced by families who have an ill child, including strained family relationships, modifications in family activities and goals, increased tasks and time commitments, increased financial burden, need for housing adaptation, social isolation, medical concerns, differences in school experiences, and repeated grieving.

It is obvious that these nine variables are not purely stressors but also psychological responses. In fact, in a recent paper, Lazarus, Delongis, Folkman, and Gruen (1985), stated that "stress is an 'unclean' variable in that as a concept it depends on the interaction of two complex systems, the environment and the person. There is no way to separate them without destroying the concept of stress as a relational and cognitively mediated phenomenon" (p. 778). Lazarus et al. also stated that the only way to understand the reciprocal relationship of person and environment (stress) is to study their temporal relations "as first one variable and then another takes on the role of antecedent" (p. 778), which supports our argument for developmental research.

Some efforts at systematically assessing parents of mentally retarded children according to the stressors just outlined have been made, most notably using the Questionnaire on Resources and Stress and its various revisions (Friedrich, Greenberg, & Crnic, 1983). Although its various factors correlate strongly with other psychosocial "outcome variables," (e.g., depression), it is important for investigators to continue to develop as clear an assessment as possible of the specific stressors to which these families have to respond. At the same time, these investigators need to realize that stressors are as much discrete events as they are the system's perception of the event (Lazarus et al., 1985).

The emphasis on perception of the stress or event, or the person's cognitions of the event, helps to bring about a very useful link between coping theory and developmental theory. The transactional theory of development, first espoused by Sameroff and Chandler (1975), emphasizes the role of parental perceptions of the child's development. For example, preterm infants who are perceived as capable by their parents do as well as full-term infants. Apparently, the stressor of having a pre-term child is viewed as manageable or expectable by the parents. Parents and infants then interact with one another in a way that maximizes the infant's future interactions with the parents. This emphasis on the cognitive appraisal of stress is shared by the cognitive theory of coping that we would like describe.

Coping

Central to the definition of coping is the assumption that stressful events have a differential impact as a result of their interaction with moderator variables. The concept of coping resources presented by Lazarus and Folkman (Folkman et al., 1979; Lazarus & Folkman, 1984) provides a useful basis for understanding the coping process and subsequent familial outcome. They delineated six types of coping resources, each of which is assumed to moderate the adverse effects of stress as appraised within the individual's cognitive–phenomenological framework. Further, some of the research previously reviewed substantiates the relevance of these resources. First, parental health and energy involve their physical and emotional well-being both prior to and during the course of a stressful event. A person who is frail, sick, tired, or otherwise debilitated has less energy to expend on coping than does a healthy, robust person. Moos and his colleagues have documented that maternal physical illness is related to greater behavior problems in the child (Holahan & Moos, 1981). Second, problem-solving skills involve both global and concrete abilities to search for and analyze information and generate various courses of action. They may include strategies that parents utilize to cope with the chronic stressor. Coping strategies are frequently thought to include problem-focused, emotion-focused, and avoidance processes, each of which may have different outcomes that are more or less successful (Lazarus & Folkman, 1984). For example, problem-focused copers may try to master and understand medical information needed to care for their child (Patterson & McCubbin, 1983). Families also have intrinsic adaptive capacities, or coping styles, of which there is an extraordinary variety (Reiss & Oliveri, 1980).

A third resource, social support, involves potentially supportive relationships that may facilitate positive adaptations, as suggested by investigators in several studies of families with retarded children (Farber, 1959; Friedrich & Friedrich, 1981). For example, Gallagher et al. (1983) described several studies of parents of handicapped children where high levels of social support—including friend, family, and intimate support—were associated with more successful parenting and less self-report of pathology. Family social environment, a type of social support, was also related to parents who were particularly adept at teaching their mentally retarded child (Baker, Sullaway, & Clark, 1982).

Fourth, material resources, including such factors as socioeconomic status (SES) and income, can have potentially powerful effects on adaptation, as shown by Farber (1970), Gath (1972), and Nihira et al. (1980). Clark, Baker, and Heifetz (1982) reported that parental SES was related to parent training proficiency at follow-up among parents of mentally retarded children participating in a behavioral parent-training program. Obviously, financial resources greatly increase coping options in almost any stressful transaction.

The fifth research area involves positive beliefs. These include such person variables as an individual's feelings of self-efficacy, greater internal locus of control, and belief in some higher purpose (e.g., religious faith). Studies of religiosity among families of retarded children (Levinson, 1976), as well as the Strom, Rees, Slaughter, and Wurster (1981) study of parents' belief in teaching their retarded child, offer some support to the importance of this resource. Further support for the importance of beliefs in general comes from the transactional developmental model (Sameroff & Chandler, 1975). These authors cited data that supports their impression that the way in which parents think about their children has an impact on what they do with their children and how these children develop. Accurate and positive beliefs are seen as the most facilitative of optimal development.

The final coping resource variable includes social skills, which refer to the ability to communicate with others in socially appropriate and effective ways. This variable is important primarily because it facilitates obtaining social support and is related to problem-solving or coping strategies.

Lazarus and Folkman (1984) also described two broad categories of constraints—personal and environmental constraints—against the use of these resources. These refer to internalized cultural values and beliefs that proscribe certain types of action or feeling and psychological deficits that are a product of the person's unique development. These might be called "personal agendas." Environmental constraints may arise due to competing demands for the same resources, especially material resources. Environments may differ in the nature and frequency of threats posed to the individual and in the breadth of options available for addressing threatening situations; or the environment may respond to people's coping efforts in ways that negate their strategies. The interaction between coping resources and coping constraints and the difficulty investigators may have in "separating" them is readily apparent. Yet assessing them together provides a more detailed perspective on the systems that are engaged in coping.

Clearly, the concepts of coping resources and constraints against using these resources have considerable utility in the study of familial adaptation to retarded children. These variables help explain why the families' differential responses to stress are not solely related to such child variables as age, appearance, and severity and type of retardation. Future research with these families must represent a more integrated perspective, assessing the relative impact and potential interaction of each of these six resources, and possibly additional resources, to the variations in family adaptational response.

CONCLUSIONS

We have discussed three conceptual models that in combination have great promise for increasing our understanding of the families of mentally retarded children: systems/ecological, developmental, and coping frameworks. In addition to their individual heuristic power, which we have already delineated, we would also like to examine briefly how they can be even more powerful—in combination.

A readily apparent synergy is between the concept of ecological levels and coping resources. The mesosystem contains those interactions within and between the various levels, of which many interactions can be viewed as supportive or facilitative. Social support, a coping resource, is a product of the interaction of the family with the individual. Material resources, another coping resource, may be derived from government support that in turn is influenced by popular and political opinion (macrosystem) regarding mentally retarded children and their families.

A developmental perspective, when added to these two frameworks, adds further understanding. Suelzle and Keenan (1981) illustrated, cross-sectionally, apparent differences in the utilization of social support as mentally retarded children get older. Friedrich et al. (1985), documented the increase in depression in mothers over a period slightly less than a year. The increase was related to changes in intimate social support, a coping resource. These two studies illustrate the additional understanding of coping by families that can be gained with a developmental perspective.

A variety of other theorists support our contention that combining at least two of these perspectives enhances our understanding of these families. For example, Reiss and Oliveri (1980) identified phases of family response to stress. These responses are affected by the family's beliefs about the social world. Although they did not study families with mentally retarded children, their research presents a model that combines developmental, systemic, and coping perspectives.

What might be a first study to utilize these perspectives with families of a retarded child? In an earlier paper (Crnic et al., 1983), we stated:

> Family functioning cannot be considered simply as a response to a
> retarded child; rather, it is more meaningful to consider familial
> adaptation as a response to the child mediated by the coping resources
> available and influenced by the family's ecological environments.
> Future investigators, if they are to add to our understanding of families
> with retarded children, must not only attempt to measure differences
> in families with and without a retarded child, but must attempt to
> account for those variables that mediate these differences within a
> comprehensive conceptual framework such as the model proposed. (p.
> 136)

If we proceed from these suggestions, it seems apparent that an appropriate investigation would be an examination of a variety of families' responses to stressors over the family life cycle. Families of mentally retarded children could not be contrasted with families of chronically ill children and both of these should be contrasted with families of non-retarded, physically healthy children. Are similar coping styles used? Are there differences between the groups in the distribution and utilization of coping resources and do they change over time? What ecological interactions are extant? Do they change over time? What type of interventions are suggested to better the outcome of these families? Are these interventions generic, or do they vary across groups and over time? Are the variables that enhance the individual functioning of the children similar? What about familial functioning?

As this chapter illustrates, the framework exists, and the data support the relevance of various components of it. Systematic investigation of all of its components is needed.

REFERENCES

Allen, D., Affleck, G., McGrade, B. J., & McQueeney, M. (1982). *Parent interactions with developmentally disabled infants: Effects of disability origin.* Paper presented at the annual meeting of the American Psychological Association, Washington, DC.

Baker, B. L., Sullaway, M. E., & Clark, D. B. (1982). *Characteristics of families with mentally retarded children: Implications for training.* Paper presented at the annual meeting of the American Association of Mental Deficiency, Boston.

Barsch, R. H. (1964). The handicapped ranking scale among parents of handicapped children. *American Journal of Public Health, 54,* 1560–1567.

Bell, R. Q., & Harper, L. V. (1977). *Child effects on adults.* Hillsdale, NJ: Erlbaum.

Bentovim, A. (1972). Emotional disturbances of handicapped preschool children and their families: Attitudes toward the child. *British Medical Journal, 3,* 579–581.

Bolstad, C. H. (1975). A behavioral comparison of handicapped and normal children within the family. *Dissertation Abstracts International, 35,* 4160B. (University Microfilms No. 79-3862).

Breiner, J., & Forehand, R. (1982). Mother-child interactions: A comparison of a clinic-referred developmentally delayed group and two non-delayed groups. *Applied Research in Mental Retardation, 3,* 175–183.

Bronfenbrenner, U. (1977). Toward an experimental ecology of human development. *American Psychologist, 32,* 513–531.

Bubolz, M. M., & Whiren, A. P. (1984). The family of the handicapped: An ecological model for policy and practice. *Family Relations, 33,* 5–12.

Clark, D. B., Baker, B. L., & Heifetz, L. J. (1982). Behavioral training for parents of mentally retarded children: Prediction of outcome. *American Journal of Mental Deficiency, 87,* 14–19.

Crnic, K., Friedrich, W. N., & Greenberg, M. T. (1983). Adaptation of families with mentally retarded children: A model of stress, coping, and family ecology. *American Journal of Mental Deficiency, 88,* 125–138.

Cunningham, C. E., Rueler, E., Blackwell, J., & Deck, J. (1981). Behavioral and linguistic developments in the interactions of normal and retarded children with their mothers. *Child Development, 52,* 62–70.

Drotar, D. (1981). Psychological perspectives in chronic childhood illness. *Journal of Pediatric Psychology, 6,* 211–228.

Eheart, B. K. (1982). Mother-child interactions with nonretarded and mentally retarded preschoolers. *American Journal of Mental Deficiency, 87,* 20–25.

Embry, L. H. (1980). Family support for handicapped preschool children at risk for abuse. *New Directions for Exceptional Children, 4,* 29–57.

Farber, B. (1959). Effects of a severely mentally retarded child on family integration. *Monographs of the Society for Research in Child Development, 24,* Whole No. 71.

Farber, B. .(1970). Notes on sociological knowledge about families with mentally retarded children. In M. Schreiber (Ed.), *Social work and mental retardation.* New York: Day.

Fewell, R. R., & Vadasy, P. F. (Eds.) (1986). *Families of handicapped children: Needs and supports across the life-span.* Austin, TX: PRO-ED.

Folkman, S., Schaefer, C., & Lazarus, R. S. (1979). Cognitive processes as mediators of stress and coping. In V. Hamilton & D. W. Warburton (Eds.), *Human stress and cognition.* New York: Wiley.

Fortier, L. M., & Wanless, R. L. (1984). Family crisis following the diagnosis of a handicapped child. *Family Relations, 33,* 13–24.

Friedrich, W. N. (1979). Predictors of the coping behavior of mothers of handicapped children. *Journal of Consulting and Clinical Psychology, 47,* 1140–1141.

Friedrich, W. N., Cohen, D. S., & Sather, (1985). *Siblings of mentally retarded children.* Unpublished manuscript, University of Washington.

Friedrich, W. N., & Friedrich, W. L. (1981). Comparison of psychosocial assets of parents with a handicapped child and their normal controls. *American Journal of Mental Deficiency, 85,* 551–553.

Friedrich, W. N., Greenberg, M. T., & Crnic, K. A. (1983). A short version of the Questionnaire on Resources and Stress. *American Journal of Mental Deficiency, 88,* 41–48.

Friedrich, W. N., Wilturner, L. T., & Cohen, D. S. (1985). Coping resources and parenting the retarded child. *American Journal of Mental Deficiency, 90,* 130–139.

Gallagher, J. J., Beckman, P., & Cross, A. H. (1983). Families of handicapped children: Sources of stress and its amelioration. *Exceptional Children, 50,* 10–20.

Garbarino, J. (1982). *Children and families in the social environment.* New York: Aldine.

Gath, A. (1972). The school age siblings of mongol children. *British Journal of Psychiatry, 123,* 161–167.

Goffman, E. (1963). *Stigma.* Englewood Cliffs, NJ: Prentice-Hall.

Holahan, C., & Moos, R. H. (1981). Social support and psychological distress: A longitudinal analysis. *Journal of Abnormal Psychology, 49,* 365–370.

Kazak, A. E., & Marvin, R. S. (1984). Differences, difficulties and adaptation: Stress and social networks in families with a handicapped child. *Family Relations, 33,* 67–77.

Kogan, K. L., Wimberger, H. C., & Bobbitt, R. A. (1969). Analysis of mother-child interaction in young mental retardates. *Child Development, 40,* 799–812.

Lazarus, R. S., DeLongis, A., Folkman, S., & Gruen, R. (1985). Stress and adaptational outcomes: The problem of confounded measures. *American Psychologist, 40,* 770–779.

Lazarus, R. S., & Folkman, S. (1984). *Stress, appraisal, and coping.* New York: Springer.

Levinson, R. M. (1976). Family crisis and adaptation: Coping with a mentally retarded child. *Dissertation Abstracts International, 36,* (University Microfilms No. 76-8221).

Litman, T. J. (1974). The family as the basic unit in health and medical care: A social behavioral overview. *Social Science and Medicine, 8,* 495–519.

Locke, H. J., & Wallace, K. M. (1959). Short marital adjustment and prediction tests: Their reliability and validity. *Marriage and Family Living, 21,* 251–255.

Mattsson, A. (1972). Long-term physical illnesses in childhood: A challenge to psychosocial adaptation. *Pediatrics, 50,* 801–811.

McCubbin, H. I., Joy, C. B., Canble, A. E., Comeau, J. K., Patterson, J. M., & Needle, R. H. (1980). Family stress and coping: A decade review. *Journal of Marriage and the Family, 42,* 855–871.

Mink, I. T., Nihira, K., & Meyers, C. E. (1983). Taxonomy of family life styles: I. Homes with TMR children. *American Journal of Mental Deficiency, 87,* 484–497.

Nihira, K., Meyers, C. E., & Mink, I. T. (1980). Home environment, family adjustment, and the development of mentally retarded children. *Applied Research in Mental Retardation, 1,* 5–24.

Nihira, K., Mink, I. T., & Meyers, C. E. (1981). Relationship between home environment and school adjustment of TMR children. *American Journal of Mental Deficiency, 86,* 8–15.

Olshansky, S. (1962). Chronic sorrow: A response to having a mentally defective child. *Social Casework, 43,* 191–193.

Patterson, J. M., & McCubbin, H. I. (1983). Chronic illness: Family stress and coping. In C. R. Figley & H. I. McCubbin (Eds.), *Stress and the family. Vol. II. Coping with catastrophe*. New York: Brunner/Mazel.

Pearlin, L. I., & Schooler, C. (1978). The structure of coping. *Journal of Health and Social Behavior, 19*, 2–21.

Reiss, D., & Oliveri, M. E. (1980). Family paradigm and family coping: A proposal for linking the family's intrinsic adaptive capacities to its responses to stress. *Family Relations, 29*, 431–444.

Rowitz, L. (1974). Social factors in mental retardation. *Social Science and Medicine, 8*, 405–412.

Rutter, M. (1983). Stress, coping, and development: Some issues and some questions. In N. Garmezy & M. Rutter (Eds.), *Stress, coping, and development in children*. New York: McGraw-Hill.

Sabbeth, B. F., & Leventhal, J. M. (1984). Marital adjustment to chronic childhood illness: A critique of the literature. *Pediatrics, 73*, 762–768.

Sameroff, A. J., & Chandler, M. I. (1975). Reproductive risk and the continuum of caretaking casualty. In F. D. Horowitz (Ed.), *Review of child development research* (Vol. 4). Chicago: the University of Chicago Press.

Schoggen, P., & Schoggen, M. (1981). Ecological factors in the prevention of psychosocial mental retardation. In M. J. Begab, H. C. Haywood, & H. L. Garber (Eds.), *Psychosocial influences in retarded performance*. Baltimore: University Park Press.

Spanier, G. (1976). Measuring dyadic adjustment: New scales for measuring the quality of marriage and other dyads. *Journal of Marriage and the Family, 38*, 15–28.

Strom, R., Rees, R., Slaughter, H., & Wurster, S. (1981). Childrearing expectations of families with atypical children. *American Journal of Orthopsychiatry, 51*, 285–296.

Suelzle, M., & Keenan, V. (1981). Changes in family support networks over the life cycle of mentally retarded persons. *American Journal of Mental Deficiency, 86*, 267–274.

Terdal, L. E., Jackson, R. H., & Garner, A. M. (1976). Mother-child interactions: A comparison between normal and developmentally delayed groups. In E. J. Mash, L. A. Hammerlynck, & L. C. Handy (Eds.), *Behavior modification and families*. New York: Brunner/Mazel.

Thoman, E. B., Becker, P. T., & Freese, M. P. (1978). Individual patterns of mother-infant interaction. In G. P. Sackett (Ed.), *Observing behavior* (Vol. 1). Baltimore: University Park Press.

Vietze, P. M., Abernathy, S. R., Ashe, M. L., & Faulstich, G. (1978). Contingency interaction between mothers and their developmentally delayed infants. In G. P. Sackett (Ed.), *Observing behavior* (Vol. 1). Baltimore: University Park Press.

Waisbren, S. E. (1980). Parents' reactions after the birth of a developmentally disabled child. *American Journal of Mental Deficiency, 84*, 345–351.

Watson, R. L., & Midlarsky E. (1979). Reactions of mothers with mentally retarded children: A social perspective. *Psychological Reports, 45*, 309–310.

Wikler, L., Wasow, M., & Hatfield, E. (1981). Chronic sorrow revisited: Parent vs. professional depiction of the adjustment of parents of mentally retarded children. *American Journal of Orthopsychiatry, 51*, 63–70.

17
The Social Networks of Children With and Without Handicaps: A Developmental Perspective

Michael Lewis and Candice Feiring
Rutgers Medical School
University of Medicine and Dentistry of New Jersey

and

Jeanne Brooks-Gunn
Educational Testing Service

The study of normal and dysfunctional development has centered largely on measuring and interpreting behavior and its change over time. Surprisingly, the contexts in which behavior occurs have been of less interest. This was acceptable as long as the situations in which behavior was observed remained few and laboratory-based; however, our ability to predict and explain human behavior is constrained by our inattention to the nature and effects of environments. Some psychologists have asserted the need for a taxonomy of the environment (Barker, 1965; Brunswick, 1956). Such a taxonomy must address who is to measure the environment and what is to be measured. In terms of the first issue, Barker argued that the environment can be described by the experimenter in objective and measurable terms. Endler and Magnusson (1974) suggested that the environment be measured by subjects' perceptual experiences. Both views are essential because the *impact* of the environment is determined by both objective characteristics and their subject-mediated transformations. Exactly how to measure external and

Acknowledgments. This research was supported by a grant from the William T. Grant Foundation, National Institute of Child Health and Human Development, Grant No. 300-77-0307 and a grant from the Bureau of Education for the Handicapped. The authors thank John Jaskir for his invaluable help in analyzing the data and Linda Wellman and Lorraine Luciano for their assistance in data collection.

subjective features, as well as their interaction, is yet to be uncovered, although psychophysics already informs us of the possibility (Woodworth & Scholesberg, 1951).

Determining the critical features of an environment is particularly important. For example, the environment may be characterized by its physical properties (e.g., temperature, area) and its location relative to a larger space, an identified function, or the subject's position (e.g., playroom, bedroom, or parents' arms). For example, location is known to influence the conversational behavior of children and parents (Freedle, & Lewis, 1977; Lewis & Cherry, 1977; Lewis & Freedle, 1973). Daily activities (e.g., washing, going to bed) or adaptive functions (e.g., protecting and nurturing others) are other distinctive dimensions of environments. Closely related are the constraints or requirements of particular environments and the affects elicited by the situation. Hypothetically, environments could be categorized based on emotions elicited, such that some are predominantly "happy" regardless of other features, whereas some are "sad" or "anxiety"-producing. Finally, the people involved in the environment cannot be neglected. Pervin (1975), among others, has explored the interrelatedness of dimensions such as these.

Each of these environmental features exerts some influence on behavior. Rather than assuming that one set is somehow better than another in accounting for the behavior of individuals, it is probably more productive to consider that some behaviors are influenced by some dimensions more than others are. To truly understand behavior in context would require constructing a complex matrix that includes environmental dimensions along one axis and particular behaviors along another. When we add the particular characteristics of the individual (e.g., handicapping condition, age, sex), this matrix becomes even more complex. Nevertheless, as Landesman-Dwyer and Butterfield (1983) demonstrated, such a model is necessary if we are to understand the role of the environment in the behavior of individuals.

Although many features of the environment can be considered to influence behavior, few would question the saliency of the social environment, particularly during infancy and early childhood. Human beings are by nature social, born relatively helpless and needing attention, care, and love from others over a relatively long childhood. Indeed, our ability to learn and to communicate symbolically requires interacting with others (Lewis & Feiring, 1978).

For many years, the mother was singled out as the most critical element in the child's social environment. Eventually, the significant roles of other family members (Lewis & Rosenblum, 1979) and peers (Lewis & Rosenblum, 1975) were recognized and explored. The child's total social network, however, extending to grandparents, aunts and uncles, cousins, parents' friends, teachers, babysitters, neighbors, service providers, and others (Cochran & Brassard, 1979) has been overlooked. When we inquire about the contribution of individuals' characteristics, such as handicaps and developmental status, to their network, we find few, if any, answers.

Social network theory and research has received the most study and attention in the field of sociology, where attributes of the social network (including size, variety of membership, density, connectedness, reciprocity,

frequency, and function of contact) have been studied in regard to the nature
of the marital relationship and social and geographic mobility patterns of
families (e.g., Lee, 1979). An extensive literature exists in which quantitative
techniques have been employed for describing and specifying the characteristics of social networks (e.g., see Holland & Leinhardt, 1979). Social networks
have also been utilized as the unit of intervention in conducting therapy
(e.g., Attneave, 1976; Pattison, Defrancisco, Wood, Frazier, & Crowder,
1975). There have been few attempts, however, to measure and describe the
broad network of people and contacts in a child's social system and to
understand the developmental influence they might have, especially in regard to young children. Currently, we have embarked on a study of social
networks to identify how the networks of nonhandicapped and handicapped
children may differ, over age, and across other child characteristics such as
sex, social class, and birth order.

SOCIAL SYSTEM THEORY

The study of social networks lends itself to a systems analysis that provides
a framework for understanding the complex nature of the social world
(Buckley, 1967). All systems can be characterized by a common set of
features. For understanding the social life of children, we have identified five
important features of social systems (Feiring & Lewis, 1978; Lewis & Feiring,
1979). First, *systems have elements*. Here, elements refer to the individuals in
the child's social network. Within the child's immediate family, for example,
elements consist of child, parents, and siblings. Beyond the immediate
family, grandparents, aunts, uncles, and cousins are included, as are nonrelated adults and peers. The number and type of elements in the nonhandicapped and handicapped child's network may differ. For example, handicapped
children are more likely than are nonhandicapped children to have only a
mother at home rather than both parents (Price-Bonham & Addison, 1978;
Reed & Reed, 1965).

A second aspect of social systems is that *elements are interrelated*. Children's
networks do not resemble a wheel with the child at the hub and the other
elements unconnected spokes to the center. Rather, the child's network is a
complex set of connections, with some elements connected to the child alone
and others connected to the child as well as to each other. Within the set of
family members, we can examine the nature and extent to which parents and
children influence one another's behavior. Lewis and his colleagues (Lewis
& Feiring, 1981; Lewis & Weinraub, 1976), Bronfenbrenner (1977), Lamb
(1979), and Parke, Power, and Gottman (1979) have discussed some of the
ways the elements within a family system may be connected and multiply
influenced. In a social network, elements can influence others through direct
interaction, such as mother–child interaction. Elements also can be connected
indirectly, a fact that often is overlooked in developmental research. Once
we consider the social network system as consisting of more than two
elements, we acknowledge that one element may be influenced by another

element vis à vis a third element or combination of elements (Lewis & Feiring, 1981). An example of an indirect influence is the husband's support of his wife and his impact on her role as a mother. Several studies confirm the importance of this particular indirect effect on the mother–child relationship (Barry, 1970; Crockenberg, 1981; Feiring & Taylor, in press). Another example of an indirect effect is the high association between severity of a child's handicap and the family's degree of social isolation from relatives, friends, and community groups (Dorner, 1975). This could reduce the connections among the elements in a handicapped child's network, compared to those of the nonhandicapped child, which in turn may influence development.

Third, social systems possess the *quality of nonadditivity*, such that knowing everything about the elements independently will not be adequate to understand the operation of the system as a whole. Elements may behave quite differently within a system than they do in isolation. For example, how an individual behaves alone may differ from how that person behaves in the presence of other family members. Clarke-Stewart (1978) observed mothers, fathers, and children in dyadic (parent–child) and triadic (mother–father–child) interactions and found that behavior in the mother–child subsystem in isolation differed significantly from the mother–child subsystem when embedded in a mother–father–child context. Similar contextual effects appear for mildly handicapped children who show more prosocial behavior when embedded in a network of nonhandicapped peers compared to one of handicapped peers (Gampel, Gottlieb, & Harrison, 1974).

Social systems are characterized further by *steady states* processes that serve to maintain and change the system in response to environmental demands. A steady state is characterized by the interplay of flexibility and stability by which a system endeavors to maintain a viable relationship among its elements and its environment. The child within the family and broader social network is influenced by the amount of flexibility and stability in the system. For example, Russell (1979) showed that families typically operate at moderate flexibility and stability, whereas families under stress (e.g., as a result of coping with a disturbed child, Olson, Russell, & Sprenkle, 1980) show either too much flexibility (chaos) or too little (rigidity). The presence of a handicapped child may alter the tuning of a family's steady state (e.g., by a need for a more consistent and predictable environment that may necessitate more regulated or rigid processes).

Finally, social systems also are viewed as *purposeful*. The family and the larger social network generally are thought to fulfill certain functions or goal-oriented activities necessary for the survival of individuals and societies. Socialization is a central goal of the family social system, accompanied by functions such as caregiving, learning, play, and nurturance. Perhaps the goals and functions of family systems may differ as a function of a child's status. For example, a nonhandicapped child may require less caregiving and participate in more learning-oriented interactions than does a retarded agemate. A systems approach permits a full exploration of the nature of the child's social environment.

SOCIAL NETWORKS

Two features are important when discussing either environmental classification or social networks: elements and functions. A matrix of people in a child's life and functional activities provides a basis for viewing social and intellectual development (Lewis, 1982; Lewis & Feiring, 1979). In Figure 1, the vertical dimension labeled P1 - Pn is the set of persons who may influence the child. The horizontal dimension, labeled F1 - Fm, consists of the functions that categorize the behavior that occurs in the child's social experience. Several different behaviors (B) comprise each function, and these may vary with such factors as the child's age and parental variables. For example, the function of caregiving (F2) includes feeding (B21) or changing the child's clothes (B22).

The matrix in Figure 1 potentially encompasses the complete array of social objects and social functions within the child's network at a given point in time. By examining the rows, one can identify which functions characterize a particular person's position in the child's social network. By examining the columns, one obtains information concerning the extent to which a particular function characterizes a child's social experience and the diversity of people who contribute to each function. Both the absolute and relative amount of time in different functions would be expected to influence the child's development. For example, a child for whom nurturance was prominent would be expected to have different developmental outcomes from a child for whom the protection function was prominent. The psychological impact of behaviors, however, also may be linked to the actual time in a given function.

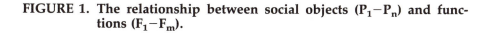

SOCIAL FUNCTIONS

		F_1	F_2	F_3	F_4	F_5	$\ldots F_m$
		PROTECTION B_{11}, B_{12}, B_{13}	CARE-GIVING B_{21}, B_{22}, B_{23}	NURTURANCE $B_{31}, B_{32} \ldots$	PLAY	EXPLORATION/LEARNING	B_{rs}
			FEEDING, CHANGING	ROCK, KISS			
P_1	SELF						
P_2	MOTHER						
P_3	FATHER						
P_4	PEER						
P_5	SIBLING						
P_6	GRANDPARENT						
P_7	AUNT						
•	•						
•	•						
•	•						
P_n							

SOCIAL OBJECTS (label at left of person column)

FIGURE 1. The relationship between social objects (P_1-P_n) and functions (F_1-F_m).

After constructing a social matrix, we must ask an important question: How do persons and functions combine or what is the distribution of social objects by social functions? Factors that constrain the form of the Person × Function distribution must also be considered. These constraints include: (a) the age of the child, (b) the family structure (such as the number of other children or the birth order of the target child), (c) cultural rules, and (d) the status of the child, for example, whether the child is handicapped or not or the type of handicapping condition.

Although investigators seldom identify this full social matrix, they have confirmed that peers and adults perform significantly different functions (Harlow & Harlow, 1965; Hartup, 1980; Lewis & Rosenblum, 1975; Mueller & Vandell, 1979). Peers are to be played with, are to practice emerging skills with, and, at an older age, for mating and cohabitation. Adults serve both caregiving and educational functions, although Edwards and Lewis (1979) reported that older peers may be especially good for educational activities. With regard to parents' functions, fathers typically differ from mothers. For example, fathers engage in more rough-and-tumble play, whereas mothers show more nurturant behavior toward their young children (Lamb, 1981; Lewis, Feiring, & Weinraub, 1981; Parke & Tinsley, 1981).

In a study of children's knowledge of the person–function relationship, Edwards and Lewis (1979) and Lecco and Lewis (1987) showed that by 3 years of age, children easily identify different functions for different people. These findings on what young children know about network members and their functions, as well as observational data on behavior of people in the network, suggest that more thorough analysis of the social matrix may yield valuable insights into the child's functional social environment.

SOCIAL NETWORKS OF FAMILIES WITH HANDICAPPED CHILDREN

Not surprisingly, the interest in the young child's social network is not limited to family systems research on nonhandicapped children. Indeed, research on handicapped children's influence upon social systems, most particularly the disruptions in families that occur in the presence of handicapped young children, has been studied since the early 1960s (Farber, 1963; Farber & Ryckman, 1965). Other investigators have focused on individual parents' reactions and adjustment to the birth of a handicapped child (Olshansky, 1962; Wolfensberger, 1970). Concomitant with early intervention and parental training programs, investigators have studied the impact of the parent (e.g., education, training, and behavioral interaction) upon the handicapped child, rather than that of the child on the parent (McAndrew, 1976; Patterson & McCubbin, 1983; Turnbull, Summers, & Bruthersun, 1986; Wilkes, 1981). Currently, both approaches are recognized as valid, with an increased emphasis on understanding individual differences in handicapped children and their families (Birenbaum, 1971; Brooks-Gunn, 1985; Turnbull et al., 1986).

At least two topics germane to social networks have been studied with young handicapped children and their families: family configuration and the size and frequency of social contacts.

Family Configuration

FAMILY STRUCTURAL CHANGE

The birth of a handicapped infant is more likely to disrupt the family structure than that of a nonhandicapped infant. Specifically, father absence due to divorce or desertion is more likely in families with a handicapped than with a nonhandicapped child (Price-Bonham & Addison, 1978; Reed & Reed, 1965). How such parental change affects the rest of the family's social network is unknown. Theoretically, the single parent experiences more child care and emotional demands than does the two-parent family. The degree to which other members of the social system provide some support to the mother, the handicapped child, or the siblings may vary as a function of the father's presence or the family size, and may differ depending on the child's status.

Even when the birth of a handicapped child does not result in an immediate change in the nuclear family structure, it is likely that a given child will experience being in a single-parent family at some point. Glick and Norton (1977) estimated that 45% of the children born in 1977 will spend part of their childhood in a single-parent family. How social networks are maintained during family structure changes is being studied in the general population (Zill & Peterson, 1982), but has been ignored for families with handicapped members. The one published study on the response to divorce in families with a handicapped child found negative effects on the psychological adjustment of nonhandicapped siblings, but not on the handicapped target child (Gallagher, Cross, & Scharfman, 1981).

Within the nuclear family, the father provides important emotional caregiving support to his wife and children. Literature in normally developing children suggests that the father's greatest impact on his child may be via an indirect route, namely his relationship with his wife (Lewis & Feiring, 1981; Lewis, Feiring, & Weinraub, 1981). Gallagher et al. (1981) found that fathers of handicapped infants helped their wives with caregiving more than did fathers of nonhandicapped children. Indeed, fathers reported that they should take more responsibility, given the additional demands associated with having a handicapped child (Briston & Gallagher, 1982; Gallagher et al., 1981). In addition to actual caregiving, a mother's perception of her husband's emotional support influences her coping and acceptance of the handicapped child (Gallagher et al., 1981). This is an example of the indirect effect of a marital relationship upon maternal behavior.

NUMBER OF SIBLINGS AND BIRTH ORDER

Parents may have fewer children after the birth of a handicapped child or may increase the spacing between children. Whether a larger sibling network is beneficial to a child, particularly a handicapped child, is not known. Some parents have reported that siblings help reduce the demands of the handicapped child on the parents (Turnbull, et al., 1986).

Regardless of birth order, the handicapped child almost always assumes the role of a younger child (Farber & Ryckman, 1965). In addition, the eldest female sibling often acts as a surrogate parent in caring for a handicapped sibling, a function that extends even into adulthood (Trevino, 1979).

Size and Number of Contacts

Extensive networks with many elements may provide parents with a large number of people upon whom to rely. In addition, these people typically perform different functions. For the handicapped child, people other than family and friends are vital; child care workers, social services personnel, and health care professionals are needed to care for the child. Such a supportive network may give parents a break for the heavy demands a handicapped child places upon them. In fact, Winton and Turnbull (1981) reported that 65% of parents view teachers as providing them with needed relief from caregiving demands as well as with educational services. In addition, frequent daily contacts may provide the handicapped child an opportunity to form close relationships with others.

The literature on handicapped children and their families indicates that data on networks are meager, and families with nonhandicapped children and those with handicapped children often differ significantly, although these differences have not been explored fully. Given the limited information, responsible public policy recommendations cannot, as yet, be made concerning how to improve handicapped children's social world or the functioning of their entire families.

NETWORKS OF NONHANDICAPPED
AND HANDICAPPED CHILDREN

We designed a short-term cross-sectional study of children's networks to delineate the nature of handicapped and nonhandicapped children's social networks at different ages.

Description and Measurement of the Social Network

Typically, the type and frequency of contact with kin and non-kin is measured through interviews and questionnaires (Bott, 1957, 1971). Additional information about the connectedness of network members (i.e., who knows whom) and the network density (the number of people who know each other compared to those who do not) often is gathered. Such research begins by determining a point of anchorage (e.g., a person, conjugal pair, nuclear family). In our study, the points of anchorage were 3- and 6-year-old children within natural families. We asked mothers about the basic attributes of their children's extended social network, using an adapted version of the Pattison Psychosocial Network Inventory (Pattison, et al., 1975). The mother listed the persons in the child's social network by category: family, relatives, friends of the parents, and friends of the child. The mother specified the child's relationship to each person (e.g., cousin, grandparent, uncle for the relatives category) and the amount of contact with each person. Contact included face-to-face, phone, or mail contact, and frequency was coded as daily, weekly, monthly, bi-yearly, or yearly. From this report, we summarized the number and the kinds of people who comprised the child's network as well as the frequency of contact with these people.

We recognize that the mother's report reflected her perception of the child's network and may not yield a totally accurate picture of the child's social contacts. We could not interview the young child for these data, nor could we rely on observation over a long period and enough situations to gather such information. The traditional questionnaire method is an efficient means of mapping the child's general social network. More important, a mother's perception of this network is likely to have significant consequences for her child.

We grouped the people in a child's network by categories, based on our theory of the young child's social world (Lewis & Feiring, 1978, 1979). We previously described variables that infants may use to construct their social world. In particular, age, gender, and familiarity are three attributes of people that infants acquire early. Whether infants actively use these characteristics to order the social array is unknown. Nonetheless, we think they provide a meaningful way of analyzing the social network data. Consequently, in the analysis to follow, people were divided into three groups: adults versus peers (i.e., age), males versus females (i.e., gender), and relatives versus nonrelatives. Although the nuclear family component of relatives may be strongly related to degree of familiarity, a comparison of relatives and nonrelatives was made because sociologists have stressed the importance of kin in defining social structure. Both sociologists and sociobiologists have argued that kin compared to non-kin have a special role to play in defining the child's primary group membership (Wilson, 1975).

SAMPLE CHARACTERISTICS

We studied a sample of 20 handicapped and 20 nonhandicapped 3-year-old children (± 3 months). There were 10 males and 10 females in each group. The handicapped children were moderately, severely, and profoundly handicapped children, and their families came from New York and New Jersey. There were 5 males and 7 females with Down syndrome; the remaining children had a wide range of handicapping conditions, such as spina bifida, neurobiological impairment, Noonan syndrome, and tuberous sclerosis. The 20 nonhandicapped children, selected from a large longitudinal study, were matched for sex and socioeconomic status (SES) with the handicapped children. In each sample, 13 families were high SES, and 7 were low SES, as determined by an adaptation of the Hollingshead scale (Feiring & Lewis, 1981).

An independent sample of 55 6-year-old (± 3 months) handicapped children (35 males, 20 females) and their mothers was studied. There were 40 high-SES and 15 low-SES families. The 6-year-old handicapped sample included 14 males and 10 females with Down syndrome; 8 males and 4 females with cerebral palsy; 5 males and one female with developmental delay; and 8 males and 5 females with other diagnoses such as hydrocephalis, Cavanons disease, quadriplegia, dysautonomia, and neurological impairments. A sample of 55 nonhandicapped 6-year-old children (also from a larger longitudinal study) was matched to the handicapped sample on sex and SES, as with the 3-year-old group. The matching technique controls for social class and sex, two variables that related significantly to nonhandicapped 3-year-old children's social networks (Lewis, Feiring, & Kotsonis, 1984).

RESULTS

In this chapter, we have focused on number of people in the social networks and daily contacts. We conducted multivariate analysis of variances for each type of network category, i.e., one for age (adults and peers); one for sex (male and female); and one for familiarity (relatives and nonrelatives) to determine whether age of child (3 and 6 years) and child status (nonhandicapped, handicapped) were significantly related to the number of people and daily contacts with network members.

Table 1 presents the number of different types of people seen by nonhandicapped and handicapped children at 3 and 6 years. All children had contact with many others besides their parents. Peers, relatives, and parents' friends were part of the child's social world. Remarkably, we detected no age effects. We did find main effects, however, for the child's handicapping condition. At both ages, nonhandicapped children saw more grandparents, $F(1, 146) = 9.79$, $p = .002$, but saw fewer aunts or uncles, $F(1, 146) = 7.47$, $p = .007$, cousins, $F(1, 146) = 10.50$, $p = .001$, other relatives, $F(1, 146) = 3.26$, $p = .07$, nonrelative adults, $F(1, 146) = 22.17$, $p = .0001$, and babysitters, $F(1, 146) = 22.47$, $p = .0001$, than did the handicapped children. Overall, nonhandicapped children had fewer nonrelated adults listed as part of their networks than did handicapped age-mates, $F(1, 146) = 16.82$, $p < .0001$.

TABLE 1 Number of People Seen by Children at 3- and 6- years

	Total no. of people				Daily contact			
	3-year olds		6-year olds		3-year olds		6-year olds	
	NH	H	NH	H	NH	H	NH	H
Grandparents	3.20	2.20	3.18	2.58	.15	.35	.16	.33
Aunts/uncles	2.75	4.70	3.18	4.67	.05	.05	.02	.25
Cousins	1.51	2.60	1.42	3.51	0	.05	0	.29
Other relatives	1.80	.80	.91	2.58	0	0	0	.05
Nonrelative/ nonrelated adults	6.65	12.75	6.56	12.47	1.35	2.30	1.16	3.35
Babysitters	.15	.95	.11	.51	0	.05	.02	.11
Male peers	3.35	3.65	2.89	3.05	.95	1.05	1.42	1.78
Female peers	3.20	2.90	2.56	2.89	.90	1.25	1.15	1.35
Nuclear family	3.53	3.25	3.53	3.29	3.53	3.29	3.53	3.25

Note: N = nonhandicapped children, H = handicapped children.

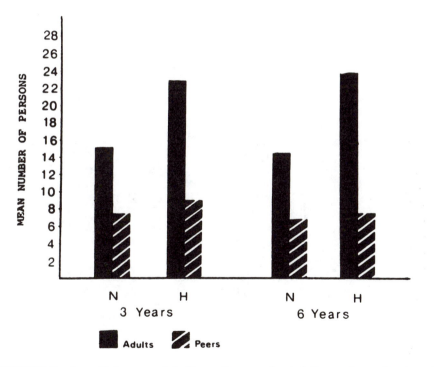

FIGURE 2. Age Category: Adults and peers for total number of network members.

For daily contact scores, the only main effect of handicap appeared for nonrelated adults. Handicapped children had more daily contact with nonrelated adults, $F(1, 146) = 13.63$, $p < .0001$, than did nonhandicapped children, an expected difference given the handicapped child's needs for special educational and medical services.

Age, Kinship, and Gender

AGE

Recall that age, kinship, familiarity, and gender are important ways of classifying the social network. Figures 2, 3, and 4 present the number of people within each category for the four subject samples. Figure 2 shows the relationship of adults to peers as a function of child's age and presence of handicap. First, the networks of all children (across handicap and age) included significantly more adults than peers, $F(1, 146) = 242.63$, $p < .01$. There was a diagnosis effect, $F(1, 146) = 17.15$, $p < .01$, such that handicapped children had more people in their social network; however, this effect is attributable entirely to the presence of more adults, rather than peers, in handicapped children's networks than in those of nonhan-

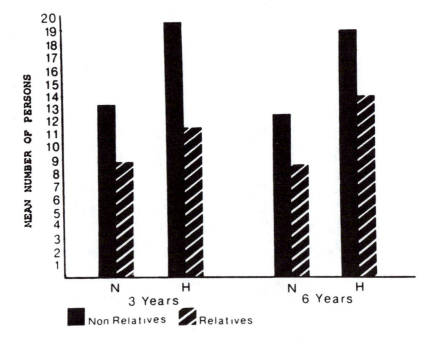

FIGURE 3. Kinship Category: Relatives and nonrelatives for total number of network members.

dicapped children $F(1, 146) = 29.97$, $p < .01$. Although there were no significant differences in the number of peers between nonhandicapped and handicapped children, the proportion of peers to adults was higher (32%) for nonhandicapped children than for handicapped children (25%), $F(1, 146) = 8.44$, $p = .004$. There were no age effects.

KINSHIP

Figure 3 presents the social network divided into relatives and nonrelatives. For all children, there were more nonrelatives than relatives, $F(1, 146) = 32.36$, $p < .01$. There was also a diagnosis effect, $F(1, 146) = 16.86$, $p < .001$, but no Diagnosis × Relative effect. Handicapped children had more relatives, $F(1, 146) = 9.23$, $p = .003$, and nonrelatives, $F(1, 146) = 12.40$, $p = .001$, than did nonhandicapped children. There were no age effects.

GENDER

Figure 4 presents the data by gender category. All children had significantly more females than males in their networks, $F(1, 146) = 83.60$, $p <$

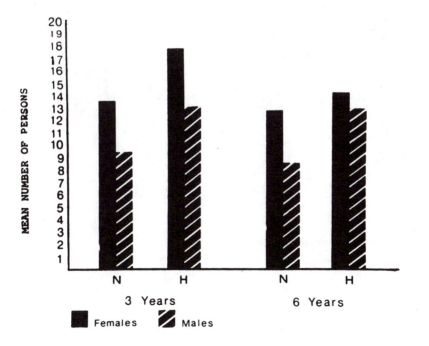

FIGURE 4. Gender Category: Males and females for total number of network members.

.001, a finding confirmed in our larger study of 117 nonhandicapped subjects (Lewis et al., 1984). There was a diagnosis effect, $F(1, 146) = 15.98$, $p < .001$, which indicates both more males and females for the handicapped children, $F (1, 146) = 12.76$, $p = .0001$ for total males; $F(1, 146) = 14.29$, $p < .0001$ for total females. No other effects were significant.

Figures 5 and 6 present the same category divisions by age and kinship for nonhandicapped and handicapped children at 3 and 6 years for the amount of daily contact. The mean frequency of daily contact shown in these figures is calculated by taking the total number of persons seen daily across all subjects in a group divided by the total number of subjects in that group.

AGE

Figure 5 shows that children's daily contact with adults and peers varied as a function of the child's status, $F(1, 146) = 7.96$, $p < .005$. Namely, nonhandicapped children had more daily contact with peers than with adults (means = 2.37 and 1.40, respectively), whereas handicapped children had more contact with adults than with peers (means = 3.88 and

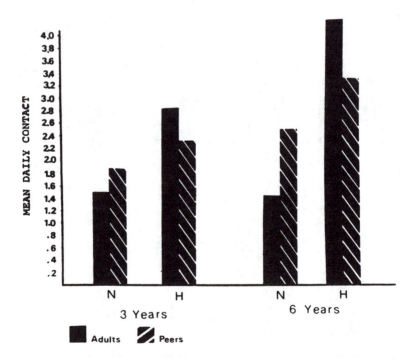

FIGURE 5. Age Category: Peers and adults for daily contact.

3.04, respectively). This effect can be further seen in the ratio of daily peer/peer plus adult contact: 56% of the nonhandicapped child's daily contact is with peers compared to only 34% of the handicapped child's daily contact, $F(1, 146) = 13.40$, $p = .0001$. This proportion also measures results in an important age effect, with 6-year-old children having proportionately more daily contact with peers than did 3-year-olds, regardless of diagnosis (35% peer contact at 3 years, 48% at 6 years, $F(1, 146) = 4.76$, $p = .03$).

KINSHIP

Figure 6 shows the daily contact by kinship. Excluding nuclear family daily contact, there was overwhelmingly more daily contact with nonrelatives than with relatives, $F(1, 146) = 98.42$, $p < .01$. There was a significant interaction between diagnosis and kinship contact, $F(1,146) = 3.66$, $p < .05$, such that handicapped children saw proportionately more kin than non-kin (means = 5% for ratio of relatives/relatives + nonrelatives for nonhandicapped and 10% for the ratio of relatives/relatives + nonrelatives for handicapped children). There was also an important age × diagnosis

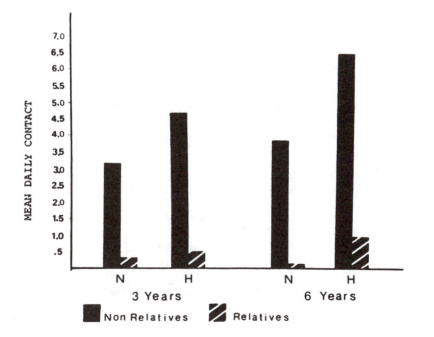

FIGURE 6. **Kinship Category: Relatives and nonrelatives for daily contact.**

effect using the proportion of kinship measure. Although nonhandicapped children saw 12% relatives at 3 years, this dropped to 6% by 6 years. Handicapped children, on the other hand, showed an increase from 5% to 12% over the same 3 year period, $F(1, 146) = 4.25$, $p = .04$. This indicates although nonhandicapped children increased proportionately their non-kin daily contacts, handicapped children spent increasingly more time with kin.

Summary

To summarize, we found 11 major characteristics of nonhandicapped and handicapped children's networks.

I. *Total Network*
   1. At both ages there were more people in the handicapped children's social networks than there were in the nonhandicapped children's networks.
   2. There were no differences in the mean number of people seen daily as a function of handicapping condition.

II. *Adult/Peer*
   3. All of the children had more adults than peers in their social networks.
   4. In their daily contacts, handicapped children saw more adults than peers, whereas nonhandicapped children were with peers more than adults.
   5. Nonhandicapped children had a higher proportion of contact with peers relative to adults than did handicapped children.
   6. With increasing age, all of the children had proportionately more daily contact with peers.

III. *Kinship*
   7. Excluding nuclear family, all the children had more non-kin than kin members in their networks.
   8. All children had more daily contact with non-kin individuals.
   9. On a daily basis, handicapped children saw proportionately more kin than did nonhandicapped children.
   10. For handicapped children the proportion of kin to non-kin daily contact increased with age, whereas this proportion decreased with age for nonhandicapped children.

IV. *Gender*
   11. For all children, there were more females than males in their social networks.

Methodological Concerns

Before developmental implications of these findings are discussed, some methodological issues relevant to data interpretation must be raised. These include the use of small sample sizes, the reliability of maternal reports, characteristics of children with handicaps, and ratio versus absolute measures.

Our small sample size reflects, in part, difficulties in locating and collecting data on handicapped children. Given the low incidence of these handicapping conditions, one check against the problems of small sample bias is to compare the matched small sample of nonhandicapped children against the larger sample of nonhandicapped children's data. If small sample bias were significant, then the two samples should differ. In this study, the sample yielded essentially the same conclusions about social networks as did the larger nonhandicapped sample.

Maternal report is always suspect. One alternative, observing children's networks, is enormously time consuming as well as intrusive and potentially biased. The potential biases associated with maternal interviews include incomplete or inaccurate memory, absence of information regarding peer contacts, and distorted reporting motivated by the need to make the family appear more socially desirable or "normal." We hope that these biases, when they do occur, operate equally and randomly for nonhandicapped and handicapped families. For this study, however, we can think of specific reasons that could contribute to differential maternal reporting. For example, mothers of handicapped children may take a greater interest in their children's activities outside the home, and their involvement in the child's daily activities may be more necessary so that they may have a more accurate picture of what their children's networks are like compared to mothers of handicapped children.

Another concern is that the social network of handicapped children may vary as a function of the type of handicapping condition. The "typical" orthopedically impaired child may have a different network contact than would the "typical" Down syndrome child. Because of our small sample size, we could not investigate this factor systematically; however, it seems obvious that the child's characteristics may contribute to the social network, and future researchers should consider this issue.

Finally, we recognize the need to measure the impact of networks on children's lives. For example, we discovered that absolute versus ratio scores yielded somewhat different pictures of adult and peer contacts. Although there were no differences in the absolute number of peers in the networks of nonhandicapped and handicapped children, the proportions of peers to adults were significantly different. Which measure best reflects the child's perception of this difference? Which measure relates best to what kind of developmental outcomes? Until we have further information, we need to explore alternative ways of characterizing social networks by comparing different network measures and their relationship to children's development.

THE SOCIAL WORLDS AND NETWORKS OF
HANDICAPPED AND NONHANDICAPPED CHILDREN

Social Network Size

The networks of handicapped children clearly are larger than those of nonhandicapped children. There are several reasons for this. First, a large number of supportive people, both professionals and family members, are needed to help the immediate family care for the handicapped child. By 3 years of age, these identified handicapped children already were participating in stimulation and remedial programs. These programs brought the handicapped children into contact with peers as well as professionals. In addition, handicapped children were in contact with extended family members, although, interestingly, these family members were not the grandparents. This may reflect some of the stress between parents and grandparents observed within the families of handicapped children (Beckman, 1983).

Although handicapped children have a larger network size than do nonhandicapped children, there are no overall differences in the mean number of people seen daily as a function of handicapping condition. These findings suggest that the enlarged size of the network of handicapped children is likely to be due to the child's contact with service personnel needed for their care and treatment; however, all of these additional people are apparently not seen on a daily basis. Thus, handicapped children may see more people, but if daily contact reflects the level of interaction (or intimacy of interaction), handicapped and nonhandicapped children appear no different on this measure. The effect of more people but not a more daily level of interaction may have negative consequences, especially for a child who may already have such problems as mental limitations, memory problems, and fears. In fact, although a larger network may help the parents manage the handicapped child's care, a smaller network, with a higher number of daily contacts, may be more positive for the handicapped child's development. Research is needed on what kinds of network characteristics best facilitate handicapped, as well as nonhandicapped, children's development.

No gender differences were found between handicapped and nonhandicapped children's networks. All children experience contact with more women than men, especially the younger children. These findings confirm the general cultural role of females as caregivers for children, regardless of the child's status.

Peers and Adults

In young American children's lives, there are usually more adults than peers. With increasing age, there is a proportionate decrease in this adult contact and an increase in peer contact. This social developmental change is associated with a new balance between central adaptive functions, achieved by a decreased need for the functions associated with adults (e.g., care and supervision) and an increased need for functions associated with peers (e.g., play and mating).

Given that handicapped children generally lag behind nonhandicapped children, we would expect a corresponding effect on social networks, including a lower proportion of peer contacts because the handicapped children have greater needs for adult-related functions. That handicapped children show a lower proportion of peer contact and do not show an increase in the proportion of peer contacts from the 3- to 6-year period suggests that handicapping conditions may affect social development through network composition.

Another explanation accounting for these differences between nonhandicapped and handicapped children may be related to societal values in general and people's response to handicapped children in particular. Until recently, handicapped children were excluded from situations that tended to promote peer interaction. Rather than developmental status accounting for the lack of peer contact, stigmatization (from within as well as from outside the family) may be limiting peer contact.

Whatever the cause of differential peer contacts, the impact vis à vis social interactions may be similar. Our study indicates that handicapped children have fewer social contacts with peers than do nonhandicapped children, and this difference increases from 3 to 6 years of age. If peer contacts provide opportunity for the practice of social skills (functions) different than those provided by adults, then handicapped children are in jeopardy for reasons not stemming *directly* from their specific handicap.

Kinship

In analyzing contact with relatives, we excluded immediate family members because the groups did not differ (see Table 1). Rather than considering how much contact with mother, father, or siblings handicapped or nonhandicapped children had, we looked at how much contact the child's other relatives provided.

Excluding the nuclear family, children had more non-kin than kin elements in their networks as well as more daily contacts with non-kin. This may reflect cultural and historical trends: Non-kin have assumed greater significance in the social life of contemporary America than they did previously or still have in some other cultures. This shift probably began with the technological–industrial revolution of the late 1800s.

Interestingly, among most animal groups, kinship determines the proximity to and amount of contact with others. For many diverse species (e.g., the Bonnet Macaque and the African Lion), the mothers exert a powerful influence on social contacts of their offspring. Our data support this, because families saw more relatives of the mother than of the father (Feiring & Lewis, 1984; Lee, 1979; Lewis & Feiring, 1983).

Finally, the findings also support a developmental shift from a family to a larger social sphere. As mentioned previously, children not only moved from reliance on adults to greater reliance on peers but increased their contacts with persons outside the kinship group. Proportionately, nonhandicapped children had a greater non-kin to kin ratio than did handicapped children. Further, although nonhandicapped children showed an increase with age in the proportion of non-kin/kin contact, handicapped children showed a decrease. Such findings suggest that handicapped children's condition affects the nature of and opportunities for social contact. Differences in the proportion of non-kin/kin members of the social network may be due to deficits in the child's skill to make contact with non-kin individuals and to deviant social status that prevents opportunity for more non-kin contact.

Overall, it appears that both handicapped and nonhandicapped children come into contact with a variety of people in their homes, play groups, schools, and neighborhoods; however, the characteristics of these social networks differ. Handicapped children may be relatively restricted by their comparative reliance on adult and kin contact, with limited peer and non-kin orientation. Handicapped children may be slower to make the shifts from adult/kin to peer/non-kin contact and may have social networks that constrain the potential for these shifts to occur.

Public policy, such as integration of handicapped children into mainstream settings, may facilitate a change in the composition of handicapped children's social network and thus provide the needed opportunity for practice of social skills with peers and non-kin. Further, such integration policy should also alter the composition of nonhandicapped children's networks, giving them more contact with handicapped individuals. As a consequence, perhaps society's stigmatization of handicapped individuals will abate, thus eliminating one factor that prevents handicapped children from participating in social experiences necessary for adaptive functioning.

REFERENCES

Attneave, C. L. (1976). Social networks as the unit of intervention. In P. J. Guerin (Ed.), *Family therapy: Theory and practice*. New York: Gardner.

Barker, R. G. (1965). Explorations in ecological psychology. *American Psychologist*, 20, 1–14.

Barry, W. A. (1970). Marriage research and conflict: An integrative review. *Psychological Bulletin*, 73(1), 41–54.

Beckman, P. J. (1983). The influence of selected child characteristics on stress in families of handicapped infants. *American Journal of Mental Deficiency*, 88, 150–156.

Birenbaum, A. (1971). The mentally retarded child in the home and the family cycle. *Journal of Health and Social Behavior*, 12, 55–65.

Bott, E. (1957). *Family and social network*. London: Tavistock Institute of Human Relations.

Bott, E. (1971). *Family and social network* (2nd ed.). New York: Free Press.

Bristol, M. M., & Gallagher, J. J. (1982). A family focus for intervention. In C. Ramey & P. Trohanis (Eds.), *Finding and educating the high-risk and handicapped infant*. Baltimore: University Park Press.

Bronfenbrenner, U. (1977). Toward an experimental ecology of human development. *American Psychologist, 32*, 513–531.

Brooks-Gunn, J. (1985). Early dyadic interactions with the handicapped: Special infants or special parents? In W. K. Frankenburg, R. P. Emde, & S. Sullivan (Eds.), *Early identification of children at risk* (pp. 103–113). New York: Plenum.

Brunswick, E. (1956). *Perception and representative design of psychological experiments*. Berkeley: University of California Press.

Buckley, W. (1967). *Sociology and modern systems theory*. New Jersey: Prentice-Hall.

Clarke-Stewart, K. A. (1978). And daddy makes three: The father's impact on mother and young child. *Child Development, 45*, 466–478.

Cochran, M. M., & Brassard, J. A. (1979). Child development and personal social networks. *Child Development, 50*, 601–616.

Crockenberg, S. B. (1981). Infant irritability, mother responsiveness and social influences on the security of infant-mother attachment. *Child Development, 52*, 857–865.

Dorner, S. (1975). The relationship of physical handicap to stress in families with an adolescent with spina bifida. *Developmental Medicine and Child Neurology, 17*, 765–776.

Edwards, C., & Lewis, M. (1979). Young children's concepts of social relations: Social functions and social objects. In M. Lewis & L. Rosenblum (Eds.), *The child and its family: The genesis of behavior (Vol. 2)*. New York: Plenum.

Endler, N. S., & Magnusson, D. (1974). Interactionism, trait psychology and situationism. *Reports from the Psychological Laboratories*. University of Stockholm, 418.

Farber, B. (1963). Interaction with retarded siblings and life goals of children. *Marriage and Family Living, 25*, 96–98.

Farber, B., & Ryckman, D. B. (1965). Effects of severely mentally retarded children on family relationships. *Mental Retardation Abstracts, 2*, 1–17.

Feiring, C., & Lewis, M. (1978). The child in the family system. *Behavioral Sciences, 23*, 225–233.

Feiring, C., & Lewis, M. (1981). Middle-class differences in the mother-child interaction and the child's cognitive development. In T. Field, A. Sostek, P. Vietze, & P. H. Leiderman (Eds.), *Culture and early interactions* (pp. 63–91). Hillsdale, NJ: Erlbaum.

Feiring, C., & Lewis, M. (1984). Changing characteristics of U.S. families: Implications for families, networks, relationships, and child development. In M. Lewis (Ed.), *Beyond the dyad*. New York: Plenum.

Feiring, C. & Taylor, J. (in press). The influence of the infant and secondary parent on maternal behavior. In N. D. Coletta & D. Belle (Eds.), *Support systems and family functioning*. Beverly Hills: Sage.

Freedle, R., & Lewis, M. (1977). Prelinguistic conversations. In M. Lewis & L. Rosenblum (Eds.), *Interaction, conversation, and the development of language: The origins of behavior* (Vol. 5). New York: Wiley.

Gallagher, J. J., Cross, A., & Scharfman, W. (1981). Parental adaptation to a young handicapped child: The father's role. *Journal of the Division of Early Childhood, 3*, 3–14.

Gampel, D. H., Gottlieb, J., & Harrison, R. H. (1974). A comparison of the classroom behaviors of special class EMR, integrated EMR, low IQ, and non-retarded children. *American Journal of Mental Deficiency, 79,* 16–21.

Glick, C. P., & Norton, A. J. (1977). Marrying, divorcing and living together in the U.S. today. *Population Bulletin, 32,* 5–20.

Harlow, H. F., & Harlow, M. K. (1965). The affectional systems. In A. M. Schrier, H. F. Harlow, & F. Stollnitz (Eds.), *Behavior of nonhuman primates* (Vol. 2). New York: Academic.

Hartup, W. (1980). Peer play and pathology: Considerations in the growth of social competence. In T. Field (Ed.), *High risk infants and children: Adult and peer interaction.* New York: Academic.

Holland, P. W., & Leinhardt, S. (Eds.). (1979). *Perspectives on social network research.* New York: Academic.

Lamb, M., (1979). The effects of the social context on dyadic social interaction. In M. Lamb, S. Suomi, & G. Stephenson (Eds.), *Social interaction analysis.* Madison: University of Wisconsin Press.

Lamb, M. E. (Ed.). (1981). *The role of the father in child development* (2nd ed.). New York: Wiley Interscience.

Landesman-Dwyer, S., & Butterfield, E. C. (1983). Mental retardation: Developmental issues in cognitive and social adaptation. In M. Lewis (Ed.), *Origins of intelligence: Infancy and early childhood* (2nd ed.) New York: Plenum.

Lecco, C., & Lewis, M. (1987). Age knowledge in children from four to thirteen years old. Manuscript in preparation.

Lee, G. R. (1979). Effects of social networks on the family. In W. R. Burr, R. Hill, F. Nye, & I. Neiss (Eds.), *Contemporary theories about the family. Vol. I, Research-based theories.* New York: Free Press.

Lewis, M. (1982). The social network systems: Toward a general theory of social development. In T. Field (Ed.), *Review of human development* (Vol. 1).

Lewis, M., & Cherry, L. (1977). Social behavior and language acquisition. In M. Lewis & L. Rosenblum (Eds.), *Interaction, conversation and the development of language: The origins of behavior* (Vol. 5). New York: Wiley.

Lewis, M., & Feiring, C. (1978). The child's social world. In R. M. Lerner & G. D. Spanier (Eds.), *Child influences on marital and family interaction: A life-span perspective.* New York: Academic.

Lewis, M., & Feiring, C. (1979). The child's social network: Social object, social functions and their relationship. In M. Lewis & L. Rosenblum (Eds.), *The child and its family.* New York: Plenum.

Lewis, M., & Feiring, C. (1981). Direct and indirect interactions in social relationships. In L. Lipsitt (Ed.), *Advances in infancy research* (Vol. 1). New York: Ablex.

Lewis, M., & Feiring, C. (1983). Some American families at dinner. In L. M. Laosa & I. E. Sigel (Ed.), *Families as learning environments for children.* New York: Plenum.

Lewis, M., Feiring, C., & Kotsonis, M. (1984). The social networks of 3-year-old children. In M. Lewis (Ed.), *Beyond the dyad.* New York: Plenum.

Lewis, M., Feiring, C., & Weinraub, M. (1981). The father as a member of the child's social network. In M. Lamb (Ed.), *The role of the father in child development* (2nd ed.), New York: Wiley.

Lewis, M., & Freedle, R. (1973). Mother-infant dyad: the cradle of meaning. In P. Pliner, L. Krames, & T. Alloway (Eds.), *Communication and affect: Language and thought.* New York: Academic.

Lewis, M., & Rosenblum, L. (Eds.) (1975). *Friendships and peer relations: The origins of behavior* (Vol. 4). New York: Wiley.

Lewis, M., & Rosenblum, L. (Eds.). (1979). *The child and its family: The genesis of behavior* (Vol. 2). New York: Plenum.

Lewis, M. & Weinraub, M. (1976). The father's role in the infant's social network. In M. E. Lamb (Ed.), *The role of the father in child development*. New York: Wiley.

McAndrew, I. (1976). Children with a handicap and their families. *Child: Care, Health, and Development, 2,* 213–237.

Mueller, E., & Vandell, D. (1979). Infant-infant interaction: A review. In J. D. Osofsky (Ed.), *Handbook of infant development*. New York: Wiley Interscience.

Olshansky, S. (1962). Chronic sorrow: A response to having a mentally defective child. *Journal of Social Casework, 43,* 190–193.

Olson, D. H., Russell, C. S., & Sprenkle, D. H. (1980). Circumplex model of marital and family systems II: Empirical studies and clinical intervention. In J. P. Vincent (Ed.), *Advances in family intervention assessment and theory*. Connecticut: JAI Press.

Parke, R. D., Power, T. G., & Gottman, J. M. (1979). Conceptualizing and qualifying influence patterns in the family triad. In M. E. Lamb, S. S. Suomi, & G. R. Stephenson (Eds.), *Social interaction analysis: Methodological issues*. Madison: University of Wisconsin Press.

Parke, R. D., & Tinsley, B. R. (1981). The father's role in infancy: Determinants of involvement in caregiving and play. In M. Lamb (Ed.), *The role of the father in child development* (2nd ed.). New York: Wiley Interscience.

Patterson, J. M., & McCubbin, H. J. (1983). The impact of family life events and changes on the health of a chronically ill child. *Family Relations, 32,* 255–264.

Pattison, M., Defrancisco, D., Wood, P., Frazier, H., & Crowder, J. (1975). A psychosocial kinship model for family therapy. *American Journal of Psychiatry, 132,* 1246–1251.

Pervin, L. (1975). Definitions, measurements and classifications of stimuli situations and environments. *Research Bulletin 75-23.* Princeton, NJ: Educational Testing Service.

Price-Bonham, S., & Addison, S. (1978). Families and mentally retarded children: Emphasis on the father. *The Family Coordinator, 3,* 221–230.

Reed, E. W., & Reed, S. C. (1965). *Mental retardation: A family study.* Philadelphia: Saunders.

Russell, C. S. (1979). Circumplex model of marital and family systems III. Empirical evaluation with families. *Family Process, 18,* 29–45.

Trevino, F. (1979). Siblings of handicapped children: Identifying those at risk. *Social Casework: The Journal of Contemporary Social Work, 60*(8), 488–492.

Turnbull, A. P., Summers, J. A., & Bruthersun, M. J. (1986). The impact of young handicapped children on families: Future research directions. In *Parents' roles in the rehabilitation of their handicapped young children.* Washington, DC: National Institute of Handicapped Research.

Wilkes, L. (1981). Chronic stress of families of mentally retarded children. *Family Relations, 30,* 281–288.

Wilson, E. O. (1975) *Sociobiology.* Cambridge: The Belknap Press of Harvard University Press.

Winton, P., & Turnbull, A. (1981). Parent involvement as viewed by parents of preschool handicapped children. *Topics in Early Childhood Special Education, 1*(3), 11–19.

Wolfensberger, W. (1970). Counseling the parents of the retarded. In A. A. Baumeister (Ed.), *Mental retardation: Appraisal, education, and rehabilitation.* Chicago: Aldine.

Woodworth, R. S., & Scholesberg, H. (1951). *Experimental psychology.* New York: Holt.

Zill, N., & Peterson, J. L. (1982). Learning to do things without help. In L. M. Laosa & I. E. Sigel (Eds.), *Families as learning environments for children.* New York: Plenum.

18

The Home Care of
Children With Developmental Disabilities:
Empirical Support for a Model of
Successful Family Coping with Stress

Marie M. Bristol

University of North Carolina at Chapel Hill

Although child outcomes are traditionally used to evaluate intervention, there is increasing recognition that long-term, positive outcomes for developmentally disabled children also depend on successful adaptation of the family units and prevention of family crises (Bristol, 1985*b*; Foster & Berger, 1979).

Problems such as divorce, marital difficulties, parental depression, and child institutionalization in these families have been documented. In families of developmentally disabled children, divorce rates may be exceptionally high (Bristol, Schopler, & McConnaughey, 1984). For families of mentally retarded children, parental suicide and desertion rates may far exceed those of parents of nonhandicapped children (Price-Bonham & Addison, 1978).

Other studies indicate that the continuing stress of coping with handicapped children's daily needs may result in clinically discernible psychological problems, especially depression, in families of disabled, chronically ill children (Bradshaw & Lawton, 1978; Tew & Lawrence, 1975). The prevalence

Acknowledgements. The author thanks Mark Appelbaum, Associate Director of the L. L. Thurstone Psychometric Laboratory, for his role in designing and interpreting the data analyses. This research was supported in part by the Special Education Program of the Department of Education, Contract Number 300-77-0309; however, the opinions expressed do not necessarily reflect the position or policy of the U.S. Department of Education and no official endorsement should be inferred.

401

estimates of depression range from over 50% in a study of mothers of physically handicapped children (McMichael, 1971) to 15% among mothers of severely handicapped infants after a 2-year home-based therapy program (Burden, 1980).

Stress in families of autistic children may be particularly acute. Parents of these children report more coping problems than do parents of children with other types of handicaps (Holroyd & McArthur, 1976). Although rates of institutionalization have been declining, many of these families still face such a crisis. Estimated rates of institutionalization for autistic individuals range from a low of 8% (Schopler, Mesibov, DeVellis, & Short, 1981) to 74% with an estimated average rate of 46% (Lotter, 1978).

There is research and clinical evidence, however, that many families adapt successfully to their developmentally disabled child, despite increased caretaking demands (Bristol, 1984; Burden, 1980; Powell & Ogle, 1985). Few systematic studies provide data about the characteristics, resources, or beliefs that enable some families to make this successful adjustment.

GENERAL FAMILY STRESS

A growing body of data helps us understand how families cope with acute or chronic stress, whether the stress is caused by physical illness, military separation, or natural disasters such as tornadoes (Cohen & Lazarus, 1979; Gallagher, Beckman, Bell, & Cross, 1983; Hill, 1958; McCubbin et al., 1980).

First, no stressful event, including the presence or care of a handicapped child, invariably causes a family crisis. In a review of family response to stressors ranging from infidelity to war separation, Hill (1958) proposed a classic ABCX model of family stress. In this model of family coping, the characteristics of the stressor (A), the family's crisis-meeting resources (B), and the family's definition of the stressor (C) interact with each other, and each contributes to the prevention or precipitation of a family crisis (X). The ABCX model has been defined and developed further by Burr (1973), Hansen and Johnson (1979), and McCubbin and Patterson (1981) to include postcrisis adaptation.

To Hill's original ABCX model, McCubbin and Patterson (1981) added the pile-up of other family stresses and hardships that make adaptation more difficult, the social and psychological resources that the family uses in managing potential crisis situations, and the range of both positive and negative outcomes possible. This broader interpretation of the classic ABCX model was tested in the present study. For simplicity, the original ABCX notation was retained.

Elements of this model of stress in "normal" families have been affirmed repeatedly in almost 30 years of sociological research (McCubbin, 1979). The relationship of selected elements of the ABCX model to family crisis and adaptation have been demonstrated in studies of war separations and reunions (Hill, 1949; McCubbin, 1979) and natural disasters (Hill & Hansen, 1962). McCubbin and his associates (McCubbin, Patterson, Wilson, & Warwick, 1979; Nevin & McCubbin, 1979) have demonstrated the utility of the A and B elements in assessing outcomes for chronically ill children and their families.

Previous investigators focused primarily on one or two components of the model and their relationship to family adaptation. In the present study, I tested the applicability of selected aspects of the entire ABCX model to predictions of successful adaptation in families of developmentally disabled children. Although no test of the overall model has been made for this population, data support the likelihood that each element may contribute to differential family adaptation.

The Stressor (A)

Both severity and duration of the stressor may affect a family's ability to cope with its impact (McCubbin et al., 1980; Rabkin & Struening, 1976). Investigators studying parents of handicapped children have reported that the amount and type of stress that parents experience vary with the type and severity of the child's handicap (Holroyd & McArthur, 1976; McCubbin et al., 1979); however, other researchers (Tew & Lawrence, 1975) have not found that the severity of the child's handicap directly affects family outcome. Specific child characteristics shown to influence parental functioning adversely are age and gender (Bristol & Schopler, 1984; Farber, 1959); caretaking demands, infant temperament, responsivity, rate of development, and infant self-stimulation (Beckman, 1983) as well as difficult personality characteristics, social obtrusiveness, dependency, and physical incapacitation of autistic children (Bristol & Schopler, 1983). The impact of such child characteristics, however, may be moderated by the family's crisis-meeting resources.

Family Resources (B)

Although there are many psychological, economic, and organizational family resources, I have focused in this chapter on only two: perceived adequacy of social support and use of specific coping strategies to manage stress.

The importance of social support networks in parenting in general has been suggested by various authors (Cochran & Brassard, 1979; Lewis, Feiring, & Weinraub, 1981) and confirmed in limited research with families of at-risk (Crnic, Friedrich, & Greenberg, 1983) and developmentally disabled children (Bristol, 1984, in press). Both the presence of a father (Beckman, 1983; Holroyd, 1974) and the support of relatives, particularly the wife's relatives (Bristol, 1985a; Farber, 1959), predict lower levels of stress in families of disabled children. In previous research I found that two variables differentiate groups of high- versus low-stress mothers of autistic children, comparable in terms of socioeconomic status (SES), severity of the child's handicap, the family demographic factors (Bristol, 1984, 1985a). The variables are maternal perception of helpfulness of spouse, immediate and extended family, friends, and other parents of handicapped children and availability of services for the children. Parents of handicapped children report that they receive less social support than do parents of nonhandicapped children (Friedrich & Friedrich, 1981).

McCubbin (1979) demonstrated that parents *actively* cope with family stress, in addition to being passive recipients of support. Parental coping patterns, together with measures of family organization and severity of the child's condition, were related to level of stress in families of children with spina bifida (Nevin & McCubbin, 1979) and to health outcomes for children with cystic fibrosis (McCubbin et al., 1979). According to the Double ABCX model, the degree of the child impairment and family resources alone cannot account for the presence or absence of a family crisis.

Family Definition of the Stressful Event (C)

As Hill (1958) noted, stressors lead to crises, depending upon the family's definition of them. He cited three ways to define the crisis-precipitating event: the objective definition of an impartial observer, the cultural definition of the community, and the subjective definition of the family. He concluded that the subjective definition was the most relevant in predicting a family crisis. He observed that if the blame for the stressful event can be placed outside the family, the stress may serve to solidify, rather than to disorganize the family. For example, a tornado is a stressful event that is not likely to precipitate a family crisis because the blame for the event is outside the family.

Although the concept of self-blame or guilt in families of disabled children has received considerable clinical and research attention, there are relatively few systematic studies relating such subjective definitions to family outcomes. Finding some broader "meaning" for interpreting a child's condition was related to better family functioning for families of children with cystic fibrosis (Venters, 1982).

Lipowski (1970) reviewed research on health outcomes and concluded that people with similar medical conditions have different outcomes depending on whether patients view the illness as a challenge or valuable experience, a punishment for real or imagined failings, or an irreparable loss or damage. Similar parental beliefs regarding their child's handicap should contribute to different family outcomes.

Family Crisis or Successful Family Adaptation (X)

In Hill's original ABCX model, the X stood for family disorganization or crisis. McCubbin (1979) pointed out, however, that any type of "stress" also may be an opportunity for growth, leading to successful adaptation rather than to family crisis. Studying successful family adaptation, not just crises, should help identify family resources and strengths that may be useful for intervention with families who do not adapt as well. For this reason, I defined the X or outcome criterion as successful adaptation instead of crisis. Three aspects of successful adaptation considered were quality of parenting, lack of maternal depression, and high marital satisfaction.

METHOD

Subjects

Fifty-two mothers of handicapped children participated in the overall study. To obtain as unbiased a sample as possible, I recruited all 62 consecutive referrals to the statewide TEACCH program who met the eligibility criteria described later. (TEACCH is the acronym for the North Carolina Program of Services for Autistic and Communication Impaired Children [Treatment and Education of Autistic and Communication Impaired Children]). All mothers who agreed to participate were interviewed ($N = 56$, 89% of those contacted), including those without telephones (contacts were made through neighbors or social service agencies), and those in remote, relatively inaccessible areas. Four mothers subsequently failed to keep their child evaluation clinic appointments, leaving 52 eligible participants. For purposes of testing the ABCX model, I restricted the sample to the 45 parents with complete data on all measures.

Eligibility criteria were: referral to TEACCH for evaluation, no previous TEACCH services, child under 10, biological child–parent relationship, English-speaking mother with at least minimal literacy level, and substantiation of the child's handicap.

Participating families represented all social status groups (Hollingshead, 1971). Mean maternal age was 31.0 years (standard deviation [SD] = 5.6, range 19 to 47), and education ranged from junior high through graduate school, with the average mother having completed high school. Fifty-two percent of the mothers were employed outside the home. Thirty-five of the mothers were married, 10 were single parents. The average number of children per family was 2.23 (SD = 1.23).

Children's mean age was 5.3 years (SD = 2.0), with a range of 2.3 to 9.7 years. Their IQs ranged from 9 to 91, with a mean of 54.0. Thirty-four of the target children were boys, 11 were girls. Twenty-seven children were autistic. The remainder ($N = 18$) had significant communication impairments, but were not autistic according to criteria for scoring the Child Autism Rating Scale (Schopler, Reichler, DeVellis, & Daly, 1980).

Procedure

Before receiving services, mothers who volunteered by telephone to participate were sent packets of self-report measures to complete prior to the first home visit. Home visits were made to collect the self-assessments and to conduct a structured interview and independent ratings. Child psychometric and family demographic data were collected by TEACCH clinical staff as part of the child's subsequent diagnostic evaluation.

Measures

To test the applicability of the ABCX model for family coping with stress, I gathered selected A, B, and C measures and used them to predict successful family adaptation (X). These measures are listed in Table 1. The choice of variables measured does not by any means exhaust the dimensions of the model. Those measured, however, do represent variables shown in previous research to influence stress or coping in families with handicapped children.

Characteristics of the Stressor (A)

For this study, the stressor was defined as the presence of a disabled child. Measures included child characteristics hypothesized to increase stress, as well as concomitant hardships (e.g., significant life events) that might have exacerbated the primary stress. These child characteristics were measured using selected scales from the Holroyd (1974) Questionnaire on Resources and Stress. The pileup of other stresses unrelated to the child was measured using the Holroyd Questionnaire on Resources and Stress, Subscale 9, Limits on Family Opportunity. This subscale assesses the extent to which a family has to pass up educational, vocational, or other self-development opportunities because of the child. In addition, all mothers completed a modified Schedule of Recent Experience (Holmes & Rahe, 1967), which measures the number of major personal, family, occupational, and financial events signifying changes in the preceding 2 years.

Family Resources (B)

COPING STRATEGIES

The Coping Health Inventory for Parents (McCubbin & Patterson, 1981), originally designed for families of chronically ill children, was adapted for use in this study of developmentally disabled children. This measure is a 45-item questionnaire designed to provide information about the specific coping responses that parents use in dealing with the chronic stress of caring for a child with special needs.

SOCIAL SUPPORT

A modified version of the Carolina Parent Support Scale (Bristol, 1979, 1985a) was used to assess parental perceptions of the availability and helpfulness of sources of support to parents of handicapped or chronically ill children. This scale measures not only the availability of support, but the perceived helpfulness of support in parenting handicapped or chronically ill children. It also covers types of support unique to parents of handicapped children, yet is brief and considers both formal and informal sources of support. *Informal sources of support* were defined as those that do not require exchange of money or participation in formal organizations. These include spouse, wife's relatives, husband's relatives, the family's own children, other unrelated children, friends, neighbors, and other parents of handicapped children. *Formal support sources* include persons and services ranging from paid babysitters to ministers and respite-care programs.

Family Definition of the Stressor (C)

The Definition Scale (Bristol & DeVellis, 1981) was used to assess parents' subjective definitions related to having a handicapped child. Three a priori scales identified (then confirmed through factor analysis with a minimum loading of .50) were: (a) a meaning/purpose scale (e.g., "Caring for my child is an opportunity to learn new skills"), (b) a self-blame scale (e.g., "My child's problems are a punishment for something someone in the family has done"), and (c) a burden/catastrophe scale (e.g., "My child's having a handicap is one of the worst possible things that could happen to our family"). Each scale contained four items.

Family Adaptation (X)

QUALITY OF PARENTING

Adaptation was assessed as it related to parenting, maternal depression, and maternal adjustment. One major concern is whether families are able and willing to maintain severely handicapped children at home, at least until they acquire sufficient skills to live elsewhere (e.g., independently or semi-independently in the community). The rate of institutionalization of children this young, however, is extremely low. An estimate of the child's prospects for staying in the home may be the degree to which family members, especially the mother, accept the child and perceive that they can cope with the problems their child presents. The Home Quality Rating Scale Factor I, Harmony of Home and Quality of Parenting (Nihira, Meyers, & Mink, 1980), was the dependent measure of family acceptance and quality of parenting. This scale consists of 26 items completed by an in-home observer after a 1.5 to 2-hour structured interview with the

TABLE 1   Independent and Dependent Measures of Family Coping with Stress (ABCX Model)

Model Components/Measure	Purpose
A. Stressor	
Standardized intelligence (choice of test determined by level of child)	To provide a measure of child's intelligence as one dimension of the severity of child's handicap
Vineland Social Maturity Scale (Doll, 1965)	To provide a measure of child's habitual or customary level of competence and independent behavior
Holroyd QRS [a] (Holroyd, 1974) Physical Incapacitation (Subscale 11) Social Obtrusiveness (Subscale 14) Difficult Personality Characteristics (Subscale 15) Limits on Family Opportunity (Subscale 9)	To provide maternal ratings of child characteristics thought to be related to stress
Child age and sex	
Modified Holmes and Rahe (1967) Schedule of Recent Experiences (Total weighted scale)—Other Family Stresses	To assess the level of general family stress in addition to that caused by the child
B. Family resources	
Coping Health Inventory for Parents (McCubbin & Patterson, 1981) I: Family Maintenance of Family Integration, Cooperation, and an Optimistic Definition of the Situation; II: Social Support/Self Esteem; III: Community Consultation and Information Seeking	To assess contribution of active coping strategies to family outcome
Carolina Parent Support Scale (Informal Support/Formal Support) (Bristol, 1979)	To assess maternal perception of helpfulness of informal supports
C. Family definition of stressor	
Definition Scale (Factors I, II, III) (Bristol, 1981) (I: Meaning; II: Self-Blame; III: Catastrophe)	To assess maternal beliefs regarding having a handicapped child
X. Family adaptation	
Short Marital Adjustment Test (weighted total score) (Locke & Wallace, 1959)	To assess marital adjustment
Community Epidemiological Survey Depression Scale (total score) (Radloff, 1977)	To assess occurrence of depressive symptoms in previous week

**TABLE 1   Independent and Dependent Measures of Family
Coping with Stress (ABCX Model)** *(Cont.)*

Model Components/Measure	Purpose
Home Quality Rating [b] Scale, Factor I (Meyers, Mink, & Nihira, 1977; Nihira, Meyers, & Mink, 1980) ("Acceptance & Quality of Parenting")	To assess family acceptance and coping with the handicapped child

[a] Questionnaire on Resources and Stress.
[b] Observer rating completed after 1.5 to 2 hours in-home interviews.

parent. The interviewer probes about the child's impact on general family habits, such as sleeping and eating, maternal and sibling coping with the child, and arguments in the family, particularly those concerned with the handicapped child. Interviewers rate families on acceptance and quality of parenting (Factor I), using seven behaviorally anchored items: growth promotion as a policy in child rearing, acceptance of the child, rejection of the child, observed ability of the parent to cope with the child, adjustment and harmony in the home, and sibling support of the handicapped child. Interrater reliability on seven families ranged from 90 to 100%, with a mean of 96%.

MATERNAL DEPRESSION SYMPTOMS

To measure maternal report of depressive symptoms, I selected the Center for Epidemiologic Studies-Depression Scale (CES-D, Radloff, 1977) because it was suitable for use with community rather than clinical samples and because it avoids the vague response options ("usually," "often," or "Have you ever had . . .") in favor of more specifically anchored responses that indicate the number of days in the past week the respondent experienced the depressive symptoms (e.g., 1 = less than one day, 4 = 5 to 7 days in the past week).

MARITAL SATISFACTION AND DEMOGRAPHIC DATA

The widely used Short Marital Adjustment Test (Locke & Wallace, 1959) was used. Demographic data included marital status, occupation and education of mother (and father where appropriate), number of children, and family income.

RESULTS

The results are based on data collected prior to the initial TEACCH evaluation of the child and before the child or parent received any intervention services. Follow-up data are now being collected.

SUCCESSFUL FAMILY ADAPTATION (X)

One objective was to determine the percentage of families adapting successfully to the stress of having a handicapped child. Two of the outcome measures, the depression (CES-D) scale (Radloff, 1977) and the Marital Adjustment Test (Locke-Wallace, 1959) provided normative data and cutoff scores that have distinguished nonclinical from clinical populations in previous studies.

Seven of the single mothers were never married, the other 3 were separated or divorced. Of the married sample, 80% of the mothers had adequate marital adjustment scores (mean = 111.6, SD = 24.4; 100 is the cutoff for "adequate"). The majority of these young married mothers, then, described themselves as happily married.

Seventy-three percent of the mothers were *not* judged at risk for depression. The remaining 27% however, had CES-Depression scores at or above the clinical cutoff of 16. The mean scores for married (mean = 12.2, SD = 10.8) and single mothers (mean = 16.6, SD = 12.2) did not differ significantly. Without comparable data on mothers of nonretarded children, the significance of this percentage cannot be determined.

No normative data were available regarding family acceptance and quality of parenting (Home Quality Rating Scale, Factor I).

Before testing the predictive utility of the ABCX model, I compared mean adaptation scores (depression, marital adjustment, and quality of parenting) for mothers of the autistic children with those for mothers of the communication-impaired children, using Student's *t*-test procedures; the scores did not differ. Thus, all families were combined into one group for analysis purposes. None of the family adaptation variables related significantly to SES in this group.

THE TOTAL ABCX MODEL

The initial analysis, then, consisted of determining the canonical correlation (Searle, 1982) of the elements in the overall model (ABCX). This provides an index of whether child characteristics, family resources, and maternal beliefs collectively predict the joint adaptation measures of maternal depression and an observer rating of parenting quality. (Marital adjustment was examined separately to avoid eliminating all single parent families from the canonical correlation.) The variables included in the canonical correlation are those listed in Table 1 (A, B, & C predictors and X, the criteria).

The overall canonical correlation of predictor variables with the criteria was .87, which, when adjusted for the large number of variables relative to subjects, yielded a canonical correlation of .81, p = .001. Thus, the ABCX model strongly predicted successful adaptation in these families of developmentally disabled children. At this point, the power of the model to predict either depression or quality of parenting alone was not known. To determine whether these separate outcomes could be predicted by the available data, separate regression tests (Sall, 1981) were conducted for each outcome variable.

The total model including child characteristics, family resources, and subjective definition significantly predicted observer ratings of quality of parenting, $F(17, 27) = 4.97$, $p < .001$, together accounting for 53% of the variance when the original R^2, .71, was adjusted for ratio of variables to subjects. Similarly, the total ABCX model also significantly predicted maternal depression, $F(17, 27) = 2.60$, $p < .01$, accounting for 38% of the variance when the original R^2, .62, was adjusted for subject:variable ratio.

The same ABC predictor variables for two-parent families ($N = 35$) indicated that child characteristics, family resources, and maternal beliefs also predicted marital adjustment, $F(17, 17) = 4.19$, $p < .01$, accounting for 61% of the variance when the original R^2 of .81 was adjusted for subject:variable ratio.

Best Predictors

The total ABCX model, then, significantly predicted each of the three measures of family adaptation.

One of the major clinical objectives of this research was to identify a limited set of data to be collected from mothers at the time of first program contact that might differentiate those families adapting successfully from those in greater need of assistance. The next question addressed, then, was which measures best predicted each adaptation outcome.

Among the problems of analyzing large data sets on a small number of subjects ($N = 45$) is the problem of capitalizing on chance if the investigators simply generated prediction equations until some significant predictors were found. To mitigate this problem, I limited analyses by first conducting tests of the significance of the overall model and only when significance was found for the overall model, proceeded to look within the model for more specific relationships.

Because the overall regression tests were significant, backward, stepwise, multiple regression equations (Draper & Smith, 1981) were generated to identify the most parsimonious combination of predictors. Beta values, F ratios, and p values for significant predictors of all three dependent measures are presented in Table 2.

Quality of Parenting (See Table 2)

The best combination of predictors of the in-home rating of quality of parenting (Home Quality Rating Scale, Factor I) accounted for 61% of the variance when the original R^2 of .69 was adjusted for subject:variable ratio, $F(8, 36) = 8.92$, $p < .0001$.

STRESSOR (A)

Families rated as providing the highest quality of parenting for their disabled child tended to have older children (range 2 to 9 years) who were more independent as measured by Vineland social quotient scores.

TABLE 2   Predictors of Quality of Maternal Parenting, Maternal Depression, and Marital Adjustment from Child Characteristics, Family Resources, and Family Definition of the Child's Handicap

Dependent variables[a], best predictors	B value	F	p
Quality of parenting (HQRS) ($n = 45$)			
Child's IQ	−0.05	3.68	.06
Social quotient	0.08	5.64	.02
Child's age	0.06	9.58	.01
Limits on opportunity	0.83	4.74	.04
Informal support	0.29	9.55	.01
Formal support	−0.17	7.43	.01
Coping Health Inventory for Parents, Factor III	0.38	16.82	.001
Self-blame	−0.44	4.51	.04
Maternal depressive symptoms (CES–D) ($n = 45$)			
Child's IQ	0.16	4.10	.05
Child's social quotient	−0.24	6.05	.02
Child's physical incapacitation	2.26	3.78	.06
Limits on family opportunities	−3.89	12.00	.001
Self-blame	1.16	4.92	.03
Other family stress	0.04	16.03	.0003
Marital adjustment (MAT) ($n = 45$)			
Child's gender	13.53	4.29	.05
Social obtrusiveness	−4.27	3.67	.07
Informal support	2.22	11.46	.002
Formal support	−1.33	8.68	.007
Coping Health Inventory, Factor I	−1.37	8.10	.009
Coping Health Inventory, Factor III	2.13	9.08	.006
Subjective meaning of handicap	2.40	5.30	.03
Self-blame	−4.69	7.99	.009
Other family stresses	−0.12	22.48	.0001

[a] Behavioral elimination procedure used for dependent variables, Quality of Parenting (Home Quality Rating Scale, Factor I [HQRS]), maternal depression (Community Epidemiological Survey Scale-Depression [CES-D]), and marital adjustment (Marital Adjustment Test [MAT]).

Families of more severely retarded children were rated higher on acceptance and quality of parenting than were those whose children were only marginally retarded (close to normal) in cognitive ability. More positively rated mothers reportedly had sacrificed more of their own educational or vocational aspirations for their child's sake (i.e., had higher scores on the Questionnaire on Resources and Stress subscale, Limits on Family Opportunity).

RESOURCES (B)

More positive ratings of acceptance and quality of parenting were also predicted by perceived helpfulness of both informal (higher scores) and formal social supports (lower scores) on the Carolina Parent Support Scale. A more active coping pattern (i.e., higher scores on the Coping Health Inventory for Parents, Subscale III) that was characterized by seeking information and services, as well as carrying out prescribed activities, significantly related to positive ratings of quality of parenting.

DEFINITION (C)

The mother's subjective definition of the child's handicap was also an important predictor of her parenting quality. Mothers who externalized the blame (i.e., had lower scores on the Self-blame subscale of the Definition Scale) were rated by the observers as adapting better to their children. (Raters were blind to maternal responses on the self-assessment measures such as depression, definition, and marital adjustment.)

Lower Levels of Maternal Depressive Syndrome (See Table 2)

The best set of predictors of maternal depressive symptoms accounted for 49% of the variance when the original R^2 of .56 was adjusted for subject:variable ratio, $F(6, 38) = 8.0$, $p < .0001$. Although the total ABCX model significantly predicted maternal depression, the components that contributed most were characteristics of the stressor (A) and subjective definition of the child's handicap (C).

STRESSOR (A)

Children who were more independent (i.e., had higher Vineland social quotients) and less physically incapacitated (i.e., had lower Questionnaire on Resources and Stress, Physical Incapacitation scores) had mothers who reported fewer depressive symptoms (i.e., lower CES-D scores). Again, mothers of more retarded children had better CES-D scores than did the mothers of the marginally normal children.

Higher scores on the measure of other family stresses (Adapted Holmes & Rahe, Life Changes) were predictive of higher levels of depressive symptoms. As in quality of parenting, greater educational or vocational sacrifices for the child (i.e., higher scores on Questionnaire on Resources and Stress, Limits on Family Opportunity) predicted a lower level of depressive symptoms.

DEFINITION (C)

Externalization of blame as indexed by lower scores on the Self-blame subscale of the Definition Scale correlated with lower levels of depressive symptoms.

Marital Adjustment (see Table 2)

The best combination of predictors of marital adjustment accounted for 64% of the variance after adjusting the original R^2 of .73, $F(9, 25) = 7.70$, $p < .0001$. The A, B, and C components contributed to the best predictors of marital adjustment.

STRESSOR (A)

Mothers of handicapped girls reported better marital adjustment (i.e., higher Locke & Wallace total weighted scores) than did mothers of boys. Children with lower social obtrusiveness scores on the Questionnaire on Resources and Stress Social Obtrusiveness subscale had parents who reported more satisfactory marital adjustment. Marital adjustment scores also were higher in families reporting fewer other family stresses.

RESOURCES (B)

As in acceptance and quality of parenting, higher Informal Support scores and lower Formal Support scores (both on the Carolina Parent Support Scale) predicted better marital adjustment (higher Locke & Wallace Marital Adjustment scores). Specific coping patterns also related to reports of more satisfactory marriages. Mothers who used coping patterns involving maintenance of family integration, cooperation, and an optimistic definition of the situation (Coping Health Inventory for Parents, Factor I) and use of community consultation, seeking information, and carrying out prescribed activities (Factor III) reported significantly happier marriages.

DEFINITION (C)

The subjective definition the mother attributed to having a handicapped child was one of the best predictors of marital adjustment. Finding a positive meaning in having a handicapped child (i.e., higher scores on the Definition Scale, Meaning subscale) as well as externalizing the blame (i.e., lower scores on the Self-blame subscale of the Definition Scale) predicted happier marriages (higher Locke & Wallace Marital Adjustment scores).

DISCUSSION

This study demonstrates that the Double ABCX model of family coping with stress is useful for predicting successful family adaptation to the stress of having a developmentally disabled child. Elements of the stressor (A), family resources (B), and family definition of the stressful event (C) did significantly predict all three measures of family adaptation (X)—quality of parenting, marital satisfaction, and lower risk for depression. As operationalized in the present study, the model appears to be a better predictor of interpersonal adaptation (quality of parenting and marital adjustment) than of intrapersonal adaptation (depression).

Best Predictors

The best predictors of the measures of family adaptation are discussed in terms of the ABC elements.

THE STRESSOR (A)

As anticipated, characteristics of the disabled child contributed significantly to prediction of adaptation, but, in some instances, the direction of effect was unexpected. As in previous studies (Bristol, 1984; Farber, 1959), boys had a more adverse effect on marital adjustment than did girls. Older children were associated with improved maternal quality of parenting, a finding similar to that of Miller and Kaplan (1982). Age effects may be curvilinear, with increased age associated with some aspects of better family functioning until mid-adolescence. Negative effects for age in studies of handicapped children appear to be found only in studies that include adolescents (Bristol & Schopler, 1984; Farber, 1959).

Such differences raise concern about the generalizability of findings from one child age or stage of family development to another. For example, in the present study, sacrifices the mother made during early years related to *decreased* reports of depression. Continued sacrifices of family opportunity over time, however, may have negative effects on the family, perhaps not detectable until the handicapped child reaches adolescence.

Another expected finding was that mothers of children who were more independent and less physically incapacitated reported fewer depressive symptoms. These findings are consistent with earlier research on families of autistic children (Bristol & Schopler, 1984) and with findings by Beckman

(1983) on the impact of caretaking demands on mothers' stress. A reduced care burden reasonably contributes to the observed greater acceptance of and quality of parenting with the child.

Less expected, however, were the findings regarding the impact of degree of retardation. The fact that mothers of the more severely retarded children reported fewer depressive symptoms and were rated as more accepting and coping better than were parents of the marginally normal children requires careful exploration. One possibility is that the finding actually reflects the prediagnostic timing of the study and the role of diagnostic ambiguity in parental coping with stress. Hansen and Johnson (1979) reviewed at length the effects of ambiguity on family communication, co-orientation, and interaction patterns. In the present study, which occurred *before* formal evaluation of the child, the more retarded children were, in all likelihood, more obviously handicapped and less apt to generate parental disagreements about whether the child was actually handicapped. Whether more severely retarded children are more or less stressful over time (after diagnosis) is an empirically testable question.

The contribution of other family stresses to the prediction of marital adjustment and number of depressive symptoms is consistent with McCubbin and Patterson's (1983) concept of the "pile-up" of stressors that increase family risk. These results provide considerable support for McCubbin and Patterson's (1983) conceptualization of a Double ABCX model.

FAMILY RESOURCES (B)

The conceptualization of family resources in the present study was limited to a consideration of the utility of perceived adequacy of formal and informal sources of support and the choice and helpfulness of specific coping strategies. Both support and coping strategies were found to be significant predictors of marital adjustment and quality of maternal parenting of the disabled child.

The importance of perceived adequacy of informal social support in predicting both quality of parenting and marital adjustment for these mothers underscores the need to study the specific *kinds* of support that contribute to successful child and family outcomes. Both intra- and extra-familial sources of support may be critical, especially in single-parent families. Work by Crnic, Greenberg, Ragozin, Robinson, and Basham (1983) and Wahler (1980) suggests the importance of type and level of informal support in parent–child interaction. The fact that both perceived helpfulness of informal and formal support *and* coping patterns made independent contributions to the prediction of quality of parenting and marital adjustment reinforces McCubbin's (1979) contention that active coping strategies play a role that goes beyond the passive receipt of support.

DEFINITION OF THE STRESSOR

The findings indicate clearly that mothers respond not only to the objective reality of the child's handicap but also to their subjective definition of that reality. Both positive and negative maternal attribution regarding the child's handicap were significant predictors of family adaptation.

Mothers who did not blame themselves or other family members for the child's handicap reported fewer depressive symptoms and happier marriages and were rated by trained observers as providing better quality of parenting for the disabled child. This provides support for the concept of "externalization of blame," an important component of the definition of the stressor in Hill's original conceptualization of the model and in Burr's (1973) and Hansen and Johnson's (1979) later explications of family stress theory.

Interestingly, it was noted that the rate of depressive symptoms found did not differ for mothers of autistic and communication-impaired children and is comparable to or lower than that found in most studies previously reviewed for mothers of *all* types of handicapped children. This consistency across types of handicapping conditions, including physical defects and genetic disorders, suggests that the depressive symptoms are *the result* of having a developmentally disabled child, not the cause of any of the disorders. Future studies should include a comparison sample of mothers of nondisabled children to assess the extent to which their levels of depression exceed those of other mothers of young children. Radloff (1977) demonstrated that mothers of preschool nondisabled children have the highest rates of depression of mothers in any child age group.

Furthermore, the mothers in this study were seen *before* their children were diagnosed or received services. It is not surprising to find depressive symptoms among parents of seriously disabled children who do not have the benefits of specially designed services nor to find unwarranted self-blame among mothers who have not yet had the biological basis for the child's disorder explained to them.

Attributing a positive meaning to having a disabled child was also a significant predictor of marital adjustment, another indication of the importance of subjective definitions of stressful events to family adaptation. This is consistent with the work of Venters (1982) and Cohen and Lazarus (1979), who repeatedly affirm the importance of attributing a positive meaning to a stressful event for successful coping and outcomes.

The finding that family resources and beliefs were as important for positive adjustment as severity of the child's handicap confirms the applicability of the Double ABCX (Hill, 1949) classic model of family coping with stress to these families of developmentally disabled children. This also provides a basis for cautious optimism regarding the home care of severely disabled children because these elements may be more amenable to intervention than is the severity of the child's condition per se.

LIMITATIONS OF THE STUDY

These correlational data, of course, can only suggest, but do not demonstrate, cause and effect relationships, and caution must be exercised in interpreting the findings. Another limitation of the study is the use of maternal self-report data, which may be subject to distortion or errors of recall. This valid concern is mitigated partially by the use of independent, objective assessment of child characteristics and in-home ratings by trained observers. It appears, however, that precisely this *subjective* aspect of maternal perception, rather than the objective dimensions of the situation, may be involved in mediating successful adaptation. How fathers' perceptions of either the child's handicaps or family adaptation agree with maternal perceptions is a potential question for future researchers.

Adaptation to stress is a process that occurs over time. Measurement of family factors over time, then, is necessary before reaching firm conclusions about successful outcomes for these families. I am presently following these families to assess the predictive utility of this model.

IMPLICATIONS FOR FUTURE RESEARCH AND CLINICAL PRACTICE

This study demonstrates that the ABCX model can be used to predict aspects of successful family adaptation to the home care of developmentally disabled children. A multivariate model is necessary to understand the complex relationship between having a handicapped child and successful family adaptation. Advances in multivariate analysis make it possible to test such multivariate models, rather than relying solely on conjecture.

The findings indicate that the total ABCX model may be a useful framework for evaluating a wider range of factors within each of the model's four dimensions. Stressors could be expanded to include long-term illness, divorce, unemployment, or age-related problems (e.g., those of adolescence). Similarly, additional family resource and definition variables can be explored within this framework. The ways to measure family adaptation also could be broadened from the measures used here. For example, assessment of familial qualities of integration and adaptability and other dimensions related both to family vulnerability and regenerative power (Burr, 1973; Hansen & Johnson, 1979) may add considerable power to the application of the ABCX model. Although the model accounted for one half to two thirds of the variance in the adaptation measures, considerable variance was not explained. The limited scope of variables used in the present study did not exhaust the possibilities of the ABCX model, and additional work remains to be done to account for the remaining variance. Similarly, the utility of this model in predicting adaptation of other family members (e.g., fathers and/or siblings) could also be explored.

The model has clear heuristic value for developing possible intervention strategies. The findings regarding the importance of support, coping strategies, and subjective beliefs suggest areas that could be targets for practitioners designing early intervention programs. The results suggest that merely changing the child's behavior may be insufficient for assisting such families, especially those with the most severely handicapped children. Although the clinical utility of many of the measures used in the present study remains to be tested, the best predictors of parents' adaptation would provide a starting point for interventionists who hope to assess initial and postintervention levels of family resources and beliefs.

The fact that clarity of the child's mental handicap related to *lower* stress, at least before formal evaluation, suggests the need for early identification of the child's handicap and/or early parent education to minimize uncertainty regarding the child. Alternatively, a nearly normal child may be a greater disappointment or may cause "false hope" for parents than does a more clearly retarded child. The contribution of unwarranted maternal self-blame to maternal depression, marital adjustment, and quality of parenting also emphasizes the need for good diagnosis and support to prevent such parental misconceptions from interfering with successful family adaptation. Perhaps teaching parents coping strategies involving seeking information, obtaining services, and carrying out prescribed activities will also increase parents' feelings of involvement, control, and effectiveness.

Results of this study indicate clearly that focusing on successful adaptation rather than merely on pathology or poor coping offers a viable avenue for future researchers and clinical practitioners. In spite of the fact that some parents were found to have significant problems, it is important to note that even before receiving specialized services, the majority of these families were coping successfully with their disabled children. There is much to be learned by exploring the ways that families successfully cope with accepting and nurturing their handicapped children.

REFERENCES

Beckman, P. B. (1983). Characteristics of handicapped infants: A study of the relationship between child characteristics and stress as reported by mothers. *American Journal of Mental Deficiency, 88,* 150–156.

Bradshaw, J., & Lawton, D. (1978). Tracing the causes of stress in families with handicapped children. *British Journal of Social Work, 8*(2), 181–192.

Bristol, M. M. (1979). Maternal coping with autistic children: The effect of child characteristics and interpersonal support (Doctoral dissertation, University of North Carolina at Chapel Hill, 1979). *Dissertation Abstracts International, 40,* 3943 A-3944A.

Bristol, M. M. (1984). Family resources and successful adaptation to autistic children. In E. Schopler & G. Mesibov (Eds.), *The effects of autism on the family.* New York: Plenum.

Bristol, M. M. (1985a). *A series of studies of social support, stress, and adaptation in families of developmentally disabled children.* Paper presented at the biennial meeting of the Society for Research in Child Development, Toronto.

Bristol, M. M. (1985b). Designing programs for young developmentally disabled children: A family systems approach to autism. *Remedial and Special Education, 4*(6), 46–53.

Bristol, M. M. (in press). Mothers of children with autism or communication disorders: Successful adaptation and the double ABCX model. *Journal of Autism and Developmental Disabilities.*

Bristol, M. M. & DeVellis, R. (1981). *The Definition Scale: Parental attributions about their special child.* Unpublished instrument, University of North Carolina.

Bristol, M. M., & Schopler, E. (1983). Coping and stress in families of autistic adolescents. In E. Schopler & G. Mesibov (Eds.), *Autistic adolescents.* New York: Plenum.

Bristol, M. M. & Schopler, E. (1984). A developmental perspective on stress and coping in families of autistic children. In J. Blacher (Ed.), *Families of severely handicapped children.* New York: Academic.

Bristol, M. M., Schopler, E., & McConnaughey, R. (1984, December). *The prevalence of separation and divorce in families of young developmentally disabled children.* Paper presented at the Handicapped Children's Early Education Program/Division for Early Childhood Annual Conference, Washington, DC.

Burden, R. L. (1980). Measuring the effects of stress on the mothers of handicapped infants: Must depression always follow? *Child Care, Health and Development, 6,* 111–125.

Burr, W. R. (1973). *Theory construction and the sociology of the family.* New York: Wiley.

Cochran, M. M., & Brassard, J. A. (1979). Child development and personal social networks. *Child Development, 50,* 601–616.

Cohen, F., & Lazarus, R. (1979). Coping with the stresses of illness. In G. C. Stone, F. Cohen, & N. Adler & Associates (Eds.), *Health psychology—A handbook.* San Francisco: Jossey-Bass.

Crnic, K., Friedrich, W., & Greenberg, M. (1983). Adaptation of families with mentally retarded children: A model of stress, coping, and family ecology. *American Journal of Mental Deficiency, 88,* 125–138.

Crnic, K., Greenberg, M., Ragozin, A. Robinson, N., & Basham, R. (1983). Effects of stress and social support on mothers and premature and full-term infants. *Child Development, 54,* 209–217.

Doll, E. A. (1965). *Vineland Social Maturity Scale: Condensed manual of directions.* Circle Pines, MN: American Guidance Service.

Draper, N., & Smith, H. (1981). *Applied regression analysis* (2nd ed.) New York: Wiley.

Farber, B. (1959). Effects of a severely retarded child on family integration. *Monographics of the Society for Research in Child Development, 24,* Serial No. 71.

Foster, M., & Berger, M. (1979). Structural family therapy: Applications in programs for preschool handicapped children. *Journal of the Division of Early Childhood, 1,* 52–58.

Friedrich, W. N., & Friedrich, W. L. (1981). Psychosocial assets of parents of handicapped and nonhandicapped children. *American Journal of Mental Deficiency, 85,* 551–553.

Gallagher, J. J., Beckman-Bell, P., & Cross, A. (1983). Families of handicapped children: Sources of stress and its amelioration. *Exceptional Children, 50* 10–19.

Hansen, D. A., & Johnson, V. A. (1979). Rethinking family stress theory: Definitional aspects. In W. Burr, R. Hill, F. I. Nye, & I. Ress (Eds.), *Contemporary theories about the family: Volume 1, Research-based theories.* New York: Free Press.

Hill, R. T. (1949). *Families under stress: Adjustment to the crises of war separation and reunion.* New York: Harper.

Hill, R. T. (1958, May). Sociology of marriage and family behavior, 1945–1956: A trend report and bibliography. *Current Sociology, 7,* 10–98.

Hill, R., & Hansen, D. (1962). The family in disaster. In G. Baker & D. Chapman (Eds.), *Man and society in disaster.* New York: Basic Books.

Hollingshead, A. B., (1971). *Four factor index of social status.* Unpublished manuscript, Yale University.

Holmes, T., & Rahe, R. (1967). The Social Readjustment Rating Scale. *Journal of Psychomatic Research, 11,* 213.

Holroyd, J. (1974). The Questionnaire on Resources and Stress: An instrument to measure family response to a handicapped member. *Journal of Community Psychology, 2,* 92–94.

Holroyd, J., & McArthur, D. (1976). Mental retardation and stress on the parents: A contrast between Down's syndrome and childhood autism. *American Journal of Mental Deficiency, 80,* 431–436.

Lewis, M., Feiring, C., & Weinraub, M. (1981). The father as a member of the child's social network. In M. E., Lamb (Ed.) *The role of the father in child development.* New York: Wiley.

Lipowski, Z. J. (1970). Physical illness, the individual, and the coping process. *Psychiatry in Medicine, 1,* 91–102.

Locke, H. J., & Wallace, K. M. (1959). Short marital-adjustment and prediction tests: Their reliability and validity. *Marriage and Family Living, 8,* 251–255.

Lotter, V. (1978). Follow-up studies. In M. Rutter & E. Schopler (Eds.), *Autism: A reappraisal of concepts and treatment.* New York: Plenum.

McCubbin, H. I. (1979). Integrating coping behavior in family stress theory. *Journal of Marriage and the Family, 42,* 237–244.

McCubbin, H. I., Jay, C. B., Cauble, A. E., Comeau, J. K., Patterson, J. M., & Needle, R. H. (1980). Family stress and coping: A decade review. *Journal of Marriage and the Family,* 855–871.

McCubbin, H. I., & Patterson, J. M. (1981). *Systematic assessment of family stress, resources, and coping.* St. Paul: University of Minnesota, Family Stress Project.

McCubbin, H. I., & Patterson, J. M. (1983). The family stress process: The double ABCX model of adjustment and adaptation. In H. I. McCubbin, M. B. Sussman, & J. M. Patterson (Eds.), *Social stress and the family: Advances and developments in family's stress theory and research.* New York: Haworth.

McCubbin, H. I., Patterson, J. M., McCubbin, M. A., Wilson, L. R., & Warwick, W. J. (1979). Parental coping and family environment: Critical factors in the home management and health status of children with cystic fibrosis. In D. Bagarozzi, T. Jurich, & J. Jackson (Eds.), *New perspectives in marriage and family therapy: Issues in theory, research and practice.* New York: Human Science Press.

McMichael, J. (1971). *Handicap: A study of physically handicapped children and their families.* London: Saples.

Miller, N., & Kaplan, P. (1982, June). *Social support and stress among mothers of handicapped children.* Paper presented at the annual meeting of the American Association on Mental Deficiency, Boston.

Nevin, R., & McCubbin, H. (1979, August). *Parental coping with physical handicaps: Social policy implications.* Paper presented at the annual meeting of the National Council of Family Relations, Boston.

Nihira, K., Meyers, C. E., & Mink, I. T. (1980). Home environment, family adjustment, and the development of mentally retarded children. *Applied Research in Mental Retardation, 1,* 5–24.

Powell, T. H., & Ogle, P. A. (1985). *Brothers and sisters—A special part of exceptional families.* Baltimore: Brookes.

Price-Bonham, S., & Addison, S. (1978). Families and mentally retarded children: Emphasis on the father. *The Family Coordinator, 27,* 221–230.

Rabkin, J., & Struening, E. (1976). Life events, stress, and illness. *Science, 194*, 1013–1020.

Radloff, L. (1977). The CES-D scale: A self-report depression scale for research in general population. *Applied Psychological Measurement, 1*, 385–401.

Sall, J. P. (1981). *SAS regression application* (Rev. ed.). Cary, NC: SAS Technical Report A-102, SAS Institute.

Schopler, E., Mesibov, G., DeVellis, R., & Short A. (1981). Treatment outcomes of autistic children and their families. In P. Mittler (Ed.), *Frontiers of knowledge in mental health, I.* (Vol. 1). Baltimore: University Park Press.

Schopler, E., Reichler, R. J., DeVellis, R. F., & Daly, K. (1980). Toward objective classification of childhood autism: Childhood Autism Rating Scale (CARS). *Journal of Autism and Developmental Disorders, 10*, 91–103.

Searle, S. R. (1982). *Linear models,* New York: Wiley.

Tew, B., & Lawrence, K. M. (1975). Mothers, brothers, and sisters of patients with spina bifida. *Developmental Medicine and Child Neurology, 15*, 69–76.

Venters, M. (1982). Familial coping with chronic and severe illness: The case of cystic fibrosis. In H. McCubbin (Ed.), *Family stress, coping and social support.* Springfield, IL: Thomas.

Wahler, R. G. (1980). The insular mother: Her problems in parent–child treatment. *Journal of Applied Behavior Analysis, 13*, 207–219.

19
Observational Research on Children, Their Parents, and Their Siblings

Zolinda Stoneman and Gene H. Brody
University of Georgia

Few would disagree that the family home is the least restrictive environment for most handicapped children. Increasing numbers of children with varying degrees and types of handicapping conditions are residing with their families throughout childhood. This fact has stimulated an increased interest in families of handicapped children, both among researchers and direct-service providers. Although a body of research focusing on these families is beginning to emerge, most of the literature on this topic continues to consist of clinical case studies and impressionistic writings (e.g., Berg, 1973; Fowle, 1969; Klein, 1972; Love, 1973; San Martino & Newman, 1974; Schild, 1964). Only a few of the researchers examining families of handicapped children have utilized observational methodologies. In this chapter we attempt to review briefly the extant observational research on families of mentally retarded children, with a particular focus on parents and siblings. In addition, a theoretical framework is presented to guide observational research efforts in this area. Preliminary observational data on parents and siblings of retarded children utilizing this framework is described.

Acknowledgements. The preliminary studies reported in this paper were supported by Biomedical Research Support Grant No. SO7 RR07025-17 awarded by the Program, Division of Research Resources, National Institutes of Health, to the University of Georgia Research Foundation, Inc. Manuscript preparation was supported in part by the National Institute of Child Health and Human Development Grant No. HD 16817-01A1, National Foundation for the March of Dimes Grant No. 12-120, and the National Institute of Child Health and Human Development Grant No. HD 06016 awarded to Emory University and Georgia State University.

In our focus on observational research with families of handicapped children, we do not want to imply that other research strategies, such as interviews, rating scales, and questionnaires, are not valuable. Rather, we believe that observational research on families with a handicapped member has lagged behind research with typical families in utilizing observational methodologies. Studies in which investigators have employed self-report data-collection strategies (where family members describe and interpret their experiences) have several limitations that have led family researchers to no longer believe that adequate information about parent–child relations, in particular, and family relations, in general, can be solely obtained through these strategies. Several converging pieces of information support this view. For example, there is little evidence that parents relate to their children as they report they do on questionnaires or interviews. Rather, the data suggest that there is often little convergence between parental self-reports and actual parent behavior (Becker & Krug, 1965; Lytton, 1971; Yarrow, 1963). Further, social and personality psychologists have demonstrated that people often behave in a manner that is discrepant from their own self-reports (Mischel, 1968). Thus, multi-method studies that include actual observations of family interaction are necessary in order to obtain realistic, reliable information about the family.

Another argument for utilizing observational methodologies in the study of families with a retarded child concerns the contextual specificity of behavior. Many previous investigators have approached research questions about the family in a global manner; that is, family members were queried about perceptions, attitudes, and behaviors without considering the context in which information was sampled. Unfortunately, this research approach has been shown to have limited value in generating replicable predictions regarding processes that govern families (Brody & Endsley, 1981). A context-free approach is being challenged by evidence that human behavior, in general, and family transactions, in particular, are dependent on context (Brody & Stoneman, 1983a, Stoneman & Brody, 1983).

A contextual approach to family research assumes that the perceptions, attitudes, and behaviors of family members cannot be understood without examining the contexts in which they occur. A context, as we define it, may be a physical setting, the presence or absence of specific persons, or a combination of settings and persons. Within the family, children and adults are viewed as adapting to existing contexts as well as contributing to the creation of new contexts through their own thoughts and actions. From this perspective, each family member is viewed as an active participant in devising strategies to adapt to family contexts as well as a contributor to the development of contexts that serve to structure family transactions.

Observational research methodologies allow actual behaviors of family members to be anchored to specific interactive contexts. These strategies also enable researchers to study the reciprocal relationships among family members as well as the reciprocal relationships between family members and specific contexts. In sum, observational methodologies permit a context-dependent approach to studying families that is, by definition, concerned with variability in family interaction patterns as well as with more stable behavior patterns that span contexts. The following two sections provide a brief summary of the extant observational research on parents and siblings of retarded children.

OBSERVATIONAL RESEARCH ON PARENTS AND THEIR RETARDED CHILDREN

Mother–child interactions

The extant observational research on interactions between retarded children and their mothers has focused primarily on studying the language environment provided for infants and young children (e.g., Berger & Cunningham, 1983; Buckhalt, Rutherford, & Goldberg, 1978; Buium, Rynders, & Turnure, 1974; Cunningham, Reuler, Blackwell, & Deck, 1981; Gutmann & Rondal, 1979; Marshall, Hegrenes, & Goldstein, 1973; Rondal, 1977; Seitz & Marcus, 1976). These studies have usually involved transcribing the verbal interactions between mothers and their handicapped children and examining parental speech parameters. This emphasis on mothers as teachers of language is not surprising because delayed language skills characterize most retarded children and are, thus, important targets for intervention. Another body of research (reviewed by Blacher & Meyers, 1983) has focused on mother–child attachment in families with handicapped infants. Investigators have utilized observational methods to study the development of eye contact (Berger & Cunningham, 1981) and mutual play (Cook & Culp, 1981) between infants with Down syndrome and their mothers. Others (Breiner & Forehand, 1982; Eheart, 1982; Filler & Bricker, 1976; Kogan, Wimberger, & Bobbitt, 1969) have focused on interactions between mothers and their handicapped preschool children.

There are several consistent findings in this literature. First, several investigators (Cunningham et al., 1981; Kogan et al., 1969; Marshall et al., 1973; Terdal, Jackson, & Garner, 1976) have found that mothers of retarded children frequently assume what might be termed a "manager" role in their interactions with their offspring. In other words, they emit high rates of commands and requests, attempting to direct the behavior of their children. In addition, these mothers ask numerous teaching questions of their children (Kogan et al., 1969). Thus, in addition to being managers of their children, mothers of retarded children appear to be actively involved in teaching.

Several investigators have studied the reciprocal interactions between mothers and their retarded offspring. Vietze, Abernathy, Ashe, and Faulstich (1978) found that developmentally delayed infants did not emit vocalizations that were contingent on maternal speech, as did nondelayed infants. Similarly, Terdal et al. (1976) have demonstrated that retarded children are less contingently responsive to their mothers' social interactions, commands, and questions than are nonhandicapped children at similar developmental levels. Cunningham et al. (1981) also found that retarded children, particularly those with low mental ages, exhibited less contingent responsiveness to their mothers than did nonretarded children.

Father–child interactions

An obvious omission in this literature are reports of observational data concerning the roles assumed by fathers of retarded children. Findings from numerous self-report studies (see Gumz & Gubrium, 1972; Peck & Stephens, 1960; Price-Bonham & Addison, 1978; Tallman, 1965), however, suggest that the roles assumed by mothers and fathers may differ. In addition, there is indication in studies of normally developing children that particularly in triadic family groupings mothers assume a managerial or overseer role in interaction with their children whereas fathers are more likely to assume a playmate role, joining in activities with their offspring (Brody, Stoneman, & Sanders, 1980; Clarke-Stewart, 1978; Stoneman & Brody, 1981). Numerous scholars and researchers have stressed the importance of fathers' contributions to child development (e.g., Lamb, 1976; Lewis, Feiring, & Weinraub, 1981; Lewis & Weinraub, 1976; Lynn, 1974) and Parke (1978) has argued for the importance of observational research focusing on paternal interaction with young retarded children, but these studies still have not been conducted.

In response to this void in the literature, Stoneman et al., (1983) conducted an observational study of family interactions that had three purposes: (a) to examine the roles assumed by mothers and fathers during in-home interactions with their young retarded and nonretarded children, (b) to study the reciprocal role interactions among family members, and (c) to explore the effects of the presence of one parent on the interactions of the other parent with his or her child.

In-home observations were completed for 16 families. Eight of these families had young children ages 4 to 7 (mean = 5.3 years) with Down Syndrome. Four of these children were male and 4 were female. Eight contrast families with young nonhandicapped children also participated. The two groups of families were matched on child age, child gender, race, family income, maternal education, and paternal education. Each group contained 7 white families and 1 black family.

Three home visits, approximately a week apart, were made to each family. During each visit, family members participated in a play session in one of the following groupings: (a) mother and child, (b) father and child, and (c) mother, father, and child. Each play session lasted 20 to 25 minutes. All observations took place in the afternoon or early evening.

At the onset of each play session, the child and his or her parent(s) were given a standard set of toys and asked to play together with any of the toys in any manner they preferred. Family members were asked to interact naturally, ignoring the observers as much as possible. Two sets of toys were used. Both sets were structurally analogous, but one set was more complex in nature and, thus, more developmentally appropriate for the nonhandicapped children.

Interactions among family members were quantified utilizing both interval recording and sequential coding procedures. Data were collected on the following roles and behaviors: teacher, manager, helper, playmate, interactor, observer, solitary activity, verbalization, positive verbal, negative verbal, touch, positive physical, negative physical, negative affect, positive affect, information-seeking, response to managing, response to teaching, and response to information seeking. Operational definitions are provided in Tables 1 and 2.

This study revealed that in dyadic interactions (mother–child, father–child), parents of children with Down syndrome assumed the manager role more frequently, emitted more positive verbal and positive physical behaviors toward their children, and touched their offspring more frequently than did parents of nonhandicapped children. Conversely, parents of nonhandicapped children interacted with their children as playmates more frequently than did parents of children with Down syndrome. Mothers of children with Down syndrome assumed the teacher role more frequently than did fathers of these children or parents of nonhandicapped children. In the triadic grouping, parents of children with Down syndrome assumed the helper, manager, and teacher roles more frequently, emitted more positive verbalizations and positive affect, and touched their children more often than did parents of the nonhandicapped children.

Looking at the children's contribution to dyadic and triadic family interactions, Stoneman et al. (1983) found that the nonhandicapped children managed their parents more frequently, assumed the playmate role with their parents more often (dyadic contexts only), and assumed the interactor role less often (triadic context only) than did children with Down syndrome. Both groups of children verbalized more and directed more negative affect toward their mothers than toward their fathers.

When child contingent responsiveness was examined, Stoneman et al. (1983) found that children with Down syndrome failed to respond to a significantly higher proportion of parental managing, teaching, and information-seeking attempts in both the dyadic and triadic contexts than did the nonhandicapped comparison children. These findings replicate the work of Terdal et al. (1976) and Cunningham et al. (1981) and extend their findings to demonstrate decreased responsiveness of Down syndrome children to fathers as well as mothers. It is interesting that in the triadic family context, both groups of children failed to respond proportionally more often to the teaching attempts of their mothers than their fathers. It is possible that fathers taking the teacher role were more novel to the children, and, thus, their teaching attempts were more interesting than the teaching attempts of mothers, or it may be that fathers are more salient teachers than mothers for other, as yet undetermined, reasons.

The final question posed by Stoneman et al. (1983) concerned the effects of the presence of one parent on the interactions of the other parent with

TABLE 1 Interval Recording Categories, Operational Definitions, and Interobserver Reliabilities

Category	Definition	Reliability
Roles		
Teacher	To explain, model, or demonstrate; to provide labels; or to question with the purpose of teaching some principle, concept, or fact.	.86
Manager	To command or request (verbally or nonverbally) another to perform or not to perform a certain behavior; to assert one's own rights, thus attempting to influence another's behavior.	.83
Helper	Any attempt to offer assistance or help to another without being commanded or requested to do so.	.82
Playmate	To engage in joint play with another family member.	.96
Interactor	To converse with another family member without being engaged in joint play.	.89
Observer	To watch or observe another person without speaking to or interacting with that person.	.95
Other behaviors		
Solitary	To engage in an activity by oneself; not talking or interacting with another.	.88
Verbalization	Spoken word or attempt to speak that is neutral in affect.	.97
Positive verbalization	Spoken word or attempt to speak that praises, reinforces, or shows appreciation for another.	.85
Negative verbalization	Spoken word or attempt to speak that involves name calling, yelling, sarcasm, teasing, or cursing.	—[a]
Touch	Physical contact with another that is neutral in affect.	.87
Positive physical	Physical contact with another such as a touch, pat, or hug done with affection.	.91
Negative physical	Physical contact with another done in a hurtful manner such as a hit, slap, or push.	.86
Negative affect	Unhappy facial expression such as associated with a frown, grimace, or crying.	.83
Positive affect	Happy facial expression such as associated with a smile, laugh, or giggle.	.80
Information-seeking	Asking another for information, preferences, or opinions. Question asked for the purpose of gaining information, rather than teaching.	.83

[a] So few negative verbalizations were observed that reliability could not be accurately determined.

TABLE 2 **Sequential Coding Categories, Operational Definitions, and Interobserver Reliabilities**

Antecendent [a]	Consequence	Definition	Reliability
Manage	Comply	To respond to a management attempt by doing what was requested.	.89
	Resist	To resist verbally or nonverbally the managing attempt of another.	.82
	No response	To ignore or give no response to the managing attempt of another.	.84
Teach	Respond	To attend to another's teaching attempts through visual attention or by making a response.	.84
	No response	Inattention to teaching. To ignore or give no response to the teaching attempt of another.	.83
Information-seeking	Provide information	Responding to another's information-seeking request by providing the desired information.	.80
	Encourage independence	Responding to an information-seeking attempt by encouraging the asker to try to solve the problem or answer the question.	.81
	No response	To ignore or give no response to an information-seeking attempt.	.87

[a] Operational definitions and reliabilities for antecedents are provided in Table 1.

his or her child (indirect, or second-order effects). In general, behaviors of all family members decreased from the parent–child dyads to the triad, as might be expected, because more individuals had to share the time available in the triadic context. It is of particular interest that fathers of both groups of children increased their use of the observer role and spent more time in solitary activities during the triadic family grouping. Mothers, on the other hand, remained involved with their children in both the dyadic and triadic contexts. This is consistent with research in the developmental literature suggesting that mothers continue to assume a managing, parenting role across family groupings, whereas in mother–father–child triads, fathers tend to defer to mothers, decreasing their interaction time with their children (Brody, Stoneman, & Sanders, 1980; Clarke-Stewart, 1978; Golinkoff & Ames, 1979; Stoneman & Brody, 1981). This study suggests that these parental role differences during triadic family contexts exist for parents of children with Down syndrome as well as for parents of nonhandicapped youngsters.

Although parents reduced their frequency of behavior from dyadic to triadic groupings, accommodating their behavior to the presence of another adult (the other parent) in the interactive setting, children's frequencies of roles and behaviors remained consistent across contexts. This finding replicates an earlier study we conducted (Stoneman & Brody, 1981), which was focused on maternal and paternal speaking patterns across family groupings, and extends those findings to families with a child who has Down syndrome.

OBSERVATIONAL RESEARCH ON
RETARDED CHILDREN AND THEIR SIBLINGS

The topic of sibling relations is of central importance to contemporary accounts of the socialization process (Bundura, 1977; Hartup, 1978; Lewis, Feiring, & Weinraub, 1981). This recent focus on siblings stems from the belief that children belong to different social systems (i.e., sibling unit, parent–child unit, as well as the peer society), each of which makes a unique contribution to the development of social, emotional, and cognitive competencies.

Siblings directly contribute to development in at least three ways: (a) by reinforcing certain patterns of behavior while discouraging others, (b) by serving as models who furnish information about the appropriateness or inappropriateness of many kinds of behaviors in different settings, and (c) by providing a forum in which children participate in the formation of rules that will govern their conduct.

Siblings also exert indirect influences on their brothers or sisters. For example, the presence of a child with special needs in a family could have a marked effect on the socialization of other, typical siblings. The child with special needs may cause the parents considerable stress that could affect the socialization practices and, thus, the quality of the relationship with the other children in the family.

Not only are siblings capable of indirectly influencing how social agents interact with a brother or sister, they are also capable of indirectly influencing what roles and responsibilities their brothers or sisters assume. For instance, children with a mentally retarded brother or sister may be more likely to spend time in helping and caregiving activities than are children without a handicapped sibling (Stoneman & Brody, 1982). It is quite possible, therefore, that siblings influence one another as much or more in an indirect manner as they do in direct manner. This should be especially true for children with siblings who have mentally handicapping conditions.

It is surprising that so little is known about how handicapped children and their nonhandicapped siblings interact. In general, in the extant research in the area, investigators have used interview or questionnaire methodologies. In some instances, the respondent has been the nonhandicapped sibling, but in most studies it has been the mother. In those instances where the nonhandicapped sibling has been interviewed, the sibling has usually been a young adult, providing retrospective information concerning childhood interactions (see Brody & Stoneman, 1983b, for a complete review of this literature). The extant research contains only a few studies in which researchers have utilized nonhandicapped comparison groups. This makes most of the findings very difficult to interpret. It is hard to know whether the form of the transactions between siblings is really different from what would occur between nonhandicapped siblings.

In addition, the extant research has taken primarily a unidirectional approach, focusing on the impact of the mentally retarded child on his or her sibling. The possible impact of nonretarded siblings on the retarded child has been largely ignored. We have posited that nonretarded siblings may create an "in-home mainstreaming" environment for the retarded sibling, providing rich opportunities for modeling and social feedback (Stoneman & Brody, 1982). This lack of emphasis on the reciprocity of sibling interactions has been accompanied by a problem-oriented research emphasis, concentrating on the potentially harmful effects of having a retarded sibling. In sum, the research on siblings of retarded children is not of uniform quality, and many important questions await future investigation.

It is obvious that a need exists for methodologically sound research in this area. In particular, there is a dearth of research *describing* sibling relations involving an atypical child. Without careful, detailed descriptions, an important phase of scientific investigation has been minimized. Skipping this phase of the inquiry process will result in theorizing about sibling interactions involving an atypical child that is likely to be simplistic and to generate controversies that produce more questions than answers. Thus, we encourage clinical and developmental researchers to conduct research with observational methodologies that paint a picture of how typical and atypical siblings reciprocally influence one another. Special efforts should be made to focus not only on interactions between siblings, but also on the indirect effects on development of being part of a sibling system in which one child is atypical. Such indirect influences might include the impact of an atypical sibling on the typical sibling's access to social networks, such as peers, as well as the indirect influence of one sibling on the other sibling's interactions with parents.

Until we understand more about the daily interactions of siblings, we are groping in the dark as we try to design interventions to improve these interactions. Intervention efforts must rest on an empirical base rather than on assumptions or untested theory. In the area of sibling relations, the level of rhetoric far outdistances the quality and quantity of the supporting data. There is much yet to be learned about nonretarded sibling interactions in general, and this body of knowledge must be the foundation for understanding interactions between handicapped children and their siblings.

Observational studies of interaction involving nonhandicapped siblings are just beginning to provide enough information to serve as a baseline against which interactions between handicapped children and their siblings can be compared. To date, most of this research has involved observations of preschool children and their toddler or infant siblings (Abramovitch, Corter, & Lando, 1979; Abramovitch, Corter, & Pepler, 1980; Lamb, 1978a, 1978b; Samuels, 1980). Overall, these studies suggest that younger siblings tend to watch, follow, and imitate their older siblings. The fact that younger siblings play with objects abandoned by their older siblings and imitate their behavior suggests that older siblings may play an important role in facilitating the young child's mastery over the inanimate environment.

In a recent study of sibling interactions between school-aged children, Brody, Stoneman, and MacKinnon (1982) examined dyadic interactions between siblings, dyadic interactions between the older sibling and his or her best friend, and the interactions that occurred when the two siblings and the older sibling's best friend played together. The children were observed playing a popular board game in their homes. This study was specifically designed to examine the roles assumed by school-aged children when interacting with a friend or younger sibling and chronicle how the roles assumed by the older sibling and his or her friend were affected by the presence of a younger sibling.

The results revealed that the older sibling assumed dominant roles (manager, teacher) in the older sibling–younger sibling dyad, an equalitarian role (playmate) in the sibling–friend interaction, and a combination of dominant and equalitarian roles (playmate, manager) in the triadic interactions. Theoretically, the role asymmetries displayed by the older sibling while participating in two different "social networks" would be advantageous to development (Brim, 1960; Bronfenbrenner, 1979). On the one hand, these children have the opportunity to practice roles associated with dominance, and on the other hand, they have the opportunity to practice roles associated with equalitarian relationships.

Because the Brody et al. (1982) was carried out within the home during only one type of play activity (a structured game), a second study was conducted that further described the role relationships of siblings in the context of their own homes while they engaged in activities of their own selection (Stoneman, Brody, & MacKinnon, 1984). The findings derived from this home-based observational investigation, in which sibling interactions were completely unstructured and the children were free to do as they pleased, were consistent with the findings of Brody et al. (1982). This suggests that the results of the Brody et al. study are robust and provide a generally accurate picture of sibling and peer interactions. In addition, sequential analyses revealed that younger siblings were more likely to accept complementary, nondominant roles from their older siblings than vice versa. This finding was not unexpected, as status, and presumably power, are allocated to children as a function of age by both parents and children themselves (Eisenstadt, 1956; Moore, 1969; Sutton-Smith & Rosenberg, 1970). Thus, low-status younger siblings would be expected to comply with the role demands of the older siblings more often than vice versa. In a subsequent study Brody, Stoneman, MacKinnon, and MacKinnon (1985) identified developmental trends in the role relationships between siblings.

A FUNCTIONAL ROLE THEORY APPROACH

There is a vast array of theoretical approaches to choose from to guide research in family relations. Our selection was guided by two biases. First, family interactions are characterized by organized response patterns, so that a given behavior gains meaning through its association with other behaviors. Thus, behaviors tend to cluster together to form organized systems. Second, family interactions are best described by a dual process, reciprocal influence model; sequential exchanges between family members have implications for each person's behavior. These two beliefs have led us to an approach we call "functional role theory." We have selected aspects of traditional role theory (Sarbin, 1954) and amalgamated with them knowledge about the reciprocal nature of human behavior.

How might the assumption of roles facilitate development, particularly between retarded children and their siblings? One could argue that in learning and practicing a role, children learn not only their own role but also the complementary roles. Effective social functioning requires children to know the expectations of complementary roles in order to coordinate behavior during social exchanges. Role assumption thus affects both cognitive and behavioral competencies. At the cognitive level, children acquire expectations regarding the appropriate role for given social contexts and expectations regarding how others are likely to behave toward them. The content of these expectations are of particular interest. If, for example, a parent places an older sibling in the role of caretaker or teacher, the sibling has to understand the requirements of the role and organize the environment so that his or her caretaking or teaching can be accomplished. Actually, there are some empirical data that suggest that being placed in the role of teacher, for example, has a faciitating influence on cognitive development (Bargh & Schul, 1980; Zajonc & Markus, 1975). Conversely, the sibling in the learner role has the opportunity to receive information and to abstract the strategies the older sibling used to organize and impart information. Whether a sibling assumes a caretaker, manager, teacher, learner, or managee role, the children are confronted with the developmental task of structuring their interpersonal expectancies and behavior consistent with the role requirements.

From our perspective, approaching the development of family relations among nonhandicapped and handicapped children from the functional role theory framework is useful because it can describe and explain behavior, and it provides suggestions for the design and implementation of intervention strategies. This perspective acknowledges the social contexts to which roles are so closely tied. Bronfenbrenner (1979) stressed that ecological settings determine the appropriateness or inappropriateness of roles: A role that is desirable in one setting can be completely inappropriate in another. Further, as a child develops, roles that were acceptable at one age are replaced by other interactive patterns more appropriate to a mature individual.

In the following section, we present two preliminary observational studies of family interaction that were based on our functional role theory approach. The studies share some characteristics. First, interactions between family members were quantified using an observational methodology. Second, all of the interactions took place within the participants' homes. Third, the observations were focused on the roles that family members assume while interacting with one another in different family contexts.

STUDY 1: SEMI-STRUCTURED OBSERVATIONS OF HANDICAPPED CHILDREN AND THEIR SIBLINGS

This study was designed to examine whether role asymmetries characterize the interactions between handicapped children and their older nonhandicapped siblings. We also wanted to ascertain how much time the sibling pairs would interact in a semi-structured play situation.

Subjects

In-home pilot observations were completed for 5 sibling pairs. Each sibling pair included a younger child who was diagnosed as being moderately mentally retarded and an older, nonhandicapped child. The handicapped children ranged from 5 to 9 years of age (mean = 6.8); the older, nonhandicapped children ranged from 8 to 13 years of age (mean = 10). The age spacing between siblings ranged from 2 to 4 years (mean = 3.2). All older, nonhandicapped siblings were firstborn, and all retarded siblings were secondborn. Both the sample of retarded children and the sample of older, nonhandicapped siblings contained 3 boys and 2 girls. One sibling pair was composed of 2 boys, and the other 4 were cross-sex sibling pairs. Three of the retarded children had Down syndrome. The other two children were diagnosed as having mental retardation due to unknown etiology. All children came from two-parent families. Three of the families were white, and 2 were black. Families were lower middle class with an average of 12 years of parental education.

Procedure

Each sibling pair was observed interacting at home. Each play session lasted 20 to 25 minutes, with only the final 15 minutes being utilized for data collection. This allowed time for the children to begin playing and to accommodate to the setting. At the onset of each play session, the children were given a standard set of toys and asked to play with the toys as they wished, as long as they did not leave the room. The children were instructed to ignore the observers as much as possible.

Two observers were present during each play session; one coded the roles and behaviors of each sibling. Observers were naive as to the purpose of the study. They did not interact with the children while data were being collected.

Sampling of Behavior

Interactions between siblings were quantified utilizing interval recording procedures similar to those reported in Stoneman, Brody, and Abbott (1983). The following roles and behaviors were sampled: amount of interaction, teaching, managing, playing/interacting, verbalizing, positive interaction, negative interaction, solitary activity, compliance with sibling management attempts, and noncompliance with sibling management attempts. Operational definitions for these roles and behaviors are similar to those presented in Tables 1 and 2.

Observer Training and Reliability

Observers were trained through the use of videotaped interactions of sibling pairs and subsequent live observations in classrooms and pilot homes until interobserver agreement levels for each role and behavior exceeded .84. During data collection observers met weekly to code new videotapes, thus providing a monitoring of interobserver reliability levels across the course of the study. Interobserver agreement for each coding category for each observer (with a criterion rater) consistently exceeded .84.

Results

The frequency of occurrence for each role and behavior for each sibling was compiled. Proportions were then created by dividing the frequency of teaching, managing, playing/interacting, verbalizing, positive interaction, and negative interaction for each sibling by the number of intervals in which interaction occurred for each sibling pair. Intervals in which the children were not interacting were not included in the proportion because the aforementioned roles and behaviors could only occur during interaction with a sibling. Proportions of solitary activity and sibling interaction were created by dividing these frequencies by the total number of coded intervals. Proportions of compliance and noncompliance to sibling management attempts were created by dividing the frequency of each of these responses by the total number of sibling management attempts.

Because of the preliminary nature of these data, they can be viewed only as being suggestive. The small number of sibling pairs, the limited amount of observation time, the absence of statistical analyses, and the heterogeneity of the target children make any conclusion tentative. During the play sessions, the sibling pairs interacted with each other frequently. Less than 14% of their time was spent in solitary activity. (Mean percentages for the roles and behaviors of interest are presented in Table 3). Consistent with earlier research with nonhandicapped sibling pairs (Brody et al., 1982; Stoneman et al., 1984), there appeared to be distinct asymmetries in the roles assumed by the older and younger siblings. The older, nonhandicapped siblings managed their younger, retarded siblings approximately 36 times as often as they were managed by their younger siblings. Similarly, the younger, handicapped children never assumed the role of teacher with their older siblings, whereas the older siblings assumed the teacher role during approximately 4% of their interactive intervals.

The younger, retarded siblings complied with only slightly more than half of their older siblings' management attempts. This appears to be a substantially lower rate of compliance than was found in the preceding study for retarded children's compliance with their parents' management attempts. Compliance with maternal and paternal management attempts averaged .77 in the dyadic situations and .74 in the triadic family grouping. As viewed through a functional role theory framework (Stoneman &

TABLE 3   Mean Percentage of Interactive Intervals Each Role
and Behavior Was Assumed by Siblings in the
Semi-Structured and Naturalistic Situations

Situation, role/behavior	Younger, handicapped sibling	Older, nonretarded sibling
Semi-structured		
Teacher	0.00[a]	3.86[a]
Manager	0.51	18.01
Playmate/interactor	23.29	23.29
Verbalization	22.65	30.66
Total sibling interaction	86.33	86.33
Naturalistic		
Teacher	0.00[a]	8.60[a]
Manager	8.10	21.51
Playmate/interactor	49.87	49.87
Verbalization	71.39	61.04
Total sibling interaction	43.88	43.88

[a] Percentage of total intervals.

Brody, 1982), complying with a management attempt of another is seen as acceptance of the reciprocal role of managee. Thus, handicapped children may be less willing to accept the manager/managee role relationship with their older siblings than with their parents. Further research utilizing a larger sample size and appropriate statistical procedures is needed to determine the replicability of these pilot findings. If they are found to be robust, future studies are needed to examine whether this difference in handicapped children's acceptance of the manager role with siblings and parents is a result of status differences between parents and siblings or whether older brothers and sisters use less effective management strategies and, thus, are more likely to be ignored or actively resisted by their younger siblings.

STUDY 2: NATURALISTIC OBSERVATIONS OF FAMILIES WITH A HANDICAPPED CHILD

The previous data-collection effort was carried out within the home during only one type of family activity, namely, play. In the ongoing home environment, however, families interact together in numerous contexts. The following set of preliminary studies was designed to examine the interactions of mothers, fathers, siblings, and retarded children during naturalistic observations in which family members were encouraged to go about their daily routines.

Subjects

Naturalistic observations were obtained for 7 families, all of whom had a child with Down syndrome who was between the ages of 4 and 8 years (mean = 5.9). Four of the children with Down syndrome were boys and 3 were girls. Five families also had one older, nonhandicapped child. These 5 families were the same families who participated in the preceding sibling pilot study. Families were all white and lower middle class. All children came from two-parent families. Naturalistic observations focusing on parent–child interactions were completed on 7 families, and observations focusing on sibling relations were completed for 5 families.

Procedure

All observations took place at the participants' homes. During two visits to the family, the parent–handicapped child interaction was the focus of observations, and interactions between siblings were the focus on two other visits (for those families in which the handicapped child had an older brother or sister living at home). Data collection during each visit lasted

30 minutes, and visits were spaced one week apart. For both the observations of parent–child interactions and sibling interactions, visits were scheduled to correspond to times when all target family members were at home. The participants were told that the observers wanted to watch their ordinary activities and were requested to go about their normal routine and to ignore the observers as much as possible.

Three observers were present during each parent–child observation, with one coder responsible for observing the mother's behavior, another for the father's behavior, and the third for the handicapped child's behavior. Two observers were present during each sibling observation, with one person responsible for coding the behavior of each sibling.

Sampling of Behavior

The same interval recording data-collection strategy employed during the semi-structured observations in Study 1 was employed during the pilot naturalistic observations. The following roles and behaviors were sampled: amount of interaction, teaching, managing, playing/interacting, and verbalizing. (See Table 1 for the operational definition of these roles and behaviors.) In addition to coding the occurrence of any of these coding categories in each 10-second interval, the observers noted the family member to whom the role or behavior was directed and the activity in which the target family member was involved.

Observer training was described in a previous section. Reliability for all roles and behaviors consistently exceeded .84.

Results

Family members engaged in a diverse array of activities during the course of these observations. Mothers did laundry, folded and sorted clothes, prepared meals, watched television, read books and magazines, and played with their children. Fathers were observed while they watched television, performed carpentry work, worked in the yard, read the newspaper and magazines, looked for lost toys, played the guitar with friends, worked on cars and motorcycles, engaged their children in play, listened to records, did paperwork at the kitchen table, and fixed snacks for their children.

The most popular activities for the siblings during the observations were watching television, eating snacks, and playing with outdoor equipment, particularly swingsets. Siblings were also observed while engaging in activities such as playing jacks, jumping rope, drawing and coloring, climbing trees, playing catch, reading, talking on the phone, playing with pets, and wrestling. Thus, these observations were made in a wide variety of contexts within the home environment.

Data on each parent's performance of the roles and behaviors of interest were reduced by computing a mean frequency for each role and behavior for the two observation sessions. Only roles and behaviors directed toward the handicapped children were included in this computation. The handicapped children's roles and behaviors toward their mothers and fathers during the two parent–child observation sessions were reduced in a similar fashion, as were siblings' behaviors and roles displayed toward each other in the two sibling-observation sessions. Proportions were created from these mean frequencies as described earlier in the semi-structured observation section.

Let us first consider the findings for the parent–child naturalistic observations. Once again, these findings are only suggestive, due to the preliminary nature of these observations. In general, mothers appeared to be engaged more with their handicapped children in the naturalistic in-home contexts than were fathers (see Table 4). Both parents were almost identical in the amount of interaction with their retarded offspring that was characterized by play, whereas mothers seemed to engage in more teaching and managing than did fathers. The finding that mothers assumed the teacher role over twice as often as fathers is consistent with the findings of the semi-structured parent–child observational study reported earlier (Stoneman et al., 1983).

It also appeared that during these observations mothers talked to their handicapped children more than fathers did and engaged their children in more positive and negative interaction than did fathers. The overall impression given by these observations was that mothers were primarily responsible for the care of their handicapped offspring, whereas fathers helped by entertaining the children and playing with them. It is important to note, however, that there was considerable variability among the fathers who participated in this study. Two of the fathers appeared to be actively

TABLE 4 Mean Percentage of Interactive Intervals Each Role and Behavior Was Assumed by Parents During Naturalistic Observations

Role/behavior	Mother	Father
Teacher	11.86[a]	5.37[a]
Manager	22.11	14.50
Playmate/interactor	45.40	49.84
Verbalizations	72.67	41.30
Positive interaction	22.79	14.96
Negative interaction	7.31	2.51
Total parent interaction	66.23	49.53

[a] Percentage of total intervals.

involved in the care of their retarded children, assuming the teacher and manager roles as frequently as did mothers.

The handicapped children complied with 72.13% of maternal managing attempts and 89.34% of paternal managing attempts. Further research may determine whether this is a reliable difference in handicapped children's assumption of the managee role with mothers and fathers. The retarded children never taught their parents, but 4.55% of their interactions with mothers and 2.32% of their interactions with fathers were characterized by management attempts.

The naturalistic observations of sibling interactions, shown in Table 3, suggest the existence of clear role asymmetries between the handicapped and nonhandicapped siblings. The latter assumed the roles of teacher and manager more frequently than did their handicapped brothers and sisters. During these preliminary observations, the siblings interacted during approximately half of the observation intervals. The majority of their interactions were characterized by verbalizations.

Naturalistic observations of sibling interactions produced very similar findings to those reported earlier in the semi-structured sibling observations. Despite the diverse situations sampled in the present set of observations, consistent role asymmetries between siblings occurred. Taken together, these observations suggest that young, handicapped children and their older siblings interact fairly frequently, and these interactions are characterized by the older, nonhandicapped siblings' assumption of managing and teaching responsibilities.

Discussion

The preliminary studies just described demonstrate the viability of observing the naturally occurring role relationships in families with retarded children. At the minimum, these studies indicate the need for expanded observational studies that chronicle the interactions between different familial subsystems. Beyond this, however, there is a pressing need to amalgamate self-reports of family functioning with observational data so that a more complete picture of each person's functioning within the family can be obtained. Finally, we hope that intensive multi-method investigations of families with a retarded child will permit us to identify patterns of family functioning that create a minimum of adjustment problems for the retarded child and each family member.

SUMMARY AND RECOMMENDATIONS

In this chapter, we have argued for the utilization of observational methodologies in research on families with retarded members. We do not believe that observational methods should replace other ways of collecting information about families. Direct observation of behavior provides an understanding of the patterns of interaction in families that cannot be obtained by any other method and, as such, complements other family research strategies such as interviews and questionnaires. In the following sections, we briefly explore the methodological ramifications of the theoretical framework presented in this chapter.

Families as systems

A functional role theory approach conceptualizes the family as a system. In this model, each subsystem—whether it be dyadic, triadic, quadric, or even larger—is an important unit of study. As such, research must move beyond the mother–child dyad, the father–child dyad, and the sibling dyad to study complex family subsystems. Observational methodologies need to be developed that can accurately provide information on multi-person family subsystems.

In addition, the spousal subsystem must not be ignored as we attempt to understand family functioning. More research is necessary before we can understand how the marital relationship impacts upon parenting, sibling relations, and overall family interaction patterns.

Indirect effects

Indirect effects refer to the influence that one family member has on the interactions of other family members. Researchers have realized that socialization practices by any social agent may vary as a function of the presence and influence of other social agents in the environment. Lamb (1978a, 1978b), for example, investigated the effects of mother and/or father presence on the interactions of infants and their preschool siblings, whereas Clarke-Stewart (1978) studied the effect of father presence on interactions between young children and their mothers. Bronfenbrenner (1979) argued for increased study of these indirect effects (or second-order effects) within the family system. Similarly, Parke (1978) cited the need for observational research with retarded children to go beyond the mother–child dyad to include both the father–child dyad and mother–father–child triad. Lewis et al., (1981) suggested that because mothers may interact more frequently with their children in dyadic settings, and fathers may more frequently interact with the child in larger family groupings (often with mothers present), the father's influence on the child may be more indirect than that of the mother. Thus, the consideration of second-order effects would seem to be very important when families with retarded members are studied.

Nonpathology models

Every family system has strengths and weaknesses, and families with retarded members are no exception. Research on families of mentally retarded children, however, has often been focused on finding family pathology "caused" by the presence of a retarded child. This research has frequently been methodologically weak, and its unidirectional focus on the handicapped child as the presumed cause of pathology in parents and siblings provides limited insight into the interactional patterns of these families. A more comprehensive research model, focusing on functional patterns within the family system, is needed. Such a model should provide an increased understanding of the mechanisms through which some families with retarded members maintain a stable, healthy family life whereas other families do not. We believe that it is more important to understand the processes by which families with retarded members adapt and thrive than it is to demonstrate that in some families the presence of a mentally retarded family member is associated with family pathology.

Extended family

In studying families with mentally retarded members, it is important to recognize that the nuclear family is often a part of a larger, extended family network. Interactions within the nuclear family are both directly and indirectly influenced by relationships with members of the extended family. Gable and Kotsch (1981) called upon researchers to include extended family networks in studies of families with handicapped members. We reaffirm that suggestion.

Developmental/lifespan emphasis

Most research on families with retarded members has been focused on families of handicapped infants. There is also considerable interest in families of handicapped preschool children. Family researchers must, however, move beyond early childhood and begin to focus on families of retarded school-age children, adolescents, and adults. Similarly, longitudinal studies of families with retarded members are needed in order to understand better the processes through which families adapt and change over time.

Changing family forms

Research on families with mentally retarded children must reflect changing societal trends. The traditional two-parent family in which the father is employed and the mother is a full-time parent and homemaker is no longer the modal American family form. Specific characteristics and role patterns of single-parent families, dual-career and dual-worker families, blended families, and joint-custody families must be acknowledged and incorporated into family research designs.

Heterogeneity of persons labeled as "mentally retarded"

In much of the extant research, investigators make an implicit assumption that mentally retarded children, as a group, are similar and, as such, are similar in their contribution to (or disruption of) family functioning. Quite the opposite is true. Even within one diagnostic category (e.g., mild mental retardation), children vary widely in temperament, compliance, social skills, personality, attractiveness, independence, and activity level as well as on many other individual difference dimensions. As the body of family research expands, it will be increasingly important for researchers to utilize methodologies that take into account individual differences among children (and adults) who are mentally retarded.

Heterogeneity of families with mentally retarded members

When thinking about families of mentally retarded children, the prototype that frequently comes to mind is a middle-class family who has a child with Down syndrome or a similar handicapping condition. This prototypical family probably also has other children who are not handicapped and who are developing in a typical fashion. Much of the theory and research related to families with handicapped members has been guided by a desire to understand the impact of a retarded child on families that fit this general prototype. These families, however, constitute only a subset of families with mentally retarded members. Consider, for example, the family living in a deprived environment with multiple children in special education classes or the teenage mother with limited skills who herself has failed to make academic progress at school and has "dropped out" to parent an infant already experiencing significant developmental delays. Theory and research methodologies need to be revamped and expanded in order to address the full range of families with mentally retarded members. Focusing on the small subset of families that fit the aforementioned prototype limits the scientific usefulness of theory as well as the generalizability of research findings.

Directionality of effect

Theoretical approaches to understanding families have often conceptualized mental retardation as being a crisis or stressor event that impinges upon the family, rather than focusing on the mentally retarded child or adult as being an integral part of the family system. Although such theories have predictive power related to family outcome variables, they are less helpful in understanding ongoing family transactional processes. The theoretical framework presented in this chapter focuses on reciprocal processes within the family system and, as such, can be helpful in understanding the ongoing transactions that occur in families with handicapped members. This emphasis on reciprocity and mutual influence is in direct contrast to the assumption of unidirectional effect, which focuses solely on the impact of the mentally retarded child or adult on other family members.

Comparison families

Many researchers of families have been interested in comparing families with mentally retarded members to other families where parents and children are nonhandicapped. Such studies require comparison families that are similar to the target families in all aspects except the presence of a mentally retarded child. Selection of appropriate comparison families is a complex research issue, with many strategies available. For example, the mentally retarded child in a family can be matched with a child of similar chronological age (CA match), mental age (MA match), or language or adaptive skills (criterion match) or matched on multiple indices. In some instances, multiple comparison groups are needed. No single comparison group strategy is appropriate for all family research. The choice of a comparison group depends on the research question to be addressed and the theoretical approach guiding the research effort. For example, researchers utilizing a functional role theory perspective (described earlier in this chapter) would tend to match comparison families based on children's CA. This strategy allows researchers to ask questions concerning family role structures at various points in the family life cycle. Some research questions, such as those focusing on intrafamily processes or on longitudinal relationships, do not need comparison families to address the specified research questions. A more thorough discussion of comparison groups in family research (with particular emphasis on families with severely handicapped children) can be found in Stoneman and Brody (1984).

CONCLUSION

More research needs to be completed before we can understand patterns of interaction in families with retarded members. We must, then, from that data base devise appropriate family intervention programs that are based on empirical observations rather than on subjective beliefs. It has been our aim in this chapter to present a discussion of theoretical and methodological issues related to studying parent and sibling interactions involving a retarded child in order to spur researchers to bring sophisticated, observational methodologies to bear on quantifying these important family interactions. It is important to reiterate, however, that our enthusiasm for observational methodologies is not intended to minimize the importance of information collected by other means. Rather, we argue for multi-method research that utilizes direct observation of family interaction as one component of an overall research plan.

REFERENCES

Abramovitch, R., Corter, C., & Lando, B. (1979). Sibling interaction in the home. *Child Development, 50,* 997–1033.

Abramovitch, R., Corter, C., & Pepler, D. J. (1980). Observations of mixed-sex sibling dyads. *Child Development, 51,* 1268–1271.

Bandura, A. *Social learning theory.* (1977). Englewood Cliffs, NJ: Prentice-Hall.

Bargh, J. A., & Schul, Y. (1980). On the cognitive benefits of teaching. *Journal of Educational Psychology, 72,* 593–604.

Becker, W. C., & Krug, R. S. (1965). The parent attitude research instrument—A research review. *Child Development, 35,* 329–365.

Berg, K. (1973). Christina loves Katherine. *Exceptional Parent, 3*(1), 35–36.

Berger, J., & Cunningham, C. C. (1981). The development of eye contact between mothers and normal vs. Down's syndrome infants. *Developmental Psychology, 17,* 678–689.

Berger, J., & Cunningham, C. C. (1983). Development of early vocal behaviors and interactions in Down's syndrome and nonhandicapped infant-mother pairs. *Developmental Psychology, 19,* 322–331.

Blacher, J., & Meyers, C. E. (1983). A review of attachment formation and disorder of handicapped children. *American Journal of Mental Deficiency, 87,* 359–371.

Breiner, J., & Forehand, R. (1982). Mother-child interactions: A comparison of a clinic-referred developmentally delayed group and two non-delayed groups. *Applied Research in Mental Retardation, 3,* 175–183.

Brim, O. G., Jr. (1960). Personality development as role-learning. In I. Isae & H. W. Stevenson (Eds.), *Personality development in children.* Austin: University of Texas Press.

Brody, G. H., & Endsley, R. C. (1981). Research children and families. Differences in approaches of child and family specialists. *Family Relations, 32,* 275–280.

Brody, G. H., & Stoneman, Z. (1983a). A contextualist framework for examining the influence of television viewing on family interactions. *Journal of Family Issues, 4*(2), 329–348.

Brody, G. H., & Stoneman, Z. (1983b). Children with atypical siblings: Socialization outcomes and clinical participation. In B. B. Lahey & A. E. Kazdin (Eds.), *Advances in clinical child psychology.* New York: Plenum.

Brody, G. H., Stoneman, Z., & MacKinnon, C. (1982). Role asymmetries in interactions between school-aged children, their younger siblings, and their friends. *Child Development, 53,* 1364–1370.

Brody, G. H., Stoneman, Z., MacKinnon, C. E., & MacKinnon, R. (1985). Role relationships and behavior among preschool-aged and school-aged sibling pairs. *Developmental Psychology, 21,* 124–129.

Brody, G. H., Stoneman, Z., & Sanders, A. K. (1980). Effects of television viewing on family interactions: An observational study. *Family Relations, 29,* 216–220.

Bronfenbrenner, U. (1979). *The ecology of human development.* Cambridge, MA: Harvard University Press.

Buckhalt, J. A., Rutherford, R. B., & Goldberg, K. E. (1978). Verbal and non-verbal interaction of mothers with their Down's syndrome and nonretarded infants. *American Journal of Mental Deficiency, 82,* 337–343.

Buium, N., Rynders, J., & Turnure, J. (1974). Early maternal linguistic environment of normal and Down's syndrome language-learning children. *American Journal of Mental Deficiency, 79,* 52–58.

Clarke-Stewart, K. A. (1978). And daddy makes three: The father's impact on mother and young child. *Child Development, 49,* 466–478.

Cook, A. S., & Culp, R. E. (1981). Mutual play of mothers with their Down's syndrome and normal infants. *International Journal of Rehabilitation Research, 4,* 542–544.

Cunningham, C. E., Reuler, E., Blackwell, J., & Deck, J. (1981). Behavioral and linguistic developments in the interactions of normal and retarded children with their mothers. *Child Development, 52,* 62–70.

Eheart, B. K. (1982). Mother-child interactions with nonretarded and mentally retarded preschoolers. *American Journal of Mental Deficiency, 87,* 20–25.

Eisenstadt, S. N. (1956). *From generation to generation.* New York: Free Press of Glencoe.

Filler, J. W., & Bricker, W. A. (1976). Teaching styles of mothers and the match-to-sample performance of their retarded preschool-age children. *American Journal of Mental Deficiency, 80,* 504–511.

Fowle, C. M. (1969). The effect of the severely retarded child on his family. *American Journal of Mental Deficiency, 73,* 468–473.

Gabel, H., & Kotsch, L. S. (1981). Extended families and young handicapped children. *Topics in Early Childhood Special Education* 1(3), 29-36.

Golinkoff, R. M., & Ames, G. J. (1979). A comparison of fathers' and mothers' speech with their young children. *Child Development, 50,* 28–32.

Gumz, E. J., & Gubrium, J. F. (1972). Comparative parental perceptions of a mentally retarded child. *American Journal of Mental Deficiency, 77,* 175–180.

Gutmann, A. J., & Rondal, J. A. (1979). Verbal operants in mothers' speech to nonretarded and Down's syndrome children matched for linguistic level. *American Journal of Mental Deficiency, 83,* 446–452.

Hartup, W. W. (1978). Peer interaction and the process of socialization. In M. J. Guralnick (Ed.), *Early intervention and the integration of handicapped and nonhandicapped children.* Baltimore: University Park Press.

Klein, S. D. (1972). Brother to sister, sister to brother: Interview with siblings of disabled children, Parts I and II. *Exceptional Parent, 21,* 10–15, 24–27.

Kogan, K. L., Wimberger, H. C., & Bobbitt, R. A. (1969). Analysis of mother-child interaction in young mental retardates. *Child Development, 40,* 799–812.

Lamb, M. E. (1976). The role of the father: An overview. In M. E. Lamb (Ed.), *The role of the father in child development.* New York: Wiley.

Lamb, M. E. (1978a). Interactions between 18-month-olds and their preschool-aged siblings. *Child Development, 49,* 51–59.

Lamb, M. E. (1978b). The development of sibling relations in infancy: A short-term longitudinal study. *Child Development, 49,* 1189–1196.

Lewis, M., Feiring, C., & Weintraub, M. (1981). The father as a member of the child's social network. In M. E. (Ed.), *The role of the father in child development.* New York: Wiley.

Lewis, M., & Weinraub, M. (1976). The father's role in the infant's social network. In M. E. Lamb (Ed.), *The role of the father in child development.* New York: Wiley.

Love, H. (1973). *The mentally retarded child and his family.* Springfield, IL: Thomas.

Lynn, D. B. (1974). *The father: His role in child development.* Monterey, CA: Brookes/Cole.

Lytton, H. (1971). Observational studies of parent-child interaction: A methodological review. *Child Development, 42,* 651–684.

Marshall, N. R., Hegrenes, J. R., & Goldstein, S. (1973). Verbal interactions: Mothers and their retarded children vs. mothers and their nonretarded children. *American Journal of Mental Deficiency, 77,* 415–419.

Mischel, W. (1968). *Personality assessment*. Englewood Cliffs, NJ: Prentice-Hall.

Moore, W. E. (1969). Social structure and behavior. In G. Lindzey & E. Aronson (Eds.), *The handbook of social psychology* (2nd ed.). Reading, MA: Addison-Wesley.

Parke, R. D. (1978). Parent-infant interaction: Progress, paradigms, and problems. In G. P. Sackett (Ed.), *Observing behavior: Theory and applications in mental retardation*. Baltimore: University Park Press.

Peck, J. R., & Stephens, W. B. (1960). A study of the relationship between the attitudes and behavior of parents and that of their mentally defective child. *American Journal of Mental Deficiency, 64*, 839–844.

Price-Bonham, S., & Addison, S. (1978). Families and the mentally retarded child: Emphasis on the father. *The Family Coordinator, 27*, 221–230.

Rondal, J. A. (1977). Maternal speech in normal and Down's syndrome children. In P. Mittler (Ed.), *Research to practice in mental retardation*. Baltimore: University Park Press.

Samuels, H. R. (1980). The effect of older sibling on infant locomotor exploration of a new environment. *Child Development, 51*, 607–609.

San Martino, M., & Newman, M. B. (1974). Siblings of retarded children. *Child Psychiatry and Human Development, 4*, 168–177.

Sarbin, T. R. (1954). Role theory. In Lindzey (Ed.), *Handbook of social psychology* (Vol. 1). Reading, MA: Addison-Wesley.

Schild, S. (1964). Counseling with parents of mentally retarded children living at home. *Social Work, 9*, 86–91.

Seitz, S., & Marcus, S. (1976). Mother-child interactions: A foundation for language development. *Exceptional Children, 43*, 445–449.

Stoneman, Z., & Brody, G. H. (1981). Two's company, three makes a difference: An examination of mothers' and fathers' speech to their young children. *Child Development, 52*, 705–707.

Stoneman, Z., & Brody, G. H. (1982). Strengths inherent in sibling interactions involving a retarded child: A functional role theory approach. In N. Stinnett, B. Chesser, J. DeFrain, & P. Knaub (Eds.), *Family strengths: Positive models for family life*. Lincoln: University of Nebraska Press.

Stoneman, Z., & Brody, G. H. (1983). Family interaction during three programs: Contextualist observations. *Journal of Family Issues, 4*, 349–366.

Stoneman, Z., & Brody, G. H. (1984). Research with families of severely handicapped children: Theoretical and methodological considerations. In J. Blacher (Ed.), *Severely handicapped young children and their families: Research in review*. New York: Academic.

Stoneman, Z., Brody, G. H., & Abbott, D. (1983). In-home observations of young Down syndrome children with their mothers and fathers. *American Journal of Mental Deficiency, 87*, 591–600.

Stoneman, Z., Brody, G. H., & MacKinnon, C. E. (1984). Naturalistic observations of children's roles and activities while playing with their siblings and friends. *Child Development, 55*, 57–72.

Sutton-Smith, B., & Rosenberg, B. G. (1970). *The sibling*. New York: Holt.

Talllman, I. (1965). Spousal role differentiation and the socialization of severely retarded children. *Journal of Marriage and the Family, 27*, 37–42.

Terdal, L. E., Jackson, R. H., & Garner, A. M. (1976). Mother-child interactions: A comparison between normal and developmentally delayed groups. In E. J. Mash, L. A. Hammerlynck, & L. C. Handy (Eds.), *Behavior modification and families*. New York: Brunner/Mazel.

Vietze, P. M., Abernathy, S. R., Ashe, M. L., & Faulstich, G. (1978). Contingent interaction between mothers and their developmentally delayed infants. In G. P. Sackett (Ed.), *Observing behavior: Theory and applications in mental retardation.* Baltimore: University Park Press.

Yarrow, M. R. (1963). Problems of methods in parent-child research. *Child Development, 34,* 215–226.

Zajonc, R. B., & Markus, G. B. (1975). Birth order and intellectual development. *Psychological Review, 82,* 74–88.

20
A Longitudinal Study of Small Family Care Placement

Richard K. Eyman
University of California, Riverside

Sharon A. Borthwick-Duffy
UCLA Mental Retardation Research Center,
Lanterman Developmental Center Research Group

Nancy L. Sheehy
St. Clare's Hospital Community Mental Health Center

Family foster care has gained popularity and visibility, although it is by no means a new alternative for community placement of mentally retarded clients. The foster care model for mentally retarded persons was introduced in the United States in the 1930s, when the first state funds were set aside to pay for care in homelike settings (Heal, Sigelman, & Switzky, 1978). Concern over the rising cost of institutionalization led the state of New York to "parole" successfully a group of institutionalized clients in family care homes (Vaux, 1935). Family care afforded a practical means of providing a more natural environment with some community involvement while reducing the need for more costly institutional care. In their review of the history of foster care for retarded individuals, Intagliata, Crosby, and Neider (1981) concluded that the current rationale for using this model remains the same (i.e., providing a family environment, opportunity for

Acknowledgements. We dedicate this chapter to the late Tzuen-Jen Lei, who directed the activities of this project from 1978 to 1980. The findings reported are a direct result of Jennie's competence and commitment to this effort. This study was supported in part by Research Grants No. HD-72947, HD-14688 and HD-04612 from the National Institute of Child Health and Human Development.

community integration, increased contact with natural families, and relatively low cost). They further concluded that although the reasons for family care placement are similar, the emphasis within the foster care setting is shifting from being merely custodial to becoming a more habilitative program. The habilitative focus does not imply that family care clients today are higher functioning than clients in past years. On the contrary, the proportion of severely and profoundly retarded persons in family care has increased since the deinstitutionalization thrust of the 1970s (Bruininks, Hill, & Thorsheim, 1980).

Small family care homes typically offer care in an unrestricted home environment. They are usually family owned and provide training in community living skills. Janicki, Jacobson, Zigman, and Lubin (Chapter 8) stated that the primary purpose of family care is "to employ the physical and social environment of the home and the psychosocial structure of the family to enhance interpersonal and group living skills." Previous investigators found that family care usually is provided for retarded people who do not have any serious behavioral or functional impairments (Eyman & Borthwick, 1980; Eyman & Call, 1977; Lei & Eyman, 1979). In a study of residential placement referrals, Lei and Eyman (1979) found that clients who were referred to family care were considerably less retarded than were those referred for institutionalization or to other types of community facilities. Although clients who have serious medical or behavioral problems rarely are placed in family care homes, clients in this setting still represent a wide range of characteristics, including all ages and levels of intelligence (Intagliata, Crosby, & Neider, 1981).

Efforts to evaluate the effects of deinstitutionalization include several studies of clients released from institutions into family care programs (Intagliata, Willer, & Wicks, 1981; Vaux, 1935; Windle, Sabagh, Brown, & Dingman, 1961). Because of the increasing reluctance by professionals and parents to place retarded children in institutions, family care homes are more likely to serve those who have never lived away from their natural families. Thus, the need arises to evaluate the adjustment of all family care clients, regardless of their placement histories.

Comparisons frequently are made across broad categories of residences (e.g., family care, board-and-care, institution), with differences noted among clients (Borthwick, Meyers, & Eyman, 1981; Eyman & Borthwick, 1980; Eyman & Call, 1977) and environments (Bjaanes, Butler, & Kelly, 1981; Eyman, Silverstein, McLain, & Miller, 1977; Felsenthal & Scheerenberger, 1978; Willer & Intagliata, 1982). As Intagliata, Willer, and Wicks (1981) cautioned, however, these comparisons and typical profiles should not lead to the incorrect conclusion that these broad classes represent homogeneous environments. In a recent study, Willer and Intagliata (1982) reported that almost as much variation exists within family care and board-and-care as does between the two settings.

Success often has been defined in terms of tenure (Intagliata, Crosby, & Neider, 1981), that is, how long a client remains with a family. Conversely, *failure* has been identified as returning to an institution (Windle, 1962). Use of this dichotomy to rate the quality of the setting or to determine client progress can be misleading because many factors may contribute to recividism and to relocation (Heal et al., 1978; Intagliata, Crosby, & Neider, 1981; McCarver & Craig, 1974). Other evaluative criteria include social worker ratings of the family care environment and of the foster parents (Intagliata, Willer, & Wicks, 1981), the emotional stability of the client (Browder, Ellis, & Neal, 1974), the home adjustment of all family members (Felsenthal & Scheerenberger, 1978), the degree to which client behavior appears normalized (Nihira & Nihira, 1975), and the length of time the family care home remains in operation (Sanderson & Crawley, 1982). Intagliata, Willer, and Wicks (1981) looked at the relationship of rated home quality to client behavior and development, additional criteria for evaluating family care success.

Most evaluations consider the interrelatedness of: client characteristics (e.g., sex, age, IQ, length of institutionalization), careprovider characteristics (e.g., age, education, marital status, experience, attitudes), and environmental characteristics (e.g., location, size of family, access to resources, atmosphere). Given the diversity of definitions of success, it is difficult to summarize the literature in terms of which client and environmental features are most influential. At first, many of the reports appear contradictory and inconclusive (McCarver & Craig, 1974). In fact, the changing composition of clients and foster family homes makes comparisons with earlier studies extremely problematic.

With the foregoing caution in mind, we offer a brief summary of the existing family care research. Windle (1962) observed a curvilinear relationship between client age and community tenure, with older and younger clients being easier to care for than adolescents. More recent reviewers, however, failed to find a clear relationship of age, IQ, or sex to stable placement in one family (Kraus, 1971; Sternlicht, 1978). Brown, Windle, and Stewart (1959) suggested that fewer years of prior institutionalization may increase the probability of stable placement, a finding partially supported by Sternlicht.

In general, careprovider characteristics have not related significantly to placement success (Penniman, 1974; Windle et al., 1961), although in one study, careprovider education differed significantly for high- and low-quality homes (Intagliata, Willer, & Wicks, 1981). These characteristics are difficult to measure objectively and have yet to be linked empirically with success criteria. After surveying a small sample of homes ($n = 18$), Scheerenberger and Felsenthal (1977) suggested that mentally retarded children in family care may be more isolated in rural settings or in settings without public transportation. Browder et al. (1974) found that 87% of the foster care clients in their sample had needs that required utilizing community resources outside the home. Accessibility of supportive services and family use of social institutions have been suggested as important variables to consider in future research (Sternlicht, 1978). In a study of the effect of community environments on adaptive behavior, Eyman, Demaine, and Lei (1979) found location and proximity of services, as well as comfort and appearance of family care and board-and-care homes to be associated with improvement in adaptive behavior.

An interesting finding of Intagliata, Willer, and Wicks (1981) was that social workers and nurses assigned different ranks of importance to various aspects of care. For example, social workers ranked encouraging independence last, whereas nurses ranked it as most important in client care. In contrast, social workers placed higher values on stability and organization of the home and on knowledge of client needs. Whether these differences were due to different professional training or to different roles played by nurses and social workers in monitoring family care homes could not be determined within the framework of the study. The differences clearly suggest, however, that perception of home quality may be "in the eye of the beholder" and that a global rating of quality may be inadequate for understanding more about the dynamics of foster care and client adjustment.

Overall, this literature is inadequate to determine the relative value of family care compared to alternative placements. The studies reviewed, however, do document considerable variation within these homes and suggest that selected characteristics of the home *may* benefit retarded children. Because of problems inherent with the type of ratings used, available samples, and the changing nature of placements over time, however, we cannot make definitive statements at this time.

The purpose of the investigation reported on in this chapter was to examine foster parent characteristics, the quality of the home environments, and the ways these variables related to changes in clients' adaptive and maladaptive behavior over 3 years. This study was limited in scope and design by constraints apparent in a real-life foster care system, together with the legal and administrative specifications under which the system operated. First, we could not determine the extent to which children with severe physical and/or medical problems could be served adequately in small family settings because the official policy is to discourage such placement and to select a convalescent residence for this population. Children with difficult-to-manage behavior generally stay only a short time in small family residences because most careproviders do not want to cope with them. We thus were limited to a natural history description of the small family care program in California as it affects handicapped children and young adults.

Under California law, small family or foster care is provided for mentally retarded and developmentally disabled people under the provision of Community Care Facilities, licensed as Small Family Homes, separately for children (under 18 years) and adults (age 18 and above) for the care and supervision of not more than six clients, excluding members of the licensee's family. The administrative vehicles for supervision of such care in California are 21 Regional Centers, which are private nonprofit corporations that have contractual access to every community care facility in a catchment area. The Regional Center used in our study covered a four-county area having a total population of about one and a quarter million people. Alternatives to institutional residence, particularly foster family homes, have been in operation in four southern counties of California for several decades. The small family home system reported on here may therefore be considered a mature program.

Out-of-home placement for children is considered only when all other available resources to work with the child and parent have been exhausted. The Regional Center generally considers placement in a small family home preferable to placement in a large or institutionalized setting, based on the face validity that such places are normalizing for a child. Generally, a child must be ambulatory (unless a special fire clearance has been granted), have no need for close medical supervision (e.g., uncontrolled seizures or diabetes), and be developmentally disabled without symptoms of a major emotional disturbance.

A small family home is usually licensed to serve children with a specific disability, age group, and sex. For example, a home may be licensed for female developmentally disabled children between 6 and 12 years of age. In addition, the careproviders determine the severity and type of a child's disability (mental retardation, cerebral palsy, epilepsy, autism, impaired hearing, impaired sight) they are willing to accept. The characteristics also considered include speech problems, toilet training, self-help skills, and types of maladaptive behavior the careproviders are prepared to handle.

METHOD AND PROCEDURE

Sample

The study sample was drawn from four counties in southern California served by 1 of 21 Regional Centers that have provided services for developmentally disabled people since 1973. Small family placement has existed in this area for over 20 years, and the Regional Center clearly prefers placing mentally retarded individuals in small family settings rather than in institutions.

In our previous research efforts, we compared clients served by this Regional Center to clients served by other California Regional Centers and by Continuing Care Services Section (CCSS). Administered by the state of California, CCSS is a state agency that was instituted to oversee releases to the community from state institutions before Regional Centers had become completely functional in assuming these responsibilities. More recently, the Regional Centers have had total control over placement of retarded clients. Because we found that these three groups did not differ significantly in age, sex, level of retardation, or adaptive behavior scores, the sample was considered representative of community-placed clients in California. The initial sample consisted of 333 mentally retarded individuals who were 21 years of age or younger in 1978. These children resided in 151 small family homes over a 3 year period. A subsample of 166 children was included in both the 1- and 2-year follow-up. These 166 clients had remained in the same house ($n = 84$ houses) over the study period. Table 1 displays selected characteristics of the study sample.

A comparison of the initial client and careprovider sample to those available for follow-up revealed no significant differences on the demographic characteristics of clients' sex, age, or level of retardation or careproviders' age, ethnicity, education, number of own children at home, or number of clients in the home.

TABLE 1   Selected Characteristics (in %) of Clients
Remaining in the Study

| | Mental retardation level | |
Age (in years)	Mild/moderate[a]	Severe/profound[b]
At initial out-of-home placement		
0 to 1	16	21
2 to 5	43	33
6 to 10	21	38
11 +	20	8
Median age	4.24	4.40
At time of initial survey in 1978		
0 to 7	9	10
8 to 11	10	3
12 to 17	37	25
18 to 21	44	62
Median age	17	19

Note. The proportions reported are almost identical to those of the total sample of 333 clients. There were 102 males and 64 females in the sample (61% and 39%, respectively).
[a] $N = 103$.
[b] $N = 63$.

Survey Instruments

THE BEHAVIOR DEVELOPMENT SURVEY (BDS)

BDS, the primary dependent variable, is a shortened version of the Adaptive Behavior Scale (ABS, Nihira, Foster, Shellhaas, & Leland, 1975), which is an extensively used, standardized behavior-rating instrument. The BDS yields the same summary factors as the ABS (Miller, 1976) and has been shown to have concurrent validity with the ABS (Pawlarczyk & Schumacher, 1983). The BDS was administered annually to all clients by their careproviders, under the supervision of their clients' caseworker, as part of the agency's routine evaluation procedure.

Five factors derived from the BDS, as well as ABS, include three factors related to adaptive behavior—Personal Self-Sufficiency, Community Self-Sufficiency, and Personal-Social Responsibility (Nihira, 1977). The other two factors measure maladaptive behavior—Personal Maladaptation and Social Maladaptation (Nihira, 1969). Because of the high correlation of the first three factors in the present sample, $r > .80$, we combined these into a single overall score for each retarded client. Accordingly, for this set of data, the major part of the variance from all domains can be indexed by a general score. Given the increased reliability of the total score, Cronbach's Alpha = .97, over the separate factor scores, average Cronbach's Alpha = .93, the summing procedure seemed warranted (Arndt, 1981). Similarly, we found that one factor accounted for the major portion of the variance (78%) for the two maladaptive factors, which were correlated .59 with each other and .94 and .84 with the total score. Also, the internal consistency reliability was higher, Cronbach's Alpha = .85, for the total score than for either of the two factor scores, Cronbach's Alpha = .83 and .66.

We used an Individual and Family Characteristics Form to record demographic and background information on clients an parental figures, through review of Regional Center files. We also included a School Behavior Development Survey, a modified version of the BDS, to measure classroom adaptive behavior. This instrument is an indirect assessment of the academic achievement of study clients in special education programs or workshops. The teacher or workshop leader provided the ratings during the first and last year of the project.

A Client Movement Update Form was used to record all relocations and the reasons for changes. Records were kept in files for the study of client movements within and out of the service system so that the length of placement could be determined.

Forty-seven children left their family care homes before two annual BDS measures were obtained. Most of these returned home to their natural families ($n = 28$); the remainder moved to a different type of community residential facility ($n \times 19$). The remaining 286 clients were assessed for at least two of the three years of this project; 247 did not change homes over the course of the study, whereas 39 moved between foster homes. Movements were attributed to the client's behavioral or health problems (30%), the unsuitability of the placement for the client's needs (28%), or closure of the facility (15%).

In examining the relocation literature to predict behavioral effects of interhome transfers on family care residents, we found conflicting reports. Relocation from large institutions to smaller facilities has been associated with behavior change, for example, increases in language use, eye contact, adaptive behavior, and participation in culturally normative activities (Conroy, Efthimiou, & Lemanowicz, 1982; Gilbert & Hemming, 1979; Hemming, Cook, Gilbert, & Lavender, 1979; Hemming, Lavender, & Pill, 1981; Weinstock, Wulkan, Colon, Coleman, & Goncalves, 1979). Negative effects, however, have also been observed, for example, lowered behavioral functioning, withdrawal, fewer initiations of social interactions, and death (Carsrud, Carsrud, Henderson, Alisch, & Fowler, 1979; Cochran, Sran, & Varano, 1977; Cohen, Conroy, Frazer, Snelbecker, & Spreat, 1977; Rago, 1976). Because all of these investigators concentrated on people who moved between facilities of drastically different sizes (i.e., from institutions to smaller units or community facilities), it is difficult to ascertain whether the observed behavioral changes were due to the move per se, the difference in environments, which would include such variables as staff-to-client ratios and caregiving practices, or an interaction of these variables; however, the findings do support the hypothesis that interfacility movement has an effect on mentally retarded residents' adjustment.

Sheehy (1983) investigated the effects of interfacility movement on behavioral development for the clients in our foster-care sample. She also considered stationary clients who experienced resident turnover within their homes (i.e., admissions and discharges of other clients). The development of these two groups was compared to that of residents who remained in the same facilities that had no resident turnover. All subjects received at least two annual BDS evaluations. Data were analyzed using an analysis of covariance design. The independent variable was the previously defined grouping factor, client movement, movement of others in the home, or no movement. The dependent measures were the final adaptive and maladaptive behavior scores, covarying for the initial score, age, and retardation level. Prior to the analysis of covariance, the three groups were compared to determine whether they differed significantly on any of the covariates. There was no significant difference betewwn groups on level of retardation; however, the three groups did differ on the client's age at the time of the first year's survey, $F(2, 264) = 6.64$, $p < .01$. A Duncan's Multiple Range Test indicated that clients in the affected-by-movement group were significantly younger than those in the other two groups.

As a final assessment of the comparability of these three groups, the clients' first-year scores on the two dependent measures, adaptive and maladaptive behavior, were tested for differences. The groups differed significantly on initial status of both adaptive and maladaptive behavior ($Fs(2, 264) = 3.18$ and 4.14, respectively, $ps < .05$); however, adaptive and maladaptive behavior scores were related to client age (i.e., given the same retardation level, an adolescent would score higher than a child). Because there were significant age differences between groups, further analyses assessed the groups' initial comparability on adaptive and maladaptive behavior scores, controlling for the age at initial testing. When the effects of the client's age were removed from the initial adaptive behavior score, the groups were no longer significantly different; however, even with the client's age controlled for, the groups were still significantly different on initial maladaptive behavior scores, ($Fs(2, 263) = 4.09$, $p < .05$). Duncan's Multiple Range Test indicated that the movement group was significantly lower scoring (or "worse") initially on maladaptive behavior. This relationship between interfacility movement and maladaptive behavior supports earlier findings (e.g., Eyman & Call, 1977; Schalock, Harper, & Genung,

1981) that clients who have behavior problems are likely to move more often.

The analysis of covariance indicated interfacility relocation did not differentially affect adaptive behavior development; however, significant differences were exhibited between groups on maladaptive behavior change, $(F (2, 260) = 4.30, p < .05)$. Compared to residents of stable environments, stationary clients affected by resident turnover exhibited a dramatic increase in maladaptive behavior, whereas moving clients exhibited fewer regressions. The dramatic results found for stationary residents of unstable family configurations, significantly different from residents of stable families, accentuate the need to separate these two stationary groups in future environmental research. Additional support for the importance of classifying research subjects into mutually exclusive groups is that in the present research we found very different exhibited behaviors for clients who moved and those who were affected by the relocation of others. Nineteen people were excluded from this study's analyses because they not only moved between facilities but were *also affected* by the interfacility movement of other clients. It is conceivable that the previously described inconsistent results between relocation studies may be due to the fact that some of the sample included people who both moved and were affected by the movement of others. A precise, unconfounded picture of the effect of relocation on behavior cannot emerge until precautions are taken that the groups studied are "pure" in composition.

Four instruments were used to obtain information about the careproviders and residential environments of the foster homes in the study. A Careprovider Questionnaire that included sociodemographic information on foster parents (e.g., number of clients as well as years of providing the type of family care) was administered to the primary careproviders of all clients in the study.

We used the Program Analysis of Service Systems (PASS 3, Wolfensberger & Glenn, 1975) to assess the quality of the home settings. Teams of specially trained raters conduct these evaluations, in which final scores represent the reconciled and negotiated consensus of opinion on each item. The Regional Center provided the specially trained rating team, which was independent of other project staff. Because of the expense involved, each home received only one PASS rating over the 3-year period.

The PASS is a 50-item scale. Flynn (1980) conducted a factor analysis and item analysis based on 256 PASS evaluations that reported four factors: Normalization of Program (19 items), Normalization of Setting (12 items), Administration (8 items), and Proximity and Access (4 items). Seven remaining items not included in these subscales were excluded from subsequent analyses. We computed the internal consistency reliabilities (Cronbach's Alpha) for each factor on our 151 foster homes: Normalization of Program = .89, Normalization of Setting = .68, Administration = .54; and Proximity and Access = .74. A factor analysis of PASS for our sample approximated the results. In both solutions, Factor 1, Normalization of Program, was a measure of the extent to which the activities of the agency and residential facility exhibit normalization philosophies, such as social integration, age-appropriate program structures, individualization, and intensity of relevant programming. Factor 2, Normalization of Setting, refers to such characteristics as appropriate size and decor, physical comfort, and congruity with the neighborhood. Factor 3, Administration, relates to public education, ties to academia, staff and manpower development, planning process, and program evaluation. The fourth factor, Proximity and Access, measures the proximity and accessibility of services to clients and their families as well as socially integrating physical resources. We adopted this scoring solution for our study.

We adapted Caldwell's Home Observation for Measurement of the Environment (HOME, Bradley & Caldwell, 1979) for these small family homes. This instrument has been used in natural homes to identify children at high risk for mental retardation (Bradley & Caldwell, 1977, 1978; Ramey, Mills, Campbell, & O'Brien, 1975) and correlates significantly with children's subsequent IQ (Bradley & Caldwell, 1979; Elardo, Bradley, & Caldwell, 1975). Based on this evidence, we viewed the HOME as a measure of the foster homes' cognitive environment.

The HOME contains 80 binary (yes/no) items answered by a trained interviewer and observer. We eliminated four direct questions that were not applicable to retarded children. The items deleted (Items 18 through 21) concerned travel outside the home (e.g., "A child has been taken by a family member on a trip more than 50 miles from home").

Although we originally intended to repeat the HOME annually for 3 years, we found such minimal variation that we decided this was not sufficient to discriminate the quality of the learning environments in these small family homes. This could reflect the fact that the HOME was designed to measure a young child's *natural* home environment. Because the family homes for developmentally disabled children all were licensed by the Regional Center to meet certain specified criteria, the careproviders are likely to maintain relatively more homogeneous environments. Based on the first year's administration, we summed the 76 items to form a total score with an internal consistency reliability (Cronbach's Alpha) of .87.

Finally, we used the Home Quality Rating Scale to measure various physical and social–psychological dimensions of the homes. This instrument, which has 20 subjectively rated items, was completed by a trained interviewer immediately after a home visit once each year. All facilities were rated once, with 129 homes measured two times and 84 homes evaluated three times.

From factor analysis of first year's data ($n = 151$), four Home Quality Rating Scale factors emerged. The first factor, Parenting Quality and Openness, contained the following items: growth promotion as a policy in client care, acceptance of the client, no evidence of rejection, coping with the client, awareness of the client's disability, adjustment of the home, harmony in the home, relationship between the client's careproviders, responses for social approval, and reliability of the interview responses. Factor 2, Support in Providing Care, consisted of: status of the secondary careprovider, significance of the secondary careprovider, and burden of care shared by others. The third factor, Quality and Safety of the Dwelling and Yard, had 4 items: the structure and appearance of the careprovider's home, safety of the client's outdoor play area, cleanliness of the interior of the careprovider's home, and interior lighting of the home. Factor 4, Size of Home and Sibling Influence, consisted of: presence of siblings, number of bedrooms in the home, and number of bathrooms in the home. Eight items that did not load sufficiently on any factor were excluded from further analyses: degree of residentiality of the street, interior of the home is not overly noisy, dominant control of careprovider, careprovider over-protection, hazards of street relative to client's ability for survival, maximum number of clients to share a bedroom, home has at least two exits, and unusual interview situation.

Internal consistency reliabilities (Cronbach's Alpha) were computed for each factor for all 3 years. These reliabilities were very high for Parenting Quality and Openness, Cronbach's Alpha = .90, and moderate for Support in Providing Care and Quality and Safety of Home, the Dwelling and Yard, Cronbach's Alphas = .73, low, Cronbach's Alpha = .49, because homes differed with respect to the number of people who lived in them.

RESULTS AND DISCUSSION

Prior independent surveys reported that foster care usually is provided for retarded persons who have no serious behavioral or functional impairments (Eyman & Borthwick, 1980; Eyman & Call, 1977; Lei & Eyman, 1979). The majority of clients in the homes studied were ambulatory (75%) toilet trained (84%); and capable of using table utensils (84%), drinking (83%), and dressing themselves adequately with or without help (82%). Most clients had no difficulty seeing (76%) or hearing (88%).

More than 90% of the clients were enrolled in special education classes or other training programs. When we compared ratings by teachers or program directors to those of careproviders, we found over 90% agreement on the three adaptive behavior factors and only moderate agreement (65%) for the maladaptive behavior scores. These results are consistent with previously reported interrater reliabilities (Miller, 1979).

Table 2 shows that family problems ($n = 84$) were given as the primary reason for out-of-home placement by the parents of our sample. The family problem most frequently recalled as the reason for placement centered on physical inability to handle the child ($n = 38$), followed by psychological pressure in the family ($n = 18$), a need for a more normal family life ($n = 18$), medical or health problem of a family member ($n = 8$), and financial or marital difficulties ($n = 2$). A number of parents gave the need for a supervised environment and special training as the major reason for out-of-home placement ($n = 47$). We also note that 24 of the children had been placed immediately after birth and had never lived at home. Other reasons in Table 2 refer to physician's recommendation ($n =$ 8) and needs to be with others of the same IQ level ($n = 3$).

TABLE 2   Reasons for Initial Out-of-Home Placement by
Individual and Family Characteristic

	No. in sample	Reasons for initial out-of-home placement[a]				
Characteristics		Family problems	Placement immediately after birth	Supervised environment and training	Other reasons	X^2
Level of mental retardation						
Mild/moderate	103	48.4	15.2	28.3	8.1	
Severe/profound	63	52.3	14.3	28.6	4.8	.76
Client's age when placed[b]						
0 to 1	29	17.2	75.9	6.9	0	
2 to 5	65	63.5	0	27.0	9.5	
6 to 10	44	53.5	2.3	37.2	7.0	108.16*
11+	28	50.0	3.6	39.3	7.1	
Mother's age[b]						
Under 30	48	50.0	20.8	16.7	12.5	
30 and over	118	50.5	12.2	33.0	4.3	8.28*
Family composition						
Both biological parents	96	57.1	6.6	29.7	6.6	
One biological parent	48	49.0	2.1	40.4	8.5	67.52**
Other	22	27.3	68.2	0	4.5	
No. of siblings						
None	17	53.4	33.3	13.3	0	
1 to 2	96	49.5	12.6	32.2	5.7	11.35
3 to 8	53	56.2	4.2	31.3	8.3	

Note. These results were almost identical to those found for the total sample of 333 clients.
[a] All numbers are row percentages, reflecting the percentage of clients with specified characteristics who were placed in foster care for the reasons listed.
[b] In years.
* $p < .01$. ** $p < .001$.

Most parents indicated they would make the same decision when interviewed as they had done at the time of placement (90%); however, about 18% of the parents indicated that they would be willing to take their child back home if reimbursed. Table 2 also shows that retardation level had no direct relationship to any reported reasons for out-of-home placement. Most retarded children placed at infancy were placed immediately after birth (76%), had never lived with their natural families (58%), and were more likely to be abandoned by young mothers (21% among mothers aged under 30 vs. 12% of mothers in the 30 to 59 age category). Many of these children have had court-appointed guardians. Significantly, more older mothers (age 30 or over) with other children at home reported the need for a more suitable environment for their retarded offspring than did younger mothers (age below 30) with no other children.

Regarding the primary caretaker in the small family home, 96% were female, with about 78% of the homes having two parents. For most foster homes, the male figure was a secondary parent. Approximately 44% of the careproviders had biological children still living at home. Most homes provided care to two or more residents, up to the maximum of six. Table 3 displays the distribution of retarded clients in relation to the number of the careprovider's own children living in the home. Nearly 60% of the careproviders had more than 5 years of experience in serving developmentally disabled clients.

The ethnicity of the careproviders differed significantly from that of the clients they served. About half of the careproviders were nonwhite (54%). Among the nonwhite careproviders, approximately 70% were black, with 9% Spanish American and 5% Oriental. Remarkably, about 60% of the careproviders were at least 50 years old. The nonwhite careproviders were

TABLE 3 Distribution of Mentally Retarded Clients and Careproviders' Own Children in the Family Care Homes

Own children	Mentally retarded clients			
	1 to 2	*3 to 4*	*5 to 6*	*Total*
0	9	38	56	103
1 to 2	7	28	22	57
3 to 4	3	3	0	6
Total	19	69	78	166

TABLE 4 Trends in Adaptive and Maladaptive Behavior Scores Over Study Period (1978 through 1980)

Study	Adaptive behavior		Maladaptive behavior	
	Mean	*SD*	*Mean*	*SD*
Initial survey (1978)	63.5	26.4	18.4	3.4
1st follow-up (1979)	65.9	25.9	18.7	3.4
2nd follow-up (1980)	70.7	26.1	18.9	3.5

Note: The means and SDs on the initial survey for the total sample ($N = 333$) were as follows: adaptive behavior mean = 62.4 ($SD = 27.1$); maladaptive behavior mean = 18.1 ($SD = 3.8$).

significantly older than were the white careproviders and were also more likely to be single.

Table 4 presents the means and standard deviations (*SD*s) of the clients' adaptive and maladaptive behavior over the period of study from 1978 to 1980. Clients definitely improved their adaptive behavior over 2 years, $t(165) = 7.44$, $p < .0001$, in contrast to the only marginal change noted for maladaptive behavior, $t(165) = 1.85$, $p < .0662$.

Table 5 shows the progress observed over a 3-year period on the adaptive and maladaptive factors by age and level of retardation of the sample. As expected, age and level of retardation related to both initial score and to change scores for adaptive behavior. Predictably, the older, less retarded residents had significantly higher initial scores than did younger, more retarded clients. A repeated measures analysis of variance on cell means, displayed in Table 5, provided significance tests on the interactions between age and change in adaptive and maladaptive behavior, in addition to level of retardation and change in adaptive and maladaptive behavior. Younger clients improved significantly more than

TABLE 5   Adaptive and Maladaptive Scores by
Client Characteristics

Characteristic	N	Initial score			Final score		
		Mean	SD	F	Mean	SD	F (165 df)
Adaptive behavior							
Age [a]							
0 to 11	28	35.1	26.5		48.0	29.6	
12 to 17	54	68.6	23.9	25.0*	76.9	24.6	15.0*
18+	84	69.6	21.3		74.2	21.3	
Level of retardation							
Mild/moderate	103	69.3	25.6	12.3*	77.0	24.3	15.5*
Severe/profound	63	55.1	24.2		61.4	24.8	
Maladaptive behavior							
Age[a]							
0 to 11	28	18.4	4.2		18.1	3.9	
12 to 17	54	18.1	2.9	.68	18.8	3.4	.25
18+	84	18.7	3.4		19.3	3.3	
Level of retardation							
Mild/moderate	103	18.5	3.2	.12	18.8	3.2	.11
Severe/profound	63	18.3	3.7		19.0	3.9	

[a] In years.
* $p = < .001$.

did older clients on adaptive behavior, $F(2, 163) = 68.25$, $p < .01$. There were no significant differences in improvement on either age or level of retardation by change in maladaptive behavior.

In contrast to adaptive behavior, maladaptive behavior was independent of clients' age or level of retardation. Furthermore, changes in maladaptive behavior on the average were very minimal. Still, there was evidence that individual clients did exhibit some change, even though mean differences for the groups were negligible.

Given these results, we proceeded with our analysis in two stages, considering adaptive behavior separately from maladaptive behavior. For Stage 1, we examined residualized gain scores for each client (i.e., controlling for the initial scores on both adaptive and maladaptive behavior). Residualized gain scores, similar to an analysis of covariance, were viewed as measures of client growth. We related residualized gain scores to client characteristics, careprovider characteristics, and evaluations of the quality of the home environment. When the relationships between variables were linear, we used correlation coefficients to examine those associations. For nonlinear relationships, notably between the careprovider's age and other variables, we recoded careprovider's age to correct this problem, so we could proceed with a regression approach. The Stage 1 analysis identified variables that appeared to have a promising relationship to residualized gain scores for adaptive and maladaptive behavior.

In Stage 2, we used two sets of path analyses to determine the relationships between those selected caretaker, client, and environmental characteristics that correlated significantly with client adaptive growth or diminishing maladaptive behavior. The objective was to determine which combination and sequence of variables are most associated with change in adaptive or in maladaptive behavior. The path analysis provides an estimate of the strength of the relationship between the careprovider characteristics, resident characteristics, and environmental ratings and the subject's final status in adaptive or maladaptive behavior. We note, however, that path analytic results do not prove causality among the variables. In addition, the path model is dependent upon a set of theoretically defined relationships. This feature has strength, but alternative models can be constructed for the same set of variables.

Each arrow in the path diagram illustrates a conditional relationship that we examined. These relationships are conditional, in that other independent variables are statistically controlled (held constant) when interpreting the association between two variables connected by an arrow. In the path diagrams given, we used one-way arrows between each determining variable and the variable theorized to be dependent. The final result is a set of standardized partial regression coefficients (also known as path coefficients) attached to the arrows. In this case, the path coefficients indicate what type of careprovider chose specified clients, who in turn seemed to benefit from any of the environmental factors by positive change in their adaptive or maladaptive behavior.

Theoretical assumptions about careprovider influences

For both adaptive and maladaptive behavior, we started with a full path model that assumed the following: that careprovider *age* and *education* would influence the *number* of clients in the home, which in turn affected the *type* of clients selected, including their initial status on adaptive or maladaptive behavior. These variables then were assumed to influence the quality of the *environment* (all factors of PASS and Home Quality Rating Scale), which in the presence of all variables contributed to subsequent changes in adaptive or maladaptive behavior. Following suggestions of Bentler (1980) and McPherson (1976), we reduced the full model and reestimated eliminating variables and paths that did *not* emerge as playing a significant role under the assumed model. By reducing the full model to a subset of variables that emerged as significant in the original path analysis, we could generate better estimates of the path coefficients, as well as obtain a more economical and interpretable solution. A more complete rationale for this approach is given by McPherson (1976).

ADAPTIVE BEHAVIOR

Among the variables that we eliminated in the reduced path model for adaptive behavior were two client characteristics that were unrelated to any other variables in this investigation: number of years in foster care and initial age at placement. Apparently, prior time in foster care or age when placed do not influence the quality of subsequent home environments or the child's future growth in adaptive behavior. In contrast, client's current level of retardation and initial adaptive behavior scores related significantly to the quality of the home and to future gains.

As noted previously, an adaptation of Caldwell's HOME had insufficient variance to relate to any of the other variables. Hence, we used the four factors of PASS and Home Quality Rating Scale (HQRS) in the full path model. Specifically, PASS Factors 3 (Administration) and 4 (Proximity and Access) and HQRS Factor 1 (Parenting Quality) related moderately to both client characteristics and client gains in adaptive behavior. In the presence of PASS Factors 3 and 4, however, the HQRS parenting factor became insignificant, and we eliminated it from the reduced model. The PASS 3 and the HQRS parenting factors were highly correlated, but because PASS 3 better predicted final adaptive behavior performance than did the HQRS Factor 1, we opted to keep PASS 3 in the reduced, final model.

Figure 1 shows the reduced path model to characterize the relationships among careprovider characteristics, initial client status, quality of the environment, and subsequent adaptive behavior performance. Note that only PASS Factor 3, Administration, and PASS Factor 4, Proximity and Access, emerged as the environmental measures significantly related to gains in adaptive behavior. For ease of interpretation, we provide only partial regression coefficients that reached significance.

Careprovider education proved to be of particular interest in Figure 1. Note that the homes of better educated careproviders scored higher on PASS Factor 3 (Administration), but lower on PASS Factor 4 (Proximity and Access). Yet both of these environmental dimensions had a significant and positive relationship with subsequent client adaptive behavior. This finding was rather puzzling given that PASS Factors 3 and 4 seem designed to measure the assimilation of the home within the larger community. Closer inspection of these factors, however, reveals some substantive differences. In particular, PASS Factor 3 is concerned with such variables as a home's ties to academia, research climate, and the planning process, which would be of greater interest to more highly educated careproviders. Conversely, PASS Factor 4 deals with such items as local proximity to community services and access to the home, which might vary across careproviders, regardless of their educational background.

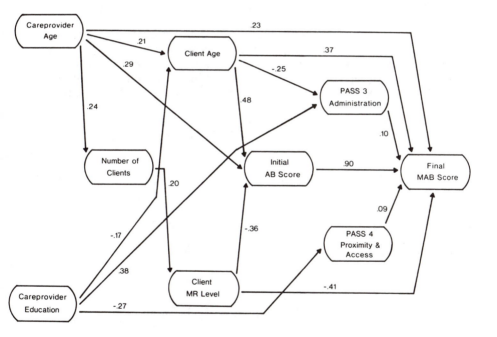

FIGURE 1. Path diagram of reduced model showing the influences of careprovider characteristics, initial client characteristics, and selected PASS facility ratings on subsequent client adaptive behavior scores. (The diagram only shows the path coefficients significant at the .05 level.)

Careproviders' age did relate to adaptive behavior performance as well as to the composition of clients in the house. For example, older foster parents tended to accommodate a larger number of clients in their homes and preferred older residents with higher adaptive behavior. In addition, less educated careproviders tended to have older clients than did better educated careproviders. Furthermore, careproviders' education had no association with residents' level of retardation or adaptive behavior competence. Overall, homes with a larger number of clients tended to be composed of more severely retarded residents. Residents' level of retardation, in turn, related to adaptive behavior performance, as expected. The coefficients were negative, indicating that greater degrees of retardation, (i.e., severe and profound) were associated with lower adaptive behavior performance. Finally, the older clients exhibited higher levels of adaptive behavior, as expected.

Overall, Figure 1 illustrates a complex set of relationships regarding client gains in adaptive behavior. Most of these relationships of selected PASS factors with changes in adaptive behavior could be expected; however, a few pertaining to careprovider education and quality of the environment were unexpected. Noteworthy is the replication of our earlier findings regarding the relationship of selected PASS factors with changes in adaptive behavior. Although these relationships may not account for a majority of the variance, they seem to be real. In addition, it can be seen from Figure 1 that the initial adaptive behavior score had a high relationship with the final score.

This high association between initial and final scores will necessarily limit the relationship of the final score with environmental variables. Hence, we would sum up Figure 1 as showing that younger clients, regardless of level of retardation, seemed to have benefited significantly in their adaptive competence in connection with positive PASS ratings on administrative and service policies (PASS Factor 3) designed to involve the home with educational institutions and the greater community. Moreover, proximity and access to community services, as well as harmony with the neighborhood (PASS Factor 4), related significantly to gains in adaptive behavior, regardless of either residents' age or level of retardation.

MALADAPTIVE BEHAVIOR

The variables eliminated in the path analysis for adaptive behavior also were unrelated to maladaptive behavior. This was not unexpected, given the higher reliability of adaptive behavior ratings in contrast to the lower reliability of maladaptive ratings and the greater degree of change in adaptive behavior in comparison to maladaptive behavior. In other words, more reliable measures have a better chance of correlating with other variables than do less reliable measures such as maladaptive behavior. Furthermore, because change in adaptive behavior was more pronounced than in maladaptive behavior, there was more variance in adaptive behavior change to be shared with other variables. Moreover, other variables associated with gains in adaptive behavior were not related to changes in maladaptive behavior. Specifically, client age, level of retardation, and all but one of the environmental ratings did not show potential for inclusion in the path analysis.

Figure 2 presents a reduced path diagram for maladaptive behavior. This diagram is much less complex than that for adaptive behavior. As noted earlier, this was because fewer predictor variables related to maladaptive behavior than to adaptive behavior and because there was only marginal change in maladaptive behavior over the study period (see Tables 3 and 4). Nevertheless, some interesting results emerged.

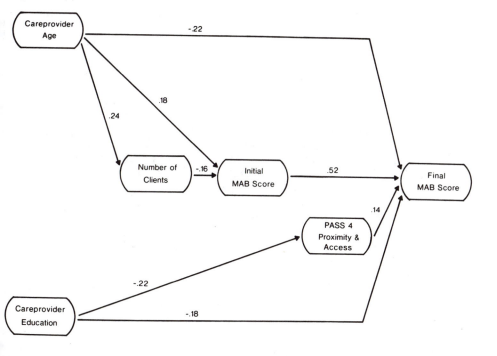

FIGURE 2. Path diagram of reduced model showing influences of care-provider characteristics, initial client characteristics, and selected PASS facility ratings on subsequent client maladaptive behavior scores. (The diagram only shows the path coefficients significant at the .05 level.)

Of the environmental ratings, only PASS Factor 4, Proximity and Access, significantly related to a *decrease* in client maladaptive behavior. Better ratings on proximity and access to community services were associated with reduced maladaptive behavior. Careprovider age and education also predicted a decline in maladaptive behavior; however, older foster parents initially selected clients with low rates of maladaptive behavior. In contrast, *less educated* foster parents seemed to provide a good environment that reduced undesirable behavior; moreover, these careproviders did not differentially select well-behaving clients. Exactly how the careproviders' education mediates their own behavior and that of the clients warrants further study.

The relationship between careprovider age and maladaptive behavior was similar to that for adaptive behavior. Older careproviders tended to have more clients in the home. Larger numbers of clients had a small but significant association with higher rates of maladaptive behavior; however, Figure 2 suggests that when the number of clients in the home is controlled, older careproviders tend to select clients with lower rates of maladaptive behavior. Finally, the initial level of maladaptive behavior related strongly to subsequent maladaptive behavior. This sequence of associations suggests that older foster parents seem to be more likely to have larger numbers of retarded residents with more maladaptive behavior. It may be that having larger numbers of retarded clients in a home hinders attempts to reduce the behavior problems of those clients.

Our findings are generally consistent with those from other studies. Quality of the home environment is decidedly related to gains in adaptive behavior. Homes that are more assimilated within their communities and relate well to educational institutions foster more growth in adaptive behavior. In earlier work, Eyman et al. (1977), Eyman, Demaine, and Lei (1979), and Eyman and Begab (1981), using different samples, found similar environmental variables significantly associated with gains in adaptive behavior for community-placed retarded individuals. Other investigators (e.g., Hull & Thompson, 1980; Intagliata, Willer, & Wicks, 1981) also found that the home environment influenced the behavior of community-placed residents.

As reported previously, clients' adaptive behavior tends to change over time more dramatically than does maladaptive behavior (Eyman, Borthwick, & Miller, 1981; Eyman et al., 1977; Eyman et al., 1979). Hence, relationships between the various independent variables and adaptive behavior are much more detectable than are such associations with maladaptive behavior, as currently indicated.

Of all the variables examined, careproviders' education demonstrated a unique association with PASS Factor 3 (Administration) and PASS Factor 4 (Proximity and Access), which in turn both related positively with subsequent clients' adaptive behavior. In other words, homes of more highly educated careproviders, scored higher on PASS Factor 3 than did homes of less educated careproviders but lower on PASS Factor 4. As noted previously, PASS Factor 3 was concerned with such variables as ties to academia, research climate, and the planning process, which should be of interest to better educated careproviders; PASS Factor 4 dealt with such items as local proximity to community services and access to the home, which represented attributes more common to less educated foster parents. The most plausible explanation for this reversal regarding careprovider education and PASS Factor 4 involves time and competing commitments of the foster parents. The fact that the better educated careroviders were heavily committed to ties to academia and the planning process suggests that they had less time available for other regional and local activities. Both of these environmental dimensions related positively to client development.

Of special interest was the replication of our earlier findings regarding the relationship of selected PASS factors with gains in adaptive behavior. Both PASS factors associated with client development in this study also significantly predicted adaptive behavior growth in a previous study using a different sample (Eyman et al., 1979). Research evidence is accumulating on the importance of specified social, intellectual, and recreational activities for developmental growth of mildly mentally retarded individuals.

Finally, older careproviders seemed to select older, high-functioning clients. They also tended to have larger numbers of clients in their homes than did younger careproviders. Disregarding careproviders' age and education, however, we found that homes with more clients tended to accommodate more severely retarded clients, who of course showed the least competence in adaptive behavior. The findings on maladaptive behavior are not as extensive as are those for adaptive behavior. To begin with, the average change in maladaptive behavior over a 2-year period was *not* significant. This finding replicates an earlier study on another sample (Eyman et al., 1981), which also found no significant trend in maladaptive behavior over time for either institution or community-based residents.

Neither clients' age nor level of retardation was related to maladaptive behavior in this sample. Other investigators have found that maladaptive behavior is related to age and level of retardation of the residents (Eyman & Call, 1977; Eyman & Borthwick, 1980; Eyman et al., 1981). We note, however, that the present study dealt with a highly selected group of children who were not as diverse in age and level of retardation as were those in previous study samples. The most interesting finding about maladaptive behavior was its relationship with PASS Factor 4 (Proximity and Access), which was associated negatively with careprovider education. It appears that maladaptive behavior decreased in homes rated high on Proximity and Access, more typical among the *less* educated careproviders. Hence, education of the foster parents indirectly predicted improvement of maladaptive behavior.

Furthermore, older careproviders accepted clients with less maladaptive behavior; however, the behavior of these residents deteriorated over time. The larger number of residents found in these homes of older foster parents may have produced a negative effect on client maladaptive behavior. An alternative explanation is that homes with a larger number of residents experience more resident turnover, which Sheehy (1983) has suggested increases maladaptive behavior. In this study, less educated careproviders seemed to provide a better environment for improving the behavior of the resident, and there was no evidence to indicate that these foster parents were only accommodating better behaved residents.

Although Intagliata, Willer, and Wicks (1981) conducted an entirely different kind of study from ours, they reported some similar findings. They noted that the careproviders they identified as low quality had less education and were more likely to report greater improvement in residents' community-living skills and behavior control compared to more educated careproviders in high quality homes. In connection with a one-time measure of abnormal behavior, however, these authors reported that clients in high quality homes of more highly educated careproviders were significantly more likely to display "normal behavior" in a number of areas than were residents of low-quality homes. In view of an inconsistent literature and lack of significant trends in clients' maladaptive behavior for the total sample of our clients, it is best to await more studies before attempting to draw conclusions from these results on maladaptive behavior.

Intagliata, Crosby, and Neider (1981) described family care as a community residential model that is in transition. They carefully noted the wide variation that exists in the purpose, character, and quality of family care environments and discussed the fact that family care homes are currently staffed by careproviders who have begun their work at different times and have different philosophies regarding client care. Moreover, the role of family care is changing. Although foster care was designed to provide "substitute" family care for a planned period, in many cases the placement becomes permanent. In other cases, family care homes serve as transitional settings in which residents acquire the self-care and community-living skills necessary for moving on to more independent-living situations within the community.

Scheerenberger (1982) recently reported a decreasing trend in the percentage of clients who were placed from institutions into family care homes, from 14.7% of all placements in 1975–1976 to 6.4% in 1981–1982. During the same period, placements to group homes (of which there are many variations in size and other characteristics) *increased*, from 15.9% of all placements to 23.5%. These fairly dramatic changes in placement patterns lead us to question the basis on which the social policy has apparently shifted. There is definitely a need for empirical studies to determine optimal placements for mentally retarded persons (Zigler & Balla, 1977). It is our hope that the findings from our family care study will contribute to this base, although we realize that additional studies will be required to verify or contradict the results reported in this chapter.

REFERENCES

Arndt, S. (1981). A general measure of adaptive behavior. *American Journal of Mental Deficiency, 85,* 554–556.

Bentler, P. M. (1980). Multivariate analysis with latent variables: Causal modeling. *Annual Review of Psychology, 31,* 419–456.

Bjaanes, A. T., Butler, E. W., & Kelly, B. R. (1981). Placement type and client functional level as factors in provision of services aimed at increasing adjustment. In R. H. Bruininks, C. E. Meyers, B. B. Sigford, & K. C. Lakin (Eds.), *Deinstitutionalization and community adjustment of mentally retarded people* (Monograph No. 4). Washington, DC: American Association on Mental Deficiency.

Borthwick, S., Meyers, C. E., & Eyman, R. K. (1981). Comparative and maladaptive behavior of mentally retarded clients of five residential settings in three western states. In R. H. Bruininks, C. E. Meyers, B. B. Sigford, & K. C. Lakin (Eds.), *Deinstitutionalization and community adjustment of mentally retarded people* (Monograph No. 4). Washington, DC: American Association on Mental Deficiency.

Bradley, R. H., & Caldwell, B. M. (1977). Home Observation for Measurement of the Environment: A validation study of screening efficiency. *American Journal of Mental Deficiency, 81,* 417–420.

Bradley, R. H., & Caldwell, B. M. (1978). Screening the environment. *American Journal of Orthopsychiatry, 48,* 114–130.

Bradley, R. H., Caldwell, B. M. (1979). Home Observation for Measurement of the Environment: A revision of the preschool scale. *American Journal of Mental Deficiency, 84,* 235–244.

Browder, J. A., Ellis, L., & Neal, J. (1974). Foster homes: Alternatives to institutions? *Mental Retardation, 12,* 33–36.

Brown, S. J., Windle, C., & Stewart, E. (1959). Statistics on a family care program. *American Journal of Mental Deficiency, 64,* 535–542.

Bruininks, R., Hill, B., & Thorsheim, M. J. (1980). *A profile of specially licensed foster homes for mentally retarded people in 1977.* Minneapolis: University of Minnesota, Department of Psychoeducational Studies.

Carsrud, A. L., Carsrud, K. B., Henderson, D. P., Alisch, C. J., & Fowler, A. V. (1979). Effects of social and environmental change on institutionalized mentally retarded persons: The relocation syndrome reconsidered. *American Journal of Mental Deficiency, 84,* 266–272.

Cochran, W. E., Sran, P. K., & Varano, G. A. (1977). The relocation syndrome in mentally retarded individuals. *Mental Retardation, 15*(2), 10–12.

Cohen, H., Conroy, J. W., Frazer, D. W., Snelbecker, G. E., [Spreat, S. (1977). Behavioral effects of interinstitutional relocation of mentally retarded residents. *American Journal of Mental Deficiency, 82,* 12–18.

Conroy, J., Efthimiou, J., & Lemanowicz, J. (1982). A matched comparison of the developmental growth of institutionalized and deinstitutionalized mentally retarded clients. *American Journal of Mental Deficiency, 86,* 581–587.

Elardo, R., Bradley, R., & Caldwell, B. M. (1975). The relation of infants' home environments to mental test performance from six to thirty-six months: A longitudinal analysis. *Child Development, 46,* 71–76.

Eyman, R. K., & Begab, M. J. (1981). Relationship between foster home environments and resident changes in adaptive behavior. In P. Mittler & J. deJong (Eds.), *Frontiers of knowledge in mental retardation* (Vol. 1). Baltimore: University Park Press.

Eyman, R. K., & Borthwick, S. A. (1980). Patterns of care for the mentally retarded. *Mental Retardation, 18,* 63–66.

Eyman, R. K., Borthwick, S. A., & Miller, C. (1981). Trends in maladaptive behavior of mentally retarded persons placed in community and institutional settings. *American Journal of Mental Deficiency, 85,* 473–479.

Eyman, R. K., & Call, T. (1977). Maladaptive behavior and community placement of mentally retarded persons. *American Journal of Mental Deficiency, 82,* 137–144.

Eyman, R. K., Demaine, G. C., & Lei, T. (1979). Relationship between community environments and resident changes in adaptive behavior: A path model. *American Journal of Mental Deficiency, 83,* 330–338.

Eyman, R. K., Silverstein, A. B., McLain, R., & Miller, C. (1977). Effects of residential settings on development. In P. Mittler (Ed.), *Research to practice in mental retardation: Care and intervention.* Baltimore: University Park Press.

Felsenthal, D., & Scheerenberger, R. C. (1978). Stability and attitudes of primary caregivers in the community. *Mental Retardation, 16,* 16–18.

Flynn, R. J. (1980). Normalization, PASS, and service quality assessment: How normalizing are current human services? In R. J. Flynn & K. E. Nitsch (Eds.), *Normalization, social integration, and community services.* Baltimore: University Park Press.

Gilbert, K. A., & Hemming, H. (1979). Environmental change and psycholinguistic ability of mentally retarded adults. *American Journal of Mental Deficiency, 83,* 453–459.

Heal, L., Sigelman, C., & Switzky, H. (1978). Research on commuity residential alternatives for the mentally retarded. In N. R. Ellis (Ed.), *International review of research in mental retardation* (Vol. 9). New York: Academic.

Hemming, H., Cook, M., Gilbert, K. A., & Lavender, A. (1979). Gaze pattern of mentally retarded adults in two contrasting environments. *American Journal of Mental Deficiency, 83,* 561–565.

Hemming, H., Lavender, T., & Pill, R. (1981). Quality of life of mentally retarded adults transferred from large institutions to new small units. *American Journal of Mental Deficiency, 80,* 157–169.

Hull, J. T., & Thompson, J. C. (1980). Predicting adaptive functioning of mentally retarded persons in community settings. *American Journal of Mental Deficiency, 85,* 253–261.

Intagliata, J., Crosby, N., & Neider, L. (1981). Foster family care for mentally retarded people: A qualitative review. In R. H. Bruininks, C. E. Meyers, B. B. Sigford, & K. C. Lakin (Eds.), *Deinstitutionalization and community adjustment of mentally retarded people* (Monograph No. 4). Washington, DC: American Association on Mental Deficiency.

Intagliata, J., Willer, B., & Wicks, N. (1981). Factors related to the quality of community adjustment in family care homes. In R. H. Bruininks, C. E. Meyers, B. B. Sigford, & L. C. Lakin (Eds.), *Deinstitutionalization and community adjustment of mentally retarded people* (Monograph No. 4). Washington, DC: American Association on Mental Deficiency.

Kraus, J. (1971). Predicting success of foster placements for school age children. *Social Work, 16,* 63–72.

Lei, T., & Eyman, R. K. (1979). Characteristics of individuals referred to services for the developmental disabled. *Mental Retardation, 17,* 196–199.

McCarver, R. B., & Craig, E. M. (1974). Placement in the community: Prognosis and outcome. In N. R. Ellis (Ed.), *International review of research in mental retardation* (Vol. 7). New York: Academic.

McPherson, J. M. (1976). *Theory trimming social science research, 5,* 95–105.

Miller, C. (1976). *The factorial structure of the behavior development survey.* Paper presented at the annual meeting of the American Associatioon on Mental Deficiency, Chicago.

Miller, C. (1979). The relationship between BDS score fluctuations and placement changes for a PMR population. In J. Duckett, C. C. Cleland, & S. H. Zucker (Eds.), *The profoundly mentally retarded.* The Western Research Conference.

Nihira, K. (1969). Factorial dimensions of adaptive behavior in adult retardates. *American Journal of Mental Deficiency, 73,* 868–878.

Nihira, K. Development of adaptive behavior in the mentally retarded. In P. Mittler (Ed)., *Research to practice in mental retardation* (Vol. II). Baltimore: University Park Press.

Nihira, K., Foster, R., Shellhaas, M., & Leland, H. (1975). *AAMD Adaptive Behavior Scale, 1975 Revision Manual.* Washington, DC: American Association on Mental Deficiency.

Nihira, L., & Nihira, K. (1975). Normalized behavior in community placement. *Mental Retardation, 13,* 9–13.

Pawlarczyk, D., & Schumacher, K. (1983). Concurrent validity of the Behavior Development Study. *American Journal of Mental Deficiency, 87,* 619–626.

Pennima, T. L. (1974). Initial screening and identification of predictors for possible use in selecting foster mothers for the mentally retarded. *Dissertation Abstracts International, 35*(6-A), 3879.

Rago, W. V. (1976). On the transfer of the PMR. *Mental Retardation, 14*(2), 27.

Ramey, C. T., Mills, P., Campbell, F. A., & O'Brien, C. (1975). Infants' home environments: A comparison of high-risk families from the general population. *American Journal of Mental Deficiency, 80,* 40–42.

Sanderson, H. W., & Crawley, M. (1982). Characteristics of successfully family-care parents. *American Journal of Mental Deficiency, 86,* 519–525.

Schalock, R. L., Harper, R. S., & Genung, T. (1981). Community integration of mentally retarded adults: Community placement and program success. *American Journal of Mental Deficiency, 85,* 478–488.

Scheerenberger, R. C. (1982). *Public residential services for the mentally retarded. 1981.* Minneapolis: University of Minnesota, Department of Psychoeducational Studies.

Scheerenberger, R. C., & Felsenthal, D. (1977). Community settings for MR persons: Satisfaction and activities. *Mental Retardation, 15*(4), 3–7.

Sheehy, N. L. (1983). The effects of a foster home's behavioral environment and family constellation on the development of mentally retarded residents. (Doctoral dissertation, Claremont Graduate School). *Dissertation Abstracts International, 44,* 1991–B.

Sternlicht, M. (1978). Variables affecting foster care placement of institutionalized retarded residents. *Mental Retardation, 1978, 16,* 25–28.

Vaux, C. L. (1935). Family care of mental defectives. *American Association on Mental Deficiency Proceedings, 40,* 168–189.

Weinstock, A., Wulken, P., Colon, C. J., Coleman, J., & Goncalves, S. (1979). Stress inoculation and interinstitutional transfer of mentally retarded individuals. *American Journal of Mental Deficiency, 83,* 385–390.

Willer, B., & Intagliata, J. (1982). Comparison of family-care and group homes as alternatives to institutions. *American Journal of Mental Deficiency, 86,* 588–595.

Windle, C. (1962). Prognosis of mental subnormals. *American Journal of Mental Deficiency, Monograph Supplement, 66,* 1–180.

Windle, C. D., Sabagh, G., Brown, S. J., & Dingman, H. F. (1961). Caretaker characteristics and placement success. *American Journal of Mental Deficiency, 65,* 739–743.

Wolfensberger, W., & Glenn, L. (1975). *PASS 3: A method for the quantitative evaluation of human services.* Toronto: National Institute on Mental Retardation.

Zigler, E., & Balla, D. A. (1977). Impact of institutional experience on the behavior and development of retarded persons. *American Journal of Mental Deficiency, 82,* 1–11.

Summary and Conclusion

21
Directions for Person–Environment Research in Mental Retardation

Nancy M. Robinson
University of Washington

Summarizing this book, which results from the Lake Wilderness Conference on the Impact of Residential Environments on Retarded Persons and Their Careproviders (August 1982) indeed presents a challenge. The investigators who contributed come from many scientific camps, with diverse interests and emphases, and they are certainly not, even after energetic discussion, of a single mind. Yet, upon reflection, we can discover amidst all this vitality some themes and structures that perhaps help to make sense of diversity and point to new research directions.

OVERALL THEMES

These chapters represent only a part of the conference. The editors of this volume, Sharon Landesman of the University of Washington's Child Development and Mental Retardation Center and Peter Vietze of the National Institute of Child Health and Human Development, set the stage for a real meeting of minds. Their goal was not to derive a single belief system but to add awareness, energy, and new direction to research that bears upon the impact of residential environments on retarded persons and their careproviders. Here are some observations from an interested bystander.

First, it is clear that *research in this area is thriving*. The chapters in this volume are interesting—important, conceptually coherent, methodologically careful and sophisticated without being overwhelmed by the weight of their own methodology. Investigators are caught up with ideas as much as with ways to study them. At a time when large segments of the field of research related to mental retardation are in the doldrums, there is in this area a sense of vigor and anticipation. In part, this ambiance seems to derive from the complementarity of ideas and approaches, complementarity that to experienced investigators suggests fruitful new directions and applications of their skills. Such insights breathe energy into one's efforts.

Second, it is also clear that the research reported here is part of the *mainstream of behavioral science* or, more particularly, developmental psychology. It is not an isolated representation of "the mental retardation research community," despite its emphasis on mentally retarded individuals. Several investigators here are as well known for their work with normally developing children and families as for their work with handicapped persons. The tools of research described in this book are primarily those of developmental psychology. The guiding theories are, as well, mainstream theories, special not in kind but only in their application to mentally retarded individuals.

Third, there is a *sense of relevance* about the work reported and discussed here. There is relevance to the welfare of retarded individuals and their families, to legislative issues and administrative decisions, to one's own professional life. This body of research can make a difference, a significant difference, directly on retarded persons, their families, and their caregivers and indirectly on society as a whole.

Fourth, one can characterize the authors of these chapters as *tolerant of complexity*. No one has presented easy answers or single-variable analyses. The interplay of multiple factors in the person–environment interaction is the object of inquiry and not considered, as it might have been in previous times, to be noisy interference. To be sure, in Chapter 3 Butterfield, suggested that the complexity of matters in the everyday world tends to preclude valid studies for at least some purposes, but this does not gainsay the point. Certainly, the advent of contemporary statistical techniques and, even more, interactional models, has made it possible to handle complex relationships previously viewed only piecemeal. This is a positive turn of affairs for investigators interested in events and trends that occur in the real world.

Finally, an important theme emerges from all of these chapters: an emphasis on enhancing the *quality of life* for retarded individuals, their families, and their careproviders. Previously, we evaluated residential settings by residents' developmental progress or achievement of "normalization." There has been little emphasis in the current set of chapters on measuring the quality of an environment by developmental gains alone (although to some extent this was the import of Eyman, Borthwick, and Sheehy's use of the Adaptive Behavior Scale as an outcome measure, see Chapter 20). Moreover, there has been no suggestion by anyone that the environment that most resembles that of nonretarded individuals is best for retarded people. As Landesman pointed out (Chapter 5), we cannot generalize from our own priorities to those that make a difference to retarded individuals. Although we ourselves may find pleasure in spacious rooms and open vistas, these distal aspects of the environment may be irrelevant for profoundly retarded individuals for whom only more proximal aspects have any significance. What, then, are some indices of the quality of life that might be examined? The following list of indicators derives in large part from hints in the chapters comprising this book:

Health

Survival, absense of disease, physical fitness, regularity of biological rhythms.

Comfort

Absence of pain, smiling, stable and positive mood.

Stereotyped Behavior

Absence of or reduction in stereotypic and self-injurious behavior.

Proximal Experience

Elements of modulated, appropriate sensory stimulation, including sensual experience.

Relationships

One or more consistent, warm, supportive relationships with careproviders who can be counted on and with friends of one's choosing.

Responses of Others

Positive regard by family and other careproviders not only toward the retarded individual but toward their own role in his or her life; satisfaction with the residential arrangement.

Focus

A sense of focus in the retarded individual's life—a reason to wake up in the morning. This may be an active daily routine, a school or recreational program, or simply an interesting proximal environment that produces a spectacle worth attending to.

Developmental Appropriateness of the Environment

None of the authors has argued that a "normalized" environment need be calibrated to the chronological age of individuals as opposed to their mental age. It is worth examining the content and organization of residential environments according to the maturity level of the retarded individuals who inhabit them. I have heard people argue (elsewhere) that music boxes for profoundly retarded adults should play adult fare such as "Swan Lake," not children's songs. Although it may be important that the music boxes appeal to the careproviders as well as to the clients, let me argue strongly for our willingness to provide to retarded individuals the objects they appreciate—dolls, trucks, puzzles, and nursery games for some; card games, television, movies, and outings to baseball games for others.

Sense of Self-Worth

For all but the most retarded individuals, a final criterion of "the good life" may be their own sense of its rightness and value. As Zetlin et al., in Chapter 13 pointed out, we cannot judge a priori whether a dependent or a more independent mode is going to bring satisfaction; there are individuals and families who are convinced that mutual dependency is right for them, and cultivate it, whereas others just as assiduously create opportunities for independence.

SUMMARY MODELS

In summarizing these chapters, I can use several models or conceptual systems to achieve coherence. Some of these are structural and inherent in the nature of research; some have been suggested by the authors themselves.

A Structural Model

Viewed rather formally, one can divide these chapters by their emphasis on the context of the field of mental retardation and residential arrangements, theoretical views of research and/or interactional processes, naturalistic or field studies, intervention and/or experimental studies, and discussions of methodology. These clusters reveal differing levels as well as kinds of emphasis.

CONTEXT

Two chapters set the stage for this volume. In Chapter 2, Bruininks, Rotegard, Lakin, and Hill described the epidemiology of mental retardation and examined in considerable detail the short-term trends in residential services in this country, particularly in the 1960s and 1970s. Meyers and Blacher described trends in residential care over much longer historical and broader geographical perspectives in Chapter 1.

THEORY

Several authors focused on the theoretical underpinnings of this field. Butterfield (Chapter 3) and Coates and Vietze (Chapter 4) discussed strategies for research, the latter authors being considerably more sanguine than the former; Bristol (Chapter 18) and Friedrich, Greenberg, and Crnic (Chapter 16) discussed models for formulating the roles of stress and coping in families with handicapped children. In Chapter 17, Lewis, Feiring, and Brooks-Gunn discussed developmental aspects of interpersonal environments of retarded and nonretarded children. Finally, Cherniss (Chapter 10) discussed a new way of looking at staff burnout, a way that is at odds with current emphasis on stress.

NATURALISTIC OR FIELD STUDIES

In a good many of the chapters in this volume, the authors reported observational and/or field studies in which they examined naturally occurring phenomena related to the care of retarded individuals. Eyman et al. (Chapter 20) discussed a large-scale California study of foster care placement, including a path analysis of factors relating to changes in adaptive behavior. Similarly, Janicki, Jacobson, Zigman, and Lubin (Chapter 8) reported a detailed study of group homes in New York State: services available in these settings; employee characteristics, attitudes, and satisfactions; and a number of systems issues. Chapter 9 by Seltzer and Seltzer dealt with attitudes of persons in various neighborhoods to community residences under different sorts of preparatory programs. Baumeister and Zaharia (Chapter 11) reported the effects of such factors as staffing patterns and economic conditions on staff turnover in a number of institutions. Sulzbacher and Steinfeld (Chapter 15) summarized evidence concerning the use ofpsychotropic medication in various residential settings. Lewis et al. (Chapter 17) examined the number of people in children's environments. Stoneman and Brody (Chapter 19) reported provocative observations of the roles assumed by retarded and nonretarded children and their parents and siblings in different configurations, including observations of siblings with their nonretarded friends, under controlled and naturally occurring conditions. (One has the vision of observers leaping over pig troughs and careening tricycles.) In Chapter 13, Zetlin, Turner, and Winik, using the participant–observer method, developed typologies of interaction of retarded individuals and their families, both those living at home and those away, those with parents and those without.

INTERVENTION AND/OR EXPERIMENT

Before-and-after observations of retarded individuals when residential patterns were changed were examined in two chapters. Felce (Chapter 6) studied the feasibility of locally based smaller units to which children and adults were moved from larger institutions in Wessex, England. Landesman (Chapter 5) used a highly original design to study the effects of moving retarded individuals from dormitory-type institutions to small, apartment-like institutions; by no means were all the changes she found in a positive direction. Baker and Clark (Chapter 12) reported the results of a program of intervention with parents of retarded children, with emphasis on the characteristics of those parents who did and did not complete, follow through, and derive benefit from the experience.

METHODOLOGY

Details of research method were emphasized by a number of authors previously cited, including Butterfield, Landesman, and Coates and Vietze. In addition Schroeder and MacLean (Chapter 14) described the phenomenon of covariation in observational/intervention research. Repp, Barton, and Brulle (Chapter 7) also discussed a number of technical issues in research in which they observed social interactions of retarded individuals and their careproviders.

LEVEL OF RETARDATION

A striking division, according to severity of subjects' handicaps, characterizes these chapters. Only a few studies covered a wide range of severity
(mostly the field studies of alternative forms of residential treatment,
namely, Eyman et al., Felce, and Janicki et al.). Aside from these, the
families studied all had mildly to moderately retarded members; studies
of community/institutional settings dealt with severely and profoundly
retarded residents. The thrust of the family-based chapters by Baker and
Clarke, Stoneman and Brody, Zetlin et al., Bristol, Lewis et al., and
Friedrich et al. was on the interaction of family members with retarded
individuals, mostly children, whose problems were of mild–moderate
degree. The thrust of the institutional/group-home chapters by Landesman, Baumeister and Zaharia, Schroeder and MacLean, Janicki et al., and
Felce were, in contrast, on more severely retarded individuals.

Although institutional care is increasingly restricted to those with se-
vere/profound impairment, multiple handicaps, and fragile health, the
data presented here demonstrate unmistakably that there are substantial
numbers of mildly retarded individuals living in alternative care arrangements, and there are substantial numbers of severely/profoundly retarded
individuals living at home. A significant achievement of the conference on
which this book is based is that these investigators were talking with one
another. Most of them could, indeed, apply with only minor adaptations
their familiar methods to the other's type of population, to the benefit of
all.

The Resource/Demands/Responsiveness Model

Still another model for examining these chapters is the model proposed
by Landesman for judging the efficacy of residential programs. She
suggested that we look at the availability of resources, the demands of the
environment (strategies required for survival and adaptation), and the
ability of individuals to perceive and respond to available aspects of the
environment. Although it is harder to categorize chapters according to this
model, I can cite some exemplars.

RESOURCES

Bruininks et al., Janicki et al., and Felce emphasized services available
in various settings; Lewis et al. directed attention to the people in the
environment.

DEMANDS

In their chapters, Zetlin et al. and Stoneman and Brody were concerned
explicitly with roles that retarded individuals are expected to play and the

contemporary roles played by other family members. Cherniss looked at the demands placed on caregivers and the need for strong commitment.

ABILITY TO RESPOND

Few of these authors looked specifically at behavioral capacities of retarded individuals or their careproviders. Eyman et al. examined adaptive behavior as an outcome; it could have been used as a predictor. Coates and Vietze suggested that we develop new means of examining the ability of even profoundly retarded individuals to respond to environmental events. Landesman examined changers versus nonchangers; Baker and Clark did the same for parents.

This model helps to settle into place the wealth of variables that can or should be included in a consideration of the person–environment interaction. As Gene Sackett pointed out, in the midst of a discussion at the conference, indeed, there are hundreds of such variables, each contributing but a small proportion of the variance of any outcome worth considering. Our research task becomes a matter of sifting through them to find those many that can be discarded from consideration and those few to which we should attend. Both Landesman and Sackett argued during the conference that we need to search for variables that make a substantial difference. Indeed, it is the spirit of this volume that big differences can and should be sought.

DEBATABLE QUESTIONS

Both in the substance of these chapters, and in the discussion in the conference room and elsewhere, two questions loomed large and remain unresolved.

Usefulness of Naturalistic Studies of Environmental Effects

One question had to do with the role of naturalistic observation as a guide to determining a course of action. Butterfield argued that unless random assignments are made between alternative treatments, there are simply so many confounds that firm conclusions are precluded. Institutions draw from different geographic sites characterized by different political and socioeconomic makeup; families who know their way around the bureaucracy obtain the favored settings for their children; retarded individuals with the most severe behavior problems are found in those settings that have the least power to transfer them elsewhere, and so on. Landesman has invented a compromise of sorts to make palatable a random-assignment method. Eyman et al. maintained that their path analysis suggests trends in effect that, if not conclusive, deserve follow-up. (One such example is their finding that older foster mothers seem to obtain more positive changes in their charges.)

One possible way out of this morass is to concentrate not on either–or outcomes but on differences in magnitude of effects. Through the use of analysis of covariance and its cousins, one should be able to take into account a substantial proportion of the naturally occurring confounds and to look, within a population, at the relationships of outcomes to variations in setting variables. One might well discover, for example, that predisposing background factors, such as social class, are considerably more important in determining outcomes with mildly than with severely handicapped individuals. (Readers are directed to Chapter 4, in particular, for Coates and Vietze's discussion relevant to this question.)

Large-Scale Empirical Study Versus The Study With Sharper Focus

Related to the first question is the utility of large-scale descriptions of current affairs versus studies with finer grain and few subjects. The old dictum that you do not know anything if you cannot control it, seemed to most of the conference participants to be going a bit too far. The heuristic value of a variety of studies was recognized and a stepwise type of progress accepted as inevitable. It was, however, noted in discussion that funding patterns and styles of research do change from time to time, partly as a result of progress, partly as a result of fashion.

QUESTIONS FOR FUTURE RESEARCH

Finally, I should like to point out some questions that were *not* raised by this group or to which, it seems to me, too little attention was devoted.

Breaking Through the Isolation of Mental Retardation Research

With only two exceptions, the presentations at this conference ignored the fact that individuals other than mentally retarded people need care. The two exceptions were Butterfield, who quoted Charles Kiesler's article about community versus institutional treatment for mental illness, and Seltzer and Seltzer, who looked at differences in acceptance of community residences for mentally retarded as opposed to mentally ill individuals. There are, in addition, many other people, both here and abroad, who live in group settings. Nonhandicapped children attend camps and boarding schools; orphans, especially in developing countries, live in orphanages; refugees live uprooted and aggregated; adolescent delinquents are placed in institutions, group homes, and foster families; abused and dependent children live in foster homes; old and chronically ill people live in various types of residences (including an increasing number of foster homes); blind and deaf children are still frequently schooled in residential institutions; even obliging college sophomores live in dormitories. It is short-sighted to restrict our efforts to mentally retarded individuals.

Cross-over Studies of Family and Institution

As I have mentioned previously, most studies of retarded individuals in family settings have been focused on mildly and moderately retarded people, many of them children; most investigators studying institutions have focused on severely and profoundly handicapped residents, mostly adults. Although there are a few exceptions in the published literature, the strong divergence represented in this book is typical of the current state of research. Surprisingly few are observational studies of parents and siblings in the presence of severely/profoundly retarded family members or of staffing patterns or group size on the adaptation of mildly retarded individuals living or working in group settings.

Individual History

We have very little information about the transition from home to residential care. The older studies of institutionalization revealed alarmingly high mortality rates in the first year of institutionalization, but those were the old institutions. What is the risk of depression today in various groups of individuals when the shift is made? Often, parents of profoundly retarded infants question the best kind of care for their children in view of the likely later need for out-of-home care. We have tended to assure parents that the best start in life is at home, the best chance for survival and vitality later on is an emotionally responsive and caring family in the early years. Is this, in fact, the case?

The Force of Individual Characteristics

Few of the authors in this volume have looked at environmental effects in terms of individual differences. Landesman delineated some retarded groups that seem more and less responsive to changes in setting and personnel; Zetlin et al. described some person–family characteristics that predispose to a conflict-ridden adaptation among mentally retarded adults in contact with their families; Baker and Clark reported individual characteristics of parents who profit less or more from intervention. Psychologists are good at looking at some kinds of individual differences, and it is a bit surprising that at this conference we heard so little about them.

Quality of Life

If we can permit ourselves to focus on such a nebulous concept as quality of life, then we need to develop sets of life-quality indicators for various sorts of people. For profoundly retarded individuals sleeping through the night might be evidence that something interesting had happened during the day; vocalizations or smiles are other indices. For mildly retarded persons, a broad variety of indicators could be added. We need to find ways to circumvent our own biases and values in this new field, but the very prospect is inviting.

Is There a Time to Cease Teaching?

Depending upon the average child's proclivity for education, somewhere between age 16 and 22, most young people "graduate" from formally mandated education. What about retarded individuals? Is there a time for careproviders to shift the priority from teaching to fostering positive adjustment? There seems to be some evidence that the period of maturation tends to be longer for retarded than nonretarded individuals, so that the answer to this question may not be a simple "normalized" response (i.e., 16 to 22 years). Some workers would maintain that because of their handicaps, retarded individuals should be taught new skills and urged to progress throughout life. Others would respond that such urging eventually implies nonacceptance of retarded adults as they "really" are. We need not take sides in this controversy, but we do need to examine it.

Finally, let me reiterate my enthusiasm for the conference and for this volume. On behalf of the participants, let me extend thanks to our sponsors, the National Institute of Child Health and Human Development and the University of Washington, and, in particular, to Drs. Vietze and Landesman. Tali Ott did a marvelous job of coordinating the affair. This volume has about it the feel of work that will make a difference.

Subject Index

A

ABCX model of family stress
  analysis of, 410–415
  discussion of study, 415–419
  elements of, 402–405
  testing of, 405–409
Absenteeism, 230
  extent of, 241–243
  related to employee withdrawal, 234–235
Adaptive behavior, 87, 104–105, 161, 331, 455–457, 459, 462–469
  see also Behaviors; Maladaptive behavior
Adaptive Behavior Scale, 87, 454–456
Adult day activity centers, 30
Alternative residential environments, 80
Anticonvulsant medication, 345–347
Applied behaviorists, 151–152
Attrition
  survival curves, 240–241
Autistic children, 278, 329, 345, 402, 417

B

Behavior Development Survey, 454–456
Behavior modification, 275–276, 278, 283, 284, 285, 344
Behavior training programs
  see Training programs
Behavioral repertoires, 86, 103, 113, 323, 340, 365
Behaviors
  antecedent setting factors
    environmental enrichment, 330–331
  changes in, 278, 282–283
  client behavior profile, 135–136
  discrete, 153–154

Behaviors (cont.)
  effects of environment on, 97–104, 165–168, 373–379
  enduring response, 153–154
  of residents, 160
  of staff, 160, 167
  rating instruments, 454–456
  recording procedures, 152–158
  studies of, 86–87
    baseline profiles, 92–97
    behavioral clusters, 105–113
    effects of moving to new environment on, 97–104
    environmental measures, 92
    observational procedures, 88–92
    subjects, 87–88
  variables affecting covariation, 328–332
  see also Adaptive behavior; Maladaptive behavior
Burnout
  definitions, 214–216
  environment leading to, 216–219
  relationship to social commitment, 219–224

C

Capital costs
  community-based residences, 144–145
Caregivers
  demographic characteristics, 70–71
    age, 466
    education, 71–72, 465, 468–469
    ethnic origin, 461
    foster parents, 457
  management attributes
    attitudes, 72

487